THE OXFORD AUTHORS

General Editor: Frank Kermode

RALPH WALDO EMERSON was born in Boston, Massachusetts, on Election Day, 25 May 1803, the fourth of eight children; only he and four brothers survived childhood. Emerson received his early education at the Boston Public Latin School, and entered Harvard in 1817. After graduating in 1821, he taught at his brother William's school in Boston. In 1825 he entered Harvard Divinity School and was accepted to preach in the following year. He accepted a position as pastor of Boston's Second Church in 1829. Though he officially resigned the pulpit three years later, Emerson continued to preach for a number of years before various Massachusetts congregations. From 1834 through the 1860s he lectured regularly in New England, on tours across the United States, and in England, where he became a good friend and corre-spondent of Carlyle. During this period he was also an active and outspoken opponent of American belligerence against Mexico, and of slavery, eventually turning against his one-time hero, Senator Daniel Webster, on the issue of the Fugitive Slave Law. Webster's 7 March 1851 speech in support of the law caused Emerson to write in his journal: 'all the drops of his blood have eyes that look downward.' His first book, *Nature*, appeared in 1836; *Essays* fol-lowed in 1841, and *Essays: Second Series* in 1844. Favourable reviews of the latter two volumes earned Emerson international acclaim. His works comprise some nine volumes of essays, two volumes of poetry, sixteen volumes of his journal, and many articles and reviews published in literary periodicals, including the trans-cendentalist journal *The Dial*, edited by Margaret Fuller, and, later, by Emerson himself. Emerson lost his first wife, Ellen Tucker, to tuberculosis in 1831. He married Lidian Jackson in 1835, and to them were born four children: Waldo (who died in 1842 at the age of 5), Ellen, Edith, and Edward. Emerson died of pneumonia on 27 April 1882 in Concord, Massachusetts.

RICHARD POIRIER is the Marius Bewley Professor of English at Rutgers University, New Jersey. He is the Editor of *Raritan*, a quarterly review, and the co-founder and Vice President of the Library of America. His books include *A World Elsewhere* (1963), *The Performing Self* (1971), *Robert Frost: The Work of Knowing* (1977), and *The Renewal of Literature* (1987).

THE OXFORD AUTHORS

RALPH WALDO EMERSON

EDITED BY

RICHARD POIRIER

Oxford   New York

OXFORD UNIVERSITY PRESS

1990

20824650

PS
1603
.P55
1990

Oxford University Press, Walton Street, Oxford OX2 6DP

Oxford New York Toronto
Delhi Bombay Calcutta Madras Karachi
Petaling Jaya Singapore Hong Kong Tokyo
Nairobi Dar es Salaam Cape Town
Melbourne Auckland

and associated companies in
Berlin Ibadan

Oxford is a trade mark of Oxford University Press

Introduction and editorial matter © Richard Poirier 1990

All rights reserved. No part of this publication may be reproduced,
stored in a retrieval system, or transmitted, in any form or by any means,
electronic, mechanical, photocopying, recording, or otherwise, without
the prior permission of Oxford University Press

This book is sold subject to the condition that it shall not, by way
of trade or otherwise, be lent, re-sold, hired out or otherwise circulated
without the publisher's prior consent in any form of binding or cover
other than that in which it is published and without a similar condition
including this condition being imposed on the subsequent purchaser

British Library Cataloguing in Publication Data
Emerson, Ralph Waldo, 1803–1882
Ralph Waldo Emerson.—(The Oxford writers).
I. Title II. Poirier, Richard, 1925–
818.309
ISBN 0–19–254193–5
ISBN 0–19–281437–0 (pbk)

Library of Congress Cataloging in Publication Data
Emerson, Ralph Waldo, 1803–1882.
[Selections. 1990]
Ralph Waldo Emerson/edited by Richard Poirier.
p. cm.—(The Oxford authors)
Includes bibliographical references.
I. Poirier, Richard. II. Title. III. Series.
PS1603.P55 1990
814'.3—dc20
ISBN 0–19–254193–5
ISBN 0–19–281437–0 (pbk).

Typeset by Promenade Graphics Ltd.
Printed in Great Britain by
Richard Clay Ltd.
Bungay, Suffolk

CONTENTS

HOLY SPIRIT LIBRARY
92 1524

INTRODUCTION

ASSESSMENTS of Emerson's place in his own culture tend to be extraordinarily at odds with one another. For the novelist John Updike there is 'something fatally faded about the works he has left us', while for the critic Harold Bloom, Emerson is 'the principal source of the American difference in poetry, criticism, and pragmatic post-philosophy'. While Irving Howe can 'wish that in the Emersonian landscape there were rather more old shoes and aunts and cousins', A. Bartlett Giamatti, speaking as Yale President to some students and their parents, claims that in the popular imagination he is 'the Lover of Nature, a sweet, sentimental Yankee Kahlil Gibran'. In reality, he says, coming closer but still far from the mark, Emerson is 'as sweet as barbed wire', and his 'greatest disservice lies in the assurances with which in subtle and in obvious ways he justified jettisoning history'.

Emerson's traces are said even by his detractors to be everywhere in American thought, representing, as the case may be, either what is best about the country—its optimism, its gregariousness, its independence of spirit—or what is worst—its tendency to ignore present ills by flattering itself as to future promise, a coldness disguised by indiscriminate *bonhomie*, an imperialism hidden even from itself by the cult of individualism. So great are the discrepancies in these assessments that one of Emerson's most ardent admirers, the philosopher Stanley Cavell, can say:

I take it for granted that Emerson and Thoreau are unknown to the culture whose thinking they helped found (I mean culturally unpossessed, unassumable among those who care for books, however possessed by shifting bands of intellectuals), in a way that it would not be thinkable for Kant and Schiller and Goethe to be unknown to the culture of Germany, or Descartes and Rousseau to France, or Locke and Hume and John Stuart Mill to England.

Emerson may well belong in this august company. And yet the terms in which on this occasion Cavell places him there beg the larger question as to whether or not he is the kind of writer who in fact ever can be 'culturally possessed' to the extent that these others presumably can be. His thinking is neither as systematic nor, finally, as available as theirs is, nor does he intend that it should be. While the titles of his essays promise to tell us about 'History' or 'Art' or 'Politics', it is impossible to come away from them with any sort of encapsulated definition, and a quotation from him about any of these or about his 'representative men' or about 'nature' can always be matched by another seriously at variance with it. 'A foolish consistency is the hobgoblin of little minds,' he writes in 'Self-Reliance', 'adored by little statesmen and philosophers and divines. With consistency a great soul has simply nothing to do . . . Speak what you think today in hard words and tomorrow speak what tomorrow thinks in hard words again, though it contradict everything you said today.' In this instance he does not even wait for tomorrow, but contradicts himself in the same essay, warning that to be too outspoken is to risk entrapment in the position you articulate and to lose the mobility essential to the free expansion of the self. 'As soon as he has acted or spoken with *éclat*,' a man, he says, 'is a committed person.' 'Committed' picks up on the previous sentence where we are told that 'the man is, as it were, clapped into jail by his consciousness'. One can expect a lot of such puns from a writer so sceptical about language, and *éclat* is yet another. A root meaning of it is 'to splinter'; he wants to suggest that even as you speak with particular force or splendour you are fracturing or dissipating your wholeness in the interest of some particular effect.

While this is apt to sound like peculiar advice from someone so frequently assertive, so ready to use 'hard words', it is altogether less so if his essays are read not for their aphoristic moments but for the rhythms and turns of a discernible voice. Emerson was one of the renowned public speakers of his time, lecturing in England, in Canada, in every part of the United States, and no fewer than eighty times in 1867 alone, all for considerable fees. John Jay Chapman, in his valuable book *Emerson and Other Essays* (1898), claims that 'It was the platform that determined Emerson's style', and that 'The pauses and hesitation, the abstraction, the searching, the balancing, the turning forward and back of the leaves of his lecture, and then the discovery, the illumination, the gleam of lightning which you saw before your eyes descend into a man of genius—all this was Emerson. He invented this way of speaking.' Oliver Wendell Holmes, describing what it was like to sit next to Emerson at the Saturday Club, a dinner club in Boston for informal literary discussion, said that 'if you have ever seen a cat picking her footsteps in wet weather, you have seen the picture of Emerson's exquisite intelligence, feeling for his phrase or epithet'.

But though Chapman and Holmes offer useful clues as to *how* we might best listen, as it were, to the writings collected here, they do not tell us why, as against the advice of Mr Updike, we should listen at all. Why read Emerson now, when there is so much else to read? One good reason, it seems to me, is that he never asks us passively to absorb his thought. Rather we are enjoined to resist it, just as he does. We are invited to think along with him in a manner always critical of the thoughts to which he seems to subscribe. 'An imaginative book,' he remarks in 'The Poet', 'renders us more service, at first, by stimulating us through its tropes, than afterward, when we arrive at the precise sense of the author.' Of Emerson it should be said that he cultivated the art of *not* arriving at intellectualized conclusions. His kind of writing does not compose itself and then wait for interpretation; rather it participates in disruptive interrogations of what is, after all, a not peculiar tendency in sentences and paragraphs to come to an end and to make a point. He is exciting because he is so full of agitated energy about the language at his disposal, and he is exemplary in his alertness to the sometimes unacceptable assumptions built into the vocabulary available to him, assumptions disclosed in the very effort at composition. Everywhere in his writing are signs of an extraordinarily rare activity of mind on the page, an extraordinary resistance to translation into the sagacities presumably appropriate to him as the sage of Concord. Emerson is not important because he needs to be retrieved by the culture he helped shape but because he enacts a mode of thinking which that culture has never dared to practise and that may, to borrow Lionel Trilling's phrase, be beyond culture.

Emerson is not an on-the-one-hand and on-the-other-hand kind of writer, arbitrating among his own contradictions. When he insists in 'Experience' that 'life is not dialectics' he means it. Life does not consist, that is, of questions and answers. Instead, as he says of 'nature' in 'Considerations by the Way', life is 'upheld by antagonism', a word which for him designates more than a response to human existence; it designates its very essence. 'Man is . . . a stupendous antagonism', as he says in 'Fate', 'a dragging together of the poles of the Universe'. 'The mind', he tells us in 'Experience', 'goes antagonizing on, and never prospers but by fits.' These fits naturally take the form of contradictions which, to borrow a phrase from his successor Wallace Stevens, occur as they occur. Something said apropos a given situation, for example, will sometimes simply nullify itself when carried over into another, different situation. So while the word 'nature' in Emerson refers to birds, flowers, and the like, it refers also—following an old distinction between *natura naturans* and *natura naturata*, which he would have known at least from Coleridge—to the power which both creates and destroys these particular things. Similarly, he sometimes opposes 'nature' to 'art', while arguing at other times, as in the essay 'Nature', that artificial life is itself natural, since 'Nature who made the mason, made the house'. In his essay on 'Plato' he claims that intellect is superior to nature, 'which it made and maketh', though earlier, in 'The Method of Nature', he had said that anything, including the mind, which refuses to 'flow with the course of nature', will be crushed.

Wordsworth's 'nature' is no less various, contradictory, and marvellous, the contradictions being a source of his poetic energy. But Emerson, though a considerable poet whose 'Uriel', 'Monadnoc', and 'Give All to Love' were especially admired by Frost, addresses us mostly in lectures and essays, forms which normally commit the writer to an effort at plain sense. What we find instead is that his prose dramatizes the workings of a mind as it functions within a word like 'nature'. His writing allows us to experience, as we do in life, the conflicting and apparently self-cancelling pulls of the word. In this way Emerson often anticipates, encompasses, and moves beyond those anxious theories that go by the name of deconstruction, one of whose principal claims to innovation depends on demonstrations that the rhetorical slippages taken for granted in poetry, or so one always assumed, belong as well to philosophical prose. Emerson writes a philosophical prose which promotes such slippages, and he thereby transforms into evidence of his own authorial presence the very tendencies in language which are alleged to discredit and dissolve it. This volatile combination of dissociative and performative rhetoric is what makes him 'the American Scholar'.

In the essay where he characterizes such a scholar, he says that 'in the right state, he is, *Man Thinking*. In the degenerative state, when the victim of society, he tends to become a mere thinker, or, still worse, the parrot of other men's thinking'. The distinction between a man thinking, engaged in an activity, and a 'mere thinker', reflecting on other men's reflections, is clear enough. So, too, I hope from the foregoing, is the relation of 'thinking' to Emerson's idea of language, not so much in the section called 'Language' in his first book *Nature*, where language is described as having a rather fixed relation to providential origins, as in subsequent writings, where it becomes increasingly a medium for transport, in every sense of that word. For if, as he says in 'The Poet', 'all language is vehicular and transitive, and is good, as ferries and horses are, for conveyance, not as farms and houses are, for homestead', then it is clear that language so conceived will move us *into* thinking by moving us *out* of thought. In this same essay, echoing an earlier remark in 'Art', he describes 'thought' as a prison: 'Every thought is also a prison; every heaven is also a prison.'

But what are we to make of the remark in the passage from 'The American Scholar' that anyone who has become 'a mere thinker' is 'the victim of society'? As a general proposition this is a familiar enough complaint of eighteenth- and nineteenth-century Romantic writers, English and Continental. And well it might have been. Unlike their American counterparts, these writers lived among the visible evidences of a culture centuries old in its potencies. Emerson's situation was by comparison notoriously thin, dispersed, and culturally timid. He knew this, and in a wonderfully exasperated entry in his journal for 10 July 1843 he turns the other cheek or, rather, turns William Ellery Channing's cheek, on the whole matter of social and literary victimizations in America:

W. E. C. railed an hour in good set terms at the usurpation of the past, at the great hoaxes of the Homers & Shakespeares, hindering the books & the men of today of their just meed. Oh certainly, I assure him, that oaks & horse-chestnuts are entirely obsolete, that the horticultural society are about to recommend the introduction of cabbages as a shade tree, so much more convenient & every way comprehensible; all grown from the seed upward to its most generous crumpled extremity within one's own short memory; past contradiction the ornament of the world, & then so good to eat, as acorn and horse-chestnuts are not. Shade-trees for breakfast!

Emerson's contempt for such efforts at 'jettisoning history', to recall Mr Giamatti's hasty allegation that he instead justified them, was accompanied by a recognition of American cultural impoverishment, a recognition nearly always lost sight of in the emphasis given only to his calls, simplified as they have been made to sound, for cultural independence. On this as on other issues one side of his multi-faceted position is usually preferred, the others dropped, and the one preferred most easily fits the stereotypic view of him. How indeed *is* his position on this score to be understood? He laments the lack of society in America and the lack of culture—'no writing is here,' he says in the *Journals* for March–April 1844, 'no redundant strength, but declamation, straining, correctness, & all other symptoms of debility.' And yet, as we have just heard, he also complains that there is too much society and that, as in the *Journals* for April–May 1846, 'I grow old, I accept conditions; thus far—no farther; to learn that we are not the first born, but the latest born; that we have no wings; that the sins of our predecessors are on us like a mountain of obstruction.'

This passage alone ought to suggest that, in Emerson's view, social and literary culture for a writer takes forms altogether less palpable and institutionalized than those imagined by Henry James, Jr. Speaking in his little book *Hawthorne* of 'the admirable and exquisite Emerson', James goes so far as to suggest that the bareness of Concord forced upon its culturally deprived inhabitants an inordinate degree of self-scrutiny. The situation in Boston, twenty miles from Concord and three hours away by coach, before the rail line connected them in 1843, was not, James would contend, much different. 'The doctrine of the supremacy of the individual to himself,' he writes, 'of his originality and, as regards his own character, unique quality, must have had a great charm for people living in a society in which introspection, thanks to the want of other entertainment, played almost the part of a social resource.' In fact, however, Emerson, like William James, his intellectual heir and Henry's brother, never recommends 'introspection', never suggests that there is a 'self' with already existing depths waiting to be plumbed. He instead counsels 'action'—'intellectual tasting of life will not supersede muscular activity', he remarks in 'Experience'—as the best way to co-ordinate individual life with the larger, impersonal energies at work in nature and traceable also in works of art.

Henry James had a familial veneration for Emerson, as did his father, the theologian-philosopher Henry James, Sr., who affectionately complained to his friend, 'Oh you man without a handle! Shall one never be able to help himself out of you, according to his needs, and be dependent only upon your fitful tippings-up?' In *Notes of a Son and Brother*, the novelist remembers Emerson visiting the family in New York's Washington Square and does so, incidentally, in phrases that testify to the power of Emerson's voice and the importance, in any effort to appreciate him, of tone:

I 'visualise' at any rate the winter firelight of our back-parlour at dusk and the great Emerson—I knew he was great, greater than any of our friends—sitting in it between my parents, before the lamps had been lighted, as a visitor consentingly housed only could have done, and affecting me the more as an apparition sinuously and, I held, elegantly slim, benevolently aquiline, and commanding a tone alien, beautifully alien, to any we heard roundabout, that he bent this benignity upon me by an invitation to draw nearer to him, off the hearth-rug, and know myself as never yet, as I was not indeed to know myself again for years, in touch with the wonder of Boston. The wonder of Boston was above all just then and there for me in the sweetness of the voice and the finish of the speech—this latter through a sort of attenuated emphasis which at the same time made sounds more important, more interesting in themselves, than by any revelation yet vouchsafed us. Was not this my first glimmer of a sense that the human tone could, in that independent and original way, be interesting? and didn't it for a long time keep me going, however unwittingly, in that faith, carrying me in fact more or less on to my day of recognising that it took much more than simply not being of New York to produce the music I had listened to. The point was that, however that might be, I had had given me there in the firelight an absolutely abiding measure. If I didn't know from that hour forth quite all it was to not utter sounds worth mentioning, I make out that I had at least the opposite knowledge. And all by the operation of those signal moments—the truth of which I find somehow reflected in the fact of my afterwards knowing one of our household rooms for the time—it must have been our only guest-chamber—as 'Mr. Emerson's room.'

For all this affecting veneration of Emerson, which carries over into James's fiction, as in the characterization of the Wentworths in *The Europeans* or of Isabel Archer in *Portrait of a Lady*, James stops well short of the hard questions about him in relation to American 'society' and the lack of it in Concord. (He is similarly superficial about Hawthorne and, in all his voluminous criticism, manages one innocuous reference to Melville.) He never asks how, in spite of—could it possibly be because of?—the lack of what he calls 'social resources', these writers managed actually to create a great national literature. This is effectively a question they asked themselves, and it is implied in Emerson's problematic use of the word 'society'. According to 'Self-Reliance', to cite another example, 'society everywhere is in conspiracy against the manhood of every one of its members'. And yet, as we saw, he at the same time repeatedly complains that he finds too little of it. In a touching entry in his journal for 27 October 1851 he recalls how 'in the rambles of last night's talk with HT [Henry Thoreau] we stated over and over again, to sadness, almost, the Eternal loneliness . . . how insular & pathetically solitary, are all the people we know!' Referring, possibly, to the resurrection of *The Dial*, he admits that 'when this annual project of a Journal returns, & I cast about to think who are to be contributors, I am struck with a feeling of great poverty; my bareness! my bareness! seems America to say'.

What was he to do about it? At times he seems to suggest that his own social diffidence only makes matters worse. His references in the *Journals*, when he was already 37, to his 'porcupine impossibility of contact with men' (14 November 1839), his long-pondered decision in 1840 not to join Brook Farm despite repeated appeals from George Ripley (he wrote at the time to Margaret Fuller that 'at the name of a society all my repulsions play, all my quills rise and sharpen'), and his critique of such communal enterprises shortly thereafter in 'New England

Reformers' are often cited, along with his devotion to the 'infinitude of the private man' (*Journals*, 7 April 1840), as evidence that in his own life he manifests the conviction that 'every man is an infinitely repellent orb, & holds his individual being on that condition' (*Journals*, 19 May 1838). And yet these colourful and quotable pieces of evidence are apt to obscure the more quotidian fact that he was for most of his life a markedly convivial and hospitable man. After his second marriage, to Lidian Jackson in 1835, their home in Concord—which he was able to purchase with the bequest from his first wife, who died in 1831—was usually crowded with visitors—some for dinner, some for tea, some overnight, many for months at a time. Thoreau lived with the Emersons off and on for close to three years before Emerson gave him the land on his property on which the Walden Pond cabin was built; Margaret Fuller was part of the household, much to the distress of Lidian, for over six weeks in 1842. For a time Emerson called almost daily on his neighbour Hawthorne, who came to suspect that Emerson wanted to appropriate him to his circle. This included Bronson Alcott (father of Louisa May), Ripley, William Ellery Channing the younger, and numerous other admirers. (Melville, living nearby in the Pittsfield, Massachusetts, farm where he finished *Moby-Dick*, a novel Emerson never mentions and probably never read, kept his distance, not wishing, as he was to say later, to 'oscillate in Emerson's rainbow'. He was far more sociable than either Hawthorne or Melville, infinitely more so than Thoreau, and sought out most of the illustrious writers of his time on his three trips to Europe, where he became especially close to Carlyle.

In the conduct of his life, he thus made the most of whatever society and culture he could find, bare as the provision might have been. It is in any case a common mistake of criticism to assume that when 'society' is disparaged on the page the word refers to some historically locatable assembly of persons and places wherein the writer is meanwhile passing time. In fact, the social disengagements a writer may recommend in poetry or prose do not necessarily occur at all in the actual life of the author. When, for example, in the most famous and often quoted passage in all of Emerson, he declares himself a transparent eyeball, it is important to keep in mind that the only place where this possibly could have occurred is in the text of *Nature* itself:

Standing on the bare ground,—my head bathed by the blithe air, and uplifted into infinite space,—all mean egotism vanishes. I become a transparent eyeball; I am nothing; I see all; the currents of the Universal Being circulate through me; I am part or parcel of God. The name of the nearest friend sounds then foreign and accidental; to be brothers, to be acquaintances,—master or servant, is then a trifle and a disturbance.

As Emerson describes the scene in which this experience is said to have occurred, his terminology makes plain that it actually had nothing to do with 'society', with persons in some culturally defined location. Rather, he is already standing, as he says, on 'the bare ground', and a few sentences earlier he describes himself as 'crossing a bare common'. If, to recall the *Journals*, America says to him 'my bareness! my bareness!', then apparently he is in need of circumstances barer still; he needs to move beyond bareness to transparency. *All* forms of mediation, including the body, are to be evaded. And yet the passage itself—the writing and reading of it, its own material coming into existence—makes it inescapably clear that the experience occurs only in the passage, only in words. Their printed visibility in itself proves that it is not possible for him to escape the mediation of language or of literature, both of which provide the precedents by which this kind of human transparency can make sense to his readers.

This is the central crux of Emerson's writing, as he himself suggests in the very first sentence of the first chapter of this, his first book: 'To go into solitude, a man needs to retire as much from his chamber as from society. I am not solitary whilst I read and write, though nobody is with me.' Here we have a crucial admission: his famous individualism is incompatible even with reading and writing, with language as it exists in culturally transmissible forms. If, together with this, individualism is threatened even by vocalized language, as in his caution against speaking with *éclat*, then his distrust of it comes close to being a disavowal. However, the style of these sentences audibly belies any such linguistic alienation. The style is polite, and socially gracious; a cultivated reader of Addison and Steele's eighteenth-century *Spectator* would be gratified by its balances. His tone confirms something inferrable from the very abundance of his literary productivity, which is that much of the energy of his writing comes from the will to overcome what he regarded as its potentially repressive power over individualism and over individualism's desire for solitude. 'Silence is a solvent that destroys personality, and gives us leave to be great and universal,' he says in 'Intellect'. Coming from this most voluble writer, who has just been praising the volubility of Socrates, such an assertion cannot obscure the evidence that in practice he finds a way to answer a central question for himself. How could 'the infinitude of the private man' be maintained and expressed even while it must submit to the mediating and shaping constraints of language?

In Emerson there can be no such thing as a single answer to such a question. But the beginnings of one may be found in what he likes to call abandonment—'the way of life is wonderful,' according to the end of 'Circles', 'it is by abandonment.' 'Abandonment' describes his habit of disavowal, his rhetorical movements of dissociation when it comes to the very things in which he conspicuously puts his trust, like language or literature or nature or even self-reliance. Of nature, to give another example, he observes in the shorter essay so titled, that 'the poet finds himself not near enough to his object. The pine-tree, the river, the bank of flowers before him, does not seem to be nature. Nature is still elsewhere.' Of literature, he writes, in his journal for 18 May 1840, that 'Criticism must be transcendental, that is, must consider literature ephemeral & easily entertain the supposition of its entire disappearance'. This is not, as in some jingoistic declaration of cultural separatism, simply to wish literature out of existence; it is to say, rather, that criticism ought to suppose that literature can be erased from consciousness by the emergence of some different form of human genius. As with his body in the opening of *Nature* or 'the bank of flowers' in the essay called 'Nature' or the speech to which, in 'Art', 'silence is a solvent', Emerson asks that literature become transparent, its language diaphanous, so as to make more immediately perceptible the power that first created it, that moves in and through it. 'Nothing', he remarks in 'Circles', 'is secure but life, transition, the energising spirit.'

Rely, that is to say, not on anything fixed or stabilized in your vocabulary but only on movements away from them, movements precipitated by desire whose object is uncertain and which, if too certainly defined, can turn your thinking about it into mere thought and thence into inertia. As a writer, much less a person, this is for him a saving principle, and it determines the disruptive energies at work in his sentences and paragraphs, and in the compellingly enigmatic turns of his poetry. Thus, in 'Self-Reliance', after some notably strong words about power as essentially a form of transition, his expenditures of rhetoric provoke in him a derisive rejoinder, a rejection of his dependence on the phrase that serves as his title:

Life only avails, not the having lived. Power ceases in the instant of repose; it resides in the moment of transition from a past to a new state, in the shooting of the gulf, in the darting of an aim. This one fact the world hates, that the soul *becomes*; for that forever degrades the past, turns all riches to poverty, all reputation to shame, confounds the saint with the rogue, shoves Jesus and Judas equally aside. Why, then, do we prate of self-reliance? Inasmuch as the soul is present there will be power not confident but agent. To talk of self-reliance is a poor external way of speaking. Speak rather of that which relies because it works and is.

With its agitated substitutions of words having to do with vocal expression—'talk', 'speak', 'prate'—this passage suggests, as do many others, a frustration with the fact that apparently any use of language may disfigure the self in the very process of expressing it. Obviously to be avoided are 'external ways of speaking', speaking in obedience to easily apprehended formulae. And avoid them he does, by the calculated opacity of that final sentence: 'Speak rather of that which relies because it works and is.' Note how the words 'self' and 'reliance' get absorbed into the word 'that', which in turn is absorbed into the word 'it', which is then immediately appropriated into its function, as in 'it works and is'. The sentence is to be experienced as it is written, and not in any clarifying translation into some other syntax. The experience is of a blur in which each of the substantives momentarily stands in place of the others, bound together with them, adhering to them, 'adhering' being a meaning of 'rely' older than the more common usage, which, as in the phrase 'rely on', suggests not adherence but dependence. The syntax approximates that only momentary achievement of simultaneous fusion among agent, action, and words which, for Emerson, *is* the self just before its transfiguring move into another transition.

It should be clear that Emerson is actually opposed to individualism in the customary or social sense in which the term is most often used. That is, he is opposed to the notion of the self as something put together by a person who is then required to express it and to ask others to confirm it as his identity. Similarly, he is opposed to literature conceived as a series of more or less discrete texts each holding in trust a source of wisdom not sufficiently available elsewhere. 'The real value of the Iliad, or the Transfiguration,' as he says in 'Art', 'is as signs of power; billows or ripples they are of the stream of tendency; tokens of the everlasting effort to produce, which even in its worst estate the soul betrays.' Persons and texts can be treated as sacred because, or rather when, they show the active workings of an aboriginal power that went into their creation. Emerson's faith resides less in any historically grounded form of human nature than in human mind, which does not recognize distinctions of time and place, of ancient and modern. Beyond the clutter of cultural accumulation, the American continent for him was a place where, freed at last from historical referentiality, the reader could 'know the awful secret of genius', as he puts it in the *Journals* for August–September 1845. 'You are here', he says, 'to become not readers of poetry but Dante, Milton, Shakespeare, Homer, Swedenborg, in the fountain through that.' He was so little an American chauvinist that in this same spirit he could say two years later that 'A good scholar will find Aristophanes & Hafiz & Rabelais full of American history'. It is likely that in these last decades of the so-called American century he would as easily find 'America' emerging on the European as on the North American continent.

CHRONOLOGY

1803   Ralph Waldo Emerson is born in Boston on Election Day (25 May), fourth child of William and Ruth Haskins Emerson.

1807   John Clarke Emerson, Ralph Waldo's elder brother, dies of tuberculosis (26 April).

1808   In November, the Emersons move into the new parsonage of the First Church, Boston, across from the Governor's Mansion.

1811   William Emerson dies on 12 May (probably of tuberculosis) in Portland, Maine, to which he had retreated a month earlier on the advice of his doctor. His sister Mary Moody Emerson, visiting the parsonage at the time of his death, stays for several months to help Ruth with the children; five have survived childhood—Ralph Waldo and four brothers.

1812   Ralph Waldo enters the Boston Public Latin School in the autumn. Studies Latin and Greek. Supplements the classical curriculum with courses in mathematics and writing at a nearby grammar school. Begins writing poetry.

1814   Mary Moody Emerson returns to Boston to help her sister-in-law manage the family. Her strong character, and strict religious temperament, with its tincture of Calvinism, will have a marked influence on her nephew Ralph Waldo, as will her writing style—idiosyncratic, often sarcastic and allusive. In November, the Emersons move into the 'Old Manse' at Concord.

1815   The Emersons move back to Boston in the spring. Ralph Waldo borrows books from the Atheneum and from friends. Reads Johnson's *Lives of the Poets*; poetry by Donne, Cowley, and others. Continues writing verse. Autumn, re-enters Boston Public Latin School with his brother Edward. Studies French at a private school.

1817   Sees President Madison speak at Boston Common (2 July). Admitted to Harvard in September, the youngest member of the class of 1821. To meet expenses, Ralph Waldo serves as an orderly to Harvard's President John Kirkland, and as a waiter.

1818   Tutors during intercessions to pay costs. Studies standard curriculum of
–19   Latin, Greek, English, History, and Rhetoric, supplemented on his own with readings in Shakespeare, Montaigne, Swift, Addison, Byron—all too 'modern' to be taught at Harvard. Decides to go by his middle name, 'Waldo'.

1820   Begins keeping a journal (25 January), which he calls 'The Wide World'. The second entry reads: 'I do hereby nominate and appoint "Imagination" the generalissimo and chief marshall of all the luckless ragamuffin Ideas which may be collected & imprisoned hereafter in these pages.' In April, delivers the poem 'Improvement' to the Pythologian

Club at Harvard: 'Ages unborn must see the muses rear / The throne of universal empire here.' Wins second prize in the Bowdoin contest for his essay on 'The Character of Socrates'.

1821   Graduates from Harvard on 21 July, thirtieth in a class of fifty-nine. Wins second prize for his Bowdoin essay on 'The Present State of Ethical Philosophy'. Takes a position teaching at his brother William's school for young ladies in Boston.

1822   November–December issue of *The Christian Disciple*, a Unitarian review, publishes Waldo's essay on religion in the Middle Ages. Continues to teach.

1823   In December, William sails for Germany to study theology and the 'higher criticism' of the Bible at the University of Gottingen. Waldo conducts the school alone in his absence.

1824   In April, writes in journal: 'In a month I shall be *legally* a man. And I deliberately dedicate my time, my talents, & my hopes to the Church.' Closes school in December. Prepares to enter Harvard Divinity School in the spring semester.

1825   In February, moves into Divinity Hall, Harvard. Eye trouble and 'rheumatism' interrupt his studies. Resumes teaching in Chelmsford, Massachusetts. In October, William returns from Germany, and, beset by religious doubts, decides against a career in the ministry. Edward sails for Europe to recover failing health.

1826   In January–March, teaches at Roxbury until 'rheumatism' confines him to his chamber. William and Edward (now back from Europe) study law, the former with a Wall Street firm, the latter with Daniel Webster's firm. In October, Waldo is licensed to preach by the Middlesex Association of Unitarian Ministers. Preaches his first sermon, on the text 'Pray Without Ceasing'. Suffers from lung trouble and travels to Charleston, South Carolina, to improve his health.

1827   Sails to St Augustine, Florida, in January for a warmer climate, and soon begins to feel stronger. Meets Achille Murat, a nephew of Napoleon and a confirmed atheist. Works on unfinished sermons he began in Charleston on the crucifixion and the atonement. Returns to Charleston in spring. Records in journal on 17 April: 'There is a pleasure in the thought that the particular tone of my mind at this moment may be new in the Universe; that the emotions of this hour may be peculiar & unexampled in the whole eternity of moral being.' Sails for Boston, where he preaches at the First Church in the pulpit once occupied by his father. Preaches in a number of New England towns. Meets Ellen Tucker in December.

1828   Edward returns to Concord suffering from fits of delusion. In July, Waldo is asked to preach temporarily at the Second Church, Boston, while the regular minister recovers his health. Becomes engaged to Ellen Tucker in December.

1829   On 11 March, Waldo is ordained minister of Boston's Second Church at a yearly salary of $1,200. Marries Ellen in September.

1830   Ellen suffers symptoms of tuberculosis, which had claimed the lives of several members of her family. In March, Waldo, Ellen, and her sister Margaret travel to Philadelphia for the milder climate. After Ellen shows signs of recovery, Waldo returns to Boston to resume his duties at the Second Church. Ellen returns in May, and the couple move into a home in Brookline, with Waldo's mother. In December, Edward, again suffering from lung trouble, sails for Puerto Rico.

1831 Ellen dies of tuberculosis on 8 February, at age 19. Waldo writes to his aunt: 'My angel is gone to heaven this morning & I am alone in the world & strangely happy. Her lungs shall no more be torn nor her head scalded by her blood nor her whole life suffer from the warfare between the force & delicacy of her soul & the weakness of her frame.' He walks to her tomb every morning.

1832 Waldo is uneasy with his performance as minister. He writes in his journal in January: 'It is the best part of the man, I sometimes think, that revolts most against his being the minister. His good revolts from official goodness.' In June, Waldo writes to the Proprietors of the Second Church requesting that he be permitted to discontinue the communion service. He is denied, and on 9 September he delivers the sermon 'The Lord's Supper', in which he announces to his congregation his resignation. Weakened by stress, he sails for Europe on Christmas Day.

1833 Sails into St Paul's Bay, Malta, in February. Travels north through Italy. Attends the Pope's Easter service in Rome. Continues to enjoy improved health. Meets Walter Savage Landor in Florence. Spends June in Paris where he visits the Jardin des Plantes, and sails to England in July. Travelling through England, meets J. S. Mill, Coleridge, Wordsworth. Meets Carlyle in Scotland, beginning lifelong friendship. Takes his first train trip, from Manchester to Liverpool. Sails for New York on 4 September. Preaches at the Second Church and to congregations in a number of New England towns. Lectures on 'The Uses of Natural History' in Boston in November.

1834 Continues itinerant preaching. Begins correspondence with Carlyle. In May, receives the first half ($11,600) of his inheritance from Ellen's estate. Edward Emerson dies in Puerto Rico in October. Waldo moves with his mother to the family home in Concord.

1835 In January, proposes by letter to Lidian Jackson of Plymouth. Lectures on 'Biography' in Boston, devoting an evening each to Michelangelo, Luther, Milton, Fox, Burke. In July, buys a house in Concord where he plans to settle with Lidian, whom he marries on 14 September. Delivers the address on Concord history for the town's bicentennial. Begins friendship with Bronson Alcott. Lectures in November on 'English Literature'.

1836 Waldo's younger brother Charles dies of tuberculosis in May. Waldo begins friendship with Margaret Fuller in July. In September, *Nature* is published in Boston by James Munroe & Co. 'The Transcendental Club', as it was later known, begins informal meetings. Waldo oversees American publication of *Sartor Resartus* at his own expense. Waldo Jr. is born on 30 October. Winter lecture series on 'The Philosophy of History'.

1837   Waldo's 'Concord Hymn' is sung at the unveiling of monument for rev-
        olutionary soldiers. Receives second half of his inheritance from Ellen's
        estate, bringing his total inheritance to $23,000; this assures him of an
        annual income of $1,200. Delivers 'American Scholar' at Harvard
        before Phi Beta Kappa Society. Begins to feel his obligations to the pul-
        pit a burden; prefers the freedom of the lectern. Begins winter lecture
        series on 'Human Culture'.

1838   In February, asks to be relieved of his duties at the East Lexington
        Church, where he had been preaching regularly since settling in Con-
        cord. Becomes a great friend of Thoreau, with whom he shares his
        walks. In May, writes a letter to President Van Buren protesting at the
        forced relocation of the Cherokee Indians. On 15 July delivers his highly
        controversial address before the Harvard Divinity School. Emerson will
        not be invited back to Harvard for some thirty years.

1839   Daughter Ellen Tucker Emerson born, 24 February. Her father writes:
        'I can hardly ask more for thee, my babe, than that name implies. Be that
        vision & remain with us, & after us.' In winter, plans with Fuller and
        others the journal that is to become *The Dial*. Begins winter lecture
        series on 'The Present Age'.

1840   The first number of *The Dial* appears on 1 July, edited by Margaret
        Fuller. Emerson will contribute to the journal regularly. Declines invi-
        tation to join the Brook Farm experiment.

1841   *Essays* is published in March. (He had considered calling it *Forest
        Essays*.) One reviewer writes that its doctrines of self-reliance and intui-
        tion, 'if acted upon, would overthrow society, and resolve the world into
        chaos'. The book is well received in London and Paris. In spring Thor-
        eau joins the Concord household, where he will remain for two years, on
        the terms that he is 'to have his board &tc. for what labor he chooses to
        do'. Daughter Edith born on 22 November.

1842   Waldo Jr. contracts scarlet fever and dies on 27 January. His father is
        devastated, writes a day later: 'Sorrow makes us all children again . . .
        The wisest knows nothing.' Lecturing in New York, meets Henry James,
        Sr. In July, succeeds Margaret Fuller as editor of *The Dial*. Hawthorne
        and his bride Sophia Peabody move into the 'Old Manse' in Concord.

1843   Intensive winter lecture series takes him to Baltimore, Philadelphia,
        New York, Brooklyn, Newark. In Washington, hears a speech by John
        C. Calhoun, the US Senator from South Carolina who had become the
        principal theorist of state rights, and spokesman for the Southern inter-
        ests. Completes a translation of Dante's *Vita Nuova*.

1844   Second son, Edward Waldo, born on 10 July. Last issue of *The Dial*,
        long financially insolvent, appears in April. Emerson buys land on the
        north shore of Walden Pond in September. Opposes the United States'
        annexation of Texas, delivers an address on emancipation in the West
        Indies. *Essays: Second Series* published in October.

1845   Enthusiastically reads an English translation of the *Bhagavadgita*. Thor-
        eau moves into his cabin on Emerson's Walden Pond property on
        Fourth of July. Emerson refuses to lecture at the New Bedford Lyceum

because they exclude blacks from membership. In December, begins a lecture course in Boston on 'Representative Men'.

1846   *Poems* published by James Munroe & Co. in December, and warmly received.

1847–8   Invited to lecture in England, Emerson sails for Liverpool in October. Sees Carlyle, Harriet Martineau, Dickens, Tennyson. Lectures in the winter from the course on 'Representative Men', and other topics, including 'Natural Aristocracy'. Sails for France in May. In Paris during the thwarted coup of 15 May. Meets Alexis de Tocqueville. Returns to England in June and lectures in London on 'The Mind and Manners of the Nineteenth Century'. Dines with Chopin, meets Mary Ann Evans (George Eliot). Returns to Boston in July.

1849   Lectures in winter, drawing on his experiences in England. Spring lecture series on 'Laws of the Intellect'. *Nature; Addresses, and Lectures* published in September.

1850   *Representative Men* published in January. Winter–spring lecture series takes him as far west as Cincinatti. Margaret Fuller Ossoli dies in September in a shipwreck off Fire Island Beach. Emerson observes, 'I have lost in her my audience.' He lectures in winter on 'The Conduct of Life'.

1851   In May, addresses the people of Concord in opposition to the Fugitive Slave Law. Speaks in various places for anti-slavery candidates of the Free-Soil Party.

1852   Co-editor of *Memoirs of Margaret Fuller Ossoli*. Lectures in winter in Montreal, Maine, St Louis, Philadelphia, and other cities.

1853   Ruth Haskins Emerson, his mother, dies in November at age 84.

1854   Speaks in New York City against the Fugitive Slave Law. On Fourth of July the Emersons drape the gates of their home in black to protest against the Kansas-Nebraska Bill, which annulled the Missouri Compromise, thus imperilling anti-slavery settlers.

1855   Continues anti-slavery addresses in New York, Philadelphia, and Boston. Speaks before the Woman's Rights Convention in Boston. Reads and much admires *Leaves of Grass*. He writes to Whitman, 'I greet you at the beginning of a great career.'

1856   Attends a June meeting for the relief of Kansas settlers menaced by pro-slavery agitators from Missouri. *English Traits* published in August. 3,000 copies sold in a month. Lectures take him through New England and as far west as Illinois. Additional printings of 1,000 copies of both series of the *Essays* prepared in Boston; *Poems* reprinted.

1857   Hears John Brown speak at Town Hall in February, and records in his journal that he 'gave a good account of himself'. Has remains of his son and mother removed to Sleepy Hollow Cemetery.

1858   Thinking of the 'cowardly' politics of Massachusetts, he writes in his journal: 'Why do we not say, We are abolitionists of the most absolute abolition, as every man that is a man must be?' Spends two weeks in August in the Adirondacks with Aggasiz, Oliver Wendell Holmes, and others.

1859   His mentally retarded brother Bulkeley dies on 27 May at age 52. Emerson is disturbed at news of the capture, trial, and execution of John Brown after his raid on the US arsenal at Harper's Ferry, Virginia. Writes in his journal: 'It is the old mistake of the slaveholder to impute the resistance . . . to some John Brown whom he has captured, and to make a personal affair of it.' He speaks at meetings for the relief of Brown's family in November and January.

1860   Lecture tour through Buffalo, Detroit, Chicago, Milwaukee, and other cities. Meets Whitman in Boston in March, and walks with him on the Common, advising him to tone down the poems he planned to insert in the next edition of *Leaves of Grass* (the 'Children of Adam' collection). Meets W. D. Howells in Concord in August. Considers Lincoln's election 'the pronunciation of the masses of America against slavery'. *Conduct of Life* published in December.

1861   Inspired by Northern unity in the wake of Fort Sumter. Writes in his journal: 'The men in search of a party, parties in search of a principle, interests and dispositions that could not fuse for want of some base,—all joyfully unite in this greatest Northern party, as the basis of Freedom. What a healthy tone exists!' Boston lecture series in April.

1862   Writes in the *Journals* for January: '*Old Age*. As we live longer, it looks as if our company were picked out to die first, and we live on in a lessening minority.' Lectures later in the same month at the Smithsonian Institution. Meets Secretary of State Seward, Senator Sumner, and Lincoln. Thoreau dies of tuberculosis 6 May. At his funeral, Emerson delivers the address 'Thoreau', later published in *Atlantic Monthly*. Publishes an article praising the Emancipation Proclamation, which has renewed his confidence in Lincoln.

1863   Aunt Mary Moody Emerson dies on 1 May, age 89. Emerson is invited in May to serve on the Board of Visitors to West Point, whose task is to review the standards of the Academy.

1864   Hawthorne dies 19 May. Emerson attends the funeral. Elected Fellow of the American Academy of Arts and Sciences. Lectures on 'American Life' in Boston and other New England towns.

1865   Writes in the *Journals* of Lee's surrender: ''Tis for the best that the rebels have been pounded instead of negociated [*sic*] into peace. They must remember it, and their inveterate brag will be humbled, if not cured.' Addresses citizens of Concord on 19 April on the death of Lincoln. Daughter Edith marries William Forbes in October.

1866   Winter–spring lecture series on 'Philosophy for the People'. Ralph Emerson Forbes, Emerson's first grandchild, born 11 July. Emerson receives honorary degree of Doctor of Law from Harvard in July.

1867   Busiest lecture year to date. Speaks in nine western states through March. *May-Day and Other Pieces* published in April. Delivers Phi Beta Kappa address at Harvard commencement—his first invitation to speak

at the University since the 1838 'Divinity School' address. Elected
Overseer of Harvard College.

1868   Brother William dies in New York City on 13 September. Emerson lec-
        tures in the autumn on 'Art', 'Poetry and Criticism', 'Historic Notes of
        Life and Letters in New England', 'Leasts and Mosts', 'Hospitality,
        Homes', 'Greatness'.

1869   Gives informal spring class at Harvard on Chaucer, Shakespeare, Jon-
        son, Bacon, and other English writers.

1870   *Society and Solitude* published in March. In April–May, delivers series of
        sixteen lectures in Harvard's Philosophy Department. Prepares intro-
        duction to an edition of Plutarch's *Morals*, long one of his favourite
        books.

1871   Repeats lecture series at Harvard Philosophy Department, but fatigue
        brings it to an early close. Embarks with family and friends on a train trip
        to California. Returns to Concord in May, and meets Bret Harte.

1872   Declining health and failing memory make spring lecture series diffi-
        cult. Fire damages Concord house in July. Friends finance a trip to Eur-
        ope, where Emerson hopes to recover his health. Sails with Ellen in late
        October for Liverpool. Sees Carlyle for the last time. Meets Ruskin and
        Browning. In Paris, Emerson is taken through the Louvre by Henry
        James, Jr. Sails to Egypt in December.

1873   Enjoys improved health. Returns to Paris in March, to London in April.
        Lands in Boston on 27 May, greeted with cheers by a large assembly
        and brass band.

1874   Nominated for position of Lord Rector, University of Glasgow, but Dis-
        raeli is elected instead. In December, publishes *Parnassus*, an anthology
        of his favourite poetry, which includes neither Poe nor Whitman.

1875   Journal entries dwindle and cease. Works on *Letters and Social Aims*
        (with assistance from Ellen and James Elliot Cabot), which is published
        in December. Speaks in April at the dedication ceremony of the Daniel
        C. French 'minute-man' statue in Concord.

1876   Poet Emma Lazarus accepts the Emersons' invitation to visit the Con-
        cord house in August. The household delights in her company.

1882   Emerson dies of pneumonia on 27 April, in Concord.

NOTE ON THE TEXT

EMERSON carefully prepared and corrected each volume of his work as it was published; revision in editions after the first is for the most part rare. For this reason, texts reprinted in this selection are generally the first editions. Exceptions are the 1849 edition of *Nature; Addresses, and Lectures* and the 1847 or second edition of *Essays: First Series*—both extensively revised. *Nature*, Emerson's first book, was published in 1836. Each of the addresses later collected with it was published in pamphlet form in the year in which it was delivered (for these dates see the chronology). Joel Porte, editor of *Emerson: Essays and Lectures* in the Library of America series, writes: 'Although other revised editions [of *Nature; Addresses, and Lectures*] appeared in later years, these were neither as carefully nor as thoroughly reworked. The late editions, moreover, represent an older, more conservative Emerson, while the 1849 edition . . . presents Emerson at the height of his creative powers.' This selection reprints the Library of America text of the 1849 edition.

Essays: First Series was first published under the title *Essays* in 1841. By 1845, the 1,500 copies printed for that edition were sold, and a number of unlicensed English editions had appeared. Emerson agreed with his publisher James Munroe that a new edition should be issued, and he began to prepare it. In 1847 a revised *Essays: First Series* appeared, so titled to distinguish it from the second volume of essays which Emerson published in 1844. Porte writes: 'Three later editions were supervised by Emerson but none was extensively revised, and despite the existence of these newer editions, printings of the 1847 edition . . . continued to appear.' The present selection uses the Library of America text of the 1847 edition. The selections from *Essays: Second Series* (1844), *Representative Men* (1850), and *Conduct of Life* (1860) included in this volume are the Library of America texts of the first editions.

Emerson delivered the sermon 'The Lord's Supper' on 19 September 1832; it first appeared in print forty-four years later in Octavius Brooks Frothingham's *Transcendentalism in New England* (1876). It was reprinted posthumously in the *Miscellanies* (1884) volume of the 'Riverside' edition, though with a number of non-authorial emendations. The text reprinted here is the Library of America text of the 1876 edition. Emerson delivered the address 'Thoreau' at a memorial service for Henry David Thoreau in May 1862. He published it in the *Atlantic Monthly* in August of the same year, and that is the text printed here. Emerson himself never collected the essay in a volume.

The texts chosen for this selection of 'Society and Solitude', 'Quotation and Originality', and 'Poetry and Imagination' are those of their first appearance in book form: for the first, *Society and Solitude* (Boston, 1870); for the latter two, *Letters and Social Aims* (Boston, 1876). Likewise, the poems here reprinted are taken from their first appearance in book form in the following volumes: *Poems* (1847), *May-Day and Other Pieces* (1867), *Selected Poems* (1876), all supervised by Emerson; *Poems* (1884)—in the 'Riverside' edition, edited by James E. Cabot—and *Poems* (1904), in the 'Centenary' edition, edited by Edward W. Emerson. The volume in which each poem first appeared is recorded below in the notes to the poetry.

The degree sign (°) indicates a note at the end of the book. More general headnotes are not cued.

NATURE; ADDRESSES, AND LECTURES (1849)

NATURE

A subtle chain of countless rings
The next unto the farthest brings;
The eye reads omens where it goes,
And speaks all languages the rose;
And, striving to be man, the worm
Mounts through all the spires of form.

Introduction

OUR age is retrospective. It builds the sepulchres of the fathers. It writes biographies, histories, and criticism. The foregoing generations beheld God and nature face to face; we, through their eyes. Why should not we also enjoy an original relation to the universe? Why should not we have a poetry and philosophy of insight and not of tradition, and a religion by revelation to us, and not the history of theirs? Embosomed for a season in nature, whose floods of life stream around and through us, and invite us by the powers they supply, to action proportioned to nature, why should we grope among the dry bones of the past, or put the living generation into masquerade out of its faded wardrobe? The sun shines to-day also. There is more wool and flax in the fields. There are new lands, new men, new thoughts. Let us demand our own works and laws and worship.

Undoubtedly we have no questions to ask which are unanswerable. We must trust the perfection of the creation so far, as to believe that whatever curiosity the order of things has awakened in our minds, the order of things can satisfy. Every man's condition is a solution in hieroglyphic to those inquiries he would put. He acts it as life, before he apprehends it as truth. In like manner, nature is already, in its forms and tendencies, describing its own design. Let us interrogate the great apparition, that shines so peacefully around us. Let us inquire, to what end is nature?

All science has one aim, namely, to find a theory of nature. We have theories of races and of functions, but scarcely yet a remote approach to an idea of creation. We are now so far from the road to truth, that religious teachers dispute and hate each other, and speculative men are esteemed unsound and frivolous. But to a sound judgment, the most abstract truth is the most practical. Whenever a true theory appears, it will be its own evidence. Its test is, that it will explain all phenomena. Now many are thought not only unexplained but inexplicable; as language, sleep, madness, dreams, beasts, sex.

Philosophically considered, the universe is composed of Nature and the Soul. Strictly speaking, therefore, all that is separate from us, all which Philosophy distinguishes as the NOT ME, that is, both nature and art, all other men and my own body, must be ranked under this name, NATURE. In enumerating the values of nature and casting up their sum, I shall use the word in both senses;—in its common and in its philosophical import. In inquiries so general as our present one, the inaccuracy is not material; no confusion of thought will occur. *Nature*, in the common sense, refers to essences unchanged by man; space, the air, the river, the leaf. *Art* is applied to the mixture of his will with the same things, as in a house, a canal, a statue, a picture. But his operations taken together are so insignificant, a little chipping, baking, patching, and washing, that in an impression so grand as that of the world on the human mind, they do not vary the result.

Chapter I

NATURE

To go into solitude, a man needs to retire as much from his chamber as from society. I am not solitary whilst I read and write, though nobody is with me. But if a man would be alone, let him look at the stars. The rays that come from those heavenly worlds, will separate between him and what he touches. One might think the atmosphere was made transparent with this design, to give man, in the heavenly bodies, the perpetual presence of the sublime. Seen in the streets of cities, how great they are! If the stars should appear one night in a thousand years, how would men believe and adore; and preserve for many generations the remembrance of the city of God which had been shown! But every night come out these envoys of beauty, and light the universe with their admonishing smile.

The stars awaken a certain reverence, because though always present, they are inaccessible; but all natural objects make a kindred impression, when the mind is open to their influence. Nature never wears a mean appearance. Neither does the wisest man extort her secret, and lose his curiosity by finding out all her perfection. Nature never became a toy to a wise spirit. The flowers, the animals, the mountains, reflected the wisdom of his best hour, as much as they had delighted the simplicity of his childhood.

When we speak of nature in this manner, we have a distinct but most poetical sense in the mind. We mean the integrity of impression made by manifold natural objects. It is this which distinguishes the stick of timber of the wood-cutter, from the tree of the poet. The charming landscape which I saw this morning, is indubitably made up of some twenty or thirty farms. Miller owns this field, Locke that, and Manning the woodland beyond. But none of them owns the landscape. There is a property in the horizon which no man has but he whose eye can integrate all the parts, that is, the poet. This is the best part of these men's farms, yet to this their warranty-deeds give no title.

To speak truly, few adult persons can see nature. Most persons do not see the sun. At least they have a very superficial seeing. The sun illuminates only the eye of the man, but shines into the eye and the heart of the child. The lover of nature is he whose inward and outward senses are still truly adjusted to each other; who has retained the spirit of infancy even into the era of manhood. His intercourse with heaven and earth, becomes part of his daily food. In the presence of nature, a wild delight runs through the man, in spite of real sorrows. Nature says,—he is my creature, and maugre all his impertinent griefs, he shall be glad with me. Not the sun or the summer alone, but every hour and season yields its tribute of delight; for every hour and change corresponds to and authorizes a different state of the mind, from breathless noon to grimmest midnight. Nature is a setting that fits equally well a comic or a mourning piece. In good health, the air is a cordial of incredible virtue. Crossing a bare common, in snow puddles, at twilight, under a clouded sky, without having in my thoughts any occurrence of special good fortune, I have enjoyed a perfect exhilaration. I am glad to the brink of fear. In the woods too, a man casts off his years, as the snake his slough, and at what period soever of life, is always a child. In the woods, is perpetual youth. Within these plantations of God, a decorum and sanctity reign, a perennial festival is dressed, and the guest sees not how he should tire of them in a thousand years. In the woods, we return to reason and faith. There I feel that nothing can befall me in life,—no disgrace, no calamity, (leaving me my eyes,) which nature cannot repair. Standing on the bare ground,—my head bathed by the blithe air, and uplifted into infinite space,—all mean egotism vanishes. I become a transparent eye-ball; I am nothing; I see all; the currents of the Universal Being circulate through me; I am part or particle of God. The name of the nearest friend sounds then foreign and accidental: to be brothers, to be acquaintances,—master or servant, is then a trifle and a disturbance. I am the lover of uncontained and immortal beauty. In the wilderness, I find something more dear and connate than in streets or villages. In the tranquil landscape, and especially in the distant line of the horizon, man beholds somewhat as beautiful as his own nature.

The greatest delight which the fields and woods minister, is the suggestion of an occult relation between man and the vegetable. I am not alone and unacknowledged. They nod to me, and I to them. The waving of the boughs in the storm, is new to me and old. It takes me by surprise, and yet is not unknown. Its effect is like that of a higher thought or a better emotion coming over me, when I deemed I was thinking justly or doing right.

Yet it is certain that the power to produce this delight, does not reside in nature, but in man, or in a harmony of both. It is necessary to use these pleasures with great temperance. For, nature is not always tricked in holiday attire, but the same scene which yesterday breathed perfume and glittered as for the frolic of the nymphs, is overspread with melancholy today. Nature always wears the colors of the spirit. To a man laboring under calamity, the heat of his own fire hath sadness in it. Then, there is a kind of contempt of the landscape felt by him who has just lost by death a dear friend. The sky is less grand as it shuts down over less worth in the population.

Chapter II

COMMODITY

WHOEVER considers the final cause of the world, will discern a multitude of uses that enter as parts into that result. They all admit of being thrown into one of the following classes; Commodity; Beauty; Language; and Discipline.

Under the general name of Commodity, I rank all those advantages which our senses owe to nature. This, of course, is a benefit which is temporary and mediate, not ultimate, like its service to the soul. Yet although low, it is perfect in its kind, and is the only use of nature which all men apprehend. The misery of man appears like childish petulance, when we explore the steady and prodigal provision that has been made for his support and delight on this green ball which floats him through the heavens. What angels invented these splendid ornaments, these rich conveniences, this ocean of air above, this ocean of water beneath, this firmament of earth between? this zodiac of lights, this tent of dropping clouds, this striped coat of climates, this fourfold year? Beasts, fire, water, stones, and corn serve him. The field is at once his floor, his work-yard, his play-ground, his garden, and his bed.

> 'More servants wait on man
> Than he'll take notice of.'°——

Nature, in its ministry to man, is not only the material, but is also the process and the result. All the parts incessantly work into each other's hands for the profit of man. The wind sows the seed; the sun evaporates the sea; the wind blows the vapor to the field; the ice, on the other side of the planet, condenses rain on this; the rain feeds the plant; the plant feeds the animal; and thus the endless circulations of the divine charity nourish man.

The useful arts are reproductions or new combinations by the wit of man, of the same natural benefactors. He no longer waits for favoring gales, but by means of steam, he realizes the fable of Æolus's bag,° and carries the two and thirty winds in the boiler of his boat. To diminish friction, he paves the road with iron bars, and, mounting a coach with a ship-load of men, animals, and merchandise behind him, he darts through the country, from town to town, like an eagle or a swallow through the air. By the aggregate of these aids, how is the face of the world changed, from the era of Noah to that of Napoleon! The private poor man hath cities, ships, canals, bridges, built for him. He goes to the post-office, and the human race run on his errands; to the book-shop, and the human race read and write of all that happens, for him; to the court-house, and nations repair his wrongs. He sets his house upon the road, and the human race go forth every morning, and shovel out the snow, and cut a path for him.

But there is no need of specifying particulars in this class of uses. The catalogue is endless, and the examples so obvious, that I shall leave them to the reader's reflection, with the general remark, that this mercenary benefit is one which has respect to a farther good. A man is fed, not that he may be fed, but that he may work.

Chapter III

BEAUTY

A NOBLER want of man is served by nature, namely, the love of Beauty.

The ancient Greeks called the world κόσμος, beauty. Such is the constitution of all things, or such the plastic power of the human eye, that the primary forms, as the sky, the mountain, the tree, the animal, give us a delight *in and for themselves*; a pleasure arising from outline, color, motion, and grouping. This seems partly owing to the eye itself. The eye is the best of artists. By the mutual action of its structure and of the laws of light, perspective is produced, which integrates every mass of objects, of what character soever, into a well colored and shaded globe, so that where the particular objects are mean and unaffecting, the landscape which they compose, is round and symmetrical. And as the eye is the best composer, so light is the first of painters. There is no object so foul that intense light will not make beautiful. And the stimulus it affords to the sense, and a sort of infinitude which it hath, like space and time, make all matter gay. Even the corpse has its own beauty. But besides this general grace diffused over nature, almost all the individual forms are agreeable to the eye, as is proved by our endless imitations of some of them, as the acorn, the grape, the pine-cone, the wheat-ear, the egg, the wings and forms of most birds, the lion's claw, the serpent, the butterfly, sea-shells, flames, clouds, buds, leaves, and the forms of many trees, as the palm.

For better consideration, we may distribute the aspects of Beauty in a threefold manner.

1. First, the simple perception of natural forms is a delight. The influence of the forms and actions in nature, is so needful to man, that, in its lowest functions, it seems to lie on the confines of commodity and beauty. To the body and mind which have been cramped by noxious work or company, nature is medicinal and restores their tone. The tradesman, the attorney comes out of the din and craft of the street, and sees the sky and the woods, and is a man again. In their eternal calm, he finds himself. The health of the eye seems to demand a horizon. We are never tired, so long as we can see far enough.

But in other hours, Nature satisfies by its loveliness, and without any mixture of corporeal benefit. I see the spectacle of morning from the hill-top over against my house, from day-break to sun-rise, with emotions which an angel might share. The long slender bars of cloud float like fishes in the sea of crimson light. From the earth, as a shore, I look out into that silent sea. I seem to partake its rapid transformations: the active enchantment reaches my dust, and I dilate and conspire with the morning wind. How does Nature deify us with a few and cheap elements! Give me health and a day, and I will make the pomp of emperors ridiculous. The dawn is my Assyria; the sun-set and moon-rise my Paphos, and unimaginable realms of faerie; broad noon shall be my England of the senses and the understanding; the night shall be my Germany of mystic philosophy and dreams.

Not less excellent, except for our less susceptibility in the afternoon, was the charm, last evening, of a January sunset. The western clouds divided and subdivided themselves into pink flakes modulated with tints of unspeakable softness; and the air had so much life and sweetness, that it was a pain to come within doors. What was it that nature would say? Was there no meaning in the live repose of the valley behind the mill, and which Homer or Shakspeare could not re-form for me in words? The leafless trees become spires of flame in the sunset, with the blue east for their back-ground, and the stars of the dead calices of flowers, and every withered stem and stubble rimed with frost, contribute something to the mute music.

The inhabitants of cities suppose that the country landscape is pleasant only half the year. I please myself with the graces of the winter scenery, and believe that we are as much touched by it as by the genial influences of summer. To the attentive eye, each moment of the year has its own beauty, and in the same field, it beholds, every hour, a picture which was never seen before, and which shall never be seen again. The heavens change every moment, and reflect their glory or gloom on the plains beneath. The state of the crop in the surrounding farms alters the expression of the earth from week to week. The succession of native plants in the pastures and roadsides, which makes the silent clock by which time tells the summer hours, will make even the divisions of the day sensible to a keen observer. The tribes of birds and insects, like the plants punctual to their time, follow each other, and the year has room for all. By water-courses, the variety is greater. In July, the blue pontederia or pickerel-weed blooms in large beds in the shallow parts of our pleasant river, and swarms with yellow butterflies in continual motion. Art cannot rival this pomp of purple and gold. Indeed the river is a perpetual gala, and boasts each month a new ornament.

But this beauty of Nature which is seen and felt as beauty, is the least part. The shows of day, the dewy morning, the rainbow, mountains, orchards in blossom, stars, moonlight, shadows in still water, and the like, if too eagerly hunted, become shows merely, and mock us with their unreality. Go out of the house to see the moon, and 't is mere tinsel; it will not please as when its light shines upon your necessary journey. The beauty that shimmers in the yellow afternoons of October, who ever could clutch it? Go forth to find it, and it is gone: 't is only a mirage as you look from the windows of diligence.

2. The presence of a higher, namely, of the spiritual element is essential to its perfection. The high and divine beauty which can be loved without effeminacy, is that which is found in combination with the human will. Beauty is the mark God sets upon virtue. Every natural action is graceful. Every heroic act is also decent, and causes the place and the bystanders to shine. We are taught by great actions that the universe is the property of every individual in it. Every rational creature has all nature for his dowry and estate. It is his, if he will. He may divest himself of it; he may creep into a corner, and abdicate his kingdom, as most men do, but he is entitled to the world by his constitution. In proportion to the energy of his thought and will, he takes up the world into himself. 'All those things for which men plough, build, or sail, obey virtue;' said Sallust. 'The winds and waves,' said Gibbon, 'are always on the side of the ablest navigators.' So are the sun and moon and all the stars of heaven. When a noble act is done,—perchance in a scene of great natural beauty; when Leonidas° and his three hundred martyrs consume one day in dying, and the sun and moon come each and look at them once in the steep defile of Thermopylæ; when Arnold Winkel-

ried,° in the high Alps, under the shadow of the avalanche, gathers in his side a sheaf of Austrian spears to break the line for his comrades; are not these heroes entitled to add the beauty of the scene to the beauty of the deed? When the bark of Columbus nears the shore of America;—before it, the beach lined with savages, fleeing out of all their huts of cane; the sea behind; and the purple mountains of the Indian Archipelago around, can we separate the man from the living picture? Does not the New World clothe his form with her palm-groves and savannahs as fit drapery? Ever does natural beauty steal in like air, and envelope great actions. When Sir Harry Vane° was dragged up the Tower-hill, sitting on a sled, to suffer death, as the champion of the English laws, one of the multitude cried out to him, 'You never sate on so glorious a seat.' Charles II., to intimidate the citizens of London, caused the patriot Lord Russel° to be drawn in an open coach, through the principal streets of the city, on his way to the scaffold. 'But,' his biographer says, 'the multitude imagined they saw liberty and virtue sitting by his side.' In private places, among sordid objects, an act of truth or heroism seems at once to draw to itself the sky as its temple, the sun as its candle. Nature stretcheth out her arms to embrace man, only let his thoughts be of equal greatness. Willingly does she follow his steps with the rose and the violet, and bend her lines of grandeur and grace to the decoration of her darling child. Only let his thoughts be of equal scope, and the frame will suit the picture. A virtuous man is in unison with her works, and makes the central figure of the visible sphere. Homer, Pindar, Socrates, Phocion, associate themselves fitly in our memory with the geography and climate of Greece. The visible heavens and earth sympathize with Jesus. And in common life, whosoever has seen a person of powerful character and happy genius, will have remarked how easily he took all things along with him,—the persons, the opinions, and the day, and nature became ancillary to a man.

3. There is still another aspect under which the beauty of the world may be viewed, namely, as it becomes an object of the intellect. Beside the relation of things to virtue, they have a relation to thought. The intellect searches out the absolute order of things as they stand in the mind of God, and without the colors of affection. The intellectual and the active powers seem to succeed each other, and the exclusive activity of the one, generates the exclusive activity of the other. There is something unfriendly in each to the other, but they are like the alternate periods of feeding and working in animals; each prepares and will be followed by the other. Therefore does beauty, which, in relation to actions, as we have seen, comes unsought, and comes because it is

unsought, remain for the apprehension and pursuit of the intellect; and then again, in its turn, of the active power. Nothing divine dies. All good is eternally reproductive. The beauty of nature reforms itself in the mind, and not for barren contemplation, but for new creation.

All men are in some degree impressed by the face of the world; some men even to delight. This love of beauty is Taste. Others have the same love in such excess, that, not content with admiring, they seek to embody it in new forms. The creation of beauty is Art.

The production of a work of art throws a light upon the mystery of humanity. A work of art is an abstract or epitome of the world. It is the result or expression of nature, in miniature. For, although the works of nature are innumerable and all different, the result or the expression of them all is similar and single. Nature is a sea of forms radically alike and even unique. A leaf, a sun-beam, a landscape, the ocean, make an analogous impression on the mind. What is common to them all,—that perfectness and harmony, is beauty. The standard of beauty is the entire circuit of natural forms,—the totality of nature; which the Italians expressed by defining beauty 'il piu nell' uno.'° Nothing is quite beautiful alone: nothing but is beautiful in the whole. A single object is only so far beautiful as it suggests this universal grace. The poet, the painter, the sculptor, the musician, the architect, seek each to concentrate this radiance of the world on one point, and each in his several work to satisfy the love of beauty which stimulates him to produce. Thus is Art, a nature passed through the alembic of man. Thus in art, does nature work through the will of a man filled with the beauty of her first works.

The world thus exists to the soul to satisfy the desire of beauty. This element I call an ultimate end. No reason can be asked or given why the soul seeks beauty. Beauty, in its largest and profoundest sense, is one expression for the universe. God is the all-fair. Truth, and goodness, and beauty, are but different faces of the same All. But beauty in nature is not ultimate. It is the herald of inward and eternal beauty, and is not alone a solid and satisfactory good. It must stand as a part, and not as yet the last or highest expression of the final cause of Nature.

Chapter IV

LANGUAGE

LANGUAGE is a third use which Nature subserves to man.

Nature is the vehicle of thought, and in a simple, double, and three-fold degree.

1. Words are signs of natural facts.
2. Particular natural facts are symbols of particular spiritual facts.
3. Nature is the symbol of spirit.

1. Words are signs of natural facts. The use of natural history is to give us aid in supernatural history: the use of the outer creation, to give us language for the beings and changes of the inward creation. Every word which is used to express a moral or intellectual fact, if traced to its root, is found to be borrowed from some material appearance. *Right* means *straight*; *wrong* means *twisted*. *Spirit* primarily means *wind*; *transgression*, the crossing of a *line*; *supercilious*, the *raising of the eyebrow*. We say the *heart* to express emotion, the *head* to denote thought; and *thought* and *emotion* are words borrowed from sensible things, and now appropriated to spiritual nature. Most of the process by which this transformation is made, is hidden from us in the remote time when language was framed; but the same tendency may be daily observed in children. Children and savages use only nouns or names of things, which they convert into verbs, and apply to analogous mental acts.

2. But this origin of all words that convey a spiritual import,—so conspicuous a fact in the history of language,—is our least debt to nature. It is not words only that are emblematic; it is things which are emblematic. Every natural fact is a symbol of some spiritual fact. Every appearance in nature corresponds to some state of the mind, and that state of the mind can only be described by presenting that natural appearance as its picture. An enraged man is a lion, a cunning man is a fox, a firm man is a rock, a learned man is a torch. A lamb is innocence; a snake is subtle spite; flowers express to us the delicate affections. Light and darkness are our familiar expression for knowledge and ignorance; and heat for love. Visible distance behind and before us, is respectively our image of memory and hope.

Who looks upon a river in a meditative hour, and is not reminded of the flux of all things? Throw a stone into the stream, and the circles that propagate themselves are the beautiful type of all influence. Man is conscious of a universal soul within or behind his individual life, wherein, as in a firmament, the natures of Justice, Truth, Love, Freedom, arise and shine. This universal soul, he calls Reason: it is not mine, or thine, or his, but we are its; we are its property and men. And the blue sky in which the private earth is buried, the sky with its eternal calm, and full of everlasting orbs, is the type of Reason. That which, intellectually considered, we call Reason, considered in relation to nature, we call Spirit. Spirit is the Creator. Spirit hath life in itself. And man in all ages and countries, embodies it in his language, as the FATHER.

It is easily seen that there is nothing lucky or capricious in these analogies, but that they are constant, and pervade nature. These are not
the dreams of a few poets, here and there, but man is an analogist, and
studies relations in all objects. He is placed in the centre of beings, and
a ray of relation passes from every other being to him. And neither can
man be understood without these objects, nor these objects without
man. All the facts in natural history taken by themselves, have no value,
but are barren, like a single sex. But marry it to human history, and it is
full of life. Whole Floras, all Linnæus' and Buffon's° volumes, are dry
catalogues of facts; but the most trivial of these facts, the habit of a
plant, the organs, or work, or noise of an insect, applied to the illustration of a fact in intellectual philosophy, or, in any way associated to
human nature, affects us in the most lively and agreeable manner. The
seed of a plant,—to what affecting analogies in the nature of man, is
that little fruit made use of, in all discourse, up to the voice of Paul, who
calls the human corpse a seed,—'It is sown a natural body;° it is raised a
spiritual body.' The motion of the earth round its axis, and round the
sun, makes the day, and the year. These are certain amounts of brute
light and heat. But is there no intent of an analogy between man's life
and the seasons? And do the seasons gain no grandeur or pathos from
that analogy? The instincts of the ant are very unimportant, considered
as the ant's; but the moment a ray of relation is seen to extend from it to
man, and the little drudge is seen to be a monitor, a little body with a
mighty heart, then all its habits, even that said to be recently observed,
that it never sleeps, become sublime.

Because of this radical correspondence between visible things and
human thoughts, savages, who have only what is necessary, converse in
figures. As we go back in history, language becomes more picturesque,
until its infancy, when it is all poetry; or all spiritual facts are represented by natural symbols. The same symbols are found to make the
original elements of all languages. It has moreover been observed, that
the idioms of all languages approach each other in passages of the
greatest eloquence and power. And as this is the first language, so is it
the last. This immediate dependence of language upon nature, this
conversion of an outward phenomenon into a type of somewhat in
human life, never loses its power to affect us. It is this which gives that
piquancy to the conversation of a strong-natured farmer or backwoodsman, which all men relish.

A man's power to connect his thought with its proper symbol, and so
to utter it, depends on the simplicity of his character, that is, upon his
love of truth, and his desire to communicate it without loss. The cor-

ruption of man is followed by the corruption of language. When simplicity of character and the sovereignty of ideas is broken up by the prevalence of secondary desires, the desire of riches, of pleasure, of power, and of praise,—and duplicity and falsehood take place of simplicity and truth, the power over nature as an interpreter of the will, is in a degree lost; new imagery ceases to be created, and old words are perverted to stand for things which are not; a paper currency is employed, when there is no bullion in the vaults. In due time, the fraud is manifest, and words lose all power to stimulate the understanding or the affections. Hundreds of writers may be found in every long-civilized nation, who for a short time believe, and make others believe, that they see and utter truths, who do not of themselves clothe one thought in its natural garment, but who feed unconsciously on the language created by the primary writers of the country, those, namely, who hold primarily on nature.

But wise men pierce this rotten diction and fasten words again to visible things; so that picturesque language is at once a commanding certificate that he who employs it, is a man in alliance with truth and God. The moment our discourse rises above the ground line of familiar facts, and is inflamed with passion or exalted by thought, it clothes itself in images. A man conversing in earnest, if he watch his intellectual processes, will find that a material image, more or less luminous, arises in his mind, cotemporaneous with every thought, which furnishes the vestment of the thought. Hence, good writing and brilliant discourse are perpetual allegories. This imagery is spontaneous. It is the blending of experience with the present action of the mind. It is proper creation. It is the working of the Original Cause through the instruments he has already made.

These facts may suggest the advantage which the country-life possesses for a powerful mind, over the artificial and curtailed life of cities. We know more from nature than we can at will communicate. Its light flows into the mind evermore, and we forget its presence. The poet, the orator, bred in the woods, whose senses have been nourished by their fair and appeasing changes, year after year, without design and without heed,—shall not lose their lesson altogether, in the roar of cities or the broil of politics. Long hereafter, amidst agitation and terror in national councils,—in the hour of revolution,—these solemn images shall reappear in their morning lustre, as fit symbols and words of the thoughts which the passing events shall awaken. At the call of a noble sentiment, again the woods wave, the pines murmur, the river rolls and shines, and the cattle low upon the mountains, as he saw and heard them in his infancy. And with these forms, the spells of persuasion, the keys of power are put into his hands.

3. We are thus assisted by natural objects in the expression of particular meanings. But how great a language to convey such pepper-corn informations! Did it need such noble races of creatures, this profusion of forms, this host of orbs in heaven, to furnish man with the dictionary and grammar of his municipal speech? Whilst we use this grand cipher to expedite the affairs of our pot and kettle, we feel that we have not yet put it to its use, neither are able. We are like travellers using the cinders of a volcano to roast their eggs. Whilst we see that it always stands ready to clothe what we would say, we cannot avoid the question, whether the characters are not significant of themselves. Have mountains, and waves, and skies, no significance but what we consciously give them, when we employ them as emblems of our thoughts? The world is emblematic. Parts of speech are metaphors, because the whole of nature is a metaphor of the human mind. The laws of moral nature answer to those of matter as face to face in a glass. 'The visible world and the relation of its parts, is the dial plate of the invisible.'° The axioms of physics translate the laws of ethics. Thus, 'the whole is greater than its part;' 'reaction is equal to action;' 'the smallest weight may be made to lift the greatest, the difference of weight being compensated by time;' and many the like propositions, which have an ethical as well as physical sense. These propositions have a much more extensive and universal sense when applied to human life, than when confined to technical use.

In like manner, the memorable words of history, and the proverbs of nations, consist usually of a natural fact, selected as a picture or parable of a moral truth. Thus; A rolling stone gathers no moss; A bird in the hand is worth two in the bush; A cripple in the right way, will beat a racer in the wrong; Make hay while the sun shines; 'T is hard to carry a full cup even; Vinegar is the son of wine; The last ounce broke the camel's back; Long-lived trees make roots first;—and the like. In their primary sense these are trivial facts, but we repeat them for the value of their analogical import. What is true of proverbs, is true of all fables, parables, and allegories.

This relation between the mind and matter is not fancied by some poet, but stands in the will of God, and so is free to be known by all men. It appears to men, or it does not appear. When in fortunate hours we ponder this miracle, the wise man doubts, if, at all other times, he is not blind and deaf;

——'Can these things be,
And overcome us like a summer's cloud,
Without our special wonder?'°

for the universe becomes transparent, and the light of higher laws than its own, shines through it. It is the standing problem which has exercised the wonder and the study of every fine genius since the world began; from the era of the Egyptians and the Brahmins, to that of Pythagoras, of Plato, of Bacon, of Leibnitz, of Swedenborg. There sits the Sphinx at the road-side, and from age to age, as each prophet comes by, he tries his fortune at reading her riddle. There seems to be a necessity in spirit to manifest itself in material forms; and day and night, river and storm, beast and bird, acid and alkali, preëxist in necessary Ideas in the mind of God, and are what they are by virtue of preceding affections, in the world of spirit. A Fact is the end or last issue of spirit. The visible creation is the terminus or the circumference of the invisible world. 'Material objects,' said a French philosopher,° 'are necessarily kinds of *scoriæ*° of the substantial thoughts of the Creator, which must always preserve an exact relation to their first origin; in other words, visible nature must have a spiritual and moral side.'

This doctrine is abstruse, and though the images of 'garment,' 'scoriæ,'° 'mirror,' &c., may stimulate the fancy, we must summon the aid of subtler and more vital expositors to make it plain. 'Every scripture is to be interpreted by the same spirit which gave it forth,'°—is the fundamental law of criticism. A life in harmony with nature, the love of truth and of virtue, will purge the eyes to understand her text. By degrees we may come to know the primitive sense of the permanent objects of nature, so that the world shall be to us an open book, and every form significant of its hidden life and final cause.

A new interest surprises us, whilst, under the view now suggested, we contemplate the fearful extent and multitude of objects; since 'every object rightly seen, unlocks a new faculty of the soul.'° That which was unconscious truth, becomes, when interpreted and defined in an object, a part of the domain of knowledge,—a new weapon in the magazine of power.

Chapter V

DISCIPLINE

IN view of the significance of nature, we arrive at once at a new fact, that nature is a discipline. This use of the world includes the preceding uses, as parts of itself.

Space, time, society, labor, climate, food, locomotion, the animals, the mechanical forces, give us sincerest lessons, day by day, whose meaning is unlimited. They educate both the Understanding and the Reason. Every property of matter is a school for the understanding,— its solidity or resistance, its inertia, its extension, its figure, its divisibility. The understanding adds, divides, combines, measures, and finds nutriment and room for its activity in this worthy scene. Meantime, Reason transfers all these lessons into its own world of thought, by perceiving the analogy that marries Matter and Mind.

1. Nature is a discipline of the understanding in intellectual truths. Our dealing with sensible objects is a constant exercise in the necessary lessons of difference, of likeness, of order, of being and seeming, of progressive arrangement; of ascent from particular to general; of combination to one end of manifold forces. Proportioned to the importance of the organ to be formed, is the extreme care with which its tuition is provided,—a care pretermitted in no single case. What tedious training, day after day, year after year, never ending, to form the common sense; what continual reproduction of annoyances, inconveniences, dilemmas; what rejoicing over us of little men; what disputing of prices, what reckonings of interest,—and all to form the Hand of the mind;—to instruct us that 'good thoughts are no better than good dreams, unless they be executed!'°

The same good office is performed by Property and its filial systems of debt and credit. Debt, grinding debt, whose iron face the widow, the orphan, and the sons of genius fear and hate;—debt, which consumes so much time, which so cripples and disheartens a great spirit with cares that seem so base, is a preceptor whose lessons cannot be forgone, and is needed most by those who suffer from it most. Moreover, property, which has been well compared to snow,—'if it fall level today, it will be blown into drifts to-morrow,'—is the surface action of internal machinery, like the index on the face of a clock. Whilst now it is the gymnastics of the understanding, it is hiving in the foresight of the spirit, experience in profounder laws.

The whole character and fortune of the individual are affected by the least inequalities in the culture of the understanding; for example, in the perception of differences. Therefore is Space, and therefore Time, that man may know that things are not huddled and lumped, but sundered and individual. A bell and a plough have each their use, and neither can do the office of the other. Water is good to drink, coal to burn, wool to wear; but wool cannot be drunk, nor water spun, nor coal eaten. The wise man shows his wisdom in separation, in gradation, and his scale of creatures and of merits is as wide as nature. The foolish have no range in their scale, but suppose every man is as every other man. What is not good they call the worst, and what is not hateful, they call the best.

In like manner, what good heed, nature forms in us! She pardons no mistakes. Her yea is yea, and her nay, nay.

The first steps in Agriculture, Astronomy, Zoölogy, (those first steps which the farmer, the hunter, and the sailor take,) teach that nature's dice are always loaded; that in her heaps and rubbish are concealed sure and useful results.

How calmly and genially the mind apprehends one after another the laws of physics! What noble emotions dilate the mortal as he enters into the counsels of the creation, and feels by knowledge the privilege to BE! His insight refines him. The beauty of nature shines in his own breast. Man is greater that he can see this, and the universe less, because Time and Space relations vanish as laws are known.

Here again we are impressed and even daunted by the immense Universe to be explored. 'What we know, is a point to what we do not know.'° Open any recent journal of science, and weigh the problems suggested concerning Light, Heat, Electricity, Magnetism, Physiology, Geology, and judge whether the interest of natural science is likely to be soon exhausted.

Passing by many particulars of the discipline of nature, we must not omit to specify two.

The exercise of the Will or the lesson of power is taught in every event. From the child's successive possession of his several senses up to the hour when he saith, 'Thy will be done!' he is learning the secret, that he can reduce under his will, not only particular events, but great classes, nay the whole series of events, and so conform all facts to his character. Nature is thoroughly mediate. It is made to serve. It receives the dominion of man as meekly as the ass on which the Saviour rode. It offers all its kingdoms to man as the raw material which he may mould into what is useful. Man is never weary of working it up. He forges the subtle and delicate air into wise and melodious words, and gives them wing as angels of persuasion and command. One after another, his victorious thought comes up with and reduces all things, until the world becomes, at last, only a realized will,—the double of the man.

2. Sensible objects conform to the premonitions of Reason and reflect the conscience. All things are moral; and in their boundless changes have an unceasing reference to spiritual nature. Therefore is nature glorious with form, color, and motion, that every globe in the

remotest heaven; every chemical change from the rudest crystal up to the laws of life; every change of vegetation from the first principle of growth in the eye of a leaf, to the tropical forest and antediluvian coalmine; every animal function from the sponge up to Hercules, shall hint or thunder to man the laws of right and wrong, and echo the Ten Commandments. Therefore is nature ever the ally of Religion: lends all her pomp and riches to the religious sentiment. Prophet and priest, David, Isaiah, Jesus, have drawn deeply from this source. This ethical character so penetrates the bone and marrow of nature, as to seem the end for which it was made. Whatever private purpose is answered by any member or part, this is its public and universal function, and is never omitted. Nothing in nature is exhausted in its first use. When a thing has served an end to the uttermost, it is wholly new for an ulterior service. In God, every end is converted into a new means. Thus the use of commodity, regarded by itself, is mean and squalid. But it is to the mind an education in the doctrine of Use, namely, that a thing is good only so far as it serves; that a conspiring of parts and efforts to the production of an end, is essential to any being. The first and gross manifestation of this truth, is our inevitable and hated training in values and wants, in corn and meat.

It has already been illustrated, that every natural process is a version of a moral sentence. The moral law lies at the centre of nature and radiates to the circumference. It is the pith and marrow of every substance, every relation, and every process. All things with which we deal, preach to us. What is a farm but a mute gospel? The chaff and the wheat, weeds and plants, blight, rain, insects, sun,—it is a sacred emblem from the first furrow of spring to the last stack which the snow of winter overtakes in the fields. But the sailor, the shepherd, the miner, the merchant, in their several resorts, have each an experience precisely parallel, and leading to the same conclusion: because all organizations are radically alike. Nor can it be doubted that this moral sentiment which thus scents the air, grows in the grain, and impregnates the waters of the world, is caught by man and sinks into his soul. The moral influence of nature Who can estimate this? Who can guess how much firmness the seabeaten rock has taught the fisherman? how much tranquillity has been reflected to man from the azure sky, over whose unspotted deeps the upon every individual is that amount of truth which it illustrates to him. winds forevermore drive flocks of stormy clouds, and leave no wrinkle or stain? how much industry and providence and affection we have caught from the pantomime of brutes? What a searching preacher of self-command is the varying phenomenon of Health!

Herein is especially apprehended the unity of Nature,—the unity in variety,—which meets us everywhere. All the endless variety of things make an identical impression. Xenophanes° complained in his old age, that, look where he would, all things hastened back to Unity. He was weary of seeing the same entity in the tedious variety of forms. The fable of Proteus° has a cordial truth. A leaf, a drop, a crystal, a moment of time is related to the whole, and partakes of the perfection of the whole. Each particle is a microcosm, and faithfully renders the likeness of the world.

Not only resemblances exist in things whose analogy is obvious, as when we detect the type of the human hand in the flipper of the fossil saurus, but also in objects wherein there is great superficial unlikeness. Thus architecture is called 'frozen music,' by De Stael and Goethe. Vitruvius° thought an architect should be a musician. 'A Gothic church,' said Coleridge, 'is a petrified religion.' Michael Angelo maintained, that, to an architect, a knowledge of anatomy is essential. In Haydn's oratorios, the notes present to the imagination not only motions, as, of the snake, the stag, and the elephant, but colors also; as the green grass. The law of harmonic sounds reappears in the harmonic colors. The granite is differenced in its laws only by the more or less of heat, from the river that wears it away. The river, as it flows, resembles the air that flows over it; the air resembles the light which traverses it with more subtile currents; the light resembles the heat which rides with it through Space. Each creature is only a modification of the other; the likeness in them is more than the difference, and their radical law is one and the same. A rule of one art, or a law of one organization, holds true throughout nature. So intimate is this Unity, that, it is easily seen, it lies under the undermost garment of nature, and betrays its source in Universal Spirit. For, it pervades Thought also. Every universal truth which we express in words, implies or supposes every other truth. *Omne verum vero consonat.*° It is like a great circle on a sphere, comprising all possible circles; which, however, may be drawn, and comprise it, in like manner. Every such truth is the absolute Ens° seen from one side. But it has innumerable sides.

The central Unity is still more conspicuous in actions. Words are finite organs of the infinite mind. They cannot cover the dimensions of what is in truth. They break, chop, and impoverish it. An action is the perfection and publication of thought. A right action seems to fill the eye, and to be related to all nature. 'The wise man, in doing one thing, does all; or, in the one thing he does rightly, he sees the likeness of all which is done rightly.'°

Words and actions are not the attributes of brute nature. They introduce us to the human form, of which all other organizations appear to
be degradations. When this appears among so many that surround it,
the spirit prefers it to all others. It says, 'From such as this, have I
drawn joy and knowledge; in such as this, have I found and beheld
myself; I will speak to it; it can speak again; it can yield me thought
already formed and alive.' In fact, the eye,—the mind,—is always
accompanied by these forms, male and female; and these are incomparably the richest informations of the power and order that lie at the
heart of things. Unfortunately, every one of them bears the marks as of
some injury; is marred and superficially defective. Nevertheless, far
different from the deaf and dumb nature around them, these all rest
like fountain-pipes on the unfathomed sea of thought and virtue
whereto they alone, of all organizations, are the entrances.

It were a pleasant inquiry to follow into detail their ministry to our
education, but where would it stop? We are associated in adolescent and
adult life with some friends, who, like skies and waters, are coextensive
with our idea; who, answering each to a certain affection of the soul,
satisfy our desire on that side; whom we lack power to put at such focal
distance from us, that we can mend or even analyze them. We cannot
choose but love them. When much intercourse with a friend has supplied us with a standard of excellence, and has increased our respect for
the resources of God who thus sends a real person to outgo our ideal;
when he has, moreover, become an object of thought, and, whilst his
character retains all its unconscious effect, is converted in the mind
into solid and sweet wisdom,—it is a sign to us that his office is closing,
and he is commonly withdrawn from our sight in a short time.

Chapter VI

IDEALISM

THUS is the unspeakable but intelligible and practicable meaning of
the world conveyed to man, the immortal pupil, in every object of sense.
To this one end of Discipline, all parts of nature conspire.

A noble doubt perpetually suggests itself, whether this end be not the
Final Cause of the Universe; and whether nature outwardly exists. It is
a sufficient account of that Appearance we call the World, that God will
teach a human mind, and so makes it the receiver of a certain number
of congruent sensations, which we call sun and moon, man and woman,
house and trade. In my utter impotence to test the authenticity of the

report of my senses, to know whether the impressions they make on me correspond with outlying objects, what difference does it make, whether Orion is up there in heaven, or some god paints the image in the firmament of the soul? The relations of parts and the end of the whole remaining the same, what is the difference, whether land and sea interact, and worlds revolve and intermingle without number or end,— deep yawning under deep, and galaxy balancing galaxy, throughout absolute space,—or, whether, without relations of time and space, the same appearances are inscribed in the constant faith of man? Whether nature enjoy a substantial existence without, or is only in the apocalypse of the mind, it is alike useful and alike venerable to me. Be it what it may, it is ideal to me, so long as I cannot try the accuracy of my senses.

The frivolous make themselves merry with the Ideal theory, as if its consequences were burlesque; as if it affected the stability of nature. It surely does not. God never jests with us, and will not compromise the end of nature, by permitting any inconsequence in its procession. Any distrust of the permanence of laws, would paralyze the faculties of man. Their permanence is sacredly respected, and his faith therein is perfect. The wheels and springs of man are all set to the hypothesis of the permanence of nature. We are not built like a ship to be tossed, but like a house to stand. It is a natural consequence of this structure, that, so long as the active powers predominate over the reflective, we resist with indignation any hint that nature is more short-lived or mutable than spirit. The broker, the wheelwright, the carpenter, the tollman, are much displeased at the intimation.

But whilst we acquiesce entirely in the permanence of natural laws, the question of the absolute existence of nature still remains open. It is the uniform effect of culture on the human mind, not to shake our faith in the stability of particular phenomena, as of heat, water, azote; but to lead us to regard nature as a phenomenon, not a substance; to attribute necessary existence to spirit; to esteem nature as an accident and an effect.

To the senses and the unrenewed understanding, belongs a sort of instinctive belief in the absolute existence of nature. In their view, man and nature are indissolubly joined. Things are ultimates, and they never look beyond their sphere. The presence of Reason mars this faith. The first effort of thought tends to relax this despotism of the senses, which binds us to nature as if we were a part of it, and shows us nature aloof, and, as it were, afloat. Until this higher agency intervened, the animal eye sees, with wonderful accuracy, sharp outlines and colored surfaces. When the eye of Reason opens, to outline and surface are at once added, grace and expression. These proceed from imagination and affection, and abate somewhat of the angular distinctness of objects. If the Reason be stimulated to more earnest vision, outlines and surfaces become transparent, and are no longer seen; causes and spirits are seen through them. The best moments of life are these delicious awakenings of the higher powers, and the reverential withdrawing of nature before its God.

Let us proceed to indicate the effects of culture. 1. Our first institution in the Ideal philosophy is a hint from nature herself.

Nature is made to conspire with spirit to emancipate us. Certain mechanical changes, a small alteration in our local position apprizes us of a dualism. We are strangely affected by seeing the shore from a moving ship, from a balloon, or through the tints of an unusual sky. The least change in our point of view, gives the whole world a pictorial air. A man who seldom rides, needs only to get into a coach and traverse his own town, to turn the street into a puppet-show. The men, the women,—talking, running, bartering, fighting,—the earnest mechanic, the lounger, the beggar, the boys, the dogs, are unrealized at once, or, at least, wholly detached from all relation to the observer, and seen as apparent, not substantial beings. What new thoughts are suggested by seeing a face of country quite familiar, in the rapid movement of the rail-road car! Nay, the most wonted objects, (make a very slight change in the point of vision,) please us most. In a camera obscura, the butcher's cart, and the figure of one of our own family amuse us. So a portrait of a well-known face gratifies us. Turn the eyes upside down, by looking at the landscape through your legs, and how agreeable is the picture, though you have seen it any time these twenty years!

In these cases, by mechanical means, is suggested the difference between the observer and the spectacle,—between man and nature. Hence arises a pleasure mixed with awe; I may say, a low degree of the sublime is felt from the fact, probably, that man is hereby apprized, that, whilst the world is a spectacle, something in himself is stable.

2. In a higher manner, the poet communicates the same pleasure. By a few strokes he delineates, as on air, the sun, the mountain, the camp, the city, the hero, the maiden, not different from what we know them, but only lifted from the ground and afloat before the eye. He unfixes the land and the sea, makes them revolve around the axis of his primary thought, and disposes them anew. Possessed himself by a heroic passion, he uses matter as symbols of it. The sensual man conforms thoughts to things; the poet conforms things to his thoughts. The one esteems nature as rooted and fast; the other, as fluid, and impresses his

being thereon. To him, the refractory world is ductile and flexible; he invests dust and stones with humanity, and makes them the words of the Reason. The Imagination may be defined to be, the use which the Reason makes of the material world. Shakspeare possesses the power of subordinating nature for the purposes of expression, beyond all poets. His imperial muse tosses the creation like a bauble from hand to hand, and uses it to embody any caprice of thought that is uppermost in his mind. The remotest spaces of nature are visited, and the farthest sundered things are brought together, by a subtle spiritual connection. We are made aware that magnitude of material things is relative, and all objects shrink and expand to serve the passion of the poet. Thus, in his sonnets, the lays of birds, the scents and dyes of flowers, he finds to be the *shadow* of his beloved; time, which keeps her from him, is his *chest*; the suspicion she has awakened, is her *ornament*;

> The ornament of beauty is Suspect,
> A crow which flies in heaven's sweetest air.°

His passion is not the fruit of chance; it swells, as he speaks, to a city, or a state.

> No, it was builded far from accident;
> It suffers not in smiling pomp, nor falls
> Under the brow of thralling discontent;
> It fears not policy, that heretic,
> That works on leases of short numbered hours,
> But all alone stands hugely politic.°

In the strength of his constancy, the Pyramids seem to him recent and transitory. The freshness of youth and love dazzles him with its resemblance to morning.

> Take those lips away
> Which so sweetly were forsworn;
> And those eyes,—the break of day,
> Lights that do mislead the morn.°

The wild beauty of this hyperbole, I may say, in passing, it would not be easy to match in literature.

This transfiguration which all material objects undergo through the passion of the poet,—this power which he exerts to dwarf the great, to magnify the small,—might be illustrated by a thousand examples from his Plays. I have before me the Tempest, and will cite only these few lines.

> ARIEL.   The strong based promontory
> Have I made shake, and by the spurs plucked up
> The pine and cedar.

Prospero calls for music to soothe the frantic Alonzo, and his companions;

> A solemn air, and the best comforter
> To an unsettled fancy, cure thy brains
> Now useless, boiled within thy skull.

Again;

> The charm dissolves apace,
> And, as the morning steals upon the night,
> Melting the darkness, so their rising senses
> Begin to chase the ignorant fumes that mantle
> Their clearer reason.
>   Their understanding
> Begins to swell: and the approaching tide
> Will shortly fill the reasonable shores
> That now lie foul and muddy.°

The perception of real affinities between events, (that is to say, of *ideal* affinities, for those only are real,) enables the poet thus to make free with the most imposing forms and phenomena of the world, and to assert the predominance of the soul.

3. Whilst thus the poet animates nature with his own thoughts, he differs from the philosopher only herein, that the one proposes Beauty as his main end; the other Truth. But the philosopher, not less than the poet, postpones the apparent order and relations of things to the empire of thought. 'The problem of philosophy,' according to Plato, 'is, for all that exists conditionally, to find a ground unconditioned and absolute.'° It proceeds on the faith that a law determines all phenomena, which being known, the phenomena can be predicted. That law, when in the mind, is an idea. Its beauty is infinite. The true philosopher and the true poet are one, and a beauty, which is truth, and a truth, which is beauty, is the aim of both. Is not the charm of one of Plato's or Aristotle's definitions, strictly like that of the Antigone of Sophocles? It is, in both cases, that a spiritual life has been imparted to nature; that the solid seeming block of matter has been pervaded and dissolved by a thought; that this feeble human being has penetrated the vast masses of nature with an informing soul, and recognised itself in their harmony, that is, seized their law. In physics, when this is attained, the memory

disburthens itself of its cumbrous catalogues of particulars, and carries centuries of observation in a single formula.

Thus even in physics, the material is degraded before the spiritual. The astronomer, the geometer, rely on their irrefragable analysis, and disdain the results of observation. The sublime remark of Euler on his law of arches, 'This will be found contrary to all experience, yet is true;'° had already transferred nature into the mind, and left matter like an outcast corpse.

4. Intellectual science has been observed to beget invariably a doubt of the existence of matter. Turgot° said, 'He that has never doubted the existence of matter, may be assured he has no aptitude for metaphysical inquiries.' It fastens the attention upon immortal necessary uncreated natures, that is, upon Ideas; and in their presence, we feel that the outward circumstance is a dream and a shade. Whilst we wait in this Olympus of gods, we think of nature as an appendix to the soul. We ascend into their region, and know that these are the thoughts of the Supreme Being. 'These are they who were set up from everlasting, from the beginning, or ever the earth was. When he prepared the heavens, they were there; when he established the clouds above, when he strengthened the fountains of the deep. Then they were by him, as one brought up with him. Of them took he counsel.'°

Their influence is proportionate. As objects of science, they are accessible to few men. Yet all men are capable of being raised by piety or by passion, into their region. And no man touches these divine natures, without becoming, in some degree, himself divine. Like a new soul, they renew the body. We become physically nimble and light-some; we tread on air; life is no longer irksome, and we think it will never be so. No man fears age or misfortune or death, in their serene company, for he is transported out of the district of change. Whilst we behold unveiled the nature of Justice and Truth, we learn the difference between the absolute and the conditional or relative. We apprehend the absolute. As it were, for the first time, *we exist*. We become immortal, for we learn that time and space are relations of matter; that, with a perception of truth, or a virtuous will, they have no affinity.

5. Finally, religion and ethics, which may be fitly called,—the practice of ideas, or the introduction of ideas into life,—have an analogous effect with all lower culture, in degrading nature and suggesting its dependence on spirit. Ethics and religion differ herein; that the one is the system of human duties commencing from man; the other, from God. Religion includes the personality of God; Ethics does not. They are one to our present design. They both put nature under foot. The

first and last lesson of religion is, 'The things that are seen, are temporal; the things that are unseen, are eternal.'° It puts an affront upon nature. It does that for the unschooled, which philosophy does for Berkeley and Viasa.° The uniform language that may be heard in the churches of the most ignorant sects, is,—'Contemn the unsubstantial shows of the world; they are vanities, dreams, shadows, unrealities; seek the realities of religion.' The devotee flouts nature. Some theosophists have arrived at a certain hostility and indignation towards matter, as the Manichean and Plotinus.° They distrusted in themselves any looking back to these flesh-pots of Egypt.° Plotinus was ashamed of his body. In short, they might all say of matter, what Michael Angelo said of external beauty, 'it is the frail and weary weed, in which God dresses the soul, which he has called into time.'°

It appears that motion, poetry, physical and intellectual science, and religion, all tend to affect our convictions of the reality of the external world. But I own there is something ungrateful in expanding too curiously the particulars of the general proposition, that all culture tends to imbue us with idealism. I have no hostility to nature, but a child's love to it. I expand and live in the warm day like corn and melons. Let us speak her fair. I do not wish to fling stones at my beautiful mother, nor soil my gentle nest. I only wish to indicate the true position of nature in regard to man, wherein to establish man, all right education tends; as the ground which to attain is the object of human life, that is, of man's connection with nature. Culture inverts the vulgar views of nature, and brings the mind to call that apparent, which it uses to call real, and that real, which it uses to call visionary. Children, it is true, believe in the external world. The belief that it appears only, is an afterthought, but with culture, this faith will as surely arise on the mind as did the first.

The advantage of the ideal theory over the popular faith, is this, that it presents the world in precisely that view which is most desirable to the mind. It is, in fact, the view which Reason, both speculative and practical, that is, philosophy and virtue, take. For, seen in the light of thought, the world always is phenomenal; and virtue subordinates it to the mind. Idealism sees the world in God. It beholds the whole circle of persons and things, of actions and events, of country and religion, not as painfully accumulated, atom after atom, act after act, in an aged creeping Past, but as one vast picture, which God paints on the instant eternity, for the contemplation of the soul. Therefore the soul holds itself off from a too trivial and microscopic study of the universal tablet. It respects the end too much, to immerse itself in the means. It sees

something more important in Christianity, than the scandals of ecclesiastical history, or the niceties of criticism; and, very incurious concerning persons or miracles, and not at all disturbed by chasms of historical
evidence, it accepts from God the phenomenon, as it finds it, as the
pure and awful form of religion in the world. It is not hot and passionate at the appearance of what it calls its own good or bad fortune, at the
union or opposition of other persons. No man is its enemy. It accepts
whatsoever befalls, as part of its lesson. It is a watcher more than a
doer, and it is a doer, only that it may the better watch.

Chapter VII

SPIRIT

IT is essential to a true theory of nature and of man, that it should contain somewhat progressive. Uses that are exhausted or that may be, and
facts that end in the statement, cannot be all that is true of this brave
lodging wherein man is harbored, and wherein all his faculties find
appropriate and endless exercise. And all the uses of nature admit of
being summed in one, which yields the activity of man an infinite scope.
Through all its kingdoms, to the suburbs and outskirts of things, it is
faithful to the cause whence it had its origin. It always speaks of Spirit.
It suggests the absolute. It is a perpetual effect. It is a great shadow
pointing always to the sun behind us.

The aspect of nature is devout. Like the figure of Jesus, she stands
with bended head, and hands folded upon the breast. The happiest
man is he who learns from nature the lesson of worship.

Of that ineffable essence which we call Spirit, he that thinks most,
will say least. We can foresee God in the coarse, and, as it were, distant
phenomena of matter; but when we try to define and describe himself,
both language and thought desert us, and we are as helpless as fools
and savages. That essence refuses to be recorded in propositions, but
when man has worshipped him intellectually, the noblest ministry of
nature is to stand as the apparition of God. It is the organ through
which the universal spirit speaks to the individual, and strives to lead
back the individual to it.

When we consider Spirit, we see that the views already presented do
not include the whole circumference of man. We must add some
related thoughts.

Three problems are put by nature to the mind; What is matter?
Whence is it? and Whereto? The first of these questions only, the ideal

theory answers. Idealism saith: matter is a phenomenon, not a substance. Idealism acquaints us with the total disparity between the evidence of our own being, and the evidence of the world's being. The one is perfect; the other, incapable of any assurance; the mind is a part of the nature of things; the world is a divine dream, from which we may presently awake to the glories and certainties of day. Idealism is a hypothesis to account for nature by other principles than those of carpentry and chemistry. Yet, if it only deny the existence of matter, it does not satisfy the demands of the spirit. It leaves God out of me. It leaves me in the splendid labyrinth of my perceptions, to wander without end. Then the heart resists it, because it balks the affections in denying substantive being to men and women. Nature is so pervaded with human life, that there is something of humanity in all, and in every particular. But this theory makes nature foreign to me, and does not account for that consanguinity which we acknowledge to it.

Let it stand, then, in the present state of our knowledge, merely as a useful introductory hypothesis, serving to apprize us of the eternal distinction between the soul and the world.

But when, following the invisible steps of thought, we come to inquire, Whence is matter? and Whereto? many truths arise to us out of the recesses of consciousness. We learn that the highest is present to the soul of man, that the dread universal essence, which is not wisdom, or love, or beauty, or power, but all in one, and each entirely, is that for which all things exist, and that by which they are; that spirit creates; that behind nature, throughout nature, spirit is present; one and not compound, it does not act upon us from without, that is, in space and time, but spiritually, or through ourselves: therefore, that spirit, that is, the Supreme Being, does not build up nature around us, but puts it forth through us, as the life of the tree puts forth new branches and leaves through the pores of the old. As a plant upon the earth, so a man rests upon the bosom of God; he is nourished by unfailing fountains, and draws, at his need, inexhaustible power. Who can set bounds to the possibilities of man? Once inhale the upper air, being admitted to behold the absolute natures of justice and truth, and we learn that man has access to the entire mind of the Creator, is himself the creator in the finite. This view, which admonishes me where the sources of wisdom and power lie, and points to virtue as to

> 'The golden key
> Which opes the palace of eternity,'°

carries upon its face the highest certificate of truth, because it animates me to create my own world through the purification of my soul.

The world proceeds from the same spirit as the body of man. It is a remoter and inferior incarnation of God, a projection of God in the unconscious. But it differs from the body in one important respect. It is not, like that, now subjected to the human will. Its serene order is inviolable by us. It is, therefore, to us, the present expositor of the divine mind. It is a fixed point whereby we may measure our departure. As we degenerate, the contrast between us and our house is more evident. We are as much strangers in nature, as we are aliens from God. We do not understand the notes of birds. The fox and the deer run away from us; the bear and tiger rend us. We do not know the uses of more than a few plants, as corn and the apple, the potato and the vine. Is not the landscape, every glimpse of which hath a grandeur, a face of him? Yet this may show us what discord is between man and nature, for you cannot freely admire a noble landscape, if laborers are digging in the field hard by. The poet finds something ridiculous in his delight, until he is out of the sight of men.

Chapter VIII

PROSPECTS

IN inquiries respecting the laws of the world and the frame of things, the highest reason is always the truest. That which seems faintly possible—it is so refined, is often faint and dim because it is deepest seated in the mind among the eternal verities. Empirical science is apt to cloud the sight, and, by the very knowledge of functions and processes, to bereave the student of the manly contemplation of the whole. The savant becomes unpoetic. But the best read naturalist who lends an entire and devout attention to truth, will see that there remains much to learn of his relation to the world, and that it is not to be learned by any addition or subtraction or other comparison of known quantities, but is arrived at by untaught sallies of the spirit, by a continual self-recovery, and by entire humility. He will perceive that there are far more excellent qualities in the student than preciseness and infallibility; that a guess is often more fruitful than an indisputable affirmation, and that a dream may let us deeper into the secret of nature than a hundred concerted experiments.

For, the problems to be solved are precisely those which the physiologist and the naturalist omit to state. It is not so pertinent to man to know all the individuals of the animal kingdom, as it is to know whence and whereto is this tyrannizing unity in his constitution, which evermore separates and classifies things, endeavoring to reduce the most diverse to one form. When I behold a rich landscape, it is less to my purpose to recite correctly the order and superposition of the strata, than to know why all thought of multitude is lost in a tranquil sense of unity. I cannot greatly honor minuteness in details, so long as there is no hint to explain the relation between things and thoughts; no ray upon the *metaphysics* of conchology, of botany, of the arts, to show the relation of the forms of flowers, shells, animals, architecture, to the mind, and build science upon ideas. In a cabinet of natural history, we become sensible of a certain occult recognition and sympathy in regard to the most unwieldly and eccentric forms of beast, fish, and insect. The American who has been confined, in his own country, to the sight of buildings designed after foreign models, is surprised on entering York Minster or St. Peter's at Rome, by the feeling that these structures are imitations also,—faint copies of an invisible archetype. Nor has science sufficient humanity, so long as the naturalist overlooks that wonderful congruity which subsists between man and the world; of which he is lord, not because he is the most subtile inhabitant, but because he is its head and heart, and finds something of himself in every great and small thing, in every mountain stratum, in every new law of color, fact of astronomy, or atmospheric influence which observation or analysis lay open. A perception of this mystery inspires the muse of George Herbert, the beautiful psalmist of the seventeenth century. The following lines are part of his little poem on Man.

> 'Man is all symmetry,
> Full of proportions, one limb to another,
> And to all the world besides.
> Each part may call the farthest, brother;
> For head with foot hath private amity,
> And both with moons and tides.
>
> 'Nothing hath got so far
> But man hath caught and kept it as his prey;
> His eyes dismount the highest star;
> He is in little all the sphere.
> Herbs gladly cure our flesh, because that they
> Find their acquaintance there.

'For us, the winds do blow,
The earth doth rest, heaven move, and fountains flow;
    Nothing we see, but means our good,
    As our delight, or as our treasure;
The whole is either our cupboard of food,
    Or cabinet of pleasure.

'The stars have us to bed:
Night draws the curtain; which the sun withdraws.
    Music and light attend our head.
    All things unto our flesh are kind,
In their descent and being; to our mind,
    In their ascent and cause.

'More servants wait on man
Than he'll take notice of. In every path,
    He treads down that which doth befriend him
    When sickness makes him pale and wan.
Oh mighty love! Man is one world, and hath
    Another to attend him.'°

The perception of this class of truths makes the attraction which draws men to science, but the end is lost sight of in attention to the means. In view of this half-sight of science, we accept the sentence of Plato,° that, 'poetry comes nearer to vital truth than history.' Every surmise and vaticination of the mind is entitled to a certain respect, and we learn to prefer imperfect theories, and sentences, which contain glimpses of truth, to digested systems which have no one valuable suggestion. A wise writer will feel that the ends of study and composition are best answered by announcing undiscovered regions of thought, and so communicating, through hope, new activity to the torpid spirit.

I shall therefore conclude this essay with some traditions of man and nature, which a certain poet° sang to me; and which, as they have always been in the world, and perhaps reappear to every bard, may be both history and prophecy.

'The foundations of man are not in matter, but in spirit. But the element of spirit is eternity. To it, therefore, the longest series of events, the oldest chronologies are young and recent. In the cycle of the universal man, from whom the known individuals proceed, centuries are points, and all history is but the epoch of one degradation.

'We distrust and deny inwardly our sympathy with nature. We own and disown our relation to it, by turns. We are, like Nebuchadnezzar,° dethroned, bereft of reason, and eating grass like an ox. But who can set limits to the remedial force of spirit?

'A man is a god in ruins. When men are innocent, life shall be longer, and shall pass into the immortal, as gently as we awake from dreams. Now, the world would be insane and rabid, if these disorganizations should last for hundreds of years. It is kept in check by death and infancy. Infancy is the perpetual Messiah, which comes into the arms of fallen men, and pleads with them to return to paradise.

'Man is the dwarf of himself. Once he was permeated and dissolved by spirit. He filled nature with his overflowing currents. Out from him sprang the sun and moon; from man, the sun; from woman, the moon. The laws of his mind, the periods of his actions externized themselves into day and night, into the year and the seasons. But, having made for himself this huge shell, his waters retired; he no longer fills the veins and veinlets; he is shrunk to a drop. He sees, that the structure still fits him, but fits him colossally. Say, rather, once it fitted him, now it corresponds to him from far and on high. He adores timidly his own work. Now is man the follower of the sun, and woman the follower of the moon. Yet sometimes he starts in his slumber, and wonders at himself and his house, and muses strangely at the resemblance betwixt him and it. He perceives that if his law is still paramount, if still he have elemental power, if his word is sterling yet in nature,° it is not conscious power, it is not inferior but superior to his will. It is Instinct'. Thus my Orphic poet sang.

At present, man applies to nature but half his force. He works on the world with his understanding alone. He lives in it, and masters it by a penny-wisdom; and he that works most in it, is but a half-man, and whilst his arms are strong and his digestion good, his mind is imbruted, and he is a selfish savage. His relation to nature, his power over it, is through the understanding; as by manure; the economic use of fire, wind, water, and the mariner's needle; steam, coal, chemical agriculture; the repairs of the human body by the dentist and the surgeon. This is such a resumption of power, as if a banished king should buy his territories inch by inch, instead of vaulting at once into his throne. Meantime, in the thick darkness, there are not wanting gleams of a better light,—occasional examples of the action of man upon nature with his entire force,—with reason as well as understanding. Such examples are; the traditions of miracles in the earliest antiquity of all nations; the history of Jesus Christ; the achievements of a principle, as in religious and political revolutions, and in the abolition of the Slave-trade; the miracles of enthusiasm, as those reported of Swedenborg, Hohenlohe, and the Shakers;° many obscure and yet contested facts, now arranged under the name of Animal Magnetism; prayer; eloquence; self-healing; and the wisdom of children. These are examples

of Reason's momentary grasp of the sceptre; the exertions of a power
which exists not in time or space, but an instantaneous in-streaming
causing power. The difference between the actual and the ideal force
of man is happily figured by the schoolmen, in saying, that the knowledge of man is an evening knowledge, *vespertina cognitio*, but that of
God is a morning knowledge, *matutina cognitio*.

The problem of restoring to the world original and eternal beauty, is
solved by the redemption of the soul. The ruin or the blank, that we see
when we look at nature, is in our own eye. The axis of vision is not
coincident with the axis of things, and so they appear not transparent
but opake. The reason why the world lacks unity, and lies broken and in
heaps, is, because man is disunited with himself. He cannot be a naturalist, until he satisfies all the demands of the spirit. Love is as much its
demand, as perception. Indeed, neither can be perfect without the
other. In the uttermost meaning of the words, thought is devout, and
devotion is thought. Deep calls unto deep.° But in actual life, the marriage is not celebrated. There are innocent men who worship God after
the tradition of their fathers, but their sense of duty has not yet
extended to the use of all their faculties. And there are patient naturalists, but they freeze their subject under the wintry light of the understanding. Is not prayer also a study of truth,—a sally of the soul into the
unfound infinite? No man ever prayed heartily, without learning something. But when a faithful thinker, resolute to detach every object from
personal relations, and see it in the light of thought, shall, at the same
time, kindle science with the fire of the holiest affections, then will God
go forth anew into the creation.

It will not need, when the mind is prepared for study, to search for
objects. The invariable mark of wisdom is to see the miraculous in the
common. What is a day? What is a year? What is summer? What is
woman? What is a child? What is sleep? To our blindness, these things
seem unaffecting. We make fables to hide the baldness of the fact and
conform it, as we say, to the higher law of the mind. But when the fact
is seen under the light of an idea, the gaudy fable fades and shrivels.
We behold the real higher law. To the wise, therefore, a fact is true
poetry, and the most beautiful of fables. These wonders are brought to
our own door. You also are a man. Man and woman, and their social
life, poverty, labor, sleep, fear, fortune, are known to you. Learn that
none of these things is superficial, but that each phenomenon has its
roots in the faculties and affections of the mind. Whilst the abstract
question occupies your intellect, nature brings it in the concrete to be
solved by your hands. It were a wise inquiry for the closet, to compare,

point by point, especially at remarkable crises in life, our daily history, with the rise and progress of ideas in the mind.

So shall we come to look at the world with new eyes. It shall answer the endless inquiry of the intellect,—What is truth? and of the affections,—What is good? by yielding itself passive to the educated Will. Then shall come to pass what my poet said; 'Nature is not fixed but fluid. Spirit alters, moulds, makes it. The immobility or bruteness of nature, is the absence of spirit; to pure spirit, it is fluid, it is volatile, it is obedient. Every spirit builds itself a house; and beyond its house a world; and beyond its world, a heaven. Know then, that the world exists for you. For you is the phenomenon perfect. What we are, that only can we see. All that Adam had, all that Cæsar could, you have and can do. Adam called his house, heaven and earth; Cæsar called his house, Rome; you perhaps call yours, a cobler's trade; a hundred acres of ploughed land; or a scholar's garret. Yet line for line and point for point, your dominion is as great as theirs, though without fine names. Build, therefore, your own world. As fast as you conform your life to the pure idea in your mind, that will unfold its great proportions. A correspondent revolution in things will attend the influx of the spirit. So fast will disagreeable appearances, swine, spiders, snakes, pests, madhouses, prisons, enemies, vanish; they are temporary and shall be no more seen. The sordor and filths of nature, the sun shall dry up, and the wind exhale. As when the summer comes from the south; the snowbanks melt, and the face of the earth becomes green before it, so shall the advancing spirit create its ornaments along its path, and carry with it the beauty it visits, and the song which enchants it; it shall draw beautiful faces, warm hearts, wise discourse, and heroic acts, around its way, until evil is no more seen. The kingdom of man over nature, which cometh not with observation,—a dominion such as now is beyond his dream of God,—he shall enter without more wonder than the blind man feels who is gradually restored to perfect sight.'

THE AMERICAN SCHOLAR

An Oration delivered before the Phi Beta Kappa Society,° *at Cambridge, August 31, 1837*

MR. PRESIDENT AND GENTLEMEN,

I GREET you on the re-commencement of our literary year. Our anniversary is one of hope, and, perhaps, not enough of labor. We do not meet for games of strength or skill, for the recitation of histories, tragedies, and odes, like the ancient Greeks; for parliaments of love and poesy, like the Troubadours; nor for the advancement of science, like our cotemporaries in the British and European capitals. Thus far, our holiday has been simply a friendly sign of the survival of the love of letters amongst a people too busy to give to letters any more. As such, it is precious as the sign of an indestructible instinct. Perhaps the time is already come, when it ought to be, and will be, something else; when the sluggard intellect of this continent will look from under its iron lids, and fill the postponed expectation of the world with something better than the exertions of mechanical skill. Our day of dependence, our long apprenticeship to the learning of other lands, draws to a close. The millions, that around us are rushing into life, cannot always be fed on the sere remains of foreign harvests. Events, actions arise, that must be sung, that will sing themselves. Who can doubt, that poetry will revive and lead in a new age, as the star in the constellation Harp,° which now flames in our zenith, astronomers announce, shall one day be the pole-star for a thousand years?

In this hope, I accept the topic which not only usage, but the nature of our association, seem to prescribe to this day,—the AMERICAN SCHOLAR. Year by year, we come up hither to read one more chapter of his biography. Let us inquire what light new days and events have thrown on his character and his hopes.

It is one of those fables,° which, out of an unknown antiquity, convey an unlooked-for wisdom, that the gods, in the beginning, divided Man into men, that he might be more helpful to himself; just as the hand was divided into fingers, the better to answer its end.

The old fable covers a doctrine ever new and sublime; that there is One Man,—present to all particular men only partially, or through one faculty; and that you must take the whole society to find the whole man. Man is not a farmer, or a professor, or an engineer, but he is all. Man is priest, and scholar, and statesman, and producer, and soldier. In the *divided* or social state, these functions are parcelled out to individuals, each of whom aims to do his stint of the joint work, whilst each other performs his. The fable implies, that the individual, to possess himself, must sometimes return from his own labor to embrace all the other laborers. But unfortunately, this original unit, this fountain of power, has been so distributed to multitudes, has been so minutely subdivided and peddled out, that it is spilled into drops, and cannot be gathered. The state of society is one in which the members have suffered amputation from the trunk, and strut about so many walking monsters,—a good finger, a neck, a stomach, an elbow, but never a man.

Man is thus metamorphosed into a thing, into many things. The planter, who is Man sent out into the field to gather food, is seldom cheered by any idea of the true dignity of his ministry. He sees his bushel and his cart, and nothing beyond, and sinks into the farmer, instead of Man on the farm. The tradesman scarcely ever gives an ideal worth to his work, but is ridden by the routine of his craft, and the soul is subject to dollars. The priest becomes a form; the attorney, a statute-book; the mechanic, a machine; the sailor, a rope of a ship.

In this distribution of functions, the scholar is the delegated intellect. In the right state, he is, *Man Thinking*. In the degenerate state, when the victim of society, he tends to become a mere thinker, or, still worse, the parrot of other men's thinking.

In this view of him, as Man Thinking, the theory of his office is contained. Him nature solicits with all her placid, all her monitory pictures; him the past instructs; him the future invites. Is not, indeed, every man a student, and do not all things exist for the student's behoof? And, finally, is not the true scholar the only true master? But the old oracle said, 'All things have two handles: beware of the wrong one.'° In life, too often, the scholar errs with mankind and forfeits his privilege. Let us see him in his school, and consider him in reference to the main influences he receives.

I. The first in time and the first in importance of the influences upon the mind is that of nature. Every day, the sun; and, after sunset, night and her stars. Ever the winds blow; ever the grass grows. Every day, men and women, conversing, beholding and beholden. The scholar is he of all men whom this spectacle most engages. He must settle its value in his mind. What is nature to him? There is never a beginning, there is never an end, to the inexplicable continuity of this web of God, but always circular power returning into itself. Therein it resembles his own spirit, whose beginning, whose ending, he never can find,—so entire, so boundless. Far, too, as her splendors shine, system on system shooting like rays, upward, downward, without centre, without circumference,—in the mass and in the particle, nature hastens to render account of herself to the mind. Classification begins. To the young mind, every thing is individual, stands by itself. By and by, it finds how to join two things, and see in them one nature; then three, then three thousand; and so, tyrannized over by its own unifying instinct, it goes on tying things together, diminishing anomalies, discovering roots running under ground, whereby contrary and remote things cohere, and flower out from one stem. It presently learns, that, since the dawn of history, there has been a constant accumulation and classifying of facts. But what is classification but the perceiving that these objects are not chaotic, and are not foreign, but have a law which is also a law of the human mind? The astronomer discovers that geometry, a pure abstraction of the human mind, is the measure of planetary motion. The chemist finds proportions and intelligible method throughout matter; and science is nothing but the finding of analogy, identity, in the most remote parts. The ambitious soul sits down before each refractory fact; one after another, reduces all strange constitutions, all new powers, to their class and their law, and goes on for ever to animate the last fibre of organization, the outskirts of nature, by insight.

Thus to him, to this school-boy under the bending dome of day, is suggested, that he and it proceed from one root; one is leaf and one is flower; relation, sympathy, stirring in every vein. And what is that Root? Is not that the soul of his soul?—A thought too bold,—a dream too wild. Yet when this spiritual light shall have revealed the law of more earthly natures,—when he has learned to worship the soul, and to see that the natural philosophy that now is, is only the first gropings of its gigantic hand, he shall look forward to an ever expanding knowledge as to a becoming creator. He shall see, that nature is the opposite of the soul, answering to it part for part. One is seal, and one is print. Its beauty is the beauty of his own mind. Its laws are the laws of his own mind. Nature then becomes to him the measure of his attainments. So much of nature as he is ignorant of, so much of his own mind does he not yet possess. And, in fine, the ancient precept, 'Know thyself,' and the modern precept, 'Study nature,' become at last one maxim.

II. The next great influence into the spirit of the scholar, is, the mind of the Past,—in whatever form, whether of literature, of art, of institutions, that mind is inscribed. Books are the best type of the influence of the past, and perhaps we shall get at the truth,—learn the amount of this influence more conveniently,—by considering their value alone.

The theory of books is noble. The scholar of the first age received into him the world around; brooded thereon; gave it the new arrangement of his own mind, and uttered it again. It came into him, life; it went out from him, truth. It came to him, short-lived actions; it went out from him, immortal thoughts. It came to him, business; it went from him, poetry. It was dead fact; now, it is quick thought. It can stand, and it can go. It now endures, it now flies, it now inspires. Precisely in proportion to the depth of mind from which it issued, so high does it soar, so long does it sing.

Or, I might say, it depends on how far the process had gone, of transmuting life into truth. In proportion to the completeness of the distillation, so will the purity and imperishableness of the product be. But none is quite perfect. As no air-pump can by any means make a perfect vacuum, so neither can any artist entirely exclude the conventional, the local, the perishable from his book, or write a book of pure thought, that shall be as efficient, in all respects, to a remote posterity, as to cotemporaries, or rather to the second age. Each age, it is found, must write its own books; or rather, each generation for the next succeeding. The books of an older period will not fit this.

Yet hence arises a grave mischief. The sacredness which attaches to the act of creation,—the act of thought,—is transferred to the record. The poet chanting, was felt to be a divine man: henceforth the chant is divine also. The writer was a just and wise spirit: henceforward it is settled, the book is perfect; as love of the hero corrupts into worship of his statue. Instantly, the book becomes noxious: the guide is a tyrant. The sluggish and perverted mind of the multitude, slow to open to the incursions of Reason, having once so opened, having once received this book, stands upon it, and makes an outcry, if it is disparaged. Colleges are built on it. Books are written on it by thinkers, not by Man Thinking; by men of talent, that is, who start wrong, who set out from accepted dogmas, not from their own sight of principles. Meek young men grow up in libraries, believing it their duty to accept the views, which Cicero, which Locke, which Bacon, have given, forgetful that Cicero, Locke, and Bacon were only young men in libraries, when they wrote these books.

Hence, instead of Man Thinking, we have the bookworm. Hence, the book-learned class, who value books, as such; not as related to nature and the human constitution, but as making a sort of Third

Estate with the world and the soul. Hence, the restorers of readings, the emendators, the bibliomaniacs of all degrees.

Books are the best of things, well used; abused, among the worst. What is the right use? What is the one end, which all means go to effect? They are for nothing but to inspire. I had better never see a book, than to be warped by its attraction clean out of my own orbit, and made a satellite instead of a system. The one thing in the world, of value, is the active soul. This every man is entitled to; this every man contains within him, although, in almost all men, obstructed, and as yet unborn. The soul active sees absolute truth; and utters truth, or creates. In this action, it is genius; not the privilege of here and there a favorite, but the sound estate of every man. In its essence, it is progressive. The book, the college, the school of art, the institution of any kind, stop with some past utterance of genius. This is good, say they,—let us hold by this. They pin me down. They look backward and not forward. But genius looks forward: the eyes of man are set in his forehead, not in his hind-head: man hopes: genius creates. Whatever talents may be, if the man create not, the pure efflux of the Deity is not his;—cinders and smoke there may be, but not yet flame. There are creative manners, there are creative actions, and creative words; manners, actions, words, that is, indicative of no custom or authority, but springing spontaneous from the mind's own sense of good and fair.

On the other part, instead of being its own seer, let it receive from another mind its truth, though it were in torrents of light, without periods of solitude, inquest, and self-recovery, and a fatal disservice is done. Genius is always sufficiently the enemy of genius by over influence. The literature of every nation bear me witness. The English dramatic poets have Shakspearized now for two hundred years.

Undoubtedly there is a right way of reading, so it be sternly subordinated. Man Thinking must not be subdued by his instruments. Books are for the scholar's idle times. When he can read God directly, the hour is too precious to be wasted in other men's transcripts of their readings. But when the intervals of darkness come, as come they must,—when the sun is hid, and the stars withdraw their shining,—we repair to the lamps which were kindled by their ray, to guide our steps to the East again, where the dawn is. We hear, that we may speak. The Arabian proverb says, 'A fig tree, looking on a fig tree, becometh fruitful.'

It is remarkable, the character of the pleasure we derive from the best books. They impress us with the conviction, that one nature wrote and the same reads. We read the verses of one of the great English poets, of Chaucer, of Marvell, of Dryden, with the most modern joy,—with a pleasure, I mean, which is in great part caused by the abstraction of all *time* from their verses. There is some awe mixed with the joy of our surprise, when this poet, who lived in some past world, two or three hundred years ago, says that which lies close to my own soul, that which I also had wellnigh thought and said. But for the evidence thence afforded to the philosophical doctrine of the identity of all minds, we should suppose some preëstablished harmony, some foresight of souls that were to be, and some preparation of stores for their future wants, like the fact observed in insects, who lay up food before death for the young grub they shall never see.

I would not be hurried by any love of system, by any exaggeration of instincts, to underrate the Book. We all know, that, as the human body can be nourished on any food, though it were boiled grass and the broth of shoes, so the human mind can be fed by any knowledge. And great and heroic men have existed, who had almost no other information than by the printed page. I only would say, that it needs a strong head to bear that diet. One must be an inventor to read well. As the proverb says, 'He that would bring home the wealth of the Indies, must carry out the wealth of the Indies.' There is then creative reading as well as creative writing. When the mind is braced by labor and invention, the page of whatever book we read becomes luminous with manifold allusion. Every sentence is doubly significant, and the sense of our author is as broad as the world. We then see, what is always true, that, as the seer's hour of vision is short and rare among heavy days and months, so is its record, perchance, the least part of his volume. The discerning will read, in his Plato or Shakspeare, only that least part,—only the authentic utterances of the oracle;—all the rest he rejects, were it never so many times Plato's and Shakspeare's.

Of course, there is a portion of reading quite indispensable to a wise man. History and exact science he must learn by laborious reading. Colleges, in like manner, have their indispensable office,—to teach elements. But they can only highly serve us, when they aim not to drill, but to create; when they gather from far every ray of various genius to their hospitable halls, and, by the concentrated fires, set the hearts of their youth on flame. Thought and knowledge are natures in which apparatus and pretension avail nothing. Gowns, and pecuniary foundations, though of towns of gold, can never countervail the least sentence or syllable of wit. Forget this, and our American colleges will recede in their public importance, whilst they grow richer every year.

III. There goes in the world a notion, that the scholar should be a recluse, a valetudinarian,—as unfit for any handiwork or public labor, as a penknife for an axe. The so-called 'practical men' sneer at speculative men, as if, because they speculate or *see*, they could do nothing. I have heard it said that the clergy,—who are always, more universally than any other class, the scholars of their day,—are addressed as women; that the rough, spontaneous conversation of men they do not hear, but only a mincing and diluted speech. They are often virtually disfranchised; and, indeed, there are advocates for their celibacy. As far as this is true of the studious classes, it is not just and wise. Action is with the scholar subordinate, but it is essential. Without it, he is not yet man. Without it, thought can never ripen into truth. Whilst the world hangs before the eye as a cloud of beauty, we cannot even see its beauty. Inaction is cowardice, but there can be no scholar without the heroic mind. The preamble of thought, the transition through which it passes from the unconscious to the conscious, is action. Only so much do I know, as I have lived. Instantly we know whose words are loaded with life, and whose not.

The world,—this shadow of the soul, or *other me*, lies wide around. Its attractions are the keys which unlock my thoughts and make me acquainted with myself. I run eagerly into this resounding tumult. I grasp the hands of those next me, and take my place in the ring to suffer and to work, taught by an instinct, that so shall the dumb abyss be vocal with speech. I pierce its order; I dissipate its fear; I dispose of it within the circuit of my expanding life. So much only of life as I know by experience, so much of the wilderness have I vanquished and planted, or so far have I extended my being, my dominion. I do not see how any man can afford, for the sake of his nerves and his nap, to spare any action in which he can partake. It is pearls and rubies to his discourse. Drudgery, calamity, exasperation, want, are instructers in eloquence and wisdom. The true scholar grudges every opportunity of action past by, as a loss of power.

It is the raw material out of which the intellect moulds her splendid products. A strange process too, this, by which experience is converted into thought, as a mulberry leaf is converted into satin. The manufacture goes forward at all hours.

The actions and events of our childhood and youth, are now matters of calmest observation. They lie like fair pictures in the air. Not so with our recent actions,—with the business which we now have in hand. On this we are quite unable to speculate. Our affections as yet circulate through it. We no more feel or know it, than we feel the feet, or the hand, or the brain of our body. The new deed is yet a part of life,—

remains for a time immersed in our unconscious life. In some contemplative hour, it detaches itself from the life like a ripe fruit, to become a thought of the mind. Instantly, it is raised, transfigured; the corruptible has put on incorruption. Henceforth it is an object of beauty, however base its origin and neighborhood. Observe, too, the impossibility of antedating this act. In its grub state, it cannot fly, it cannot shine, it is a dull grub. But suddenly, without observation, the selfsame thing unfurls beautiful wings, and is an angel of wisdom. So is there no fact, no event, in our private history, which shall not, sooner or later, lose its adhesive, inert form, and astonish us by soaring from our body into the empyrean. Cradle and infancy, school and playground, the fear of boys, and dogs, and ferules, the love of little maids and berries, and many another fact that once filled the whole sky, are gone already; friend and relative, profession and party, town and country, nation and world, must also soar and sing.

Of course, he who has put forth his total strength in fit actions, has the richest return of wisdom. I will not shut myself out of this globe of action, and transplant an oak into a flower-pot, there to hunger and pine; nor trust the revenue of some single faculty, and exhaust one vein of thought, much like those Savoyards,° who, getting their livelihood by carving shepherds, shepherdesses, and smoking Dutchmen, for all Europe, went out one day to the mountain to find stock, and discovered that they had whittled up the last of their pine-trees. Authors we have, in numbers, who have written out their vein, and who, moved by a commendable prudence, sail for Greece or Palestine, follow the trapper into the prairie, or ramble round Algiers, to replenish their merchantable stock.

If it were only for a vocabulary, the scholar would be covetous of action. Life is our dictionary. Years are well spent in country labors; in town,—in the insight into trades and manufactures; in frank intercourse with many men and women; in science; in art; to the one end of mastering in all their facts a language by which to illustrate and embody our perceptions. I learn immediately from any speaker how much he has already lived, through the poverty or the splendor of his speech. Life lies behind us as the quarry from whence we get tiles and copestones for the masonry of to-day. This is the way to learn grammar. Colleges and books only copy the language which the field and the work-yard made.

But the final value of action, like that of books, and better than books, is, that it is a resource. That great principle of Undulation in nature, that shows itself in the inspiring and expiring of the breath; in desire and satiety; in the ebb and flow of the sea; in day and night; in heat and cold; and as yet more deeply ingrained in every atom and every fluid, is known to us under the name of Polarity,—these 'fits of easy transmission and reflection,' as Newton called them, are the law of nature because they are the law of spirit.

The mind now thinks; now acts; and each fit reproduces the other. When the artist has exhausted his materials, when the fancy no longer paints, when thoughts are no longer apprehended, and books are a weariness,—he has always the resource *to live*. Character is higher than intellect. Thinking is the function. Living is the functionary. The stream retreats to its source. A great soul will be strong to live, as well as strong to think. Does he lack organ or medium to impart his truths? He can still fall back on this elemental force of living them. This is a total act. Thinking is a partial act. Let the grandeur of justice shine in his affairs. Let the beauty of affection cheer his lowly roof. Those 'far from fame,' who dwell and act with him, will feel the force of his constitution in the doings and passages of the day better than it can be measured by any public and designed display. Time shall teach him, that the scholar loses no hour which the man lives. Herein he unfolds the sacred germ of his instinct, screened from influence. What is lost in seemliness is gained in strength. Not out of those, on whom systems of education have exhausted their culture, comes the helpful giant to destroy the old or to build the new, but out of unhandselled savage nature, out of terrible Druids and Berserkirs,° come at last Alfred° and Shakspeare.

I hear therefore with joy whatever is beginning to be said of the dignity and necessity of labor to every citizen. There is virtue yet in the hoe and the spade, for learned as well as for unlearned hands. And labor is everywhere welcome; always we are invited to work; only be this limitation observed, that a man shall not for the sake of wider activity sacrifice any opinion to the popular judgments and modes of action.

I have now spoken of the education of the scholar by nature, by books, and by action. It remains to say somewhat of his duties.

They are such as become Man Thinking. They may all be comprised in self-trust. The office of the scholar is to cheer, to raise, and to guide men by showing them facts amidst appearances. He plies the slow, unhonored, and unpaid task of observation. Flamsteed and Herschel,° in their glazed observatories, may catalogue the stars with the praise of all men, and, the results being splendid and useful, honor is sure. But he, in his private observatory, cataloguing obscure and nebulous stars of the human mind, which as yet no man has thought of as such,—watching days and months, sometimes, for a few facts; correcting still his old records;—must relinquish display and immediate fame. In the long period of his preparation, he must betray often an ignorance and shiftlessness in popular arts, incurring the disdain of the able who shoulder him aside. Long he must stammer in his speech; often forego the living for the dead. Worse yet, he must accept,—how often! poverty and solitude. For the ease and pleasure of treading the old road, accepting the fashions, the education, the religion of society, he takes the cross of making his own, and, of course, the self-accusation, the faint heart, the frequent uncertainty and loss of time, which are the nettles and tangling vines in the way of the self-relying and self-directed; and the state of virtual hostility in which he seems to stand to society, and especially to educated society. For all this loss and scorn, what offset? He is to find consolation in exercising the highest functions of human nature. He is one, who raises himself from private considerations, and breathes and lives on public and illustrious thoughts. He is the world's eye. He is the world's heart. He is to resist the vulgar prosperity that retrogrades ever to barbarism, by preserving and communicating heroic sentiments, noble biographies, melodious verse, and the conclusions of history. Whatsoever oracles the human heart, in all emergencies, in all solemn hours, has uttered as its commentary on the world of actions,—these he shall receive and impart. And whatsoever new verdict Reason from her inviolable seat pronounces on the passing men and events of to-day,—this he shall hear and promulgate.

These being his functions, it becomes him to feel all confidence in himself, and to defer never to the popular cry. He and he only knows the world. The world of any moment is the merest appearance. Some great decorum, some fetish of a government, some ephemeral trade, or war, or man, is cried up by half mankind and cried down by the other half, as if all depended on this particular up or down. The odds are that the whole question is not worth the poorest thought which the scholar has lost in listening to the controversy. Let him not quit his belief that a popgun is a popgun, though the ancient and honorable of the earth affirm it to be the crack of doom. In silence, in steadiness, in severe abstraction, let him hold by himself; add observation to observation, patient of neglect, patient of reproach; and bide his own time,—happy enough, if he can satisfy himself alone, that this day he has seen something truly. Success treads on every right step. For the instinct is sure, that prompts him to tell his brother what he thinks. He then learns, that in going down into the secrets of his own mind, he has descended into the secrets of all minds. He learns that he who has mastered any law in his private thoughts, is master to that extent of all men whose language he speaks, and of all into whose language his own can be translated. The poet, in utter solitude remembering his spontaneous thoughts and recording them, is found to have recorded that, which men in crowded cities find true for them also. The orator distrusts at first the fitness of his frank confessions,—his want of knowledge of the persons he addresses,—until he finds that he is the complement of his hearers;— that they drink his words because he fulfils for them their own nature; the deeper he dives into his privatest, secretest presentiment, to his wonder he finds, this is the most acceptable, most public, and univer- sally true. The people delight in it; the better part of every man feels, This is my music; this is myself.

In self-trust, all the virtues are comprehended. Free should the scholar be,—free and brave. Free even to the definition of freedom, 'without any hindrance that does not arise out of his own constitution.' Brave; for fear is a thing, which a scholar by his very function puts behind him. Fear always springs from ignorance. It is a shame to him if his tranquillity, amid dangerous times, arise from the presumption, that, like children and women, his is a protected class; or if he seek a temporary peace by the diversion of his thoughts from politics or vexed questions, hiding his head like an ostrich in the flowering bushes, peep- ing into microscopes, and turning rhymes, as a boy whistles to keep his courage up. So is the danger a danger still; so is the fear worse. Man- like let him turn and face it. Let him look into its eye and search its nature, inspect its origin,—see the whelping of this lion,—which lies no great way back; he will then find in himself a perfect comprehension of its nature and extent; he will have made his hands meet on the other side, and can henceforth defy it, and pass on superior. The world is his, who can see through its pretension. What deafness, what stone-blind custom, what overgrown error you behold, is there only by suffer- ance,—by your sufferance. See it to be a lie, and you have already dealt it its mortal blow.

Yes, we are the cowed,—we the trustless. It is a mischievous notion that we are come late into nature; that the world was finished a long time ago. As the world was plastic and fluid in the hands of God, so it is ever to so much of his attributes as we bring to it. To ignorance and sin, it is flint. They adapt themselves to it as they may; but in proportion as a man has any thing in him divine, the firmament flows before him and takes his signet and form. Not he is great who can alter matter, but he who can alter my state of mind. They are the kings of the world who give the color of their present thought to all nature and all art, and persuade men by the cheerful serenity of their carrying the matter, that this thing which they do, is the apple which the ages have desired to pluck, now at last ripe, and inviting nations to the harvest. The great man makes the great thing. Wherever Macdonald sits, there is the head of the table. Linnæus makes botany the most alluring of studies, and wins it from the farmer and the herb-woman; Davy, chemistry; and Cuvier,° fossils. The day is always his, who works in it with serenity and great aims. The unstable estimates of men crowd to him whose mind is filled with a truth, as the heaped waves of the Atlantic follow the moon.

For this self-trust, the reason is deeper than can be fathomed,—darker than can be enlightened. I might not carry with me the feeling of my audience in stating my own belief. But I have already shown the ground of my hope, in adverting to the doctrine that man is one. I believe man has been wronged; he has wronged himself. He has almost lost the light, that can lead him back to his prerogatives. Men are become of no account. Men in history, men in the world of to-day are bugs, are spawn, and are called 'the mass' and 'the herd'. In a century, in a millennium, one or two men; that is to say,—one or two approximations to the right state of every man. All the rest behold in the hero or the poet their own green and crude being,—ripened; yes, and are content to be less, so *that* may attain to its full stature. What a testimony,—full of grandeur, full of pity, is borne to the demands of his own nature, by the poor clansman, the poor partisan, who rejoices in the glory of his chief. The poor and the low find some amends to their immense moral capacity, for their acquiescence in a political and social inferiority. They are content to be brushed like flies from the path of a great person, so that justice shall be done by him to that common nature which it is the dearest desire of all to see enlarged and glorified. They sun themselves in the great man's light, and feel it to be their own element. They cast the dignity of man from their downtrod selves upon the shoulders of a hero, and will perish to add one drop of blood to make that great heart beat, those giant sinews combat and conquer. He lives for us, and we live in him.

Men such as they are, very naturally seek money or power; and power because it is as good as money,—the 'spoils,' so called, 'of office.' And why not? for they aspire to the highest, and this, in their sleep-walking, they dream is highest. Wake them, and they shall quit the false good, and leap to the true, and leave governments to clerks and desks. This revolution is to be wrought by the gradual domestication of the idea of Culture. The main enterprise of the world for splendor, for extent, is the upbuilding of a man. Here are the materials strown along the ground. The private life of one man shall be a more illustrious monarchy,—more formidable to its enemy, more sweet and serene in its influence to its friend, than any kingdom in history. For a man, rightly viewed, comprehendeth the particular natures of all men. Each philosopher, each bard, each actor, has only done for me, as by a delegate, what one day I can do for myself. The books which once we valued more than the apple of the eye, we have quite exhausted. What is that but saying, that we have come up with the point of view which the universal mind took through the eyes of one scribe; we have been that man, and have passed on. First, one; then, another; we drain all cisterns, and, waxing greater by all these supplies, we crave a better and more abundant food. The man has never lived that can feed us ever. The human mind cannot be enshrined in a person, who shall set a barrier on any one side to this unbounded, unboundable empire. It is one central fire, which, flaming now out of the lips of Etna, lightens the capes of Sicily; and, now out of the throat of Vesuvius, illuminates the towers and vineyards of Naples. It is one light which beams out of a thousand stars. It is one soul which animates all men.

But I have dwelt perhaps tediously upon this abstraction of the Scholar. I ought not to delay longer to add what I have to say, of nearer reference to the time and to this country.

Historically, there is thought to be a difference in the ideas which predominate over successive epochs, and there are data for marking the genius of the Classic, of the Romantic, and now of the Reflective or Philosophical age. With the views I have intimated of the oneness or the identity of the mind through all individuals, I do not much dwell on these differences. In fact, I believe each individual passes through all three. The boy is a Greek; the youth, romantic; the adult, reflective. I deny not, however, that a revolution in the leading idea may be distinctly enough traced.

Our age is bewailed as the age of Introversion. Must that needs be evil? We, it seems, are critical; we are embarrassed with second thoughts; we cannot enjoy any thing for hankering to know whereof the pleasure consists; we are lined with eyes; we see with our feet; the time is infected with Hamlet's unhappiness,—

'Sicklied o'er with the pale cast of thought.'°

Is it so bad then? Sight is the last thing to be pitied. Would we be blind? Do we fear lest we should outsee nature and God, and drink truth dry? I look upon the discontent of the literary class, as a mere announcement of the fact, that they find themselves not in the state of mind of their fathers, and regret the coming state as untried; as a boy dreads the water before he has learned that he can swim. If there is any period one would desire to be born in,—is it not the age of Revolution; when the old and the new stand side by side, and admit of being compared; when the energies of all men are searched by fear and by hope; when the historic glories of the old, can be compensated by the rich possibilities of the new era? This time, like all times, is a very good one, if we but know what to do with it.

I read with joy some of the auspicious signs of the coming days, as they glimmer already through poetry and art, through philosophy and science, through church and state.

One of these signs is the fact, that the same movement which effected the elevation of what was called the lowest class in the state, assumed in literature a very marked and as benign an aspect. Instead of the sublime and beautiful; the near, the low, the common, was explored and poetized. That, which had been negligently trodden under foot by those who were harnessing and provisioning themselves for long journeys into far countries, is suddenly found to be richer than all foreign parts. The literature of the poor, the feelings of the child, the philosophy of the street, the meaning of household life, are the topics of the time. It is a great stride. It is a sign,—is it not? of new vigor, when the extremities are made active, when currents of warm life run into the hands and the feet. I ask not for the great, the remote, the romantic; what is doing in Italy or Arabia; what is Greek art, or Provençal minstrelsy; I embrace the common, I explore and sit at the feet of the familiar, the low. Give me insight into to-day, and you may have the antique and future worlds. What would we really know the meaning of? The meal in the firkin; the milk in the pan; the ballad in the street; the news of the boat; the glance of the eye; the form and the gait of the body;—show me the ultimate reason of these matters; show me the sublime presence of the highest spiritual cause lurking, as always it does lurk, in these suburbs and extremities of nature; let me see every trifle bristling with the polarity that ranges it instantly on an eternal law; and the shop, the plough, and the leger, referred to the like cause by which light undulates and poets sing;—and the world lies no longer a dull miscellany and lumber-room, but has form and order; there is no trifle; there is no puzzle; but one design unites and animates the farthest pinnacle and the lowest trench.

This idea has inspired the genius of Goldsmith, Burns, Cowper, and, in a newer time, of Goethe, Wordsworth, and Carlyle. This idea they have differently followed and with various success. In contrast with their writing, the style of Pope, of Johnson, of Gibbon, looks cold and pedantic. This writing is blood-warm. Man is surprised to find that things near are not less beautiful and wondrous than things remote. The near explains the far. The drop is a small ocean. A man is related to all nature. This perception of the worth of the vulgar is fruitful in discoveries. Goethe, in this very thing the most modern of the moderns, has shown us, as none ever did, the genius of the ancients.

There is one man of genius, who has done much for this philosophy of life, whose literary value has never yet been rightly estimated;—I mean Emanuel Swedenborg. The most imaginative of men, yet writing with the precision of a mathematician, he endeavored to engraft a purely philosophical Ethics on the popular Christianity of his time. Such an attempt, of course, must have difficulty, which no genius could surmount. But he saw and showed the connection between nature and the affections of the soul. He pierced the emblematic or spiritual character of the visible, audible, tangible world. Especially did his shade-loving muse hover over and interpret the lower parts of nature; he showed the mysterious bond that allies moral evil to the foul material forms, and has given in epical parables a theory of insanity, of beasts, of unclean and fearful things.

Another sign of our times, also marked by an analogous political movement, is, the new importance given to the single person. Every thing that tends to insulate the individual,—to surround him with barriers of natural respect, so that each man shall feel the world is his, and man shall treat with man as a sovereign state with a sovereign state;— tends to true union as well as greatness. 'I learned,' said the melancholy Pestalozzi,° 'that no man in God's wide earth is either willing or able to help any other man.' Help must come from the bosom alone. The scholar is that man who must take up into himself all the ability of the time, all the contributions of the past, all the hopes of the future. He must be an university of knowledges. If there be one lesson more than another, which should pierce his ear, it is, The world is nothing, the man is all; in yourself is the law of all nature, and you know not yet how a globule of sap ascends; in yourself slumbers the whole of Reason; it is for you to know all, it is for you to dare all. Mr. President and Gentlemen, this confidence in the unsearched might of man belongs, by all motives, by all prophecy, by all preparation, to the American Scholar. We have listened too long to the courtly muses of Europe. The spirit of the American freeman is already suspected to be timid, imitative, tame. Public and private avarice make the air we breathe thick and fat. The scholar is decent, indolent, complaisant. See already the tragic consequence. The mind of this country, taught to aim at low objects, eats upon itself. There is no work for any but the decorous and the complaisant. Young men of the fairest promise, who begin life upon our shores, inflated by the mountain winds, shined upon by all the stars of God, find the earth below not in unison with these,—but are hindered from action by the disgust which the principles on which business is managed inspire, and turn drudges, or die of disgust,—some of them suicides. What is the remedy? They did not yet see, and thousands of young men as hopeful now crowding to the barriers for the career, do not yet see, that, if the single man plant himself indomitably on his instincts, and there abide, the huge world will come round to him. Patience,—patience;—with the shades of all the good and great for company; and for solace, the perspective of your own infinite life; and for work, the study and the communication of principles, the making those instincts prevalent, the conversion of the world. Is it not the chief disgrace in the world, not to be an unit;—not to be reckoned one character;—not to yield that peculiar fruit which each man was created to bear, but to be reckoned in the gross, in the hundred, or the thousand, of the party, the section, to which we belong; and our opinion predicted geographically, as the north, or the south? Not so, brothers and friends,—please God, ours shall not be so. We will walk on our own feet; we will work with our own hands; we will speak our own minds. The study of letters shall be no longer a name for pity, for doubt, and for sensual indulgence. The dread of man and the love of man shall be a wall of defence and a wreath of joy around all. A nation of men will for the first time exist, because each believes himself inspired by the Divine Soul which also inspires all men.

AN ADDRESS

Delivered before the Senior Class in Divinity College,
Cambridge, Sunday Evening, July 15, 1838

IN this refulgent summer, it has been a luxury to draw the breath of life. The grass grows, the buds burst, the meadow is spotted with fire and gold in the tint of flowers. The air is full of birds, and sweet with the breath of the pine, the balm-of-Gilead, and the new hay. Night brings no gloom to the heart with its welcome shade. Through the transparent darkness the stars pour their almost spiritual rays. Man under them seems a young child, and his huge globe a toy. The cool night bathes the world as with a river, and prepares his eyes again for the crimson dawn. The mystery of nature was never displayed more happily. The corn and the wine have been freely dealt to all creatures, and the never-broken silence with which the old bounty goes forward, has not yielded yet one word of explanation. One is constrained to respect the perfection of this world, in which our senses converse. How wide; how rich; what invitation from every property it gives to every faculty of man! In its fruitful soils; in its navigable sea; in its mountains of metal and stone; in its forests of all woods; in its animals; in its chemical ingredients; in the powers and path of light, heat, attraction, and life, it is well worth the pith and heart of great men to subdue and enjoy it. The planters, the mechanics, the inventors, the astronomers, the builders of cities, and the captains, history delights to honor.

But when the mind opens, and reveals the laws which traverse the universe, and make things what they are, then shrinks the great world at once into a mere illustration and fable of this mind. What am I? and What is? asks the human spirit with a curiosity new-kindled, but never to be quenched. Behold these outrunning laws, which our imperfect apprehension can see tend this way and that, but not come full circle. Behold these infinite relations, so like, so unlike; many, yet one. I would study, I would know, I would admire forever. These works of thought have been the entertainments of the human spirit in all ages.

A more secret, sweet, and overpowering beauty appears to man when his heart and mind open to the sentiment of virtue. Then he is instructed in what is above him. He learns that his being is without bound; that, to the good, to the perfect, he is born, low as he now lies in evil and weakness. That which he venerates is still his own, though he has not realized it yet. *He ought.* He knows the sense of that grand word, though his analysis fails entirely to render account of it. When in innocency, or when by intellectual perception, he attains to say,—'I love the Right; Truth is beautiful within and without, forevermore. Virtue, I am thine: save me: use me: thee will I serve, day and night, in great, in small, that I may be not virtuous, but virtue;'—then is the end of the creation answered, and God is well pleased.

The sentiment of virtue is a reverence and delight in the presence of certain divine laws. It perceives that this homely game of life we play, covers, under what seem foolish details, principles that astonish. The child amidst his baubles, is learning the action of light, motion, gravity, muscular force; and in the game of human life, love, fear, justice, appetite, man, and God, interact. These laws refuse to be adequately stated. They will not be written out on paper, or spoken by the tongue. They elude our persevering thought; yet we read them hourly in each other's faces, in each other's actions, in our own remorse. The moral traits which are all globed into every virtuous act and thought,—in speech, we must sever, and describe or suggest by painful enumeration of many particulars. Yet, as this sentiment is the essence of all religion, let me guide your eye to the precise objects of the sentiment, by an enumeration of some of those classes of facts in which this element is conspicuous.

The intuition of the moral sentiment is an insight of the perfection of the laws of the soul. These laws execute themselves. They are out of time, out of space, and not subject to circumstance. Thus; in the soul of man there is a justice whose retributions are instant and entire. He who does a good deed, is instantly ennobled. He who does a mean deed, is by the action itself contracted. He who puts off impurity, thereby puts on purity. If a man is at heart just, then in so far is he God; the safety of God, the immortality of God, the majesty of God do enter into that man with justice. If a man dissemble, deceive, he deceives himself, and goes out of acquaintance with his own being. A man in the view of absolute goodness, adores, with total humility. Every step so downward, is a step upward. The man who renounces himself, comes to himself.

See how this rapid intrinsic energy worketh everywhere, righting wrongs, correcting appearances, and bringing up facts to a harmony with thoughts. Its operation in life, though slow to the senses, is, at last, as sure as in the soul. By it, a man is made the Providence to himself, dispensing good to his goodness, and evil to his sin. Character is always known. Thefts never enrich; alms never impoverish; murder will speak out of stone walls. The least admixture of a lie,—for example, the taint of vanity, the least attempt to make a good impression, a favorable appearance,—will instantly vitiate the effect. But speak the truth, and all nature and all spirits help you with unexpected furtherance. Speak the truth, and all things alive or brute are vouchers, and the very roots of the grass underground there, do seem to stir and move to bear you witness. See again the perfection of the Law as it applies itself to the affections, and becomes the law of society. As we are, so we associate. The good, by affinity, seek the good; the vile, by affinity, the vile. Thus of their own volition, souls proceed into heaven, into hell.

These facts have always suggested to man the sublime creed, that the world is not the product of manifold power, but of one will, of one mind; and that one mind is everywhere active, in each ray of the star, in each wavelet of the pool; and whatever opposes that will, is everywhere balked and baffled, because things are made so, and not otherwise. Good is positive. Evil is merely privative, not absolute: it is like cold, which is the privation of heat. All evil is so much death or nonentity. Benevolence is absolute and real. So much benevolence as a man hath, so much life hath he. For all things proceed out of this same spirit, which is differently named love, justice, temperance, in its different applications, just as the ocean receives different names on the several shores which it washes. All things proceed out of the same spirit, and all things conspire with it. Whilst a man seeks good ends, he is strong by the whole strength of nature. In so far as he roves from these ends, he bereaves himself of power, of auxiliaries; his being shrinks out of all remote channels, he becomes less and less, a mote, a point, until absolute badness is absolute death.

The perception of this law of laws awakens in the mind a sentiment which we call the religious sentiment, and which makes our highest happiness. Wonderful is its power to charm and to command. It is a mountain air. It is the embalmer of the world. It is myrrh and storax, and chlorine and rosemary. It makes the sky and the hills sublime, and the silent song of the stars is it. By it, is the universe made safe and habitable, not by science or power. Thought may work cold and intransitive in things, and find no end or unity; but the dawn of the sentiment of virtue on the heart, gives and is the assurance that Law is sovereign over all natures; and the worlds, time, space, eternity, do seem to break out into joy.

This sentiment is divine and deifying. It is the beatitude of man. It makes him illimitable. Through it, the soul first knows itself. It corrects the capital mistake of the infant man, who seeks to be great by following the great, and hopes to derive advantages *from another*,—by showing the fountain of all good to be in himself, and that he, equally with every man, is an inlet into the deeps of Reason. When he says, 'I ought'; when love warms him; when he chooses, warned from on high, the good and great deed; then, deep melodies wander through his soul from Supreme Wisdom. Then he can worship, and be enlarged by his worship; for he can never go behind this sentiment. In the sublimest flights of the soul, rectitude is never surmounted, love is never outgrown.

This sentiment lies at the foundation of society, and successively creates all forms of worship. The principle of veneration never dies out. Man fallen into superstition, into sensuality, is never quite without the visions of the moral sentiment. In like manner, all the expressions of this sentiment are sacred and permanent in proportion to their purity. The expressions of this sentiment affect us more than all other compositions. The sentences of the oldest time, which ejaculate this piety, are still fresh and fragrant. This thought dwelled always deepest in the minds of men in the devout and contemplative East; not alone in Palestine, where it reached its purest expression, but in Egypt, in Persia, in India, in China. Europe has always owed to oriental genius, its divine impulses. What these holy bards said, all sane men found agreeable and true. And the unique impression of Jesus upon mankind, whose name is not so much written as ploughed into the history of this world, is proof of the subtle virtue of this infusion.

Meantime, whilst the doors of the temple stand open, night and day, before every man, and the oracles of this truth cease never, it is guarded by one stern condition; this, namely; it is an intuition. It cannot be received at second hand. Truly speaking, it is not instruction, but provocation, that I can receive from another soul. What he announces, I must find true in me, or wholly reject; and on his word, or as his second, be he who he may, I can accept nothing. On the contrary, the absence of this primary faith is the presence of degradation. As is the flood so is the ebb. Let this faith depart, and the very words it spake, and the things it made, become false and hurtful. Then falls the church, the state, art, letters, life. The doctrine of the divine nature being forgotten, a sickness infects and dwarfs the constitution. Once man was all; now he is an appendage, a nuisance. And because the indwelling Supreme Spirit cannot wholly be got rid of, the doctrine of it suffers this perversion, that the divine nature is attributed to one or two persons, and denied to all the rest, and denied with fury. The doctrine of inspiration is lost; the base doctrine of the majority of voices, usurps the place of the doctrine of the soul. Miracles, prophecy, poetry; the

ideal life, the holy life, exist as ancient history merely; they are not in
the belief, nor in the aspiration of society; but, when suggested, seem
ridiculous. Life is comic or pitiful, as soon as the high ends of being
fade out of sight, and man becomes near-sighted, and can only attend
to what addresses the senses.

These general views, which, whilst they are general, none will contest, find abundant illustration in the history of religion, and especially
in the history of the Christian church. In that, all of us have had our
birth and nurture. The truth contained in that, you, my young friends,
are now setting forth to teach. As the Cultus, or established worship
of the civilized world, it has great historical interest for us. Of its
blessed words, which have been the consolation of humanity, you
need not that I should speak. I shall endeavor to discharge my duty to
you, on this occasion, by pointing out two errors in its administration,
which daily appear more gross from the point of view we have just
now taken.

Jesus Christ belonged to the true race of prophets. He saw with open
eye the mystery of the soul. Drawn by its severe harmony, ravished with
its beauty, he lived in it, and had his being there. Alone in all history, he
estimated the greatness of man. One man was true to what is in you and
me. He saw that God incarnates himself in man, and evermore goes
forth anew to take possession of his world. He said, in this jubilee of
sublime emotion, 'I am divine. Through me, God acts; through me,
speaks. Would you see God, see me; or, see thee, when thou also think-
est as I now think.' But what a distortion did his doctrine and memory
suffer in the same, in the next, and the following ages! There is no doctrine of the Reason which will bear to be taught by the Understanding.
The understanding caught this high chant from the poet's lips, and
said, in the next age, 'This was Jehovah come down out of heaven. I will
kill you, if you say he was a man.' The idioms of his language, and
the figures of his rhetoric, have usurped the place of his truth; and
churches are not built on his principles, but on his tropes. Christianity
became a Mythus, as the poetic teaching of Greece and of Egypt,
before. He spoke of miracles; for he felt that man's life was a miracle,
and all that man doth, and he knew that this daily miracle shines, as the
character ascends. But the word Miracle, as pronounced by Christian
churches, gives a false impression; it is Monster. It is not one with the
blowing clover and the falling rain.

He felt respect for Moses and the prophets; but no unfit tenderness
at postponing their initial revelations, to the hour and the man that now
is; to the eternal revelation in the heart. Thus was he a true man.

Having seen that the law in us is commanding, he would not suffer it to be commanded. Boldly, with hand, and heart, and life, he declared it was God. Thus is he, as I think, the only soul in history who has appreciated the worth of a man.

1. In this point of view we become very sensible of the first defect of historical Christianity. Historical Christianity has fallen into the error that corrupts all attempts to communicate religion. As it appears to us, and as it has appeared for ages, it is not the doctrine of the soul, but an exaggeration of the personal, the positive, the ritual. It has dwelt, it dwells, with noxious exaggeration about the *person* of Jesus. The soul knows no persons. It invites every man to expand to the full circle of the universe, and will have no preferences but those of spontaneous love. But by this eastern monarchy of a Christianity, which indolence and fear have built, the friend of man is made the injurer of man. The manner in which his name is surrounded with expressions, which were once sallies of admiration and love, but are now petrified into official titles, kills all generous sympathy and liking. All who hear me, feel, that the language that describes Christ to Europe and America, is not the style of friendship and enthusiasm to a good and noble heart, but is appropriated and formal,—paints a demigod, as the Orientals or the Greeks would describe Osiris or Apollo. Accept the injurious impositions of our early catachetical instruction, and even honesty and self-denial were but splendid sins, if they did not wear the Christian name. One would rather be

'A pagan, suckled in a creed outworn,'°

than to be defrauded of his manly right in coming into nature, and finding not names and places, not land and professions, but even virtue and truth foreclosed and monopolized. You shall not be a man even. You shall not own the world; you shall not dare, and live after the infinite Law that is in you, and in company with the infinite Beauty which heaven and earth reflect to you in all lovely forms; but you must subordinate your nature to Christ's nature; you must accept our interpretations; and take his portrait as the vulgar draw it.

That is always best which gives me to myself. The sublime is excited in me by the great stoical doctrine, Obey thyself. That which shows God in me, fortifies me. That which shows God out of me, makes me a wart and a wen. There is no longer a necessary reason for my being. Already the long shadows of untimely oblivion creep over me, and I shall decease forever.

The divine bards are the friends of my virtue, of my intellect, of my strength. They admonish me, that the gleams which flash across my mind, are not mine, but God's; that they had the like, and were not disobedient to the heavenly vision.° So I love them. Noble provocations go out from them, inviting me to resist evil; to subdue the world; and to Be. And thus by his holy thoughts, Jesus serves us, and thus only. To aim to convert a man by miracles, is a profanation of the soul. A true conversion, a true Christ, is now, as always, to be made, by the reception of beautiful sentiments. It is true that a great and rich soul, like his, falling among the simple, does so preponderate, that, as his did, it names the world. The world seems to them to exist for him, and they have not yet drunk so deeply of his sense, as to see that only by coming again to themselves, or to God in themselves, can they grow forevermore. It is a low benefit to give me something; it is a high benefit to enable me to do somewhat of myself. The time is coming when all men will see, that the gift of God to the soul is not a vaunting, overpowering, excluding sanctity, but a sweet, natural goodness, a goodness like thine and mine, and that so invites thine and mine to be and to grow.

The injustice of the vulgar tone of preaching is not less flagrant to Jesus, than to the souls which it profanes. The preachers do not see that they make his gospel not glad, and shear him of the locks of beauty and the attributes of heaven. When I see a majestic Epaminondas,° or Washington; when I see among my contemporaries, a true orator, an upright judge, a dear friend; when I vibrate to the melody and fancy of a poem; I see beauty that is to be desired. And so lovely, and with yet more entire consent of my human being, sounds in my ear the severe music of the bards that have sung of the true God in all ages. Now do not degrade the life and dialogues of Christ out of the circle of this charm, by insulation and peculiarity. Let them lie as they befel, alive and warm, part of human life, and of the landscape, and of the cheerful day.

2. The second defect of the traditionary and limited way of using the mind of Christ is a consequence of the first; this, namely; that the Moral Nature, that Law of laws, whose revelations introduce greatness,—yea, God himself, into the open soul, is not explored as the fountain of the established teaching in society. Men have come to speak of the revelation as somewhat long ago given and done, as if God were dead. The injury to faith throttles the preacher; and the goodliest of institutions becomes an uncertain and inarticulate voice.

It is very certain that it is the effect of conversation with the beauty of the soul, to beget a desire and need to impart to others the same knowledge and love. If utterance is denied, the thought lies like a burden on the man. Always the seer is a sayer. Somehow his dream is told: somehow he publishes it with solemn joy: sometimes with pencil on canvas; sometimes with chisel on stone; sometimes in towers and aisles of granite, his soul's worship is builded; sometimes in anthems of indefinite music; but clearest and most permanent, in words.

The man enamored of this excellency, becomes its priest or poet. The office is coeval with the world. But observe the condition, the spiritual limitation of the office. The spirit only can teach. Not any profane man, not any sensual, not any liar, not any slave can teach, but only he can give, who has; he only can create, who is. The man on whom the soul descends, through whom the soul speaks, alone can teach. Courage, piety, love, wisdom, can teach; and every man can open his door to these angels, and they shall bring him the gift of tongues. But the man who aims to speak as books enable, as synods use, as the fashion guides, and as interest commands, babbles. Let him hush.

To this holy office, you propose to devote yourselves. I wish you may feel your call in throbs of desire and hope. The office is the first in the world. It is of that reality, that it cannot suffer the deduction of any falsehood. And it is my duty to say to you, that the need was never greater of new revelation than now. From the views I have already expressed, you will infer the sad conviction, which I share, I believe, with numbers, of the universal decay and now almost death of faith in society. The soul is not preached. The Church seems to totter to its fall, almost all life extinct. On this occasion, any complaisance would be criminal, which told you, whose hope and commission it is to preach the faith of Christ, that the faith of Christ is preached.

It is time that this ill-suppressed murmur of all thoughtful men against the famine of our churches; this moaning of the heart because it is bereaved of the consolation, the hope, the grandeur, that come alone out of the culture of the moral nature; should be heard through the sleep of indolence, and over the din of routine. This great and perpetual office of the preacher is not discharged. Preaching is the expression of the moral sentiment in application to the duties of life. In how many churches, by how many prophets, tell me, is man made sensible that he is an infinite Soul; that the earth and heavens are passing into his mind; that he is drinking forever the soul of God? Where now sounds the persuasion, that by its very melody imparadises my heart, and so affirms its own origin in heaven? Where shall I hear words such as in elder ages drew men to leave all and follow,—father and mother, house and land, wife and child? Where shall I hear these august laws of moral being so pronounced, as to fill my ear, and I feel ennobled by the offer of my uttermost action and passion? The test of the true faith, certainly, should be its power to charm and command the soul, as the laws of nature control the activity of the hands,—so commanding that we find pleasure and honor in obeying. The faith should blend with the light of rising and of setting suns, with the flying cloud, the singing bird, and the breath of flowers. But now the priest's Sabbath has lost the splendor of nature; it is unlovely; we are glad when it is done; we can make, we do make, even sitting in our pews, a far better, holier, sweeter, for ourselves.

Whenever the pulpit is usurped by a formalist, then is the worshipper defrauded and disconsolate. We shrink as soon as the prayers begin, which do not uplift, but smite and offend us. We are fain to wrap our cloaks about us, and secure, as best we can, a solitude that hears not. I once heard a preacher who sorely tempted me to say, I would go to church no more. Men go, thought I, where they are wont to go, else had no soul entered the temple in the afternoon. A snow storm was falling around us. The snow storm was real; the preacher merely spectral; and the eye felt the sad contrast in looking at him, and then out of the window behind him, into the beautiful meteor of the snow. He had lived in vain. He had no one word intimating that he had laughed or wept, was married or in love, had been commended, or cheated, or chagrined. If he had ever lived and acted, we were none the wiser for it. The capital secret of his profession, namely, to convert life into truth, he had not learned. Not one fact in all his experience, had he yet imported into his doctrine. This man had ploughed, and planted, and talked, and bought, and sold; he had read books; he had eaten and drunken; his head aches; his heart throbs; he smiles and suffers; yet was there not a surmise, a hint, in all the discourse, that he had ever lived at all. Not a line did he draw out of real history. The true preacher can be known by this, that he deals out to the people his life,—life passed through the fire of thought. But of the bad preacher, it could not be told from his sermon, what age of the world he fell in; whether he had a father or a child; whether he was a freeholder or a pauper; whether he was a citizen or a countryman; or any other fact of his biography. It seemed strange that the people should come to church. It seemed as if their houses were very unentertaining, that they should prefer this thoughtless clamor. It shows that there is a commanding attraction in the moral sentiment, that can lend a faint tint of light to dulness and ignorance, coming in its name and place. The good hearer is sure he has been touched sometimes; is sure there is somewhat to be reached, and some word that can reach it. When he listens to these vain words, he comforts himself by their relation to his remembrance of better hours, and so they clatter and echo unchallenged.

I am not ignorant that when we preach unworthily, it is not always quite in vain. There is a good ear, in some men, that draws supplies to virtue out of very indifferent nutriment. There is poetic truth concealed in all the commonplaces of prayer and of sermons, and though foolishly spoken, they may be wisely heard; for, each is some select expression that broke out in a moment of piety from some stricken or jubilant soul, and its excellency made it remembered. The prayers and even the dogmas of our church, are like the zodiac of Denderah, and the astronomical monuments of the Hindoos, wholly insulated from anything now extant in the life and business of the people. They mark the height to which the waters once rose. But this docility is a check upon the mischief from the good and devout. In a large portion of the community, the religious service gives rise to quite other thoughts and emotions. We need not chide the negligent servant. We are struck with pity, rather, at the swift retribution of his sloth. Alas for the unhappy man that is called to stand in the pulpit, and *not* give bread of life. Everything that befalls, accuses him. Would he ask contributions for the missions, foreign or domestic? Instantly his face is suffused with shame, to propose to his parish, that they should send money a hundred or a thousand miles, to furnish such poor fare as they have at home, and would do well to go the hundred or the thousand miles to escape. Would he urge people to a godly way of living;—and can he ask a fellow-creature to come to Sabbath meetings, when he and they all know what is the poor uttermost they can hope for therein? Will he invite them privately to the Lord's Supper? He dares not. If no heart warm this rite, the hollow, dry, creaking formality is too plain, than that he can face a man of wit and energy, and put the invitation without terror. In the street, what has he to say to the bold village blasphemer? The village blasphemer sees fear in the face, form, and gait of the minister.

Let me not taint the sincerity of this plea by any oversight of the claims of good men. I know and honor the purity and strict conscience of numbers of the clergy. What life the public worship retains, it owes to the scattered company of pious men, who minister here and there in the churches, and who, sometimes accepting with too great tenderness the tenet of the elders, have not accepted from others, but from their own heart, the genuine impulses of virtue, and so still command our love and awe, to the sanctity of character. Moreover, the exceptions are not so much to be found in a few eminent preachers, as in the better hours, the truer inspirations of all,—nay, in the sincere moments of every man. But with whatever exception, it is still true, that tradition characterizes the preaching of this country; that it comes out of the memory, and not out of the soul; that it aims at what is usual, and not at what is necessary and eternal; that thus, historical Christianity destroys the power of preaching, by withdrawing it from the exploration of the moral nature of man, where the sublime is, where are the resources of astonishment and power. What a cruel injustice it is to that Law, the joy of the whole earth, which alone can make thought dear and rich; that Law whose fatal sureness the astronomical orbits poorly emulate, that it is travestied and depreciated, that it is behooted and behowled, and not a trait, not a word of it articulated. The pulpit in losing sight of this Law, loses its reason, and gropes after it knows not what. And for want of this culture, the soul of the community is sick and faithless. It wants nothing so much as a stern, high, stoical, Christian discipline, to make it know itself and the divinity that speaks through it. Now man is ashamed of himself; he skulks and sneaks through the world, to be tolerated, to be pitied, and scarcely in a thousand years does any man dare to be wise and good, and so draw after him the tears and blessings of his kind.

Certainly there have been periods when, from the inactivity of the intellect on certain truths, a greater faith was possible in names and persons. The Puritans in England and America, found in the Christ of the Catholic Church, and in the dogmas inherited from Rome, scope for their austere piety, and their longings for civil freedom. But their creed is passing away, and none arises in its room. I think no man can go with his thoughts about him, into one of our churches, without feeling, that what hold the public worship had on men is gone, or going. It has lost its grasp on the affection of the good, and the fear of the bad. In the country, neighborhoods, half parishes are *signing off*,—to use the local term. It is already beginning to indicate character and religion to withdraw from the religious meetings. I have heard a devout person,° who prized the Sabbath, say in bitterness of heart, 'On Sundays, it seems wicked to go to church.' And the motive, that holds the best there, is now only a hope and a waiting. What was once a mere circumstance, that the best and the worst men in the parish, the poor and the rich, the learned and the ignorant, young and old, should meet one day as fellows in one house, in sign of an equal right in the soul,—has come to be a paramount motive for going thither.

My friends, in these two errors, I think, I find the causes of a decaying church and a wasting unbelief. And what greater calamity can fall upon a nation, than the loss of worship? Then all things go to decay.

Genius leaves the temple, to haunt the senate, or the market. Literature becomes frivolous. Science is cold. The eye of youth is not lighted by the hope of other worlds, and age is without honor. Society lives to trifles, and when men die, we do not mention them.

And now, my brothers, you will ask, What in these desponding days can be done by us? The remedy is already declared in the ground of our complaint of the Church. We have contrasted the Church with the Soul. In the soul, then, let the redemption be sought. Wherever a man comes, there comes revolution. The old is for slaves. When a man comes, all books are legible, all things transparent, all religions are forms. He is religious. Man is the wonderworker. He is seen amid miracles. All men bless and curse. He saith yea and nay, only. The stationariness of religion; the assumption that the age of inspiration is past, that the Bible is closed; the fear of degrading the character of Jesus by representing him as a man; indicate with sufficient clearness the falsehood of our theology. It is the office of a true teacher to show us that God is, not was; that He speaketh, not spake. The true Christianity,—a faith like Christ's in the infinitude of man,—is lost. None believeth in the soul of man, but only in some man or person old and departed. Ah me! no man goeth alone. All men go in flocks to this saint or that poet, avoiding the God who seeth in secret.° They cannot see in secret; they love to be blind in public. They think society wiser than their soul, and know not that one soul, and their soul, is wiser than the whole world. See how nations and races flit by on the sea of time, and leave no ripple to tell where they floated or sunk, and one good soul shall make the name of Moses, or of Zeno, or of Zoroaster,° reverend forever. None assayeth the stern ambition to be the Self of the nation, and of nature, but each would be an easy secondary to some Christian scheme, or sectarian connection, or some eminent man. Once leave your own knowledge of God, your own sentiment, and take secondary knowledge, as St. Paul's, or George Fox's,° or Swedenborg's, and you get wide from God with every year this secondary form lasts, and if, as now, for centuries,—the chasm yawns to that breadth, that men can scarcely be convinced there is in them anything divine.

Let me admonish you, first of all, to go alone; to refuse the good models, even those which are sacred in the imagination of men, and dare to love God without mediator or veil. Friends enough you shall find who will hold up to your emulation Wesleys and Oberlins,° Saints and Prophets. Thank God for these good men, but say, 'I also am a man.' Imitation cannot go above its model. The imitator dooms himself to hopeless mediocrity. The inventor did it, because it was natural to him, and so in him it has a charm. In the imitator, something else is natural, and he bereaves himself of his own beauty, to come short of another man's.

Yourself a newborn bard of the Holy Ghost,—cast behind you all conformity, and acquaint men at first hand with Deity. Look to it first and only, that fashion, custom, authority, pleasure, and money, are nothing to you,—are not bandages over your eyes, that you cannot see,—but live with the privilege of the immeasurable mind. Not too anxious to visit periodically all families and each family in your parish connection,—when you meet one of these men or women, be to them a divine man; be to them thought and virtue; let their timid aspirations find in you a friend; let their trampled instincts be genially tempted out in your atmosphere; let their doubts know that you have doubted, and their wonder feel that you have wondered. By trusting your own heart, you shall gain more confidence in other men. For all our penny-wisdom, for all our soul-destroying slavery to habit, it is not to be doubted, that all men have sublime thoughts; that all men value the few real hours of life; they love to be heard; they love to be caught up into the vision of principles. We mark with light in the memory the few interviews we have had, in the dreary years of routine and of sin, with souls that made our souls wiser; that spoke what we thought; that told us what we knew; that gave us leave to be what we inly were. Discharge to men the priestly office, and, present or absent, you shall be followed with their love as by an angel.

And, to this end, let us not aim at common degrees of merit. Can we not leave, to such as love it, the virtue that glitters for the commendation of society, and ourselves pierce the deep solitudes of absolute ability and worth? We easily come up to the standard of goodness in society. Society's praise can be cheaply secured, and almost all men are content with those easy merits; but the instant effect of conversing with God, will be, to put them away. There are persons who are not actors, not speakers, but influences; persons too great for fame, for display; who disdain eloquence; to whom all we call art and artist, seems too nearly allied to show and by-ends, to the exaggeration of the finite and selfish, and loss of the universal. The orators, the poets, the commanders encroach on us only as fair women do, by our allowance and homage. Slight them by preoccupation of mind, slight them, as you can well afford to do, by high and universal aims, and they instantly feel that you have right, and that it is in lower places that they must shine. They also feel your right; for they with you are open to the influx of the all-knowing Spirit, which annihilates before its broad noon the little shades and gradations of intelligence in the compositions we call wiser and wisest.

In such high communion, let us study the grand strokes of rectitude: a bold benevolence, an independence of friends, so that not the unjust wishes of those who love us, shall impair our freedom, but we shall resist for truth's sake the freest flow of kindness, and appeal to sympathies far in advance; and,—what is the highest form in which we know this beautiful element,—a certain solidity of merit, that has nothing to do with opinion, and which is so essentially and manifestly virtue, that it is taken for granted, that the right, the brave, the generous step will be taken by it, and nobody thinks of commending it. You would compliment a coxcomb doing a good act, but you would not praise an angel. The silence that accepts merit as the most natural thing in the world, is the highest applause. Such souls, when they appear, are the Imperial Guard of Virtue, the perpetual reserve, the dictators of fortune. One needs not praise their courage,—they are the heart and soul of nature. O my friends, there are resources in us on which we have not drawn. There are men who rise refreshed on hearing a threat; men to whom a crisis which intimidates and paralyzes the majority,— demanding not the faculties of prudence and thrift, but comprehension, immovableness, the readiness of sacrifice,—comes graceful and beloved as a bride. Napoleon said of Massena,° that he was not himself until the battle began to go against him; then, when the dead began to fall in ranks around him, awoke his powers of combination, and he put on terror and victory as a robe. So it is in rugged crises, in unweariable endurance, and in aims which put sympathy out of question, that the angel is shown. But these are heights that we can scarce remember and look up to, without contrition and shame. Let us thank God that such things exist.

And now let us do what we can to rekindle the smouldering, nigh quenched fire on the altar. The evils of the church that now is are manifest. The question returns, What shall we do? I confess, all attempts to project and establish a Cultus with new rites and forms, seem to me vain. Faith makes us, and not we it, and faith makes its own forms. All attempts to contrive a system are as cold as the new worship introduced by the French to the goddess of Reason,—to-day, pasteboard and fillagree, and ending to-morrow in madness and murder. Rather let the breath of new life be breathed by you through the forms already existing. For, if once you are alive, you shall find they shall become plastic and new. The remedy to their deformity is, first, soul, and second, soul, and evermore, soul. A whole popedom of forms, one pulsation of virtue can uplift and vivify. Two inestimable advantages Christianity has given us; first; the Sabbath, the jubilee of the whole world; whose light dawns welcome alike into the closet of the philosopher, into the garret of toil, and into prison cells, and everywhere suggests, even to the vile, the dignity of spiritual being. Let it stand forevermore, a temple, which new love, new faith, new sight shall restore to more than its first splendor to mankind. And secondly, the institution of preaching,—the speech of man to men,—essentially the most flexible of all organs, of all forms. What hinders that now, everywhere, in pulpits, in lecture-rooms, in houses, in fields, wherever the invitation of men or your own occasions lead you, you speak the very truth, as your life and conscience teach it, and cheer the waiting, fainting hearts of men with new hope and new revelation?

I look for the hour when that supreme Beauty, which ravished the souls of those eastern men, and chiefly of those Hebrews, and through their lips spoke oracles to all time, shall speak in the West also. The Hebrew and Greek Scriptures contain immortal sentences, that have been bread of life to millions. But they have no epical integrity; are fragmentary; are not shown in their order to the intellect. I look for the new Teacher, that shall follow so far those shining laws, that he shall see them come full circle; shall see their rounding complete grace; shall see the world to be the mirror of the soul; shall see the identity of the law of gravitation with purity of heart; and shall show that the Ought, that Duty, is one thing with Science, with Beauty, and with Joy.

THE CONSERVATIVE

A Lecture delivered at the Masonic Temple, Boston, December 9, 1841

THE two parties which divide the state, the party of Conservatism and that of Innovation, are very old, and have disputed the possession of the world ever since it was made. This quarrel is the subject of civil history. The conservative party established the reverend hierarchies and monarchies of the most ancient world. The battle of patrician and plebeian, of parent state and colony, of old usage and accommodation to new facts, of the rich and the poor, reappears in all countries and times. The war rages not only in battlefields, in national councils, and ecclesiastical synods, but agitates every man's bosom with opposing advantages every hour. On rolls the old world meantime, and now one, now the other gets the day, and still the fight renews itself as if for the first time, under new names and hot personalities.

Such an irreconcilable antagonism, of course, must have a correspondent depth of seat in the human constitution. It is the opposition of Past and Future, of Memory and Hope, of the Understanding and the Reason. It is the primal antagonism, the appearance in trifles of the two poles of nature.

There is a fragment of old fable which seems somehow to have been dropped from the current mythologies, which may deserve attention, as it appears to relate to this subject.

Saturn° grew weary of sitting alone, or with none but the great Uranus or Heaven beholding him, and he created an oyster. Then he would act again, but he made nothing more, but went on creating the race of oysters. Then Uranus cried, 'a new work, O Saturn! the old is not good again.'

Saturn replied. 'I fear. There is not only the alternative of making and not making, but also of unmaking. Seest thou the great sea, how it ebbs and flows? so is it with me; my power ebbs; and if I put forth my hands, I shall not do, but undo. Therefore I do what I have done; I hold what I have got; and so I resist Night and Chaos.'

'O Saturn,' replied Uranus, 'thou canst not hold thine own, but by making more. Thy oysters are barnacles and cockles, and with the next flowing of the tide, they will be pebbles and sea-foam.'

'I see,' rejoins Saturn, 'thou art in league with Night, thou art become an evil eye; thou spakest from love; now thy words smite me with hatred. I appeal to Fate, must there not be rest?'—'I appeal to Fate also,' said Uranus, 'must there not be motion?'—But Saturn was silent, and went on making oysters for a thousand years.

After that, the word of Uranus came into his mind like a ray of the sun, and he made Jupiter; and then he feared again; and nature froze, the things that were made went backward, and, to save the world, Jupiter slew his father Saturn.

This may stand for the earliest account of a conversation on politics between a Conservative and a Radical, which has come down to us. It is ever thus. It is the counteraction of the centripetal and the centrifugal forces. Innovation is the salient energy; Conservatism the pause on the last movement. 'That which is was made by God,' saith Conservatism. 'He is leaving that, he is entering this other;' rejoins Innovation.

There is always a certain meanness in the argument of conservatism, joined with a certain superiority in its fact. It affirms because it holds. Its fingers clutch the fact, and it will not open its eyes to see a better fact. The castle, which conservatism is set to defend, is the actual state of things, good and bad. The project of innovation is the best possible state of things. Of course, conservatism always has the worst of the argument, is always apologizing, pleading a necessity, pleading that to change would be to deteriorate; it must saddle itself with the mountain-ous load of the violence and vice of society, must deny the possibility of good, deny ideas, and suspect and stone the prophet; whilst innovation is always in the right, triumphant, attacking, and sure of final success. Conservatism stands on man's confessed limitations; reform on his indisputable infinitude; conservatism on circumstance; liberalism on power; one goes to make an adroit member of the social frame; the other to postpone all things to the man himself; conservatism is debon-nair and social; reform is individual and imperious. We are reformers in spring and summer; in autumn and winter, we stand by the old; reformers in the morning, conservers at night. Reform is affirmative, conservatism negative; conservatism goes for comfort, reform for truth. Conservatism is more candid to behold another's worth; reform more disposed to maintain and increase its own. Conservatism makes no poetry, breathes no prayer, has no invention; it is all memory. Reform has no gratitude, no prudence, no husbandry. It makes a great differ-ence to your figure and to your thought, whether your foot is advancing or receding. Conservatism never puts the foot forward; in the hour when it does that, it is not establishment, but reform. Conservatism tends to universal seeming and treachery, believes in a negative fate; believes that men's temper governs them; that for me, it avails not to trust in principles; they will fail me; I must bend a little; it distrusts nature; it thinks there is a general law without a particular application,— law for all that does not include any one. Reform in its antagonism inclines to asinine resistance, to kick with hoofs; it runs to egotism and bloated self-conceit; it runs to a bodiless pretension, to unnatural refining and elevation, which ends in hypocrisy and sensual reaction.

And so whilst we do not go beyond general statements, it may be safely affirmed of these two metaphysical antagonists, that each is a good half, but an impossible whole. Each exposes the abuses of the other, but in a true society, in a true man, both must combine. Nature does not give the crown of its approbation, namely, beauty, to any action or emblem or actor, but to one which combines both these elements; not to the rock which resists the waves from age to age, nor to the wave which lashes incessantly the rock, but the superior beauty is with the oak which stands with its hundred arms against the storms of a century, and grows every year like a sapling; or the river which ever flowing, yet is found in the same bed from age to age; or, greatest of all, the man who has subsisted for years amid the changes of nature, yet has distanced himself, so that when you remember what he was, and see what he is, you say, what strides! what a disparity is here!

Throughout nature the past combines in every creature with the present. Each of the convolutions of the sea-shell, each node and spine marks one year of the fish's life, what was the mouth of the shell for one season, with the addition of new matter by the growth of the animal, becoming an ornamental node. The leaves and a shell of soft wood are all that the vegetation of this summer has made, but the solid columnar stem, which lifts that bank of foliage into the air to draw the eye and to cool us with its shade, is the gift and legacy of dead and buried years.

In nature, each of these elements being always present, each theory has a natural support. As we take our stand on Necessity, or on Ethics, shall we go for the conservative, or for the reformer. If we read the world historically, we shall say, Of all the ages, the present hour and circumstance is the cumulative result; this is the best throw of the dice of nature that has yet been, or that is yet possible. If we see it from the side of Will, or the Moral Sentiment, we shall accuse the Past and the Present, and require the impossible of the Future.

But although this bifold fact lies thus united in real nature, and so united that no man can continue to exist in whom both these elements do not work, yet men are not philosophers, but are rather very foolish children, who, by reason of their partiality, see everything in the most absurd manner, and are the victims at all times of the nearest object.

There is even no philosopher who is a philosopher at all times. Our experience, our perception is conditioned by the need to acquire in parts and in succession, that is, with every truth a certain falsehood. As this is the invariable method of our training, we must give it allowance, and suffer men to learn as they have done for six millenniums, a word at a time, to pair off into insane parties, and learn the amount of truth each knows, by the denial of an equal amount of truth. For the present, then, to come at what sum is attainable to us, we must even hear the parties plead as parties.

That which is best about conservatism, that which, though it cannot be expressed in detail, inspires reverence in all, is the Inevitable. There is the question not only, what the conservative says for himself? but, why must he say it? What insurmountable fact binds him to that side? Here is the fact which men call Fate, and fate in dread degrees, fate behind fate, not to be disposed of by the consideration that the Conscience commands this or that, but necessitating the question, whether the faculties of man will play him true in resisting the facts of universal experience? For although the commands of the Conscience are *essentially* absolute, they are *historically* limitary. Wisdom does not seek a literal rectitude, but an useful, that is, a conditioned one, such a one as the faculties of man and the constitution of things will warrant. The reformer, the partisan loses himself in driving to the utmost some specialty of right conduct, until his own nature and all nature resist him; but Wisdom attempts nothing enormous and disproportioned to its powers, nothing which it cannot perform or nearly perform. We have all a certain intellection or presentiment of reform existing in the mind, which does not yet descend into the character, and those who throw themselves blindly on this lose themselves. Whatever they attempt in that direction, fails, and reacts suicidally on the actor himself. This is the penalty of having transcended nature. For the existing world is not a dream, and cannot with impunity be treated as a dream; neither is it a disease; but it is the ground on which you stand, it is the mother of whom you were born. Reform converses with possibilities, perchance with impossibilities; but here is sacred fact. This also was true, or it could not be: it had life in it, or it could not have existed; it has life in it, or it could not continue. Your schemes may be feasible, or may not be, but this has the endorsement of nature and a long friendship and cohabitation with the powers of nature. This will stand until a better cast of the dice is made. The contest between the Future and the Past is one between Divinity entering, and Divinity departing. You are welcome to try your experiments, and, if you can, to displace the actual order by that ideal republic you announce, for nothing but God will expel God. But plainly the burden of proof must lie with the projector. We hold to this, until you can demonstrate something better.

The system of property and law goes back for its origin to barbarous and sacred times; it is the fruit of the same mysterious cause as the mineral or animal world. There is a natural sentiment and prepossession in favor of age, of ancestors, of barbarous and aboriginal usages, which is a homage to the element of necessity and divinity which is in them. The respect for the old names of places, of mountains, and streams, is universal. The Indian and barbarous name can never be supplanted without loss. The ancients tell us that the gods loved the Ethiopians for their stable customs; and the Egyptians and Chaldeans,° whose origin could not be explored, passed among the junior tribes of Greece and Italy for sacred nations.

Moreover, so deep is the foundation of the existing social system, that it leaves no one out of it. We may be partial, but Fate is not. All men have their root in it. You who quarrel with the arrangements of society, and are willing to embroil all, and risk the indisputable good that exists, for the chance of better, live, move, and have your being in this, and your deeds contradict your words every day. For as you cannot jump from the ground without using the resistance of the ground, nor put out the boat to sea, without shoving from the shore, nor attain liberty without rejecting obligation, so you are under the necessity of using the Actual order of things, in order to disuse it; to live by it, whilst you wish to take away its life. The past has baked your loaf, and in the strength of its bread you would break up the oven. But you are betrayed by your own nature. You also are conservatives. However men please to style themselves, I see no other than a conservative party. You are not only identical with us in your needs, but also in your methods and aims. You quarrel with my conservatism, but it is to build up one of your own; it will have a new beginning, but the same course and end, the same trials, the same passions; among the lovers of the new I observe that there is a jealousy of the newest, and that the seceder from the seceder is as damnable as the pope himself.

On these and the like grounds of general statement, conservatism plants itself without danger of being displaced. Especially before this *personal* appeal, the innovator must confess his weakness, must confess that no man is to be found good enough to be entitled to stand champion for the principle. But when this great tendency comes to practical encounters, and is challenged by young men, to whom it is no abstraction, but a fact of hunger, distress, and exclusion from opportunities, it must needs seem injurious. The youth, of course, is an innovator by the fact of his birth. There he stands, newly born on the planet, a universal beggar, with all the reason of things, one would say, on his side. In his first consideration how to feed, clothe, and warm himself, he is met by warnings on every hand, that this thing and that thing have owners, and he must go elsewhere. Then he says; If I am born into the earth, where is my part? have the goodness, gentlemen of this world, to show me my wood-lot, where I may fell my wood, my field where to plant my corn, my pleasant ground where to build my cabin.

'Touch any wood, or field, or house-lot, on your peril', cry all the gentlemen of this world; 'but you may come and work in ours, for us, and we will give you a piece of bread.'

And what is that peril?

Knives and muskets, if we meet you in the act; imprisonment, if we find you afterward.

And by what authority, kind gentlemen?

By our law.

And your law,—is it just?

As just for you as it was for us. We wrought for others under this law, and got our lands so.

I repeat the question, Is your law just?

Not quite just, but necessary. Moreover, it is juster now than it was when we were born; we have made it milder and more equal.

I will none of your law, returns the youth; it encumbers me. I cannot understand, or so much as spare time to read that needless library of your laws. Nature has sufficiently provided me with rewards and sharp penalties, to bind me not to transgress. Like the Persian noble of old,° I ask 'that I may neither command nor obey'. I do not wish to enter into your complex social system. I shall serve those whom I can, and they who can will serve me. I shall seek those whom I love, and shun those whom I love not, and what more can all your laws render me?

With equal earnestness and good faith, replies to this plaintiff an upholder of the establishment, a man of many virtues:

Your opposition is feather-brained and overfine. Young man, I have no skill to talk with you, but look at me; I have risen early and sat late, and toiled honestly, and painfully for very many years. I never dreamed about methods; I laid my bones to, and drudged for the good I possess; it was not got by fraud, nor by luck, but by work, and you must show me a warrant like these stubborn facts in your own fidelity and labor, before I suffer you, on the faith of a few fine words, to ride into my estate, and claim to scatter it as your own.

Now you touch the heart of the matter, replies the reformer. To that fidelity and labor, I pay homage. I am unworthy to arraign your manner of living, until I too have been tried. But I should be more unworthy, if I did not tell you why I cannot walk in your steps. I find this vast network, which you call property, extended over the whole planet. I cannot occupy the bleakest crag of the White Hills or the Alleghany Range, but some man or corporation steps up to me to show me that it is his. Now, though I am very peaceable, and on my private account could well enough die, since it appears there was some mistake in my creation, and that I have been *mis*sent to this earth, where all the seats were already taken,—yet I feel called upon in behalf of rational nature, which I represent, to declare to you my opinion, that, if the Earth is yours, so also is it mine. All your aggregate existences are less to me a fact than is my own; as I am born to the earth, so the Earth is given to me, what I want of it to till and to plant; nor could I, without pusillanimity, omit to claim so much. I must not only have a name to live, I must live. My genius leads me to build a different manner of life from any of yours. I cannot then spare you the whole world. I love you better. I must tell you the truth practically; and take that which you call yours. It is God's world and mine; yours as much as you want, mine as much as I want. Besides, I know your ways; I know the symptoms of the disease. To the end of your power, you will serve this lie which cheats you. Your want is a gulf which the possession of the broad earth would not fill. Yonder sun in heaven you would pluck down from shining on the universe, and make him a property and privacy, if you could; and the moon and the north star you would quickly have occasion for in your closet and bed-chamber. What you do not want for use, you crave for ornament, and what your convenience could spare, your pride cannot.

On the other hand, precisely the defence which was set up for the British Constitution, namely, that with all its admitted defects, rotten boroughs and monopolies, it worked well, and substantial justice was somehow done; the wisdom and the worth did get into parliament, and every interest did by right, or might, or sleight, get represented;—the same defence is set up for the existing institutions. They are not the best; they are not just; and in respect to you, personally, O brave young man! they cannot be justified. They have, it is most true, left you no acre for your own, and no law but our law, to the ordaining of which, you were no party. But they do answer the end, they are really friendly to the good; unfriendly to the bad; they second the industrious, and the kind; they foster genius. They really have so much flexibility as to afford your talent and character, on the whole, the same chance of demonstration and success which they might have, if there was no law and no property.

It is trivial and merely superstitious to say that nothing is given you, no outfit, no exhibition; for in this institution of *credit*, which is as universal as honesty and promise in the human countenance, always some neighbor stands ready to be bread and land and tools and stock to the young adventurer. And if in any one respect they have come short, see what ample retribution of good they have made. They have lost no time and spared no expense to collect libraries, museums, galleries, colleges, palaces, hospitals, observatories, cities. The ages have not been idle, nor kings slack, nor the rich niggardly. Have we not atoned for this small offence (which we could not help) of leaving you no right in the soil, by this splendid indemnity of ancestral and national wealth? Would you have been born like a gipsy in a hedge, and preferred your freedom on a heath, and the range of a planet which had no shed or boscage to cover you from sun and wind,—to this towered and citied world? to this world of Rome, and Memphis, and Constantinople, and Vienna, and Paris, and London, and New York? For thee Naples, Florence, and Venice, for thee the fair Mediterranean, the sunny Adriatic; for thee both Indies smile; for thee the hospitable North opens its heated palaces under the polar circle; for thee roads have been cut in every direction across the land, and fleets of floating palaces with every security for strength, and provision for luxury, swim by sail and by steam through all the waters of this world. Every island for thee has a town; every town a hotel. Though thou wast born landless, yet to thy industry and thrift and small condescension to the established usage,— scores of servants are swarming in every strange place with cap and knee to thy command, scores, nay hundreds and thousands, for thy wardrobe, thy table, thy chamber, thy library, thy leisure; and every whim is anticipated and served by the best ability of the whole population of each country. The king on the throne governs for thee, and the judge judges; the barrister pleads, the farmer tills, the joiner hammers, the postman rides. Is it not exaggerating a trifle to insist on a formal acknowledgment of your claims, when these substantial advantages have been secured to you? Now can your children be educated, your labor turned to their advantage, and its fruits secured to them after your death. It is frivolous to say, you have no acre, because you have not a mathematically measured piece of land. Providence takes care that you shall have a place, that you are waited for, and come accredited; and, as soon as you put your gift to use, you shall have acre or acre's worth according to your exhibition of desert,—acre, if you need land;—acre's worth, if you prefer to draw, or carve, or make shoes, or wheels, to the tilling of the soil.

Besides, it might temper your indignation at the supposed wrong which society has done you, to keep the question before you, how society got into this predicament? Who put things on this false basis? No single man, but all men. No man voluntarily and knowingly; but it is the result of that degree of culture there is in the planet. The order of things is as good as the character of the population permits. Consider it as the work of a great and beneficent and progressive necessity, which, from the first pulsation of the first animal life, up to the present high culture of the best nations, has advanced thus far. Thank the rude fostermother though she has taught you a better wisdom than her own, and has set hopes in your heart which shall be history in the next ages. You are yourself the result of this manner of living, this foul compromise, this vituperated Sodom. It nourished you with care and love on its breast, as it had nourished many a lover of the right, and many a poet, and prophet, and teacher of men. Is it so irremediably bad? Then again, if the mitigations are considered, do not all the mischiefs virtually vanish? The form is bad, but see you not how every personal character reacts on the form, and makes it new? A strong person makes the law and custom null before his own will. Then the principle of love and truth reappears in the strictest courts of fashion and property. Under the richest robes, in the darlings of the selectest circles of European or American aristocracy, the strong heart will beat with love of mankind, with impatience of accidental distinctions, with the desire to achieve its own fate, and make every ornament it wears authentic and real.

Moreover, as we have already shown that there is no pure reformer, so it is to be considered that there is no pure conservative, no man who from the beginning to the end of his life maintains the defective institutions; but he who sets his face like a flint against every novelty, when approached in the confidence of conversation, in the presence of friendly and generous persons, has also his gracious and relenting motions, and espouses for the time the cause of man; and even if this be a shortlived emotion, yet the remembrance of it in private hours mitigates his selfishness and compliance with custom.

The Friar Bernard° lamented in his cell on Mount Cenis the crimes of mankind, and rising one morning before day from his bed of moss and dry leaves, he gnawed his roots and berries, drank of the spring, and set forth to go to Rome to reform the corruption of mankind. On his way he encountered many travellers who greeted him courteously; and the cabins of the peasants and the castles of the lords supplied his few wants. When he came at last to Rome, his piety and good will easily introduced him to many families of the rich, and on the first day he saw and talked with gentle mothers with their babes at their breasts, who told him how much love they bore their children, and how they were perplexed in their daily walk lest they should fail in their duty to them. 'What!' he said, 'and this on rich embroidered carpets, on marble floors, with cunning sculpture, and carved wood, and rich pictures, and piles of books about you?'—'Look at our pictures and books,' they said, 'and we will tell you, good Father, how we spent the last evening. These are stories of godly children and holy families and romantic sacrifices made in old or in recent times by great and not mean persons; and last evening, our family was collected, and our husbands and brothers discoursed sadly on what we could save and give in the hard times.' Then came in the men, and they said, 'What cheer, brother? Does thy convent want gifts?' Then the friar Bernard went home swiftly with other thoughts than he brought, saying, 'This way of life is wrong, yet these Romans, whom I prayed God to destroy, are lovers, they are lovers; what can I do?'

The reformer concedes that these mitigations exist, and that, if he proposed comfort, he should take sides with the establishment. Your words are excellent, but they do not tell the whole. Conservatism is affluent and openhanded, but there is a cunning juggle in riches. I observe that they take somewhat for everything they give. I look bigger, but am less; I have more clothes, but am not so warm; more armor, but less courage; more books, but less wit. What you say of your planted, builded and decorated world, is true enough, and I gladly avail myself of its convenience; yet I have remarked that what holds in particular, holds in general, that the plant Man does not require for his most glorious flowering this pomp of preparation and convenience, but the thoughts of some beggarly Homer who strolled, God knows when, in the infancy and barbarism of the old world, the gravity and sense of some slave Moses who leads away his fellow slaves from their masters; the contemplation of some Scythian Anacharsis; the erect, formidable valor of some Dorian townsmen in the town of Sparta; the vigor of Clovis the Frank, and Alfred the Saxon, and Alaric the Goth, and Mahomet, Ali, and Omar the Arabians, Saladin the Curd, and Othman the Turk,° sufficed to build what you call society, on the spot and in the instant when the sound mind in a sound body appeared. Rich and fine is your dress, O conservatism! your horses are of the best blood; your roads are well cut and well paved; your pantry is full of meats and your cellar of wines, and a very good state and condition are you for gentlemen and ladies to live under; but every one of these goods steals away a drop of my blood. I want the necessity of supplying my own wants. All this costly culture of yours is not necessary. Greatness does not need it. Yonder peasant, who sits neglected there in a corner, carries a whole revolution of man and nature in his head, which shall be a sacred history to some future ages. For man is the end of nature; nothing so easily organizes itself in every part of the universe as he; no moss, no lichen is so easily born; and he takes along with him and puts out from himself the whole apparatus of society and condition *extempore*, as an army encamps in a desert, and where all was just now blowing sand, creates a white city in an hour, a government, a market, a place for feasting, for conversation, and for love.

These considerations, urged by those whose characters and whose fortunes are yet to be formed, must needs command the sympathy of all reasonable persons. But beside that charity which should make all adult persons interested for the youth, and engage them to see that he has a free field and fair play on his entrance into life, we are bound to see that the society, of which we compose a part, does not permit the formation or continuance of views and practices injurious to the honor and welfare of mankind. The objection to conservatism, when embodied in a party, is, that in its love of acts, it hates principles; it lives in the senses, not in truth; it sacrifices to despair; it goes for availableness in its candidate, not for worth; and for expediency in its measures, and not for the right. Under pretence of allowing for friction, it makes so many additions and supplements to the machine of society, that it will play smoothly and softly, but will no longer grind any grist.

The conservative party in the universe concedes that the radical would talk sufficiently to the purpose, if we were still in the garden of Eden; he legislates for man as he ought to be; his theory is right, but he makes no allowance for friction; and this omission makes his whole doctrine false. The idealist retorts, that the conservative falls into a far more noxious error in the other extreme. The conservative assumes sickness as a necessity, and his social frame is a hospital, his total legislation is for the present distress, a universe in slippers and flannels, with bib and papspoon, swallowing pills and herb-tea. Sickness gets organized as well as health, the vice as well as the virtue. Now that a vicious system of trade has existed so long, it has stereotyped itself in the human generation, and misers are born. And now that sickness has got such a foothold, leprosy has grown cunning, has got into the ballot-box; the lepers outvote the clean; society has resolved itself into a Hospital Committee, and all its laws are quarantine. If any man resist, and set up a foolish hope he has entertained as good against the general despair, society frowns on him, shuts him out of her opportunities, her granaries, her refectories, her water and bread, and will serve him a sexton's turn. Conservatism takes as low a view of every part of human action and passion. Its religion is just as bad; a lozenge for the sick; a dolorous tune to beguile the distemper; mitigations of pain by pillows and anodynes; always mitigations, never remedies; pardons for sin, funeral honors,—never self-help, renovation, and virtue. Its social and political action has no better aim; to keep out wind and weather, to bring the day and year about, and make the world last our day; not to sit on the world and steer it; not to sink the memory of the past in the glory of a new and more excellent creation; a timid cobbler and patcher, it degrades whatever it touches. The cause of education is urged in this country with the utmost earnestness,—on what ground? why on this, that the people have the power, and if they are not instructed to sympathize with the intelligent, reading, trading, and governing class, inspired with a taste for the same competitions and prizes, they will upset the fair pageant of Judicature, and perhaps lay a hand on the sacred muniments of wealth itself, and new distribute the land. Religion is taught in the same spirit. The contractors who were building a road out of Baltimore, some years ago, found the Irish laborers quarrelsome and refractory, to a degree that embarrassed the agents, and seriously interrupted the progress of the work. The corporation were advised to call off the police, and build a Catholic chapel; which they did; the priest presently restored order, and the work went on prosperously. Such hints, be sure, are too valuable to be lost. If you do not value the Sabbath, or other religious institutions, give yourself no concern about maintaining them. They have already acquired a market value as conservators of property; and if priest and church-member should fail, the chambers of commerce and the presidents of the Banks, the very innholders and landlords of the county would muster with fury to their support.

Of course, religion in such hands loses its essence. Instead of that reliance, which the soul suggests on the eternity of truth and duty, men are misled into a reliance on institutions, which, the moment they cease to be the instantaneous creations of the devout sentiment, are worthless. Religion among the low becomes low. As it loses its truth, it loses credit with the sagacious. They detect the falsehood of the preaching, but when they say so, all good citizens cry, Hush; do not weaken the state, do not take off the strait jacket from dangerous persons. Every honest fellow must keep up the hoax the best he can; must patronize providence and piety, and wherever he sees anything that will keep men amused, schools or churches or poetry, or picture-galleries or music, or what not, he must cry 'Hist-a-boy,' and urge the game on. What a compliment we pay to the good SPIRIT with our superserviceable zeal!

But not to balance reasons for and against the establishment any longer, and if it still be asked in this necessity of partial organization, which party on the whole has the highest claims on our sympathy? I bring it home to the private heart, where all such questions must have their final arbitrement. How will every strong and generous mind choose its ground,—with the defenders of the old? or with the seekers of the new? Which is that state which promises to edify a great, brave, and beneficent man; to throw him on his resources, and tax the strength of his character? On which part will each of us find himself in the hour of health and of aspiration?

I understand well the respect of mankind for war, because that breaks up the Chinese stagnation of society, and demonstrates the personal merits of all men. A state of war or anarchy, in which law has little force, is so far valuable, that it puts every man on trial. The man of principle is known as such, and even in the fury of faction is respected. In the civil wars of France, Montaigne° alone, among all the French gentry, kept his castle gates unbarred, and made his personal integrity as good at least as a regiment. The man of courage and resources is shown, and the effeminate and base person. Those who rise above war, and those who fall below it, it easily discriminates, as well as those, who, accepting its rude conditions, keep their own head by their own sword.

But in peace and a commercial state we depend, not as we ought, on our knowledge and all men's knowledge that we are honest men, but we cowardly lean on the virtue of others. For it is always at last the virtue of some men in the society, which keeps the law in any reverence and power. Is there not something shameful that I should owe my peaceful occupancy of my house and field, not to the knowledge of my countrymen that I am useful, but to their respect for sundry other reputable persons, I know not whom, whose joint virtues still keep the law in good odor?

It will never make any difference to a hero what the laws are. His greatness will shine and accomplish itself unto the end, whether they second him or not. If he have earned his bread by drudgery, and in the narrow and crooked ways which were all an evil law had left him, he will make it at least honorable by his expenditure. Of the past he will take no heed; for its wrongs he will not hold himself responsible: he will say, all the meanness of my progenitors shall not bereave me of the power to make this hour and company fair and fortunate. Whatsoever streams of power and commodity flow to me, shall of me acquire healing virtue, and become fountains of safety. Cannot I too descend a Redeemer into nature? Whosoever hereafter shall name my name, shall not record a malefactor, but a benefactor in the earth. If there be power in good intention, in fidelity, and in toil, the north wind shall be purer, the stars in heaven shall glow with a kindlier beam, that I have lived. I am primarily engaged to myself to be a public servant of all the gods, to demonstrate to all men that there is intelligence and good will at the heart of things, and ever higher and yet higher leadings. These are my engagements; how can your law further or hinder me in what I shall do to men? On the other hand, these dispositions establish their relations to me. Wherever there is worth, I shall be greeted. Wherever there are men, are the objects of my study and love. Sooner or later all men will be my friends, and will testify in all methods the energy of their regard. I cannot thank your law for my protection. I protect it. It is not in its power to protect me. It is my business to make myself revered. I depend on my honor, my labor, and my dispositions, for my place in the affections of mankind, and not on any conventions or parchments of yours.

But if I allow myself in derelictions, and become idle and dissolute, I quickly come to love the protection of a strong law, because I feel no title in myself to my advantages. To the intemperate and covetous person no love flows; to him mankind would pay no rent, no dividend, if force were once relaxed; nay, if they could give their verdict, they would say, that his self-indulgence and his oppression deserved punishment from society, and not that rich board and lodging he now enjoys. The law acts then as a screen of his unworthiness, and makes him worse the longer it protects him.

In conclusion, to return from this alternation of partial views, to the high platform of universal and necessary history, it is a happiness for mankind that innovation has got on so far, and has so free a field before it. The boldness of the hope men entertain transcends all former experience. It calms and cheers them with the picture of a simple and equal life of truth and piety. And this hope flowered on what tree? It was not imported from the stock of some celestial plant, but grew here on the wild crab of conservatism. It is much that this old and vituperated system of things has borne so fair a child. It predicts that amidst a planet peopled with conservatives, one Reformer may yet be born.

THE METHOD OF NATURE

*An Oration delivered before the Society of the Adelphi, in Waterville College, Maine,
August 11, 1841*

GENTLEMEN,

Let us exchange congratulations on the enjoyments and the promises of this literary anniversary. The land we live in has no interest so dear, if it knew its want, as the fit consecration of days of reason and thought. Where there is no vision, the people perish.° The scholars are the priests of that thought which establishes the foundations of the earth. No matter what is their special work or profession, they stand for the spiritual interest of the world, and it is a common calamity if they neglect their post in a country where the material interest is so predominant as it is in America. We hear something too much of the results of machinery, commerce, and the useful arts. We are a puny and a fickle folk. Avarice, hesitation, and following, are our diseases. The rapid wealth which hundreds in the community acquire in trade, or by the incessant expansions of our population and arts, enchants the eyes of all the rest; the luck of one is the hope of thousands, and the bribe acts like the neighborhood of a gold mine to impoverish the farm, the school, the church, the house, and the very body and feature of man.

I do not wish to look with sour aspect at the industrious manufacturing village, or the mart of commerce. I love the music of the waterwheel; I value the railway; I feel the pride which the sight of a ship inspires; I look on trade and every mechanical craft as education also. But let me discriminate what is precious herein. There is in each of these works an act of invention, an intellectual step, or short series of steps taken; that act or step is the spiritual act; all the rest is mere repetition of the same a thousand times. And I will not be deceived into admiring the routine of handicrafts and mechanics, how splendid soever the result, any more than I admire the routine of the scholars or clerical class. That splendid results ensue from the labors of stupid men, is the fruit of higher laws than their will, and the routine is not to be praised for it. I would not have the laborer sacrificed to the result,— I would not have the laborer sacrificed to my convenience and pride, nor to that of a great class of such as me. Let there be worse cotton and better men. The weaver should not be bereaved of his superiority to his work, and his knowledge that the product or the skill is of no value, except so far as it embodies his spiritual prerogatives. If I see nothing to admire in the unit, shall I admire a million units? Men stand in awe of the city, but do not honor any individual citizen; and are continually yielding to this dazzling result of numbers, that which they would never yield to the solitary example of any one.

Whilst the multitude of men degrade each other, and give currency to desponding doctrines, the scholar must be a bringer of hope, and must reinforce man against himself. I sometimes believe that our literary anniversaries will presently assume a greater importance, as the eyes of men open to their capabilities. Here, a new set of distinctions, a new order of ideas, prevail. Here, we set a bound to the respectability of wealth, and a bound to the pretensions of the law and the church. The bigot must cease to be a bigot to-day. Into our charmed circle, power cannot enter; and the sturdiest defender of existing institutions feels the terrific inflammability of this air which condenses heat in every corner that may restore to the elements the fabrics of ages. Nothing solid is secure; every thing tilts and rocks. Even the scholar is not safe; he too is searched and revised. Is his learning dead? Is he living in his memory? The power of mind is not mortification, but life. But come forth, thou curious child! hither, thou loving, all-hoping poet! hither, thou tender, doubting heart, who hast not yet found any place in the world's market fit for thee; any wares which thou couldst buy or sell,—so large is thy love and ambition,—thine and not theirs is the hour. Smooth thy brow, and hope and love on, for the kind heaven justifies thee, and the whole world feels that thou art in the right.

We ought to celebrate this hour by expressions of manly joy. Not thanks, not prayer seem quite the highest or truest name for our communication with the infinite,—but glad and conspiring reception,—reception that becomes giving in its turn, as the receiver is only the All-Giver in part and in infancy. I cannot,—nor can any man,—speak precisely of things so sublime, but it seems to me, the wit of man, his strength, his grace, his tendency, his art, is the grace and the presence of God. It is beyond explanation. When all is said and done, the rapt saint is found the only logician. Not exhortation, not argument becomes our lips, but pæans of joy and praise. But not of adulation: we are too nearly related in the deep of the mind to that we honor. It is God in us which checks the language of petition by a grander thought. In the bottom of the heart, it is said; 'I am, and by me, O child! this fair body and world of thine stands and grows. I am; all things are mine: and all mine are thine.'

The festival of the intellect, and the return to its source, cast a strong light on the always interesting topics of Man and Nature. We are forcibly reminded of the old want. There is no man; there hath never been. The Intellect still asks that a man may be born. The flame of life flickers feebly in human breasts. We demand of men a richness and universality we do not find. Great men do not content us. It is their solitude, not their force, that makes them conspicuous. There is somewhat indigent and tedious about them. They are poorly tied to one thought. If they are prophets, they are egotists; if polite and various, they are shallow. How tardily men arrive at any result! how tardily they pass from it to another! The crystal sphere of thought is as concentrical as the geological structure of the globe. As our soils and rocks lie in strata, concentric strata, so do all men's thinkings run laterally, never vertically. Here comes by a great inquisitor with auger and plumb-line, and will bore an Artesian well through our conventions and theories, and pierce to the core of things. But as soon as he probes the crust, behold gimlet, plumb-line, and philosopher take a lateral direction, in spite of all resistance, as if some strong wind took everything off its feet, and if you come month after month to see what progress our reformer has made,—not an inch has he pierced,—you still find him with new words in the old place, floating about in new parts of the same old vein or crust. The new book says, 'I will give you the key to nature,' and we expect to go like a thunderbolt to the centre. But the thunder is a surface phenomenon, makes a skin-deep cut, and so does the sage. The wedge turns out to be a rocket. Thus a man lasts but a very little while, for his monomania becomes insupportably tedious in a few months. It is so with every book and person: and yet—and yet—we do not take up a new book, or meet a new man, without a pulse-beat of expectation. And this invincible hope of a more adequate interpreter is the sure prediction of his advent.

In the absence of man, we turn to nature, which stands next. In the divine order, intellect is primary; nature, secondary; it is the memory of the mind. That which once existed in intellect as pure law, has now taken body as Nature. It existed already in the mind in solution; now, it has been precipitated, and the bright sediment is the world. We can never be quite strangers or inferiors in nature. It is flesh of our flesh, and bone of our bone. But we no longer hold it by the hand; we have lost our miraculous power; our arm is no more as strong as the frost; nor our will equivalent to gravity and the elective attractions. Yet we can use nature as a convenient standard, and the meter of our rise and fall. It has this advantage as a witness, it cannot be debauched. When man curses, nature still testifies to truth and love. We may, therefore, safely study the mind in nature, because we cannot steadily gaze on it in mind; as we explore the face of the sun in a pool, when our eyes cannot brook his direct splendors.

It seems to me, therefore, that it were some suitable pæan, if we should piously celebrate this hour by exploring the *method of nature*. Let us see *that*, as nearly as we can, and try how far it is transferable to the literary life. Every earnest glance we give to the realities around us, with intent to learn, proceeds from a holy impulse, and is really songs of praise. What difference can it make whether it take the shape of exhortation, or of passionate exclamation, or of scientific statement? These are forms merely. Through them we express, at last, the fact, that God has done thus or thus.

In treating a subject so large, in which we must necessarily appeal to the intuition, and aim much more to suggest, than to describe, I know it is not easy to speak with the precision attainable on topics of less scope. I do not wish in attempting to paint a man, to describe an air-fed, unimpassioned, impossible ghost. My eyes and ears are revolted by any neglect of the physical facts, the limitations of man. And yet one who conceives the true order of nature, and beholds the visible as proceeding from the invisible, cannot state his thought, without seeming to those who study the physical laws, to do them some injustice. There is an intrinsic defect in the organ. Language overstates. Statements of the infinite are usually felt to be unjust to the finite, and blasphemous. Empedocles° undoubtedly spoke a truth of thought, when he said, 'I am God;' but the moment it was out of his mouth, it became a lie to the ear; and the world revenged itself for the seeming arrogance, by the good story about his shoe. How can I hope for better hap in my attempts to enunciate spiritual facts? Yet let us hope, that as far as we receive the truth, so far shall we be felt by every true person to say what is just.

The method of nature: who could ever analyze it? That rushing stream will not stop to be observed. We can never surprise nature in a corner; never find the end of a thread; never tell where to set the first stone. The bird hastens to lay her egg: the egg hastens to be a bird. The wholeness we admire in the order of the world, is the result of infinite distribution. Its smoothness is the smoothness of the pitch of the cataract. Its permanence is a perpetual inchoation. Every natural fact is an emanation, and that from which it emanates is an emanation also, and from every emanation is a new emanation. If anything could stand still, it would be crushed and dissipated by the torrent it resisted, and if it were a mind, would be crazed; as insane persons are those who hold fast to one thought, and do not flow with the course of nature. Not the cause, but an ever novel effect, nature descends always from above. It is unbroken obedience. The beauty of these fair objects is imported into them from a metaphysical and eternal spring. In all animal and vegetable forms, the physiologist concedes that no chemistry, no mechanics, can account for the facts, but a mysterious principle of life must be assumed, which not only inhabits the organ, but makes the organ.

How silent, how spacious, what room for all, yet without place to insert an atom,—in graceful succession, in equal fulness, in balanced beauty, the dance of the hours goes forward still. Like an odor of incense, like a strain of music, like a sleep, it is inexact and boundless. It will not be dissected, nor unravelled, nor shown. Away profane philosopher! seekest thou in nature the cause? This refers to that, and that to the next, and the next to the third, and everything refers. Thou must ask in another mood, thou must feel it and love it, thou must behold it in a spirit as grand as that by which it exists, ere thou canst know the law. Known it will not be, but gladly beloved and enjoyed.

The simultaneous life throughout the whole body, the equal serving of innumerable ends without the least emphasis or preference to any, but the steady degradation of each to the success of all, allows the understanding no place to work. Nature can only be conceived as existing to a universal and not to a particular end, to a universe of ends, and not to one,—a work of *ecstasy*, to be represented by a circular movement, as intention might be signified by a straight line of definite length. Each effect strengthens every other. There is no revolt in all the kingdoms from the commonweal: no detachment of an individual. Hence the catholic character which makes every leaf an exponent of the world. When we behold the landscape in a poetic spirit, we do not reckon individuals. Nature knows neither palm nor oak, but only vegetable life, which sprouts into forests, and festoons the globe with a garland of grasses and vines.

That no single end may be selected, and nature judged thereby, appears from this, that if man himself be considered as the end, and it be assumed that the final cause of the world is to make holy or wise or beautiful men, we see that it has not succeeded. Read alternately in natural and in civil history, a treatise of astronomy, for example, with a volume of French *Memoires pour servir.*° When we have spent our wonder in computing this wasteful hospitality with which boon nature turns off new firmaments without end into her wide common, as fast as the madrepores make coral,—suns and planets hospitable to souls,— and then shorten the sight to look into this court of Louis Quatorze, and see the game that is played there,—duke and marshal, abbé and madame,—a gambling table where each is laying traps for the other, where the end is ever by some lie or fetch to outwit your rival and ruin him with this solemn fop in wig and stars,—the king; one can hardly help asking if this planet is a fair specimen of the so generous astronomy, and if so, whether the experiment have not failed, and whether it be quite worth while to make more, and glut the innocent space with so poor an article.

I think we feel not much otherwise if, instead of beholding foolish nations, we take the great and wise men, the eminent souls, and narrowly inspect their biography. None of them seen by himself—and his performance compared with his promise or idea, will justify the cost of that enormous apparatus of means by which this spotted and defective person was at last procured.

To questions of this sort, nature replies, 'I grow'. All is nascent, infant. When we are dizzied with the arithmetic of the savant toiling to compute the length of her line, the return of her curve, we are steadied by the perception that a great deal is doing; that all seems just begun; remote aims are in active accomplishment. We can point nowhere to anything final; but tendency appears on all hands: planet, system, constellation, total nature is growing like a field of maize in July; is becoming somewhat else; is in rapid metamorphosis. The embryo does not more strive to be man, than yonder burr of light we call a nebula tends to be a ring, a comet, a globe, and parent of new stars. Why should not then these messieurs of Versailles strut and plot for tabourets and ribbons, for a season, without prejudice to their faculty to run on better errands by and by?

But nature seems further to reply, 'I have ventured so great a stake as my success, in no single creature. I have not yet arrived at any end. The gardener aims to produce a fine peach or pear, but my aim is the health of the whole tree,—root, stem, leaf, flower, and seed,—and by no means the pampering of a monstrous pericarp° at the expense of all the other functions.'

In short, the spirit and peculiarity of that impression nature makes on us, is this, that it does not exist to any one or to any number of particular ends, but to numberless and endless benefit; that there is in it no private will, no rebel leaf or limb, but the whole is oppressed by one superincumbent tendency, obeys that redundancy or excess of life which in conscious beings we call *ecstasy*.

With this conception of the genius or method of nature, let us go back to man. It is true, he pretends to give account of himself to himself, but, at last, what has he to recite but the fact that there is a Life not to be described or known otherwise than by possession? What account can he give of his essence more than *so it was to be*? The *royal* reason, the Grace of God seems the only description of our multiform but ever identical fact. There is virtue, there is genius, there is success, or there is not. There is the incoming or the receding of God: that is all we can affirm; and we can show neither how nor why. Self-accusation, remorse, and the didactic morals of self-denial and strife with sin, is a view we are constrained by our constitution to take of the fact seen from the platform of action; but seen from the platform of intellection, there is nothing for us but praise and wonder.

The termination of the world in a man, appears to be the last victory of intelligence. The universal does not attract us until housed in an individual. Who heeds the waste abyss of possibility? The ocean is everywhere the same, but it has no character until seen with the shore or the ship. Who would value any number of miles of Atlantic brine bounded by lines of latitude and longitude? Confine it by granite rocks, let it wash a shore where wise men dwell, and it is filled with expression; and the point of greatest interest is where the land and water meet. So must we admire in man, the form of the formless, the concentration of the vast, the house of reason, the cave of memory. See the play of thoughts! what nimble gigantic creatures are these! what saurians, what palaiotheria° shall be named with these agile movers? The great Pan of old, who was clothed in a leopard skin to signify the beautiful variety of things, and the firmament, his coat of stars,—was but the representative of thee, O rich and various Man! thou palace of sight and sound, carrying in thy senses the morning and the night and the unfathomable galaxy; in thy brain, the geometry of the City of God; in thy heart, the bower of love and the realms of right and wrong. An individual man is a fruit which it cost all the foregoing ages to form and ripen. The history of the genesis or the old mythology repeats itself in the experience of every child. He too is a demon or god thrown into a particular chaos, where he strives ever to lead things from disorder into order. Each individual soul is such, in virtue of its being a power to translate the world into some particular language of its own; if not into a picture, a statue, or a dance,—why, then, into a trade, an art, a science, a mode of living, a conversation, a character, an influence. You admire pictures, but it is as impossible for you to paint a right picture, as for grass to bear apples. But when the genius comes, it makes fingers: it is pliancy, and the power of transferring the affair in the street into oils and colors. Raphael must be born, and Salvator° must be born.

There is no attractiveness like that of a new man. The sleepy nations are occupied with their political routine. England, France and America read Parliamentary Debates, which no high genius now enlivens; and nobody will read them who trusts his own eye: only they who are deceived by the popular repetition of distinguished names. But when Napoleon unrolls his map, the eye is commanded by original power. When Chatham leads the debate, men may well listen, because they must listen. A man, a personal ascendancy is the only great phenomenon. When nature has work to be done, she creates a genius to do it. Follow the great man, and you shall see what the world has at heart in these ages. There is no omen like that.

But what strikes us in the fine genius is that which belongs of right to every one. A man should know himself for a necessary actor. A link was wanting between two craving parts of nature, and he was hurled into being as the bridge over that yawning need, the mediator betwixt two else unmarriageable facts. His two parents held each of one of the wants, and the union of foreign constitutions in him enables him to do gladly and gracefully what the assembled human race could not have sufficed to do. He knows his materials; he applies himself to his work; he cannot read, or think, or look, but he unites the hitherto separated strands into a perfect cord. The thoughts he delights to utter are the reason of his incarnation. Is it for him to account himself cheap and superfluous, or to linger by the wayside for opportunities? Did he not come into being because something must be done which he and no other is and does? If only he *sees*, the world will be visible enough. He need not study where to stand, nor to put things in favorable lights; in him is the light, from him all things are illuminated, to their centre. What patron shall he ask for employment and reward? Hereto was he born, to deliver the thought of his heart from the universe to the universe, to do an office which nature could not forego, nor he be discharged from rendering, and then immerge again into the holy silence and eternity out of which as a man he arose. God is rich, and many more men than one he harbors in his bosom, biding their time and the needs and the beauty of all. Is not this the theory of every man's genius or faculty? Why then goest thou as some Boswell or listening worshipper to this saint or to that? That is the only lese-majesty. Here art thou with whom so long the universe travailed in labor; darest thou think meanly of thyself whom the stalwart Fate brought forth to unite his ragged sides, to shoot the gulf, to reconcile the irreconcilable?

Whilst a necessity so great caused the man to exist, his health and erectness consist in the fidelity with which he transmits influences from the vast and universal to the point on which his genius can act. The ends are momentary: they are vents for the current of inward life which increases as it is spent. A man's wisdom is to know that all ends are momentary, that the best end must be superseded by a better. But there is a mischievous tendency in him to transfer his thought from the life to the ends, to quit his agency and rest in his acts: the tools run away with the workman, the human with the divine. I conceive a man as always spoken to from behind, and unable to turn his head and see the speaker. In all the millions who have heard the voice, none ever saw the face. As children in their play run behind each other, and seize one by the ears and make him walk before them, so is the spirit our unseen pilot. That well-known voice speaks in all languages, governs all men, and none ever caught a glimpse of its form. If the man will exactly obey it, it will adopt him, so that he shall not any longer separate it from himself in his thought, he shall seem to be it, he shall be it. If he listen with insatiable ears, richer and greater wisdom is taught him, the sound swells to a ravishing music, he is borne away as with a flood, he becomes careless of his food and of his house, he is the fool of ideas, and leads a heavenly life. But if his eye is set on the things to be done, and not on the truth that is still taught, and for the sake of which the things are to be done, then the voice grows faint, and at last is but a humming in his ears. His health and greatness consist in his being the channel through which heaven flows to earth, in short, in the fulness in which an ecstatical state takes place in him. It is pitiful to be an artist, when, by forbearing to be artists, we might be vessels filled with the divine overflowings, enriched by the circulations of omniscience and omnipresence. Are there not moments in the history of heaven when the human race was not counted by individuals, but was only the Influenced, was God in distribution, God rushing into multiform benefit? It is sublime to receive, sublime to love, but this lust of imparting as from *us*, this desire to be loved, the wish to be recognized as individuals,—is finite, comes of a lower strain.

Shall I say, then, that, as far as we can trace the natural history of the soul, its health consists in the fulness of its reception,—call it piety, call it veneration—in the fact, that enthusiasm is organized therein. What is best in any work of art, but that part which the work itself seems to require and do; that which the man cannot do again, that which flows from the hour and the occasion, like the eloquence of men in a tumultuous debate? It was always the theory of literature, that the word of a poet was authoritative and final. He was supposed to be the mouth of a divine wisdom. We rather envied his circumstance than his talent. We too could have gladly prophesied standing in that place. We so quote our Scriptures; and the Greeks so quoted Homer, Theognis, Pindar, and the rest. If the theory has receded out of modern criticism, it is because we have not had poets. Whenever they appear, they will redeem their own credit.

This ecstatical state seems to direct a regard to the whole and not to the parts; to the cause and not to the ends; to the tendency, and not to the act. It respects genius and not talent; hope, and not possession: the anticipation of all things by the intellect, and not the history itself; art, and not works of art; poetry, and not experiment; virtue, and not duties.

There is no office or function of man but is rightly discharged by this divine method, and nothing that is not noxious to him if detached from its universal relations. Is it his work in the world to study nature, or the laws of the world? Let him beware of proposing to himself any end. Is it for use? nature is debased, as if one looking at the ocean can remember only the price of fish. Or is it for pleasure? he is mocked: there is a certain infatuating air in woods and mountains which draws on the idler to want and misery. There is something social and intrusive in the nature of all things; they seek to penetrate and overpower, each the nature of every other creature, and itself alone in all modes and throughout space and spirit to prevail and possess. Every star in heaven is discontented and insatiable. Gravitation and chemistry cannot content them. Ever they woo and court the eye of every beholder. Every man who comes into the world they seek to fascinate and possess, to pass into his mind, for they desire to republish themselves in a more delicate world than that they occupy. It is not enough that they are Jove, Mars, Orion, and the North Star, in the gravitating firmament: they would have such poets as Newton, Herschel and Laplace, that they may re-exist and re-appear in the finer world of rational souls, and fill that realm with their fame. So is it with all immaterial objects. These beautiful basilisks set their brute, glorious eyes on the eye of every child, and, if they can, cause their nature to pass through his wondering eyes into him, and so all things are mixed.

Therefore man must be on his guard against this cup of enchantments, and must look at nature with a supernatural eye. By piety alone, by conversing with the cause of nature, is he safe and commands it. And because all knowledge is assimilation to the object of knowledge, as the power or genius of nature is ecstatic, so must its science or the description of it be. The poet must be a rhapsodist: his inspiration a sort of bright casualty: his will in it only the surrender of will to the Universal Power, which will not be seen face to face, but must be received and sympathetically known. It is remarkable that we have out of the deeps of antiquity in the oracles ascribed to the half fabulous Zoroaster,° a statement of this fact, which every lover and seeker of truth will recognize. 'It is not proper,' said Zoroaster, 'to understand the Intelligible with vehemence, but if you incline your mind, you will apprehend it: not too earnestly, but bringing a pure and inquiring eye. You will not understand it as when understanding some particular thing, but with the flower of the mind. Things divine are not attainable by mortals who understand sensual things, but only the light-armed arrive at the summit.'

And because ecstasy is the law and cause of nature, therefore you cannot interpret it in too high and deep a sense. Nature represents the best meaning of the wisest man. Does the sunset landscape seem to you the palace of Friendship,—those purple skies and lovely waters the amphitheatre dressed and garnished only for the exchange of thought and love of the purest souls? It is that. All other meanings which base men have put on it are conjectural and false. You cannot bathe twice in the same river, said Heraclitus;° and I add, a man never sees the same object twice: with his own enlargement the object acquires new aspects.

Does not the same law hold for virtue? It is vitiated by too much will. He who aims at progress, should aim at an infinite, not at a special benefit. The reforms whose fame now fills the land with Temperance, Anti-Slavery, Non-Resistance, No Government, Equal Labor, fair and generous as each appears, are poor bitter things when prosecuted for themselves as an end. To every reform, in proportion to its energy, early disgusts are incident, so that the disciple is surprised at the very hour of his first triumphs, with chagrins, and sickness, and a general distrust: so that he shuns his associates, hates the enterprise which lately seemed so fair, and meditates to cast himself into the arms of that society and manner of life which he had newly abandoned with so much pride and hope. Is it that he attached the value of virtue to some particular practices, as, the denial of certain appetites in certain specified indulgences, and, afterward, found himself still as wicked and as far from happiness in that abstinence, as he had been in the abuse? But the soul can be appeased not by a deed but by a tendency. It is in a hope that she feels her wings. You shall love rectitude and not the disuse of money or the avoidance of trade: an unimpeded mind, and not a monkish diet; sympathy and usefulness, and not hoeing or coopering. Tell me not how great your project is, the civil liberation of the world, its conversion into a Christian church, the establishment of public education, cleaner diet, a new division of labor and of land, laws of love for laws of property;—I say to you plainly there is no end to which your practical faculty can aim, so sacred or so large, that, if pursued for itself, will not at last become carrion and an offence to the nostril. The imaginative faculty of the soul must be fed with objects immense and eternal. Your end should be one inapprehensible to the senses: then will it be a god always approached,—never touched; always giving health. A man adorns himself with prayer and love, as an aim adorns an action. What is strong but goodness, and what is energetic but the presence of a brave man? The doctrine in vegetable physiology of the *presence*, or the general influence of any substance over and above its chemical influence, as of an alkali or a living plant, is more predicable of man. You need not speak to me, I need not go where you are, that you should exert magnetism on me. Be you only whole and sufficient, and I shall feel you in every part of my life and fortune, and I can as easily dodge the gravitation of the globe as escape your influence.

But there are other examples of this total and supreme influence, besides Nature and the conscience. 'From the poisonous tree, the world,' say the Brahmins, 'two species of fruit are produced, sweet as the waters of life, Love or the society of beautiful souls, and Poetry, whose taste is like the immortal juice of Vishnu.' What is Love, and why is it the chief good, but because it is an overpowering enthusiasm? Never self-possessed or prudent, it is all abandonment. Is it not a certain admirable wisdom, preferable to all other advantages, and whereof all others are only secondaries and indemnities, because this is that in which the individual is no longer his own foolish master, but inhales an odorous and celestial air, is wrapped round with awe of the object, blending for the time that object with the real and only good, and consults every omen in nature with tremulous interest. When we speak truly,—is not he only unhappy who is not in love? his fancied freedom and self-rule—is it not so much death? He who is in love is wise and is becoming wiser, sees newly every time he looks at the object beloved, drawing from it with his eyes and his mind those virtues which it possesses. Therefore if the object be not itself a living and expanding soul, he presently exhausts it. But the love remains in his mind, and the wisdom it brought him; and it craves a new and higher object. And the reason why all men honor love, is because it looks up and not down; aspires and not despairs.

And what is Genius but finer love, a love impersonal, a love of the flower and perfection of things, and a desire to draw a new picture or copy of the same? It looks to the cause and life: it proceeds from within outward, whilst Talent goes from without inward. Talent finds its models, methods, and ends, in society, exists for exhibition, and goes to the soul only for power to work. Genius is its own end, and draws its means and the style of its architecture from within, going abroad only for audience, and spectator, as we adapt our voice and phrase to the distance and character of the ear we speak to. All your learning of all literatures would never enable you to anticipate one of its thoughts or expressions, and yet each is natural and familiar as household words. Here about us coils forever the ancient enigma, so old and so unutterable. Behold! there is the sun, and the rain, and the rocks: the old sun, the old stones. How easy were it to describe all this fitly; yet no word can pass. Nature is a mute, and man, her articulate speaking brother, lo! he also is a mute. Yet when Genius arrives, its speech is like a river; it has no straining to describe, more than there is straining in nature to exist. When thought is best, there is most of it. Genius sheds wisdom like perfume, and advertises us that it flows out of a deeper source than the foregoing silence, that it knows so deeply and speaks so musically, because it is itself a mutation of the thing it describes. It is sun and moon and wave and fire in music, as astronomy is thought and harmony in masses of matter.

What is all history but the work of ideas, a record of the incomputable energy which his infinite aspirations infuse into man? Has any thing grand and lasting been done? Who did it? Plainly not any man, but all men: it was the prevalence and inundation of an idea. What brought the pilgrims here? One man says, civil liberty; another, the desire of founding a church; and a third, discovers that the motive force was plantation and trade. But if the Puritans could rise from the dust, they could not answer. It is to be seen in what they were, and not in what they designed; it was the growth and expansion of the human race, and resembled herein the sequent Revolution, which was not begun in Concord, or Lexington, or Virginia, but was the overflowing of the sense of natural right in every clear and active spirit of the period. Is a man boastful and knowing, and his own master?—we turn from him without hope: but let him be filled with awe and dread before the Vast and the Divine, which uses him glad to be used, and our eye is riveted to the chain of events. What a debt is ours to that old religion which, in the childhood of most of us, still dwelt like a sabbath morning in the country of New England, teaching privation, self-denial and sorrow! A man was born not for prosperity, but to suffer for the benefit of others, like the noble rock-maple which all around our villages bleeds for the service of man. Not praise, not men's acceptance of our doing, but the spirit's holy errand through us absorbed the thought. How dignified was this! How all that is called talents and success, in our noisy capitals, becomes buzz and din before this man-worthiness! How our friendships and the complaisances we use, shame us now! Shall we not quit our companions, as if they were thieves and pot-companions, and betake ourselves to some desert cliff of mount Katahdin, some unvisited recess in Moosehead Lake, to bewail our innocency and to recover it, and with it the power to communicate again with these sharers of a more sacred idea?

And what is to replace for us the piety of that race? We cannot have theirs: it glides away from us day by day, but we also can bask in the great morning which rises forever out of the eastern sea, and be ourselves the children of the light. I stand here to say, Let us worship the mighty and transcendent Soul. It is the office, I doubt not, of this age to annul that adulterous divorce which the superstition of many ages has effected between the intellect and holiness. The lovers of goodness have been one class, the students of wisdom another, as if either could exist in any purity without the other. Truth is always holy, holiness always wise. I will that we keep terms with sin, and a sinful literature and society, no longer, but live a life of discovery and performance. Accept the intellect, and it will accept us. Be the lowly ministers of that pure omniscience, and deny it not before men. It will burn up all profane literature, all base current opinions, all the false powers of the world, as in a moment of time. I draw from nature the lesson of an intimate divinity. Our health and reason as men needs our respect to this fact, against the heedlessness and against the contradiction of society. The sanity of man needs the poise of this immanent force. His nobility needs the assurance of this inexhaustible reserved power. How great soever have been its bounties, they are a drop to the sea whence they flow. If you say, 'the acceptance of the vision is also the act of God:'—I shall not seek to penetrate the mystery, I admit the force of what you say. If you ask, 'How can any rules be given for the attainment of gifts so sublime?' I shall only remark that the solicitations of this spirit, as long as there is life, are never forborne. Tenderly, tenderly, they woo and court us from every object in nature, from every fact in life, from every thought in the mind. The one condition coupled with the gift of truth is its use. That man shall be learned who reduceth his learning to practice. Emanuel Swedenborg° affirmed that it was opened to him, 'that the spirits who knew truth in this life, but did it not, at death shall lose their knowledge.' 'If knowledge,' said Ali the Caliph,° 'calleth unto practice, well; if not, it goeth away.' The only way into nature is to enact our best insight. Instantly we are higher poets, and can speak a deeper law. Do what you know, and perception is converted into character, as islands and continents were built by invisible infusories, or, as these forest leaves absorb light, electricity, and volatile gases, and the gnarled oak to live a thousand years is the arrest and fixation of the most volatile and ethereal currents. The doctrine of this Supreme Presence is a cry of joy and exultation. Who shall dare think he has come late into nature, or has missed anything excellent in the past, who seeth the admirable stars of possibility, and the yet untouched continent of hope glittering with all its mountains in the vast West? I praise with wonder this great reality, which seems to drown all things in the deluge of its light. What man seeing this, can lose it from his thoughts, or entertain a meaner subject? The entrance of this into his mind seems to be the birth of man. We cannot describe the natural history of the soul, but we know that it is divine. I cannot tell if these wonderful qualities which house to-day in this mortal frame, shall ever re-assemble in equal activity in a similar frame, or whether they have before had a natural history like that of this body you see before you; but this one thing I know, that these qualities did not now begin to exist, cannot be sick with my sickness, nor buried in any grave; but that they circulate through the Universe: before the world was, they were. Nothing can bar them out, or shut them in, but they penetrate the ocean and land, space and time, form and essence, and hold the key to universal nature. I draw from this faith courage and hope. All things are known to the soul. It is not to be surprised by any communication. Nothing can be greater than it. Let those fear and those fawn who will. The soul is in her native realm, and it is wider than space, older than time, wide as hope, rich as love. Pusillanimity and fear she refuses with a beautiful scorn: they are not for her who putteth on her coronation robes, and goes out through universal love to universal power.

THE TRANSCENDENTALIST

A Lecture read at the Masonic Temple, Boston, January, 1842°

THE first thing we have to say respecting what are called *new views* here in New England, at the present time, is, that they are not new, but the very oldest of thoughts cast into the mould of these new times. The light is always identical in its composition, but it falls on a great variety of objects, and by so falling is first revealed to us, not in its own form, for it is formless, but in theirs; in like manner, thought only appears in the objects it classifies. What is popularly called Transcendentalism among us, is Idealism; Idealism as it appears in 1842. As thinkers, mankind have ever divided into two sects, Materialists and Idealists; the first class founding on experience, the second on consciousness; the first class beginning to think from the data of the senses, the second class perceive that the senses are not final, and say, the senses give us representations of things, but what are the things themselves, they cannot tell. The materialist insists on facts, on history, on the force of circumstances, and the animal wants of man; the idealist on the power of Thought and of Will, on inspiration, on miracle, on individual culture. These two modes of thinking are both natural, but the idealist contends that his way of thinking is in higher nature. He concedes all that the other affirms, admits the impressions of sense, admits their coherency, their use and beauty, and then asks the materialist for his grounds of assurance that things are as his senses represent them. But I, he says, affirm facts not affected by the illusions of sense, facts which are of the same nature as the faculty which reports them, and not liable to doubt; facts which in their first appearance to us assume a native superiority to material facts, degrading these into a language by which the first are to be spoken; facts which it only needs a retirement from the senses to discern. Every materialist will be an idealist; but an idealist can never go backward to be a materialist.

The idealist, in speaking of events, sees them as spirits. He does not deny the sensuous fact: by no means; but he will not see that alone. He does not deny the presence of this table, this chair, and the walls of this room, but he looks at these things as the reverse side of the tapestry, as the *other end*, each being a sequel or completion of a spiritual fact which nearly concerns him. This manner of looking at things, transfers every object in nature from an independent and anomalous position without there, into the consciousness. Even the materialist Condillac,° perhaps the most logical expounder of materialism, was constrained to say, 'Though we should soar into the heavens, though we should sink into the abyss, we never go out of ourselves; it is always our own thought that we perceive.' What more could an idealist say?

The materialist, secure in the certainty of sensation, mocks at fine-spun theories, at star-gazers and dreamers, and believes that his life is solid, that he at least takes nothing for granted, but knows where he stands, and what he does. Yet how easy it is to show him, that he also is a phantom walking and working amid phantoms, and that he need only ask a question or two beyond his daily questions, to find his solid universe growing dim and impalpable before his sense. The sturdy capitalist, no matter how deep and square on blocks of Quincy granite he lays the foundations of his banking-house or Exchange, must set it, at last, not on a cube corresponding to the angles of his structure, but on a mass of unknown materials and solidity, red-hot or white-hot, perhaps at the core, which rounds off to an almost perfect sphericity, and lies floating in soft air, and goes spinning away, dragging bank and banker with it at a rate of thousands of miles the hour, he knows not whither,—a bit of bullet, now glimmering, now darkling through a small cubic space on the edge of an unimaginable pit of emptiness. And this wild balloon, in which his whole venture is embarked, is a just symbol of his whole state and faculty. One thing, at least, he says is certain, and does not give me the headache, that figures do not lie; the multiplication table has been hitherto found unimpeachable truth; and, moreover, if I put a gold eagle in my safe, I find it again to-morrow;—but for these thoughts, I know not whence they are. They change and pass away. But ask him why he believes that an uniform experience will continue uniform, or on what grounds he founds his faith in his figures, and he will perceive that his mental fabric is built up on just as strange and quaking foundations as his proud edifice of stone.

In the order of thought, the materialist takes his departure from the external world, and esteems a man as one product of that. The idealist takes his departure from his consciousness, and reckons the world an appearance. The materialist respects sensible masses, Society, Government, social art, and luxury, every establishment, every mass, whether majority of numbers, or extent of space, or amount of objects, every social action. The idealist has another measure, which is metaphysical, namely, the *rank* which things themselves take in his consciousness; not at all, the size or appearance. Mind is the only reality, of which men and all other natures are better or worse reflectors. Nature, literature, history, are only subjective phenomena. Although in his action overpowered by the laws of action, and so, warmly coöperating with men, even preferring them to himself, yet when he speaks scientifically, or after the order of thought, he is constrained to degrade persons into representatives of truths. He does not respect labor, or the products of labor, namely, property, otherwise than as a manifold symbol, illustrating with wonderful fidelity of details the laws of being; he does not respect government, except as far as it reiterates the law of his mind; nor the church; nor charities; nor arts, for themselves; but hears, as at a vast distance, what they say, as if his consciousness would speak to him through a pantomimic scene. His thought,—that is the Universe. His experience inclines him to behold the procession of facts you call the world, as flowing perpetually outward from an invisible, unsounded centre in himself, centre alike of him and of them, and necessitating him to regard all things as having a subjective or relative existence, relative to that aforesaid Unknown Centre of him.

From this transfer of the world into the consciousness, this beholding of all things in the mind, follow easily his whole ethics. It is simpler to be self-dependent. The height, the deity of man is, to be self-sustained, to need no gift, no foreign force. Society is good when it does not violate me; but best when it is likest to solitude. Everything real is self-existent. Everything divine shares the self-existence of Deity. All that you call the world is the shadow of that substance which you are, the perpetual creation of the powers of thought, of those that are dependent and of those that are independent of your will. Do not cumber yourself with fruitless pains to mend and remedy remote effects; let the soul be erect, and all things will go well. You think me the child of my circumstances: I make my circumstance. Let any thought or motive of mine be different from that they are, the difference will transform my condition and economy. I—this thought which is called I,—is the mould into which the world is poured like melted wax. The mould is invisible, but the world betrays the shape of the mould. You call it the power of circumstance, but it is the power of me. Am I in harmony with myself? my position will seem to you just and commanding. Am I vicious and insane? my fortunes will seem to you obscure and descending. As I am, so shall I associate, and, so shall I act; Cæsar's history will paint out Cæsar. Jesus acted so, because he thought so. I do not wish to overlook or to gainsay any reality; I say, I make my circumstance: but if you ask me, Whence am I? I feel like other men my relation to that Fact which cannot be spoken, or defined, nor even thought, but which exists, and will exist.

The Transcendentalist adopts the whole connection of spiritual doctrine. He believes in miracle, in the perpetual openness of the human mind to new influx of light and power; he believes in inspiration, and in ecstasy. He wishes that the spiritual principle should be suffered to demonstrate itself to the end, in all possible applications to the state of man, without the admission of anything unspiritual; that is, anything positive, dogmatic, personal. Thus, the spiritual measure of inspiration is the depth of the thought, and never, who said it? And so he resists all attempts to palm other rules and measures on the spirit than its own.

In action, he easily incurs the charge of antinomianism by his avowal that he, who has the Lawgiver, may with safety not only neglect, but even contravene every written commandment. In the play of Othello, the expiring Desdemona absolves her husband of the murder, to her attendant Emilia. Afterwards, when Emilia charges him with the crime, Othello exclaims,

> 'You heard her say herself it was not I.'°

Emilia replies,

> 'The more angel she, and thou the blacker devil.'°

Of this fine incident, Jacobi,° the Transcendental moralist, makes use, with other parallel instances, in his reply to Fichte.° Jacobi, refusing all measure of right and wrong except the determinations of the private spirit, remarks that there is no crime but has sometimes been a virtue. 'I,' he says, 'am that atheist, that godless person who, in opposition to an imaginary doctrine of calculation, would lie as the dying Desdemona lied; would lie and deceive, as Pylades when he personated Orestes; would assassinate like Timoleon; would perjure myself like Epaminondas, and John de Witt; I would resolve on suicide like Cato;° I would commit sacrilege with David; yea, and pluck ears of corn on the Sabbath, for no other reason than that I was fainting for lack of food. For, I have assurance in myself, that, in pardoning these faults according to the letter, man exerts the sovereign right which the majesty of his being confers on him; he sets the seal of his divine nature to the grace he accords.'*

In like manner, if there is anything grand and daring in human thought or virtue, any reliance on the vast, the unknown; any presentiment; any extravagance of faith, the spiritualist adopts it as most in nature. The oriental mind has always tended to this largeness. Buddh-

---

* Coleridge's Translation.

ism is an expression of it. The Buddhist who thanks no man, who says, 'do not flatter your benefactors,' but who, in his conviction that every good deed can by no possibility escape its reward, will not deceive the benefactor by pretending that he has done more than he should, is a Transcendentalist.

You will see by this sketch that there is no such thing as a Transcendental *party*; that there is no pure Transcendentalist; that we know of none but prophets and heralds of such a philosophy; that all who by strong bias of nature have leaned to the spiritual side in doctrine, have stopped short of their goal. We have had many harbingers and forerunners; but of a purely spiritual life, history has afforded no example. I mean, we have yet no man who has leaned entirely on his character, and eaten angels' food; who, trusting to his sentiments, found life made of miracles; who, working for universal aims, found himself fed, he knew not how; clothed, sheltered, and weaponed, he knew not how, and yet it was done by his own hands. Only in the instinct of the lower animals, we find the suggestion of the methods of it, and something higher than our understanding. The squirrel hoards nuts, and the bee gathers honey, without knowing what they do, and they are thus provided for without selfishness or disgrace.

Shall we say, then, that Transcendentalism is the Saturnalia or excess of Faith; the presentiment of a faith proper to man in his integrity, excessive only when his imperfect obedience hinders the satisfaction of his wish. Nature is transcendental, exists primarily, necessarily, ever works and advances, yet takes no thought for the morrow. Man owns the dignity of the life which throbs around him in chemistry, and tree, and animal, and in the involuntary functions of his own body; yet he is balked when he tries to fling himself into this enchanted circle, where all is done without degradation. Yet genius and virtue predict in man the same absence of private ends, and of condescension to circumstances, united with every trait and talent of beauty and power.

This way of thinking, falling on Roman times, made Stoic philosophers; falling on despotic times, made patriot Catos and Brutuses; falling on superstitious times, made prophets and apostles; on popish times, made protestants and ascetic monks, preachers of Faith against the preachers of Works; on prelatical times, made Puritans and Quakers; and falling on Unitarian and commercial times, makes the peculiar shades of Idealism which we know.

It is well known to most of my audience, that the Idealism of the present day acquired the name of Transcendental, from the use of that term by Immanuel Kant, of Konigsberg, who replied to the skeptical philosophy of Locke,° which insisted that there was nothing in the intellect which was not previously in the experience of the senses, by showing that there was a very important class of ideas, or imperative forms, which did not come by experience, but through which experience was acquired; that these were intuitions of the mind itself; and he denominated them *Transcendental* forms. The extraordinary profoundness and precision of that man's thinking have given vogue to his nomenclature, in Europe and America, to that extent, that whatever belongs to the class of intuitive thought, is popularly called at the present day *Transcendental*.

Although, as we have said, there is no pure Transcendentalist, yet the tendency to respect the intuitions, and to give them, at least in our creed, all authority over our experience, has deeply colored the conversation and poetry of the present day; and the history of genius and of religion in these times, though impure, and as yet not incarnated in any powerful individual, will be the history of this tendency.

It is a sign of our times, conspicuous to the coarsest observer, that many intelligent and religious persons withdraw themselves from the common labors and competitions of the market and the caucus, and betake themselves to a certain solitary and critical way of living, from which no solid fruit has yet appeared to justify their separation. They hold themselves aloof: they feel the disproportion between their faculties and the work offered them, and they prefer to ramble in the country and perish of ennui, to the degradation of such charities and such ambitions as the city can propose to them. They are striking work, and crying out for somewhat worthy to do! What they do, is done only because they are overpowered by the humanities that speak on all sides; and they consent to such labor as is open to them, though to their lofty dream the writing of Iliads or Hamlets, or the building of cities or empires seems drudgery.

Now every one must do after his kind, be he asp or angel, and these must. The question, which a wise man and a student of modern history will ask, is, what that kind is? And truly, as in ecclesiastical history we take so much pains to know what the Gnostics, what the Essenes, what the Manichees, and what the Reformers° believed, it would not misbecome us to inquire nearer home, what these companions and contemporaries of ours think and do, at least so far as these thoughts and actions appear to be not accidental and personal, but common to many, and the inevitable flower of the Tree of Time. Our American literature and spiritual history are, we confess, in the optative mood; but whoso knows these seething brains, these admirable radicals, these unsocial worshippers, these talkers who talk the sun and moon away, will believe that this heresy cannot pass away without leaving its mark.

They are lonely; the spirit of their writing and conversation is lonely; they repel influences; they shun general society; they incline to shut themselves in their chamber in the house, to live in the country rather than in the town, and to find their tasks and amusements in solitude. Society, to be sure, does not like this very well; it saith, Whoso goes to walk alone, accuses the whole world; he declareth all to be unfit to be his companions; it is very uncivil, nay, insulting; Society will retaliate. Meantime, this retirement does not proceed from any whim on the part of these separators; but if any one will take pains to talk with them, he will find that this part is chosen both from temperament and from principle; with some unwillingness, too, and as a choice of the less of two evils; for these persons are not by nature melancholy, sour, and unsocial,—they are not stockish or brute,—but joyous; susceptible, affectionate; they have even more than others a great wish to be loved. Like the young Mozart, they are rather ready to cry ten times a day, 'But are you sure you love me?' Nay, if they tell you their whole thought, they will own that love seems to them the last and highest gift of nature; that there are persons whom in their hearts they daily thank for existing,—persons whose faces are perhaps unknown to them, but whose fame and spirit have penetrated their solitude,—and for whose sake they wish to exist. To behold the beauty of another character, which inspires a new interest in our own; to behold the beauty lodged in a human being, with such vivacity of apprehension, that I am instantly forced home to inquire if I am not deformity itself: to behold in another the expression of a love so high that it assures itself,—assures itself also to me against every possible casualty except my unworthiness;—these are degrees on the scale of human happiness, to which they have ascended; and it is a fidelity to this sentiment which has made common association distasteful to them. They wish a just and even fellowship, or none. They cannot gossip with you, and they do not wish, as they are sincere and religious, to gratify any mere curiosity which you may entertain. Like fairies, they do not wish to be spoken of. Love me, they say, but do not ask who is my cousin and my uncle. If you do not need to hear my thought, because you can read it in my face and behavior, then I will tell it you from sunrise to sunset. If you cannot divine it, you would not understand what I say. I will not molest myself for you. I do not wish to be profaned.

And yet, it seems as if this loneliness, and not this love, would prevail in their circumstances, because of the extravagant demand they make on human nature. That, indeed, constitutes a new feature in their portrait, that they are the most exacting and extortionate critics. Their quarrel with every man they meet, is not with his kind, but with his degree. There is not enough of him,—that is the only fault. They prolong their privilege of childhood in this wise, of doing nothing,—but making immense demands on all the gladiators in the lists of action and fame. They make us feel the strange disappointment which overcasts every human youth. So many promising youths, and never a finished man! The profound nature will have a savage rudeness; the delicate one will be shallow, or the victim of sensibility; the richly accomplished will have some capital absurdity; and so every piece has a crack. 'T is strange, but this masterpiece is a result of such an extreme delicacy, that the most unobserved flaw in the boy will neutralize the most aspiring genius, and spoil the work. Talk with a seaman of the hazards to life in his profession, and he will ask you, 'Where are the old sailors? do you not see that all are young men?' And we, on this sea of human thought, in like manner inquire, Where are the old idealists? where are they who represented to the last generation that extravagant hope, which a few happy aspirants suggest to ours? In looking at the class of counsel, and power, and wealth, and at the matronage of the land, amidst all the prudence and all the triviality, one asks, Where are they who represented genius, virtue, the invisible and heavenly world, to these? Are they dead,—taken in early ripeness to the gods,—as ancient wisdom foretold their fate? Or did the high idea die out of them, and leave their unperfumed body as its tomb and tablet, announcing to all that the celestial inhabitant, who once gave them beauty, had departed? Will it be better with the new generation? We easily predict a fair future to each new candidate who enters the lists, but we are frivolous and volatile, and by low aims and ill example do what we can to defeat this hope. Then these youths bring us a rough but effectual aid. By their unconcealed dissatisfaction, they expose our poverty, and the insignificance of man to man. A man is a poor limitary benefactor. He ought to be a shower of benefits—a great influence, which should never let his brother go, but should refresh old merits continually with new ones; so that, though absent, he should never be out of my mind, his name never far from my lips; but if the earth should open at my side, or my last hour were come, his name should be the prayer I should utter to the Universe. But in our experience, man is cheap, and friendship wants its deep sense. We affect to dwell with our friends in their absence, but we do not; when deed, word, or letter comes not, they let us go. These exacting children advertise us of our wants. There is no compliment, no smooth speech with them; they pay you only this one compliment, of insatiable expectation; they aspire, they severely exact, and if they only stand fast in this watchtower, and persist in demanding unto the end, and without end, then are they terrible friends, whereof poet and priest cannot choose but stand in awe; and what if they eat clouds, and drink wind, they have not been without service to the race of man.

With this passion for what is great and extraordinary, it cannot be wondered at, that they are repelled by vulgarity and frivolity in people. They say to themselves, It is better to be alone than in bad company. And it is really a wish to be met,—the wish to find society for their hope and religion,—which prompts them to shun what is called society. They feel that they are never so fit for friendship, as when they have quitted mankind, and taken themselves to friend. A picture, a book, a favorite spot in the hills or the woods, which they can people with the fair and worthy creation of the fancy, can give them often forms so vivid, that these for the time shall seem real, and society the illusion.

But their solitary and fastidious manners not only withdraw them from the conversation, but from the labors of the world; they are not good citizens, not good members of society; unwillingly they bear their part of the public and private burdens; they do not willingly share in the public charities, in the public religious rites, in the enterprises of education, of missions foreign or domestic, in the abolition of the slave-trade, or in the temperance society. They do not even like to vote. The philanthropists inquire whether Transcendentalism does not mean sloth: they had as lief hear that their friend is dead, as that he is a Transcendentalist; for then is he paralyzed, and can never do anything for humanity. What right, cries the good world, has the man of genius to retreat from work, and indulge himself? The popular literary creed seems to be, 'I am a sublime genius; I ought not therefore to labor.' But genius is the power to labor better and more availably. Deserve thy genius: exalt it. The good, the illuminated, sit apart from the rest, censuring their dulness and vices, as if they thought that, by sitting very grand in their chairs, the very brokers, attorneys, and congressmen would see the error of their ways, and flock to them. But the good and wise must learn to act, and carry salvation to the combatants and demagogues in the dusty arena below.

On the part of these children, it is replied, that life and their faculty seem to them gifts too rich to be squandered on such trifles as you propose to them. What you call your fundamental institutions, your great and holy causes, seem to them great abuses, and, when nearly seen, paltry matters. Each 'Cause,' as it is called,—say Abolition, Temperance, say Calvinism, or Unitarianism,—becomes speedily a little shop, where the article, let it have been at first never so subtle and ethereal, is now made up into portable and convenient cakes, and retailed in small quantities to suit purchasers. You make very free use of these words 'great' and 'holy', but few things appear to them such. Few persons have any magnificence of nature to inspire enthusiasm, and the philanthropies and charities have a certain air of quackery. As to the general course of living, and the daily employments of men, they cannot see much virtue in these, since they are parts of this vicious circle; and, as no great ends are answered by the men, there is nothing noble in the arts by which they are maintained. Nay, they have made the experiment, and found that, from the liberal professions to the coarsest manual labor, and from the courtesies of the academy and the college to the conventions of the cotillon-room and the morning call, there is a spirit of cowardly compromise and seeming, which intimates a frightful skepticism, a life without love, and an activity without an aim.

Unless the action is necessary, unless it is adequate, I do not wish to perform it. I do not wish to do one thing but once. I do not love routine. Once possessed of the principle, it is equally easy to make four or forty thousand applications of it. A great man will be content to have indicated in any the slightest manner his perception of the reigning Idea of his time, and will leave to those who like it the multiplication of examples. When he has hit the white, the rest may shatter the target. Every thing admonishes us how needlessly long life is. Every moment of a hero so raises and cheers us, that a twelve-month is an age. All that the brave Xanthus brings home from his wars, is the recollection that, at the storming of Samos, 'in the heat of the battle, Pericles smiled on me, and passed on to another detachment.'° It is the quality of the moment, not the number of days, of events, or of actors, that imports.

New, we confess, and by no means happy, is our condition: if you want the aid of our labor, we ourselves stand in greater want of the labor. We are miserable with inaction. We perish of rest and rust: but we do not like your work.

'Then,' says the world, 'show me your own.'

'We have none.'

'What will you do, then?' cries the world.

'We will wait.'

'How long?'

'Until the Universe rises up and calls us to work.'

'But whilst you wait, you grow old and useless.'

'Be it so: I can sit in a corner and *perish*, (as you call it,) but I will not move until I have the highest command. If no call should come for years, for centuries, then I know that the want of the Universe is the attestation of faith by my abstinence. Your virtuous projects, so called, do not cheer me. I know that which shall come will cheer me. If I cannot work, at least I need not lie. All that is clearly due to-day is not to lie. In other places, other men have encountered sharp trials, and have behaved themselves well. The martyrs were sawn asunder, or hung alive on meat-hooks. Cannot we screw our courage to patience and truth, and without complaint, or even with good-humor, await our turn of action in the Infinite Counsels?'

But, to come a little closer to the secret of these persons, we must say, that to them it seems a very easy matter to answer the objections of the man of the world, but not so easy to dispose of the doubts and objections that occur to themselves. They are exercised in their own spirit with queries, which acquaint them with all adversity, and with the trials of the bravest heroes. When I asked them concerning their private experience, they answered somewhat in this wise: It is not to be denied that there must be some wide difference between my faith and other faith; and mine is a certain brief experience, which surprised me in the highway or in the market, in some place, at some time,—whether in the body or out of the body, God knoweth,—and made me aware that I had played the fool with fools all this time, but that law existed for me and for all; that to me belonged trust, a child's trust and obedience, and the worship of ideas, and I should never be fool more. Well, in the space of an hour, probably, I was let down from this height; I was at my old tricks, the selfish member of a selfish society. My life is superficial, takes no root in the deep world; I ask, When shall I die, and be relieved of the responsibility of seeing an Universe which I do not use? I wish to exchange this flash-of-lightning faith for continuous daylight, this fever-glow for a benign climate.

These two states of thought diverge every moment, and stand in wild contrast. To him who looks at his life from these moments of illumination, it will seem that he skulks and plays a mean, shiftless, and subaltern part in the world. That is to be done which he has not skill to do, or to be said which others can say better, and he lies by, or occupies his hands with some plaything, until his hour comes again. Much of our reading, much of our labor, seems mere waiting: it was not that we were born for. Any other could do it as well, or better. So little skill enters into these works, so little do they mix with the divine life, that it really signifies little what we do, whether we turn a grindstone, or ride, or run, or make fortunes, or govern the state. The worst feature of this double consciousness is, that the two lives, of the understanding and of the soul, which we lead, really show very little relation to each other, never meet and measure each other: one prevails now, all buzz and din; and the other prevails then, all infinitude and paradise; and, with the progress of life, the two discover no greater disposition to reconcile themselves. Yet, what is my faith? What am I? What but a thought of serenity and independence, an abode in the deep blue sky? Presently the clouds shut down again; yet we retain the belief that this petty web we weave will at last be overshot and reticulated with veins of the blue, and that the moments will characterize the days. Patience, then, is for us, is it not? Patience, and still patience. When we pass, as presently we shall, into some new infinitude, out of this Iceland of negations, it will please us to reflect that, though we had few virtues or consolations, we bore with our indigence, nor once strove to repair it with hypocrisy or false heat of any kind.

But this class are not sufficiently characterized, if we omit to add that they are lovers and worshippers of Beauty. In the eternal trinity of Truth, Goodness, and Beauty, each in its perfection including the three, they prefer to make Beauty the sign and head. Something of the same taste is observable in all the moral movements of the time, in the religious and benevolent enterprises. They have a liberal, even an æsthetic spirit. A reference to Beauty in action sounds, to be sure, a little hollow and ridiculous in the ears of the old church. In politics, it has often sufficed, when they treated of justice, if they kept the bounds of selfish calculation. If they granted restitution, it was prudence which granted it. But the justice which is now claimed for the black, and the pauper, and the drunkard is for Beauty,—is for a necessity to the soul of the agent, not of the beneficiary. I say, this is the tendency, not yet the realization. Our virtue totters and trips, does not yet walk firmly. Its representatives are austere; they preach and denounce; their rectitude is not yet a grace. They are still liable to that slight taint of burlesque which, in our strange world, attaches to the zealot. A saint should be as dear as the apple of the eye. Yet we are tempted to smile, and we flee from the working to the speculative reformer, to escape that same slight ridicule. Alas for these days of derision and criticism! We call the Beautiful the highest, because it appears to us the golden mean, escaping the dowdiness of the good, and the heartlessness of the true.—They are lovers of nature also, and find an indemnity in the inviolable order of the world for the violated order and grace of man.

There is, no doubt, a great deal of well-founded objection to be spoken or felt against the sayings and doings of this class, some of whose traits we have selected; no doubt, they will lay themselves open to criticism and to lampoons, and as ridiculous stories will be to be told of them as of any. There will be cant and pretension; there will be subtilty and moon-shine. These persons are of unequal strength, and do not all prosper. They complain that everything around them must be denied; and if feeble, it takes all their strength to deny, before they can begin to lead their own life. Grave seniors insist on their respect to this institution, and that usage; to an obsolete history; to some vocation, or college, or etiquette, or beneficiary, or charity, or morning or evening call, which they resist, as what does not concern them. But it costs such sleepless nights, alienations and misgivings,—they have so many moods about it;—these old guardians never change *their* minds; they have but one mood on the subject, namely, that Antony is very perverse,—that it is quite as much as Antony can do, to assert his rights, abstain from what he thinks foolish, and keep his temper. He cannot help the reaction of this injustice in his own mind. He is braced-up and stilted; all freedom and flowing genius, all sallies of wit and frolic nature are quite out of the question; it is well if he can keep from lying, injustice, and suicide. This is no time for gaiety and grace. His strength and spirits are wasted in rejection. But the strong spirits overpower those around them without effort. Their thought and emotion comes in like a flood, quite withdraws them from all notice of these carping critics; they surrender themselves with glad heart to the heavenly guide, and only by implication reject the clamorous nonsense of the hour. Grave seniors talk to the deaf,—church and old book mumble and ritualize to an unheeding, preöccupied and advancing mind, and thus they by happiness of greater momentum lose no time, but take the right road at first.

But all these of whom I speak are not proficients; they are novices; they only show the road in which man should travel, when the soul has greater health and prowess. Yet let them feel the dignity of their charge, and deserve a larger power. Their heart is the ark in which the fire is concealed, which shall burn in a broader and universal flame. Let them obey the Genius then most when his impulse is wildest; then most when he seems to lead to uninhabitable desarts of thought and life; for the path which the hero travels alone is the highway of health and benefit to mankind. What is the privilege and nobility of our nature, but its persistency, through its power to attach itself to what is permanent?

Society also has its duties in reference to this class, and must behold them with what charity it can. Possibly some benefit may yet accrue from them to the state. In our Mechanics' Fair, there must be not only bridges, ploughs, carpenters' planes, and baking troughs, but also some few finer instruments,—raingauges, thermometers, and telescopes; and in society, besides farmers, sailors, and weavers, there must be a few persons of purer fire kept specially as gauges and meters of character; persons of a fine, detecting instinct, who betray the smallest accumulations of wit and feeling in the bystander. Perhaps too there might be room for the exciters and monitors; collectors of the heavenly spark with power to convey the electricity to others. Or, as the storm-tossed vessel at sea speaks the frigate or 'line packet' to learn its longitude, so it may not be without its advantage that we should now and then encounter rare and gifted men, to compare the points of our spiritual compass, and verify our bearings from superior chronometers.

Amidst the downward tendency and proneness of things, when every voice is raised for a new road or another statute, or a subscription of stock, for an improvement in dress, or in dentistry, for a new house or a larger business, for a political party, or the division of an estate,—will you not tolerate one or two solitary voices in the land, speaking for thoughts and principles not marketable or perishable? Soon these improvements and mechanical inventions will be superseded; these modes of living lost out of memory; these cities rotted, ruined by war, by new inventions, by new seats of trade, or the geologic changes:—all gone, like the shells which sprinkle the seabeach with a white colony to-day, forever renewed to be forever destroyed. But the thoughts which these few hermits strove to proclaim by silence, as well as by speech, not only by what they did, but by what they forbore to do, shall abide in beauty and strength, to reorganize themselves in nature, to invest themselves anew in other, perhaps higher endowed and happier mixed clay than ours, in fuller union with the surrounding system.

ESSAYS: FIRST SERIES
(1847)

HISTORY

There is no great and no small
To the Soul that maketh all:
And where it cometh, all things are;
And it cometh everywhere.

———

I am owner of the sphere,
Of the seven stars and the solar year,
Of Cæsar's hand, and Plato's brain,
Of Lord Christ's heart, and Shakspeare's strain.

THERE is one mind common to all individual men. Every man is an inlet to the same and to all of the same. He that is once admitted to the right of reason is made a freeman of the whole estate. What Plato has thought, he may think; what a saint has felt, he may feel; what at any time has befallen any man, he can understand. Who hath access to this universal mind is a party to all that is or can be done, for this is the only and sovereign agent.

Of the works of this mind history is the record. Its genius is illustrated by the entire series of days. Man is explicable by nothing less than all his history. Without hurry, without rest, the human spirit goes forth from the beginning to embody every faculty, every thought, every emotion, which belongs to it in appropriate events. But the thought is always prior to the fact; all the facts of history preëxist in the mind as laws. Each law in turn is made by circumstances predominant, and the limits of nature give power to but one at a time. A man is the whole encyclopædia of facts. The creation of a thousand forests is in one acorn, and Egypt, Greece, Rome, Gaul, Britain, America, lie folded already in the first man. Epoch after epoch, camp, kingdom, empire, republic, democracy, are merely the application of his manifold spirit to the manifold world.

This human mind wrote history, and this must read it. The Sphinx must solve her own riddle. If the whole of history is in one man, it is all to be explained from individual experience. There is a relation between the hours of our life and the centuries of time. As the air I breathe is drawn from the great repositories of nature, as the light on my book is yielded by a star a hundred millions of miles distant, as the poise of my body depends on the equilibrium of centrifugal and centripetal forces, so the hours should be instructed by the ages, and the ages explained by the hours. Of the universal mind each individual man is one more incarnation. All its properties consist in him. Each new fact in his private experience flashes a light on what great bodies of men have done, and the crises of his life refer to national crises. Every revolution was first a thought in one man's mind, and when the same thought occurs to another man, it is the key to that era. Every reform was once a private opinion, and when it shall be a private opinion again, it will solve the problem of the age. The fact narrated must correspond to something in me to be credible or intelligible. We as we read must become Greeks, Romans, Turks, priest and king, martyr and executioner, must fasten these images to some reality in our secret experience, or we shall learn nothing rightly. What befell Asdrubal or Cæsar Borgia° is as much an illustration of the mind's powers and depravations as what has befallen us. Each new law and political movement has meaning for you. Stand before each of its tablets and say, 'Under this mask did my Proteus nature hide itself'. This remedies the defect of our too great nearness to ourselves. This throws our actions into perspective: and as crabs, goats, scorpions, the balance, and the waterpot lose their meanness when hung as signs in the zodiac, so I can see my own vices without heat in the distant persons of Solomon, Alcibiades, and Catiline.°

It is the universal nature which gives worth to particular men and things. Human life as containing this is mysterious and inviolable, and we hedge it round with penalties and laws. All laws derive hence their ultimate reason; all express more or less distinctly some command of this supreme, illimitable essence. Property also holds of the soul, covers great spiritual facts, and instinctively we at first hold to it with swords and laws, and wide and complex combinations. The obscure consciousness of this fact is the light of all our day, the claim of claims; the plea for education, for justice, for charity, the foundation of friendship and love, and of the heroism and grandeur which belong to acts of self-reliance. It is remarkable that involuntarily we always read as superior beings. Universal history, the poets, the romancers, do not in their stateliest pictures—in the sacerdotal, the imperial palaces, in the triumphs of will or of genius—anywhere lose our ear, anywhere make us feel that we intrude, that this is for better men; but rather is it true, that in their grandest strokes we feel most at home. All that Shakspeare says of the king, yonder slip of a boy that reads in the corner feels to be true of himself. We sympathize in the great moments of history, in the great

discoveries, the great resistances, the great prosperities of men;—
because there law was enacted, the sea was searched, the land was
found, or the blow was struck *for us*, as we ourselves in that place would
have done or applauded.

We have the same interest in condition and character. We honor the
rich, because they have externally the freedom, power, and grace which
we feel to be proper to man, proper to us. So all that is said of the wise
man by Stoic, or oriental or modern essayist, describes to each reader
his own idea, describes his unattained but attainable self. All literature
writes the character of the wise man. Books, monuments, pictures,
conversation, are portraits in which he finds the lineaments he is forming. The silent and the eloquent praise him and accost him, and he is
stimulated wherever he moves as by personal allusions. A true aspirant,
therefore, never needs look for allusions personal and laudatory in discourse. He hears the commendation, not of himself, but more sweet, of
that character he seeks, in every word that is said concerning character,
yea, further, in every fact and circumstance,—in the running river and
the rustling corn. Praise is looked, homage tendered, love flows from
mute nature, from the mountains and the lights of the firmament.

These hints, dropped as it were from sleep and night, let us use in
broad day. The student is to read history actively and not passively; to
esteem his own life the text, and books the commentary. Thus compelled, the Muse of history will utter oracles, as never to those who do
not respect themselves. I have no expectation that any man will read
history aright, who thinks that what was done in a remote age, by men
whose names have resounded far, has any deeper sense than what he is
doing to-day.

The world exists for the education of each man. There is no age or
state of society or mode of action in history, to which there is not somewhat corresponding in his life. Every thing tends in a wonderful manner to abbreviate itself and yield its own virtue to him. He should see
that he can live all history in his own person. He must sit solidly at
home, and not suffer himself to be bullied by kings or empires, but
know that he is greater than all the geography and all the government of
the world; he must transfer the point of view from which history is
commonly read, from Rome and Athens and London to himself, and
not deny his conviction that he is the court, and if England or Egypt
have any thing to say to him, he will try the case; if not, let them for ever
be silent. He must attain and maintain that lofty sight where facts yield
their secret sense, and poetry and annals are alike. The instinct of the
mind, the purpose of nature, betrays itself in the use we make of the

signal narrations of history. Time dissipates to shining ether the solid angularity of facts. No anchor, no cable, no fences, avail to keep a fact a fact. Babylon, Troy, Tyre, Palestine, and even early Rome, are passing already into fiction. The Garden of Eden, the sun standing still in Gibeon, is poetry thenceforward to all nations. Who cares what the fact was, when we have made a constellation of it to hang in heaven an immortal sign? London and Paris and New York must go the same way. 'What is History,' said Napoleon, 'but a fable agreed upon?' This life of ours is stuck round with Egypt, Greece, Gaul, England, War, Colonization, Church, Court, and Commerce, as with so many flowers and wild ornaments grave and gay. I will not make more account of them. I believe in Eternity. I can find Greece, Asia, Italy, Spain, and the Islands,—the genius and creative principle of each and of all eras in my own mind.

We are always coming up with the emphatic facts of history in our private experience, and verifying them here. All history becomes subjective; in other words, there is properly no history; only biography. Every mind must know the whole lesson for itself,—must go over the whole ground. What it does not see, what it does not live, it will not know. What the former age has epitomized into a formula or rule for manipular convenience, it will lose all the good of verifying for itself, by means of the wall of that rule. Somewhere, sometime, it will demand and find compensation for that loss by doing the work itself. Ferguson° discovered many things in astronomy which had long been known. The better for him.

History must be this or it is nothing. Every law which the state enacts indicates a fact in human nature; that is all. We must in ourselves see the necessary reason of every fact,—see how it could and must be. So stand before every public and private work; before an oration of Burke, before a victory of Napoleon, before a martyrdom of Sir Thomas More, of Sidney, of Marmaduke Robinson,° before a French Reign of Terror, and a Salem hanging of witches, before a fanatic Revival, and the Animal Magnetism in Paris, or in Providence. We assume that we under like influence should be alike affected, and should achieve the like; and we aim to master intellectually the steps, and reach the same height or the same degradation, that our fellow, our proxy, has done.

All inquiry into antiquity,—all curiosity respecting the Pyramids, the excavated cities, Stonehenge, the Ohio Circles,° Mexico, Memphis,— is the desire to do away this wild, savage, and preposterous There or Then, and introduce in its place the Here and the Now. Belzoni° digs and measures in the mummy-pits and pyramids of Thebes, until he can see the end of the difference between the monstrous work and himself. When he has satisfied himself, in general and in detail, that it was made by such a person as he, so armed and so motived, and to ends to which he himself should also have worked, the problem is solved; his thought lives along the whole line of temples and sphinxes and catacombs, passes through them all with satisfaction, and they live again to the mind, or are *now*.

A Gothic cathedral affirms that it was done by us, and not done by us. Surely it was by man, but we find it not in our man. But we apply ourselves to the history of its production. We put ourselves into the place and state of the builder. We remember the forest-dwellers, the first temples, the adherence to the first type, and the decoration of it as the wealth of the nation increased; the value which is given to wood by carving led to the carving over the whole mountain of stone of a cathedral. When we have gone through this process, and added thereto the Catholic Church, its cross, its music, its processions, its Saints' days and image-worship, we have, as it were, been the man that made the minster; we have seen how it could and must be. We have the sufficient reason.

The difference between men is in their principle of association. Some men classify objects by color and size and other accidents of appearance; others by intrinsic likeness, or by the relation of cause and effect. The progress of the intellect is to the clearer vision of causes, which neglects surface differences. To the poet, to the philosopher, to the saint, all things are friendly and sacred, all events profitable, all days holy, all men divine. For the eye is fastened on the life, and slights the circumstance. Every chemical substance, every plant, every animal in its growth, teaches the unity of cause, the variety of appearance.

Upborne and surrounded as we are by this all-creating nature, soft and fluid as a cloud or the air, why should we be such hard pedants, and magnify a few forms? Why should we make account of time, or of magnitude, or of figure? The soul knows them not, and genius, obeying its law, knows how to play with them as a young child plays with gray-beards and in churches. Genius studies the causal thought, and, far back in the womb of things, sees the rays parting from one orb, that diverge ere they fall by infinite diameters. Genius watches the monad through all his masks as he performs the metempsychosis of nature. Genius detects through the fly, through the caterpillar, through the grub, through the egg, the constant individual; through countless individuals, the fixed species; through many species, the genus; through all genera, the steadfast type; through all the kingdoms of organized life, the eternal unity. Nature is a mutable cloud, which is always and never the same. She casts the same thought into troops of forms, as a poet makes twenty fables with one moral. Through the bruteness and toughness of matter, a subtle spirit bends all things to its own will. The adamant streams into soft but precise form before it, and, whilst I look at it, its outline and texture are changed again. Nothing is so fleeting as form; yet never does it quite deny itself. In man we still trace the remains or hints of all that we esteem badges of servitude in the lower races; yet in him they enhance his nobleness and grace; as Io, in Æschylus, transformed to a cow, offends the imagination; but how changed, when as Isis in Egypt she meets Osiris-Jove, a beautiful woman, with nothing of the metamorphosis left but the lunar horns as the splendid ornament of her brows!

The identity of history is equally intrinsic, the diversity equally obvious. There is at the surface infinite variety of things; at the centre there is simplicity of cause. How many are the acts of one man in which we recognize the same character! Observe the sources of our information in respect to the Greek genius. We have the *civil history* of that people, as Herodotus, Thucydides, Xenophon, and Plutarch have given it; a very sufficient account of what manner of persons they were, and what they did. We have the same national mind expressed for us again in their *literature*, in epic and lyric poems, drama, and philosophy; a very complete form. Then we have it once more in their *architecture*, a beauty as of temperance itself, limited to the straight line and the square,—a builded geometry. Then we have it once again in *sculpture*, the 'tongue on the balance of expression,'° a multitude of forms in the utmost freedom of action, and never transgressing the ideal serenity; like votaries performing some religious dance before the gods, and, though in convulsive pain or mortal combat, never daring to break the figure and decorum of their dance. Thus, of the genius of one remarkable people, we have a fourfold representation: and to the senses what more unlike than an ode of Pindar,° a marble centaur, the peristyle of the Parthenon, and the last actions of Phocion?°

Every one must have observed faces and forms which, without any resembling feature, make a like impression on the beholder. A particular picture or copy of verses, if it do not awaken the same train of images, will yet superinduce the same sentiment as some wild mountain walk, although the resemblance is nowise obvious to the senses, but is occult and out of the reach of the understanding. Nature is an endless combination and repetition of a very few laws. She hums the old well-known air through innumerable variations.

Nature is full of a sublime family likeness throughout her works; and delights in startling us with resemblances in the most unexpected quarters. I have seen the head of an old sachem of the forest, which at once reminded the eye of a bald mountain summit, and the furrows of the brow suggested the strata of the rock. There are men whose manners have the same essential splendor as the simple and awful sculpture on the friezes of the Parthenon, and the remains of the earliest Greek art. And there are compositions of the same strain to be found in the books of all ages. What is Guido's Rospigliosi Aurora° but a morning thought, as the horses in it are only a morning cloud. If any one will but take pains to observe the variety of actions to which he is equally inclined in certain moods of mind, and those to which he is averse, he will see how deep is the chain of affinity.

A painter told me that nobody could draw a tree without in some sort becoming a tree; or draw a child by studying the outlines of its form merely,—but, by watching for a time his motions and plays, the painter enters into his nature, and can then draw him at will in every attitude. So Roos° 'entered into the inmost nature of a sheep.' I knew a draughtsman employed in a public survey, who found that he could not sketch the rocks until their geological structure was first explained to him. In a certain state of thought is the common origin of very diverse works. It is the spirit and not the fact that is identical. By a deeper apprehension, and not primarily by a painful acquisition of many manual skills, the artist attains the power of awakening other souls to a given activity.

It has been said, that 'common souls pay with what they do; nobler souls with that which they are.' And why? Because a profound nature awakens in us by its actions and words, by its very looks and manners, the same power and beauty that a gallery of sculpture, or of pictures, addresses.

Civil and natural history, the history of art and of literature, must be explained from individual history, or must remain words. There is nothing but is related to us, nothing that does not interest us,—kingdom, college, tree, horse, or iron shoe, the roots of all things are in man. Santa Croce and the Dome of St. Peter's are lame copies after a divine model. Strasburg Cathedral is a material counterpart of the soul of Erwin of Steinbach.° The true poem is the poet's mind; the true ship is the ship-builder. In the man, could we lay him open, we should see the reason for the last flourish and tendril of his work; as every spine and tint in the sea-shell pre-ëxist in the secreting organs of the fish. The whole of heraldry and of chivalry is in courtesy. A man of fine manners shall pronounce your name with all the ornament that titles of nobility could ever add.

The trivial experience of every day is always verifying some old prediction to us, and converting into things the words and signs which we had heard and seen without heed. A lady, with whom I was riding in the forest, said to me, that the woods always seemed to her *to wait*, as if the genii who inhabit them suspended their deeds until the wayfarer has passed onward: a thought which poetry has celebrated in the dance of the fairies, which breaks off on the approach of human feet. The man who has seen the rising moon break out of the clouds at midnight has been present like an archangel at the creation of light and of the world. I remember one summer day, in the fields, my companion pointed out to me a broad cloud, which might extend a quarter of a mile parallel to the horizon, quite accurately in the form of a cherub as painted over churches,—a round block in the centre, which it was easy to animate with eyes and mouth, supported on either side by wide-stretched symmetrical wings. What appears once in the atmosphere may appear often, and it was undoubtedly the archetype of that familiar ornament. I have seen in the sky a chain of summer lightning which at once showed to me that the Greeks drew from nature when they painted the thunder-bolt in the hand of Jove. I have seen a snow-drift along the sides of the stone wall which obviously gave the idea of the common architectural scroll to abut a tower.

By surrounding ourselves with the original circumstances, we invent anew the orders and the ornaments of architecture, as we see how each people merely decorated its primitive abodes. The Doric temple preserves the semblance of the wooden cabin in which the Dorian dwelt. The Chinese pagoda is plainly a Tartar tent. The Indian and Egyptian temples still betray the mounds and subterranean houses of their forefathers. 'The custom of making houses and tombs in the living rock,' says Heeren,° in his Researches on the Ethiopians, 'determined very naturally the principal character of the Nubian Egyptian architecture to the colossal form which it assumed. In these caverns, already prepared by nature, the eye was accustomed to dwell on huge shapes and masses, so that, when art came to the assistance of nature, it could not move on a small scale without degrading itself. What would statues of the usual size, or neat porches and wings, have been, associated with those gigantic halls before which only Colossi could sit as watchmen, or lean on the pillars of the interior?'

The Gothic church plainly originated in a rude adaptation of the forest trees with all their boughs to a festal or solemn arcade, as the bands about the cleft pillars still indicate the green withes that tied them. No one can walk in a road cut through pine woods, without being struck with the architectural appearance of the grove, especially in winter, when the bareness of all other trees shows the low arch of the Saxons. In the woods in a winter afternoon one will see as readily the origin of the stained glass window, with which the Gothic cathedrals are adorned, in the colors of the western sky seen through the bare and crossing branches of the forest. Nor can any lover of nature enter the old piles of Oxford and the English cathedrals, without feeling that the forest overpowered the mind of the builder, and that his chisel, his saw, and plane still reproduced its ferns, its spikes of flowers, its locust, elm, oak, pine, fir, and spruce.

The Gothic cathedral is a blossoming in stone subdued by the insatiable demand of harmony in man. The mountain of granite blooms into an eternal flower, with the lightness and delicate finish, as well as the aerial proportions and perspective, of vegetable beauty.

In like manner, all public facts are to be individualized, all private facts are to be generalized. Then at once History becomes fluid and true, and Biography deep and sublime. As the Persian imitated in the slender shafts and capitals of his architecture the stem and flower of the lotus and palm, so the Persian court in its magnificent era never gave over the nomadism of its barbarous tribes, but travelled from Ecbatana, where the spring was spent, to Susa in summer, and to Babylon for the winter.

In the early history of Asia and Africa, Nomadism and Agriculture are the two antagonist facts. The geography of Asia and of Africa necessitated a nomadic life. But the nomads were the terror of all those whom the soil, or the advantages of a market, had induced to build towns. Agriculture, therefore, was a religious injunction, because of the perils of the state from nomadism. And in these late and civil countries of England and America, these propensities still fight out the old battle in the nation and in the individual. The nomads of Africa were constrained to wander by the attacks of the gad-fly, which drives the cattle mad, and so compels the tribe to emigrate in the rainy season, and to drive off the cattle to the higher sandy regions. The nomads of Asia follow the pasturage from month to month. In America and Europe, the nomadism is of trade and curiosity; a progress, certainly, from the gad-fly of Astaboras° to the Anglo and Italo-mania of Boston Bay. Sacred cities, to which a periodical religious pilgrimage was enjoined, or stringent laws and customs, tending to invigorate the national bond, were the check on the old rovers; and the cumulative values of long residence are the restraints on the itineracy of the present day. The antagonism of the two tendencies is not less active in individuals, as the love of adventure or the love of repose happens to predominate. A man of rude health and flowing spirits has the faculty of rapid domestication, lives in his wagon, and roams through all latitudes as easily as a Calmuc. At sea, or in the forest, or in the snow, he sleeps as warm, dines with as good appetite, and associates as happily, as beside his own chimneys. Or perhaps his facility is deeper seated, in the increased range of his faculties of observation, which yield him points of interest wherever fresh objects meet his eyes. The pastoral nations were needy and hungry to desperation; and this intellectual nomadism, in its excess, bankrupts the mind, through the dissipation of power on a miscellany of objects. The home-keeping wit, on the other hand, is that continence or content which finds all the elements of life in its own soil; and which has its own perils of monotony and deterioration, if not stimulated by foreign infusions.

Every thing the individual sees without him corresponds to his states of mind, and every thing is in turn intelligible to him, as his onward thinking leads him into the truth to which that fact or series belongs.

The primeval world,—the Fore-World, as the Germans say,—I can dive to it in myself as well as grope for it with researching fingers in catacombs, libraries, and the broken reliefs and torsos of ruined villas.

What is the foundation of that interest all men feel in Greek history, letters, art, and poetry, in all its periods, from the Heroic or Homeric age down to the domestic life of the Athenians and Spartans, four or five centuries later? What but this, that every man passes personally through a Grecian period. The Grecian state is the era of the bodily nature, the perfection of the senses,—of the spiritual nature unfolded in strict unity with the body. In it existed those human forms which supplied the sculptor with his models of Hercules, Phœbus, and Jove; not like the forms abounding in the streets of modern cities, wherein the face is a confused blur of features, but composed of incorrupt, sharply defined, and symmetrical features, whose eye-sockets are so formed that it would be impossible for such eyes to squint, and take furtive glances on this side and on that, but they must turn the whole head. The manners of that period are plain and fierce. The reverence exhibited is for personal qualities, courage, address, self-command, justice, strength, swiftness, a loud voice, a broad chest. Luxury and elegance are not known. A sparse population and want make every man his own valet, cook, butcher, and soldier, and the habit of supplying his own needs educates the body to wonderful performances. Such are the

Agamemnon and Diomed of Homer, and not far different is the picture
Xenophon gives of himself and his compatriots in the Retreat of the
Ten Thousand. 'After the army had crossed the river Teleboas in
Armenia, there fell much snow, and the troops lay miserably on the
ground covered with it. But Xenophon arose naked, and, taking an axe,
began to split wood; whereupon others rose and did the like'.°
Throughout his army exists a boundless liberty of speech. They quarrel
for plunder, they wrangle with the generals on each new order, and
Xenophon is as sharp-tongued as any, and sharper-tongued than most,
and so gives as good as he gets. Who does not see that this is a gang of
great boys, with such a code of honor and such lax discipline as great
boys have?

The costly charm of the ancient tragedy, and indeed of all the old
literature, is, that the persons speak simply,—speak as persons who
have great good sense without knowing it, before yet the reflective habit
has become the predominant habit of the mind. Our admiration of the
antique is not admiration of the old, but of the natural. The Greeks are
not reflective, but perfect in their senses and in their health, with the
finest physical organization in the world. Adults acted with the simplicity and grace of children. They made vases, tragedies, and statues,
such as healthy senses should,—that is, in good taste. Such things have
continued to be made in all ages, and are now, wherever a healthy phys-
ique exists; but, as a class, from their superior organization, they have
surpassed all. They combine the energy of manhood with the engaging
unconsciousness of childhood. The attraction of these manners is that
they belong to man, and are known to every man in virtue of his being
once a child; besides that there are always individuals who retain these
characteristics. A person of child-like genius and inborn energy is still a
Greek, and revives our love of the Muse of Hellas. I admire the love of
nature in the Philoctetes.° In reading those fine apostrophes to sleep, to
the stars, rocks, mountains, and waves, I feel time passing away as an
ebbing sea. I feel the eternity of man, the identity of his thought. The
Greek had, it seems, the same fellow-beings as I. The sun and moon,
water and fire, met his heart precisely as they meet mine. Then the
vaunted distinction between Greek and English, between Classic and
Romantic schools, seems superficial and pedantic. When a thought of
Plato becomes a thought to me,—when a truth that fired the soul of
Pindar fires mine, time is no more. When I feel that we two meet in a
perception, that our two souls are tinged with the same hue, and do, as
it were, run into one, why should I measure degrees of latitude, why
should I count Egyptian years?

The student interprets the age of chivalry by his own age of chivalry, and the days of maritime adventure and circumnavigation by quite parallel miniature experiences of his own. To the sacred history of the world, he has the same key. When the voice of a prophet out of the deeps of antiquity merely echoes to him a sentiment of his infancy, a prayer of his youth, he then pierces to the truth through all the confusion of tradition and the caricature of institutions.

Rare, extravagant spirits come by us at intervals, who disclose to us new facts in nature. I see that men of God have, from time to time, walked among men and made their commission felt in the heart and soul of the commonest hearer. Hence, evidently, the tripod, the priest, the priestess inspired by the divine afflatus.

Jesus astonishes and overpowers sensual people. They cannot unite him to history, or reconcile him with themselves. As they come to revere their intuitions and aspire to live holily, their own piety explains every fact, every word.

How easily these old worships of Moses, of Zoroaster, of Menu,° of Socrates, domesticate themselves in the mind. I cannot find any antiquity in them. They are mine as much as theirs.

I have seen the first monks and anchorets without crossing seas or centuries. More than once some individual has appeared to me with such negligence of labor and such commanding contemplation, a haughty beneficiary, begging in the name of God, as made good to the nineteenth century Simeon the Stylite, the Thebais,° and the first Capuchins.

The priestcraft of the East and West, of the Magian, Brahmin, Druid, and Inca, is expounded in the individual's private life. The cramping influence of a hard formalist on a young child in repressing his spirits and courage, paralyzing the understanding, and that without producing indignation, but only fear and obedience, and even much sympathy with the tyranny,—is a familiar fact explained to the child when he becomes a man, only by seeing that the oppressor of his youth is himself a child tyrannized over by those names and words and forms, of whose influence he was merely the organ to the youth. The fact teaches him how Belus° was worshipped, and how the Pyramids were built, better than the discovery by Champollion° of the names of all the workmen and the cost of every tile. He finds Assyria and the Mounds of Cholula at his door, and himself has laid the courses.

Again, in that protest which each considerate person makes against the superstition of his times, he repeats step for step the part of old reformers, and in the search after truth finds like them new perils to virtue. He learns again what moral vigor is needed to supply the girdle of a superstition. A great licentiousness treads on the heels of a reformation. How many times in the history of the world has the Luther of the day had to lament the decay of piety in his own household! 'Doctor,' said his wife to Martin Luther, one day, 'how is it that, whilst subject to papacy, we prayed so often and with such fervor, whilst now we pray with the utmost coldness and very seldom?'

The advancing man discovers how deep a property he has in literature,—in all fable as well as in all history. He finds that the poet was no odd fellow who described strange and impossible situations, but that universal man wrote by his pen a confession true for one and true for all. His own secret biography he finds in lines wonderfully intelligible to him, dotted down before he was born. One after another he comes up in his private adventures with every fable of Æsop, of Homer, of Hafiz, of Ariosto,° of Chaucer, of Scott, and verifies them with his own head and hands.

The beautiful fables of the Greeks, being proper creations of the imagination and not of the fancy, are universal verities. What a range of meanings and what perpetual pertinence has the story of Prometheus! Beside its primary value as the first chapter of the history of Europe, (the mythology thinly veiling authentic facts, the invention of the mechanic arts, and the migration of colonies,) it gives the history of religion with some closeness to the faith of later ages. Prometheus is the Jesus of the old mythology. He is the friend of man; stands between the unjust 'justice' of the Eternal Father and the race of mortals, and readily suffers all things on their account. But where it departs from the Calvinistic Christianity, and exhibits him as the defier of Jove, it represents a state of mind which readily appears wherever the doctrine of Theism is taught in a crude, objective form, and which seems the self-defence of man against this untruth, namely, a discontent with the believed fact that a God exists, and a feeling that the obligation of reverence is onerous. It would steal, if it could, the fire of the Creator, and live apart from him, and independent of him. The Prometheus Vinctus is the romance of skepticism. Not less true to all time are the details of that stately apologue. Apollo kept the flocks of Admetus, said the poets. When the gods come among men, they are not known. Jesus was not; Socrates and Shakspeare were not. Antæus was suffocated by the gripe of Hercules, but every time he touched his mother earth, his strength was renewed. Man is the broken giant, and, in all his weakness, both his body and his mind are invigorated by habits of conversation with nature. The power of music, the power of poetry to unfix,

and, as it were, clap wings to solid nature, interprets the riddle of
Orpheus. The philosophical perception of identity through endless
mutations of form makes him know the Proteus. What else am I who
laughed or wept yesterday, who slept last night like a corpse, and this
morning stood and ran? And what see I on any side but the transmig-
rations of Proteus? I can symbolize my thought by using the name of any
creature, of any fact, because every creature is man agent or patient.
Tantalus is but a name for you and me. Tantalus means the impossibility of drinking the waters of thought which are always gleaming and
waving within sight of the soul. The transmigration of souls is no fable.
I would it were; but men and women are only half human. Every animal
of the barn-yard, the field, and the forest, of the earth and of the waters
that are under the earth, has contrived to get a footing and to leave the
print of its features and form in some one or other of these upright,
heaven-facing speakers. Ah! brother, stop the ebb of thy soul,—ebbing
downward into the forms into whose habits thou hast now for many
years slid. As near and proper to us is also that old fable of the Sphinx,
who was said to sit in the road-side and put riddles to every passenger.
If the man could not answer, she swallowed him alive. If he could solve
the riddle, the Sphinx was slain. What is our life but an endless flight of
winged facts or events! In splendid variety these changes come, all putting questions to the human spirit. Those men who cannot answer by a
superior wisdom these facts or questions of time, serve them. Facts
encumber them, tyrannize over them, and make the men of routine the
men of *sense*, in whom a literal obedience to facts has extinguished
every spark of that light by which man is truly man. But if the man is
true to his better instincts or sentiments, and refuses the dominion of
facts, as one that comes of a higher race, remains fast by the soul and
sees the principle, then the facts fall aptly and supple into their places;
they know their master, and the meanest of them glorifies him.

See in Goethe's Helena the same desire that every word should be a
thing. These figures, he would say, these Chirons, Griffins, Phorkyas,
Helen, and Leda,° are somewhat, and do exert a specific influence on
the mind. So far then are they eternal entities, as real to-day as in the
first Olympiad. Much revolving them, he writes out freely his humor,
and gives them body to his own imagination. And although that poem
be as vague and fantastic as a dream, yet is it much more attractive than
the more regular dramatic pieces of the same author, for the reason
that it operates a wonderful relief to the mind from the routine of customary images,—awakens the reader's invention and fancy by the wild

freedom of the design, and by the unceasing succession of brisk shocks of surprise.

The universal nature, too strong for the petty nature of the bard, sits on his neck and writes through his hand; so that when he seems to vent a mere caprice and wild romance, the issue is an exact allegory. Hence Plato said that 'poets utter great and wise things which they do not themselves understand.'° All the fictions of the Middle Age explain themselves as a masked or frolic expression of that which in grave earnest the mind of that period toiled to achieve. Magic, and all that is ascribed to it, is a deep presentiment of the powers of science. The shoes of swiftness, the sword of sharpness, the power of subduing the elements, of using the secret virtues of minerals, of understanding the voices of birds, are the obscure efforts of the mind in a right direction. The preternatural prowess of the hero, the gift of perpetual youth, and the like, are alike the endeavour of the human spirit 'to bend the shows of things to the desires of the mind.'°

In Perceforest and Amadis de Gaul,° a garland and a rose bloom on the head of her who is faithful, and fade on the brow of the inconstant. In the story of the Boy and the Mantle,° even a mature reader may be surprised with a glow of virtuous pleasure at the triumph of the gentle Genelas; and, indeed, all the postulates of elfin annals,—that the fairies do not like to be named; that their gifts are capricious and not to be trusted; that who seeks a treasure must not speak; and the like,—I find true in Concord, however they might be in Cornwall or Bretagne.

Is it otherwise in the newest romance? I read the Bride of Lammermoor.° Sir William Ashton is a mask for a vulgar temptation, Ravenswood Castle a fine name for proud poverty, and the foreign mission of state only a Bunyan disguise for honest industry. We may all shoot a wild bull that would toss the good and beautiful, by fighting down the unjust and sensual. Lucy Ashton is another name for fidelity, which is always beautiful and always liable to calamity in this world.

But along with the civil and metaphysical history of man, another history goes daily forward,—that of the external world,—in which he is not less strictly implicated. He is the compend of time; he is also the correlative of nature. His power consists in the multitude of his affinities, in the fact that his life is intertwined with the whole chain of organic and inorganic being. In old Rome the public roads beginning at the Forum proceeded north, south, east, west, to the centre of every province of the empire, making each market-town of Persia, Spain, and Britain pervious to the soldiers of the capital: so out of the human heart go, as it were, highways to the heart of every object in nature, to reduce it under the dominion of man. A man is a bundle of relations, a knot of roots, whose flower and fruitage is the world. His faculties refer to natures out of him, and predict the world he is to inhabit, as the fins of the fish foreshow that water exists, or the wings of an eagle in the egg presuppose air. He cannot live without a world. Put Napoleon in an island prison, let his faculties find no men to act on, no Alps to climb, no stake to play for, and he would beat the air and appear stupid. Transport him to large countries, dense population, complex interests, and antagonist power, and you shall see that the man Napoleon, bounded, that is, by such a profile and outline, is not the virtual Napoleon. This is but Talbot's shadow;

> 'His substance is not here:
> For what you see is but the smallest part
> And least proportion of humanity;
> But were the whole frame here,
> It is of such a spacious, lofty pitch,
> Your roof were not sufficient to contain it.'°
>   *Henry VI.*

Columbus needs a planet to shape his course upon. Newton and Laplace need myriads of ages and thick-strewn celestial areas. One may say a gravitating solar system is already prophesied in the nature of Newton's mind. Not less does the brain of Davy or of Gay-Lussac,° from childhood exploring the affinities and repulsions of particles, anticipate the laws of organization. Does not the eye of the human embryo predict the light? the ear of Handel predict the witchcraft of harmonic sound? Do not the constructive fingers of Watt, Fulton, Whittemore, Arkwright,° predict the fusible, hard, and temperable texture of metals, the properties of stone, water, and wood? Do not the lovely attributes of the maiden child predict the refinements and decorations of civil society? Here also we are reminded of the action of man on man. A mind might ponder its thought for ages, and not gain so much self-knowledge as the passion of love shall teach it in a day. Who knows himself before he has been thrilled with indignation at an outrage, or has heard an eloquent tongue, or has shared the throb of thousands in a national exultation or alarm? No man can antedate his experience, or guess what faculty or feeling a new object shall unlock, any more than he can draw to-day the face of a person whom he shall see to-morrow for the first time.

I will not now go behind the general statement to explore the reason of this correspondency. Let it suffice that in the light of these two facts, namely, that the mind is One, and that nature is its correlative, history is to be read and written.

Thus in all ways does the soul concentrate and reproduce its treasures for each pupil. He, too, shall pass through the whole cycle of experience. He shall collect into a focus the rays of nature. History no longer shall be a dull book. It shall walk incarnate in every just and wise man. You shall not tell me by languages and titles a catalogue of the volumes you have read. You shall make me feel what periods you have lived. A man shall be the Temple of Fame. He shall walk, as the poets have described that goddess, in a robe painted all over with wonderful events and experiences;—his own form and features by their exalted intelligence shall be that variegated vest. I shall find in him the Fore-world; in his childhood the Age of Gold; the Apples of Knowledge; the Argonautic Expedition; the calling of Abraham; the building of the Temple; the Advent of Christ; Dark Ages; the Revival of Letters; the Reformation; the discovery of new lands; the opening of new sciences, and new regions in man. He shall be the priest of Pan, and bring with him into humble cottages the blessing of the morning stars and all the recorded benefits of heaven and earth.

Is there somewhat overweening in this claim? Then I reject all I have written, for what is the use of pretending to know what we know not? But it is the fault of our rhetoric that we cannot strongly state one fact without seeming to belie some other. I hold our actual knowledge very cheap. Hear the rats in the wall, see the lizard on the fence, the fungus under foot, the lichen on the log. What do I know sympathetically, morally, of either of these worlds of life? As old as the Caucasian man,—perhaps older,—these creatures have kept their counsel beside him, and there is no record of any word or sign that has passed from one to the other. What connection do the books show between the fifty or sixty chemical elements, and the historical eras? Nay, what does history yet record of the metaphysical annals of man? What light does it shed on those mysteries which we hide under the names Death and Immortality? Yet every history should be written in a wisdom which divined the range of our affinities and looked at facts as symbols. I am ashamed to see what a shallow village tale our so-called History is. How many times we must say Rome, and Paris, and Constantinople! What does Rome know of rat and lizard? What are Olympiads and Consulates to these neighbouring systems of being? Nay, what food or experience or succour have they for the Esquimaux seal-hunter, for the Kanàka in his canoe, for the fisherman, the stevedore, the porter?

Broader and deeper we must write our annals,—from an ethical reformation, from an influx of the ever new, ever sanative conscience,—if we would trulier express our central and wide-related nature, instead of this old chronology of selfishness and pride to which we have too long lent our eyes. Already that day exists for us, shines in on us at unawares, but the path of science and of letters is not the way into nature. The idiot, the Indian, the child, and unschooled farmer's boy, stand nearer to the light by which nature is to be read, than the dissector or the antiquary.

SELF-RELIANCE°

'Ne te quæsiveris extra'.

———

'Man is his own star; and the soul that can
Render an honest and a perfect man,
Commands all light, all influence, all fate;
Nothing to him falls early or too late.
Our acts our angels are, or good or ill,
Our fatal shadows that walk by us still'.
Epilogue to Beaumont and Fletcher's
Honest Man's Fortune

———

Cast the bantling on the rocks,
Suckle him with the she-wolf's teat;
Wintered with the hawk and fox,
Power and speed be hands and feet.

I READ the other day some verses written by an eminent painter which
were original and not conventional. The soul always hears an admoni-
tion in such lines, let the subject be what it may. The sentiment they
instil is of more value than any thought they may contain. To believe
your own thought, to believe that what is true for you in your private
heart is true for all men,—that is genius. Speak your latent conviction,
and it shall be the universal sense; for the inmost in due time becomes
the outmost,—and our first thought is rendered back to us by the trumpets of the Last Judgment. Familiar as the voice of the mind is to each,
the highest merit we ascribe to Moses, Plato, and Milton is, that they
set at naught books and traditions, and spoke not what men but what
they thought. A man should learn to detect and watch that gleam of
light which flashes across his mind from within, more than the lustre of
the firmament of bards and sages. Yet he dismisses without notice his
thought, because it is his. In every work of genius we recognize our own
rejected thoughts: they come back to us with a certain alienated majesty. Great works of art have no more affecting lesson for us than this.
They teach us to abide by our spontaneous impression with good-

humored inflexibility then most when the whole cry of voices is on the other side. Else, to-morrow a stranger will say with masterly good sense precisely what we have thought and felt all the time, and we shall be forced to take with shame our own opinion from another.

There is a time in every man's education when he arrives at the conviction that envy is ignorance; that imitation is suicide; that he must take himself for better, for worse, as his portion; that though the wide universe is full of good, no kernel of nourishing corn can come to him but through his toil bestowed on that plot of ground which is given to him to till. The power which resides in him is new in nature, and none but he knows what that is which he can do, nor does he know until he has tried. Not for nothing one face, one character, one fact, makes much impression on him, and another none. This sculpture in the memory is not without preëstablished harmony. The eye was placed where one ray should fall, that it might testify of that particular ray. We but half express ourselves, and are ashamed of that divine idea which each of us represents. It may be safely trusted as proportionate and of good issues, so it be faithfully imparted, but God will not have his work made manifest by cowards. A man is relieved and gay when he has put his heart into his work and done his best; but what he has said or done otherwise, shall give him no peace. It is a deliverance which does not deliver. In the attempt his genius deserts him; no muse befriends; no invention, no hope.

Trust thyself: every heart vibrates to that iron string. Accept the place the divine providence has found for you, the society of your contemporaries, the connection of events. Great men have always done so, and confided themselves childlike to the genius of their age, betraying their perception that the absolutely trustworthy was seated at their heart, working through their hands, predominating in all their being. And we are now men, and must accept in the highest mind the same transcendent destiny; and not minors and invalids in a protected corner, not cowards fleeing before a revolution, but guides, redeemers, and benefactors, obeying the Almighty effort, and advancing on Chaos and the Dark.

What pretty oracles nature yields us on this text, in the face and behaviour of children, babes, and even brutes! That divided and rebel mind, that distrust of a sentiment because our arithmetic has computed the strength and means opposed to our purpose, these have not. Their mind being whole, their eye is as yet unconquered, and when we look in their faces, we are disconcerted. Infancy conforms to nobody: all conform to it, so that one babe commonly makes four or five out of the adults who prattle and play to it. So God has armed youth and puberty and manhood no less with its own piquancy and charm, and made it enviable and gracious and its claims not to be put by, if it will stand by itself. Do not think the youth has no force, because he cannot speak to you and me. Hark! in the next room his voice is sufficiently clear and emphatic. It seems he knows how to speak to his contemporaries. Bashful or bold, then, he will know how to make us seniors very unnecessary.

The nonchalance of boys who are sure of a dinner, and would disdain as much as a lord to do or say aught to conciliate one, is the healthy attitude of human nature. A boy is in the parlour what the pit is in the playhouse; independent, irresponsible, looking out from his corner on such people and facts as pass by, he tries and sentences them on their merits, in the swift, summary way of boys, as good, bad, interesting, silly, eloquent, troublesome. He cumbers himself never about consequences, about interests: he gives an independent, genuine verdict. You must court him: he does not court you. But the man is, as it were, clapped into jail by his consciousness. As soon as he has once acted or spoken with eclat, he is a committed person, watched by the sympathy or the hatred of hundreds, whose affections must now enter into his account. There is no Lethe° for this. Ah, that he could pass again into his neutrality! Who can thus avoid all pledges, and having observed, observe again from the same unaffected, unbiased, unbribable, unaffrighted innocence, must always be formidable. He would utter opinions on all passing affairs, which being seen to be not private, but necessary, would sink like darts into the ear of men, and put them in fear.

These are the voices which we hear in solitude, but they grow faint and inaudible as we enter into the world. Society everywhere is in conspiracy against the manhood of every one of its members. Society is a joint-stock company, in which the members agree, for the better securing of his bread to each shareholder, to surrender the liberty and culture of the eater. The virtue in most request is conformity. Self-reliance is its aversion. It loves not realities and creators, but names and customs.

Whoso would be a man must be a nonconformist. He who would gather immortal palms must not be hindered by the name of goodness, but must explore if it be goodness. Nothing is at last sacred but the integrity of your own mind. Absolve you to yourself, and you shall have the suffrage of the world. I remember an answer which when quite young I was prompted to make to a valued adviser, who was wont to importune me with the dear old doctrines of the church. On my saying, What have I to do with the sacredness of traditions, if I live wholly from within? my friend suggested,—'But these impulses may be from below, not from above.' I replied, 'They do not seem to me to be such; but if I am the Devil's child, I will live then from the Devil.' No law can be sacred to me but that of my nature. Good and bad are but names very readily transferable to that or this; the only right is what is after my constitution, the only wrong what is against it. A man is to carry himself in the presence of all opposition, as if every thing were titular and ephemeral but he. I am ashamed to think how easily we capitulate to badges and names, to large societies and dead institutions. Every decent and well-spoken individual affects and sways me more than is right. I ought to go upright and vital, and speak the rude truth in all ways. If malice and vanity wear the coat of philanthropy, shall that pass? If an angry bigot assumes this bountiful cause of Abolition, and comes to me with his last news from Barbadoes,° why should I not say to him, 'Go love thy infant; love thy wood-chopper: be good-natured and modest: have that grace; and never varnish your hard, uncharitable ambition with this incredible tenderness for black folk a thousand miles off. Thy love afar is spite at home'. Rough and graceless would be such greeting, but truth is handsomer than the affectation of love. Your goodness must have some edge to it,—else it is none. The doctrine of hatred must be preached as the counteraction of the doctrine of love when that pules and whines. I shun father and mother and wife and brother, when my genius calls me.° I would write on the lintels of the door-post,° *Whim*. I hope it is somewhat better than whim at last, but we cannot spend the day in explanation. Expect me not to show cause why I seek or why I exclude company. Then, again, do not tell me, as a good man did to-day, of my obligation to put all poor men in good situations. Are they *my* poor? I tell thee, thou foolish philanthropist, that I grudge the dollar, the dime, the cent, I give to such men as do not belong to me and to whom I do not belong. There is a class of persons to whom by all spiritual affinity I am bought and sold; for them I will go to prison, if need be; but your miscellaneous popular charities; the education at college of fools; the building of meeting-houses to the vain end to which many now stand; alms to sots; and the thousandfold Relief Societies;—though I confess with shame I sometimes succumb and give the dollar, it is a wicked dollar which by and by I shall have the manhood to withhold.

Virtues are, in the popular estimate, rather the exception than the rule. There is the man *and* his virtues. Men do what is called a good action, as some piece of courage or charity, much as they would pay a fine in expiation of daily non-appearance on parade. Their works are done as an apology or extenuation of their living in the world,—as invalids and the insane pay a high board. Their virtues are penances. I do not wish to expiate, but to live. My life is for itself and not for a spectacle. I much prefer that it should be of a lower strain, so it be genuine and equal, than that it should be glittering and unsteady. I wish it to be sound and sweet, and not to need diet and bleeding. I ask primary evidence that you are a man, and refuse this appeal from the man to his actions. I know that for myself it makes no difference whether I do or forbear those actions which are reckoned excellent. I cannot consent to pay for a privilege where I have intrinsic right. Few and mean as my gifts may be, I actually am, and do not need for my own assurance or the assurance of my fellows any secondary testimony.

What I must do is all that concerns me, not what the people think. This rule, equally arduous in actual and in intellectual life, may serve for the whole distinction between greatness and meanness. It is the harder, because you will always find those who think they know what is your duty better than you know it. It is easy in the world to live after the world's opinion; it is easy in solitude to live after our own; but the great man is he who in the midst of the crowd keeps with perfect sweetness the independence of solitude.

The objection to conforming to usages that have become dead to you is, that it scatters your force. It loses your time and blurs the impression of your character. If you maintain a dead church, contribute to a dead Bible-society, vote with a great party either for the government or against it, spread your table like base housekeepers,—under all these screens I have difficulty to detect the precise man you are. And, of course, so much force is withdrawn from your proper life. But do your work, and I shall know you. Do your work, and you shall reinforce yourself. A man must consider what a blindman's-buff is this game of conformity. If I know your sect, I anticipate your argument. I hear a preacher announce for his text and topic the expediency of one of the institutions of his church. Do I not know beforehand that not possibly can he say a new and spontaneous word? Do I not know that, with all this ostentation of examining the grounds of the institution, he will do no such thing? Do I not know that he is pledged to himself not to look but at one side,—the permitted side, not as a man, but as a parish minister? He is a retained attorney, and these airs of the bench are the emptiest affectation. Well, most men have bound their eyes with one or another handkerchief, and attached themselves to some one of these communities of opinion. This conformity makes them not false in a few particulars, authors of a few lies, but false in all particulars. Their every truth is not quite true. Their two is not the real two, their four not the real four; so that every word they say chagrins us, and we know not where to begin to set them right. Meantime nature is not slow to equip us in the prison-uniform of the party to which we adhere. We come to wear one cut of face and figure, and acquire by degrees the gentlest asinine expression. There is a mortifying experience in particular, which does not fail to wreak itself also in the general history; I mean 'the foolish face of praise,'° the forced smile which we put on in company where we do not feel at ease in answer to conversation which does not interest us. The muscles, not spontaneously moved, but moved by a low usurping wilfulness, grow tight about the outline of the face with the most disagreeable sensation.

For nonconformity the world whips you with its displeasure. And therefore a man must know how to estimate a sour face. The bystanders look askance on him in the public street or in the friend's parlour. If this aversation had its origin in contempt and resistance like his own, he might well go home with a sad countenance; but the sour faces of the multitude, like their sweet faces, have no deep cause, but are put on and off as the wind blows and a newspaper directs. Yet is the discontent of the multitude more formidable than that of the senate and the college. It is easy enough for a firm man who knows the world to brook the rage of the cultivated classes. Their rage is decorous and prudent, for they are timid as being very vulnerable themselves. But when to their feminine rage the indignation of the people is added, when the ignorant and the poor are aroused, when the unintelligent brute force that lies at the bottom of society is made to growl and mow, it needs the habit of magnanimity and religion to treat it godlike as a trifle of no concernment.

The other terror that scares us from self-trust is our consistency; a reverence for our past act or word, because the eyes of others have no other data for computing our orbit than our past acts, and we are loath to disappoint them.

But why should you keep your head over your shoulder? Why drag about this corpse of your memory, lest you contradict somewhat you have stated in this or that public place? Suppose you should contradict yourself; what then? It seems to be a rule of wisdom never to rely on your memory alone, scarcely even in acts of pure memory, but to bring the past for judgment into the thousand-eyed present, and live ever in a new day. In your metaphysics you have denied personality to the Deity: yet when the devout motions of the soul come, yield to them heart and life, though they should clothe God with shape and color. Leave your theory, as Joseph his coat in the hand of the harlot, and flee.°

A foolish consistency is the hobgoblin of little minds, adored by little statesmen and philosophers and divines. With consistency a great soul has simply nothing to do. He may as well concern himself with his shadow on the wall. Speak what you think now in hard words, and to-morrow speak what to-morrow thinks in hard words again, though it contradict every thing you said to-day.—'Ah, so you shall be sure to be misunderstood.'—Is it so bad, then, to be misunderstood? Pythagoras was misunderstood, and Socrates, and Jesus, and Luther, and Copernicus, and Galileo, and Newton, and every pure and wise spirit that ever took flesh. To be great is to be misunderstood.

I suppose no man can violate his nature. All the sallies of his will are rounded in by the law of his being, as the inequalities of Andes and Himmaleh are insignificant in the curve of the sphere. Nor does it matter how you gauge and try him. A character is like an acrostic or Alexandrian stanza;°—read it forward, backward, or across, it still spells the same thing. In this pleasing, contrite wood-life which God allows me, let me record day by day my honest thought without prospect or retrospect, and, I cannot doubt, it will be found symmetrical, though I mean it not, and see it not. My book should smell of pines and resound with the hum of insects. The swallow over my window should interweave that thread or straw he carries in his bill into my web also. We pass for what we are. Character teaches above our wills. Men imagine that they communicate their virtue or vice only by overt actions, and do not see that virtue or vice emit a breath every moment.

There will be an agreement in whatever variety of actions, so they be each honest and natural in their hour. For of one will, the actions will be harmonious, however unlike they seem. These varieties are lost sight of at a little distance, at a little height of thought. One tendency unites them all. The voyage of the best ship is a zigzag line of a hundred tacks. See the line from a sufficient distance, and it straightens itself to the average tendency. Your genuine action will explain itself, and will explain your other genuine actions. Your conformity explains nothing. Act singly, and what you have already done singly will justify you now. Greatness appeals to the future. If I can be firm enough to-day to do right, and scorn eyes, I must have done so much right before as to defend me now. Be it how it will, do right now. Always scorn appearances, and you always may. The force of character is cumulative. All the foregone days of virtue work their health into this. What makes the majesty of the heroes of the senate and the field, which so fills the imagination? The consciousness of a train of great days and victories behind. They shed an united light on the advancing actor. He is attended as by a visible escort of angels. That is it which throws thunder into Chatham's voice, and dignity into Washington's port, and America into Adams's eye.° Honor is venerable to us because it is no ephemeris. It is always ancient virtue. We worship it to-day because it is not of to-day. We love it and pay it homage, because it is not a trap for our love and homage, but is self-dependent, self-derived, and therefore of an old immaculate pedigree, even if shown in a young person.

I hope in these days we have heard the last of conformity and consistency. Let the words be gazetted° and ridiculous henceforward. Instead of the gong for dinner, let us hear a whistle from the Spartan fife. Let us never bow and apologize more. A great man is coming to eat at my house. I do not wish to please him; I wish that he should wish to please me. I will stand here for humanity, and though I would make it kind, I would make it true. Let us affront and reprimand the smooth mediocrity and squalid contentment of the times, and hurl in the face of custom, and trade, and office, the fact which is the upshot of all history, that there is a great responsible Thinker and Actor working wherever a man works; that a true man belongs to no other time or place, but is the centre of things. Where he is, there is nature. He measures you, and all men, and all events. Ordinarily, every body in society reminds us of somewhat else, or of some other person. Character, reality, reminds you of nothing else; it takes place of the whole creation. The man must be so much, that he must make all circumstances indifferent. Every true man is a cause, a country, and an age; requires infinite spaces and numbers and time fully to accomplish his design;—and posterity seem to follow his steps as a train of clients. A man Cæsar is born, and for ages after we have a Roman Empire. Christ is born, and millions of minds so grow and cleave to his genius, that he is confounded with virtue and the possible of man. An institution is the lengthened shadow of one man; as, Monachism, of the Hermit Antony; the Reformation, of Luther; Quakerism, of Fox; Methodism, of Wesley; Abolition, of Clarkson. Scipio, Milton called 'the height of Rome';° and all history resolves itself very easily into the biography of a few stout and earnest persons.

Let a man then know his worth, and keep things under his feet. Let him not peep or steal, or skulk up and down with the air of a charity-boy, a bastard, or an interloper, in the world which exists for him. But the man in the street, finding no worth in himself which corresponds to the force which built a tower or sculptured a marble god, feels poor when he looks on these. To him a palace, a statue, or a costly book have an alien and forbidding air, much like a gay equipage, and seem to say like that, 'Who are you, Sir?' Yet they all are his, suitors for his notice, petitioners to his faculties that they will come out and take possession. The picture waits for my verdict: it is not to command me, but I am to settle its claims to praise. That popular fable of the sot° who was picked up dead drunk in the street, carried to the duke's house, washed and dressed and laid in the duke's bed, and, on his waking, treated with all obsequious ceremony like the duke, and assured that he had been insane, owes its popularity to the fact, that it symbolizes so well the state of man, who is in the world a sort of sot, but now and then wakes up, exercises his reason, and finds himself a true prince.

Our reading is mendicant and sycophantic. In history, our imagination plays us false. Kingdom and lordship, power and estate, are a gaudier vocabulary than private John and Edward in a small house and common day's work; but the things of life are the same to both; the sum total of both is the same. Why all this deference to Alfred, and Scanderbeg, and Gustavus?° Suppose they were virtuous; did they wear out virtue? As great a stake depends on your private act to-day, as followed their public and renowned steps. When private men shall act with original views, the lustre will be transferred from the actions of kings to those of gentlemen.

The world has been instructed by its kings, who have so magnetized the eyes of nations. It has been taught by this colossal symbol the mutual reverence that is due from man to man. The joyful loyalty with which men have everywhere suffered the king, the noble, or the great proprietor to walk among them by a law of his own, make his own scale of men and things, and reverse theirs, pay for benefits not with money but with honor, and represent the law in his person, was the hieroglyphic by which they obscurely signified their consciousness of their own right and comeliness, the right of every man.

The magnetism which all original action exerts is explaincd when we inquire the reason of self-trust. Who is the Trustee? What is the aboriginal Self, on which a universal reliance may be grounded? What is the nature and power of that science-baffling star, without parallax, without calculable elements, which shoots a ray of beauty even into trivial and impure actions, if the least mark of independence appear? The inquiry leads us to that source, at once the essence of genius, of virtue, and of life, which we call Spontaneity or Instinct. We denote this primary wisdom as Intuition, whilst all later teachings are tuitions. In that deep force, the last fact behind which analysis cannot go, all things find their

common origin. For, the sense of being which in calm hours rises, we
know not how, in the soul, is not diverse from things, from space, from
light, from time, from man, but one with them, and proceeds obviously
from the same source whence their life and being also proceed. We first
share the life by which things exist, and afterwards see them as appearances in nature, and forget that we have shared their cause. Here is the
fountain of action and of thought. Here are the lungs of that inspiration
which giveth man wisdom, and which cannot be denied without impiety
and atheism. We lie in the lap of immense intelligence, which makes us
receivers of its truth and organs of its activity. When we discern justice,
when we discern truth, we do nothing of ourselves, but allow a passage
to its beams. If we ask whence this comes, if we seek to pry into the soul
that causes, all philosophy is at fault. Its presence or its absence is all we
can affirm. Every man discriminates between the voluntary acts of his
mind, and his involuntary perceptions, and knows that to his involuntary perceptions a perfect faith is due. He may err in the expression of
them, but he knows that these things are so, like day and night, not to
be disputed. My wilful actions and acquisitions are but roving;—the
idlest reverie, the faintest native emotion, command my curiosity and
respect. Thoughtless people contradict as readily the statement of perceptions as of opinions, or rather much more readily; for, they do not
distinguish between perception and notion. They fancy that I choose to
see this or that thing. But perception is not whimsical, but fatal. If I see
a trait, my children will see it after me, and in course of time, all mankind,—although it may chance that no one has seen it before me. For
my perception of it is as much a fact as the sun.

The relations of the soul to the divine spirit are so pure, that it is profane to seek to interpose helps. It must be that when God speaketh he
should communicate, not one thing, but all things; should fill the world
with his voice; should scatter forth light, nature, time, souls, from the
centre of the present thought; and new date and new create the whole.
Whenever a mind is simple, and receives a divine wisdom, old things
pass away,—means, teachers, texts, temples fall; it lives now, and
absorbs past and future into the present hour. All things are made
sacred by relation to it,—one as much as another. All things are dissolved to their centre by their cause, and, in the universal miracle, petty
and particular miracles disappear. If, therefore, a man claims to know
and speak of God, and carries you backward to the phraseology of some
old mouldered nation in another country, in another world, believe him
not. Is the acorn better than the oak which is its fulness and completion?
Is the parent better than the child into whom he has cast his ripened

being? Whence, then, this worship of the past? The centuries are conspirators against the sanity and authority of the soul. Time and space are but physiological colors which the eye makes, but the soul is light; where it is, is day; where it was, is night; and history is an impertinence and an injury, if it be any thing more than a cheerful apologue or parable of my being and becoming.

Man is timid and apologetic; he is no longer upright; he dares not say 'I think,' 'I am,' but quotes some saint or sage. He is ashamed before the blade of grass or the blowing rose. These roses under my window make no reference to former roses or to better ones; they are for what they are; they exist with God to-day. There is no time to them. There is simply the rose; it is perfect in every moment of its existence. Before a leaf-bud has burst, its whole life acts; in the full-blown flower there is no more; in the leafless root there is no less. Its nature is satisfied, and it satisfies nature, in all moments alike. But man postpones or remembers; he does not live in the present, but with reverted eye laments the past, or, heedless of the riches that surround him, stands on tiptoe to foresee the future. He cannot be happy and strong until he too lives with nature in the present, above time.

This should be plain enough. Yet see what strong intellects dare not yet hear God himself, unless he speak the phraseology of I know not what David, or Jeremiah, or Paul. We shall not always set so great a price on a few texts, on a few lives. We are like children who repeat by rote the sentences of grandames and tutors, and, as they grow older, of the men of talents and character they chance to see,—painfully recollecting the exact words they spoke; afterwards, when they come into the point of view which those had who uttered these sayings, they understand them, and are willing to let the words go; for, at any time, they can use words as good when occasion comes. If we live truly, we shall see truly. It is as easy for the strong man to be strong, as it is for the weak to be weak. When we have new perception, we shall gladly disburden the memory of its hoarded treasures as old rubbish. When a man lives with God, his voice shall be as sweet as the murmur of the brook and the rustle of the corn.

And now at last the highest truth on this subject remains unsaid; probably cannot be said; for all that we say is the far-off remembering of the intuition. That thought, by what I can now nearest approach to say it, is this. When good is near you, when you have life in yourself, it is not by any known or accustomed way; you shall not discern the footprints of any other; you shall not see the face of man; you shall not hear any name;—the way, the thought, the good, shall be wholly strange and new. It shall exclude example and experience. You take the way from man, not to man. All persons that ever existed are its forgotten ministers. Fear and hope are alike beneath it. There is somewhat low even in hope. In the hour of vision, there is nothing that can be called gratitude, nor properly joy. The soul raised over passion beholds identity and eternal causation, perceives the self-existence of Truth and Right, and calms itself with knowing that all things go well. Vast spaces of nature, the Atlantic Ocean, the South Sea,—long intervals of time, years, centuries,—are of no account. This which I think and feel underlay every former state of life and circumstances, as it does underlie my present, and what is called life, and what is called death.

Life only avails, not the having lived. Power ceases in the instant of repose; it resides in the moment of transition from a past to a new state, in the shooting of the gulf, in the darting to an aim. This one fact the world hates, that the soul *becomes*; for that for ever degrades the past, turns all riches to poverty, all reputation to a shame, confounds the saint with the rogue, shoves Jesus and Judas equally aside. Why, then, do we prate of self-reliance? Inasmuch as the soul is present, there will be power not confident but agent. To talk of reliance is a poor external way of speaking. Speak rather of that which relies, because it works and is. Who has more obedience than I masters me, though he should not raise his finger. Round him I must revolve by the gravitation of spirits. We fancy it rhetoric, when we speak of eminent virtue. We do not yet see that virtue is Height, and that a man or a company of men, plastic and permeable to principles, by the law of nature must overpower and ride all cities, nations, kings, rich men, poets, who are not.

This is the ultimate fact which we so quickly reach on this, as on every topic, the resolution of all into the ever-blessed ONE. Self-existence is the attribute of the Supreme Cause, and it constitutes the measure of good by the degree in which it enters into all lower forms. All things real are so by so much virtue as they contain. Commerce, husbandry, hunting, whaling, war, eloquence, personal weight, are somewhat, and engage my respect as examples of its presence and impure action. I see the same law working in nature for conservation and growth. Power is in nature the essential measure of right. Nature suffers nothing to remain in her kingdoms which cannot help itself. The genesis and maturation of a planet, its poise and orbit, the bended tree recovering itself from the strong wind, the vital resources of every animal and vegetable, are demonstrations of the self-sufficing, and therefore self-relying soul.

Thus all concentrates: let us not rove; let us sit at home with the cause. Let us stun and astonish the intruding rabble of men and books and institutions, by a simple declaration of the divine fact. Bid the invaders take the shoes from off their feet, for God is here within.° Let our simplicity judge them, and our docility to our own law demonstrate the poverty of nature and fortune beside our native riches.

But now we are a mob. Man does not stand in awe of man, nor is his genius admonished to stay at home, to put itself in communication with the internal ocean, but it goes abroad to beg a cup of water of the urns of other men. We must go alone. I like the silent church before the service begins, better than any preaching. How far off, how cool, how chaste the persons look, begirt each one with a precinct or sanctuary! So let us always sit. Why should we assume the faults of our friend, or wife, or father, or child, because they sit around our hearth, or are said to have the same blood? All men have my blood, and I have all men's. Not for that will I adopt their petulance or folly, even to the extent of being ashamed of it. But your isolation must not be mechanical, but spiritual, that is, must be elevation. At times the whole world seems to be in conspiracy to importune you with emphatic trifles. Friend, client, child, sickness, fear, want, charity, all knock at once at thy closet door, and say,—'Come out unto us.'° But keep thy state; come not into their confusion. The power men possess to annoy me, I give them by a weak curiosity. No man can come near me but through my act. 'What we love that we have, but by desire we bereave ourselves of the love.'°

If we cannot at once rise to the sanctities of obedience and faith, let us at least resist our temptations; let us enter into the state of war, and wake Thor and Woden,° courage and constancy, in our Saxon breasts. This is to be done in our smooth times by speaking the truth. Check this lying hospitality and lying affection. Live no longer to the expectation of these deceived and deceiving people with whom we converse. Say to them, O father, O mother, O wife, O brother, O friend, I have lived with you after appearances hitherto. Henceforward I am the truth's. Be it known unto you that henceforward I obey no law less than the eternal law. I will have no covenants but proximities. I shall endeavour to nourish my parents, to support my family, to be the chaste husband of one wife,—but these relations I must fill after a new and unprecedented way. I appeal from your customs. I must be myself. I cannot break myself any longer for you, or you. If you can love me for what I am, we shall be the happier. If you cannot, I will still seek to deserve that you should. I will not hide my tastes or aversions. I will so trust that what is deep is holy, that I will do strongly before the sun and moon whatever inly rejoices me, and the heart appoints. If you are noble, I will love you; if you are not, I will not hurt you and myself by hypocritical attentions. If you are true, but not in the same truth with me, cleave to your companions; I will seek my own. I do this not selfishly, but humbly and truly. It is alike your interest, and mine, and all men's, however long we have dwelt in lies, to live in truth. Does this sound harsh to-day? You will soon love what is dictated by your nature as well as mine, and, if we follow the truth, it will bring us out safe at last.—But so you may give these friends pain. Yes, but I cannot sell my liberty and my power, to save their sensibility. Besides, all persons have their moments of reason, when they look out into the region of absolute truth; then will they justify me, and do the same thing.

The populace think that your rejection of popular standards is a rejection of all standard, and mere antinomianism; and the bold sensualist will use the name of philosophy to gild his crimes. But the law of consciousness abides. There are two confessionals, in one or the other of which we must be shriven. You may fulfil your round of duties by clearing yourself in the *direct*, or in the *reflex* way. Consider whether you have satisfied your relations to father, mother, cousin, neighbour, town, cat, and dog; whether any of these can upbraid you. But I may also neglect this reflex standard, and absolve me to myself. I have my own stern claims and perfect circle. It denies the name of duty to many offices that are called duties. But if I can discharge its debts, it enables me to dispense with the popular code. If any one imagines that this law is lax, let him keep its commandment one day.

And truly it demands something godlike in him who has cast off the common motives of humanity, and has ventured to trust himself for a taskmaster. High be his heart, faithful his will, clear his sight, that he may in good earnest be doctrine, society, law, to himself, that a simple purpose may be to him as strong as iron necessity is to others!

If any man consider the present aspects of what is called by distinction *society*, he will see the need of these ethics. The sinew and heart of man seem to be drawn out, and we are become timorous, desponding whimperers. We are afraid of truth, afraid of fortune, afraid of death, and afraid of each other. Our age yields no great and perfect persons. We want men and women who shall renovate life and our social state, but we see that most natures are insolvent, cannot satisfy their own wants, have an ambition out of all proportion to their practical force, and do lean and beg day and night continually. Our housekeeping is mendicant, our arts, our occupations, our marriages, our religion, we have not chosen, but society has chosen for us. We are parlour soldiers. We shun the rugged battle of fate, where strength is born.

If our young men miscarry in their first enterprises, they lose all heart. If the young merchant fails, men say he is *ruined*. If the finest genius studies at one of our colleges, and is not installed in an office within one year afterwards in the cities or suburbs of Boston or New York, it seems to his friends and to himself that he is right in being disheartened, and in complaining the rest of his life. A sturdy lad from New Hampshire or Vermont, who in turn tries all the professions, who *teams it, farms it, peddles*, keeps a school, preaches, edits a newspaper, goes to Congress, buys a township, and so forth, in successive years, and always, like a cat, falls on his feet, is worth a hundred of these city dolls. He walks abreast with his days, and feels no shame in not 'studying a profession,' for he does not postpone his life, but lives already. He has not one chance, but a hundred chances. Let a Stoic open the resources of man, and tell men they are not leaning willows, but can and must detach themselves; that with the exercise of self-trust, new powers shall appear; that a man is the word made flesh, born to shed healing to the nations,° that he should be ashamed of our compassion, and that the moment he acts from himself, tossing the laws, the books, idolatries, and customs out of the window, we pity him no more, but thank and revere him,—and that teacher shall restore the life of man to splendor, and make his name dear to all history.

It is easy to see that a greater self-reliance must work a revolution in all the offices and relations of men; in their religion; in their education; in their pursuits; their modes of living; their association; in their property; in their speculative views.

1. In what prayers do men allow themselves! That which they call a holy office is not so much as brave and manly. Prayer looks abroad and asks for some foreign addition to come through some foreign virtue, and loses itself in endless mazes of natural and supernatural, and mediatorial and miraculous. Prayer that craves a particular commodity,—any thing less than all good,—is vicious. Prayer is the contemplation of the facts of life from the highest point of view. It is the soliloquy of a beholding and jubilant soul. It is the spirit of God pronouncing his works good. But prayer as a means to effect a private end is meanness and theft. It supposes dualism and not unity in nature and consciousness. As soon as the man is at one with God, he will not beg. He will then see prayer in all action.° The prayer of the farmer kneeling in his field to weed it, the prayer of the rower kneeling with the stroke of his oar, are true prayers heard throughout nature, though for cheap ends. Caratach, in Fletcher's Bonduca, when admonished to inquire the mind of the god Audate, replies,—

'His hidden meaning lies in our endeavours;
Our valors are our best gods'.°

Another sort of false prayers are our regrets. Discontent is the want of self-reliance: it is infirmity of will. Regret calamities, if you can thereby help the sufferer; if not, attend your own work, and already the evil begins to be repaired. Our sympathy is just as base. We come to them who weep foolishly, and sit down and cry for company, instead of imparting to them truth and health in rough electric shocks, putting them once more in communication with their own reason. The secret of fortune is joy in our hands. Welcome evermore to gods and men is the self-helping man. For him all doors are flung wide: him all tongues greet, all honors crown, all eyes follow with desire. Our love goes out to him and embraces him, because he did not need it. We solicitously and apologetically caress and celebrate him, because he held on his way and scorned our disapprobation. The gods love him because men hated him. 'To the persevering mortal,' said Zoroaster, 'the blessed Immortals are swift.'°

As men's prayers are a disease of the will, so are their creeds a disease of the intellect. They say with those foolish Israelites, 'Let not God speak to us, lest we die. Speak thou, speak any man with us, and we will obey'.° Everywhere I am hindered of meeting God in my brother, because he has shut his own temple doors, and recites fables merely of his brother's, or his brother's brother's God. Every new mind is a new classification. If it prove a mind of uncommon activity and power, a Locke, a Lavoisier, a Hutton, a Bentham, a Fourier,° it imposes its classification on other men, and lo! a new system. In proportion to the depth of the thought, and so to the number of the objects it touches and brings within reach of the pupil, is his complacency. But chiefly is this apparent in creeds and churches, which are also classifications of some powerful mind acting on the elemental thought of duty, and man's relation to the Highest. Such is Calvinism, Quakerism, Swedenborgism. The pupil takes the same delight in subordinating every thing to the new terminology, as a girl who has just learned botany in seeing a new earth and new seasons thereby. It will happen for a time, that the pupil will find his intellectual power has grown by the study of his master's mind. But in all unbalanced minds, the classification is idolized, passes for the end, and not for a speedily exhaustible means, so that the walls of the system blend to their eye in the remote horizon with the walls of the universe; the luminaries of heaven seem to them hung on the arch their master built. They cannot imagine how you aliens have any right to see,—how you can see; 'It must be somehow that you stole the light from us.' They do not yet perceive, that light, unsystematic, indomitable, will break into any cabin, even into theirs. Let them chirp awhile and call it their own. If they are honest and do well, presently their neat new pinfold will be too strait and low, will crack, will lean, will rot and vanish, and the immortal light, all young and joyful, million-orbed, million-colored, will beam over the universe as on the first morning.

2. It is for want of self-culture that the superstition of Travelling, whose idols are Italy, England, Egypt, retains its fascination for all educated Americans. They who made England, Italy, or Greece venerable in the imagination did so by sticking fast where they were, like an axis of the earth. In manly hours, we feel that duty is our place. The soul is no traveller; the wise man stays at home, and when his necessities, his duties, on any occasion call him from his house, or into foreign lands, he is at home still, and shall make men sensible by the expression of his countenance, that he goes the missionary of wisdom and virtue, and visits cities and men like a sovereign, and not like an interloper or a valet.

I have no churlish objection to the circumnavigation of the globe, for the purposes of art, of study, and benevolence, so that the man is first domesticated, or does not go abroad with the hope of finding somewhat greater than he knows. He who travels to be amused, or to get somewhat which he does not carry, travels away from himself, and grows old even in youth among old things. In Thebes, in Palmyra, his will and mind have become old and dilapidated as they. He carries ruins to ruins.

Travelling is a fool's paradise. Our first journeys discover to us the indifference of places. At home I dream that at Naples, at Rome, I can be intoxicated with beauty, and lose my sadness. I pack my trunk, embrace my friends, embark on the sea, and at last wake up in Naples, and there beside me is the stern fact, the sad self, unrelenting, identical, that I fled from. I seek the Vatican, and the palaces. I affect to be intoxicated with sights and suggestions, but I am not intoxicated. My giant goes with me wherever I go.

3. But the rage of travelling is a symptom of a deeper unsoundness affecting the whole intellectual action. The intellect is vagabond, and our system of education fosters restlessness. Our minds travel when our bodies are forced to stay at home. We imitate; and what is imitation but the travelling of the mind? Our houses are built with foreign taste; our shelves are garnished with foreign ornaments; our opinions, our

tastes, our faculties, lean, and follow the Past and the Distant. The soul created the arts wherever they have flourished. It was in his own mind that the artist sought his model. It was an application of his own thought to the thing to be done and the conditions to be observed. And why need we copy the Doric or the Gothic model? Beauty, convenience, grandeur of thought, and quaint expression are as near to us as to any, and if the American artist will study with hope and love the precise thing to be done by him, considering the climate, the soil, the length of the day, the wants of the people, the habit and form of the government, he will create a house in which all these will find themselves fitted, and taste and sentiment will be satisfied also.

Insist on yourself; never imitate. Your own gift you can present every moment with the cumulative force of a whole life's cultivation; but of the adopted talent of another, you have only an extemporaneous, half possession. That which each can do best, none but his Maker can teach him. No man yet knows what it is, nor can, till that person has exhibited it. Where is the master who could have taught Shakspeare? Where is the master who could have instructed Franklin, or Washington, or Bacon, or Newton? Every great man is a unique. The Scipionism of Scipio is precisely that part he could not borrow. Shakspeare will never be made by the study of Shakspeare. Do that which is assigned you, and you cannot hope too much or dare too much. There is at this moment for you an utterance brave and grand as that of the colossal chisel of Phidias,° or trowel of the Egyptians, or the pen of Moses, or Dante, but different from all these. Not possibly will the soul all rich, all eloquent, with thousand-cloven tongue, deign to repeat itself; but if you can hear what these patriarchs say, surely you can reply to them in the same pitch of voice; for the ear and the tongue are two organs of one nature. Abide in the simple and noble regions of thy life, obey thy heart, and thou shalt reproduce the Foreworld again.

4. As our Religion, our Education, our Art look abroad, so does our spirit of society. All men plume themselves on the improvement of society, and no man improves.

Society never advances. It recedes as fast on one side as it gains on the other. It undergoes continual changes; it is barbarous, it is civilized, it is christianized, it is rich, it is scientific; but this change is not amelioration. For every thing that is given, something is taken. Society acquires new arts, and loses old instincts. What a contrast between the well-clad, reading, writing, thinking American, with a watch, a pencil, and a bill of exchange in his pocket, and the naked New Zealander, whose property is a club, a spear, a mat, and an undivided twentieth of a shed to sleep under! But compare the health of the two men, and you shall see that the white man has lost his aboriginal strength. If the traveller tell us truly, strike the savage with a broad axe, and in a day or two the flesh shall unite and heal as if you struck the blow into soft pitch, and the same blow shall send the white to his grave.

The civilized man has built a coach, but has lost the use of his feet. He is supported on crutches, but lacks so much support of muscle. He has a fine Geneva watch, but he fails of the skill to tell the hour by the sun. A Greenwich nautical almanac he has, and so being sure of the information when he wants it, the man in the street does not know a star in the sky. The solstice he does not observe; the equinox he knows as little; and the whole bright calendar of the year is without a dial in his mind. His note-books impair his memory; his libraries overload his wit; the insurance-office increases the number of accidents; and it may be a question whether machinery does not encumber; whether we have not lost by refinement some energy, by a Christianity entrenched in establishments and forms, some vigor of wild virtue. For every Stoic was a Stoic; but in Christendom where is the Christian?

There is no more deviation in the moral standard than in the standard of height or bulk. No greater men are now than ever were. A singular equality may be observed between the great men of the first and of the last ages; nor can all the science, art, religion, and philosophy of the nineteenth century avail to educate greater men than Plutarch's heroes, three or four and twenty centuries ago. Not in time is the race progressive. Phocion, Socrates, Anaxagoras, Diogenes,° are great men, but they leave no class. He who is really of their class will not be called by their name, but will be his own man, and, in his turn, the founder of a sect. The arts and inventions of each period are only its costume, and do not invigorate men. The harm of the improved machinery may compensate its good. Hudson and Behring accomplished so much in their fishing-boats, as to astonish Parry and Franklin,° whose equipment exhausted the resources of science and art. Galileo, with an opera-glass, discovered a more splendid series of celestial phenomena than any one since. Columbus found the New World in an undecked boat. It is curious to see the periodical disuse and perishing of means and machinery, which were introduced with loud laudation a few years or centuries before. The great genius returns to essential man. We reckoned the improvements of the art of war among the triumphs of science, and yet Napoleon conquered Europe by the bivouac, which consisted of falling back on naked valor, and disencumbering it of all aids. The Emperor held it impossible to make a perfect army, says Las

Casas,° 'without abolishing our arms, magazines, commissaries, and carriages, until, in imitation of the Roman custom, the soldier should receive his supply of corn, grind it in his hand-mill, and bake his bread himself.'

Society is a wave. The wave moves onward, but the water of which it is composed does not. The same particle does not rise from the valley to the ridge. Its unity is only phenomenal. The persons who make up a nation to-day, next year die, and their experience with them.

And so the reliance on Property, including the reliance on governments which protect it, is the want of self-reliance. Men have looked away from themselves and at things so long, that they have come to esteem the religious, learned, and civil institutions as guards of property, and they deprecate assaults on these, because they feel them to be assaults on property. They measure their esteem of each other by what each has, and not by what each is. But a cultivated man becomes ashamed of his property, out of new respect for his nature. Especially he hates what he has, if he see that it is accidental,—came to him by inheritance, or gift, or crime; then he feels that it is not having; it does not belong to him, has no root in him, and merely lies there, because no revolution or no robber takes it away. But that which a man is does always by necessity acquire, and what the man acquires is living property, which does not wait the beck of rulers, or mobs, or revolutions, or fire, or storm, or bankruptcies, but perpetually renews itself wherever the man breathes. 'Thy lot or portion of life,' said the Caliph Ali,° 'is seeking after thee; therefore be at rest from seeking after it.' Our dependence on these foreign goods leads us to our slavish respect for numbers. The political parties meet in numerous conventions; the greater the concourse, and with each new uproar of announcement, The delegation from Essex! The Democrats from New Hampshire! The Whigs of Maine! the young patriot feels himself stronger than before by a new thousand of eyes and arms. In like manner the reformers summon conventions, and vote and resolve in multitude. Not so, O friends! will the God deign to enter and inhabit you, but by a method precisely the reverse. It is only as a man puts off all foreign support, and stands alone, that I see him to be strong and to prevail. He is weaker by every recruit to his banner. Is not a man better than a town? Ask nothing of men, and in the endless mutation, thou only firm column must presently appear the upholder of all that surrounds thee. He who knows that power is inborn, that he is weak because he has looked for good out of him and elsewhere, and so perceiving, throws himself unhesitatingly on his thought, instantly rights himself, stands in the erect position, commands his limbs, works miracles; just as a man who stands on his feet is stronger than a man who stands on his head.

So use all that is called Fortune. Most men gamble with her, and gain all, and lose all, as her wheel rolls. But do thou leave as unlawful these winnings, and deal with Cause and Effect, the chancellors of God. In the Will work and acquire, and thou hast chained the wheel of Chance, and shalt sit hereafter out of fear from her rotations. A political victory, a rise of rents, the recovery of your sick, or the return of your absent friend, or some other favorable event, raises your spirits, and you think good days are preparing for you. Do not believe it. Nothing can bring you peace but yourself. Nothing can bring you peace but the triumph of principles.

THE OVER-SOUL

'But souls that of his own good life partake,
He loves as his own self; dear as his eye
They are to Him: He 'll never them forsake:
When they shall die, then God himself shall die:
They live, they live in blest eternity.'°

Henry More

———

Space is ample, east and west,
But two cannot go abreast,
Cannot travel in it two:
Yonder masterful cuckoo
Crowds every egg out of the nest,
Quick or dead, except its own;
A spell is laid on sod and stone,
Night and Day 've been tampered with,
Every quality and pith
Surcharged and sultry with a power
That works its will on age and hour.

THERE is a difference between one and another hour of life, in their authority and subsequent effect. Our faith comes in moments; our vice is habitual. Yet there is a depth in those brief moments which constrains us to ascribe more reality to them than to all other experiences. For this reason, the argument which is always forthcoming to silence those who conceive extraordinary hopes of man, namely, the appeal to experience, is for ever invalid and vain. We give up the past to the objector, and yet we hope. He must explain this hope. We grant that human life is mean; but how did we find out that it was mean? What is the ground of this uneasiness of ours; of this old discontent? What is the universal sense of want and ignorance, but the fine inuendo by which the soul makes its enormous claim? Why do men feel that the natural history of man has never been written, but he is always leaving behind what you have said of him, and it becomes old, and books of metaphysics worthless? The philosophy of six thousand years has not searched the chambers and magazines of the soul. In its experiments there has always remained, in the last analysis, a residuum it could not resolve.

Man is a stream whose source is hidden. Our being is descending into us from we know not whence. The most exact calculator has no prescience that somewhat incalculable may not balk the very next moment. I am constrained every moment to acknowledge a higher origin for events than the will I call mine.

As with events, so is it with thoughts. When I watch that flowing river, which, out of regions I see not, pours for a season its streams into me, I see that I am a pensioner; not a cause, but a surprised spectator of this ethereal water; that I desire and look up, and put myself in the attitude of reception, but from some alien energy the visions come.

The Supreme Critic on the errors of the past and the present, and the only prophet of that which must be, is that great nature in which we rest, as the earth lies in the soft arms of the atmosphere; that Unity, that Over-soul, within which every man's particular being is contained and made one with all other; that common heart, of which all sincere conversation is the worship, to which all right action is submission; that overpowering reality which confutes our tricks and talents, and constrains every one to pass for what he is, and to speak from his character, and not from his tongue, and which evermore tends to pass into our thought and hand, and become wisdom, and virtue, and power, and beauty. We live in succession, in division, in parts, in particles. Meantime within man is the soul of the whole; the wise silence; the universal beauty, to which every part and particle is equally related; the eternal ONE. And this deep power in which we exist, and whose beatitude is all accessible to us, is not only self-sufficing and perfect in every hour, but the act of seeing and the thing seen, the seer and the spectacle, the subject and the object, are one. We see the world piece by piece, as the sun, the moon, the animal, the tree; but the whole, of which these are the shining parts, is the soul. Only by the vision of that Wisdom can the horoscope of the ages be read, and by falling back on our better thoughts, by yielding to the spirit of prophecy which is innate in every man, we can know what it saith. Every man's words, who speaks from that life, must sound vain to those who do not dwell in the same thought on their own part. I dare not speak for it. My words do not carry its august sense; they fall short and cold. Only itself can inspire whom it will, and behold! their speech shall be lyrical, and sweet, and universal as the rising of the wind. Yet I desire, even by profane words, if I may not use sacred, to indicate the heaven of this deity, and to report what hints I have collected of the transcendent simplicity and energy of the Highest Law.

If we consider what happens in conversation, in reveries, in remorse, in times of passion, in surprises, in the instructions of dreams, wherein often we see ourselves in masquerade,—the droll disguises only magnifying and enhancing a real element, and forcing it on our distinct notice,—we shall catch many hints that will broaden and lighten into knowledge of the secret of nature. All goes to show that the soul in man is not an organ, but animates and exercises all the organs; is not a function, like the power of memory, of calculation, of comparison, but uses these as hands and feet; is not a faculty, but a light; is not the intellect or the will, but the master of the intellect and the will; is the background of our being, in which they lie,—an immensity not possessed and that cannot be possessed. From within or from behind, a light shines through us upon things, and makes us aware that we are nothing, but the light is all. A man is the façade of a temple wherein all wisdom and all good abide. What we commonly call man, the eating, drinking, planting, counting man, does not, as we know him, represent himself, but misrepresents himself. Him we do not respect, but the soul, whose organ he is, would he let it appear through his action, would make our knees bend. When it breathes through his intellect, it is genius; when it breathes through his will, it is virtue; when it flows through his affection, it is love. And the blindness of the intellect begins, when it would be something of itself. The weakness of the will begins, when the individual would be something of himself. All reform aims, in some one particular, to let the soul have its way through us; in other words, to engage us to obey.

Of this pure nature every man is at some time sensible. Language cannot paint it with his colors. It is too subtile. It is undefinable, unmeasurable, but we know that it pervades and contains us. We know that all spiritual being is in man. A wise old proverb says, 'God comes to see us without bell;' that is, as there is no screen or ceiling between our heads and the infinite heavens, so is there no bar or wall in the soul where man, the effect, ceases, and God, the cause, begins. The walls are taken away. We lie open on one side to the deeps of spiritual nature, to the attributes of God. Justice we see and know, Love, Freedom, Power. These natures no man ever got above, but they tower over us, and most in the moment when our interests tempt us to wound them.

The sovereignty of this nature whereof we speak is made known by its independency of those limitations which circumscribe us on every hand. The soul circumscribes all things. As I have said, it contradicts all experience. In like manner it abolishes time and space. The influence of the senses has, in most men, overpowered the mind to that degree, that the walls of time and space have come to look real and insurmountable; and to speak with levity of these limits is, in the world, the sign of insanity. Yet time and space are but inverse measures of the force of the soul. The spirit sports with time,—

> 'Can crowd eternity into an hour,
> Or stretch an hour to eternity.'°

We are often made to feel that there is another youth and age than that which is measured from the year of our natural birth. Some thoughts always find us young, and keep us so. Such a thought is the love of the universal and eternal beauty. Every man parts from that contemplation with the feeling that it rather belongs to ages than to mortal life. The least activity of the intellectual powers redeems us in a degree from the conditions of time. In sickness, in languor, give us a strain of poetry, or a profound sentence, and we are refreshed; or produce a volume of Plato, or Shakspeare, or remind us of their names, and instantly we come into a feeling of longevity. See how the deep, divine thought reduces centuries, and millenniums, and makes itself present through all ages. Is the teaching of Christ less effective now than it was when first his mouth was opened? The emphasis of facts and persons in my thought has nothing to do with time. And so, always, the soul's scale is one; the scale of the senses and the understanding is another. Before the revelations of the soul, Time, Space, and Nature shrink away. In common speech, we refer all things to time, as we habitually refer the immensely sundered stars to one concave sphere. And so we say that the Judgment is distant or near, that the Millennium approaches, that a day of certain political, moral, social reforms is at hand, and the like, when we mean, that, in the nature of things, one of the facts we contemplate is external and fugitive, and the other is permanent and connate with the soul. The things we now esteem fixed shall, one by one, detach themselves, like ripe fruit, from our experience, and fall. The wind shall blow them none knows whither.° The landscape, the figures, Boston, London, are facts as fugitive as any institution past, or any whiff of mist or smoke, and so is society, and so is the world. The soul looketh steadily forwards, creating a world before her, leaving worlds behind her. She has no dates, nor rites, nor persons, nor specialties, nor men. The soul knows only the soul; the web of events is the flowing robe in which she is clothed.

After its own law and not by arithmetic is the rate of its progress to be computed. The soul's advances are not made by gradation, such as can be represented by motion in a straight line; but rather by ascension of state, such as can be represented by metamorphosis,—from the egg to the worm, from the worm to the fly. The growths of genius are of a certain *total* character, that does not advance the elect individual first over John, then Adam, then Richard, and give to each the pain of discovered inferiority, but by every throe of growth the man expands there where he works, passing, at each pulsation, classes, populations, of men. With each divine impulse the mind rends the thin rinds of the visible and finite, and comes out into eternity, and inspires and expires its air. It converses with truths that have always been spoken in the world, and becomes conscious of a closer sympathy with Zeno and Arrian,° than with persons in the house.

This is the law of moral and of mental gain. The simple rise as by specific levity, not into a particular virtue, but into the region of all the virtues. They are in the spirit which contains them all. The soul requires purity, but purity is not it; requires justice, but justice is not that; requires beneficence, but is somewhat better; so that there is a kind of descent and accommodation felt when we leave speaking of moral nature, to urge a virtue which it enjoins. To the well-born child, all the virtues are natural, and not painfully acquired. Speak to his heart, and the man becomes suddenly virtuous.

Within the same sentiment is the germ of intellectual growth, which obeys the same law. Those who are capable of humility, of justice, of love, of aspiration, stand already on a platform that commands the sciences and arts, speech and poetry, action and grace. For whoso dwells in this moral beatitude already anticipates those special powers which men prize so highly. The lover has no talent, no skill, which passes for quite nothing with his enamoured maiden, however little she may possess of related faculty; and the heart which abandons itself to the Supreme Mind finds itself related to all its works, and will travel a royal road to particular knowledges and powers. In ascending to this primary and aboriginal sentiment, we have come from our remote station on the circumference instantaneously to the centre of the world, where, as in the closet of God, we see causes, and anticipate the universe, which is but a slow effect.

One mode of the divine teaching is the incarnation of the spirit in a form,—in forms, like my own. I live in society; with persons who answer to thoughts in my own mind, or express a certain obedience to the great instincts to which I live. I see its presence to them. I am certified of a common nature; and these other souls, these separated selves, draw me as nothing else can. They stir in me the new emotions we call passion; of love, hatred, fear, admiration, pity; thence comes conversation, competition, persuasion, cities, and war. Persons are supplementary to the primary teaching of the soul. In youth we are mad for persons. Childhood and youth see all the world in them. But the larger experience of man discovers the identical nature appearing through them all. Persons themselves acquaint us with the impersonal. In all conversation between two persons, tacit reference is made, as to a third party, to a common nature. That third party or common nature is not social; it is impersonal; is God. And so in groups where debate is earnest, and especially on high questions, the company become aware that the thought rises to an equal level in all bosoms, that all have a spiritual property in what was said, as well as the sayer. They all become wiser than they were. It arches over them like a temple, this unity of thought, in which every heart beats with nobler sense of power and duty, and thinks and acts with unusual solemnity. All are conscious of attaining to a higher self-possession. It shines for all. There is a certain wisdom of humanity which is common to the greatest men with the lowest, and which our ordinary education often labors to silence and obstruct. The mind is one, and the best minds, who love truth for its own sake, think much less of property in truth. They accept it thankfully everywhere, and do not label or stamp it with any man's name, for it is theirs long beforehand, and from eternity. The learned and the studious of thought have no monopoly of wisdom. Their violence of direction in some degree disqualifies them to think truly. We owe many valuable observations to people who are not very acute or profound, and who say the thing without effort, which we want and have long been hunting in vain. The action of the soul is oftener in that which is felt and left unsaid, than in that which is said in any conversation. It broods over every society, and they unconsciously seek for it in each other. We know better than we do. We do not yet possess ourselves, and we know at the same time that we are much more. I feel the same truth how often in my trivial conversation with my neighbours, that somewhat higher in each of us overlooks this by-play, and Jove nods to Jove from behind each of us.

Men descend to meet. In their habitual and mean service to the world, for which they forsake their native nobleness, they resemble those Arabian sheiks, who dwell in mean houses, and affect an external poverty, to escape the rapacity of the Pacha, and reserve all their display of wealth for their interior and guarded retirements.

As it is present in all persons, so it is in every period of life. It is adult already in the infant man. In my dealing with my child, my Latin and Greek, my accomplishments and my money stead me nothing; but as much soul as I have avails. If I am wilful, he sets his will against mine, one for one, and leaves me, if I please, the degradation of beating him by my superiority of strength. But if I renounce my will, and act for the soul, setting that up as umpire between us two, out of his young eyes looks the same soul; he reveres and loves with me.

The soul is the perceiver and revealer of truth. We know truth when we see it, let skeptic and scoffer say what they choose. Foolish people ask you, when you have spoken what they do not wish to hear, 'How do you know it is truth, and not an error of your own?' We know truth when we see it, from opinion, as we know when we are awake that we are awake. It was a grand sentence of Emanuel Swedenborg,° which would alone indicate the greatness of that man's perception,—'It is no proof of a man's understanding to be able to confirm whatever he pleases; but to be able to discern that what is true is true, and that what is false is false, this is the mark and character of intelligence.' In the book I read, the good thought returns to me, as every truth will, the image of the whole soul. To the bad thought which I find in it, the same soul becomes a discerning, separating sword, and lops it away. We are wiser than we know. If we will not interfere with our thought, but will act entirely, or see how the thing stands in God, we know the particular thing, and every thing, and every man. For the Maker of all things and all persons stands behind us, and casts his dread omniscience through us over things.

But beyond this recognition of its own in particular passages of the individual's experience, it also reveals truth. And here we should seek to reinforce ourselves by its very presence, and to speak with a worthier, loftier strain of that advent. For the soul's communication of truth is the highest event in nature, since it then does not give somewhat from itself, but it gives itself, or passes into and becomes that man whom it enlightens; or, in proportion to that truth he receives, it takes him to itself.

We distinguish the announcements of the soul, its manifestations of its own nature, by the term *Revelation*. These are always attended by the emotion of the sublime. For this communication is an influx of the Divine mind into our mind. It is an ebb of the individual rivulet before the flowing surges of the sea of life. Every distinct apprehension of this central commandment agitates men with awe and delight. A thrill passes through all men at the reception of new truth, or at the performance of a great action, which comes out of the heart of nature. In these communications, the power to see is not separated from the will to do, but the insight proceeds from obedience, and the obedience proceeds from a joyful perception. Every moment when the individual feels himself invaded by it is memorable. By the necessity of our constitution, a certain enthusiasm attends the individual's consciousness of that divine presence. The character and duration of this enthusiasm varies with the state of the individual, from an ecstasy and trance and prophetic inspiration,—which is its rarer appearance,—to the faintest glow of virtuous emotion, in which form it warms, like our household fires, all the families and associations of men, and makes society possible. A certain tendency to insanity has always attended the opening of the religious sense in men, as if they had been 'blasted with excess of light.'° The trances of Socrates, the 'union' of Plotinus, the vision of Porphyry, the conversion of Paul, the aurora of Behmen,° the convulsions of George Fox and his Quakers, the illumination of Swedenborg, are of this kind. What was in the case of these remarkable persons a ravishment has, in innumerable instances in common life, been exhibited in less striking manner. Everywhere the history of religion betrays a tendency to enthusiasm. The rapture of the Moravian and Quietist; the opening of the internal sense of the Word, in the language of the New Jerusalem Church;° the *revival* of the Calvinistic churches; the *experiences* of the Methodists, are varying forms of that shudder of awe and delight with which the individual soul always mingles with the universal soul.

The nature of these revelations is the same; they are perceptions of the absolute law. They are solutions of the soul's own questions. They do not answer the questions which the understanding asks. The soul answers never by words, but by the thing itself that is inquired after.

Revelation is the disclosure of the soul. The popular notion of a revelation is, that it is a telling of fortunes. In past oracles of the soul, the understanding seeks to find answers to sensual questions, and undertakes to tell from God how long men shall exist, what their hands shall do, and who shall be their company, adding names, and dates, and places. But we must pick no locks. We must check this low curiosity. An answer in words is delusive; it is really no answer to the questions you ask. Do not require a description of the countries towards which you sail. The description does not describe them to you, and to-morrow you arrive there, and know them by inhabiting them. Men ask concerning the immortality of the soul, the employments of heaven, the state of the sinner, and so forth. They even dream that Jesus has left replies to precisely these interrogatories. Never a moment did that sublime spirit speak in their *patois*.° To truth, justice, love, the attributes of the soul, the idea of immutableness is essentially associated. Jesus, living in these moral sentiments, heedless of sensual fortunes, heeding only the manifestations of these, never made the separation of the idea of duration from the essence of these attributes, nor uttered a syllable concerning the duration of the soul. It was left to his disciples to sever duration from the moral elements, and to teach the immortality of the soul as a doctrine, and maintain it by evidences. The moment the doctrine of the immortality is separately taught, man is already fallen. In the flowing of love, in the adoration of humility, there is no question of continuance. No inspired man ever asks this question, or condescends to these evidences. For the soul is true to itself, and the man in whom it is shed abroad cannot wander from the present, which is infinite, to a future which would be finite.

These questions which we lust to ask about the future are a confession of sin. God has no answer for them. No answer in words can reply to a question of things. It is not in an arbitrary 'decree of God,' but in the nature of man, that a veil shuts down on the facts of to-morrow; for the soul will not have us read any other cipher than that of cause and effect. By this veil, which curtains events, it instructs the children of men to live in to-day. The only mode of obtaining an answer to these questions of the senses is to forego all low curiosity, and, accepting the tide of being which floats us into the secret of nature, work and live, work and live, and all unawares the advancing soul has built and forged for itself a new condition, and the question and the answer are one.

By the same fire, vital, consecrating, celestial, which burns until it shall dissolve all things into the waves and surges of an ocean of light, we see and know each other, and what spirit each is of. Who can tell the grounds of his knowledge of the character of the several individuals in his circle of friends? No man. Yet their acts and words do not disappoint him. In that man, though he knew no ill of him, he put no trust. In that other, though they had seldom met, authentic signs had yet passed, to signify that he might be trusted as one who had an interest in his own character. We know each other very well,—which of us has been just to himself, and whether that which we teach or behold is only an aspiration, or is our honest effort also.

We are all discerners of spirits. That diagnosis lies aloft in our life or unconscious power. The intercourse of society,—its trade, its religion, its friendships, its quarrels,—is one wide, judicial investigation of character. In full court, or in small committee, or confronted face to face, accuser and accused, men offer themselves to be judged. Against their will they exhibit those decisive trifles by which character is read. But who judges? and what? Not our understanding. We do not read them by learning or craft. No; the wisdom of the wise man consists herein, that he does not judge them; he lets them judge themselves, and merely reads and records their own verdict.

By virtue of this inevitable nature, private will is overpowered, and, maugre our efforts or our imperfections, your genius will speak from you, and mine from me. That which we are, we shall teach, not voluntarily, but involuntarily. Thoughts come into our minds by avenues which we never left open, and thoughts go out of our minds through avenues which we never voluntarily opened. Character teaches over our head. The infallible index of true progress is found in the tone the man takes. Neither his age, nor his breeding, nor company, nor books, nor actions, nor talents, nor all together, can hinder him from being deferential to a higher spirit than his own. If he have not found his home in God, his manners, his forms of speech, the turn of his sentences, the build, shall I say, of all his opinions, will involuntarily confess it, let him brave it out how he will. If he have found his centre, the Deity will shine through him, through all the disguises of ignorance, of ungenial temperament, of unfavorable circumstance. The tone of seeking is one, and the tone of having is another.

The great distinction between teachers sacred or literary,—between poets like Herbert, and poets like Pope,—between philosophers like Spinoza, Kant, and Coleridge, and philosophers like Locke, Paley, Mackintosh, and Stewart,°—between men of the world, who are reckoned accomplished talkers, and here and there a fervent mystic, prophesying, half insane under the infinitude of his thought,—is, that one class speak *from within*, or from experience, as parties and possessors of the fact; and the other class, *from without*, as spectators merely, or perhaps as acquainted with the fact on the evidence of third persons. It is of no use to preach to me from without. I can do that too easily myself. Jesus speaks always from within, and in a degree that transcends all others. In that is the miracle. I believe beforehand that it ought so to be. All men stand continually in the expectation of the appearance of such a teacher. But if a man do not speak from within the veil, where the word is one with that it tells of, let him lowly confess it.

The same Omniscience flows into the intellect, and makes what we call genius. Much of the wisdom of the world is not wisdom, and the most illuminated class of men are no doubt superior to literary fame, and are not writers. Among the multitude of scholars and authors, we feel no hallowing presence; we are sensible of a knack and skill rather than of inspiration; they have a light, and know not whence it comes, and call it their own; their talent is some exaggerated faculty, some overgrown member, so that their strength is a disease. In these instances the intellectual gifts do not make the impression of virtue, but almost of vice; and we feel that a man's talents stand in the way of his advancement in truth. But genius is religious. It is a larger imbibing of the common heart. It is not anomalous, but more like, and not less like other men. There is, in all great poets, a wisdom of humanity which is superior to any talents they exercise. The author, the wit, the partisan, the fine gentleman, does not take place of the man. Humanity shines in Homer, in Chaucer, in Spenser, in Shakspeare, in Milton. They are content with truth. They use the positive degree. They seem frigid and phlegmatic to those who have been spiced with the frantic passion and violent coloring of inferior, but popular writers. For they are poets by the free course which they allow to the informing soul, which through their eyes beholds again, and blesses the things which it hath made. The soul is superior to its knowledge; wiser than any of its works. The great poet makes us feel our own wealth, and then we think less of his compositions. His best communication to our mind is to teach us to despise all he has done. Shakspeare carries us to such a lofty strain of intelligent activity, as to suggest a wealth which beggars his own; and we then feel that the splendid works which he has created, and which in other hours we extol as a sort of self-existent poetry, take no stronger hold of real nature than the shadow of a passing traveller on the rock. The inspiration which uttered itself in Hamlet and Lear could utter things as good from day to day, for ever. Why, then, should I make account of Hamlet and Lear, as if we had not the soul from which they fell as syllables from the tongue?

This energy does not descend into individual life on any other condition than entire possession. It comes to the lowly and simple; it comes to whomsoever will put off what is foreign and proud; it comes as insight; it comes as serenity and grandeur. When we see those whom it inhabits, we are apprized of new degrees of greatness. From that inspiration the man comes back with a changed tone. He does not talk with men with an eye to their opinion. He tries them. It requires of us to be plain and true. The vain traveller attempts to embellish his life by quoting my lord, and the prince, and the countess, who thus said or did to *him*. The ambitious vulgar show you their spoons, and brooches, and rings, and preserve their cards and compliments. The more cultivated, in their account of their own experience, cull out the pleasing, poetic circumstance,—the visit to Rome, the man of genius they saw, the brilliant friend they know; still further on, perhaps, the gorgeous landscape, the mountain lights, the mountain thoughts, they enjoyed yesterday,—and so seek to throw a romantic color over their life. But the soul that ascends to worship the great God is plain and true; has no rose-color, no fine friends, no chivalry, no adventures; does not want admiration; dwells in the hour that now is, in the earnest experience of the common day,—by reason of the present moment and the mere trifle having become porous to thought, and bibulous of the sea of light.

Converse with a mind that is grandly simple, and literature looks like word-catching. The simplest utterances are worthiest to be written, yet are they so cheap, and so things of course, that, in the infinite riches of the soul, it is like gathering a few pebbles off the ground, or bottling a little air in a phial, when the whole earth and the whole atmosphere are ours. Nothing can pass there, or make you one of the circle, but the casting aside your trappings, and dealing man to man in naked truth, plain confession, and omniscient affirmation.

Souls such as these treat you as gods would; walk as gods in the earth, accepting without any admiration your wit, your bounty, your virtue even,—say rather your act of duty, for your virtue they own as their proper blood, royal as themselves, and over-royal, and the father of the gods. But what rebuke their plain fraternal bearing casts on the mutual flattery with which authors solace each other and wound themselves! These flatter not. I do not wonder that these men go to see Cromwell, and Christina, and Charles the Second, and James the First, and the Grand Turk. For they are, in their own elevation, the fellows of kings, and must feel the servile tone of conversation in the world. They must always be a godsend to princes, for they confront them, a king to a king, without ducking or concession, and give a high nature the refreshment and satisfaction of resistance, of plain humanity, of even companionship, and of new ideas. They leave them wiser and superior men. Souls like these make us feel that sincerity is more excellent than flattery. Deal so plainly with man and woman, as to constrain the utmost sincerity, and destroy all hope of trifling with you. It is the highest compliment you can pay. Their 'highest praising,' said Milton, 'is not flattery, and their plainest advice is a kind of praising.'°

Ineffable is the union of man and God in every act of the soul. The simplest person, who in his integrity worships God, becomes God; yet for ever and ever the influx of this better and universal self is new and unsearchable. It inspires awe and astonishment. How dear, how soothing to man, arises the idea of God, peopling the lonely place, effacing the scars of our mistakes and disappointments! When we have broken our god of tradition, and ceased from our god of rhetoric, then may God fire the heart with his presence. It is the doubling of the heart itself, nay, the infinite enlargement of the heart with a power of growth to a new infinity on every side. It inspires in man an infallible trust. He has not the conviction, but the sight, that the best is the true, and may in that thought easily dismiss all particular uncertainties and fears, and adjourn to the sure revelation of time, the solution of his private riddles. He is sure that his welfare is dear to the heart of being. In the presence of law to his mind, he is overflowed with a reliance so universal, that it sweeps away all cherished hopes and the most stable projects of mortal condition in its flood. He believes that he cannot escape from his good. The things that are really for thee gravitate to thee. You are running to seek your friend. Let your feet run, but your mind need not. If you do not find him, will you not acquiesce that it is best you should not find him? for there is a power, which, as it is in you, is in him also, and could therefore very well bring you together, if it were for the best. You are preparing with eagerness to go and render a service to which your talent and your taste invite you, the love of men and the hope of fame. Has it not occurred to you, that you have no right to go, unless you are equally willing to be prevented from going? O, believe, as thou livest, that every sound that is spoken over the round world, which thou oughtest to hear, will vibrate on thine ear! Every proverb, every book, every byword that belongs to thee for aid or comfort, shall surely come home through open or winding passages. Every friend whom not thy fantastic will, but the great and tender heart in thee craveth, shall lock thee in his embrace. And this, because the heart in thee is the heart of all; not a valve, not a wall, not an intersection is there anywhere in nature, but one blood rolls uninterruptedly an endless circulation through all men, as the water of the globe is all one sea, and, truly seen, its tide is one.

Let man, then, learn the revelation of all nature and all thought to his heart; this, namely; that the Highest dwells with him; that the sources of nature are in his own mind, if the sentiment of duty is there. But if he would know what the great God speaketh, he must 'go into his closet and shut the door,'° as Jesus said. God will not make himself manifest to cowards. He must greatly listen to himself, withdrawing himself from all the accents of other men's devotion. Even their prayers are hurtful to him, until he have made his own. Our religion vulgarly stands on numbers of believers. Whenever the appeal is made—no matter how indirectly—to numbers, proclamation is then and there made, that religion is not. He that finds God a sweet, enveloping thought to him never counts his company. When I sit in that presence, who shall dare to come in? When I rest in perfect humility, when I burn with pure love, what can Calvin or Swedenborg say?

It makes no difference whether the appeal is to numbers or to one. The faith that stands on authority is not faith. The reliance on authority measures the decline of religion, the withdrawal of the soul. The position men have given to Jesus, now for many centuries of history, is a position of authority. It characterizes themselves. It cannot alter the eternal facts. Great is the soul, and plain. It is no flatterer, it is no follower; it never appeals from itself. It believes in itself. Before the immense possibilities of man, all mere experience, all past biography, however spotless and sainted, shrinks away. Before that heaven which our presentiments foreshow us, we cannot easily praise any form of life we have seen or read of. We not only affirm that we have few great men, but, absolutely speaking, that we have none; that we have no history, no record of any character or mode of living, that entirely contents us. The saints and demigods whom history worships we are constrained to accept with a grain of allowance. Though in our lonely hours we draw a new strength out of their memory, yet, pressed on our attention, as they are by the thoughtless and customary, they fatigue and invade. The soul gives itself, alone, original, and pure, to the Lonely, Original, and Pure, who, on that condition, gladly inhabits, leads, and speaks through it. Then is it glad, young, and nimble. It is not wise, but it sees through all things. It is not called religious, but it is innocent. It calls the light its own, and feels that the grass grows and the stone falls by a law inferior to, and dependent on, its nature. Behold, it saith, I am born into the great, the universal mind. I, the imperfect, adore my own Perfect. I am somehow receptive of the great soul, and thereby I do overlook the sun and the stars, and feel them to be the fair accidents and effects which change and pass. More and more the surges of everlasting nature enter into me, and I become public and human in my regards and actions. So come I to live in thoughts, and act with energies, which are immortal. Thus revering the soul, and learning, as the ancient° said, that 'its beauty is immense,' man will come to see that the world is the perennial miracle which the soul worketh, and be less astonished at particular wonders; he will learn that there is no profane history; that all history is sacred; that the universe is represented in an atom, in a moment of time. He will weave no longer a spotted life of shreds and patches, but he will live with a divine unity. He will cease from what is base and frivolous in his life, and be content with all places and with any service he can render. He will calmly front the morrow in the negligency of that trust which carries God with it, and so hath already the whole future in the bottom of the heart.

CIRCLES

Nature centres into balls,
And her proud ephemerals,
Fast to surface and outside,
Scan the profile of the sphere;
Knew they what that signified,
A new genesis were here.

THE eye is the first circle; the horizon which it forms is the second; and throughout nature this primary figure is repeated without end. It is the highest emblem in the cipher of the world. St. Augustine described° the nature of God as a circle whose centre was everywhere, and its circumference nowhere. We are all our lifetime reading the copious sense of this first of forms. One moral we have already deduced,° in considering the circular or compensatory character of every human action. Another analogy we shall now trace; that every action admits of being outdone. Our life is an apprenticeship to the truth, that around every circle another can be drawn; that there is no end in nature, but every end is a beginning; that there is always another dawn risen on midnoon,° and under every deep a lower deep opens.

This fact, as far as it symbolizes the moral fact of the Unattainable, the flying Perfect, around which the hands of man can never meet, at once the inspirer and the condemner of every success, may conveniently serve us to connect many illustrations of human power in every department.

There are no fixtures in nature. The universe is fluid and volatile. Permanence is but a word of degrees. Our globe seen by God is a transparent law, not a mass of facts. The law dissolves the fact and holds it fluid. Our culture is the predominance of an idea which draws after it this train of cities and institutions. Let us rise into another idea: they will disappear. The Greek sculpture is all melted away, as if it had been statues of ice; here and there a solitary figure or fragment remaining, as we see flecks and scraps of snow left in cold dells and mountain clefts, in June and July. For the genius that created it creates now somewhat else. The Greek letters last a little longer, but are already passing under the same sentence, and tumbling into the inevitable pit which the creation of new thought opens for all that is old. The new continents are built out of the ruins of an old planet; the new races fed out of the decomposition of the foregoing. New arts destroy the old. See the investment of capital in aqueducts made useless by hydraulics; fortifications, by gunpowder; roads and canals, by railways; sails, by steam; steam, by electricity.

You admire this tower of granite, weathering the hurts of so many ages. Yet a little waving hand built this huge wall, and that which builds is better than that which is built. The hand that built can topple it down much faster. Better than the hand, and nimbler, was the invisible thought which wrought through it; and thus ever, behind the coarse effect, is a fine cause, which, being narrowly seen, is itself the effect of a finer cause. Every thing looks permanent until its secret is known. A rich estate appears to women a firm and lasting fact; to a merchant, one easily created out of any materials, and easily lost. An orchard, good tillage, good grounds, seem a fixture, like a gold mine, or a river, to a citizen; but to a large farmer, not much more fixed than the state of the crop. Nature looks provokingly stable and secular, but it has a cause like all the rest; and when once I comprehend that, will these fields stretch so immovably wide, these leaves hang so individually considerable? Permanence is a word of degrees. Every thing is medial. Moons are no more bounds to spiritual power than bat-balls.

The key to every man is his thought. Sturdy and defying though he look, he has a helm which he obeys, which is the idea after which all his facts are classified. He can only be reformed by showing him a new idea which commands his own. The life of man is a self-evolving circle, which, from a ring imperceptibly small, rushes on all sides outwards to new and larger circles, and that without end. The extent to which this generation of circles, wheel without wheel, will go, depends on the force or truth of the individual soul. For it is the inert effort of each thought, having formed itself into a circular wave of circumstance,—as, for instance, an empire, rules of an art, a local usage, a religious rite,—to heap itself on that ridge, and to solidify and hem in the life. But if the soul is quick and strong, it bursts over that boundary on all sides, and expands another orbit on the great deep, which also runs up into a high wave, with attempt again to stop and to bind. But the heart refuses to be imprisoned; in its first and narrowest pulses, it already tends outward with a vast force, and to immense and innumerable expansions.

Every ultimate fact is only the first of a new series. Every general law only a particular fact of some more general law presently to disclose itself. There is no outside, no inclosing wall, no circumference to us. The man finishes his story,—how good! how final! how it puts a new face on all things! He fills the sky. Lo! on the other side rises also a man, and draws a circle around the circle we had just pronounced the outline of the sphere. Then already is our first speaker not man, but only a first speaker. His only redress is forthwith to draw a circle outside of his antagonist. And so men do by themselves. The result of to-day, which haunts the mind and cannot be escaped, will presently be abridged into a word, and the principle that seemed to explain nature will itself be included as one example of a bolder generalization. In the thought of to-morrow there is a power to upheave all thy creed, all the creeds, all the literatures, of the nations, and marshal thee to a heaven which no epic dream has yet depicted. Every man is not so much a workman in the world, as he is a suggestion of that he should be. Men walk as prophecies of the next age.

Step by step we scale this mysterious ladder: the steps are actions; the new prospect is power. Every several result is threatened and judged by that which follows. Every one seems to be contradicted by the new; it is only limited by the new. The new statement is always hated by the old, and, to those dwelling in the old, comes like an abyss of skepticism. But the eye soon gets wonted to it, for the eye and it are effects of one cause; then its innocency and benefit appear, and presently, all its energy spent, it pales and dwindles before the revelation of the new hour.

Fear not the new generalization. Does the fact look crass and material, threatening to degrade thy theory of spirit? Resist it not; it goes to refine and raise thy theory of matter just as much.

There are no fixtures to men, if we appeal to consciousness. Every man supposes himself not to be fully understood; and if there is any truth in him, if he rests at last on the divine soul, I see not how it can be otherwise. The last chamber, the last closet, he must feel, was never opened; there is always a residuum unknown, unanalyzable. That is, every man believes that he has a greater possibility.

Our moods do not believe in each other. To-day I am full of thoughts, and can write what I please. I see no reason why I should not have the same thought, the same power of expression, to-morrow. What I write, whilst I write it, seems the most natural thing in the world; but yesterday I saw a dreary vacuity in this direction in which now I see so much; and a month hence, I doubt not, I shall wonder who he was that wrote so many continuous pages. Alas for this infirm faith, this will not strenuous, this vast ebb of a vast flow! I am God in nature; I am a weed by the wall.

The continual effort to raise himself above himself, to work a pitch above his last height, betrays itself in a man's relations. We thirst for approbation, yet cannot forgive the approver. The sweet of nature is love; yet, if I have a friend, I am tormented by my imperfections. The love of me accuses the other party. If he were high enough to slight me, then could I love him, and rise by my affection to new heights. A man's growth is seen in the successive choirs of his friends. For every friend whom he loses for truth, he gains a better. I thought, as I walked in the woods and mused on my friends, why should I play with them this game of idolatry? I know and see too well, when not voluntarily blind, the speedy limits of persons called high and worthy. Rich, noble, and great they are by the liberality of our speech, but truth is sad. O blessed Spirit, whom I forsake for these, they are not thou! Every personal consideration that we allow costs us heavenly state. We sell the thrones of angels for a short and turbulent pleasure.

How often must we learn this lesson? Men cease to interest us when we find their limitations. The only sin is limitation. As soon as you once come up with a man's limitations, it is all over with him. Has he talents? has he enterprise? has he knowledge? it boots not. Infinitely alluring and attractive was he to you yesterday, a great hope, a sea to swim in; now, you have found his shores, found it a pond, and you care not if you never see it again.

Each new step we take in thought reconciles twenty seemingly discordant facts, as expressions of one law. Aristotle and Plato are reckoned the respective heads of two schools. A wise man will see that Aristotle Platonizes. By going one step farther back in thought, discordant opinions are reconciled, by being seen to be two extremes of one principle, and we can never go so far back as to preclude a still higher vision.

Beware when the great God lets loose a thinker on this planet. Then all things are at risk. It is as when a conflagration has broken out in a great city, and no man knows what is safe, or where it will end. There is not a piece of science, but its flank may be turned to-morrow; there is not any literary reputation, not the so-called eternal names of fame, that may not be revised and condemned. The very hopes of man, the thoughts of his heart, the religion of nations, the manners and morals of mankind, are all at the mercy of a new generalization. Generalization is always a new influx of the divinity into the mind. Hence the thrill that attends it.

Valor consists in the power of self-recovery, so that a man cannot have his flank turned, cannot be out-generalled, but put him where you will, he stands. This can only be by his preferring truth to his past apprehension of truth; and his alert acceptance of it, from whatever quarter; the intrepid conviction that his laws, his relations to society, his Christianity, his world, may at any time be superseded and decease.

There are degrees in idealism. We learn first to play with it academically, as the magnet was once a toy. Then we see in the heyday of youth and poetry that it may be true, that it is true in gleams and fragments. Then, its countenance waxes stern and grand, and we see that it must be true. It now shows itself ethical and practical. We learn that God IS; that he is in me; and that all things are shadows of him. The idealism of Berkeley is only a crude statement of the idealism of Jesus, and that again is a crude statement of the fact, that all nature is the rapid efflux of goodness executing and organizing itself. Much more obviously is history and the state of the world at any one time directly dependent on the intellectual classification then existing in the minds of men. The things which are dear to men at this hour are so on account of the ideas which have emerged on their mental horizon, and which cause the present order of things as a tree bears its apples. A new degree of culture would instantly revolutionize the entire system of human pursuits.

Conversation is a game of circles. In conversation we pluck up the *termini* which bound the common of silence on every side. The parties are not to be judged by the spirit they partake and even express under this Pentecost.° To-morrow they will have receded from this high-water mark. To-morrow you shall find them stooping under the old pack-saddles. Yet let us enjoy the cloven flame whilst it glows on our walls. When each new speaker strikes a new light, emancipates us from the oppression of the last speaker, to oppress us with the greatness and exclusiveness of his own thought, then yields us to another redeemer, we seem to recover our rights, to become men. O, what truths profound and executable only in ages and orbs are supposed in the announcement of every truth! In common hours, society sits cold and statuesque. We all stand waiting, empty,—knowing, possibly, that we can be full, surrounded by mighty symbols which are not symbols to us, but prose and trivial toys. Then cometh the god, and converts the statues into fiery men, and by a flash of his eye burns up the veil which shrouded all things, and the meaning of the very furniture, of cup and saucer, of chair and clock and tester, is manifest. The facts which loomed so large in the fogs of yesterday,—property, climate, breeding, personal beauty, and the like, have strangely changed their proportions. All that we reckoned settled shakes and rattles; and literatures, cities, climates, religions, leave their foundations, and dance before our eyes. And yet here again see the swift circumspection! Good as is discourse, silence is better, and shames it. The length of the discourse indicates the distance of thought betwixt the speaker and the hearer. If they were at a perfect understanding in any part, no words would be necessary thereon. If at one in all parts, no words would be suffered.

Literature is a point outside of our hodiernal circle, through which a new one may be described. The use of literature is to afford us a platform whence we may command a view of our present life, a purchase by which we may move it. We fill ourselves with ancient learning, install ourselves the best we can in Greek, in Punic, in Roman houses, only that we may wiselier see French, English, and American houses and modes of living. In like manner, we see literature best from the midst of wild nature, or from the din of affairs, or from a high religion. The field cannot be well seen from within the field. The astronomer must have his diameter of the earth's orbit as a base to find the parallax of any star.

Therefore we value the poet. All the argument and all the wisdom is not in the encyclopædia, or the treatise on metaphysics, or the Body of Divinity, but in the sonnet or the play. In my daily work I incline to repeat my old steps, and do not believe in remedial force, in the power of change and reform. But some Petrarch or Ariosto, filled with the new wine of his imagination, writes me an ode or a brisk romance, full of daring thought and action. He smites and arouses me with his shrill tones, breaks up my whole chain of habits, and I open my eye on my own possibilities. He claps wings to the sides of all the solid old lumber of the world, and I am capable once more of choosing a straight path in theory and practice.

We have the same need to command a view of the religion of the world. We can never see Christianity from the catechism:—from the pastures, from a boat in the pond, from amidst the songs of wood-birds, we possibly may. Cleansed by the elemental light and wind, steeped in the sea of beautiful forms which the field offers us, we may chance to cast a right glance back upon biography. Christianity is rightly dear to the best of mankind, yet was there never a young philosopher whose breeding had fallen into the Christian church, by whom that brave text of Paul's was not specially prized:—'Then shall also the Son be subject unto Him who put all things under him, that God may be all in all.'° Let the claims and virtues of persons be never so great and welcome, the instinct of man presses eagerly onward to the impersonal and illimitable, and gladly arms itself against the dogmatism of bigots with this generous word out of the book itself.

The natural world may be conceived of as a system of concentric circles, and we now and then detect in nature slight dislocations, which apprize us that this surface on which we now stand is not fixed, but

sliding. These manifold tenacious qualities, this chemistry and vegetation, these metals and animals, which seem to stand there for their
own sake, are means and methods only,—are words of God, and as
fugitive as other words. Has the naturalist or chemist learned his craft,
who has explored the gravity of atoms and the elective affinities, who
has not yet discerned the deeper law whereof this is only a partial or
approximate statement, namely, that like draws to like; and that the
goods which belong to you gravitate to you, and need not be pursued
with pains and cost? Yet is that statement approximate also, and not
final. Omnipresence is a higher fact. Not through subtle, subterranean
channels need friend and fact be drawn to their counterpart, but,
rightly considered, these things proceed from the eternal generation of
the soul. Cause and effect are two sides of one fact.

The same law of eternal procession ranges all that we call the virtues, and extinguishes each in the light of a better. The great man will
not be prudent in the popular sense; all his prudence will be so much
deduction from his grandeur. But it behooves each to see, when he
sacrifices prudence, to what god he devotes it; if to ease and pleasure,
he had better be prudent still; if to a great trust, he can well spare his
mule and panniers who has a winged chariot instead. Geoffrey draws
on his boots to go through the woods, that his feet may be safer from
the bite of snakes; Aaron never thinks of such a peril. In many years
neither is harmed by such an accident. Yet it seems to me, that, with
every precaution you take against such an evil, you put yourself into
the power of the evil. I suppose that the highest prudence is the lowest
prudence. Is this too sudden a rushing from the centre to the verge of
our orbit? Think how many times we shall fall back into pitiful calcula-
tions before we take up our rest in the great sentiment, or make the
verge of to-day the new centre. Besides, your bravest sentiment is
familiar to the humblest men. The poor and the low have their way of
expressing the last facts of philosophy as well as you. 'Blessed be
nothing,' and 'the worse things are, the better they are,' are proverbs
which express the transcendentalism of common life.

One man's justice is another's injustice; one man's beauty, another's
ugliness; one man's wisdom, another's folly; as one beholds the same
objects from a higher point. One man thinks justice consists in paying
debts, and has no measure in his abhorrence of another who is very
remiss in this duty, and makes the creditor wait tediously. But that
second man has his own way of looking at things; asks himself which
debt must I pay first, the debt to the rich, or the debt to the poor? the
debt of money, or the debt of thought to mankind, of genius to nature?

For you, O broker! there is no other principle but arithmetic. For me, commerce is of trivial import; love, faith, truth of character, the aspiration of man, these are sacred; nor can I detach one duty, like you, from all other duties, and concentrate my forces mechanically on the payment of moneys. Let me live onward; you shall find that, though slower, the progress of my character will liquidate all these debts without injustice to higher claims. If a man should dedicate himself to the payment of notes, would not this be injustice? Does he owe no debt but money? And are all claims on him to be postponed to a landlord's or a banker's?

There is no virtue which is final; all are initial. The virtues of society are vices of the saint. The terror of reform is the discovery that we must cast away our virtues, or what we have always esteemed such, into the same pit that has consumed our grosser vices.

> 'Forgive his crimes, forgive his virtues too,
> Those smaller faults, half converts to the right'.°

It is the highest power of divine moments that they abolish our contritions also. I accuse myself of sloth and unprofitableness day by day; but when these waves of God flow into me, I no longer reckon lost time. I no longer poorly compute my possible achievement by what remains to me of the month or the year; for these moments confer a sort of omnipresence and omnipotence which asks nothing of duration, but sees that the energy of the mind is commensurate with the work to be done, without time.

And thus, O circular philosopher, I hear some reader exclaim, you have arrived at a fine Pyrrhonism, at an equivalence and indifferency of all actions, and would fain teach us that, *if we are true*, forsooth, our crimes may be lively stones out of which we shall construct the temple of the true God!°

I am not careful to justify myself. I own I am gladdened by seeing the predominance of the saccharine principle throughout vegetable nature, and not less by beholding in morals that unrestrained inundation of the principle of good into every chink and hole that selfishness has left open, yea, into selfishness and sin itself; so that no evil is pure, nor hell itself without its extreme satisfactions. But lest I should mislead any when I have my own head and obey my whims, let me remind the reader that I am only an experimenter. Do not set the least value on what I do, or the least discredit on what I do not, as if I pretended to settle any thing as true or false. I unsettle all things. No facts are to me sacred; none are profane; I simply experiment, an endless seeker, with no Past at my back.

Yet this incessant movement and progression which all things partake could never become sensible to us but by contrast to some principle of fixture or stability in the soul. Whilst the eternal generation of circles proceeds, the eternal generator abides. That central life is somewhat superior to creation, superior to knowledge and thought, and contains all its circles. For ever it labors to create a life and thought as large and excellent as itself; but in vain; for that which is made instructs how to make a better.

Thus there is no sleep, no pause, no preservation, but all things renew, germinate, and spring. Why should we import rags and relics into the new hour? Nature abhors the old, and old age seems the only disease; all others run into this one. We call it by many names,—fever, intemperance, insanity, stupidity, and crime; they are all forms of old age; they are rest, conservatism, appropriation, inertia, not newness, not the way onward. We grizzle every day. I see no need of it. Whilst we converse with what is above us, we do not grow old, but grow young. Infancy, youth, receptive, aspiring, with religious eye looking upward, counts itself nothing, and abandons itself to the instruction flowing from all sides. But the man and woman of seventy assume to know all, they have outlived their hope, they renounce aspiration, accept the actual for the necessary, and talk down to the young. Let them, then, become organs of the Holy Ghost; let them be lovers; let them behold truth; and their eyes are uplifted, their wrinkles smoothed, they are perfumed again with hope and power. This old age ought not to creep on a human mind. In nature every moment is new; the past is always swallowed and forgotten; the coming only is sacred. Nothing is secure but life, transition, the energizing spirit. No love can be bound by oath or covenant to secure it against a higher love. No truth so sublime but it may be trivial to-morrow in the light of new thoughts. People wish to be settled; only as far as they are unsettled is there any hope for them.

Life is a series of surprises. We do not guess to-day the mood, the pleasure, the power of to-morrow, when we are building up our being. Of lower states,—of acts of routine and sense,—we can tell somewhat; but the masterpieces of God, the total growths and universal movements of the soul, he hideth; they are incalculable. I can know that truth is divine and helpful; but how it shall help me I can have no guess, for *so to be* is the sole inlet of *so to know*. The new position of the advancing man has all the powers of the old, yet has them all new. It carries in its bosom all the energies of the past, yet is itself an exhalation of the morning. I cast away in this new moment all my once hoarded knowledge, as vacant and vain. Now, for the first time, seem I to know any thing rightly. The simplest words,—we do not know what they mean, except when we love and aspire.

The difference between talents and character is adroitness to keep the old and trodden round, and power and courage to make a new road to new and better goals. Character makes an overpowering present; a cheerful, determined hour, which fortifies all the company, by making them see that much is possible and excellent that was not thought of. Character dulls the impression of particular events. When we see the conqueror, we do not think much of any one battle or success. We see that we had exaggerated the difficulty. It was easy to him. The great man is not convulsible or tormentable; events pass over him without much impression. People say sometimes, 'See what I have overcome; see how cheerful I am; see how completely I have triumphed over these black events.' Not if they still remind me of the black event. True conquest is the causing the calamity to fade and disappear, as an early cloud of insignificant result in a history so large and advancing.

The one thing which we seek with insatiable desire is to forget ourselves, to be surprised out of our propriety, to lose our sempiternal memory, and to do something without knowing how or why; in short, to draw a new circle. Nothing great was ever achieved without enthusiasm.° The way of life is wonderful: it is by abandonment. The great moments of history are the facilities of performance through the strength of ideas, as the works of genius and religion. 'A man,' said Oliver Cromwell, 'never rises so high as when he knows not whither he is going.' Dreams and drunkenness, the use of opium and alcohol are the semblance and counterfeit of this oracular genius, and hence their dangerous attraction for men. For the like reason, they ask the aid of wild passions, as in gaming and war, to ape in some manner these flames and generosities of the heart.

INTELLECT

Go, speed the stars of Thought
On to their shining goals;—
The sower scatters broad his seed,
The wheat thou strew'st be souls.

EVERY substance is negatively electric to that which stands above it in the chemical tables, positively to that which stands below it. Water dissolves wood, and iron, and salt; air dissolves water; electric fire dissolves air, but the intellect dissolves fire, gravity, laws, method, and the subtlest unnamed relations of nature, in its resistless menstruum. Intellect lies behind genius, which is intellect constructive. Intellect is the simple power anterior to all action or construction. Gladly would I unfold in calm degrees a natural history of the intellect, but what man has yet been able to mark the steps and boundaries of that transparent essence? The first questions are always to be asked, and the wisest doctor is gravelled by the inquisitiveness of a child. How can we speak of the action of the mind under any divisions, as of its knowledge, of its ethics, of its works, and so forth, since it melts will into perception, knowledge into act? Each becomes the other. Itself alone is. Its vision is not like the vision of the eye, but is union with the things known.

Intellect and intellection signify to the common ear consideration of abstract truth. The considerations of time and place, of you and me, of profit and hurt, tyrannize over most men's minds. Intellect separates the fact considered from *you*, from all local and personal reference, and discerns it as if it existed for its own sake. Heraclitus looked upon the affections as dense and colored mists.° In the fog of good and evil affections, it is hard for man to walk forward in a straight line. Intellect is void of affection, and sees an object as it stands in the light of science, cool and disengaged. The intellect goes out of the individual, floats over its own personality, and regards it as a fact, and not as *I* and *mine*. He who is immersed in what concerns person or place cannot see the problem of existence. This the intellect always ponders. Nature shows all things formed and bound. The intellect pierces the form, overleaps the wall, detects intrinsic likeness between remote things, and reduces all things into a few principles.

The making a fact the subject of thought raises it. All that mass of mental and moral phenomena, which we do not make objects of voluntary thought, come within the power of fortune; they constitute the circumstance of daily life; they are subject to change, to fear, and hope. Every man beholds his human condition with a degree of melancholy. As a ship aground is battered by the waves, so man, imprisoned in mortal life, lies open to the mercy of coming events. But a truth, separated by the intellect, is no longer a subject of destiny. We behold it as a god upraised above care and fear. And so any fact in our life, or any record of our fancies or reflections, disentangled from the web of our unconsciousness, becomes an object impersonal and immortal. It is the past restored, but embalmed. A better art than that of Egypt has taken fear and corruption out of it. It is eviscerated of care. It is offered for science. What is addressed to us for contemplation does not threaten us, but makes us intellectual beings.

The growth of the intellect is spontaneous in every expansion. The mind that grows could not predict the times, the means, the mode of that spontaneity. God enters by a private door into every individual. Long prior to the age of reflection is the thinking of the mind. Out of darkness, it came insensibly into the marvellous light of to-day. In the period of infancy it accepted and disposed of all impressions from the surrounding creation after its own way. Whatever any mind doth or saith is after a law; and this native law remains over it after it has come to reflection or conscious thought. In the most worn, pedantic, introverted self-tormenter's life, the greatest part is incalculable by him, unforeseen, unimaginable, and must be, until he can take himself up by his own ears. What am I? What has my will done to make me that I am? Nothing. I have been floated into this thought, this hour, this connection of events, by secret currents of might and mind, and my ingenuity and wilfulness have not thwarted, have not aided to an appreciable degree.

Our spontaneous action is always the best. You cannot, with your best deliberation and heed, come so close to any question as your spontaneous glance shall bring you, whilst you rise from your bed, or walk abroad in the morning after meditating the matter before sleep on the previous night. Our thinking is a pious reception. Our truth of thought is therefore vitiated as much by too violent direction given by our will, as by too great negligence. We do not determine what we will think. We only open our senses, clear away, as we can, all obstruction from the fact, and suffer the intellect to see. We have little control over our thoughts. We are the prisoners of ideas. They catch us up for moments into their heaven, and so fully engage us, that we take no thought for the morrow,° gaze like children, without an effort to make them our own. By and by we fall out of that rapture, bethink us where we have been, what we have seen, and repeat, as truly as we can, what we have beheld. As far as we can recall these ecstasies, we carry away in the ineffaceable memory the result, and all men and all the ages confirm it. It is called Truth. But the moment we cease to report, and attempt to correct and contrive, it is not truth.

If we consider what persons have stimulated and profited us, we shall perceive the superiority of the spontaneous or intuitive principle over the arithmetical or logical. The first contains the second, but virtual and latent. We want, in every man, a long logic; we cannot pardon the absence of it, but it must not be spoken. Logic is the procession or pro-portionate unfolding of the intuition; but its virtue is as silent method; the moment it would appear as propositions, and have a separate value, it is worthless.

In every man's mind, some images, words, and facts remain, without effort on his part to imprint them, which others forget, and afterwards these illustrate to him important laws. All our progress is an unfolding, like the vegetable bud. You have first an instinct, then an opinion, then a knowledge, as the plant has root, bud, and fruit. Trust the instinct to the end, though you can render no reason. It is vain to hurry it. By trusting it to the end, it shall ripen into truth, and you shall know why you believe.

Each mind has its own method. A true man never acquires after col-lege rules. What you have aggregated in a natural manner surprises and delights when it is produced. For we cannot oversee each other's secret. And hence the differences between men in natural endowment are insignificant in comparison with their common wealth. Do you think the porter and the cook have no anecdotes, no experiences, no wonders for you? Every body knows as much as the savant. The walls of rude minds are scrawled all over with facts, with thoughts. They shall one day bring a lantern and read the inscriptions. Every man, in the degree in which he has wit and culture, finds his curiosity inflamed concerning the modes of living and thinking of other men, and especially of those classes whose minds have not been subdued by the drill of school education.

This instinctive action never ceases in a healthy mind, but becomes richer and more frequent in its informations through all states of cul-ture. At last comes the era of reflection, when we not only observe, but take pains to observe; when we of set purpose sit down to consider an abstract truth; when we keep the mind's eye open, whilst we converse, whilst we read, whilst we act, intent to learn the secret law of some class of facts.

What is the hardest task in the world? To think. I would put myself in the attitude to look in the eye an abstract truth, and I cannot. I blench and withdraw on this side and on that. I seem to know what he meant who said, No man can see God face to face and live.° For example, a man explores the basis of civil government. Let him intend his mind without respite, without rest, in one direction. His best heed long time avails him nothing. Yet thoughts are flitting before him. We all but apprehend, we dimly forebode the truth. We say, I will walk abroad, and the truth will take form and clearness to me. We go forth, but cannot find it. It seems as if we needed only the stillness and composed attitude of the library to seize the thought. But we come in, and are as far from it as at first. Then, in a moment, and unannounced, the truth appears. A certain, wandering light appears, and is the distinction, the principle, we wanted. But the oracle comes, because we had previously laid siege to the shrine. It seems as if the law of the intellect resembled that law of nature by which we now inspire, now expire the breath; by which the heart now draws in, then hurls out the blood,—the law of undulation. So now you must labor with your brains, and now you must forbear your activity, and see what the great Soul showeth.

The immortality of man is as legitimately preached from the intellections as from the moral volitions. Every intellection is mainly prospective. Its present value is its least. Inspect what delights you in Plutarch, in Shakspeare, in Cervantes. Each truth that a writer acquires is a lantern, which he turns full on what facts and thoughts lay already in his mind, and behold, all the mats and rubbish which had littered his garret become precious. Every trivial fact in his private biography becomes an illustration of this new principle, revisits the day, and delights all men by its piquancy and new charm. Men say, Where did he get this? and think there was something divine in his life. But no; they have myriads of facts just as good, would they only get a lamp to ransack their attics withal.

We are all wise. The difference between persons is not in wisdom but in art. I knew, in an academical club, a person who always deferred to me, who, seeing my whim for writing, fancied that my experiences had somewhat superior; whilst I saw that his experiences were as good as mine. Give them to me, and I would make the same use of them. He held the old; he holds the new; I had the habit of tacking together the old and the new, which he did not use to exercise. This may hold in the great examples. Perhaps if we should meet Shakspeare, we should not be conscious of any steep inferiority; no: but of a great equality,—only that he possessed a strange skill of using, of classifying, his facts, which we lacked. For, notwithstanding our utter incapacity to produce any thing like Hamlet and Othello, see the perfect reception this wit, and immense knowledge of life, and liquid eloquence find in us all.

If you gather apples in the sunshine, or make hay, or hoe corn, and then retire within doors, and shut your eyes, and press them with your hand, you shall still see apples hanging in the bright light, with boughs and leaves thereto, or the tasselled grass, or the corn-flags, and this for five or six hours afterwards. There lie the impressions on the retentive organ, though you knew it not. So lies the whole series of natural images with which your life has made you acquainted in your memory, though you know it not, and a thrill of passion flashes light on their dark chamber, and the active power seizes instantly the fit image, as the word of its momentary thought.

It is long ere we discover how rich we are. Our history, we are sure, is quite tame: we have nothing to write, nothing to infer. But our wiser years still run back to the despised recollections of childhood, and always we are fishing up some wonderful article out of that pond; until, by and by, we begin to suspect that the biography of the one foolish person we know is, in reality, nothing less than the miniature paraphrase of the hundred volumes of the Universal History.

In the intellect constructive, which we popularly designate by the word Genius, we observe the same balance of two elements as in intellect receptive. The constructive intellect produces thoughts, sentences, poems, plans, designs, systems. It is the generation of the mind, the marriage of thought with nature. To genius must always go two gifts, the thought and the publication. The first is revelation, always a miracle, which no frequency of occurrence or incessant study can ever familiarize, but which must always leave the inquirer stupid with wonder. It is the advent of truth into the world, a form of thought now, for the first time, bursting into the universe, a child of the old eternal soul, a piece of genuine and immeasurable greatness. It seems, for the time, to inherit all that has yet existed, and to dictate to the unborn. It affects every thought of man, and goes to fashion every institution. But to make it available, it needs a vehicle or art by which it is conveyed to men. To be communicable, it must become picture or sensible object. We must learn the language of facts. The most wonderful inspirations die with their subject, if he has no hand to paint them to the senses. The ray of light passes invisible through space, and only when it falls on an object is it seen. When the spiritual energy is directed on something outward, then it is a thought. The relation between it and you first makes you, the value of you, apparent to me. The rich, inventive genius of the painter must be smothered and lost for want of the power of drawing, and in our happy hours we should be inexhaustible poets, if once we could break through the silence into adequate rhyme. As all men have some access to primary truth, so all have some art or power of communication in their head, but only in the artist does it descend into the hand. There is an inequality, whose laws we do not yet know, between two men and between two moments of the same man, in respect to this faculty. In common hours, we have the same facts as in the uncommon or inspired, but they do not sit for their portraits; they are not detached, but lie in a web. The thought of genius is spontaneous; but the power of picture or expression, in the most enriched and flowing nature, implies a mixture of will, a certain control over the spontaneous states, without which no production is possible. It is a conversion of all nature into the rhetoric of thought, under the eye of judgment, with a strenuous exercise of choice. And yet the imaginative vocabulary seems to be spontaneous also. It does not flow from experience only or mainly, but from a richer source. Not by any conscious imitation of particular forms are the grand strokes of the painter executed, but by repairing to the fountain-head of all forms in his mind. Who is the first drawing-master? Without instruction we know very well the ideal of the human form. A child knows if an arm or a leg be distorted in a picture, if the attitude be natural or grand, or mean, though he has never received any instruction in drawing, or heard any conversation on the subject, nor can himself draw with correctness a single feature. A good form strikes all eyes pleasantly, long before they have any science on the subject, and a beautiful face sets twenty hearts in palpitation, prior to all consideration of the mechanical proportions of the features and head. We may owe to dreams some light on the fountain of this skill; for, as soon as we let our will go, and let the unconscious states ensue, see what cunning draughtsmen we are! We entertain ourselves with wonderful forms of men, of women, of animals, of gardens, of woods, and of monsters, and the mystic pencil wherewith we then draw has no awkwardness or inexperience, no meagreness or poverty; it can design well, and group well; its composition is full of art, its colors are well laid on, and the whole canvas which it paints is life-like, and apt to touch us with terror, with tenderness, with desire, and with grief. Neither are the artist's copies from experience ever mere copies, but always touched and softened by tints from this ideal domain.

The conditions essential to a constructive mind do not appear to be so often combined but that a good sentence or verse remains fresh and memorable for a long time. Yet when we write with ease, and come out into the free air of thought, we seem to be assured that nothing is easier than to continue this communication at pleasure. Up, down, around, the kingdom of thought has no inclosures, but the Muse makes us free of her city. Well, the world has a million writers. One would think, then, that good thought would be as familiar as air and water, and the gifts of each new hour would exclude the last. Yet we can count all our good books; nay, I remember any beautiful verse for twenty years. It is true that the discerning intellect of the world is always much in advance of the creative, so that there are many competent judges of the best book, and few writers of the best books. But some of the conditions of intellectual construction are of rare occurrence. The intellect is a whole, and demands integrity in every work. This is resisted equally by a man's devotion to a single thought, and by his ambition to combine too many.

Truth is our element of life, yet if a man fasten his attention on a single aspect of truth, and apply himself to that alone for a long time, the truth becomes distorted and not itself, but falsehood; herein resembling the air, which is our natural element, and the breath of our nostrils, but if a stream of the same be directed on the body for a time, it causes cold, fever, and even death. How wearisome the grammarian, the phrenologist, the political or religious fanatic, or indeed any possessed mortal whose balance is lost by the exaggeration of a single topic. It is incipient insanity. Every thought is a prison also. I cannot see what you see, because I am caught up by a strong wind, and blown so far in one direction that I am out of the hoop of your horizon.

Is it any better, if the student, to avoid this offence, and to liberalize himself, aims to make a mechanical whole of history, or science, or philosophy, by a numerical addition of all the facts that fall within his vision? The world refuses to be analyzed by addition and subtraction. When we are young, we spend much time and pains in filling our notebooks with all definitions of Religion, Love, Poetry, Politics, Art, in the hope that, in the course of a few years, we shall have condensed into our encyclopædia the net value of all the theories at which the world has yet arrived. But year after year our tables get no completeness, and at last we discover that our curve is a parabola, whose arcs will never meet.

Neither by detachment, neither by aggregation, is the integrity of the intellect transmitted to its works, but by a vigilance which brings the intellect in its greatness and best state to operate every moment. It must have the same wholeness which nature has. Although no diligence can rebuild the universe in a model, by the best accumulation or disposition of details, yet does the world reappear in miniature in every event, so that all the laws of nature may be read in the smallest fact. The intellect must have the like perfection in its apprehension and in its works. For this reason, an index or mercury of intellectual proficiency is the perception of identity. We talk with accomplished persons who appear to be strangers in nature. The cloud, the tree, the turf, the bird are not theirs, have nothing of them: the world is only their lodging and table. But the poet, whose verses are to be spheral and complete, is one whom Nature cannot deceive, whatsoever face of strangeness she may put on. He feels a strict consanguinity, and detects more likeness than variety in all her changes. We are stung by the desire for new thought; but when we receive a new thought, it is only the old thought with a new face, and though we make it our own, we instantly crave another; we are not really enriched. For the truth was in us before it was reflected to us from natural objects; and the profound genius will cast the likeness of all creatures into every product of his wit.

But if the constructive powers are rare, and it is given to few men to be poets, yet every man is a receiver of this descending holy ghost, and may well study the laws of its influx. Exactly parallel is the whole rule of intellectual duty to the rule of moral duty. A self-denial, no less austere than the saint's, is demanded of the scholar. He must worship truth, and forego all things for that, and choose defeat and pain, so that his treasure in thought is thereby augmented.

God offers to every mind its choice between truth and repose. Take which you please,—you can never have both. Between these, as a pendulum, man oscillates. He in whom the love of repose predominates will accept the first creed, the first philosophy, the first political party he meets,—most likely his father's. He gets rest, commodity, and reputation; but he shuts the door of truth. He in whom the love of truth predominates will keep himself aloof from all moorings, and afloat. He will abstain from dogmatism, and recognize all the opposite negations, between which, as walls, his being is swung. He submits to the inconvenience of suspense and imperfect opinion, but he is a candidate for truth, as the other is not, and respects the highest law of his being.

The circle of the green earth he must measure with his shoes, to find the man who can yield him truth. He shall then know that there is somewhat more blessed and great in hearing than in speaking. Happy is the hearing man; unhappy the speaking man. As long as I hear truth, I am bathed by a beautiful element, and am not conscious of any limits to my nature. The suggestions are thousandfold that I hear and see. The waters of the great deep have ingress and egress to the soul. But if I speak, I define, I confine, and am less. When Socrates speaks, Lysis and Menexenus° are afflicted by no shame that they do not speak. They also are good. He likewise defers to them, loves them, whilst he speaks. Because a true and natural man contains and is the same truth which an eloquent man articulates: but in the eloquent man, because he can articulate it, it seems something the less to reside, and he turns to these silent beautiful with the more inclination and respect. The ancient sentence said, Let us be silent, for so are the gods. Silence is a solvent that destroys personality, and gives us leave to be great and universal. Every man's progress is through a succession of teachers, each of whom seems at the time to have a superlative influence, but it at last gives place to a new. Frankly let him accept it all. Jesus says, Leave father, mother, house and lands, and follow me.° Who leaves all, receives more. This is as true intellectually as morally. Each new mind we approach seems to require an abdication of all our past and present possessions. A new doctrine seems, at first, a subversion of all our opinions, tastes, and manner of living. Such has Swedenborg, such has Kant, such has Coleridge, such has Hegel or his interpreter Cousin,° seemed to many young men in this country. Take thankfully and heartily all they can give. Exhaust them, wrestle with them, let them not go until their blessing be won, and, after a short season, the dismay will be overpast, the excess of influence withdrawn, and they will be no longer an alarming meteor, but one more bright star shining serenely in your heaven, and blending its light with all your day.

But whilst he gives himself up unreservedly to that which draws him, because that is his own, he is to refuse himself to that which draws him not, whatsoever fame and authority may attend it, because it is not his own. Entire self-reliance belongs to the intellect. One soul is a counterpoise of all souls, as a capillary column of water is a balance for the sea. It must treat things, and books, and sovereign genius, as itself also a sovereign. If Æschylus be that man he is taken for, he has not yet done his office, when he has educated the learned of Europe for a thousand years. He is now to approve himself a master of delight to me also. If he cannot do that, all his fame shall avail him nothing with me. I were a fool not to sacrifice a thousand Æschyluses to my intellectual integrity. Especially take the same ground in regard to abstract truth, the science of the mind. The Bacon, the Spinoza, the Hume, Schelling, Kant, or whosoever propounds to you a philosophy of the mind, is only a more or less awkward translator of things in your consciousness, which you have also your way of seeing, perhaps of denominating. Say, then, instead of too timidly poring into his obscure sense, that he has not succeeded in rendering back to you your consciousness. He has not succeeded; now let another try. If Plato cannot, perhaps Spinoza will. If Spinoza cannot, then perhaps Kant. Anyhow, when at last it is done, you will find it is no recondite, but a simple, natural, common state, which the writer restores to you.

But let us end these didactics. I will not, though the subject might provoke it, speak to the open question between Truth and Love. I shall not presume to interfere in the old politics of the skies;—'The cherubim know most; the seraphim love most.'° The gods shall settle their own quarrels. But I cannot recite, even thus rudely, laws of the intellect, without remembering that lofty and sequestered class of men who have been its prophets and oracles, the high-priesthood of the pure reason, the *Trismegisti*,° the expounders of the principles of thought from age to age. When, at long intervals, we turn over their abstruse pages, wonderful seems the calm and grand air of these few, these great spiritual lords, who have walked in the world,—these of the old religion,—dwelling in a worship which makes the sanctities of Christianity look *parvenues* and popular; for 'persuasion is in soul, but necessity is in intellect.'° This band of grandees, Hermes, Heraclitus, Empedocles, Plato, Plotinus, Olympiodorus, Proclus, Synesius, and the rest, have somewhat so vast in their logic, so primary in their thinking, that it seems antecedent to all the ordinary distinctions of rhetoric and literature, and to be at once poetry, and music, and dancing, and astronomy, and mathematics. I am present at the sowing of the seed of the world. With a geometry of sunbeams, the soul lays the foundations of nature. The truth and grandeur of their thought is proved by its scope and applicability, for it commands the entire schedule and inventory of things for its illustration. But what marks its elevation, and has even a comic look to us, is the innocent serenity with which these babe-like Jupiters sit in their clouds, and from age to age prattle to each other, and to no contemporary. Well assured that their speech is intelligible, and the most natural thing in the world, they add thesis to thesis, without a moment's heed of the universal astonishment of the human race below, who do not comprehend their plainest argument; nor do they ever relent so much as to insert a popular or explaining sentence; nor testify the least displeasure or petulance at the dulness of their amazed auditory. The angels are so enamoured of the language that is spoken in heaven, that they will not distort their lips with the hissing and unmusical dialects of men, but speak their own, whether there be any who understand it or not.

ART

Give to barrows, trays, and pans
Grace and glimmer of romance;
Bring the moonlight into noon
Hid in gleaming piles of stone;
On the city's paved street
Plant gardens lined with lilac sweet;
Let spouting fountains cool the air,
Singing in the sun-baked square;
Let statue, picture, park, and hall,
Ballad, flag, and festival,
The past restore, the day adorn,
And make each morrow a new morn.
So shall the drudge in dusty frock
Spy behind the city clock
Retinues of airy kings,
Skirts of angels, starry wings,
His fathers shining in bright fables,
His children fed at heavenly tables.
'T is the privilege of Art
Thus to play its cheerful part,
Man in Earth to acclimate,
And bend the exile to his fate,
And, moulded of one element
With the days and firmament,
Teach him on these as stairs to climb,
And live on even terms with Time;
Whilst upper life the slender rill
Of human sense doth overfill.

BECAUSE the soul is progressive, it never quite repeats itself, but in every act attempts the production of a new and fairer whole. This appears in works both of the useful and the fine arts, if we employ the popular distinction of works according to their aim, either at use or beauty. Thus in our fine arts, not imitation, but creation is the aim. In landscapes, the painter should give the suggestion of a fairer creation than we know. The details, the prose of nature he should omit, and give us only the spirit and splendor. He should know that the landscape has beauty for his eye, because it expresses a thought which is to him good: and this, because the same power which sees through his eyes, is seen in that spectacle; and he will come to value the expression of nature, and not nature itself, and so exalt in his copy, the features that please him. He will give the gloom of gloom, and the sunshine of sunshine. In a portrait, he must inscribe the character, and not the features, and must esteem the man who sits to him as himself only an imperfect picture or likeness of the aspiring original within.

What is that abridgment and selection we observe in all spiritual activity, but itself the creative impulse? for it is the inlet of that higher illumination which teaches to convey a larger sense by simpler symbols. What is a man but nature's finer success in self-explication? What is a man but a finer and compacter landscape than the horizon figures,— nature's eclecticism? and what is his speech, his love of painting, love of nature, but a still finer success? all the weary miles and tons of space and bulk left out, and the spirit or moral of it contracted into a musical word, or the most cunning stroke of the pencil?

But the artist must employ the symbols in use in his day and nation, to convey his enlarged sense to his fellow-men. Thus the new in art is always formed out of the old. The Genius of the Hour sets his ineffaceable seal on the work, and gives it an inexpressible charm for the imagination. As far as the spiritual character of the period overpowers the artist, and finds expression in his work, so far it will retain a certain grandeur, and will represent to future beholders the Unknown, the Inevitable, the Divine. No man can quite exclude this element of Necessity from his labor. No man can quite emancipate himself from his age and country, or produce a model in which the education, the religion, the politics, usages, and arts, of his times shall have no share. Though he were never so original, never so wilful and fantastic, he cannot wipe out of his work every trace of the thoughts amidst which it grew. The very avoidance betrays the usage he avoids. Above his will, and out of his sight, he is necessitated, by the air he breathes, and the idea on which he and his contemporaries live and toil, to share the manner of his times, without knowing what that manner is. Now that which is inevitable in the work has a higher charm than individual talent can ever give, inasmuch as the artist's pen or chisel seems to have been held and guided by a gigantic hand to inscribe a line in the history of the human race. This circumstance gives a value to the Egyptian hieroglyphics, to the Indian, Chinese, and Mexican idols, however gross and shapeless. They denote the height of the human soul in that hour, and were not fantastic, but sprung from a necessity as deep as the world. Shall I now add, that the whole extant product of the plastic arts has herein its highest value, *as history*; as a stroke drawn in the portrait of that fate, perfect and beautiful, according to whose ordinations all beings advance to their beatitude?

Thus, historically viewed, it has been the office of art to educate the perception of beauty. We are immersed in beauty, but our eyes have no clear vision. It needs, by the exhibition of single traits, to assist and lead the dormant taste. We carve and paint, or we behold what is carved and painted, as students of the mystery of Form. The virtue of art lies in detachment, in sequestering one object from the embarrassing variety. Until one thing comes out from the connection of things, there can be enjoyment, contemplation, but no thought. Our happiness and unhappiness are unproductive. The infant lies in a pleasing trance, but his individual character and his practical power depend on his daily progress in the separation of things, and dealing with one at a time. Love and all the passions concentrate all existence around a single form. It is the habit of certain minds to give an all-excluding fulness to the object, the thought, the word, they alight upon, and to make that for the time the deputy of the world. These are the artists, the orators, the leaders of society. The power to detach, and to magnify by detaching, is the essence of rhetoric in the hands of the orator and the poet. This rhetoric, or power to fix the momentary eminency of an object,—so remarkable in Burke, in Byron, in Carlyle,—the painter and sculptor exhibit in color and in stone. The power depends on the depth of the artist's insight of that object he contemplates. For every object has its roots in central nature, and may of course be so exhibited to us as to represent the world. Therefore, each work of genius is the tyrant of the hour, and concentrates attention on itself. For the time, it is the only thing worth naming to do that,—be it a sonnet, an opera, a landscape, a statue, an oration, the plan of a temple, of a campaign, or of a voyage of discovery. Presently we pass to some other object, which rounds itself into a whole, as did the first; for example, a well-laid garden: and nothing seems worth doing but the laying out of gardens. I should think fire the best thing in the world, if I were not acquainted with air, and water, and earth. For it is the right and property of all natural objects, of all genuine talents, of all native properties whatsoever, to be for their moment the top of the world. A squirrel leaping from bough to bough, and making the wood but one wide tree for his pleasure, fills the eye not less than a lion,—is beautiful, self-sufficing, and stands then and there for nature. A good ballad draws my ear and heart whilst I listen, as much as an epic has done before. A dog, drawn by a master, or a litter of pigs, satisfies, and is a reality not less than the frescoes of Angelo. From this succession of excellent objects, we learn at last the immensity of the world, the opulence of human nature, which can run out to infinitude in any direction. But I also learn that what astonished and fascinated me in the first work astonished me in the second work also; that excellence of all things is one.

The office of painting and sculpture seems to be merely initial. The best pictures can easily tell us their last secret. The best pictures are rude draughts of a few of the miraculous dots and lines and dyes which make up the ever-changing 'landscape with figures' amidst which we dwell. Painting seems to be to the eye what dancing is to the limbs. When that has educated the frame to self-possession, to nimbleness, to grace, the steps of the dancing-master are better forgotten; so painting teaches me the splendor of color and the expression of form, and, as I see many pictures and higher genius in the art, I see the boundless opulence of the pencil, the indifferency in which the artist stands free to choose out of the possible forms. If he can draw every thing, why draw any thing? and then is my eye opened to the eternal picture which nature paints in the street with moving men and children, beggars, and fine ladies, draped in red, and green, and blue, and gray; long-haired, grizzled, white-faced, black-faced, wrinkled, giant, dwarf, expanded, elfish,—capped and based by heaven, earth, and sea.

A gallery of sculpture teaches more austerely the same lesson. As picture teaches the coloring, so sculpture the anatomy of form. When I have seen fine statues, and afterwards enter a public assembly, I understand well what he meant who said, 'When I have been reading Homer, all men look like giants.' I too see that painting and sculpture are gymnastics of the eye, its training to the niceties and curiosities of its function. There is no statue like this living man, with his infinite advantage over all ideal sculpture, of perpetual variety. What a gallery of art have I here! No mannerist made these varied groups and diverse original single figures. Here is the artist himself improvising, grim and glad, at his block. Now one thought strikes him, now another, and with each moment he alters the whole air, attitude, and expression of his clay. Away with your nonsense of oil and easels, of marble and chisels: except to open your eyes to the masteries of eternal art, they are hypocritical rubbish.

The reference of all production at last to an aboriginal Power explains the traits common to all works of the highest art,—that they are universally intelligible; that they restore to us the simplest states of mind; and are religious. Since what skill is therein shown is the reappearance of the original soul, a jet of pure light, it should produce a similar impression to that made by natural objects. In happy hours, nature appears to us one with art; art perfected,—the work of genius. And the individual, in whom simple tastes and susceptibility to all the great human influences overpower the accidents of a local and special culture, is the best critic of art. Though we travel the world over to find the beautiful, we must carry it with us, or we find it not. The best of beauty is a finer charm than skill in surfaces, in outlines, or rules of art can ever teach, namely, a radiation from the work of art of human character,—a wonderful expression through stone, or canvas, or musical sound, of the deepest and simplest attributes of our nature, and therefore most intelligible at last to those souls which have these attributes. In the sculptures of the Greeks, in the masonry of the Romans, and in the pictures of the Tuscan and Venetian masters, the highest charm is the universal language they speak. A confession of moral nature, of purity, love, and hope, breathes from them all. That which we carry to them, the same we bring back more fairly illustrated in the memory. The traveller who visits the Vatican, and passes from chamber to chamber through galleries of statues, vases, sarcophagi, and candelabra, through all forms of beauty, cut in the richest materials, is in danger of forgetting the simplicity of the principles out of which they all sprung, and that they had their origin from thoughts and laws in his own breast. He studies the technical rules on these wonderful remains, but forgets that these works were not always thus constellated; that they are the contributions of many ages and many countries; that each came out of the solitary workshop of one artist, who toiled perhaps in ignorance of the existence of other sculpture, created his work without other model, save life, household life, and the sweet and smart of personal relations, of beating hearts, and meeting eyes, of poverty, and necessity, and hope, and fear. These were his inspirations, and these are the effects he carries home to your heart and mind. In proportion to his force, the artist will find in his work an outlet for his proper character. He must not be in any manner pinched or hindered by his material, but through his necessity of imparting himself the adamant will be wax in his hands, and will allow an adequate communication of himself, in his full stature and proportion. He need not cumber himself with a conventional nature and culture, nor ask what is the mode in Rome or in Paris, but that house, and weather, and manner of living which poverty and the fate of birth have made at once so odious and so dear, in the gray, unpainted wood cabin, on the corner of a New Hampshire farm, or in the log-hut of the backwoods, or in the narrow lodging where he has endured the constraints and seeming of a city poverty, will serve as

well as any other condition as the symbol of a thought which pours itself
indifferently through all.

I remember, when in my younger days I had heard of the wonders of
Italian painting, I fancied the great pictures would be great strangers;
some surprising combination of color and form; a foreign wonder, barbaric pearl and gold,° like the spontoons and standards of the militia,
which play such pranks in the eyes and imaginations of school-boys. I
was to see and acquire I knew not what. When I came at last to Rome,
and saw with eyes the pictures, I found that genius left to novices the
gay and fantastic and ostentatious, and itself pierced directly to the simple and true; that it was familiar and sincere; that it was the old, eternal
fact I had met already in so many forms,—unto which I lived; that it was
the plain *you and me* I knew so well,—had left at home in so many conversations. I had the same experience already in a church at Naples.
There I saw that nothing was changed with me but the place, and said
to myself,—'Thou foolish child, hast thou come out hither, over four
thousand miles of salt water, to find that which was perfect to thee there
at home?'—that fact I saw again in the Academmia at Naples, in the
chambers of sculpture, and yet again when I came to Rome, and to the
paintings of Raphael, Angelo, Sacchi, Titian,° and Leonardo da Vinci.
'What, old mole! workest thou in the earth so fast?'° It had travelled by
my side: that which I fancied I had left in Boston was here in the Vatican, and again at Milan, and at Paris, and made all travelling ridiculous
as a treadmill. I now require this of all pictures, that they domesticate
me, not that they dazzle me. Pictures must not be too picturesque.
Nothing astonishes men so much as common-sense and plain dealing.
All great actions have been simple, and all great pictures are.

The Transfiguration, by Raphael, is an eminent example of this
peculiar merit. A calm, benignant beauty shines over all this picture,
and goes directly to the heart. It seems almost to call you by name. The
sweet and sublime face of Jesus is beyond praise, yet how it disappoints
all florid expectations! This familiar, simple, home-speaking countenance is as if one should meet a friend. The knowledge of picture-
dealers has its value, but listen not to their criticism when your heart is
touched by genius. It was not painted for them, it was painted for you;
for such as had eyes capable of being touched by simplicity and lofty
emotions.

Yet when we have said all our fine things about the arts, we must end
with a frank confession, that the arts, as we know them, are but initial.
Our best praise is given to what they aimed and promised, not to the
actual result. He has conceived meanly of the resources of man, who

believes that the best age of production is past. The real value of the
Iliad, or the Transfiguration, is as signs of power; billows or ripples
they are of the stream of tendency; tokens of the everlasting effort to
produce, which even in its worst estate the soul betrays. Art has not yet
come to its maturity, if it do not put itself abreast with the most potent
influences of the world, if it is not practical and moral, if it do not stand
in connection with the conscience, if it do not make the poor and
uncultivated feel that it addresses them with a voice of lofty cheer.
There is higher work for Art than the arts. They are abortive births of
an imperfect or vitiated instinct. Art is the need to create; but in its
essence, immense and universal, it is impatient of working with lame or
tied hands, and of making cripples and monsters, such as all pictures
and statues are. Nothing less than the creation of man and nature is its
end. A man should find in it an outlet for his whole energy. He may
paint and carve only as long as he can do that. Art should exhilarate,
and throw down the walls of circumstance on every side, awakening in
the beholder the same sense of universal relation and power which the
work evinced in the artist, and its highest effect is to make new artists.

Already History is old enough to witness the old age and disappearance of particular arts. The art of sculpture is long ago perished to any
real effect. It was originally a useful art, a mode of writing, a savage's
record of gratitude or devotion, and among a people possessed of a
wonderful perception of form this childish carving was refined to the
utmost splendor of effect. But it is the game of a rude and youthful
people, and not the manly labor of a wise and spiritual nation. Under an
oak-tree loaded with leaves and nuts, under a sky full of eternal eyes, I
stand in a thoroughfare; but in the works of our plastic arts, and
especially of sculpture, creation is driven into a corner. I cannot hide
from myself that there is a certain appearance of paltriness, as of toys,
and the trumpery of a theatre, in sculpture. Nature transcends all our
moods of thought, and its secret we do not yet find. But the gallery
stands at the mercy of our moods, and there is a moment when it
becomes frivolous. I do not wonder that Newton, with an attention
habitually engaged on the paths of planets and suns, should have wondered what the Earl of Pembroke° found to admire in 'stone dolls.'
Sculpture may serve to teach the pupil how deep is the secret of form,
how purely the spirit can translate its meanings into that eloquent dialect. But the statue will look cold and false before that new activity
which needs to roll through all things, and is impatient of counterfeits,
and things not alive. Picture and sculpture are the celebrations and fes-
tivities of form. But true art is never fixed, but always flowing. The

sweetest music is not in the oratorio, but in the human voice when it speaks from its instant life tones of tenderness, truth, or courage. The oratorio has already lost its relation to the morning, to the sun, and the earth, but that persuading voice is in tune with these. All works of art should not be detached, but extempore performances. A great man is a new statue in every attitude and action. A beautiful woman is a picture which drives all beholders nobly mad. Life may be lyric or epic, as well as a poem or a romance.

A true announcement of the law of creation, if a man were found worthy to declare it, would carry art up into the kingdom of nature, and destroy its separate and contrasted existence. The fountains of invention and beauty in modern society are all but dried up. A popular novel, a theatre, or a ball-room makes us feel that we are all paupers in the almshouse of this world, without dignity, without skill, or industry. Art is as poor and low. The old tragic Necessity, which lowers on the brows even of the Venuses and the Cupids of the antique, and furnishes the sole apology for the intrusion of such anomalous figures into nature,— namely, that they were inevitable; that the artist was drunk with a passion for form which he could not resist, and which vented itself in these fine extravagances,—no longer dignifies the chisel or the pencil. But the artist and the connoisseur now seek in art the exhibition of their talent, or an asylum from the evils of life. Men are not well pleased with the figure they make in their own imaginations, and they flee to art, and convey their better sense in an oratorio, a statue, or a picture. Art makes the same effort which a sensual prosperity makes; namely, to detach the beautiful from the useful, to do up the work as unavoidable, and, hating it, pass on to enjoyment. These solaces and compensations, this division of beauty from use, the laws of nature do not permit. As soon as beauty is sought, not from religion and love, but for pleasure, it degrades the seeker. High beauty is no longer attainable by him in canvas or in stone, in sound, or in lyrical construction; an effeminate, prudent, sickly beauty, which is not beauty, is all that can be formed; for the hand can never execute any thing higher than the character can inspire.

The art that thus separates is itself first separated. Art must not be a superficial talent, but must begin farther back in man. Now men do not see nature to be beautiful, and they go to make a statue which shall be. They abhor men as tasteless, dull, and inconvertible, and console themselves with color-bags, and blocks of marble. They reject life as prosaic, and create a death which they call poetic. They despatch the day's weary chores, and fly to voluptuous reveries. They eat and drink, that they may afterwards execute the ideal. Thus is art vilified; the name conveys to the mind its secondary and bad senses; it stands in the imagination as somewhat contrary to nature, and struck with death from the first. Would it not be better to begin higher up,—to serve the ideal before they eat and drink; to serve the ideal in eating and drinking, in drawing the breath, and in the functions of life? Beauty must come back to the useful arts, and the distinction between the fine and the useful arts be forgotten. If history were truly told, if life were nobly spent, it would be no longer easy or possible to distinguish the one from the other. In nature, all is useful, all is beautiful. It is therefore beautiful, because it is alive, moving, reproductive; it is therefore useful, because it is symmetrical and fair. Beauty will not come at the call of a legislature, nor will it repeat in England or America its history in Greece. It will come, as always, unannounced, and spring up between the feet of brave and earnest men. It is in vain that we look for genius to reiterate its miracles in the old arts; it is its instinct to find beauty and holiness in new and necessary facts, in the field and road-side, in the shop and mill. Proceeding from a religious heart it will raise to a divine use the railroad, the insurance office, the joint-stock company, our law, our primary assemblies, our commerce, the galvanic battery, the electric jar, the prism, and the chemist's retort, in which we seek now only an economical use. Is not the selfish and even cruel aspect which belongs to our great mechanical works,—to mills, railways, and machinery,—the effect of the mercenary impulses which these works obey? When its errands are noble and adequate, a steamboat bridging the Atlantic between Old and New England, and arriving at its ports with the punctuality of a planet, is a step of man into harmony with nature. The boat at St. Petersburgh, which plies along the Lena° by magnetism, needs little to make it sublime. When science is learned in love, and its powers are wielded by love, they will appear the supplements and continuations of the material creation.

ESSAYS: SECOND SERIES
(1844)

THE POET

A moody child and wildly wise
Pursued the game with joyful eyes,
Which chose, like meteors, their way,
And rived the dark with private ray:
They overleapt the horizon's edge,
Searched with Apollo's privilege;
Through man, and woman, and sea, and star,
Saw the dance of nature forward far;
Through worlds, and races, and terms, and times,
Saw musical order, and pairing rhymes.

THOSE who are esteemed umpires of taste, are often persons who have acquired some knowledge of admired pictures or sculptures, and have an inclination for whatever is elegant; but if you inquire whether they are beautiful souls, and whether their own acts are like fair pictures, you learn that they are selfish and sensual. Their cultivation is local, as if you should rub a log of dry wood in one spot to produce fire, all the rest remaining cold. Their knowledge of the fine arts is some study of rules and particulars, or some limited judgment of color or form, which is exercised for amusement or for show. It is a proof of the shallowness of the doctrine of beauty, as it lies in the minds of our amateurs, that men seem to have lost the perception of the instant dependence of form upon soul. There is no doctrine of forms in our philosophy. We were put into our bodies, as fire is put into a pan, to be carried about; but there is no accurate adjustment between the spirit and the organ, much less is the latter the germination of the former. So in regard to other forms, the intellectual men do not believe in any essential dependence of the material world on thought and volition. Theologians think it a pretty air-castle to talk of the spiritual meaning of a ship or a cloud, of a city or a contract, but they prefer to come again to the solid ground of historical evidence; and even the poets are contented with a civil and conformed manner of living, and to write poems from the fancy, at a safe distance from their own experience. But the highest minds of the world have never ceased to explore the double meaning, or, shall I say, the quadruple, or the centuple, or much more manifold meaning, of every sensuous fact: Orpheus, Empedocles, Heraclitus, Plato, Plutarch, Dante, Swedenborg,° and the masters of sculpture, picture, and poetry. For we are not pans and barrows, nor even porters of the fire and torch-bearers, but children of the fire, made of it, and only the same divinity transmuted, and at two or three removes, when we know least about it. And this hidden truth, that the fountains whence all this river of Time, and its creatures, floweth, are intrinsically ideal and beautiful, draws us to the consideration of the nature and functions of the Poet, or the man of Beauty, to the means and materials he uses, and to the general aspect of the art in the present time.

The breadth of the problem is great, for the poet is representative. He stands among partial men for the complete man, and apprises us not of his wealth, but of the commonwealth. The young man reveres men of genius, because, to speak truly, they are more himself than he is. They receive of the soul as he also receives, but they more. Nature enhances her beauty, to the eye of loving men, from their belief that the poet is beholding her shows at the same time. He is isolated among his contemporaries, by truth and by his art, but with this consolation in his pursuits, that they will draw all men sooner or later. For all men live by truth, and stand in need of expression. In love, in art, in avarice, in politics, in labor, in games, we study to utter our painful secret. The man is only half himself, the other half is his expression.

Notwithstanding this necessity to be published, adequate expression is rare. I know not how it is that we need an interpreter; but the great majority of men seem to be minors, who have not yet come into possession of their own, or mutes, who cannot report the conversation they have had with nature. There is no man who does not anticipate a supersensual utility in the sun, and stars, earth, and water. These stand and wait to render him a peculiar service.° But there is some obstruction, or some excess of phlegm in our constitution, which does not suffer them to yield the due effect. Too feeble fall the impressions of nature on us to make us artists. Every touch should thrill. Every man should be so much an artist, that he could report in conversation what had befallen him. Yet, in our experience, the rays or appulses have sufficient force to arrive at the senses, but not enough to reach the quick, and compel the reproduction of themselves in speech. The poet is the person in whom these powers are in balance, the man without impediment, who sees and handles that which others dream of, traverses the whole scale of experience, and is representative of man, in virtue of being the largest power to receive and to impart.

For the Universe has three children, born at one time, which reappear, under different names, in every system of thought, whether they be called cause, operation, and effect; or, more poetically, Jove,

Pluto, Neptune; or, theologically, the Father, the Spirit, and the Son; but which we will call here, the Knower, the Doer, and the Sayer. These stand respectively for the love of truth, for the love of good, and for the love of beauty. These three are equal. Each is that which he is essentially, so that he cannot be surmounted or analyzed, and each of these three has the power of the others latent in him, and his own patent.

The poet is the sayer, the namer, and represents beauty. He is a sovereign, and stands on the centre. For the world is not painted, or adorned, but is from the beginning beautiful; and God has not made some beautiful things, but Beauty is the creator of the universe. Therefore the poet is not any permissive potentate, but is emperor in his own right. Criticism is infested with a cant of materialism, which assumes that manual skill and activity is the first merit of all men, and disparages such as say and do not, overlooking the fact, that some men, namely, poets, are natural sayers, sent into the world to the end of expression, and confounds them with those whose province is action, but who quit it to imitate the sayers. But Homer's words are as costly and admirable to Homer, as Agamemnon's victories are to Agamemnon. The poet does not wait for the hero or the sage, but, as they act and think primarily, so he writes primarily what will and must be spoken, reckoning the others, though primaries also, yet, in respect to him, secondaries and servants; as sitters or models in the studio of a painter, or as assistants who bring building materials to an architect.

For poetry was all written before time was, and whenever we are so finely organized that we can penetrate into that region where the air is music, we hear those primal warblings, and attempt to write them down, but we lose ever and anon a word, or a verse, and substitute something of our own, and thus miswrite the poem. The men of more delicate ear write down these cadences more faithfully, and these transcripts, though imperfect, become the songs of the nations. For nature is as truly beautiful as it is good, or as it is reasonable, and must as much appear, as it must be done, or be known. Words and deeds are quite indifferent modes of the divine energy. Words are also actions, and actions are a kind of words.

The sign and credentials of the poet are, that he announces that which no man foretold. He is the true and only doctor; he knows and tells; he is the only teller of news, for he was present and privy to the appearance which he describes. He is a beholder of ideas, and an utterer of the necessary and causal. For we do not speak now of men of poetical talents, or of industry and skill in metre, but of the true poet. I took part in a conversation the other day, concerning a recent writer of lyrics, a man of subtle mind, whose head appeared to be a music-box of delicate tunes and rhythms, and whose skill, and command of language, we could not sufficiently praise. But when the question arose, whether he was not only a lyrist, but a poet, we were obliged to confess that he is plainly a contemporary, not an eternal man. He does not stand out of our low limitations, like a Chimborazo under the line,° running up from the torrid base through all the climates of the globe, with belts of the herbage of every latitude on its high and mottled sides; but this genius is the landscape-garden of a modern house, adorned with fountains and statues, with well-bred men and women standing and sitting in the walks and terraces. We hear, through all the varied music, the ground-tone of conventional life. Our poets are men of talents who sing, and not the children of music. The argument is secondary, the finish of the verses is primary.

For it is not metres, but a metre-making argument, that makes a poem,—a thought so passionate and alive, that, like the spirit of a plant or an animal, it has an architecture of its own, and adorns nature with a new thing. The thought and the form are equal in the order of time, but in the order of genesis the thought is prior to the form. The poet has a new thought: he has a whole new experience to unfold; he will tell us how it was with him, and all men will be the richer in his fortune. For, the experience of each new age requires a new confession, and the world seems always waiting for its poet. I remember, when I was young, how much I was moved one morning by tidings that genius had appeared in a youth who sat near me at table. He had left his work, and gone rambling none knew whither, and had written hundreds of lines, but could not tell whether that which was in him was therein told: he could tell nothing but that all was changed,—man, beast, heaven, earth, and sea. How gladly we listened! how credulous! Society seemed to be compromised. We sat in the aurora of a sunrise which was to put out all the stars. Boston seemed to be at twice the distance it had the night before, or was much farther than that. Rome,—what was Rome? Plutarch and Shakspeare were in the yellow leaf,° and Homer no more should be heard of. It is much to know that poetry has been written this very day, under this very roof, by your side. What! that wonderful spirit has not expired! these stony moments are still sparkling and animated! I had fancied that the oracles were all silent, and nature had spent her fires, and behold! all night, from every pore, these fine auroras have been streaming. Every one has some interest in the advent of the poet, and no one knows how much it may concern him. We know that the secret of the world is profound, but who or what shall be our interpreter, we know not. A mountain ramble, a new style of face, a new person, may put the key into our hands. Of course, the value of genius to us is in the veracity of its report. Talent may frolic and juggle; genius realizes and adds. Mankind, in good earnest, have availed so far in understanding themselves and their work, that the foremost watchman on the peak announces his news. It is the truest word ever spoken, and the phrase will be the fittest, most musical, and the unerring voice of the world for that time.

All that we call sacred history attests that the birth of a poet is the principal event in chronology. Man, never so often deceived, still watches for the arrival of a brother who can hold him steady to a truth, until he has made it his own. With what joy I begin to read a poem, which I confide in as an inspiration! And now my chains are to be broken; I shall mount above these clouds and opaque airs in which I live,—opaque, though they seem transparent,—and from the heaven of truth I shall see and comprehend my relations. That will reconcile me to life, and renovate nature, to see trifles animated by a tendency, and to know what I am doing. Life will no more be a noise; now I shall see men and women, and know the signs by which they may be discerned from fools and satans. This day shall be better than my birth-day: then I became an animal: now I am invited into the science of the real. Such is the hope, but the fruition is postponed. Oftener it falls, that this winged man, who will carry me into the heaven, whirls me into the clouds, then leaps and frisks about with me from cloud to cloud, still affirming that he is bound heavenward; and I, being myself a novice, am slow in perceiving that he does not know the way into the heavens, and is merely bent that I should admire his skill to rise, like a fowl or a flying fish, a little way from the ground or the water; but the all-piercing, all-feeding, and ocular air of heaven, that man shall never inhabit. I tumble down again soon into my old nooks, and lead the life of exaggerations as before, and have lost my faith in the possibility of any guide who can lead me thither where I would be.

But leaving these victims of vanity, let us, with new hope, observe how nature, by worthier impulses, has ensured the poet's fidelity to his office of announcement and affirming, namely, by the beauty of things, which becomes a new, and higher beauty, when expressed. Nature offers all her creatures to him as a picture-language. Being used as a type, a second wonderful value appears in the object, far better than its old value, as the carpenter's stretched cord, if you hold your ear close enough, is musical in the breeze. 'Things more excellent than every image,' says Jamblichus,° 'are expressed through images.' Things admit

of being used as symbols, because nature is a symbol, in the whole, and
in every part. Every line we can draw in the sand, has expression; and
there is no body without its spirit or genius. All form is an effect of
character; all condition, of the quality of the life; all harmony, of health;
(and, for this reason, a perception of beauty should be sympathetic, or
proper only to the good.) The beautiful rests on the foundations of the
necessary. The soul makes the body, as the wise Spenser teaches:—

> 'So every spirit, as it is most pure,
> And hath in it the more of heavenly light,
> So it the fairer body doth procure
> To habit in, and it more fairly dight,
> With cheerful grace and amiable sight.
> For, of the soul, the body form doth take,
> For soul is form, and doth the body make.'°

Here we find ourselves, suddenly, not in a critical speculation, but in a
holy place, and should go very warily and reverently. We stand before
the secret of the world, there where Being passes into Appearance, and
Unity into Variety.

The Universe is the externisation of the soul. Wherever the life is,
that bursts into appearance around it. Our science is sensual, and
therefore superficial. The earth, and the heavenly bodies, physics, and
chemistry, we sensually treat, as if they were self-existent; but these are
the retinue of that Being we have. 'The mighty heaven,' said Proclus,°
'exhibits, in its transfigurations, clear images of the splendor of intellectual perceptions; being moved in conjunction with the unapparent
periods of intellectual natures.' Therefore, science always goes abreast
with the just elevation of the man, keeping step with religion and metaphysics; or, the state of science is an index of our self-knowledge. Since
everything in nature answers to a moral power, if any phenomenon
remains brute and dark, it is that the corresponding faculty in the
observer is not yet active.

No wonder, then, if these waters be so deep, that we hover over them
with a religious regard. The beauty of the fable proves the importance
of the sense; to the poet, and to all others; or, if you please, every man is
so far a poet as to be susceptible of these enchantments of nature: for
all men have the thoughts whereof the universe is the celebration. I find
that the fascination resides in the symbol. Who loves nature? Who does
not? Is it only poets, and men of leisure and cultivation, who live with
her? No; but also hunters, farmers, grooms, and butchers, though they
express their affection in their choice of life, and not in their choice of

words. The writer wonders what the coachman or the hunter values in riding, in horses, and dogs. It is not superficial qualities. When you talk with him, he holds these at as slight a rate as you. His worship is sympathetic; he has no definitions, but he is commanded in nature, by the living power which he feels to be there present. No imitation, or playing of these things, would content him; he loves the earnest of the north-wind, of rain, of stone, and wood, and iron. A beauty not explicable, is dearer than a beauty which we can see to the end of. It is nature the symbol, nature certifying the supernatural, body overflowed by life, which he worships, with coarse, but sincere rites.

The inwardness, and mystery, of this attachment, drives men of every class to the use of emblems. The schools of poets, and philosophers, are not more intoxicated with their symbols, than the populace with theirs. In our political parties, compute the power of badges and emblems. See the great ball which they roll from Baltimore to Bunker hill! In the political processions, Lowell goes in a loom, and Lynn in a shoe, and Salem in a ship. Witness the cider-barrel, the log-cabin, the hickory-stick, the palmetto,° and all the cognizances of party. See the power of national emblems. Some stars, lilies, leopards, a crescent, a lion, an eagle, or other figure, which came into credit God knows how, on an old rag of bunting, blowing in the wind, on a fort, at the ends of the earth, shall make the blood tingle under the rudest, or the most conventional exterior. The people fancy they hate poetry, and they are all poets and mystics!

Beyond this universality of the symbolic language, we are apprised of the divineness of this superior use of things, whereby the world is a temple, whose walls are covered with emblems, pictures, and commandments of the Deity, in this, that there is no fact in nature which does not carry the whole sense of nature; and the distinctions which we make in events, and in affairs, of low and high, honest and base, disappear when nature is used as a symbol. Thought makes every thing fit for use. The vocabulary of an omniscient man would embrace words and images excluded from polite conversation. What would be base, or even obscene, to the obscene, becomes illustrious, spoken in a new connexion of thought. The piety of the Hebrew prophets purges their grossness. The circumcision is an example of the power of poetry to raise the low and offensive. Small and mean things serve as well as great symbols. The meaner the type by which a law is expressed, the more pungent it is, and the more lasting in the memories of men: just as we choose the smallest box, or case, in which any needful utensil can be carried. Bare lists of words are found suggestive, to an imaginative and excited mind; as it is related of Lord Chatham, that he was accustomed to read in Bailey's Dictionary,° when he was preparing to speak in Parliament. The poorest experience is rich enough for all the purposes of expressing thought. Why covet a knowledge of new facts? Day and night, house and garden, a few books, a few actions, serve us as well as would all trades and all spectacles. We are far from having exhausted the significance of the few symbols we use. We can come to use them yet with a terrible simplicity. It does not need that a poem should be long. Every word was once a poem. Every new relation is a new word. Also, we use defects and deformities to a sacred purpose, so expressing our sense that the evils of the world are such only to the evil eye. In the old mythology, mythologists observe, defects are ascribed to divine natures, as lameness to Vulcan, blindness to Cupid, and the like, to signify exuberances.

For, as it is dislocation and detachment from the life of God, that makes things ugly, the poet, who re-attaches things to nature and the Whole,—re-attaching even artificial things, and violations of nature, to nature, by a deeper insight,—disposes very easily of the most disagreeable facts. Readers of poetry see the factory-village, and the railway, and fancy that the poetry of the landscape is broken up by these; for these works of art are not yet consecrated in their reading; but the poet sees them fall within the great Order not less than the bee-hive, or the spider's geometrical web. Nature adopts them very fast into her vital circles, and the gliding train of cars she loves like her own. Besides, in a centred mind, it signifies nothing how many mechanical inventions you exhibit. Though you add millions, and never so surprising, the fact of mechanics has not gained a grain's weight. The spiritual fact remains unalterable, by many or by few particulars; as no mountain is of any appreciable height to break the curve of the sphere. A shrewd country-boy goes to the city for the first time, and the complacent citizen is not satisfied with his little wonder. It is not that he does not see all the fine houses, and know that he never saw such before, but he disposes of them as easily as the poet finds place for the railway. The chief value of the new fact, is to enhance the great and constant fact of Life, which can dwarf any and every circumstance, and to which the belt of wampum, and the commerce of America, are alike.

The world being thus put under the mind for verb and noun, the poet is he who can articulate it. For, though life is great, and fascinates, and absorbs,—and though all men are intelligent of the symbols through which it is named,—yet they cannot originally use them. We are symbols, and inhabit symbols; workman, work, and tools, words and things, birth and death, all are emblems; but we sympathize with the symbols, and, being infatuated with the economical uses of things, we do not know that they are thoughts. The poet, by an ulterior intellectual perception, gives them a power which makes their old use forgotten, and puts eyes, and a tongue, into every dumb and inanimate object. He perceives the independence of the thought on the symbol, the stability of the thought, the accidency and fugacity of the symbol. As the eyes of Lyncæus° were said to see through the earth, so the poet turns the world to glass, and shows us all things in their right series and procession. For, through that better perception, he stands one step nearer to things, and sees the flowing or metamorphosis; perceives that thought is multiform; that within the form of every creature is a force impelling it to ascend into a higher form; and, following with his eyes the life, uses the forms which express that life, and so his speech flows with the flowing of nature. All the facts of the animal economy, sex, nutriment, gestation, birth, growth, are symbols of the passage of the world into the soul of man, to suffer there a change, and reappear a new and higher fact. He uses forms according to the life, and not according to the form. This is true science. The poet alone knows astronomy, chemistry, vegetation, and animation, for he does not stop at these facts, but employs them as signs. He knows why the plain, or meadow of space, was strown with these flowers we call suns, and moons, and stars; why the great deep is adorned with animals, with men, and gods; for, in every word he speaks he rides on them as the horses of thought.

By virtue of this science the poet is the Namer, or Language-maker, naming things sometimes after their appearance, sometimes after their essence, and giving to every one its own name and not another's, thereby rejoicing the intellect, which delights in detachment or boundary. The poets made all the words, and therefore language is the archives of history, and, if we must say it, a sort of tomb of the muses. For, though the origin of most of our words is forgotten, each word was at first a stroke of genius, and obtained currency, because for the moment it symbolized the world to the first speaker and to the hearer. The etymologist finds the deadest word to have been once a brilliant picture. Language is fossil poetry. As the limestone of the continent consists of infinite masses of the shells of animalcules, so language is made up of images, or tropes, which now, in their secondary use, have long ceased to remind us of their poetic origin. But the poet names the thing because he sees it, or comes one step nearer to it than any other. This expression, or naming, is not art, but a second nature, grown out of the first, as a leaf out of a tree. What we call nature, is a certain

self-regulated motion, or change; and nature does all things by her own
hands, and does not leave another to baptise her, but baptises herself;
and this through the metamorphosis again. I remember that a certain
poet described it to me thus:

Genius is the activity which repairs the decays of things, whether
wholly or partly of a material and finite kind. Nature, through all her
kingdoms, insures herself. Nobody cares for planting the poor fungus:
so she shakes down from the gills of one agaric countless spores, any
one of which, being preserved, transmits new billions of spores to-
morrow or next day. The new agaric of this hour has a chance which
the old one had not. This atom of seed is thrown into a new place, not
subject to the accidents which destroyed its parent two rods off. She
makes a man; and having brought him to ripe age, she will no longer
run the risk of losing this wonder at a blow, but she detaches from him
a new self, that the kind may be safe from accidents to which the individual is exposed. So when the soul of the poet has come to ripeness of
thought, she detaches and sends away from it its poems or songs,—a
fearless, sleepless, deathless progeny, which is not exposed to the accidents of the weary kingdom of time: a fearless, vivacious offspring, clad
with wings (such was the virtue of the soul out of which they came),
which carry them fast and far, and infix them irrecoverably into the
hearts of men. These wings are the beauty of the poet's soul. The
songs, thus flying immortal from their mortal parent, are pursued by
clamorous flights of censures, which swarm in far greater numbers, and
threaten to devour them; but these last are not winged. At the end of a
very short leap they fall plump down, and rot, having received from the
souls out of which they came no beautiful wings. But the melodies of
the poet ascend, and leap, and pierce into the deeps of infinite time.

So far the bard taught me, using his freer speech. But nature has a
higher end, in the production of new individuals, than security, namely,
ascension, or, the passage of the soul into higher forms. I knew, in my
younger days, the sculptor who made the statue of the youth which
stands in the public garden. He was, as I remember, unable to tell
directly, what made him happy, or unhappy, but by wonderful indirections he could tell. He rose one day, according to his habit, before the
dawn, and saw the morning break, grand as the eternity out of which it
came, and, for many days after, he strove to express this tranquillity,
and, lo! his chisel had fashioned out of marble the form of a beautiful
youth, Phosphorus,° whose aspect is such, that, it is said, all persons

who look on it become silent. The poet also resigns himself to his mood, and that thought which agitated him is expressed, but *alter idem*,° in a manner totally new. The expression is organic, or, the new type which things themselves take when liberated. As, in the sun, objects paint their images on the retina of the eye, so they, sharing the aspiration of the whole universe, tend to paint a far more delicate copy of their essence in his mind. Like the metamorphosis of things into higher organic forms, is their change into melodies. Over everything stands its dæmon, or soul, and, as the form of the thing is reflected by the eye, so the soul of the thing is reflected by a melody. The sea, the mountain-ridge, Niagara, and every flower-bed, pre-exist, or super-exist, in pre-cantations, which sail like odors in the air, and when any man goes by with an ear sufficiently fine, he overhears them, and endeavors to write down the notes, without diluting or depraving them. And herein is the legitimation of criticism, in the mind's faith, that the poems are a corrupt version of some text in nature, with which they ought to be made to tally. A rhyme in one of our sonnets should not be less pleasing than the iterated nodes of a sea-shell, or the resembling difference of a group of flowers. The pairing of the birds is an idyl, not tedious as our idyls are; a tempest is a rough ode, without falsehood or rant: a summer, with its harvest sown, reaped, and stored, is an epic song, subordinating how many admirably executed parts. Why should not the symmetry and truth that modulate these, glide into our spirits, and we participate the invention of nature?

This insight, which expresses itself by what is called Imagination, is a very high sort of seeing, which does not come by study, but by the intellect being where and what it sees, by sharing the path, or circuit of things through forms, and so making them translucid to others. The path of things is silent. Will they suffer a speaker to go with them? A spy they will not suffer; a lover, a poet, is the transcendency of their own nature,—him they will suffer. The condition of true naming, on the poet's part, is the resigning himself to the divine *aura* which breathes through forms, and accompanying that.

It is a secret which every intellectual man quickly learns, that, beyond the energy of his possessed and conscious intellect, he is capable of a new energy (as of an intellect doubled on itself), by abandonment to the nature of things; that, beside his privacy of power as an individual man, there is a great public power, on which he can draw, by unlocking, at all risks, his human doors, and suffering the ethereal tides to roll and circulate through him: then he is caught up into the life of the Universe, his speech is thunder, his thought is law, and his words are universally intelligible as the plants and animals. The poet knows that he speaks adequately, then, only when he speaks somewhat wildly, or, 'with the flower of the mind;' not with the intellect, used as an organ, but with the intellect released from all service, and suffered to take its direction from its celestial life; or, as the ancients were wont to express themselves, not with intellect alone, but with the intellect inebriated by nectar. As the traveller who has lost his way, throws his reins on his horse's neck, and trusts to the instinct of the animal to find his road, so must we do with the divine animal who carries us through this world. For if in any manner we can stimulate this instinct, new passages are opened for us into nature, the mind flows into and through things hardest and highest, and the metamorphosis is possible.

This is the reason why bards love wine, mead, narcotics, coffee, tea, opium, the fumes of sandal-wood and tobacco, or whatever other species of animal exhilaration. All men avail themselves of such means as they can, to add this extraordinary power to their normal powers; and to this end they prize conversation, music, pictures, sculpture, dancing, theatres, travelling, war, mobs, fires, gaming, politics, or love, or science, or animal intoxication, which are several coarser or finer *quasi*-mechanical substitutes for the true nectar, which is the ravishment of the intellect by coming nearer to the fact. These are auxiliaries to the centrifugal tendency of a man, to his passage out into free space, and they help him to escape the custody of that body in which he is pent up, and of that jail-yard of individual relations in which he is enclosed. Hence a great number of such as were professionally expressors of Beauty, as painters, poets, musicians, and actors, have been more than others wont to lead a life of pleasure and indulgence; all but the few who received the true nectar; and, as it was a spurious mode of attaining freedom, as it was an emancipation not into the heavens, but into the freedom of baser places, they were punished for that advantage they won, by a dissipation and deterioration. But never can any advantage be taken of nature by a trick. The spirit of the world, the great calm presence of the creator, comes not forth to the sorceries of opium or of wine. The sublime vision comes to the pure and simple soul in a clean and chaste body. That is not an inspiration which we owe to narcotics, but some counterfeit excitement and fury. Milton says, that the lyric poet may drink wine and live generously, but the epic poet, he who shall sing of the gods, and their descent unto men, must drink water out of a wooden bowl.° For poetry is not 'Devil's wine,' but God's wine. It is with this as it is with toys. We fill the hands and nurseries of our children with all manner of dolls, drums, and horses, withdrawing their eyes from the plain face and sufficing objects of nature, the sun, and moon, the animals, the water, and stones, which should be their toys. So the poet's habit of living should be set on a key so low and plain, that the common influences should delight him. His cheerfulness should be the gift of the sunlight; the air should suffice for his inspiration, and he should be tipsy with water. That spirit which suffices quiet hearts, which seems to come forth to such from every dry knoll of sere grass, from every pine-stump, and half-imbedded stone, on which the dull March sun shines, comes forth to the poor and hungry, and such as are of simple taste. If thou fill thy brain with Boston and New York, with fashion and covetousness, and wilt stimulate thy jaded senses with wine and French coffee, thou shalt find no radiance of wisdom in the lonely waste of the pine-woods.

If the imagination intoxicates the poet, it is not inactive in other men. The metamorphosis excites in the beholder an emotion of joy. The use of symbols has a certain power of emancipation and exhilaration for all men. We seem to be touched by a wand, which makes us dance and run about happily, like children. We are like persons who come out of a cave or cellar into the open air. This is the effect on us of tropes, fables, oracles, and all poetic forms. Poets are thus liberating gods. Men have really got a new sense, and found within their world, another world, or nest of worlds; for, the metamorphosis once seen, we divine that it does not stop. I will not now consider how much this makes the charm of algebra and the mathematics, which also have their tropes, but it is felt in every definition; as, when Aristotle defines *space* to be an immovable vessel, in which things are contained;—or, when Plato defines a *line* to be a flowing point; or, *figure* to be a bound of solid; and many the like. What a joyful sense of freedom we have, when Vitruvius° announces the old opinion of artists, that no architect can build any house well, who does not know something of anatomy. When Socrates, in Charmides,° tells us that the soul is cured of its maladies by certain incantations, and that these incantations are beautiful reasons, from which temperance is generated in souls; when Plato calls the world an animal; and Timæus affirms that the plants also are animals; or affirms a man to be a heavenly tree, growing with his root, which is his head, upward; and, as George Chapman, following him, writes,—

> 'So in our tree of man, whose nervie root
> Springs in his top;'°

when Orpheus speaks of hoariness as 'that white flower which marks extreme old age;' when Proclus calls the universe the statue of the intellect; when Chaucer, in his praise° of 'Gentilesse,' compares good blood in mean condition to fire, which, though carried to the darkest house betwixt this and the mount of Caucasus, will yet hold its natural office, and burn as bright as if twenty thousand men did it behold; when John saw,° in the apocalypse, the ruin of the world through evil, and the stars fall from heaven, as the figtree casteth her untimely fruit; when Æsop reports the whole catalogue of common daily relations through the masquerade of birds and beasts;—we take the cheerful hint of the immortality of our essence, and its versatile habit and escapes, as when the gypsies say, 'it is in vain to hang them, they cannot die.'

The poets are thus liberating gods. The ancient British bards had for the title of their order, 'Those who are free throughout the world.' They are free, and they make free. An imaginative book renders us much more service at first, by stimulating us through its tropes, than afterward, when we arrive at the precise sense of the author. I think nothing is of any value in books, excepting the transcendental and extraordinary. If a man is inflamed and carried away by his thought, to that degree that he forgets the authors and the public, and heeds only this one dream, which holds him like an insanity, let me read his paper, and you may have all the arguments and histories and criticism. All the value which attaches to Pythagoras, Paracelsus, Cornelius Agrippa, Cardan, Kepler, Swedenborg, Schelling, Oken,° or any other who introduces questionable facts into his cosmogony, as angels, devils, magic, astrology, palmistry, mesmerism, and so on, is the certificate we have of departure from routine, and that here is a new witness. That also is the best success in conversation, the magic of liberty, which puts the world, like a ball, in our hands. How cheap even the liberty then seems; how mean to study, when an emotion communicates to the intellect the power to sap and upheave nature: how great the perspective! nations, times, systems, enter and disappear, like threads in tapestry of large figure and many colors; dream delivers us to dream, and, while the drunkenness lasts, we will sell our bed, our philosophy, our religion, in our opulence.

There is good reason why we should prize this liberation. The fate of the poor shepherd, who, blinded and lost in the snow-storm, perishes in a drift within a few feet of his cottage door, is an emblem of the state of man. On the brink of the waters of life and truth, we are miserably dying. The inaccessibleness of every thought but that we are in, is wonderful. What if you come near to it,—you are as remote, when you are nearest, as when you are farthest. Every thought is also a prison; every heaven is also a prison. Therefore we love the poet, the inventor, who in any form, whether in an ode, or in an action, or in looks and behavior, has yielded us a new thought. He unlocks our chains, and admits us to a new scene.

This emancipation is dear to all men, and the power to impart it, as it must come from greater depth and scope of thought, is a measure of intellect. Therefore all books of the imagination endure, all which ascend to that truth, that the writer sees nature beneath him, and uses it as his exponent. Every verse or sentence, possessing this virtue, will take care of its own immortality. The religions of the world are the ejaculations of a few imaginative men.

But the quality of the imagination is to flow, and not to freeze. The poet did not stop at the color, or the form, but read their meaning; neither may he rest in this meaning, but he makes the same objects exponents of his new thought. Here is the difference betwixt the poet and the mystic, that the last nails a symbol to one sense, which was a true sense for a moment, but soon becomes old and false. For all symbols are fluxional; all language is vehicular and transitive, and is good, as ferries and horses are, for conveyance, not as farms and houses are, for homestead. Mysticism consists in the mistake of an accidental and individual symbol for an universal one. The morning-redness happens to be the favorite meteor to the eyes of Jacob Behmen,° and comes to stand to him for truth and faith; and he believes should stand for the same realities to every reader. But the first reader prefers as naturally the symbol of a mother and child, or a gardener and his bulb, or a jeweller polishing a gem. Either of these, or of a myriad more, are equally good to the person to whom they are significant. Only they must be held lightly, and be very willingly translated into the equivalent terms which others use. And the mystic must be steadily told,—All that you say is just as true without the tedious use of that symbol as with it. Let us have a little algebra, instead of this trite rhetoric,—universal signs, instead of these village symbols,—and we shall both be gainers. The history of hierarchies seems to show, that all religious error consisted in making the symbol too stark and solid, and, at last, nothing but an excess of the organ of language.

Swedenborg, of all men in the recent ages, stands eminently for the translator of nature into thought. I do not know the man in history to whom things stood so uniformly for words. Before him the metamorphosis continually plays. Everything on which his eye rests, obeys the impulses of moral nature. The figs become grapes whilst he eats them. When some of his angels affirmed a truth, the laurel twig which they held blossomed in their hands. The noise which, at a distance, appeared like gnashing and thumping, on coming nearer was found to be the voice of disputants. The men, in one of his visions, seen in heavenly light, appeared like dragons, and seemed in darkness: but, to each other, they appeared as men, and, when the light from heaven shone into their cabin, they complained of the darkness, and were compelled to shut the window that they might see.

There was this perception in him, which makes the poet or seer, an object of awe and terror, namely, that the same man, or society of men, may wear one aspect to themselves and their companions, and a different aspect to higher intelligences. Certain priests, whom he describes as conversing very learnedly together, appeared to the children, who were at some distance, like dead horses: and many the like misappearances. And instantly the mind inquires, whether these fishes under the bridge, yonder oxen in the pasture, those dogs in the yard, are immutably fishes, oxen, and dogs, or only so appear to me, and perchance to themselves appear upright men; and whether I appear as a man to all eyes. The Bramins and Pythagoras propounded the same question, and if any poet has witnessed the transformation, he doubtless found it in harmony with various experiences. We have all seen changes as considerable in wheat and caterpillars. He is the poet, and shall draw us with love and terror, who sees, through the flowing vest, the firm nature, and can declare it.

I look in vain for the poet whom I describe. We do not, with sufficient plainness, or sufficient profoundness, address ourselves to life, nor dare we chaunt our own times and social circumstance. If we filled the day with bravery, we should not shrink from celebrating it. Time and nature yield us many gifts, but not yet the timely man, the new religion, the reconciler, whom all things await. Dante's praise is, that he dared to write his autobiography in colossal cipher, or into universality. We have yet had no genius in America, with tyrannous eye, which knew the value of our incomparable materials, and saw, in the barbarism and materialism of the times, another carnival of the same gods whose picture he so much admires in Homer; then in the middle age; then in Calvinism. Banks and tariffs, the newspaper and caucus, methodism and unitarianism, are flat and dull to dull people, but rest on the same foundations of wonder as the town of Troy, and the temple of Delphos, and are as swiftly passing away. Our logrolling, our stumps and their politics, our fisheries, our Negroes, and Indians, our boasts, and our repudiations, the wrath of rogues, and the pusillanimity of honest men, the northern trade, the southern planting, the western clearing,

Oregon, and Texas, are yet unsung. Yet America is a poem in our eyes; its ample geography dazzles the imagination, and it will not wait long for metres. If I have not found that excellent combination of gifts in my countrymen which I seek, neither could I aid myself to fix the idea of the poet by reading now and then in Chalmers's collection° of five centuries of English poets. These are wits, more than poets, though there have been poets among them. But when we adhere to the ideal of the poet, we have our difficulties even with Milton and Homer. Milton is too literary, and Homer too literal and historical.

But I am not wise enough for a national criticism, and must use the old largeness a little longer, to discharge my errand from the muse to the poet concerning his art.

Art is the path of the creator to his work. The paths, or methods, are ideal and eternal, though few men ever see them, not the artist himself for years, or for a lifetime, unless he come into the conditions. The painter, the sculptor, the composer, the epic rhapsodist, the orator, all partake one desire, namely, to express themselves symmetrically and abundantly, not dwarfishly and fragmentarily. They found or put themselves in certain conditions, as, the painter and sculptor before some impressive human figures; the orator, into the assembly of the people; and the others, in such scenes as each has found exciting to his intellect; and each presently feels the new desire. He hears a voice, he sees a beckoning. Then he is apprised, with wonder, what herds of dæmons hem him in. He can no more rest; he says, with the old painter, 'By God, it is in me, and must go forth of me.' He pursues a beauty, half seen, which flies before him. The poet pours out verses in every solitude. Most of the things he says are conventional, no doubt; but by and by he says something which is original and beautiful. That charms him. He would say nothing else but such things. In our way of talking, we say, 'That is yours, this is mine;' but the poet knows well that it is not his; that it is as strange and beautiful to him as to you; he would fain hear the like eloquence at length. Once having tasted this immortal ichor, he cannot have enough of it, and, as an admirable creative power exists in these intellections, it is of the last importance that these things get spoken. What a little of all we know is said! What drops of all the sea of our science are baled up! and by what accident it is that these are exposed, when so many secrets sleep in nature! Hence the necessity of speech and song; hence these throbs and heartbeatings in the orator, at the door of the assembly, to the end, namely, that thought may be ejaculated as Logos, or Word.

Doubt not, O poet, but persist. Say, 'It is in me, and shall out.' Stand there, baulked and dumb, stuttering and stammering, hissed and hooted, stand and strive, until, at last, rage draw out of thee that *dream*-power which every night shows thee is thine own; a power transcending all limit and privacy, and by virtue of which a man is the conductor of the whole river of electricity. Nothing walks, or creeps, or grows, or exists, which must not in turn arise and walk before him as exponent of his meaning. Comes he to that power, his genius is no longer exhaustible. All the creatures, by pairs and by tribes, pour into his mind as into a Noah's ark, to come forth again to people a new world. This is like the stock of air for our respiration, or for the combustion of our fireplace, not a measure of gallons, but the entire atmosphere if wanted. And therefore the rich poets, as Homer, Chaucer, Shakspeare, and Raphael, have obviously no limits to their works, except the limits of their lifetime, and resemble a mirror carried through the street, ready to render an image of every created thing.

O poet! a new nobility is conferred in groves and pastures, and not in castles, or by the sword-blade, any longer. The conditions are hard, but equal. Thou shalt leave the world, and know the muse only. Thou shalt not know any longer the times, customs, graces, politics, or opinions of men, but shalt take all from the muse. For the time of towns is tolled from the world by funereal chimes, but in nature the universal hours are counted by succeeding tribes of animals and plants, and by growth of joy on joy. God wills also that thou abdicate a manifold and duplex life, and that thou be content that others speak for thee. Others shall be thy gentlemen, and shall represent all courtesy and worldly life for thee; others shall do the great and resounding actions also. Thou shalt lie close hid with nature, and canst not be afforded to the Capitol or the Exchange. The world is full of renunciations and apprenticeships, and this is thine: thou must pass for a fool and a churl for a long season. This is the screen and sheath in which Pan has protected his well-beloved flower, and thou shalt be known only to thine own, and they shall console thee with tenderest love. And thou shalt not be able to rehearse the names of thy friends in thy verse, for an old shame before the holy ideal. And this is the reward: that the ideal shall be real to thee, and the impressions of the actual world shall fall like summer rain, copious, but not troublesome, to thy invulnerable essence. Thou shalt have the whole land for thy park and manor, the sea for thy bath and navigation, without tax and without envy; the woods and the rivers thou shalt own; and thou shalt possess that wherein others are only tenants and boarders. Thou true land-lord! sea-lord! air-lord! Wherever snow falls, or water flows, or birds fly, wherever day and night meet in twi-

light, wherever the blue heaven is hung by clouds, or sown with stars,
wherever are forms with transparent boundaries, wherever are outlets
into celestial space, wherever is danger, and awe, and love, there is
Beauty, plenteous as rain, shed for thee, and though thou shouldest
walk the world over, thou shalt not be able to find a condition inoppor-
tune or ignoble.

EXPERIENCE

The lords of life, the lords of life,—
I saw them pass,
In their own guise,
Like and unlike,
Portly and grim,
Use and Surprise,
Surface and Dream,
Succession swift, and spectral Wrong,
Temperament without a tongue,
And the inventor of the game
Omnipresent without name;—
Some to see, some to be guessed,
They marched from east to west:
Little man, least of all,
Among the legs of his guardians tall,
Walked about with puzzled look:—
Him by the hand dear nature took;
Dearest nature, strong and kind,
Whispered, 'Darling, never mind!
Tomorrow they will wear another face,
The founder thou! these are thy race!'

WHERE do we find ourselves? In a series of which we do not know the extremes, and believe that it has none. We wake and find ourselves on a stair; there are stairs below us, which we seem to have ascended; there are stairs above us, many a one, which go upward and out of sight. But the Genius which, according to the old belief, stands at the door by which we enter, and gives us the lethe to drink,° that we may tell no tales, mixed the cup too strongly, and we cannot shake off the lethargy now at noonday. Sleep lingers all our lifetime about our eyes, as night hovers all day in the boughs of the fir-tree. All things swim and glitter. Our life is not so much threatened as our perception. Ghostlike we glide through nature, and should not know our place again. Did our birth fall in some fit of indigence and frugality in nature, that she was so sparing of her fire and so liberal of her earth, that it appears to us that we lack the affirmative principle, and though we have health and reason, yet we have no superfluity of spirit for new creation? We have enough to live and bring the year about, but not an ounce to impart or to invest. Ah that our Genius were a little more of a genius! We are like

millers on the lower levels of a stream, when the factories above them
have exhausted the water. We too fancy that the upper people must
have raised their dams.

If any of us knew what we were doing, or where we are going, then
when we think we best know! We do not know today whether we are
busy or idle. In times when we thought ourselves indolent, we have
afterwards discovered, that much was accomplished, and much was
begun in us. All our days are so unprofitable while they pass, that 'tis
wonderful where or when we ever got anything of this which we call
wisdom, poetry, virtue. We never got it on any dated calendar day.
Some heavenly days must have been intercalated somewhere, like those
that Hermes won° with dice of the Moon, that Osiris might be born. It
is said, all martyrdoms looked mean when they were suffered. Every
ship is a romantic object, except that we sail in. Embark, and the
romance quits our vessel, and hangs on every other sail in the horizon.
Our life looks trivial, and we shun to record it. Men seem to have
learned of the horizon the art of perpetual retreating and reference.
'Yonder uplands are rich pasturage, and my neighbor has fertile
meadow, but my field,' says the querulous farmer, 'only holds the world
together.' I quote another man's saying; unluckily, that other withdraws
himself in the same way, and quotes me. 'Tis the trick of nature thus to
degrade today; a good deal of buzz, and somewhere a result slipped
magically in. Every roof is agreeable to the eye, until it is lifted; then
we find tragedy and moaning women, and hard-eyed husbands, and
deluges of lethe, and the men ask, 'What's the news?' as if the old were
so bad. How many individuals can we count in society? how many
actions? how many opinions? So much of our time is preparation, so
much is routine, and so much retrospect, that the pith of each man's
genius contracts itself to a very few hours. The history of literature—
take the net result of Tiraboschi, Warton, or Schlegel,°—is a sum of
very few ideas, and of very few original tales,—all the rest being vari-
ation of these. So in this great society wide lying around us, a critical
analysis would find very few spontaneous actions. It is almost all custom
and gross sense. There are even few opinions, and these seem organic
in the speakers, and do not disturb the universal necessity.

What opium is instilled into all disaster! It shows formidable as we
approach it, but there is at last no rough rasping friction, but the most
slippery sliding surfaces. We fall soft on a thought. *Ate Dea* is gentle,

> 'Over men's heads walking aloft,
> With tender feet treading so soft.'°

People give and bemoan themselves, but it is not half so bad with them as they say. There are moods in which we court suffering, in the hope that here, at least, we shall find reality, sharp peaks and edges of truth. But it turns out to be scene-painting and counterfeit. The only thing grief has taught me, is to know how shallow it is. That, like all the rest, plays about the surface, and never introduces me into the reality, for contact with which, we would even pay the costly price of sons and lovers. Was it Boscovich° who found out that bodies never come in contact? Well, souls never touch their objects. An innavigable sea washes with silent waves between us and the things we aim at and converse with. Grief too will make us idealists. In the death of my son, now more than two years ago, I seem to have lost a beautiful estate,—no more. I cannot get it nearer to me. If tomorrow I should be informed of the bankruptcy of my principal debtors, the loss of my property would be a great inconvenience to me, perhaps, for many years; but it would leave me as it found me,—neither better nor worse. So is it with this calamity: it does not touch me: some thing which I fancied was a part of me, which could not be torn away without tearing me, nor enlarged without enriching me, falls off from me, and leaves no scar. It was caducous. I grieve that grief can teach me nothing, nor carry me one step into real nature. The Indian who was laid under a curse, that the wind should not blow on him, nor water flow to him, nor fire burn him, is a type of us all.° The dearest events are summer-rain, and we the Para coats° that shed every drop. Nothing is left us now but death. We look to that with a grim satisfaction, saying, there at least is reality that will not dodge us.

I take this evanescence and lubricity of all objects, which lets them slip through our fingers then when we clutch hardest, to be the most unhandsome part of our condition. Nature does not like to be observed, and likes that we should be her fools and playmates. We may have the sphere for our cricketball, but not a berry for our philosophy. Direct strokes she never gave us power to make; all our blows glance, all our hits are accidents. Our relations to each other are oblique and casual.

Dream delivers us to dream, and there is no end to illusion. Life is a train of moods like a string of beads, and, as we pass through them, they prove to be many-colored lenses which paint the world their own hue, and each shows only what lies in its focus. From the mountain you see the mountain. We animate what we can, and we see only what we animate. Nature and books belong to the eyes that see them. It depends on the mood of the man, whether he shall see the sunset or the fine poem. There are always sunsets, and there is always genius; but only a few

hours so serene that we can relish nature or criticism. The more or less
depends on structure or temperament. Temperament is the iron wire on
which the beads are strung. Of what use is fortune or talent to a cold and
defective nature? Who cares what sensibility or discrimination a man has
at some time shown, if he falls asleep in his chair? or if he laugh and
giggle? or if he apologize? or is affected with egotism? or thinks of his dollar? or cannot go by food? or has gotten a child in his boyhood? Of what
use is genius, if the organ is too convex or too concave, and cannot find a
focal distance within the actual horizon of human life? Of what use, if the
brain is too cold or too hot, and the man does not care enough for
results, to stimulate him to experiment, and hold him up in it? or if the
web is too finely woven, too irritable by pleasure and pain, so that life
stagnates from too much reception, without due outlet? Of what use to
make heroic vows of amendment, if the same old lawbreaker is to keep
them? What cheer can the religious sentiment yield, when that is suspected to be secretly dependent on the seasons of the year, and the state
of the blood? I knew a witty physician who found theology in the biliary
duct, and used to affirm that if there was disease in the liver, the man
became a Calvinist, and if that organ was sound, he became a Unitarian.
Very mortifying is the reluctant experience that some unfriendly excess
or imbecility neutralizes the promise of genius. We see young men who
owe us a new world, so readily and lavishly they promise, but they never
acquit the debt; they die young and dodge the account: or if they live,
they lose themselves in the crowd.

Temperament also enters fully into the system of illusions, and shuts
us in a prison of glass which we cannot see. There is an optical illusion
about every person we meet. In truth, they are all creatures of given
temperament, which will appear in a given character, whose boundaries
they will never pass: but we look at them, they seem alive, and we presume there is impulse in them. In the moment it seems impulse; in the
year, in the lifetime, it turns out to be a certain uniform tune which the
revolving barrel of the music-box must play. Men resist the conclusion
in the morning, but adopt it as the evening wears on, that temper prevails over everything of time, place, and condition, and is inconsumable
in the flames of religion. Some modifications the moral sentiment avails
to impose, but the individual texture holds its dominion, if not to bias
the moral judgments, yet to fix the measure of activity and of enjoyment.

I thus express the law as it is read from the platform of ordinary life,
but must not leave it without noticing the capital exception. For temperament is a power which no man willingly hears any one praise but

himself. On the platform of physics, we cannot resist the contracting influences of so-called science. Temperament puts all divinity to rout. I know the mental proclivity of physicians. I hear the chuckle of the phrenologists. Theoretic kidnappers and slave-drivers, they esteem each man the victim of another, who winds him round his finger by knowing the law of his being, and by such cheap signboards as the color of his beard, or the slope of his occiput, reads the inventory of his fortunes and character. The grossest ignorance does not disgust like this impudent knowingness. The physicians say, they are not materialists; but they are:—Spirit is matter reduced to an extreme thinness: O *so* thin!—But the definition of *spiritual* should be, *that which is its own evidence.* What notions do they attach to love! what to religion! One would not willingly pronounce these words in their hearing, and give them the occasion to profane them. I saw a gracious gentleman who adapts his conversation to the form of the head of the man he talks with! I had fancied that the value of life lay in its inscrutable possibilities; in the fact that I never know, in addressing myself to a new individual, what may befall me. I carry the keys of my castle in my hand, ready to throw them at the feet of my lord, whenever and in what disguise soever he shall appear. I know he is in the neighborhood hidden among vagabonds. Shall I preclude my future, by taking a high seat, and kindly adapting my conversation to the shape of heads? When I come to that, the doctors shall buy me for a cent.——'But, sir, medical history; the report to the Institute; the proven facts!'—I distrust the facts and the inferences. Temperament is the veto or limitation-power in the constitution, very justly applied to restrain an opposite excess in the constitution, but absurdly offered as a bar to original equity. When virtue is in presence, all subordinate powers sleep. On its own level, or in view of nature, temperament is final. I see not, if one be once caught in this trap of so-called sciences, any escape for the man from the links of the chain of physical necessity. Given such an embryo, such a history must follow. On this platform, one lives in a sty of sensualism, and would soon come to suicide. But it is impossible that the creative power should exclude itself. Into every intelligence there is a door which is never closed, through which the creator passes. The intellect, seeker of absolute truth, or the heart, lover of absolute good, intervenes for our succor, and at one whisper of these high powers, we awake from ineffectual struggles with this nightmare. We hurl it into its own hell, and cannot again contract ourselves to so base a state.

The secret of the illusoriness is in the necessity of a succession of

moods or objects. Gladly we would anchor, but the anchorage is quicksand. This onward trick of nature is too strong for us: *Pero si muove*.°
When, at night, I look at the moon and stars, I seem stationary, and they to hurry. Our love of the real draws us to permanence, but health of body consists in circulation, and sanity of mind in variety or facility of association. We need change of objects. Dedication to one thought is quickly odious. We house with the insane, and must humor them; then conversation dies out. Once I took such delight in Montaigne, that I thought I should not need any other book; before that, in Shakspeare; then in Plutarch; then in Plotinus;° at one time in Bacon; afterwards in Goethe; even in Bettine;° but now I turn the pages of either of them languidly, whilst I still cherish their genius. So with pictures; each will bear an emphasis of attention once, which it cannot retain, though we fain would continue to be pleased in that manner. How strongly I have felt of pictures, that when you have seen one well, you must take your leave of it; you shall never see it again. I have had good lessons from pictures, which I have since seen without emotion or remark. A deduction must be made from the opinion, which even the wise express of a new book or occurrence. Their opinion gives me tidings of their mood, and some vague guess at the new fact, but is nowise to be trusted as the lasting relation between that intellect and that thing. The child asks, 'Mamma, why don't I like the story as well as when you told it me yesterday?' Alas, child, it is even so with the oldest cherubim of knowledge. But will it answer thy question to say, Because thou wert born to a whole, and this story is a particular? The reason of the pain this discovery causes us (and we make it late in respect to works of art and intellect), is the plaint of tragedy which murmurs from it in regard to persons, to friendship and love.

That immobility and absence of elasticity which we find in the arts, we find with more pain in the artist. There is no power of expansion in men. Our friends early appear to us as representatives of certain ideas, which they never pass or exceed. They stand on the brink of the ocean of thought and power, but they never take the single step that would bring them there. A man is like a bit of Labrador spar,° which has no lustre as you turn it in your hand, until you come to a particular angle; then it shows deep and beautiful colors. There is no adaptation or universal applicability in men, but each has his special talent, and the mastery of successful men consists in adroitly keeping themselves where and when that turn shall be oftenest to be practised. We do what we must, and call it by the best names we can, and would fain have the praise of having intended the result which ensues. I cannot recall any form of man who is not superfluous sometimes. But is not this pitiful? Life is not worth the taking, to do tricks in.

Of course, it needs the whole society, to give the symmetry we seek. The parti-colored wheel must revolve very fast to appear white. Something is learned too by conversing with so much folly and defect. In fine, whoever loses, we are always of the gaining party. Divinity is behind our failures and follies also. The plays of children are nonsense, but very educative nonsense. So it is with the largest and solemnest things, with commerce, government, church, marriage, and so with the history of every man's bread, and the ways by which he is to come by it. Like a bird which alights nowhere, but hops perpetually from bough to bough, is the Power which abides in no man and in no woman, but for a moment speaks from this one, and for another moment from that one.

*   *   *

But what help from these fineries or pedantries? What help from thought? Life is not dialectics. We, I think, in these times, have had lessons enough of the futility of criticism. Our young people have thought and written much on labor and reform, and for all that they have written, neither the world nor themselves have got on a step. Intellectual tasting of life will not supersede muscular activity. If a man should consider the nicety of the passage of a piece of bread down his throat, he would starve. At Education-Farm,° the noblest theory of life sat on the noblest figures of young men and maidens, quite powerless and melancholy. It would not rake or pitch a ton of hay; it would not rub down a horse; and the men and maidens it left pale and hungry. A political orator wittily compared our party promises to western roads, which opened stately enough, with planted trees on either side, to tempt the traveller, but soon became narrow and narrower, and ended in a squirrel-track, and ran up a tree. So does culture with us; it ends in head-ache. Unspeakably sad and barren does life look to those, who a few months ago were dazzled with the splendor of the promise of the times. 'There is now no longer any right course of action, nor any self-devotion left among the Iranis.'° Objections and criticism we have had our fill of. There are objections to every course of life and action, and the practical wisdom infers an indifferency, from the omnipresence of objection. The whole frame of things preaches indifference. Do not craze yourself with thinking, but go about your business anywhere. Life is not intellectual or critical, but sturdy. Its chief good is for well-mixed people who can enjoy what they find, without question. Nature hates peeping, and our mothers speak her very sense when they say, 'Children, eat your victuals, and say no more of it.' To fill the hour,—that is happiness; to fill the hour, and leave no crevice for a repentance or an approval. We live amid surfaces, and the true art of life is to skate well on them. Under the oldest mouldiest conventions, a man of native force prospers just as well as in the newest world, and that by skill of handling and treatment. He can take hold anywhere. Life itself is a mixture of power and form, and will not bear the least excess of either. To finish the moment, to find the journey's end in every step of the road, to live the greatest number of good hours, is wisdom. It is not the part of men, but of fanatics, or of mathematicians, if you will, to say, that, the shortness of life considered, it is not worth caring whether for so short a duration we were sprawling in want, or sitting high. Since our office is with moments, let us husband them. Five minutes of today are worth as much to me, as five minutes in the next millennium. Let us be poised, and wise, and our own, today. Let us treat the men and women well: treat them as if they were real: perhaps they are. Men live in their fancy, like drunkards whose hands are too soft and tremulous for successful labor. It is a tempest of fancies, and the only ballast I know, is a respect to the present hour. Without any shadow of doubt, amidst this vertigo of shows and politics, I settle myself ever the firmer in the creed, that we should not postpone and refer and wish, but do broad justice where we are, by whomsoever we deal with, accepting our actual companions and circumstances, however humble or odious, as the mystic officials to whom the universe has delegated its whole pleasure for us. If these are mean and malignant, their contentment, which is the last victory of justice, is a more satisfying echo to the heart, than the voice of poets and the casual sympathy of admirable persons. I think that however a thoughtful man may suffer from the defects and absurdities of his company, he cannot without affectation deny to any set of men and women, a sensibility to extraordinary merit. The coarse and frivolous have an instinct of superiority, if they have not a sympathy, and honor it in their blind capricious way with sincere homage.

The fine young people despise life, but in me, and in such as with me are free from dyspepsia, and to whom a day is a sound and solid good, it is a great excess of politeness to look scornful and to cry for company. I am grown by sympathy a little eager and sentimental, but leave me alone, and I should relish every hour and what it brought me, the potluck of the day, as heartily as the oldest gossip in the bar-room. I am thankful for small mercies. I compared notes with one of my friends who expects everything of the universe, and is disappointed when anything is less than the best, and I found that I begin at the other extreme, expecting nothing, and am always full of thanks for moderate goods. I accept the clangor and jangle of contrary tendencies. I find my account in sots and bores also. They give a reality to the circumjacent picture, which such a vanishing meteorous appearance can ill spare. In the morning I awake, and find the old world, wife, babes, and mother, Concord and Boston, the dear old spiritual world, and even the dear old devil not far off. If we will take the good we find, asking no questions, we shall have heaping measures. The great gifts are not got by analysis. Everything good is on the highway. The middle region of our being is the temperate zone. We may climb into the thin and cold realm of pure geometry and lifeless science, or sink into that of sensation. Between these extremes is the equator of life, of thought, of spirit, of poetry,—a narrow belt. Moreover, in popular experience, everything good is on the highway. A collector peeps into all the picture-shops of Europe, for a landscape of Poussin, a crayon-sketch of Salvator; but the Transfiguration, the Last Judgment, the Communion of St. Jerome,° and what are as transcendent as these, are on the walls of the Vatican, the Uffizii, or the Louvre, where every footman may see them; to say nothing of nature's pictures in every street, of sunsets and sunrises every day, and the sculpture of the human body never absent. A collector recently bought at public auction, in London, for one hundred and fifty-seven guineas, an autograph of Shakspeare: but for nothing a school-boy can read Hamlet, and can detect secrets of highest concernment yet unpublished therein. I think I will never read any but the commonest books,—the Bible, Homer, Dante, Shakspeare, and Milton. Then we are impatient of so public a life and planet, and run hither and thither for nooks and secrets. The imagination delights in the wood-craft of Indians, trappers, and bee-hunters. We fancy that we are strangers, and not so intimately domesticated in the planet as the wild man, and the wild beast and bird. But the exclusion reaches them also; reaches the climbing, flying, gliding, feathered and four-footed man. Fox and woodchuck, hawk and snipe, and bittern, when nearly seen, have no more root in the deep world than man, and are just such superficial tenants of the globe. Then the new molecular philosophy shows astronomical interspaces betwixt atom and atom, shows that the world is all outside: it has no inside.

The mid-world is best. Nature, as we know her, is no saint. The lights of the church, the ascetics, Gentoos and Grahamites,° she does not distinguish by any favor. She comes eating and drinking and sinning. Her darlings, the great, the strong, the beautiful, are not children of our law, do not come out of the Sunday School, nor weigh their food, nor punctually keep the commandments. If we will be strong with her strength, we must not harbor such disconsolate consciences, borrowed too from the consciences of other nations. We must set up the strong present tense against all the rumors of wrath, past or to come. So many things are unsettled which it is of the first importance to settle,—and, pending their settlement, we will do as we do. Whilst the debate goes forward on the equity of commerce, and will not be closed for a century or two, New and Old England may keep shop. Law of copyright and international copyright is to be discussed, and, in the interim, we will sell our books for the most we can. Expediency of literature, reason of literature, lawfulness of writing down a thought, is questioned; much is to say on both sides, and, while the fight waxes hot, thou, dearest scholar, stick to thy foolish task, add a line every hour, and between whiles add a line. Right to hold land, right of property, is disputed, and the conventions convene, and before the vote is taken, dig away in your garden, and spend your earnings as a waif or godsend to all serene and beautiful purposes. Life itself is a bubble and a skepticism, and a sleep within a sleep.° Grant it, and as much more as they will,—but thou, God's darling! heed thy private dream: thou wilt not be missed in the scorning and skepticism: there are enough of them: stay there in thy closet, and toil, until the rest are agreed what to do about it. Thy sickness, they say, and thy puny habit, require that thou do this or avoid that, but know that thy life is a flitting state, a tent for a night, and do thou, sick or well, finish that stint. Thou art sick, but shalt not be worse, and the universe, which holds thee dear, shall be the better.

Human life is made up of the two elements, power and form, and the proportion must be invariably kept, if we would have it sweet and sound. Each of these elements in excess makes a mischief as hurtful as its defect. Everything runs to excess: every good quality is noxious, if unmixed, and, to carry the danger to the edge of ruin, nature causes each man's peculiarity to superabound. Here, among the farms, we adduce the scholars as examples of this treachery. They are nature's victims of expression. You who see the artist, the orator, the poet, too near, and find their life no more excellent than that of mechanics or farmers, and themselves victims of partiality, very hollow and haggard, and pronounce them failures,—not heroes, but quacks,—conclude very reasonably, that these arts are not for man, but are disease. Yet nature will not bear you out. Irresistible nature made men such, and makes legions more of such, every day. You love the boy reading in a book, gazing at a drawing, or a cast: yet what are these millions who read and behold, but incipient writers and sculptors? Add a little more of that quality which now reads and sees, and they will seize the pen and chisel. And if one remembers how innocently he began to be an artist, he perceives that nature joined with his enemy. A man is a golden impossibility. The line he must walk is a hair's breadth. The wise through excess of wisdom is made a fool.

How easily, if fate would suffer it, we might keep forever these beautiful limits, and adjust ourselves, once for all, to the perfect calculation of the kingdom of known cause and effect. In the street and in the newspapers, life appears so plain a business, that manly resolution and adherence to the multiplication-table through all weathers, will insure success. But ah! presently comes a day, or is it only a half-hour, with its angel-whispering,—which discomfits the conclusions of nations and of years! Tomorrow again, everything looks real and angular, the habitual standards are reinstated, common sense is as rare as genius,—is the basis of genius, and experience is hands and feet to every enterprise;— and yet, he who should do his business on this understanding, would be quickly bankrupt. Power keeps quite another road than the turnpikes of choice and will, namely, the subterranean and invisible tunnels and channels of life. It is ridiculous that we are diplomatists, and doctors, and considerate people: there are no dupes like these. Life is a series of surprises, and would not be worth taking or keeping, if it were not. God delights to isolate us every day, and hide from us the past and the future. We would look about us, but with grand politeness he draws down before us an impenetrable screen of purest sky, and another behind us of purest sky. 'You will not remember,' he seems to say, 'and you will not expect.' All good conversation, manners, and action, come from a spontaneity which forgets usages, and makes the moment great. Nature hates calculators; her methods are saltatory and impulsive. Man lives by pulses; our organic movements are such; and the chemical and ethereal agents are undulatory and alternate; and the mind goes antagonizing on, and never prospers but by fits. We thrive by casualties. Our chief experiences have been casual. The most attractive class of people are those who are powerful obliquely, and not by the direct stroke: men of genius, but not yet accredited: one gets the cheer of their light, without paying too great a tax. Theirs is the beauty of the bird, or the morning light, and not of art. In the thought of genius there is always a surprise; and the moral sentiment is well called 'the newness,' for it is never other; as new to the oldest intelligence as to the young child,—'the kingdom that cometh without observation.'° In like manner, for practical success, there must not be too much design. A man will not be observed in doing that which he can do best. There is a certain magic about his properest action, which stupefies your powers of observation, so that though it is done before you, you wist not of it. The art of life has a pudency, and will not be exposed. Every man is an impossibility, until he is born; every thing impossible, until we see a success. The ardors of piety agree at last with the coldest skepticism,—that nothing is of us or our works,—that all is of God. Nature will not spare us the smallest leaf of laurel. All writing comes by the grace of God, and all doing and having. I would gladly be moral, and keep due metes and bounds, which I dearly love, and allow the most to the will of man, but I have set my heart on honesty in this chapter, and I can see nothing at last, in success or failure, than more or less of vital force supplied from the Eternal. The results of life are uncalculated and uncalculable. The years teach much which the days never know. The persons who compose our company, converse, and come and go, and design and execute many things, and somewhat comes of it all, but an unlooked for result. The individual is always mistaken. He designed many things, and drew in other persons as coadjutors, quarrelled with some or all, blundered much, and something is done; all are a little advanced, but the individual is always mistaken. It turns out somewhat new, and very unlike what he promised himself.

The ancients, struck with this irreducibleness of the elements of human life to calculation, exalted Chance into a divinity, but that is to stay too long at the spark,—which glitters truly at one point,—but the universe is warm with the latency of the same fire. The miracle of life which will not be expounded, but will remain a miracle, introduces a new element. In the growth of the embryo, Sir Everard Home,° I think, noticed that the evolution was not from one central point, but co-active from three or more points. Life has no memory. That which proceeds in succession might be remembered, but that which is coexistent, or ejaculated from a deeper cause, as yet far from being conscious, knows not its own tendency. So is it with us, now skeptical, or without unity, because immersed in forms and effects all seeming to be of equal yet hostile value, and now religious, whilst in the reception of spiritual law. Bear with these distractions, with this coetaneous growth of the parts: they will one day be *members*, and obey one will. On that one will, on that secret cause, they nail our attention and hope. Life is hereby melted into an expectation or a religion. Underneath the inharmonious and trivial particulars, is a musical perfection, the Ideal journeying always with us, the heaven without rent or seam. Do but observe the mode of our illumination. When I converse with a profound mind, or if at any time being alone I have good thoughts, I do not at once arrive at satisfactions, as when, being thirsty, I drink water, or go to the fire, being cold: no! but I am at first apprised of my vicinity to a new and excellent region of life. By persisting to read or to think, this region gives further sign of itself, as it were in flashes of light, in sudden discoveries of its profound beauty and repose, as if the clouds that covered it parted at intervals, and showed the approaching traveller the inland mountains, with the tranquil eternal meadows spread at their base, whereon flocks graze, and shepherds pipe and dance. But every insight from this realm of thought is felt as initial, and promises a sequel. I do not make it; I arrive there, and behold what was there already. I make! O no! I clap my hands in infantine joy and amazement, before the first opening to me of this august magnificence, old with the love and homage of innumerable ages, young with the life of life, the sunbright Mecca of the desert. And what a future it opens! I feel a new heart beating with the love of the new beauty. I am ready to die out of nature, and be born again into this new yet unapproachable America I have found in the West.

> 'Since neither now nor yesterday began
> These thoughts, which have been ever, nor yet can
> A man be found who their first entrance knew.'°

If I have described life as a flux of moods, I must now add, that there is that in us which changes not, and which ranks all sensations and states of mind. The consciousness in each man is a sliding scale, which identifies him now with the First Cause, and now with the flesh of his body; life above life, in infinite degrees. The sentiment from which it sprung determines the dignity of any deed, and the question ever is, not, what you have done or forborne, but, at whose command you have done or forborne it.

Fortune, Minerva, Muse, Holy Ghost,—these are quaint names, too narrow to cover this unbounded substance. The baffled intellect must still kneel before this cause, which refuses to be named,—ineffable cause, which every fine genius has essayed to represent by some emphatic symbol, as, Thales by water, Anaximenes by air, Anaxagoras by (Νοῦς) thought, Zoroaster° by fire, Jesus and the moderns by love: and the metaphor of each has become a national religion. The Chinese Mencius° has not been the least successful in his generalization. 'I fully understand language,' he said, 'and nourish well my vast-flowing vigor.'—'I beg to ask what you call vast-flowing vigor?'—said his companion. 'The explanation,' replies Mencius, 'is difficult. This vigor is supremely great, and in the highest degree unbending. Nourish it correctly, and do it no injury, and it will fill up the vacancy between heaven and earth. This vigor accords with and assists justice and reason, and leaves no hunger.'—In our more correct writing, we give to this generalization the name of Being, and thereby confess that we have arrived as far as we can go. Suffice it for the joy of the universe, that we have not arrived at a wall, but at interminable oceans. Our life seems not present, so much as prospective; not for the affairs on which it is wasted, but as a hint of this vast-flowing vigor. Most of life seems to be mere advertisement of faculty: information is given us not to sell ourselves cheap; that we are very great. So, in particulars, our greatness is always in a tendency or direction, not in an action. It is for us to believe in the rule, not in the exception. The noble are thus known from the ignoble. So in accepting the leading of the sentiments, it is not what we believe concerning the immortality of the soul, or the like, but *the universal impulse to believe*, that is the material circumstance, and is the principal fact in the history of the globe. Shall we describe this cause as that which works directly? The spirit is not helpless or needful of mediate organs. It has plentiful powers and direct effects. I am explained without explaining, I am felt without acting, and where I am not. Therefore all just persons are satisfied with their own praise. They refuse to explain themselves, and are content that new actions should do them that office. They believe that we communicate without speech, and above speech, and that no right action of ours is quite unaffecting to our friends, at whatever distance; for the influence of action is not to be measured by miles. Why should I fret myself, because a circumstance has occurred, which hinders my presence where I was expected? If I am not at the meeting, my presence where I am, should be as useful to the commonwealth of friendship and wisdom, as would be my presence in that place. I exert the same quality of power in all places. Thus journeys the mighty Ideal before us; it never was known to fall into the rear. No man ever came to an experience which was satiating, but his good is tidings of a better. Onward and onward! In liberated moments, we know that a new picture of life and duty is already possible; the elements already exist in many minds around you, of a doctrine of life which shall transcend any written record we have. The new statement will comprise the skepticisms, as well as the faiths of society, and out of unbeliefs a creed shall be formed. For, skepticisms are not gratuitous or lawless, but are limitations of the affirmative statement, and the new philosophy must take them in, and make affirmations outside of them, just as much as it must include the oldest beliefs.

It is very unhappy, but too late to be helped, the discovery we have made, that we exist. That discovery is called the Fall of Man. Ever afterwards, we suspect our instruments. We have learned that we do not see directly, but mediately, and that we have no means of correcting these colored and distorting lenses which we are, or of computing the amount of their errors. Perhaps these subject-lenses have a creative power; perhaps there are no objects. Once we lived in what we saw; now, the rapaciousness of this new power, which threatens to absorb all things, engages us. Nature, art, persons, letters, religions,—objects, successively tumble in, and God is but one of its ideas. Nature and literature are subjective phenomena; every evil and every good thing is a shadow which we cast. The street is full of humiliations to the proud. As the fop contrived to dress his bailiffs in his livery, and make them wait on his guests at table, so the chagrins which the bad heart gives off as bubbles, at once take form as ladies and gentlemen in the street, shopmen or barkeepers in hotels, and threaten or insult whatever is threatenable and insultable in us. 'Tis the same with our idolatries. People forget that it is the eye which makes the horizon, and the rounding mind's eye which makes this or that man a type or representative of humanity with the name of hero or saint. Jesus the 'providential man,' is a good man on whom many people are agreed that these optical laws shall take effect. By love on one part, and by forbearance to press objection on the other part, it is for a time settled, that we will look at him in the centre of the horizon, and ascribe to him the properties that will attach to any man so seen. But the longest love or aversion has a speedy term. The great and crescive self, rooted in absolute nature, supplants all relative existence, and ruins the kingdom of mortal friendship and love. Marriage (in what is called the spiritual world) is impossible, because of the inequality between every subject and every object. The subject is the receiver of Godhead, and at every comparison must feel his being enhanced by that cryptic might. Though not in energy, yet by presence, this magazine of substance cannot be otherwise than felt: nor can any force of intellect attribute to the object the proper deity which sleeps or wakes forever in every subject. Never can love make consciousness and ascription equal in force. There will be the same gulf between every me and thee, as between the original and the picture. The universe is the bride of the soul. All private sympathy is partial. Two human beings are like globes, which can touch only in a point, and, whilst they remain in contact, all other points of each of the spheres are inert; their turn must also come, and the longer a particular union lasts, the more energy of appetency the parts not in union acquire.

Life will be imaged, but cannot be divided nor doubled. Any invasion of its unity would be chaos. The soul is not twin-born, but the only begotten, and though revealing itself as child in time, child in appearance, is of a fatal and universal power, admitting no co-life. Every day, every act betrays the ill-concealed deity. We believe in ourselves, as we do not believe in others. We permit all things to ourselves, and that which we call sin in others, is experiment for us. It is an instance of our faith in ourselves, that men never speak of crime as lightly as they think: or, every man thinks a latitude safe for himself, which is nowise to be indulged to another. The act looks very differently on the inside, and on the outside; in its quality, and in its consequences. Murder in the murderer is no such ruinous thought as poets and romancers will have it; it does not unsettle him, or fright him from his ordinary notice of trifles: it is an act quite easy to be contemplated, but in its sequel, it turns out to be a horrible jangle and confounding of all relations. Especially the crimes that spring from love, seem right and fair from the actor's point of view, but, when acted, are found destructive of society. No man at last believes that he can be lost, nor that the crime in him is as black as in the felon. Because the intellect qualifies in our own case the moral judgments. For there is no crime to the intellect. That is antinomian or hypernomian, and judges law as well as fact. 'It is worse than a crime, it is a blunder,' said Napoleon, speaking the language of the intellect. To it, the world is a problem in mathematics or the science of quantity, and it leaves out praise and blame, and all weak emotions. All stealing is comparative. If you come to absolutes, pray who does not steal? Saints are sad, because they behold sin, (even when they speculate,) from the point of view of the conscience, and not of the intellect; a confusion of thought. Sin seen from the thought, is a diminution or *less*: seen from the conscience or will, it is pravity or *bad*. The intellect names it shade, absence of light, and no essence. The conscience must feel it as essence, essential evil. This it is not: it has an objective existence, but no subjective.

Thus inevitably does the universe wear our color, and every object fall successively into the subject itself. The subject exists, the subject enlarges; all things sooner or later fall into place. As I am, so I see; use what language we will, we can never say anything but what we are; Hermes, Cadmus,° Columbus, Newton, Buonaparte, are the mind's ministers. Instead of feeling a poverty when we encounter a great man, let us treat the new comer like a travelling geologist, who passes through our estate, and shows us good slate, or limestone, or anthracite, in our brush pasture. The partial action of each strong mind in one direction, is a telescope for the objects on which it is pointed. But every other part of knowledge is to be pushed to the same extravagance, ere the soul attains her due sphericity. Do you see that kitten chasing so prettily her own tail? If you could look with her eyes, you might see her surrounded with hundreds of figures performing complex dramas, with tragic and comic issues, long conversations, many characters, many ups and downs of fate,—and meantime it is only puss and her tail. How long before our masquerade will end its noise of tamborines, laughter, and shouting, and we shall find it was a solitary performance?—A subject and an object,—it takes so much to make the galvanic circuit complete, but magnitude adds nothing. What imports it whether it is Kepler and the sphere; Columbus and America; a reader and his book; or puss with her tail?

It is true that all the muses and love and religion hate these developments, and will find a way to punish the chemist, who publishes in the parlor the secrets of the laboratory. And we cannot say too little of our constitutional necessity of seeing things under private aspects, or saturated with our humors. And yet is the God the native of these bleak rocks. That need makes in morals the capital virtue of self-trust. We must hold hard to this poverty, however scandalous, and by more vigorous self-recoveries, after the sallies of action, possess our axis more firmly. The life of truth is cold, and so far mournful; but it is not the slave of tears, contritions, and perturbations. It does not attempt another's work, nor adopt another's facts. It is a main lesson of wisdom to know your own from another's. I have learned that I cannot dispose of other people's facts; but I possess such a key to my own, as persuades me against all their denials, that they also have a key to theirs. A sympathetic person is placed in the dilemma of a swimmer among drowning men, who all catch at him, and if he give so much as a leg or a finger, they will drown him. They wish to be saved from the mischiefs of their vices, but not from their vices. Charity would be wasted on this poor waiting on the symptoms. A wise and hardy physician will say, *Come out of that*, as the first condition of advice.

In this our talking America, we are ruined by our good nature and listening on all sides. This compliance takes away the power of being greatly useful. A man should not be able to look other than directly and forthright. A preoccupied attention is the only answer to the importunate frivolity of other people: an attention, and to an aim which makes their wants frivolous. This is a divine answer, and leaves no appeal, and no hard thoughts. In Flaxman's drawing° of the Eumenides of Æschylus, Orestes supplicates Apollo, whilst the Furies sleep on the threshold. The face of the god expresses a shade of regret and compassion, but calm with the conviction of the irreconcilableness of the two spheres. He is born into other politics, into the eternal and beautiful. The man at his feet asks for his interest in turmoils of the earth, into which his nature cannot enter. And the Eumenides there lying express pictorially this disparity. The god is surcharged with his divine destiny.

Illusion, Temperament, Succession, Surface, Surprise, Reality, Subjectiveness,—these are threads on the loom of time, these are the lords of life. I dare not assume to give their order, but I name them as I find them in my way. I know better than to claim any completeness for my picture. I am a fragment, and this is a fragment of me. I can very confidently announce one or another law, which throws itself into relief and form, but I am too young yet by some ages to compile a code. I gossip for my hour concerning the eternal politics. I have seen many fair pictures not in vain. A wonderful time I have lived in. I am not the novice I was fourteen, nor yet seven years ago. Let who will ask, where is the fruit? I find a private fruit sufficient. This is a fruit,—that I should not ask for a rash effect from meditations, counsels, and the hiving of truths. I should feel it pitiful to demand a result on this town and county, an overt effect on the instant month and year. The effect is deep and secular as the cause. It works on periods in which mortal lifetime is lost. All I know is reception; I am and I have: but I do not get, and when I have fancied I had gotten anything, I found I did not. I worship with wonder the great Fortune. My reception has been so large, that I am not annoyed by receiving this or that superabundantly. I say to the Genius, if he will pardon the proverb, *In for a mill, in for a million*. When I receive a new gift, I do not macerate my body to make the account square, for, if I should die, I could not make the account square. The benefit overran the merit the first day, and has overran the merit ever since. The merit itself, so-called, I reckon part of the receiving.

Also, that hankering after an overt or practical effect seems to me an apostasy. In good earnest, I am willing to spare this most unnecessary deal of doing. Life wears to me a visionary face. Hardest, roughest action is visionary also. It is but a choice between soft and turbulent dreams. People disparage knowing and the intellectual life, and urge doing. I am very content with knowing, if only I could know. That is an august entertainment, and would suffice me a great while. To know a little, would be worth the expense of this world. I hear always the law of Adrastia, 'that every soul which had acquired any truth, should be safe from harm until another period.'°

I know that the world I converse with in the city and in the farms, is not the world I *think*. I observe that difference, and shall observe it. One day, I shall know the value and law of this discrepance. But I have not found that much was gained by manipular attempts to realize the world of thought. Many eager persons successively make an experiment in this way, and make themselves ridiculous. They acquire democratic manners, they foam at the mouth, they hate and deny. Worse, I observe, that, in the history of mankind, there is never a solitary example of success,—taking their own tests of success. I say this polemically, or in reply to the inquiry, why not realize your world? But far be from me the despair which prejudges the law by a paltry empiricism,—since there never was a right endeavor, but it succeeded. Patience and patience, we shall win at the last. We must be very suspicious of the deceptions of the element of time. It takes a good deal of time to eat or to sleep, or to earn a hundred dollars, and a very little time to entertain a hope and an insight which becomes the light of our life. We dress our garden, eat our dinners, discuss the household with our wives, and these things make no impression, are forgotten next week; but in the solitude to which every man is always returning, he has a sanity and revelations, which in his passage into new worlds he will carry with him. Never mind the ridicule, never mind the defeat: up again, old heart!—it seems to say,—there is victory yet for all justice; and the true romance which the world exists to realize, will be the transformation of genius into practical power.

NATURE

The rounded world is fair to see,
Nine times folded in mystery:
Though baffled seers cannot impart
The secret of its laboring heart,
Throb thine with Nature's throbbing breast,
And all is clear from east to west.
Spirit that lurks each form within
Beckons to spirit of its kin;
Self-kindled every atom glows,
And hints the future which it owes.

THERE are days which occur in this climate, at almost any season of the year, wherein the world reaches its perfection, when the air, the heavenly bodies, and the earth, make a harmony, as if nature would indulge her offspring; when, in these bleak upper sides of the planet, nothing is to desire that we have heard of the happiest latitudes, and we bask in the shining hours of Florida and Cuba; when everything that has life gives sign of satisfaction, and the cattle that lie on the ground seem to have great and tranquil thoughts. These halcyons may be looked for with a little more assurance in that pure October weather, which we distinguish by the name of the Indian Summer. The day, immeasurably long, sleeps over the broad hills and warm wide fields. To have lived through all its sunny hours, seems longevity enough. The solitary places do not seem quite lonely. At the gates of the forest, the surprised man of the world is forced to leave his city estimates of great and small, wise and foolish. The knapsack of custom falls off his back with the first step he makes into these precincts. Here is sanctity which shames our religions, and reality which discredits our heroes. Here we find nature to be the circumstance which dwarfs every other circumstance, and judges like a god all men that come to her. We have crept out of our close and crowded houses into the night and morning, and we see what majestic beauties daily wrap us in their bosom. How willingly we would escape the barriers which render them comparatively impotent, escape the sophistication and second thought, and suffer nature to intrance us. The tempered light of the woods is like a perpetual morning, and is stimulating and heroic. The anciently reported spells of these places creep on us. The stems of pines, hemlocks, and oaks, almost gleam like iron on the excited eye. The incommunicable trees begin to persuade us to live with them, and quit our life of solemn trifles. Here no history, or church, or state, is interpolated on the divine sky and the immortal year. How easily we might walk onward into the opening landscape, absorbed by new pictures, and by thoughts fast succeeding each other, until by degrees the recollection of home was crowded out of the mind, all memory obliterated by the tyranny of the present, and we were led in triumph by nature.

These enchantments are medicinal, they sober and heal us. These are plain pleasures, kindly and native to us. We come to our own, and make friends with matter, which the ambitious chatter of the schools would persuade us to despise. We never can part with it; the mind loves its old home: as water to our thirst, so is the rock, the ground, to our eyes, and hands, and feet. It is firm water: it is cold flame: what health, what affinity! Ever an old friend, ever like a dear friend and brother, when we chat affectedly with strangers, comes in this honest face, and takes a grave liberty with us, and shames us out of our nonsense. Cities give not the human senses room enough. We go out daily and nightly to feed the eyes on the horizon, and require so much scope, just as we need water for our bath. There are all degrees of natural influence, from these quarantine powers of nature, up to her dearest and gravest ministrations to the imagination and the soul. There is the bucket of cold water from the spring, the wood-fire to which the chilled traveller rushes for safety,—and there is the sublime moral of autumn and of noon. We nestle in nature, and draw our living as parasites from her roots and grains, and we receive glances from the heavenly bodies, which call us to solitude, and foretell the remotest future. The blue zenith is the point in which romance and reality meet. I think, if we should be rapt away into all that we dream of heaven, and should converse with Gabriel and Uriel,° the upper sky would be all that would remain of our furniture.

It seems as if the day was not wholly profane, in which we have given heed to some natural object. The fall of snowflakes in a still air, preserving to each crystal its perfect form; the blowing of sleet over a wide sheet of water, and over plains, the waving rye-field, the mimic waving of acres of houstonia,° whose innumerable florets whiten and ripple before the eye; the reflections of trees and flowers in glassy lakes; the musical steaming odorous south wind, which converts all trees to wind-harps; the crackling and spurting of hemlock in the flames; or of pine logs, which yield glory to the walls and faces in the sittingroom,—these are the music and pictures of the most ancient religion. My house stands in low land, with limited outlook, and on the skirt of the village.

But I go with my friend to the shore of our little river, and with one stroke of the paddle, I leave the village politics and personalities, yes, and the world of villages and personalities behind, and pass into a delicate realm of sunset and moonlight, too bright almost for spotted man to enter without novitiate and probation. We penetrate bodily this incredible beauty; we dip our hands in this painted element: our eyes are bathed in these lights and forms. A holiday, a villeggiatura,° a royal revel, the proudest, most heart-rejoicing festival that valor and beauty, power and taste, ever decked and enjoyed, establishes itself on the instant. These sunset clouds, these delicately emerging stars, with their private and ineffable glances, signify it and proffer it. I am taught the poorness of our invention, the ugliness of towns and palaces. Art and luxury have early learned that they must work as enhancement and sequel to this original beauty. I am over-instructed for my return. Henceforth I shall be hard to please. I cannot go back to toys. I am grown expensive and sophisticated. I can no longer live without elegance: but a countryman shall be my master of revels.° He who knows the most, he who knows what sweets and virtues are in the ground, the waters, the plants, the heavens, and how to come at these enchantments, is the rich and royal man. Only as far as the masters of the world have called in nature to their aid, can they reach the height of magnificence. This is the meaning of their hanging-gardens, villas, garden-houses, islands, parks, and preserves, to back their faulty personality with these strong accessories. I do not wonder that the landed interest should be invincible in the state with these dangerous auxiliaries. These bribe and invite; not kings, not palaces, not men, not women, but these tender and poetic stars, eloquent of secret promises. We heard what the rich man said, we knew of his villa, his grove, his wine, and his company, but the provocation and point of the invitation came out of these beguiling stars. In their soft glances, I see what men strove to realize in some Versailles, or Paphos, or Ctesiphon.° Indeed, it is the magical lights of the horizon, and the blue sky for the background, which save all our works of art, which were otherwise bawbles. When the rich tax the poor with servility and obsequiousness, they should consider the effect of men reputed to be the possessors of nature, on imaginative minds. Ah! if the rich were rich as the poor fancy riches! A boy hears a military band play on the field at night, and he has kings and queens, and famous chivalry palpably before him. He hears the echoes of a horn in a hill country, in the Notch Mountains,° for example, which converts the mountains into an Æolian harp, and this supernatural *tiralira* restores to him the Dorian mythology, Apollo, Diana, and all divine hunters and huntresses. Can a musical note be so lofty, so haughtily beautiful! To the poor young poet, thus fabulous is his picture of society; he is loyal; he respects the rich; they are rich for the sake of his imagination; how poor his fancy would be, if they were not rich! That they have some highfenced grove, which they call a park; that they live in larger and better-garnished saloons than he has visited, and go in coaches, keeping only the society of the elegant, to watering-places, and to distant cities, are the groundwork from which he has delineated estates of romance, compared with which their actual possessions are shanties and paddocks. The muse herself betrays her son, and enhances the gifts of wealth and well-born beauty, by a radiation out of the air, and clouds, and forests that skirt the road,—a certain haughty favor, as if from patrician genii to patricians, a kind of aristocracy in nature, a prince of the power of the air.°

The moral sensibility which makes Edens and Tempes° so easily, may not be always found, but the material landscape is never far off. We can find these enchantments without visiting the Como Lake, or the Madeira Islands.° We exaggerate the praises of local scenery. In every landscape, the point of astonishment is the meeting of the sky and the earth, and that is seen from the first hillock as well as from the top of the Alleghanies. The stars at night stoop down over the brownest, homeliest common, with all the spiritual magnificence which they shed on the Campagna,° or on the marble deserts of Egypt. The uprolled clouds and the colors of morning and evening, will transfigure maples and alders. The difference between landscape and landscape is small, but there is great difference in the beholders. There is nothing so wonderful in any particular landscape, as the necessity of being beautiful under which every landscape lies. Nature cannot be surprised in undress. Beauty breaks in everywhere.

But it is very easy to outrun the sympathy of readers on this topic, which schoolmen called *natura naturata*,° or nature passive. One can hardly speak directly of it without excess. It is as easy to broach in mixed companies what is called 'the subject of religion.' A susceptible person does not like to indulge his tastes in this kind, without the apology of some trivial necessity: he goes to see a wood-lot, or to look at the crops, or to fetch a plant or a mineral from a remote locality, or he carries a fowling piece, or a fishing-rod. I suppose this shame must have a good reason. A dilettantism in nature is barren and unworthy. The fop of fields is no better than his brother of Broadway. Men are naturally hunters and inquisitive of wood-craft, and I suppose that such a gazetteer as wood-cutters and Indians should furnish facts for, would take place in the most sumptuous drawingrooms of all the 'Wreaths' and 'Flora's chaplets'° of the bookshops; yet ordinarily, whether we are too clumsy for so subtle a topic, or from whatever cause, as soon as men begin to write on nature, they fall into euphuism. Frivolity is a most unfit tribute to Pan, who ought to be represented in the mythology as the most continent of gods. I would not be frivolous before the admirable reserve and prudence of time, yet I cannot renounce the right of returning often to this old topic. The multitude of false churches accredits the true religion. Literature, poetry, science, are the homage of man to this unfathomed secret, concerning which no sane man can affect an indifference or incuriosity. Nature is loved by what is best in us. It is loved as the city of God, although, or rather because there is no citizen. The sunset is unlike anything that is underneath it: it wants men. And the beauty of nature must always seem unreal and mocking, until the landscape has human figures, that are as good as itself. If there were good men, there would never be this rapture in nature. If the king is in the palace, nobody looks at the walls. It is when he is gone, and the house is filled with grooms and gazers, that we turn from the people, to find relief in the majestic men that are suggested by the pictures and the architecture. The critics who complain of the sickly separation of the beauty of nature from the thing to be done, must consider that our hunting of the picturesque is inseparable from our protest against false society. Man is fallen; nature is erect, and serves as a differential thermometer,° detecting the presence or absence of the divine sentiment in man. By fault of our dulness and selfishness, we are looking up to nature, but when we are convalescent, nature will look up to us. We see the foaming brook with compunction: if our own life flowed with the right energy, we should shame the brook. The stream of zeal sparkles with real fire, and not with reflex rays of sun and moon. Nature may be as selfishly studied as trade. Astronomy to the selfish becomes astrology; psychology, mesmerism (with intent to show where our spoons are gone); and anatomy and physiology, become phrenology and palmistry.

But taking timely warning, and leaving many things unsaid on this topic, let us not longer omit our homage to the Efficient Nature, *natura naturans*, the quick cause, before which all forms flee as the driven snows, itself secret, its works driven before it in flocks and multitudes, (as the ancient represented nature by Proteus,° a shepherd,) and in undescribable variety. It publishes itself in creatures, reaching from particles and spicula, through transformation on transformation to the highest symmetries, arriving at consummate results without a shock or a leap. A little heat, that is, a little motion, is all that differences the bald, dazzling white, and deadly cold poles of the earth from the prolific tropical climates. All changes pass without violence, by reason of the two cardinal conditions of boundless space and boundless time. Geology has initiated us into the secularity of nature, and taught us to disuse our dame-school measures, and exchange our Mosaic and Ptolemaic schemes for her large style. We knew nothing rightly, for want of perspective. Now we learn what patient periods must round themselves before the rock is formed, then before the rock is broken, and the first lichen race has disintegrated the thinnest external plate into soil, and opened the door for the remote Flora, Fauna, Ceres, and Pomona,° to come in. How far off yet is the trilobite! how far the quadruped! how inconceivably remote is man! All duly arrive, and then race after race of men. It is a long way from granite to the oyster; farther yet to Plato, and the preaching of the immortality of the soul. Yet all must come, as surely as the first atom has two sides.

Motion or change, and identity or rest, are the first and second secrets of nature: Motion and Rest. The whole code of her laws may be written on the thumbnail, or the signet of a ring. The whirling bubble on the surface of a brook, admits us to the secret of the mechanics of the sky. Every shell on the beach is a key to it. A little water made to rotate in a cup explains the formation of the simpler shells; the addition of matter from year to year, arrives at last at the most complex forms; and yet so poor is nature with all her craft, that, from the beginning to the end of the universe, she has but one stuff,—but one stuff with its two ends, to serve up all her dream-like variety. Compound it how she will, star, sand, fire, water, tree, man, it is still one stuff, and betrays the same properties.

Nature is always consistent, though she feigns to contravene her own laws. She keeps her laws, and seems to transcend them. She arms and equips an animal to find its place and living in the earth, and, at the same time, she arms and equips another animal to destroy it. Space exists to divide creatures; but by clothing the sides of a bird with a few feathers, she gives him a petty omnipresence. The direction is forever onward, but the artist still goes back for materials, and begins again with the first elements on the most advanced stage: otherwise, all goes to ruin. If we look at her work, we seem to catch a glance of a system in transition. Plants are the young of the world, vessels of health and vigor; but they grope ever upward towards consciousness; the trees are imperfect men, and seem to bemoan their imprisonment, rooted in the ground. The animal is the novice and probationer of a more advanced order. The men, though young, having tasted the first drop from the cup of thought, are already dissipated: the maples and ferns are still uncorrupt; yet no doubt, when they come to consciousness, they too will curse and swear. Flowers so strictly belong to youth, that we adult men soon come to feel, that their beautiful generations concern not us: we have had our day; now let the children have theirs. The flowers jilt us, and we are old bachelors with our ridiculous tenderness.

Things are so strictly related, that according to the skill of the eye, from any one object the parts and properties of any other may be predicted. If we had eyes to see it, a bit of stone from the city wall would certify us of the necessity that man must exist, as readily as the city. That identity makes us all one, and reduces to nothing great intervals on our customary scale. We talk of deviations from natural life, as if artificial life were not also natural. The smoothest curled courtier in the boudoirs of a palace has an animal nature, rude and aboriginal as a white bear, omnipotent to its own ends, and is directly related, there amid essences and billetsdoux, to Himmaleh mountain-chains, and the axis of the globe. If we consider how much we are nature's, we need not be superstitious about towns, as if that terrific or benefic force did not find us there also, and fashion cities. Nature who made the mason, made the house. We may easily hear too much of rural influences. The cool disengaged air of natural objects, makes them enviable to us, chafed and irritable creatures with red faces, and we think we shall be as grand as they, if we camp out and eat roots; but let us be men instead of woodchucks, and the oak and the elm shall gladly serve us, though we sit in chairs of ivory on carpets of silk.

This guiding identity runs through all the surprises and contrasts of the piece, and characterizes every law. Man carries the world in his head, the whole astronomy and chemistry suspended in a thought. Because the history of nature is charactered in his brain, therefore is he the prophet and discoverer of her secrets. Every known fact in natural science was divined by the presentiment of somebody, before it was actually verified. A man does not tie his shoe without recognising laws which bind the farthest regions of nature: moon, plant, gas, crystal, are concrete geometry and numbers. Common sense knows its own, and recognises the fact at first sight in chemical experiment. The common sense of Franklin, Dalton, Davy, and Black,° is the same common sense which made the arrangements which now it discovers.

If the identity expresses organized rest, the counter action runs also into organization. The astronomers said, 'Give us matter, and a little motion, and we will construct the universe. It is not enough that we should have matter, we must also have a single impulse, one shove to launch the mass, and generate the harmony of the centrifugal and centripetal forces. Once heave the ball from the hand, and we can show how all this mighty order grew.'—'A very unreasonable postulate,' said the metaphysicians, 'and a plain begging of the question. Could you not prevail to know the genesis of projection, as well as the continuation of it?' Nature, meanwhile, had not waited for the discussion, but, right or wrong, bestowed the impulse, and the balls rolled. It was no great affair, a mere push, but the astronomers were right in making much of it, for there is no end to the consequences of the act. That famous aboriginal push propagates itself through all the balls of the system, and through every atom of every ball, through all the races of creatures, and through the history and performances of every individual. Exaggeration is in the course of things. Nature sends no creature, no man into the world, without adding a small excess of his proper quality. Given the planet, it is still necessary to add the impulse; so, to every creature nature added a little violence of direction in its proper path, a shove to put it on its way; in every instance, a slight generosity, a drop too much. Without electricity the air would rot, and without this violence of direction, which men and women have, without a spice of bigot and fanatic, no excitement, no efficiency. We aim above the mark, to hit the mark. Every act hath some falsehood of exaggeration in it. And when now and then comes along some sad, sharp-eyed man, who sees how paltry a game is played, and refuses to play, but blabs the secret;—how then? is the bird flown? O no, the wary Nature sends a new troop of fairer forms, of lordlier youths, with a little more excess of direction to hold them fast to their several aim; makes them a little wrong-headed in that direction in which they are rightest, and on goes the game again with new whirl, for a generation or two more. The child with his sweet pranks, the fool of his senses, commanded by every sight and sound, without any power to compare and rank his sensations, abandoned to a whistle or a painted chip, to a lead dragoon, or a gingerbread-dog, individualizing everything, generalizing nothing, delighted with every new thing, lies down at night overpowered by the fatigue, which this day of continual pretty madness has incurred. But Nature has answered her purpose with the curly, dimpled lunatic. She has tasked every faculty, and has secured the symmetrical growth of the bodily frame, by all these attitudes and exertions,—an end of the first importance, which could not be trusted to any care less perfect than her own. This glitter, this opaline lustre plays round the top of every toy to his eye, to ensure his fidelity, and he is deceived to his good. We are made alive and kept alive by the same arts. Let the stoics say what they please, we do not eat for the good of living, but because the meat is savory and the appetite is keen. The vegetable life does not content itself with casting from the flower or the tree a single seed, but it fills the air and earth with a prodigality of seeds, that, if thousands perish, thousands may plant themselves, that hundreds may come up, that tens may live to maturity, that, at least, one may replace the parent. All things betray the same calculated profusion. The excess of fear with which the animal frame is hedged round, shrinking from cold, starting at sight of a snake, or at a sudden noise, protects us, through a multitude of groundless alarms, from some one real danger at last. The lover seeks in marriage his private felicity and perfection, with no prospective end; and nature hides in his happiness her own end, namely, progeny, or the perpetuity of the race.

But the craft with which the world is made, runs also into the mind and character of men. No man is quite sane; each has a vein of folly in his composition, a slight determination of blood to the head, to make sure of holding him hard to some one point which nature had taken to heart. Great causes are never tried on their merits; but the cause is reduced to particulars to suit the size of the partizans, and the contention is ever hottest on minor matters. Not less remarkable is the overfaith of each man in the importance of what he has to do or say. The poet, the prophet, has a higher value for what he utters than any hearer, and therefore it gets spoken. The strong, self-complacent Luther declares° with an emphasis, not to be mistaken, that 'God himself cannot do without wise men.' Jacob Behmen and George Fox° betray their egotism in the pertinacity of their controversial tracts, and James Naylor° once suffered himself to be worshipped as the Christ. Each prophet comes presently to identify himself with his thought, and to esteem his hat and shoes sacred. However this may discredit such persons with the judicious, it helps them with the people, as it gives heat, pungency, and publicity to their words. A similar experience is not infrequent in private life. Each young and ardent person writes a diary, in which, when the hours of prayer and penitence arrive, he inscribes his soul. The pages thus written are, to him, burning and fragrant: he reads them on his knees by midnight and by the morning star; he wets them with his tears: they are sacred; too good for the world, and hardly yet to be shown to the dearest friend. This is the man-child that is born to the soul, and her life still circulates in the babe. The umbilical cord has not yet been cut. After some time has elapsed, he begins to wish to admit his friend to this hallowed experience, and with hesitation, yet with firmness, exposes the pages to his eye. Will they not burn his eyes?

The friend coldly turns them over, and passes from the writing to conversation, with easy transition, which strikes the other party with astonishment and vexation. He cannot suspect the writing itself. Days and nights of fervid life, of communion with angels of darkness and of light, have engraved their shadowy characters on that tear-stained book. He suspects the intelligence or the heart of his friend. Is there then no friend? He cannot yet credit that one may have impressive experience, and yet may not know how to put his private fact into literature; and perhaps the discovery that wisdom has other tongues and ministers than we, that though we should hold our peace, the truth would not the less be spoken, might check injuriously the flames of our zeal. A man can only speak, so long as he does not feel his speech to be partial and inadequate. It is partial, but he does not see it to be so, whilst he utters it. As soon as he is released from the instinctive and particular, and sees its partiality, he shuts his mouth in disgust. For, no man can write anything, who does not think that what he writes is for the time the history of the world; or do anything well, who does not esteem his work to be of importance. My work may be of none, but I must not think it of none, or I shall not do it with impunity.

In like manner, there is throughout nature something mocking, something that leads us on and on, but arrives nowhere, keeps no faith with us. All promise outruns the performance. We live in a system of approximations. Every end is prospective of some other end, which is also temporary; a round and final success nowhere. We are encamped in nature, not domesticated. Hunger and thirst lead us on to eat and to drink; but bread and wine, mix and cook them how you will, leave us hungry and thirsty, after the stomach is full. It is the same with all our arts and performances. Our music, our poetry, our language itself are not satisfactions, but suggestions. The hunger for wealth, which reduces the planet to a garden, fools the eager pursuer. What is the end sought? Plainly to secure the ends of good sense and beauty, from the intrusion of deformity or vulgarity of any kind. But what an operose method! What a train of means to secure a little conversation! This palace of brick and stone, these servants, this kitchen, these stables, horses and equipage, this bank-stock, and file of mortgages; trade to all the world, country-house and cottage by the waterside, all for a little conversation, high, clear, and spiritual! Could it not be had as well by beggars on the highway? No, all these things came from successive efforts of these beggars to remove friction from the wheels of life, and give opportunity. Conversation, character, were the avowed ends; wealth was good as it appeased the animal cravings, cured the smoky chimney, silenced the creaking door, brought friends together in a warm and quiet room, and kept the children and the dinner-table in a different apartment. Thought, virtue, beauty, were the ends; but it was known that men of thought and virtue sometimes had the head-ache, or wet feet, or could lose good time whilst the room was getting warm in winter days. Unluckily, in the exertions necessary to remove these inconveniences, the main attention has been diverted to this object; the old aims have been lost sight of, and to remove friction has come to be the end. That is the ridicule of rich men, and Boston, London, Vienna, and now the governments generally of the world, are cities and governments of the rich, and the masses are not men, but *poor men*, that is, men who would be rich; this is the ridicule of the class, that they arrive with pains and sweat and fury nowhere; when all is done, it is for nothing. They are like one who has interrupted the conversation of a company to make his speech, and now has forgotten what he went to say. The appearance strikes the eye everywhere of an aimless society, of aimless nations. Were the ends of nature so great and cogent, as to exact this immense sacrifice of men?

Quite analogous to the deceits in life, there is, as might be expected, a similar effect on the eye from the face of external nature. There is in woods and waters a certain enticement and flattery, together with a failure to yield a present satisfaction. This disappointment is felt in every landscape. I have seen the softness and beauty of the summer-clouds floating feathery overhead, enjoying, as it seemed, their height and privilege of motion, whilst yet they appeared not so much the drapery of this place and hour, as forelooking to some pavilions and gardens of festivity beyond. It is an odd jealousy: but the poet finds himself not near enough to his object. The pine-tree, the river, the bank of flowers before him, does not seem to be nature. Nature is still elsewhere. This or this is but outskirt and far-off reflection and echo of the triumph that has passed by, and is now at its glancing splendor and heyday, perchance in the neighboring fields, or, if you stand in the field, then in the adjacent woods. The present object shall give you this sense of stillness that follows a pageant which has just gone by. What splendid distance, what recesses of ineffable pomp and loveliness in the sunset! But who can go where they are, or lay his hand or plant his foot thereon? Off they fall from the round world forever and ever. It is the same among the men and women, as among the silent trees; always a referred existence, an absence, never a presence and satisfaction. Is it, that beauty can never be grasped? in persons and in landscape is equally inaccessible? The accepted and betrothed lover has lost the wildest charm of his maiden in her acceptance of him. She was heaven whilst he pursued her as a star: she cannot be heaven, if she stoops to such a one as he.

What shall we say of this omnipresent appearance of that first projectile impulse, of this flattery and baulking of so many well-meaning creatures? Must we not suppose somewhere in the universe a slight treachery and derision? Are we not engaged to a serious resentment of this use that is made of us? Are we tickled trout,° and fools of nature? One look at the face of heaven and earth lays all petulance at rest, and soothes us to wiser convictions. To the intelligent, nature converts itself into a vast promise, and will not be rashly explained. Her secret is untold. Many and many an Œdipus arrives: he has the whole mystery teeming in his brain. Alas! the same sorcery has spoiled his skill; no syllable can he shape on his lips. Her mighty orbit vaults like the fresh rainbow into the deep, but no archangel's wing was yet strong enough to follow it, and report of the return of the curve. But it also appears, that our actions are seconded and disposed to greater conclusions than we designed. We are escorted on every hand through life by spiritual agents, and a beneficent purpose lies in wait for us. We cannot bandy words with nature, or deal with her as we deal with persons. If we measure our individual forces against hers, we may easily feel as if we were the sport of an insuperable destiny. But if, instead of identifying ourselves with the work, we feel that the soul of the workman streams through us, we shall find the peace of the morning dwelling first in our hearts, and the fathomless powers of gravity and chemistry, and, over them, of life, preëxisting within us in their highest form.

The uneasiness which the thought of our helplessness in the chain of causes occasions us, results from looking too much at one condition of nature, namely, Motion. But the drag is never taken from the wheel. Wherever the impulse exceeds, the Rest or Identity insinuates its compensation. All over the wide fields of earth grows the prunella or self-heal. After every foolish day we sleep off the fumes and furies of its hours; and though we are always engaged with particulars, and often enslaved to them, we bring with us to every experiment the innate universal laws. These, while they exist in the mind as ideas, stand around us in nature forever embodied, a present sanity to expose and cure the insanity of men. Our servitude to particulars betrays into a hundred foolish expectations. We anticipate a new era from the invention of a locomotive, or a balloon; the new engine brings with it the old checks. They say that by electro-magnetism, your sallad shall be grown from the seed, whilst your fowl is roasting for dinner: it is a symbol of our modern aims and endeavors,—of our condensation and acceleration of objects: but nothing is gained: nature cannot be cheated: man's life is but seventy sallads long, grow they swift or grow they slow. In these checks and impossibilities, however, we find our advantage, not less than in the impulses. Let the victory fall where it will, we are on that side. And the knowledge that we traverse the whole scale of being, from the centre to the poles of nature, and have some stake in every possibility, lends that sublime lustre to death, which philosophy and religion have too outwardly and literally striven to express in the popular doctrine of the immortality of the soul. The reality is more excellent than the report. Here is no ruin, no discontinuity, no spent ball. The divine circulations never rest nor linger. Nature is the incarnation of a thought, and turns to a thought again, as ice becomes water and gas. The world is mind precipitated, and the volatile essence is forever escaping again into the state of free thought. Hence the virtue and pungency of the influence on the mind, of natural objects, whether inorganic or organized. Man imprisoned, man crystallized, man vegetative, speaks to man impersonated. That power which does not respect quantity, which makes the whole and the particle its equal channel, delegates its smile to the morning, and distils its essence into every drop of rain. Every moment instructs, and every object: for wisdom is infused into every form. It has been poured into us as blood; it convulsed us as pain; it slid into us as pleasure; it enveloped us in dull, melancholy days, or in days of cheerful labor; we did not guess its essence, until after a long time.

POLITICS

Gold and iron are good
To buy iron and gold;
All earth's fleece and food
For their like are sold.
Boded Merlin wise,
Proved Napoleon great,—
Nor kind nor coinage buys
Aught above its rate.
Fear, Craft, and Avarice
Cannot rear a State.
Out of dust to build
What is more than dust,—
Walls Amphion piled
Phœbus stablish must.
When the Muses nine
With the Virtues meet,
Find to their design
An Atlantic seat,
By green orchard boughs
Fended from the heat,
Where the statesman ploughs
Furrow for the wheat;
When the Church is social worth,
When the state-house is the hearth,
Then the perfect State is come,
The republican at home.

In dealing with the State, we ought to remember that its institutions are
not aboriginal, though they existed before we were born: that they are
not superior to the citizen: that every one of them was once the act of a
single man: every law and usage was a man's expedient to meet a particular case: that they all are imitable, all alterable; we may make as
good; we may make better. Society is an illusion to the young citizen. It
lies before him in rigid repose, with certain names, men, and institutions, rooted like oak-trees to the centre, round which all arrange
themselves the best they can. But the old statesman knows that society
is fluid; there are no such roots and centres; but any particle may suddenly become the centre of the movement, and compel the system to
gyrate round it, as every man of strong will, like Pisistratus, or Crom-

well, does for a time, and every man of truth, like Plato, or Paul, does forever. But politics rest on necessary foundations, and cannot be treated with levity. Republics abound in young civilians, who believe that the laws make the city, that grave modifications of the policy and modes of living, and employments of the population, that commerce, education, and religion, may be voted in or out; and that any measure, though it were absurd, may be imposed on a people, if only you can get sufficient voices to make it a law. But the wise know that foolish legislation is a rope of sand, which perishes in the twisting; that the State must follow, and not lead the character and progress of the citizen; the strongest usurper is quickly got rid of; and they only who build on Ideas, build for eternity; and that the form of government which prevails, is the expression of what cultivation exists in the population which permits it. The law is only a memorandum. We are superstitious, and esteem the statute somewhat: so much life as it has in the character of living men, is its force. The statute stands there to say, yesterday we agreed so and so, but how feel ye this article today? Our statute is a currency, which we stamp with our own portrait: it soon becomes unrecognizable, and in process of time will return to the mint. Nature is not democratic, nor limited-monarchical, but despotic, and will not be fooled or abated of any jot of her authority, by the pertest of her sons: and as fast as the public mind is opened to more intelligence, the code is seen to be brute and stammering. It speaks not articulately, and must be made to. Meantime the education of the general mind never stops. The reveries of the true and simple are prophetic. What the tender poetic youth dreams, and prays, and paints today, but shuns the ridicule of saying aloud, shall presently be the resolutions of public bodies, then shall be carried as grievance and bill of rights through conflict and war, and then shall be triumphant law and establishment for a hundred years, until it gives place, in turn, to new prayers and pictures. The history of the State sketches in coarse outline the progress of thought, and follows at a distance the delicacy of culture and of aspiration.

The theory of politics, which has possessed the mind of men, and which they have expressed the best they could in their laws and in their revolutions, considers persons and property as the two objects for whose protection government exists. Of persons, all have equal rights, in virtue of being identical in nature. This interest, of course, with its whole power demands a democracy. Whilst the rights of all as persons are equal, in virtue of their access to reason, their rights in property are very unequal. One man owns his clothes, and another owns a county. This accident, depending, primarily, on the skill and virtue of the parties, of which there is every degree, and, secondarily, on patrimony, falls unequally, and its rights, of course, are unequal. Personal rights, universally the same, demand a government framed on the ratio of the census: property demands a government framed on the ratio of owners and of owning. Laban, who has flocks and herds, wishes them looked after by an officer on the frontiers, lest the Midianites shall drive them off, and pays a tax to that end. Jacob has no flocks or herds, and no fear of the Midianites, and pays no tax to the officer.° It seemed fit that Laban and Jacob should have equal rights to elect the officer, who is to defend their persons, but that Laban, and not Jacob, should elect the officer who is to guard the sheep and cattle. And, if question arise whether additional officers or watch-towers should be provided, must not Laban and Isaac, and those who must sell part of their herds to buy protection for the rest, judge better of this, and with more right, than Jacob, who, because he is a youth and a traveller, eats their bread and not his own.

In the earliest society the proprietors made their own wealth, and so long as it comes to the owners in the direct way, no other opinion would arise in any equitable community, than that property should make the law for property, and persons the law for persons.

But property passes through donation or inheritance to those who do not create it. Gift, in one case, makes it as really the new owner's, as labor made it the first owner's: in the other case, of patrimony, the law makes an ownership, which will be valid in each man's view according to the estimate which he sets on the public tranquillity.

It was not, however, found easy to embody the readily admitted principle, that property should make law for property, and persons for persons: since persons and property mixed themselves in every transaction. At last it seemed settled, that the rightful distinction was, that the proprietors should have more elective franchise than non-proprietors, on the Spartan principle of 'calling that which is just, equal; not that which is equal, just.'°

That principle no longer looks so self-evident as it appeared in former times, partly, because doubts have arisen whether too much weight had not been allowed in the laws, to property, and such a structure given to our usages, as allowed the rich to encroach on the poor, and to keep them poor; but mainly, because there is an instinctive sense, however obscure and yet inarticulate, that the whole constitution of property, on its present tenures, is injurious, and its influence on persons deteriorating and degrading; that truly, the only interest for the consideration of the State, is persons: that property will always follow persons; that the highest end of government is the culture of men: and if men can be educated, the institutions will share their improvement, and the moral sentiment will write the law of the land.

If it be not easy to settle the equity of this question, the peril is less when we take note of our natural defences. We are kept by better guards than the vigilance of such magistrates as we commonly elect. Society always consists, in greatest part, of young and foolish persons. The old, who have seen through the hypocrisy of courts and statesmen, die, and leave no wisdom to their sons. They believe their own newspaper, as their fathers did at their age. With such an ignorant and deceivable majority, States would soon run to ruin, but that there are limitations, beyond which the folly and ambition of governors cannot go. Things have their laws, as well as men; and things refuse to be trifled with. Property will be protected. Corn will not grow, unless it is planted and manured; but the farmer will not plant or hoe it, unless the chances are a hundred to one, that he will cut and harvest it. Under any forms, persons and property must and will have their just sway. They exert their power, as steadily as matter its attraction. Cover up a pound of earth never so cunningly, divide and subdivide it; melt it to liquid, convert it to gas; it will always weigh a pound: it will always attract and resist other matter, by the full virtue of one pound weight;—and the attributes of a person, his wit and his moral energy, will exercise, under any law or extinguishing tyranny, their proper force,—if not overtly, then covertly; if not for the law, then against it; with right, or by might.

The boundaries of personal influence it is impossible to fix, as persons are organs of moral or supernatural force. Under the dominion of an idea, which possesses the minds of multitudes, as civil freedom, or the religious sentiment, the powers of persons are no longer subjects of calculation. A nation of men unanimously bent on freedom, or conquest, can easily confound the arithmetic of statists, and achieve extravagant actions, out of all proportion to their means; as, the Greeks, the Saracens, the Swiss, the Americans, and the French have done.

In like manner, to every particle of property belongs its own attraction. A cent is the representative of a certain quantity of corn or other commodity. Its value is in the necessities of the animal man. It is so much warmth, so much bread, so much water, so much land. The law may do what it will with the owner of property, its just power will still attach to the cent. The law may in a mad freak say, that all shall have power except the owners of property: they shall have no vote. Nevertheless, by a higher law, the property will, year after year, write every statute that respects property. The non-proprietor will be the scribe of the proprietor. What the owners wish to do, the whole power of property will do, either through the law, or else in defiance of it. Of course, I speak of all the property, not merely of the great estates. When the rich are outvoted, as frequently happens, it is the joint treasury of the poor which exceeds their accumulations. Every man owns something, if it is only a cow, or a wheelbarrow, or his arms, and so has that property to dispose of.

The same necessity which secures the rights of person and property against the malignity or folly of the magistrate, determines the form and methods of governing, which are proper to each nation, and to its habit of thought, and nowise transferable to other states of society. In this country, we are very vain of our political institutions, which are singular in this, that they sprung, within the memory of living men, from the character and condition of the people, which they still express with sufficient fidelity,—and we ostentatiously prefer them to any other in history. They are not better, but only fitter for us. We may be wise in asserting the advantage in modern times of the democratic form, but to other states of society, in which religion consecrated the monarchical, that and not this was expedient. Democracy is better for us, because the religious sentiment of the present time accords better with it. Born democrats, we are nowise qualified to judge of monarchy, which, to our fathers living in the monarchical idea, was also relatively right. But our institutions, though in coincidence with the spirit of the age, have not any exemption from the practical defects which have discredited other forms. Every actual State is corrupt. Good men must not obey the laws too well. What satire on government can equal the severity of censure conveyed in the word *politic*, which now for ages has signified *cunning*, intimating that the State is a trick?

The same benign necessity and the same practical abuse appear in the parties into which each State divides itself, of opponents and defenders of the administration of the government. Parties are also founded on instincts, and have better guides to their own humble aims than the sagacity of their leaders. They have nothing perverse in their origin, but rudely mark some real and lasting relation. We might as wisely reprove the east wind, or the frost, as a political party, whose members, for the most part, could give no account of their position, but stand for the defence of those interests in which they find themselves. Our quarrel with them begins, when they quit this deep natural ground at the bidding of some leader, and, obeying personal considerations, throw themselves into the maintenance and defence of points, nowise belonging to their system. A party is perpetually corrupted by personality. Whilst we absolve the association from dishonesty, we cannot extend the same charity to their leaders. They reap the rewards of the docility and zeal of the masses which they direct. Ordinarily, our parties are parties of circumstance, and not of principle; as, the planting interest in conflict with the commercial; the party of capitalists, and that of operatives; parties which are identical in their moral character, and which can easily change ground with each other, in the support of many of their measures. Parties of principle, as, religious sects, or the party of free-trade, of universal suffrage, of abolition of slavery, of abolition of capital punishment, degenerate into personalities, or would inspire enthusiasm. The vice of our leading parties in this country (which may be cited as a fair specimen of these societies of opinion) is, that they do not plant themselves on the deep and necessary grounds to which they are respectively entitled, but lash themselves to fury in the carrying of some local and momentary measure, nowise useful to the commonwealth. Of the two great parties, which, at this hour, almost share the nation between them, I should say, that, one has the best cause, and the other contains the best men. The philosopher, the poet, or the religious man, will, of course, wish to cast his vote with the democrat, for free-trade, for wide suffrage, for the abolition of legal cruelties in the penal code, and for facilitating in every manner the access of the young and the poor to the sources of wealth and power. But he can rarely accept the persons whom the so-called popular party propose to him as representatives of these liberalities. They have not at heart the ends which give to the name of democracy what hope and virtue are in it. The spirit of our American radicalism is destructive and aimless: it is not loving; it has no ulterior and divine ends; but is destructive only out of hatred and selfishness. On the other side, the conservative party, composed of the most moderate, able, and cultivated part of the population, is timid, and merely defensive of property. It vindicates no right, it aspires to no real good, it brands no crime, it proposes no generous policy, it does not build, nor write, nor cherish the arts, nor foster religion, nor establish schools, nor encourage science, nor emancipate the slave, nor befriend the poor, or the Indian, or the immigrant. From neither party, when in power, has the world any benefit to expect in science, art, or humanity, at all commensurate with the resources of the nation.

I do not for these defects despair of our republic. We are not at the mercy of any waves of chance. In the strife of ferocious parties, human nature always finds itself cherished, as the children of the convicts at Botany Bay° are found to have as healthy a moral sentiment as other children. Citizens of feudal states are alarmed at our democratic institutions lapsing into anarchy; and the older and more cautious among ourselves are learning from Europeans to look with some terror at our turbulent freedom. It is said that in our license of construing the Constitution, and in the despotism of public opinion, we have no anchor; and one foreign observer thinks he has found the safeguard in the sanctity of Marriage among us;° and another thinks he has found it in our Calvinism. Fisher Ames° expressed the popular security more wisely, when he compared a monarchy and a republic, saying, 'that a monarchy is a merchantman, which sails well, but will sometimes strike on a rock, and go to the bottom; whilst a republic is a raft, which would never sink, but then your feet are always in water.' No forms can have any dangerous importance, whilst we are befriended by the laws of things. It makes no difference how many tons weight of atmosphere presses on our heads, so long as the same pressure resists it within the lungs. Augment the mass a thousand fold, it cannot begin to crush us, as long as reaction is equal to action. The fact of two poles, of two forces, centripetal and centrifugal, is universal, and each force by its own activity develops the other. Wild liberty develops iron conscience. Want of liberty, by strengthening law and decorum, stupefies conscience. 'Lynch-law' prevails only where there is greater hardihood and self-subsistency in the leaders. A mob cannot be a permanency: everybody's interest requires that it should not exist, and only justice satisfies all.

We must trust infinitely to the beneficent necessity which shines through all laws. Human nature expresses itself in them as characteristically as in statues, or songs, or railroads, and an abstract of the codes of nations would be a transcript of the common conscience. Governments have their origin in the moral identity of men. Reason for one is seen to be reason for another, and for every other. There is a middle measure which satisfies all parties, be they never so many, or so resolute for their own. Every man finds a sanction for his simplest claims and deeds in decisions of his own mind, which he calls Truth and Holiness. In these decisions all the citizens find a perfect agreement, and only in these; not in what is good to eat, good to wear, good use of time, or what amount of land, or of public aid, each is entitled to claim. This truth and justice men presently endeavor to make application of, to the measuring of land, the apportionment of service, the protection of life and property. Their first endeavors, no doubt, are very awkward. Yet absolute right is the first governor; or, every government is an impure theocracy. The idea, after which each community is aiming to make and mend its law, is, the will of the wise man. The wise man, it cannot find in nature, and it makes awkward but earnest efforts to secure his government by contrivance; as, by causing the entire people to give their voices on every measure; or, by a double choice to get the representation of the whole; or, by a selection of the best citizens; or, to secure the advantages of efficiency and internal peace, by confiding the government to one, who may himself select his agents. All forms of government symbolize an immortal government, common to all dynasties and independent of numbers, perfect where two men exist, perfect where there is only one man.

Every man's nature is a sufficient advertisement to him of the character of his fellows. My right and my wrong, is their right and their wrong. Whilst I do what is fit for me, and abstain from what is unfit, my neighbor and I shall often agree in our means, and work together for a time to one end. But whenever I find my dominion over myself not sufficient for me, and undertake the direction of him also, I overstep the truth, and come into false relations to him. I may have so much more skill or strength than he, that he cannot express adequately his sense of wrong, but it is a lie, and hurts like a lie both him and me. Love and nature cannot maintain the assumption: it must be executed by a practical lie, namely, by force. This undertaking for another, is the blunder which stands in colossal ugliness in the governments of the world. It is the same thing in numbers, as in a pair, only not quite so intelligible. I can see well enough a great difference between my setting myself down to a self-control, and my going to make somebody else act after my views: but when a quarter of the human race assume to tell me what I must do, I may be too much disturbed by the circumstances to see so clearly the absurdity of their command. Therefore, all public ends look vague and quixotic beside private ones. For, any laws but those which men make for themselves, are laughable. If I put myself in the place of my child, and we stand in one thought, and see that things are thus or thus, that perception is law for him and me. We are both there, both act. But if, without carrying him into the thought, I look over into his plot, and, guessing how it is with him, ordain this or that, he will never obey me. This is the history of governments,—one man does something which is to bind another. A man who cannot be acquainted with me, taxes me; looking from afar at me, ordains that a part of my labor shall go to this or that whimsical end, not as I, but as he happens to fancy. Behold the consequence. Of all debts, men are least willing to pay the taxes. What a satire is this on government! Everywhere they think they get their money's worth, except for these.

Hence, the less government we have, the better,—the fewer laws, and the less confided power. The antidote to this abuse of formal

Government, is, the influence of private character, the growth of the Individual; the appearance of the principal to supersede the proxy; the appearance of the wise man, of whom the existing government, is, it must be owned, but a shabby imitation. That which all things tend to educe, which freedom, cultivation, intercourse, revolutions, go to form and deliver, is character; that is the end of nature, to reach unto this coronation of her king. To educate the wise man, the State exists; and with the appearance of the wise man, the State expires. The appearance of character makes the State unnecessary. The wise man is the State. He needs no army, fort, or navy,—he loves men too well; no bribe, or feast, or palace, to draw friends to him; no vantage ground, no favorable circumstance. He needs no library, for he has not done thinking; no church, for he is a prophet; no statute book, for he has the lawgiver; no money, for he is value; no road, for he is at home where he is; no experience, for the life of the creator shoots through him, and looks from his eyes. He has no personal friends, for he who has the spell to draw the prayer and piety of all men unto him, needs not husband and educate a few, to share with him a select and poetic life. His relation to men is angelic; his memory is myrrh to them; his presence, frankincense and flowers.

We think our civilization near its meridian, but we are yet only at the cock-crowing and the morning star. In our barbarous society the influence of character is in its infancy. As a political power, as the rightful lord who is to tumble all rulers from their chairs, its presence is hardly yet suspected. Malthus and Ricardo quite omit it; the Annual Register is silent; in the Conversations' Lexicon,° it is not set down; the President's Message, the Queen's Speech, have not mentioned it; and yet it is never nothing. Every thought which genius and piety throw into the world, alters the world. The gladiators in the lists of power feel, through all their frocks of force and simulation, the presence of worth. I think the very strife of trade and ambition are confession of this divinity; and successes in those fields are the poor amends, the fig-leaf with which the shamed soul attempts to hide its nakedness. I find the like unwilling homage in all quarters. It is because we know how much is due from us, that we are impatient to show some petty talent as a substitute for worth. We are haunted by a conscience of this right to grandeur of character, and are false to it. But each of us has some talent, can do somewhat useful, or graceful, or formidable, or amusing, or lucrative. That we do, as an apology to others and to ourselves, for not reaching the mark of a good and equal life. But it does not satisfy *us*, whilst we thrust it on the notice of our companions. It may throw dust in their eyes, but does not smooth our own brow, or give us the tranquillity of the strong when we walk abroad. We do penance as we go. Our talent is a sort of expiation, and we are constrained to reflect on our splendid moment, with a certain humiliation, as somewhat too fine, and not as one act of many acts, a fair expression of our permanent energy. Most persons of ability meet in society with a kind of tacit appeal. Each seems to say, 'I am not all here.' Senators and presidents have climbed so high with pain enough, not because they think the place specially agreeable, but as an apology for real worth, and to vindicate their manhood in our eyes. This conspicuous chair is their compensation to themselves for being of a poor, cold, hard nature. They must do what they can. Like one class of forest animals, they have nothing but a prehensile tail: climb they must, or crawl. If a man found himself so rich-natured that he could enter into strict relations with the best persons, and make life serene around him by the dignity and sweetness of his behavior, could he afford to circumvent the favor of the caucus and the press, and covet relations so hollow and pompous, as those of a politician? Surely nobody would be a charlatan, who could afford to be sincere.

The tendencies of the times favor the idea of self-government, and leave the individual, for all code, to the rewards and penalties of his own constitution, which work with more energy than we believe, whilst we depend on artificial restraints. The movement in this direction has been very marked in modern history. Much has been blind and discreditable, but the nature of the revolution is not affected by the vices of the revolters; for this is a purely moral force. It was never adopted by any party in history, neither can be. It separates the individual from all party, and unites him, at the same time, to the race. It promises a recognition of higher rights than those of personal freedom, or the security of property. A man has a right to be employed, to be trusted, to be loved, to be revered. The power of love, as the basis of a State, has never been tried. We must not imagine that all things are lapsing into confusion, if every tender protestant be not compelled to bear his part in certain social conventions: nor doubt that roads can be built, letters carried, and the fruit of labor secured, when the government of force is at an end. Are our methods now so excellent that all competition is hopeless? Could not a nation of friends even devise better ways? On the other hand, let not the most conservative and timid fear anything from a premature surrender of the bayonet, and the system of force. For, according to the order of nature, which is quite superior to our will, it stands thus; there will always be a government of force, where men are selfish; and when they are pure enough to abjure the code of force, they will be wise enough to see how these public ends of the post-office, of the highway, of commerce, and the exchange of property, of museums and libraries, of institutions of art and science, can be answered.

We live in a very low state of the world, and pay unwilling tribute to governments founded on force. There is not, among the most religious and instructed men of the most religious and civil nations, a reliance on the moral sentiment, and a sufficient belief in the unity of things to persuade them that society can be maintained without artificial restraints, as well as the solar system; or that the private citizen might be reasonable, and a good neighbor, without the hint of a jail or a confiscation. What is strange too, there never was in any man sufficient faith in the power of rectitude, to inspire him with the broad design of renovating the State on the principle of right and love. All those who have pretended this design, have been partial reformers, and have admitted in some manner the supremacy of the bad State. I do not call to mind a single human being who has steadily denied the authority of the laws, on the simple ground of his own moral nature. Such designs, full of genius and full of fate as they are, are not entertained except avowedly as air-pictures. If the individual who exhibits them, dare to think them practicable, he disgusts scholars and churchmen; and men of talent, and women of superior sentiments, cannot hide their contempt. Not the less does nature continue to fill the heart of youth with suggestions of this enthusiasm, and there are now men,—if indeed I can speak in the plural number,—more exactly, I will say, I have just been conversing with one man, to whom no weight of adverse experience will make it for a moment appear impossible, that thousands of human beings might exercise towards each other the grandest and simplest sentiments, as well as a knot of friends, or a pair of lovers.

NOMINALIST AND REALIST

In countless upward-striving waves
The moon-drawn tide-wave strives;
In thousand far-transplanted grafts
The parent fruit survives;
So, in the new-born millions,
The perfect Adam lives.
Not less are summer-mornings dear
To every child they wake,
And each with novel life his sphere
Fills for his proper sake.

I CANNOT often enough say, that a man is only a relative and representative nature. Each is a hint of the truth, but far enough from being that truth, which yet he quite newly and inevitably suggests to us. If I seek it in him, I shall not find it. Could any man conduct into me the pure stream of that which he pretends to be! Long afterwards, I find that quality elsewhere which he promised me. The genius of the Platonists, is intoxicating to the student, yet how few particulars of it can I detach from all their books. The man momentarily stands for the thought, but will not bear examination; and a society of men will cursorily represent well enough a certain quality and culture, for example, chivalry or beauty of manners, but separate them, and there is no gentleman and no lady in the group. The least hint sets us on the pursuit of a character, which no man realizes. We have such exorbitant eyes, that on seeing the smallest arc, we complete the curve, and when the curtain is lifted from the diagram which it seemed to veil, we are vexed to find that no more was drawn, than just that fragment of an arc which we first beheld. We are greatly too liberal in our construction of each other's faculty and promise. Exactly what the parties have already done, they shall do again; but that which we inferred from their nature and inception, they will not do. That is in nature, but not in them. That happens in the world, which we often witness in a public debate. Each of the speakers expresses himself imperfectly: no one of them hears much that another says, such is the preoccupation of mind of each; and the audience, who have only to hear and not to speak, judge very wisely and superiorly how wrongheaded and unskilful is each of the debaters to his own affair. Great men or men of great gifts you shall easily find, but symmetrical men never. When I meet a pure intellectual force, or a

generosity of affection, I believe, here then is man; and am presently
mortified by the discovery, that this individual is no more available to
his own or to the general ends, than his companions; because the power
which drew my respect, is not supported by the total symphony of his
talents. All persons exist to society by some shining trait of beauty or
utility, which they have. We borrow the proportions of the man from
that one fine feature, and finish the portrait symmetrically; which is
false; for the rest of his body is small or deformed. I observe a person
who makes a good public appearance, and conclude thence the perfection of his private character, on which this is based; but he has no private character. He is a graceful cloak or lay-figure for holidays. All our
poets, heroes, and saints, fail utterly in some one or in many parts to
satisfy our idea, fail to draw our spontaneous interest, and so leave us
without any hope of realization but in our own future. Our exaggeration
of all fine characters arises from the fact, that we identify each in turn
with the soul. But there are no such men as we fable; no Jesus, nor
Pericles, nor Cæsar, nor Angelo, nor Washington, such as we have
made. We consecrate a great deal of nonsense, because it was allowed
by great men. There is none without his foible. I verily believe if an
angel should come to chaunt the chorus of the moral law, he would eat
too much gingerbread, or take liberties with private letters, or do some
precious atrocity. It is bad enough, that our geniuses cannot do anything useful, but it is worse that no man is fit for society, who has fine
traits. He is admired at a distance, but he cannot come near without
appearing a cripple. The men of fine parts protect themselves by solitude, or by courtesy, or by satire, or by an acid worldly manner, each
concealing, as he best can, his incapacity for useful association, but they
want either love or self-reliance.

Our native love of reality joins with this experience to teach us a little
reserve, and to dissuade a too sudden surrender to the brilliant qualities
of persons. Young people admire talents or particular excellences; as
we grow older, we value total powers and effects, as, the impression,
the quality, the spirit of men and things. The genius is all. The man,—
it is his system: we do not try a solitary word or act, but his habit. The
acts which you praise, I praise not, since they are departures from his
faith, and are mere compliances. The magnetism which arranges tribes
and races in one polarity, is alone to be respected; the men are steel-
filings. Yet we unjustly select a particle, and say, 'O steel-filing number
one! what heart-drawings I feel to thee! what prodigious virtues are
these of thine! how constitutional to thee, and incommunicable.' Whilst
we speak, the loadstone is withdrawn; down falls our filing in a heap

with the rest, and we continue our mummery to the wretched shaving. Let us go for universals; for the magnetism, not for the needles. Human life and its persons are poor empirical pretensions. A personal influence is an *ignis fatuus*. If they say, it is great, it is great; if they say, it is small, it is small; you see it, and you see it not, by turns; it borrows all its size from the momentary estimation of the speakers: the Will-of-the-wisp vanishes, if you go too near, vanishes if you go too far, and only blazes at one angle. Who can tell if Washington be a great man, or no? Who can tell if Franklin be? Yes, or any but the twelve, or six, or three great gods of fame? And they, too, loom and fade before the eternal.

We are amphibious creatures, weaponed for two elements, having two sets of faculties, the particular and the catholic. We adjust our instrument for general observation, and sweep the heavens as easily as we pick out a single figure in the terrestrial landscape. We are practically skilful in detecting elements, for which we have no place in our theory, and no name. Thus we are very sensible of an atmospheric influence in men and in bodies of men, not accounted for in an arithmetical addition of all their measurable properties. There is a genius of a nation, which is not to be found in the numerical citizens, but which characterizes the society. England, strong, punctual, practical, well-spoken England, I should not find, if I should go to the island to seek it. In the parliament, in the playhouse, at dinner-tables, I might see a great number of rich, ignorant, book-read, conventional, proud men,—many old women,—and not anywhere the Englishman who made the good speeches, combined the accurate engines, and did the bold and nervous deeds. It is even worse in America, where, from the intellectual quickness of the race, the genius of the country is more splendid in its promise, and more slight in its performance. Webster cannot do the work of Webster. We conceive distinctly enough the French, the Spanish, the German genius, and it is not the less real, that perhaps we should not meet in either of those nations, a single individual who corresponded with the type. We infer the spirit of the nation in great measure from the language, which is a sort of monument, to which each forcible individual in a course of many hundred years has contributed a stone. And, universally, a good example of this social force, is the veracity of language, which cannot be debauched. In any controversy concerning morals, an appeal may be made with safety to the sentiments, which the language of the people expresses. Proverbs, words, and grammar inflections convey the public sense with more purity and precision, than the wisest individual.

In the famous dispute with the Nominalists, the Realists had a good deal of reason. General ideas are essences. They are our gods: they round and ennoble the most partial and sordid way of living. Our proclivity to details cannot quite degrade our life, and divest it of poetry. The day-laborer is reckoned as standing at the foot of the social scale, yet he is saturated with the laws of the world. His measures are the hours; morning and night, solstice and equinox, geometry, astronomy, and all the lovely accidents of nature play through his mind. Money, which represents the prose of life, and which is hardly spoken of in parlors without an apology, is, in its effects and laws, as beautiful as roses. Property keeps the accounts of the world, and is always moral. The property will be found where the labor, the wisdom, and the virtue have been in nations, in classes, and (the whole life-time considered, with the compensations) in the individual also. How wise the world appears, when the laws and usages of nations are largely detailed, and the completeness of the municipal system is considered! Nothing is left out. If you go into the markets, and the custom-houses, the insurers' and notaries' offices, the offices of sealers of weights and measures, of inspection of provisions,—it will appear as if one man had made it all. Wherever you go, a wit like your own has been before you, and has realized its thought. The Eleusinian mysteries,° the Egyptian architecture, the Indian astronomy, the Greek sculpture, show that there always were seeing and knowing men in the planet. The world is full of masonic ties, of guilds, of secret and public legions of honor; that of scholars, for example; and that of gentlemen fraternizing with the upper class of every country and every culture.

I am very much struck in literature by the appearance, that one person wrote all the books; as if the editor of a journal planted his body of reporters in different parts of the field of action, and relieved some by others from time to time; but there is such equality and identity both of judgment and point of view in the narrative, that it is plainly the work of one all-seeing, all-hearing gentleman. I looked into Pope's Odyssey° yesterday: it is as correct and elegant after our canon of today, as if it were newly written. The modernness of all good books seems to give me an existence as wide as man. What is well done, I feel as if I did; what is ill-done, I reck not of. Shakspeare's passages of passion (for example, in Lear and Hamlet) are in the very dialect of the present year. I am faithful again to the whole over the members in my use of books. I find the most pleasure in reading a book in a manner least flattering to the author. I read Proclus, and sometimes Plato, as I might read a dictionary, for a mechanical help to the fancy and the imagination. I read for the lustres, as if one should use a fine picture in a chromatic experiment, for its rich colors. 'Tis not Proclus, but a piece of nature and fate that I explore. It is a greater joy to see the author's author, than himself. A higher pleasure of the same kind I found lately at a concert, where I went to hear Handel's Messiah.° As the master overpowered the littleness and incapableness of the performers, and made them conductors of his electricity, so it was easy to observe what efforts nature was making through so many hoarse, wooden, and imperfect persons, to produce beautiful voices, fluid and soul-guided men and women. The genius of nature was paramount at the oratorio.

This preference of the genius to the parts is the secret of that deification of art, which is found in all superior minds. Art, in the artist, is proportion, or, a habitual respect to the whole by an eye loving beauty in details. And the wonder and charm of it is the sanity in insanity which it denotes. Proportion is almost impossible to human beings. There is no one who does not exaggerate. In conversation, men are encumbered with personality, and talk too much. In modern sculpture, picture, and poetry, the beauty is miscellaneous; the artist works here and there, and at all points, adding and adding, instead of unfolding the unit of his thought. Beautiful details we must have, or no artist: but they must be means and never other. The eye must not lose sight for a moment of the purpose. Lively boys write to their ear and eye, and the cool reader finds nothing but sweet jingles in it. When they grow older, they respect the argument.

We obey the same intellectual integrity, when we study in exceptions the law of the world. Anomalous facts, as the never quite obsolete rumors of magic and demonology, and the new allegations of phrenologists and neurologists, are of ideal use. They are good indications. Homœopathy is insignificant as an art of healing, but of great value as criticism on the hygeia or medical practice of the time. So with Mesmerism, Swedenborgism, Fourierism, and the Millennial Church;° they are poor pretensions enough, but good criticism on the science, philosophy, and preaching of the day. For these abnormal insights of the adepts, ought to be normal, and things of course.

All things show us, that on every side we are very near to the best. It seems not worth while to execute with too much pains some one intellectual, or æsthetical, or civil feat, when presently the dream will scatter, and we shall burst into universal power. The reason of idleness and of crime is the deferring of our hopes. Whilst we are waiting, we beguile the time with jokes, with sleep, with eating, and with crimes.

Thus we settle it in our cool libraries, that all the agents with which we deal are subalterns, which we can well afford to let pass, and life will be simpler when we live at the centre, and flout the surfaces. I wish to speak with all respect of persons, but sometimes I must pinch myself to keep awake, and preserve the due decorum. They melt so fast into each other, that they are like grass and trees, and it needs an effort to treat them as individuals. Though the uninspired man certainly finds persons a conveniency in household matters, the divine man does not respect them: he sees them as a rack of clouds, or a fleet of ripples which the wind drives over the surface of the water. But this is flat rebellion. Nature will not be Buddhist: she resents generalizing, and insults the philosopher in every moment with a million of fresh particulars. It is all idle talking: as much as a man is a whole, so is he also a part; and it were partial not to see it. What you say in your pompous distribution only distributes you into your class and section. You have not got rid of parts by denying them, but are the more partial. You are one thing, but nature is *one thing and the other thing*, in the same moment. She will not remain orbed in a thought, but rushes into persons; and when each person, inflamed to a fury of personality, would conquer all things to his poor crotchet, she raises up against him another person, and by many persons incarnates again a sort of whole. She will have all. Nick Bottom° cannot play all the parts, work it how he may: there will be somebody else, and the world will be round. Everything must have its flower or effort at the beautiful, coarser or finer according to its stuff. They relieve and recommend each other, and the sanity of society is a balance of a thousand insanities. She punishes abstractionists, and will only forgive an induction which is rare and casual. We like to come to a height of land and see the landscape, just as we value a general remark in conversation. But it is not the intention of nature that we should live by general views. We fetch fire and water, run about all day among the shops and markets, and get our clothes and shoes made and mended, and are the victims of these details, and once in a fortnight we arrive perhaps at a rational moment. If we were not thus infatuated, if we saw the real from hour to hour, we should not be here to write and to read, but should have been burned or frozen long ago. She would never get anything done, if she suffered admirable Crichtons, and universal geniuses. She loves better a wheelwright who dreams all night of wheels, and a groom who is part of his horse: for she is full of work, and these are her hands. As the frugal farmer takes care that his cattle shall eat down the rowan, and swine shall eat the waste of his house, and poultry shall pick the crumbs, so our economical mother despatches a new genius and habit of mind into every district and condition of existence, plants an eye wherever a new ray of light can fall, and gathering up into some man every property in the universe, establishes thousandfold occult mutual attractions among her offspring, that all this wash and waste of power may be imparted and exchanged.

Great dangers undoubtedly accrue from this incarnation and distribution of the godhead, and hence nature has her maligners, as if she were Circe; and Alphonso of Castille° fancied he could have given useful advice. But she does not go unprovided; she has hellebore° at the bottom of the cup. Solitude would ripen a plentiful crop of despots. The recluse thinks of men as having his manner, or as not having his manner; and as having degrees of it, more and less. But when he comes into a public assembly, he sees that men have very different manners from his own, and in their way admirable. In his childhood and youth, he has had many checks and censures, and thinks modestly enough of his own endowment. When afterwards he comes to unfold it in propitious circumstance, it seems the only talent: he is delighted with his success, and accounts himself already the fellow of the great. But he goes into a mob, into a banking-house, into a mechanic's shop, into a mill, into a laboratory, into a ship, into a camp, and in each new place he is no better than an idiot: other talents take place, and rule the hour. The rotation which whirls every leaf and pebble to the meridian, reaches to every gift of man, and we all take turns at the top.

For nature, who abhors mannerism, has set her heart on breaking up all styles and tricks, and it is so much easier to do what one has done before, than to do a new thing, that there is a perpetual tendency to a set mode. In every conversation, even the highest, there is a certain trick, which may be soon learned by an acute person, and then that particular style continued indefinitely. Each man, too, is a tyrant in tendency, because he would impose his idea on others; and their trick is their natural defence. Jesus would absorb the race; but Tom Paine or the coarsest blasphemer helps humanity by resisting this exuberance of power. Hence the immense benefit of party in politics, as it reveals faults of character in a chief, which the intellectual force of the persons, with ordinary opportunity, and not hurled into aphelion by hatred, could not have seen. Since we are all so stupid, what benefit that there should be two stupidities! It is like that brute advantage so essential to astronomy, of having the diameter of the earth's orbit for a base of its triangles. Democracy is morose, and runs to anarchy, but in the state, and in the schools, it is indispensable to resist the consolidation of all men into a few men. If John was perfect, why are you and I alive? As long as any man exists, there is some need of him; let him fight for his own. A new poet has appeared; a new character approached us; why should we refuse to eat bread, until we have found his regiment and section in our old army-files? Why not a new man? Here is a new enterprise of Brook Farm, of Skeneateles, of Northampton: why so impatient to baptise them Essenes, or Port-Royalists, or Shakers,° or by any known and effete name? Let it be a new way of living. Why have only two or three ways of life, and not thousands? Every man is wanted, and no man is wanted much. We came this time for condiments, not for corn. We want the great genius only for joy; for one star more in our constellation, for one tree more in our grove. But he thinks we wish to belong to him, as he wishes to occupy us. He greatly mistakes us. I think I have done well, if I have acquired a new word from a good author; and my business with him is to find my own, though it were only to melt him down into an epithet or an image for daily use.

'Into paint will I grind thee, my bride!'°

To embroil the confusion, and make it impossible to arrive at any general statement, when we have insisted on the imperfection of individuals, our affections and our experience urge that every individual is entitled to honor, and a very generous treatment is sure to be repaid. A recluse sees only two or three persons, and allows them all their room; they spread themselves at large. The man of state looks at many, and compares the few habitually with others, and these look less. Yet are they not entitled to this generosity of reception? and is not munificence the means of insight? For though gamesters say, that the cards beat all the players, though they were never so skilful, yet in the contest we are now considering, the players are also the game, and share the power of the cards. If you criticise a fine genius, the odds are that you are out of your reckoning, and, instead of the poet, are censuring your own caricature of him. For there is somewhat spheral and infinite in every man, especially in every genius, which, if you can come very near him, sports with all your limitations. For, rightly, every man is a channel through which heaven floweth, and, whilst I fancied I was criticizing him, I was censuring or rather terminating my own soul. After taxing Goethe as a courtier, artificial, unbelieving, worldly, —I took up this book of Helena, and found him an Indian of the wilderness, a piece of pure nature like an apple or an oak, large as morning or night, and virtuous as a briar-rose.

But care is taken that the whole tune shall be played. If we were not kept among surfaces, every thing would be large and universal: now the excluded attributes burst in on us with the more brightness, that they have been excluded. 'Your turn now, my turn next,' is the rule of the game. The universality being hindered in its primary form, comes in the secondary form of *all sides*: the points come in succession to the meridian, and by the speed of rotation, a new whole is formed. Nature keeps herself whole, and her representation complete in the experience of each mind. She suffers no seat to be vacant in her college. It is the secret of the world that all things subsist, and do not die, but only retire a little from sight, and afterwards return again. Whatever does not concern us, is concealed from us. As soon as a person is no longer related to our present well-being, he is concealed, or *dies*, as we say. Really, all things and persons are related to us, but according to our nature, they act on us not at once, but in succession, and we are made aware of their presence one at a time. All persons, all things which we have known, are here present, and many more than we see; the world is full. As the ancient said, the world is a *plenum* or solid; and if we saw all things that really surround us, we should be imprisoned and unable to move. For, though nothing is impassable to the soul, but all things are pervious to it, and like highways, yet this is only whilst the soul does not see them. As soon as the soul sees any object, it stops before that object. Therefore, the divine Providence, which keeps the universe open in every direction to the soul, conceals all the furniture and all the persons that do not concern a particular soul, from the senses of that individual. Through solidest eternal things, the man finds his road, as if they did not subsist, and does not once suspect their being. As soon as he needs a new object, suddenly he beholds it, and no longer attempts to pass through it, but takes another way. When he has exhausted for the time the nourishment to be drawn from any one person or thing, that object is withdrawn from his observation, and though still in his immediate neighborhood, he does not suspect its presence.

Nothing is dead: men feign themselves dead, and endure mock funerals and mournful obituaries, and there they stand looking out of the window, sound and well, in some new and strange disguise. Jesus is not dead: he is very well alive: nor John, nor Paul, nor Mahomet, nor Aristotle; at times we believe we have seen them all, and could easily tell the names under which they go.

If we cannot make voluntary and conscious steps in the admirable science of universals, let us see the parts wisely, and infer the genius of nature from the best particulars with a becoming charity. What is best in each kind is an index of what should be the average of that thing. Love shows me the opulence of nature, by disclosing to me in my friend a hidden wealth, and I infer an equal depth of good in every other direction. It is commonly said by farmers, that a good pear or apple costs no more time or pains to rear, than a poor one; so I would have no work of art, no speech, or action, or thought, or friend, but the best.

The end and the means, the gamester and the game,—life is made up of the intermixture and reaction of these two amicable powers, whose marriage appears beforehand monstrous, as each denies and tends to abolish the other. We must reconcile the contradictions as we can, but their discord and their concord introduce wild absurdities into our thinking and speech. No sentence will hold the whole truth, and the only way in which we can be just, is by giving ourselves the lie; Speech is better than silence; silence is better than speech;—All things are in contact; every atom has a sphere of repulsion;—Things are, and are not, at the same time;—and the like. All the universe over, there is but one thing, this old Two-Face, creator-creature, mind-matter, right-wrong, of which any proposition may be affirmed or denied. Very fitly, therefore, I assert, that every man is a partialist, that nature secures him as an instrument by self-conceit, preventing the tendencies to religion and science; and now further assert, that, each man's genius being nearly and affectionately explored, he is justified in his individuality, as his nature is found to be immense; and now I add, that every man is a universalist also, and, as our earth, whilst it spins on its own axis, spins all the time around the sun through the celestial spaces, so the least of its rational children, the most dedicated to his private affair, works out, though as it were under a disguise, the universal problem. We fancy men are individuals; so are pumpkins; but every pumpkin in the field, goes through every point of pumpkin history. The rabid democrat, as soon as he is senator and rich man, has ripened beyond possibility of sincere radicalism, and unless he can resist the sun, he must be conservative the remainder of his days. Lord Eldon° said in his old age, 'that, if he were to begin life again, he would be damned but he would begin as agitator.'

We hide this universality, if we can, but it appears at all points. We are as ungrateful as children. There is nothing we cherish and strive to draw to us, but in some hour we turn and rend it. We keep a running fire of sarcasm at ignorance and the life of the senses; then goes by, perchance, a fair girl, a piece of life, gay and happy, and making the commonest offices beautiful, by the energy and heart with which she does them, and seeing this, we admire and love her and them, and say, 'Lo! a genuine creature of the fair earth, not dissipated, or too early ripened by books, philosophy, religion, society, or care!' insinuating a treachery and contempt for all we had so long loved and wrought in ourselves and others.

If we could have any security against moods! If the profoundest prophet could be holden to his words, and the hearer who is ready to sell all and join the crusade, could have any certificate that tomorrow his prophet shall not unsay his testimony! But the Truth sits veiled there on the Bench, and never interposes an adamantine syllable; and the most sincere and revolutionary doctrine, put as if the ark of God were carried forward some furlongs, and planted there for the succor of the world, shall in a few weeks be coldly set aside by the same speaker, as morbid; 'I thought I was right, but I was not,'—and the same immeasurable credulity demanded for new audacities. If we were not of all opinions! if we did not in any moment shift the platform on which we stand, and look and speak from another! if there could be any regulation, any 'one-hour-rule,' that a man should never leave his point of view, without sound of trumpet. I am always insincere, as always knowing there are other moods.

How sincere and confidential we can be, saying all that lies in the mind, and yet go away feeling that all is yet unsaid, from the incapacity of the parties to know each other, although they use the same words! My companion assumes to know my mood and habit of thought, and we go on from explanation to explanation, until all is said which words can, and we leave matters just as they were at first, because of that vicious assumption. Is it that every man believes every other to be an incurable partialist, and himself an universalist? I talked yesterday with a pair of philosophers: I endeavored to show my good men that I love everything by turns, and nothing long; that I loved the centre, but doated on the superficies; that I loved man, if men seemed to me mice and rats; that I revered saints, but woke up glad that the old pagan world stood its ground, and died hard; that I was glad of men of every gift and nobility, but would not live in their arms. Could they but once understand, that I loved to know that they existed, and heartily wished them Godspeed, yet, out of my poverty of life and thought, had no word or welcome for them when they came to see me, and could well consent to their living in Oregon, for any claim I felt on them, it would be a great satisfaction.

NEW ENGLAND REFORMERS

A lecture read before the Society in Amory Hall, on Sunday, 3 March, 1844

WHOEVER has had opportunity of acquaintance with society in New England, during the last twenty-five years, with those middle and with those leading sections that may constitute any just representation of the character and aim of the community, will have been struck with the great activity of thought and experimenting. His attention must be commanded by the signs that the Church, or religious party, is falling from the church nominal, and is appearing in temperance and non-resistance societies, in movements of abolitionists and of socialists, and in very significant assemblies, called Sabbath and Bible Conventions,—composed of ultraists, of seekers, of all the soul of the soldiery of dissent, and meeting to call in question the authority of the Sabbath, of the priesthood, and of the church. In these movements, nothing was more remarkable than the discontent they begot in the movers. The spirit of protest and of detachment, drove the members of these Conventions to bear testimony against the church, and immediately afterward, to declare their discontent with these Conventions, their independence of their colleagues, and their impatience of the methods whereby they were working. They defied each other, like a congress of kings, each of whom had a realm to rule, and a way of his own that made concert unprofitable. What a fertility of projects for the salvation of the world! One apostle thought all men should go to farming; and another, that no man should buy or sell: that the use of money was the cardinal evil; another, that the mischief was in our diet, that we eat and drink damnation. These made unleavened bread, and were foes to the death to fermentation. It was in vain urged by the housewife, that God made yeast, as well as dough, and loves fermentation just as dearly as he loves vegetation; that fermentation develops the saccharine element in the grain, and makes it more palatable and more digestible. No; they wish the pure wheat, and will die but it shall not ferment. Stop, dear nature, these incessant advances of thine; let us scotch these ever-rolling wheels! Others attacked the system of agriculture, the use of animal manures in farming; and the tyranny of man over brute nature; these abuses polluted his food. The ox must be taken from the plough, and the horse from the cart, the hundred acres of the farm must be spaded, and the man must walk wherever boats and locomotives will not carry him. Even the insect world was to be defended,—that had been too long neglected, and a society for the protection of ground-worms, slugs, and mosquitos was to be incorporated without delay. With these appeared the adepts of homœopathy, of hydropathy, of mesmerism, of phrenology, and their wonderful theories of the Christian miracles! Others assailed particular vocations, as that of the lawyer, that of the merchant, of the manufacturer, of the clergyman, of the scholar. Others attacked the institution of marriage, as the fountain of social evils. Others devoted themselves to the worrying of churches and meetings for public worship; and the fertile forms of antinomianism among the elder puritans, seemed to have their match in the plenty of the new harvest of reform.

With this din of opinion and debate, there was a keener scrutiny of institutions and domestic life than any we had known, there was sincere protesting against existing evils, and there were changes of employment dictated by conscience. No doubt, there was plentiful vaporing, and cases of backsliding might occur. But in each of these movements emerged a good result, a tendency to the adoption of simpler methods, and an assertion of the sufficiency of the private man. Thus it was directly in the spirit and genius of the age, what happened in one instance, when a church censured° and threatened to excommunicate one of its members, on account of the somewhat hostile part to the church, which his conscience led him to take in the anti-slavery business; the threatened individual immediately excommunicated the church in a public and formal process. This has been several times repeated: it was excellent when it was done the first time, but, of course, loses all value when it is copied. Every project in the history of reform, no matter how violent and surprising, is good, when it is the dictate of a man's genius and constitution, but very dull and suspicious when adopted from another. It is right and beautiful in any man to say, 'I will take this coat, or this book, or this measure of corn of yours,'—in whom we see the act to be original, and to flow from the whole spirit and faith of him; for then that taking will have a giving as free and divine: but we are very easily disposed to resist the same generosity of speech, when we miss originality and truth to character in it.

There was in all the practical activities of New England, for the last quarter of a century, a gradual withdrawal of tender consciences from the social organizations. There is observable throughout, the contest between mechanical and spiritual methods, but with a steady tendency of the thoughtful and virtuous to a deeper belief and reliance on spiritual facts.

In politics, for example, it is easy to see the progress of dissent. The country is full of rebellion; the country is full of kings. Hands off! let there be no control and no interference in the administration of the affairs of this kingdom of me. Hence the growth of the doctrine and of the party of Free Trade,° and the willingness to try that experiment, in the face of what appear incontestable facts. I confess, the motto of the Globe newspaper° is so attractive to me, that I can seldom find much appetite to read what is below it in its columns, 'The world is governed too much.' So the country is frequently affording solitary examples of resistance to the government, solitary nullifiers, who throw themselves on their reserved rights; nay, who have reserved all their rights; who reply to the assessor, and to the clerk of court, that they do not know the State; and embarrass the courts of law, by non-juring, and the commander-in-chief of the militia, by non-resistance.

The same disposition to scrutiny and dissent appeared in civil, festive, neighborly, and domestic society. A restless, prying, conscientious criticism broke out in unexpected quarters. Who gave me the money with which I bought my coat? Why should professional labor and that of the counting-house be paid so disproportionately to the labor of the porter, and woodsawyer? This whole business of Trade gives me to pause and think, as it constitutes false relations between men; inasmuch as I am prone to count myself relieved of any responsibility to behave well and nobly to that person whom I pay with money, whereas if I had not that commodity, I should be put on my good behavior in all companies, and man would be a benefactor to man, as being himself his only certificate that he had a right to those aids and services which each asked of the other. Am I not too protected a person? is there not a wide disparity between the lot of me and the lot of thee, my poor brother, my poor sister? Am I not defrauded of my best culture in the loss of those gymnastics which manual labor and the emergencies of poverty constitute? I find nothing healthful or exalting in the smooth conventions of society; I do not like the close air of saloons. I begin to suspect myself to be a prisoner, though treated with all this courtesy and luxury. I pay a destructive tax in my conformity.

The same insatiable criticism may be traced in the efforts for the reform of Education. The popular education has been taxed with a want of truth and nature. It was complained that an education to things was not given. We are students of words: we are shut up in schools, and colleges, and recitation-rooms, for ten or fifteen years, and come out at last with a bag of wind, a memory of words, and do not know a thing. We cannot use our hands, or our legs, or our eyes, or our arms. We do not know an edible root in the woods, we cannot tell our course by the stars, nor the hour of the day by the sun. It is well if we can swim and skate. We are afraid of a horse, of a cow, of a dog, of a snake, of a spider. The Roman rule was, to teach a boy nothing that he could not learn standing. The old English rule was, 'All summer in the field, and all winter in the study.' And it seems as if a man should learn to plant, or to fish, or to hunt, that he might secure his subsistence at all events, and not be painful to his friends and fellow men. The lessons of science should be experimental also. The sight of the planet through a telescope, is worth all the course on astronomy: the shock of the electric spark in the elbow, out-values all the theories; the taste of the nitrous oxide, the firing of an artificial volcano, are better than volumes of chemistry.

One of the traits of the new spirit, is the inquisition it fixed on our scholastic devotion to the dead languages. The ancient languages, with great beauty of structure, contain wonderful remains of genius, which draw, and always will draw, certain likeminded men,—Greek men, and Roman men, in all countries, to their study; but by a wonderful drowsiness of usage, they had exacted the study of *all* men. Once (say two centuries ago), Latin and Greek had a strict relation to all the science and culture there was in Europe, and the Mathematics had a momentary importance at some era of activity in physical science. These things became stereotyped as *education*, as the manner of men is. But the Good Spirit never cared for the colleges, and though all men and boys were now drilled in Latin, Greek, and Mathematics, it had quite left these shells high and dry on the beach, and was now creating and feeding other matters at other ends of the world. But in a hundred high schools and colleges, this warfare against common sense still goes on. Four, or six, or ten years, the pupil is parsing Greek and Latin, and as soon as he leaves the University, as it is ludicrously called, he shuts those books for the last time. Some thousands of young men are graduated at our colleges in this country every year, and the persons who, at forty years, still read Greek, can all be counted on your hand. I never met with ten. Four or five persons I have seen who read Plato.

But is not this absurd, that the whole liberal talent of this country should be directed in its best years on studies which lead to nothing? What was the consequence? Some intelligent persons said or thought; 'Is that Greek and Latin some spell to conjure with, and not words of reason? If the physician, the lawyer, the divine, never use it to come at their ends, I need never learn it to come at mine. Conjuring is gone out of fashion, and I will omit this conjugating, and go straight to affairs.'

So they jumped the Greek and Latin, and read law, medicine, or sermons, without it. To the astonishment of all, the self-made men took even ground at once with the oldest of the regular graduates, and in a few months the most conservative circles of Boston and New York had quite forgotten who of their gownsmen was college-bred, and who was not.

One tendency appears alike in the philosophical speculation, and in the rudest democratical movements, through all the petulance and all the puerility, the wish, namely, to cast aside the superfluous, and arrive at short methods, urged, as I suppose, by an intuition that the human spirit is equal to all emergencies, alone, and that man is more often injured than helped by the means he uses.

I conceive this gradual casting off of material aids, and the indication of growing trust in the private, self-supplied powers of the individual, to be the affirmative principle of the recent philosophy: and that it is feeling its own profound truth, and is reaching forward at this very hour to the happiest conclusions. I readily concede that in this, as in every period of intellectual activity, there has been a noise of denial and protest; much was to be resisted, much was to be got rid of by those who were reared in the old, before they could begin to affirm and to construct. Many a reformer perishes in his removal of rubbish,—and that makes the offensiveness of the class. They are partial; they are not equal to the work they pretend. They lose their way; in the assault on the kingdom of darkness, they expend all their energy on some accidental evil, and lose their sanity and power of benefit. It is of little moment that one or two, or twenty errors of our social system be corrected, but of much that the man be in his senses.

The criticism and attack on institutions which we have witnessed, has made one thing plain, that society gains nothing whilst a man, not himself renovated, attempts to renovate things around him: he has become tediously good in some particular, but negligent or narrow in the rest; and hypocrisy and vanity are often the disgusting result.

It is handsomer to remain in the establishment better than the establishment, and conduct that in the best manner, than to make a sally against evil by some single improvement, without supporting it by a total regeneration. Do not be so vain of your one objection. Do you think there is only one? Alas! my good friend, there is no part of society or of life better than any other part. All our things are right and wrong together. The wave of evil washes all our institutions alike. Do you complain of our Marriage? Our marriage is no worse than our education, our diet, our trade, our social customs. Do you complain of the laws of Property? It is a pedantry to give such importance to them. Can we not play the game of life with these counters, as well as with those; in the institution of property, as well as out of it. Let into it the new and renewing principle of love, and property will be universality. No one gives the impression of superiority to the institution, which he must give who will reform it. It makes no difference what you say: you must make me feel that you are aloof from it; by your natural and supernatural advantages, do easily see to the end of it,—do see how man can do without it. Now all men are on one side. No man deserves to be heard against property. Only Love, only an Idea, is against property, as we hold it.

I cannot afford to be irritable and captious, nor to waste all my time in attacks. If I should go out of church whenever I hear a false sentiment, I could never stay there five minutes. But why come out? the street is as false as the church, and when I get to my house, or to my manners, or to my speech, I have not got away from the lie. When we see an eager assailant of one of these wrongs, a special reformer, we feel like asking him, What right have you, sir, to your one virtue? Is virtue piecemeal? This is a jewel amidst the rags of a beggar.

In another way the right will be vindicated. In the midst of abuses, in the heart of cities, in the aisles of false churches, alike in one place and in another,—wherever, namely, a just and heroic soul finds itself, there it will do what is next at hand, and by the new quality of character it shall put forth, it shall abrogate that old condition, law or school in which it stands, before the law of its own mind.

If partiality was one fault of the movement party, the other defect was their reliance on Association. Doubts such as those I have intimated, drove many good persons to agitate the questions of social reform. But the revolt against the spirit of commerce, the spirit of aristocracy, and the inveterate abuses of cities, did not appear possible to individuals; and to do battle against numbers, they armed themselves with numbers, and against concert, they relied on new concert.

Following, or advancing beyond the ideas of St. Simon, of Fourier, and of Owen,° three communities have already been formed in Massachusetts on kindred plans, and many more in the country at large. They aim to give every member a share in the manual labor, to give an equal reward to labor and to talent, and to unite a liberal culture with an education to labor. The scheme offers, by the economies of associated labor and expense, to make every member rich, on the same amount of property, that, in separate families, would leave every member poor. These new associations are composed of men and women of superior talents and sentiments: yet it may easily be questioned, whether such a community will draw, except in its beginnings, the able and the good; whether those who have energy, will not prefer their chance of superiority and power in the world, to the humble certainties of the association; whether such a retreat does not promise to become an assylum to those who have tried and failed, rather than a field to the strong; and whether the members will not necessarily be fractions of men, because each finds that he cannot enter it, without some compromise. Friendship and association are very fine things, and a grand phalanx of the best of the human race, banded for some catholic object: yes, excellent; but remember that no society can ever be so large as one man. He in his friendship, in his natural and momentary associations, doubles or multiplies himself; but in the hour in which he mortgages himself to two or ten or twenty, he dwarfs himself below the stature of one.

But the men of less faith could not thus believe, and to such, concert appears the sole specific of strength. I have failed, and you have failed, but perhaps together we shall not fail. Our housekeeping is not satisfactory to us, but perhaps a phalanx, a community, might be. Many of us have differed in opinion, and we could find no man who could make the truth plain, but possibly a college, or an ecclesiastical council might. I have not been able either to persuade my brother or to prevail on myself, to disuse the traffic or the potation of brandy, but perhaps a pledge of total abstinence might effectually restrain us. The candidate my party votes for is not to be trusted with a dollar, but he will be honest in the Senate, for we can bring public opinion to bear on him. Thus concert was the specific in all cases. But concert is neither better nor worse, neither more nor less potent than individual force. All the men in the world cannot make a statue walk and speak, cannot make a drop of blood, or a blade of grass, any more than one man can. But let there be one man, let there be truth in two men, in ten men, then is concert for the first time possible, because the force which moves the world is a new quality, and can never be furnished by adding whatever quantities of a different kind. What is the use of the concert of the false and the disunited? There can be no concert in two, where there is no concert in one. When the individual is not *individual*, but is dual; when his thoughts look one way, and his actions another; when his faith is traversed by his habits; when his will, enlightened by reason, is warped by his sense; when with one hand he rows, and with the other backs water, what concert can be?

I do not wonder at the interest these projects inspire. The world is awaking to the idea of union, and these experiments show what it is thinking of. It is and will be magic. Men will live and communicate, and plough, and reap, and govern, as by added ethereal power, when once they are united; as in a celebrated experiment, by expiration and respiration exactly together, four persons lift a heavy man from the ground by the little finger only, and without sense of weight. But this union must be inward, and not one of covenants, and is to be reached by a reverse of the methods they use. The union is only perfect, when all the uniters are isolated. It is the union of friends who live in different streets or towns. Each man, if he attempts to join himself to others, is on all sides cramped and diminished of his proportion; and the stricter the union, the smaller and the more pitiful he is. But leave him alone, to recognize in every hour and place the secret soul, he will go up and down doing the works of a true member, and, to the astonishment of all, the work will be done with concert, though no man spoke. Government will be adamantine without any governor. The union must be ideal in actual individualism.

I pass to the indication in some particulars of that faith in man, which the heart is preaching to us in these days, and which engages the more regard, from the consideration, that the speculations of one generation are the history of the next following.

In alluding just now to our system of education, I spoke of the deadness of its details. But it is open to graver criticism than the palsy of its members: it is a system of despair. The disease with which the human mind now labors, is want of faith. Men do not believe in a power of education. We do not think we can speak to divine sentiments in man, and we do not try. We renounce all high aims. We believe that the defects of so many perverse and so many frivolous people, who make up society, are organic, and society is a hospital of incurables. A man of good sense but of little faith, whose compassion seemed to lead him to church as often as he went there, said to me; 'that he liked to have concerts, and fairs, and churches, and other public amusements go on.' I am afraid the remark is too honest, and comes from the same origin as the maxim of the tyrant, 'If you would rule the world quietly, you must keep it amused.' I notice too, that the ground on which eminent public servants urge the claims of popular education is fear: 'This country is filling up with thousands and millions of voters, and you must educate them to keep them from our throats.' We do not believe that any education, any system of philosophy, any influence of genius, will ever give depth of insight to a superficial mind. Having settled ourselves into this infidelity, our skill is expended to procure alleviations, diversion, opiates. We adorn the victim with manual skill, his tongue with languages, his body with inoffensive and comely manners. So have we cunningly hid the tragedy of limitation and inner death we cannot avert. Is it strange that society should be devoured by a secret melancholy, which breaks through all its smiles, and all its gayety and games?

But even one step farther our infidelity has gone. It appears that some doubt is felt by good and wise men, whether really the happiness and probity of men is increased by the culture of the mind in those disciplines to which we give the name of education. Unhappily, too, the doubt comes from scholars, from persons who have tried these methods. In their experience, the scholar was not raised by the sacred thoughts amongst which he dwelt, but used them to selfish ends. He was a profane person, and became a showman, turning his gifts to a marketable use, and not to his own sustenance and growth. It was found that the intellect could be independently developed, that is, in separation from the man, as any single organ can be invigorated, and the result was monstrous. A canine appetite for knowledge was generated, which must still be fed, but was never satisfied, and this knowledge not being directed on action, never took the character of substantial, humane truth, blessing those whom it entered. It gave the scholar certain powers of expression, the power of speech, the power of poetry, of literary art, but it did not bring him to peace, or to beneficence.

When the literary class betray a destitution of faith, it is not strange that society should be disheartened and sensualized by unbelief. What remedy? Life must be lived on a higher plane. We must go up to a higher platform, to which we are always invited to ascend; there, the whole aspect of things changes. I resist the skepticism of our education, and of our educated men. I do not believe that the differences of opinion and character in men are organic. I do not recognize, beside the class of the good and the wise, a permanent class of skeptics, or a class of conservatives, or of malignants, or of materialists. I do not believe in two classes. You remember the story° of the poor woman who importuned King Philip of Macedon to grant her justice, which Philip refused: the woman exclaimed, 'I appeal': the king, astonished, asked to whom she appealed: the woman replied, 'from Philip drunk to Philip sober.' The text will suit me very well. I believe not in two classes of men, but in man in two moods, in Philip drunk and Philip sober. I think, according to the good-hearted word of Plato, 'Unwillingly the soul is deprived of truth.'° Iron conservative, miser, or thief, no man is, but by a supposed necessity, which he tolerates by shortness or torpidity of sight. The soul lets no man go without some visitations and holy-days of a diviner presence. It would be easy to show, by a narrow scanning of any man's biography, that we are not so wedded to our paltry performances of every kind, but that every man has at intervals the grace to scorn his performances, in comparing them with his belief of what he should do, that he puts himself on the side of his enemies, listening gladly to what they say of him, and accusing himself of the same things.

What is it men love in Genius, but its infinite hope, which degrades all it has done? Genius counts all its miracles poor and short. Its own idea it never executed. The Iliad, the Hamlet, the Doric column, the Roman arch, the Gothic minster, the German anthem, when they are ended, the master casts behind him. How sinks the song in the waves of melody which the universe pours over his soul! Before that gracious Infinite, out of which he drew these few strokes, how mean they look, though the praises of the world attend them. From the triumphs of his art, he turns with desire to this greater defeat. Let those admire who will. With silent joy he sees himself to be capable of a beauty that eclipses all which his hands have done, all which human hands have ever done.

Well, we are all the children of genius, the children of virtue,—and feel their inspirations in our happier hours. Is not every man sometimes a radical in politics? Men are conservatives when they are least vigorous, or when they are most luxurious. They are conservatives after dinner, or before taking their rest; when they are sick, or aged: in the morning, or when their intellect or their conscience have been aroused, when they hear music, or when they read poetry, they are radicals. In the circle of the rankest tories that could be collected in England, Old or New, let a powerful and stimulating intellect, a man of great heart and mind, act on them, and very quickly these frozen conservators will yield to the friendly influence, these hopeless will begin to hope, these haters will begin to love, these immovable statues will begin to spin and revolve. I cannot help recalling the fine anecdote which Warton relates of Bishop Berkeley, when he was preparing to leave England, with his plan of planting the gospel among the American savages. 'Lord Bathurst told me, that the members of the Scriblerus club, being met at his house at dinner, they agreed to rally Berkeley,° who was also his guest, on his scheme at Bermudas. Berkeley, having listened to the many lively things they had to say, begged to be heard in his turn, and displayed his plan with such an astonishing and animating force of eloquence and enthusiasm, that they were struck dumb, and, after some pause, rose up all together with earnestness, exclaiming, "Let us set out with him immediately." ' Men in all ways are better than they seem.

They like flattery for the moment, but they know the truth for their own. It is a foolish cowardice which keeps us from trusting them, and speaking to them rude truth. They resent your honesty for an instant, they will thank you for it always. What is it we heartily wish of each other? Is it to be pleased and flattered? No, but to be convicted and exposed, to be shamed out of our nonsense of all kinds, and made men of, instead of ghosts and phantoms. We are weary of gliding ghostlike through the world, which is itself so slight and unreal. We crave a sense of reality, though it come in strokes of pain. I explain so,—by this manlike love of truth,—those excesses and errors into which souls of great vigor, but not equal insight, often fall. They feel the poverty at the bottom of all the seeming affluence of the world. They know the speed with which they come straight through the thin masquerade, and conceive a disgust at the indigence of nature: Rousseau, Mirabeau, Charles Fox,° Napoleon, Byron,—and I could easily add names nearer home, of raging riders, who drive their steeds so hard, in the violence of living to forget its illusion: they would know the worst, and tread the floors of hell. The heroes of ancient and modern fame, Cimon, Themistocles, Alcibiades,° Alexander, Cæsar, have treated life and fortune as a game to be well and skilfully played, but the stake not to be so valued, but that any time, it could be held as a trifle light as air, and thrown up. Cæsar, just before the battle of Pharsalia, discourses with the Egyptian priest, concerning the fountains of the Nile, and offers to quit the army, the empire, and Cleopatra, if he will show him those mysterious sources.

The same magnanimity shows itself in our social relations, in the preference, namely, which each man gives to the society of superiors over that of his equals. All that a man has, will he give for right relations with his mates. All that he has, will he give for an erect demeanour in every company and on each occasion. He aims at such things as his neighbors prize, and gives his days and nights, his talents and his heart, to strike a good stroke, to acquit himself in all men's sight as a man. The consideration of an eminent citizen, of a noted merchant, of a man of mark in his profession; naval and military honor, a general's commission, a marshal's baton, a ducal coronet, the laurel of poets, and, anyhow procured, the acknowledgment of eminent merit, have this lustre for each candidate, that they enable him to walk erect and unashamed, in the presence of some persons, before whom he felt himself inferior. Having raised himself to this rank, having established his equality with class after class, of those with whom he would live well, he still finds certain others, before whom he cannot possess himself, because they have somewhat fairer, somewhat grander, somewhat purer, which extorts homage of him. Is his ambition pure? then, will his laurels and his possessions seem worthless: instead of avoiding these men who make his fine gold dim, he will cast all behind him, and seek their society only, woo and embrace this his humiliation and mortification, until he shall know why his eye sinks, his voice is husky, and his brilliant talents are paralyzed in this presence. He is sure that the soul which gives the lie to all things, will tell none. His constitution will not mislead him. If it cannot carry itself as it ought, high and unmatchable in the presence of any man, if the secret oracles whose whisper makes the sweetness and dignity of his life, do here withdraw and accompany him no longer, it is time to undervalue what he has valued, to dispossess himself of what he has acquired, and with Cæsar to take in his hand the army, the empire, and Cleopatra, and say, 'All these will I relinquish, if you will show me the fountains of the Nile.' Dear to us are those who love us, the swift moments we spend with them are a compensation for a great deal of misery; they enlarge our life;—but dearer are those who reject us as unworthy, for they add another life: they build a heaven before us, whereof we had not dreamed, and thereby supply to us new powers out of the recesses of the spirit, and urge us to new and unattempted performances.

As every man at heart wishes the best and not inferior society, wishes to be convicted of his error, and to come to himself, so he wishes that the same healing should not stop in his thought, but should penetrate his will or active power. The selfish man suffers more from his selfishness, than he from whom that selfishness withholds some important benefit. What he most wishes is to be lifted to some higher platform, that he may see beyond his present fear the transalpine good, so that his fear, his coldness, his custom may be broken up like fragments of ice, melted and carried away in the great stream of good will. Do you ask my aid? I also wish to be a benefactor. I wish more to be a benefactor and servant, than you wish to be served by me, and surely the greatest good fortune that could befall me, is precisely to be so moved by you that I should say, 'Take me and all mine, and use me and mine freely to your ends'! for, I could not say it, otherwise than because a great enlargement had come to my heart and mind, which made me superior to my fortunes. Here we are paralyzed with fear; we hold on to our little properties, house and land, office and money, for the bread which they have in our experience yielded us, although we confess, that our being does not flow through them. We desire to be made great, we desire to be touched with that fire which shall command this ice to stream, and make our existence a benefit. If therefore we start objections to your project, O friend of the slave, or friend of the poor, or of the race, understand well, that it is because we wish to drive you to drive us into your measures. We wish to hear ourselves confuted. We are haunted with a belief that you have a secret, which it would highliest advantage us to learn, and we would force you to impart it to us, though it should bring us to prison, or to worse extremity.

Nothing shall warp me from the belief, that every man is a lover of truth. There is no pure lie, no pure malignity in nature. The entertainment of the proposition of depravity is the last profligacy and profanation. There is no skepticism, no atheism but that. Could it be received into common belief, suicide would unpeople the planet. It has had a name to live in some dogmatic theology, but each man's innocence and his real liking of his neighbor, have kept it a dead letter. I remember standing at the polls one day, when the anger of the political contest gave a certain grimness to the faces of the independent electors, and a good man at my side looking on the people, remarked, 'I am satisfied that the largest part of these men, on either side, mean to vote right.' I suppose, considerate observers looking at the masses of men, in their blameless, and in their equivocal actions, will assent, that in spite of selfishness and frivolity, the general purpose in the great number of persons is fidelity. The reason why any one refuses his assent to your opinion, or his aid to your benevolent design, is in you: he refuses to accept you as a bringer of truth, because, though you think you have it, he feels that you have it not. You have not given him the authentic sign.

If it were worth while to run into details this general doctrine of the latent but ever soliciting Spirit, it would be easy to adduce illustration in particulars of a man's equality to the church, of his equality to the state, and of his equality to every other man. It is yet in all men's memory, that, a few years ago, the liberal churches complained, that the Calvinistic church denied to them the name of Christian. I think the complaint was confession: a religious church would not complain. A religious man like Behmen, Fox, or Swedenborg, is not irritated by wanting the sanction of the church, but the church feels the accusation of his presence and belief.

It only needs, that a just man should walk in our streets, to make it appear how pitiful and inartificial a contrivance is our legislation. The man whose part is taken, and who does not wait for society in anything, has a power which society cannot choose but feel. The familiar experiment, called the hydrostatic paradox, in which a capillary column of water balances the ocean, is a symbol of the relation of one man to the whole family of men. The wise Dandini,° on hearing the lives of Socrates, Pythagoras, and Diogenes read, 'judged them to be great men every way, excepting, that they were too much subjected to the reverence of the laws, which to second and authorize, true virtue must abate very much of its original vigor.'

And as a man is equal to the church, and equal to the state, so he is equal to every other man. The disparities of power in men are superficial; and all frank and searching conversation, in which a man lays himself open to his brother, apprizes each of their radical unity. When two persons sit and converse in a thoroughly good understanding, the remark is sure to be made, See how we have disputed about words! Let a clear, apprehensive mind, such as every man knows among his friends, converse with the most commanding poetic genius, I think, it would appear that there was no inequality such as men fancy between them; that a perfect understanding, a like receiving, a like perceiving, abolished differences, and the poet would confess, that his creative imagination gave him no deep advantage, but only the superficial one, that he could express himself, and the other could not; that his advantage was a knack, which might impose on indolent men, but could not impose on lovers of truth; for they know the tax of talent, or, what a price of greatness the power of expression too often pays. I believe it is the conviction of the purest men, that the net amount of man and man does not much vary. Each is incomparably superior to his companion in some faculty. His want of skill in other directions, has added to his fitness for his own work. Each seems to have some compensation yielded to him by his infirmity, and every hindrance operates as a concentration of his force.

These and the like experiences intimate, that man stands in strict connexion with a higher fact never yet manifested. There is power over and behind us, and we are the channels of its communications. We seek to say thus and so, and over our head some spirit sits, which contradicts what we say. We would persuade our fellow to this or that; another self within our eyes dissuades him. That which we keep back, this reveals. In vain we compose our faces and our words; it holds uncontrollable communication with the enemy, and he answers civilly to us, but believes the spirit. We exclaim, 'There's a traitor in the house!' but at last it appears that he is the true man, and I am the traitor. This open channel to the highest life is the first and last reality, so subtle, so quiet, yet so tenacious, that although I have never expressed the truth, and although I have never heard the expression of it from any other, I know that the whole truth is here for me. What if I cannot answer your questions? I am not pained that I cannot frame a reply to the question, What is the operation we call Providence? There lies the unspoken thing, present, omnipresent. Every time we converse, we seek to translate it into speech, but whether we hit, or whether we miss, we have the fact. Every discourse is an approximate answer: but it is of small consequence, that we do not get it into verbs and nouns, whilst it abides for contemplation forever.

If the auguries of the prophesying heart shall make themselves good in time, the man who shall be born, whose advent men and events prepare and foreshow, is one who shall enjoy his connexion with a higher life, with the man within man; shall destroy distrust by his trust, shall use his native but forgotten methods, shall not take counsel of flesh and blood, but shall rely on the Law alive and beautiful, which works over our heads and under our feet. Pitiless, it avails itself of our success, when we obey it, and of our ruin, when we contravene it. Men are all secret believers in it, else, the word justice would have no meaning: they believe that the best is the true; that right is done at last; or chaos would come. It rewards actions after their nature, and not after the design of the agent. 'Work,' it saith to man, 'in every hour, paid or unpaid, see only that thou work, and thou canst not escape the reward: whether thy work be fine or coarse, planting corn, or writing epics, so only it be honest work, done to thine own approbation, it shall earn a reward to the senses as well as to the thought: no matter, how often defeated, you are born to victory. The reward of a thing well done, is to have done it.'

As soon as a man is wonted to look beyond surfaces, and to see how this high will prevails without an exception or an interval, he settles himself into serenity. He can already rely on the laws of gravity, that every stone will fall where it is due; the good globe is faithful, and carries us securely through the celestial spaces, anxious or resigned: we need not interfere to help it on, and he will learn, one day, the mild lesson they teach, that our own orbit is all our task, and we need not assist the administration of the universe. Do not be so impatient to set the town right concerning the unfounded pretensions and the false reputation of certain men of standing. They are laboring harder to set the town right concerning themselves, and will certainly succeed. Suppress for a few days your criticism on the insufficiency of this or that teacher or experimenter, and he will have demonstrated his insufficiency to all men's eyes. In like manner, let a man fall into the divine circuits, and he is enlarged. Obedience to his genius is the only liberating influence. We wish to escape from subjection, and a sense of inferiority,—and we make self-denying ordinances, we drink water, we eat grass, we refuse the laws, we go to jail: it is all in vain; only by obedience to his genius;

only by the freest activity in the way constitutional to him, does an angel seem to arise before a man, and lead him by the hand out of all the wards of the prison.

That which befits us, embosomed in beauty and wonder as we are, is cheerfulness and courage, and the endeavor to realize our aspirations. The life of man is the true romance, which, when it is valiantly conducted, will yield the imagination a higher joy than any fiction. All around us, what powers are wrapped up under the coarse mattings of custom, and all wonder prevented. It is so wonderful to our neurologists that a man can see without his eyes, that it does not occur to them, that it is just as wonderful, that he should see with them; and that is ever the difference between the wise and the unwise: the latter wonders at what is unusual, the wise man wonders at the usual. Shall not the heart which has received so much, trust the Power by which it lives? May it not quit other leadings, and listen to the Soul that has guided it so gently, and taught it so much, secure that the future will be worthy of the past?

REPRESENTATIVE MEN
(1850)

PLATO; OR, THE PHILOSOPHER

AMONG books, Plato only is entitled to Omar's° fanatical compliment to the Koran, when he said, 'Burn the libraries; for, their value is in this book.' These sentences contain the culture of nations; these are the corner-stone of schools; these are the fountain-head of literatures. A discipline it is in logic, arithmetic, taste, symmetry, poetry, language, rhetoric, ontology, morals, or practical wisdom. There was never such range of speculation. Out of Plato come all things that are still written and debated among men of thought. Great havoc makes he among our originalities. We have reached the mountain from which all these drift boulders were detached. The Bible of the learned for twenty-two hundred years, every brisk young man, who says in succession fine things to each reluctant generation,—Boethius, Rabelais, Erasmus, Bruno, Locke, Rousseau, Alfieri,° Coleridge,—is some reader of Plato, translating into the vernacular, wittily, his good things. Even the men of grander proportion suffer some deduction from the misfortune (shall I say?) of coming after this exhausting generalizer. St. Augustine, Copernicus, Newton, Behmen,° Swedenborg, Goethe, are likewise his debtors, and must say after him. For it is fair to credit the broadest generalizer with all the particulars deducible from his thesis.

Plato is philosophy, and philosophy, Plato,—at once the glory and the shame of mankind, since neither Saxon nor Roman have availed to add any idea to his categories. No wife, no children had he, and the thinkers of all civilized nations are his posterity, and are tinged with his mind. How many great men Nature is incessantly sending up out of night, to be *his men*,—Platonists! the Alexandrians, a constellation of genius; the Elizabethans, not less; Sir Thomas More, Henry More, John Hales, John Smith, Lord Bacon, Jeremy Taylor, Ralph Cudworth, Sydenham, Thomas Taylor; Marcilius Ficinus, and Picus Mirandola.° Calvinism is in his Phædo: Christianity is in it. Mahometanism draws all its philosophy, in its handbook of morals, the Akhlak-y-Jalaly, from him. Mysticism finds in Plato all its texts. This citizen of a town in Greece is no villager nor patriot. An Englishman reads and says, 'how English!' a German,—'how Teutonic!' an Italian,—'how Roman and how Greek!' As they say that Helen of Argos, had that universal beauty that every body felt related to her, so Plato seems, to a reader in New England, an American genius. His broad humanity transcends all sectional lines.

This range of Plato instructs us what to think of the vexed question concerning his reputed works,—what are genuine, what spurious. It is singular that wherever we find a man higher, by a whole head, than any of his contemporaries, it is sure to come into doubt, what are his real works. Thus, Homer, Plato, Raffaelle, Shakspeare. For these men magnetise their contemporaries, so that their companions can do for them what they can never do for themselves; and the great man does thus live in several bodies, and write, or paint, or act, by many hands: and, after some time, it is not easy to say what is the authentic work of the master, and what is only of his school.

Plato, too, like every great man, consumed his own times. What is a great man, but one of great affinities, who takes up into himself all arts, sciences, all knowables, as his food? He can spare nothing; he can dispose of every thing. What is not good for virtue, is good for knowledge. Hence his contemporaries tax him with plagiarism. But the inventor only knows how to borrow; and society is glad to forget the innumerable laborers who ministered to this architect, and reserves all its gratitude for him. When we are praising Plato, it seems we are praising quotations from Solon, and Sophron, and Philolaus.° Be it so. Every book is a quotation; and every house is a quotation out of all forests, and mines, and stone quarries; and every man is a quotation from all his ancestors. And this grasping inventor puts all nations under contribution.

Plato absorbed the learning of his times,—Philolaus, Timæus, Heraclitus, Parmenides,° and what else; then his master, Socrates; and, finding himself still capable of a larger synthesis,—beyond all example then or since,—he travelled into Italy, to gain what Pythagoras had for him; then into Egypt, and perhaps still farther east, to import the other element, which Europe wanted, into the European mind. This breadth entitles him to stand as the representative of philosophy. He says, in the Republic, 'Such a genius as philosophers must of necessity have, is wont but seldom, in all its parts, to meet in one man; but its different parts generally spring up in different persons.'° Every man, who would do any thing well, must come to it from a higher ground. A philosopher must be more than a philosopher. Plato is clothed with the powers of a poet, stands upon the highest place of the poet, and, (though I doubt he wanted the decisive gift of lyric expression,) mainly is not a poet, because he chose to use the poetic gift to an ulterior purpose.

Great geniuses have the shortest biographies. Their cousins can tell you nothing about them. They lived in their writings, and so their house and street life was trivial and commonplace. If you would know their tastes and complexions, the most admiring of their readers most resembles them. Plato, especially, has no external biography. If he had lover, wife, or children, we hear nothing of them. He ground them all into paint.° As a good chimney burns its smoke, so a philosopher converts the value of all his fortunes into his intellectual performances.

He was born 430,° A.C., about the time of the death of Pericles; was of patrician connection in his times and city; and is said to have had an early inclination for war; but, in his twentieth year, meeting with Socrates, was easily dissuaded from this pursuit, and remained for ten years his scholar, until the death of Socrates. He then went to Megara; accepted the invitations of Dion and of Dionysius, to the court of Sicily; and went thither three times, though very capriciously treated. He travelled into Italy; then into Egypt, where he stayed a long time; some say three,—some say thirteen years. It is said, he went farther, into Babylonia: this is uncertain. Returning to Athens, he gave lessons, in the Academy, to those whom his fame drew thither; and died, as we have received it, in the act of writing, at eighty-one years.

But the biography of Plato is interior. We are to account for the supreme elevation of this man, in the intellectual history of our race,— how it happens that, in proportion to the culture of men, they become his scholars; that, as our Jewish Bible has implanted itself in the table-talk and household life of every man and woman in the European and American nations, so the writings of Plato have preoccupied every school of learning, every lover of thought, every church, every poet,— making it impossible to think, on certain levels, except through him. He stands between the truth and every man's mind, and has almost impressed language, and the primary forms of thought, with his name and seal. I am struck, in reading him, with the extreme modernness of his style and spirit. Here is the germ of that Europe we know so well, in its long history of arts and arms: here are all its traits, already discernible in the mind of Plato,—and in none before him. It has spread itself since into a hundred histories, but has added no new element. This perpetual modernness is the measure of merit, in every work of art; since the author of it was not misled by any thing short-lived or local, but abode by real and abiding traits. How Plato came thus to be Europe, and philosophy, and almost literature, is the problem for us to solve.

This could not have happened, without a sound, sincere, and catholic man, able to honor, at the same time, the ideal, or laws of the mind, and fate, or the order of nature. The first period of a nation, as of an individual, is the period of unconscious strength. Children cry, scream, and stamp with fury, unable to express their desires. As soon as they can speak and tell their want, and the reason of it, they become gentle. In adult life, whilst the perceptions are obtuse, men and women talk vehemently and superlatively, blunder and quarrel: their manners are full of desperation; their speech is full of oaths. As soon as, with culture, things have cleared up a little, and they see them no longer in lumps and masses, but accurately distributed, they desist from that weak vehemence, and explain their meaning in detail. If the tongue had not been framed for articulation, man would still be a beast in the forest. The same weakness and want, on a higher plane, occurs daily in the education of ardent young men and women. 'Ah! you don't understand me; I have never met with any one who comprehends me:' and they sigh and weep, write verses, and walk alone,—fault of power to express their precise meaning. In a month or two, through the favor of their good genius, they meet some one so related as to assist their volcanic estate; and, good communication being once established, they are thenceforward good citizens. It is ever thus. The progress is to accuracy, to skill, to truth, from blind force.

There is a moment, in the history of every nation, when, proceeding out of this brute youth, the perceptive powers reach their ripeness, and have not yet become microscopic: so that man, at that instant, extends across the entire scale; and, with his feet still planted on the immense forces of night, converses, by his eyes and brain, with solar and stellar creation. That is the moment of adult health, the culmination of power.

Such is the history of Europe, in all points; and such in philosophy. Its early records, almost perished, are of the immigrations from Asia, bringing with them the dreams of barbarians; a confusion of crude notions of morals, and of natural philosophy, gradually subsiding, through the partial insight of single teachers.

Before Pericles, came the Seven Wise Masters;° and we have the beginnings of geometry, metaphysics, and ethics: then the partialists,— deducing the origin of things from flux or water, or from air, or from fire, or from mind. All mix with these causes mythologic pictures. At last, comes Plato, the distributor, who needs no barbaric paint, or tattoo, or whooping; for he can define. He leaves with Asia the vast and superlative; he is the arrival of accuracy and intelligence. 'He shall be as a god to me, who can rightly divide and define.'°

This defining is philosophy. Philosophy is the account which the human mind gives to itself of the constitution of the world. Two cardinal facts lie forever at the base; the one, and the two.—1. Unity, or Identity; and, 2. Variety. We unite all things, by perceiving the law which pervades them; by perceiving the superficial differences, and the profound resemblances. But every mental act,—this very perception of identity or oneness, recognizes the difference of things. Oneness and otherness. It is impossible to speak, or to think, without embracing both.

The mind is urged to ask for one cause of many effects; then for the cause of that; and again the cause, diving still into the profound: self-assured that it shall arrive at an absolute and sufficient one,—a one that shall be all. 'In the midst of the sun is the light, in the midst of the light is truth, and in the midst of truth is the imperishable being,' say the Vedas.° All philosophy, of east and west, has the same centripetence. Urged by an opposite necessity, the mind returns from the one, to that which is not one, but other or many; from cause to effect; and affirms the necessary existence of variety, the self-existence of both, as each is involved in the other. These strictly-blended elements it is the problem of thought to separate, and to reconcile. Their existence is mutually contradictory and exclusive; and each so fast slides into the other, that we can never say what is one, and what it is not. The Proteus is as nimble in the highest as in the lowest grounds, when we contemplate the one, the true, the good,—as in the surfaces and extremities of matter.

In all nations, there are minds which incline to dwell in the conception of the fundamental Unity. The raptures of prayer and ecstasy of devotion lose all being in one Being. This tendency finds its highest expression in the religious writings of the East, and chiefly, in the Indian Scriptures, in the Vedas, the Bhagavat Geeta, and the Vishnu Purana. Those writings contain little else than this idea, and they rise to pure and sublime strains in celebrating it.

The Same, the Same: friend and foe are of one stuff; the plough-man, the plough, and the furrow, are of one stuff; and the stuff is such, and so much, that the variations of form are unimportant. 'You are fit,' (says the supreme Krishna to a sage,) 'to apprehend that you are not distinct from me. That which I am, thou art, and that also is this world, with its gods, and heroes, and mankind. Men contemplate distinctions, because they are stupefied with ignorance.' 'The words *I* and *mine* constitute ignorance. What is the great end of all, you shall now learn from me. It is soul,—one in all bodies, pervading, uniform, perfect, preëminent over nature, exempt from birth, growth, and decay, omnipresent, made up of true knowledge, independent, unconnected with unrealities, with name, species, and the rest, in time past, present, and to come. The knowledge that this spirit, which is essentially one, is in one's own, and in all other bodies, is the wisdom of one who knows the unity of things. As one diffusive air, passing through the perforations of a flute, is distinguished as the notes of a scale, so the nature of the Great Spirit is single, though its forms be manifold, arising from the consequences of acts. When the difference of the investing form, as that of god, or the rest, is destroyed, there is no distinction.' 'The whole world is but a manifestation of Vishnu, who is identical with all things, and is to be regarded by the wise, as not differing from, but as the same as themselves. I neither am going nor coming; nor is my dwelling in any one place; nor art thou, thou; nor are others, others; nor am I, I.'° As if he had said, 'All is for the soul, and the soul is Vishnu; and animals and stars are transient paintings; and light is whitewash; and durations are deceptive; and form is imprisonment; and heaven itself a decoy.' That which the soul seeks is resolution into being, above form, out of Tartarus,° and out of heaven,—liberation from nature.

If speculation tends thus to a terrific unity, in which all things are absorbed, action tends directly backwards to diversity. The first is the course or gravitation of mind; the second is the power of nature. Nature is the manifold. The unity absorbs, and melts or reduces. Nature opens and creates. These two principles reappear and interpenetrate all things, all thought; the one, the many. One is being; the other, intellect: one is necessity; the other, freedom: one, rest; the other, motion: one, power; the other, distribution: one, strength; the other, pleasure: one, consciousness; the other, definition: one, genius; the other, talent: one, earnestness; the other, knowledge: one, possession; the other, trade: one, caste; the other, culture: one, king; the other, democracy: and, if we dare carry these generalizations a step higher, and name the last tendency of both, we might say, that the end of the one is escape from organization,— pure science; and the end of the other is the highest instrumentality, or use of means, or executive deity.

Each student adheres, by temperament and by habit, to the first or to the second of these gods of the mind. By religion, he tends to unity; by intellect, or by the senses, to the many. A too rapid unification, and an excessive appliance to parts and particulars, are the twin dangers of speculation.

To this partiality the history of nations corresponded. The country of unity, of immovable institutions, the seat of a philosophy delighting in abstractions, of men faithful in doctrine and in practice to the idea of a deaf, unimplorable, immense fate, is Asia; and it realizes this faith in the social institution of caste. On the other side, the genius of Europe is active and creative: it resists caste by culture; its philosophy was a discipline; it is a land of arts, inventions, trade, freedom. If the East loved infinity, the West delighted in boundaries.

European civility is the triumph of talent, the extension of system, the sharpened understanding, adaptive skill, delight in forms, delight in manifestation, in comprehensible results. Pericles, Athens, Greece, had been working in this element with the joy of genius not yet chilled by any foresight of the detriment of an excess. They saw before them no sinister political economy; no ominous Malthus;° no Paris or London; no pitiless subdivision of classes,—the doom of the pinmakers, the doom of the weavers, of dressers, of stockingers, of carders, of spinners, of colliers; no Ireland; no Indian caste, superinduced by the efforts of Europe to throw it off. The understanding was in its health and prime. Art was in its splendid novelty. They cut the Pentelican marble° as if it were snow, and their perfect works in architecture and sculpture seemed things of course, not more difficult than the completion of a new ship at the Medford yards, or new mills at Lowell.° These things are in course, and may be taken for granted. The Roman legion, Byzantine legislation, English trade, the saloons of Versailles, the cafés of Paris, the steam-mill, steamboat, steam-coach, may all be seen in perspective; the town-meeting, the ballot-box, the newspaper and cheap press.

Meantime, Plato, in Egypt and in eastern pilgrimages, imbibed the idea of one Deity, in which all things are absorbed. The unity of Asia, and the detail of Europe; the infinitude of the Asiatic soul, and the defining, result-loving, machine-making, surface-seeking, opera-going Europe,—Plato came to join, and by contact, to enhance the energy of each. The excellence of Europe and Asia are in his brain. Metaphysics and natural philosophy expressed the genius of Europe; he substructs the religion of Asia, as the base.

In short, a balanced soul was born, perceptive of the two elements. It is as easy to be great as to be small. The reason why we do not at once believe in admirable souls, is because they are not in our experience. In actual life, they are so rare, as to be incredible; but, primarily, there is not only no presumption against them, but the strongest presumption in favor of their appearance. But whether voices were heard in the sky, or not; whether his mother or his father dreamed that the infant man-child was the son of Apollo; whether a swarm of bees settled on his lips, or not; a man who could see two sides of a thing was born. The wonderful synthesis so familiar in nature; the upper and the under side of the medal of Jove; the union of impossibilities, which reappears in every object; its real and its ideal power,—was now, also, transferred entire to the consciousness of a man.

The balanced soul came. If he loved abstract truth, he saved himself by propounding the most popular of all principles, the absolute good, which rules rulers, and judges the judge. If he made transcendental distinctions, he fortified himself by drawing all his illustrations from sources disdained by orators and polite conversers; from mares and puppies; from pitchers and soup-ladles; from cooks and criers; the shops of potters, horse-doctors, butchers, and fishmongers. He cannot forgive in himself a partiality, but is resolved that the two poles of thought shall appear in his statement. His argument and his sentence are self-poised and spherical. The two poles appear; yes, and become two hands, to grasp and appropriate their own.

Every great artist has been such by synthesis. Our strength is transitional, alternating; or, shall I say, a thread of two strands. The sea-shore, sea seen from shore, shore seen from sea; the taste of two metals in contact; and our enlarged powers at the approach and at the departure of a friend; the experience of poetic creativeness, which is not found in staying at home, nor yet in travelling, but in transitions from one to the other, which must therefore be adroitly managed to present as much transitional surface as possible; this command of two elements must explain the power and the charm of Plato. Art expresses the one, or the same by the different. Thought seeks to know unity in unity; poetry to show it by variety; that is, always by an object or symbol. Plato keeps the two vases, one of æther and one of pigment, at his side, and invariably uses both. Things added to things, as statistics, civil history, are inventories. Things used as language are inexhaustibly attractive. Plato turns incessantly the obverse and the reverse of the medal of Jove.

To take an example:—The physical philosophers had sketched each his theory of the world; the theory of atoms, of fire, of flux, of spirit; theories mechanical and chemical in their genius. Plato, a master of mathematics, studious of all natural laws and causes, feels these, as second causes, to be no theories of the world, but bare inventories and lists. To the study of nature he therefore prefixes the dogma,—'Let us declare the cause which led the Supreme Ordainer to produce and compose the universe. He was good; and he who is good has no kind of envy. Exempt from envy, he wished that all things should be as much as possible like himself. Whosoever, taught by wise men, shall admit this as the prime cause of the origin and foundation of the world, will be in the truth.'° 'All things are for the sake of the good, and it is the cause of every thing beautiful.'° This dogma animates and impersonates his philosophy.

The synthesis which makes the character of his mind appears in all his talents. Where there is great compass of wit, we usually find excellencies that combine easily in the living man, but in description appear incompatible. The mind of Plato is not to be exhibited by a Chinese catalogue, but is to be apprehended by an original mind in the exercise of its original power. In him the freest abandonment is united with the precision of a geometer. His daring imagination gives him the more solid grasp of facts; as the birds of highest flight have the strongest alar bones.° His patrician polish, his intrinsic elegance, edged by an irony so subtle that it stings and paralyses, adorn the soundest health and strength of frame. According to the old sentence, 'If Jove should descend to the earth, he would speak in the style of Plato.'

With this palatial air, there is, for the direct aim of several of his works, and running through the tenor of them all, a certain earnestness, which mounts, in the Republic, and in the Phædo, to piety. He has been charged with feigning sickness at the time of the death of Socrates. But the anecdotes that have come down from the times attest his manly interference before the people in his master's behalf, since even the savage cry of the assembly to Plato is preserved; and the indignation towards popular government, in many of his pieces, expresses a personal exasperation. He has a probity, a native reverence for justice and honor, and a humanity which makes him tender for the superstitions of the people. Add to this, he believes that poetry, prophecy, and the high insight, are from a wisdom of which man is not master; that the gods never philosophize; but, by a celestial mania, these miracles are accomplished. Horsed on these winged steeds, he sweeps the dim regions, visits worlds which flesh cannot enter: he saw the souls in pain; he hears the doom of the judge; he beholds the penal metempsychosis; the Fates, with the rock and shears; and hears the intoxicating hum of their spindle.

But his circumspection never forsook him. One would say, he had read the inscription on the gates of Busyrane,—'Be bold;' and on the second gate,—'Be bold, be bold, and evermore be bold:' and then again had paused well at the third gate,—'Be not too bold.'° His strength is like the momentum of a falling planet; and his discretion, the return of its due and perfect curve,—so excellent is his Greek love of boundary, and his skill in definition. In reading logarithms, one is not more secure, than in following Plato in his flights. Nothing can be colder than his head, when the lightnings of his imagination are playing in the sky. He has finished his thinking, before he brings it to the reader; and he abounds in the surprises of a literary master. He has that opulence which furnishes, at every turn, the precise weapon he needs. As the rich man wears no more garments, drives no more horses, sits in no more chambers, than the poor,—but has that one dress, or equipage, or instrument, which is fit for the hour and the need; so Plato, in his plenty, is never restricted, but has the fit word. There is, indeed, no weapon in all the armory of wit which he did not possess and use,— epic, analysis, mania, intuition, music, satire, and irony, down to the customary and polite. His illustrations are poetry, and his jests illustrations. Socrates' profession° of obstetric art is good philosophy; and his finding that word 'cookery,' and 'adulatory art,' for rhetoric, in the Gorgias, does us a substantial service still. No orator can measure in effect with him who can give good nicknames.

What moderation, and understatement, and checking his thunder in mid volley! He has good-naturedly furnished the courtier and citizen with all that can be said against the schools. 'For philosophy is an elegant thing, if any one modestly meddles with it; but, if he is conversant with it more than is becoming, it corrupts the man.'° He could well afford to be generous,—he, who from the sunlike centrality and reach of his vision, had a faith without cloud. Such as his perception, was his speech: he plays with the doubt, and makes the most of it: he paints and quibbles; and by and by comes a sentence that moves the sea and land. The admirable earnest comes not only at intervals, in the perfect yes and no of the dialogue, but in bursts of light. 'I, therefore, Callicles, am persuaded by these accounts, and consider how I may exhibit my soul before the judge in a healthy condition. Wherefore, disregarding the honors that most men value, and looking to the truth, I shall endeavor in reality to live as virtuously as I can; and, when I die, to die so. And I invite all other men, to the utmost of my power; and you, too, I in turn invite to this contest, which, I affirm, surpasses all contests here.'°

He is a great average man; one who, to the best thinking, adds a proportion and equality in his faculties, so that men see in him their own dreams and glimpses made available, and made to pass for what they are. A great common sense is his warrant and qualification to be the world's interpreter. He has reason, as all the philosophic and poetic class have: but he has, also, what they have not,—this strong solving sense to reconcile his poetry with the appearances of the world, and build a bridge from the streets of cities to the Atlantis. He omits never this graduation, but slopes his thought, however picturesque the precipice on one side, to an access from the plain. He never writes in ecstasy, or catches us up into poetic raptures.

*   *   *

Plato apprehended the cardinal facts. He could prostrate himself on the earth, and cover his eyes, whilst he adored that which cannot be numbered, or gauged, or known, or named: that of which every thing can be affirmed and denied: that 'which is entity and nonentity.' He called it super-essential. He even stood ready, as in the Parmenides, to demonstrate that it was so,—that this Being exceeded the limits of intellect. No man ever more fully acknowledged the Ineffable. Having paid his homage, as for the human race, to the Illimitable, he then stood erect, and for the human race affirmed, 'And yet things are knowable!'—that is, the Asia in his mind was first heartily honored,—the ocean of love and power, before form, before will, before knowledge, the Same, the Good, the One; and now, refreshed and empowered by this worship, the instinct of Europe, namely, culture, returns; and he cries, Yet things are knowable! They are knowable, because, being from one, things correspond. There is a scale: and the correspondence of heaven to earth, of matter to mind, of the part to the whole, is our guide. As there is a science of stars, called astronomy; a science of quantities, called mathematics; a science of qualities, called chemistry; so there is a science of sciences,—I call it Dialectic,—which is the Intellect discriminating the false and the true. It rests on the observation of identity and diversity; for, to judge, is to unite to an object the notion which belongs to it. The sciences, even the best,—mathematics, and astronomy,—are like sportsmen, who seize whatever prey offers, even without being able to make any use of it. Dialectic must teach the use of them. 'This is of that rank that no intellectual man will enter on any study for its own sake, but only with a view to advance himself in that one sole science which embraces all.'

'The essence or peculiarity of man is to comprehend a whole; or that which, in the diversity of sensations, can be comprised under a rational unity.' 'The soul which has never perceived the truth, cannot pass into the human form.'° I announce to men the Intellect. I announce the good of being interpenetrated by the mind that made nature: this benefit, namely, that it can understand nature, which it made and maketh. Nature is good, but intellect is better: as the law-giver is before the law-receiver. I give you joy, O sons of men! that truth is altogether wholesome; that we have hope to search out what might be the very self of every thing. The misery of man is to be baulked of the sight of essence, and to be stuffed with conjectures: but the supreme good is reality; the supreme beauty is reality; and all virtue and all felicity depend on this science of the real: for courage is nothing else than knowledge: the fairest fortune that can befall man, is to be guided by his dæmon to that which is truly his own. This also is the essence of justice,—to attend every one his own: nay, the notion of virtue is not to be arrived at, except through direct contemplation of the divine essence. Courage, then! for, 'the persuasion that we must search that which we do not know, will render us, beyond comparison, better, braver, and more industrious, than if we thought it impossible to discover what we do not know, and useless to search for it.' He secures a position not to be commanded, by his passion for reality; valuing philosophy only as it is the pleasure of conversing with real being.

Thus, full of the genius of Europe, he said, *Culture.* He saw the institutions of Sparta, and recognized more genially, one would say, than any since, the hope of education. He delighted in every accomplishment, in every graceful and useful and truthful performance; above all, in the splendors of genius and intellectual achievement. 'The whole of life, O Socrates, said Glauco, is, with the wise, the measure of hearing such discourses as these.'° What a price he sets on the feats of talent, on the powers of Pericles, of Isocrates,° of Parmenides! What price, above price, on the talents themselves! He called the several faculties, gods, in his beautiful personation. What value he gives to the art of gymnastic in education; what to geometry; what to music; what to astronomy, whose appeasing and medicinal power he celebrates! In the Timæus, he indicates the highest employment of the eyes. 'By us it is asserted, that God invented and bestowed sight on us for this purpose,—that, on surveying the circles of intelligence in the heavens, we might properly employ those of our own minds, which, though disturbed when compared with the others that are uniform, are still allied to their circulations; and that, having thus learned, and being naturally possessed of a correct reasoning faculty, we might, by imitating the uniform revolutions of divinity, set right our own wanderings and blunders.'° And in the Republic,— 'By each of these disciplines, a certain organ of the soul is both purified and reanimated, which is blinded and buried by studies of another kind; an organ better worth saving than ten thousand eyes, since truth is perceived by this alone.'°

He said, Culture; but he first admitted its basis, and gave immeasurably the first place to advantages of nature. His patrician tastes laid stress on the distinctions of birth. In the doctrine of the organic character and disposition is the origin of caste. 'Such as were fit to govern, into their composition the informing Deity mingled gold: into the military, silver; iron and brass for husbandmen and artificers.' The East confirms itself, in all ages, in this faith. The Koran is explicit on this point of caste. 'Men have their metal, as of gold and silver. Those of you who were the worthy ones in the state of ignorance, will be the worthy ones in the state of faith, as soon as you embrace it.' Plato was not less firm. 'Of the five orders of things, only four can be taught to the generality of men.' In the Republic,° he insists on the temperaments of the youth, as first of the first.

A happier example of the stress laid on nature, is in the dialogue with the young Theages, who wishes to receive lessons from Socrates. Socrates declares that, if some have grown wise by associating with him, no thanks are due to him; but, simply, whilst they were with him, they grew wise, not because of him; he pretends not to know the way of it. 'It is adverse to many, nor can those be benefited by associating with me, whom the Dæmon opposes; so that it is not possible for me to live with these. With many, however, he does not prevent me from conversing, who yet are not at all benefited by associating with me. Such, O Theages, is the association with me; for, if it pleases the God, you will make great and rapid proficiency: you will not, if he does not please. Judge whether it is not safer to be instructed by some one of those who have power over the benefit which they impart to men, than by me, who benefit or not, just as it may happen.'° As if he had said, 'I have no system. I cannot be answerable for you. You will be what you must. If there is love between us, inconceivably delicious and profitable will our intercourse be; if not, your time is lost, and you will only annoy me. I shall seem to you stupid, and the reputation I have, false. Quite above us, beyond the will of you or me, is this secret affinity or repulsion laid. All my good is magnetic, and I educate, not by lessons, but by going about my business.'

He said, Culture; he said, Nature: and he failed not to add, 'There is also the divine.' There is no thought in any mind, but it quickly tends to convert itself into a power, and organizes a huge instrumentality of means. Plato, lover of limits, loved the illimitable, saw the enlargement and nobility which come from truth itself and good itself, and attempted, as if on the part of the human intellect, once for all, to do it adequate homage,—homage fit for the immense soul to receive, and yet homage becoming the intellect to render. He said, then, 'Our faculties run out into infinity, and return to us thence. We can define but a little way; but here is a fact which will not be skipped, and which to shut our eyes upon is suicide. All things are in a scale; and, begin where we will, ascend and ascend. All things are symbolical; and what we call results are beginnings.'

A key to the method and completeness of Plato is his twice bisected line. After he has illustrated the relation between the absolute good and true, and the forms of the intelligible world, he says:—'Let there be a line cut in two unequal parts. Cut again each of these two parts,—one representing the visible, the other the intelligible world,—and these two new sections, representing the bright part and the dark part of these worlds, you will have, for one of the sections of the visible world,—images, that is, both shadows and reflections; for the other section, the objects of these images,—that is, plants, animals, and the works of art and nature. Then divide the intelligible world in like manner; the one section will be of opinions and hypotheses, and the other section, of truths.'° To these four sections, the four operations of the soul correspond,—conjecture, faith, understanding, reason. As every pool reflects the image of the sun, so every thought and thing restores us an image and creature of the supreme Good. The universe is perforated by a million channels for his activity. All things mount and mount.

All his thought has this ascension; in Phædrus, teaching that beauty is the most lovely of all things, exciting hilarity, and shedding desire and confidence through the universe, wherever it enters; and it enters, in some degree, into all things: but that there is another, which is as much more beautiful than beauty, as beauty is than chaos; namely, wisdom, which our wonderful organ of sight cannot reach unto, but which, could it be seen, would ravish us with its perfect reality. He has the same regard to it as the source of excellence in works of art. 'When an artificer, in the fabrication of any work, looks to that which always subsists according *to the same*; and, employing a model of this kind, expresses its idea and power in his work; it must follow, that his production should be beautiful. But when he beholds that which is born and dies, it will be far from beautiful.'°

Thus ever: the Banquet° is a teaching in the same spirit, familiar now to all the poetry, and to all the sermons of the world, that the love of the sexes is initial; and symbolizes, at a distance, the passion of the soul for that immense lake of beauty it exists to seek. This faith in the Divinity is never out of mind, and constitutes the limitation of all his dogmas. Body cannot teach wisdom;—God only.° In the same mind, he constantly affirms that virtue cannot be taught; that it is not a science, but an inspiration; that the greatest goods are produced to us through mania, and are assigned to us by a divine gift.

This leads me to that central figure, which he has established in his Academy, as the organ through which every considered opinion shall be announced, and whose biography he has likewise so labored, that the historic facts are lost in the light of Plato's mind. Socrates and Plato are the double star, which the most powerful instruments will not entirely separate. Socrates, again, in his traits and genius, is the best example of that synthesis which constitutes Plato's extraordinary power. Socrates, a man of humble stem, but honest enough; of the commonest history; of a personal homeliness so remarkable, as to be a cause of wit in others,—the rather that his broad good nature and exquisite taste for a joke invited the sally, which was sure to be paid. The players personated him on the stage; the potters copied his ugly face on their stone jugs. He was a cool fellow, adding to his humor a perfect temper, and a knowledge of his man, be he who he might whom he talked with, which laid the companion open to certain defeat in any debate,—and in debate he immoderately delighted. The young men are prodigiously fond of him, and invite him to their feasts, whither he goes for conversation. He can drink, too; has the strongest head in Athens; and, after leaving the whole party under the table, goes away, as if nothing had happened, to begin new dialogues with somebody that is sober. In short, he was what our country-people call *an old one.*

He affected a good many citizen-like tastes, was monstrously fond of Athens, hated trees, never willingly went beyond the walls, knew the old characters, valued the bores and philistines, thought every thing in Athens a little better than any thing in any other place. He was plain as a Quaker in habit and speech, affected low phrases, and illustrations from cocks and quails, soup-pans and sycamore-spoons, grooms and farriers, and unnameable offices,—especially if he talked with any superfine person. He had a Franklin-like wisdom. Thus, he showed one who was afraid to go on foot to Olympia, that it was no more than his daily walk within doors, if continuously extended, would easily reach.

Plain old uncle as he was, with his great ears,—an immense talker,— the rumor ran, that, on one or two occasions, in the war with Bœotia, he had shown a determination which had covered the retreat of a troop; and there was some story that, under cover of folly, he had, in the city government, when one day he chanced to hold a seat there, evinced a courage in opposing singly the popular voice, which had well-nigh ruined him. He is very poor; but then he is hardy as a soldier, and can live on a few olives; usually, in the strictest sense, on bread and water, except when entertained by his friends. His necessary expenses were exceedingly small, and no one could live as he did. He wore no under garment; his upper garment was the same for summer and winter; and he went barefooted; and it is said that, to procure the pleasure, which he loves, of talking at his ease all day with the most elegant and cultivated young men, he will now and then return to his shop, and carve statues, good or bad, for sale. However that be, it is certain that he had grown to delight in nothing else than this conversation; and that, under his hypocritical pretence of knowing nothing, he attacks and brings down all the fine speakers, all the fine philosophers of Athens, whether natives, or strangers from Asia Minor and the islands. Nobody can refuse to talk with him, he is so honest, and really curious to know; a man who was willingly confuted, if he did not speak the truth, and who willingly confuted others, asserting what was false; and not less pleased when confuted than when confuting; for he thought not any evil happened to men, of such a magnitude as false opinion respecting the just and unjust. A pitiless disputant, who knows nothing, but the bounds of whose conquering intelligence no man had ever reached; whose temper was imperturbable; whose dreadful logic was always leisurely and sportive; so careless and ignorant, as to disarm the wariest, and draw them, in the pleasantest manner, into horrible doubts and confusion. But he always knew the way out; knew it, yet would not tell it. No escape; he drives them to terrible choices by his dilemmas, and tosses the Hippiases and Gorgiases,° with their grand reputations, as a boy tosses his balls. The tyrannous realist!—Meno° has discoursed a thousand times, at length, on virtue, before many companies, and very well, as it appeared to him; but, at this moment, he cannot even tell what it is,—this cramp-fish of a Socrates has so bewitched him.

This hard-headed humorist, whose strange conceits, drollery, and *bonhommie*, diverted the young patricians, whilst the rumor of his sayings and quibbles gets abroad every day, turns out, in the sequel, to have a probity as invincible as his logic, and to be either insane, or, at least, under cover of this play, enthusiastic in his religion. When accused before the judges of subverting the popular creed, he affirms the immortality of the soul, the future reward and punishment; and, refusing to recant, in a caprice of the popular government, was condemned to die, and sent to the prison. Socrates entered the prison, and took away all ignominy from the place, which could not be a prison, whilst he was there. Crito bribed the jailer; but Socrates would not go out by treachery. 'Whatever inconvenience ensue, nothing is to be preferred before justice. These things I hear like pipes and drums, whose sound makes me deaf to every thing you say.'° The fame of this prison, the fame of the discourses there, and the drinking of the hemlock, are one of the most precious passages in the history of the world.

The rare coincidence, in one ugly body, of the droll and the martyr, the keen street and market debater with the sweetest saint known to any history at that time, had forcibly struck the mind of Plato, so capacious of these contrasts; and the figure of Socrates, by a necessity, placed itself in the foreground of the scene, as the fittest dispenser of the intellectual treasures he had to communicate. It was a rare fortune, that this Æsop of the mob, and this robed scholar, should meet, to make each other immortal in their mutual faculty. The strange synthesis, in the character of Socrates, capped the synthesis in the mind of Plato. Moreover, by this means, he was able, in the direct way, and without envy, to avail himself of the wit and weight of Socrates, to which unquestionably his own debt was great; and these derived again their principal advantage from the perfect art of Plato.

It remains to say, that the defect of Plato in power is only that which results inevitably from his quality. He is intellectual in his aim; and, therefore, in expression, literary. Mounting into heaven, diving into the pit, expounding the laws of the state, the passion of love, the remorse of crime, the hope of the parting soul,—he is literary, and never otherwise. It is almost the sole deduction from the merit of Plato, that his writings have not,—what is, no doubt, incident to this regnancy of intellect in his work,—the vital authority which the screams of prophets and the sermons of unlettered Arabs and Jews possess. There is an interval; and to cohesion, contact is necessary.

I know not what can be said in reply to this criticism, but that we have come to a fact in the nature of things: an oak is not an orange. The qualities of sugar remain with sugar, and those of salt, with salt.

In the second place, he has not a system. The dearest defenders and disciples are at fault. He attempted a theory of the universe, and his theory is not complete or self-evident. One man thinks he means this; and another, that: he has said one thing in one place, and the reverse of it in another place. He is charged with having failed to make the transition from ideas to matter. Here is the world, sound as a nut, perfect, not the smallest piece of chaos left, never a stitch nor an end, not a mark of haste, or botching, or second thought; but the theory of the world is a thing of shreds and patches.

The longest wave is quickly lost in the sea. Plato would willingly have a Platonism, a known and accurate expression for the world, and it should be accurate. It shall be the world passed through the mind of Plato,—nothing less. Every atom shall have the Platonic tinge; every atom, every relation or quality you knew before, you shall know again, and find here, but now ordered; not nature, but art. And you shall feel that Alexander indeed overran, with men and horses, some countries of the planet; but countries, and things of which countries are made, elements, planet itself, laws of planet and of men, have passed through this man as bread into his body, and become no longer bread, but body: so all this mammoth morsel has become Plato. He has clapped copyright on the world. This is the ambition of individualism. But the mouthful proves too large. *Boa constrictor* has good will to eat it, but he is foiled. He falls abroad in the attempt; and biting, gets strangled: the bitten world holds the biter fast by his own teeth. There he perishes: unconquered nature lives on, and forgets him. So it fares with all: so must it fare with Plato. In view of eternal nature, Plato turns out to be philosophical exercitations. He argues on this side, and on that. The acutest German, the lovingest disciple, could never tell what Platonism was; indeed, admirable texts can be quoted on both sides of every great question from him.

These things we are forced to say, if we must consider the effort of Plato, or of any philosopher, to dispose of Nature,—which will not be disposed of. No power of genius has ever yet had the smallest success in explaining existence. The perfect enigma remains. But there is an injustice in assuming this ambition for Plato. Let us not seem to treat with flippancy his venerable name. Men, in proportion to their intellect, have admitted his transcendant claims. The way to know him, is to compare him, not with nature, but with other men. How many ages have gone by, and he remains unapproached! A chief structure of human wit, like Karnac,° or the mediæval cathedrals, or the Etrurian remains,° it requires all the breadth of human faculty to know it. I think it is trueliest seen, when seen with the most respect. His sense deepens, his merits multiply, with study. When we say, here is a fine collection of fables; or, when we praise the style; or the common sense; or arithmetic; we speak as boys, and much of our impatient criticism of the dialectic, I suspect, is no better. The criticism is like our impatience of miles, when we are in a hurry; but it is still best that a mile should have seventeen hundred and sixty yards. The great-eyed Plato proportioned the lights and shades after the genius of our life.

PLATO: NEW READINGS

THE publication, in Mr. Bohn's 'Serial Library,'° of the excellent translations of Plato, which we esteem one of the chief benefits the cheap press has yielded, gives us an occasion to take hastily a few more notes of the elevation and bearings of this fixed star; or, to add a bulletin, like the journals, of *Plato at the latest dates*.

Modern science, by the extent of its generalization, has learned to indemnify the student of man for the defects of individuals, by tracing growth and ascent in races; and, by the simple expedient of lighting up the vast background, generates a feeling of complacency and hope. The human being has the saurian and the plant in his rear. His arts and sciences, the easy issue of his brain, look glorious when prospectively beheld from the distant brain of ox, crocodile, and fish. It seems as if nature, in regarding the geologic night behind her, when, in five or six millenniums, she had turned out five or six men, as Homer, Phidias, Menu,° and Columbus, was no wise discontented with the result. These samples attested the virtue of the tree. These were a clear amelioration of trilobite and saurus, and a good basis for further proceeding. With this artist, time and space are cheap, and she is insensible to what you say of tedious preparation. She waited tranquilly the flowing periods of paleontology, for the hour to be struck when man should arrive. Then periods must pass before the motion of the earth can be suspected; then before the map of the instincts and the cultivable powers can be drawn. But as of races, so the succession of individual men is fatal and beautiful, and Plato has the fortune, in the history of mankind, to mark an epoch.

Plato's fame does not stand on a syllogism, or on any masterpieces of the Socratic reasoning, or on any thesis, as, for example, the immortality of the soul. He is more than an expert, or a schoolman, or a geometer, or the prophet of a peculiar message. He represents the privilege of the intellect, the power, namely, of carrying up every fact to successive platforms, and so disclosing, in every fact, a germ of expansion. These expansions are in the essence of thought. The naturalist would never help us to them by any discoveries of the extent of the universe, but is as poor, when cataloguing the resolved nebula of Orion, as when measuring the angles of an acre. But the Republic of Plato, by these expansions, may be said to require, and so to anticipate, the astronomy of Laplace.° The expansions are organic. The mind does not create what it perceives, any more than the eye creates the rose. In ascribing to Plato the merit of announcing them, we only say, here was a more complete man, who could apply to nature the whole scale of the senses, the understanding, and the reason. These expansions, or extensions, consist in continuing the spiritual sight where the horizon falls on our natural vision, and, by this second sight, discovering the long lines of law which shoot in every direction. Everywhere he stands on a path which has no end, but runs continuously round the universe. Therefore, every word becomes an exponent of nature. Whatever he looks upon discloses a second sense, and ulterior senses. His perception of the generation of contraries, of death out of life, and life out of death,— that law by which, in nature, decomposition is recomposition, and putrefaction and cholera are only signals of a new creation;° his discernment of the little in the large, and the large in the small; studying the state in the citizen, and the citizen in the state; and leaving it doubtful whether he exhibited the Republic as an allegory on the education of the private soul; his beautiful definitions of ideas, of time, of form, of figure, of the line, sometimes hypothetically given, as his defining of virtue, courage, justice, temperance; his love of the apologue, and his apologues themselves; the cave of Trophonius; the ring of Gyges; the charioteer and two horses; the golden, silver, brass, and iron temperaments; Theuth and Thamus; and the visions of Hades and the Fates,°—fables which have imprinted themselves in the human memory like the signs of the zodiac; his soliform eye and his boniform° soul; his doctrine of assimilation; his doctrine of reminiscence; his clear vision of the laws of return, or reaction, which secure instant justice throughout the universe, instanced every where, but specially in the doctrine, 'what comes from God to us, returns from us to God,' and in Socrates' belief that the laws below are sisters of the laws above.

More striking examples are his moral conclusions. Plato affirms the coincidence of science and virtue; for vice can never know itself and virtue; but virtue knows both itself and vice. The eye attested that justice was best, as long as it was profitable; Plato affirms that it is profitable throughout; that the profit is intrinsic, though the just conceal his justice from gods and men; that it is better to suffer injustice, than to do it;° that the sinner ought to covet punishment;° that the lie was more hurtful than homicide;° and that ignorance, or the involuntary lie, was more calamitous than involuntary homicide; that the soul is unwillingly deprived of true opinions; and that no man sins willingly;° that the order or proceeding of nature was from the mind to the body; and, though a sound body cannot restore an unsound mind, yet a good soul can, by its virtue, render the body the best possible.° The intelligent have a right over the ignorant, namely, the right of instructing them. The right of punishment of one out of tune, is to make him play in tune; the fine which the good, refusing to govern, ought to pay, is, to be governed by a worse man;° that his guards shall not handle gold and silver, but shall be instructed that there is gold and silver in their souls, which will make men willing to give them every thing which they need.°

This second sight explains the stress laid on geometry. He saw that the globe of earth was not more lawful and precise than was the supersensible; that a celestial geometry was in place there, as a logic of lines and angles here below; that the world was throughout mathematical; the proportions are constant of oxygen, azote, and lime; there is just so much water, and slate, and magnesia; not less are the proportions constant of the moral elements.

This eldest Goethe, hating varnish and falsehood, delighted in revealing the real at the base of the accidental; in discovering connection, continuity, and representation, everywhere; hating insulation; and appears like the god of wealth among the cabins of vagabonds, opening power and capability in every thing he touches. Ethical science was new and vacant, when Plato could write thus:—'Of all whose arguments are left to the men of the present time, no one has ever yet condemned injustice, or praised justice, otherwise than as respects the repute, honors, and emoluments arising therefrom; while, as respects either of them in itself, and subsisting by its own power in the soul of the possessor, and concealed both from gods and men, no one has yet sufficiently investigated, either in poetry or prose writings,—how, namely, that the one is the greatest of all the evils that the soul has within it, and justice the greatest good.'°

His definition of ideas, as what is simple, permanent, uniform, and self-existent, forever discriminating them from the notions of the understanding, marks an era in the world. He was born to behold the self-evolving power of spirit, endless generator of new ends; a power which is the key at once to the centrality and the evanescence of things. Plato is so centred, that he can well spare all his dogmas. Thus the fact of knowledge and ideas reveals to him the fact of eternity; and the doctrine of reminiscence he offers as the most probable particular explication.° Call that fanciful,—it matters not: the connection between our knowledge and the abyss of being is still real, and the explication must be not less magnificent.

He has indicated every eminent point in speculation. He wrote on the scale of the mind itself, so that all things have symmetry in his tablet. He put in all the past, without weariness, and descended into detail with a courage like that he witnessed in nature. One would say, that his forerunners had mapped out each a farm, or a district, or an island, in intellectual geography, but that Plato first drew the sphere. He domesticates the soul in nature: man is the microcosm. All the circles of the visible heaven represent as many circles in the rational soul. There is no lawless particle, and there is nothing casual in the action of the human mind. The names of things, too, are fatal, following the nature of things. All the gods of the Pantheon are, by their names, significant of a profound sense. The gods are the ideas. Pan is speech, or manifestation; Saturn, the contemplative; Jove, the regal soul; and Mars, passion. Venus is proportion; Calliope, the soul of the world; Aglaia, intellectual illustration.°

*   *   *

These thoughts, in sparkles of light, had appeared often to pious and to poetic souls; but this well-bred, all-knowing Greek geometer comes with command, gathers them all up into rank and gradation, the Euclid of holiness, and marries the two parts of nature. Before all men, he saw the intellectual values of the moral sentiment. He describes his own ideal, when he paints° in Timæus a god leading things from disorder into order. He kindled a fire so truly in the centre, that we see the sphere illuminated, and can distinguish poles, equator, and lines of latitude, every arc and node: a theory so averaged, so modulated, that you would say, the winds of ages had swept through this rhythmic structure, and not that it was the brief extempore blotting of one short-lived scribe. Hence it has happened that a very well-marked class of souls, namely, those who delight in giving a spiritual, that is, an ethico-intellectual expression to every truth, by exhibiting an ulterior end which is yet legitimate to it, are said to Platonise. Thus, Michel Angelo is a Platonist, in his sonnets. Shakspeare is a Platonist, when he writes, 'Nature is made better by no mean, but nature makes that mean,' or,

> 'He, that can endure
> To follow with allegiance a fallen lord,
> Does conquer him that did his master conquer,
> And earns a place in the story.'°

Hamlet is a pure Platonist, and 'tis the magnitude only of Shakspeare's proper genius that hinders him from being classed as the most eminent of this school. Swedenborg, throughout his prose poem of 'Conjugal Love,' is a Platonist.

His subtlety commended him to men of thought. The secret of his popular success is the moral aim, which endeared him to mankind. 'Intellect,' he said, 'is king of heaven and of earth;' but, in Plato, intellect is always moral. His writings have also the sempiternal youth of poetry. For their arguments, most of them, might have been couched in sonnets: and poetry has never soared higher than in the Timæus and the Phædrus. As the poet, too, he is only contemplative. He did not, like Pythagoras, break himself with an institution. All his painting in the Republic must be esteemed mythical, with intent to bring out, sometimes in violent colors, his thought. You cannot institute, without peril of charlatanism.

It was a high scheme, his absolute privilege for the best, (which, to make emphatic, he expressed by community of women,) as the premium which he would set on grandeur. There shall be exempts of two kinds: first, those who by demerit have put themselves below protection,—outlaws; and secondly, those who by eminence of nature and desert are out of the reach of your rewards: let such be free of the city, and above the law. We confide them to themselves; let them do with us as they will. Let none presume to measure the irregularities of Michel Angelo and Socrates by village scales.

In his eighth book of the Republic, he throws a little mathematical dust in our eyes. I am sorry to see him, after such noble superiorities, permitting the lie to governors. Plato plays Providence a little with the baser sort, as people allow themselves with their dogs and cats.

MONTAIGNE; OR, THE SKEPTIC

EVERY fact is related on one side to sensation, and, on the other, to morals. The game of thought is, on the appearance of one of these two sides, to find the other: given the upper, to find the under side. Nothing so thin, but has these two faces; and, when the observer has seen the obverse, he turns it over to see the reverse. Life is a pitching of this penny,—heads or tails. We never tire of this game, because there is still a slight shudder of astonishment at the exhibition of the other face, at the contrast of the two faces. A man is flushed with success, and bethinks himself what this good luck signifies. He drives his bargain in the street; but it occurs, that he also is bought and sold. He sees the beauty of a human face, and searches the cause of that beauty, which must be more beautiful. He builds his fortunes, maintains the laws, cherishes his children; but he asks himself, why? and whereto? This head and this tail are called, in the language of philosophy, Infinite and Finite; Relative and Absolute; Apparent and Real; and many fine names beside.

Each man is born with a predisposition to one or the other of these sides of nature; and, it will easily happen that men will be found devoted to one or the other. One class has the perception of difference, and is conversant with facts and surfaces; cities and persons; and the bringing certain things to pass;—the men of talent and action. Another class have the perception of identity, and are men of faith and philosophy, men of genius.

Each of these riders drives too fast. Plotinus believes only in philosophers; Fenelon, in saints; Pindar° and Byron, in poets. Read the haughty language in which Plato and the Platonists speak of all men who are not devoted to their own shining abstractions: other men are rats and mice. The literary class is usually proud and exclusive. The correspondence of Pope and Swift describes mankind around them as monsters; and that of Goethe and Schiller, in our own time, is scarcely more kind.

It is easy to see how this arrogance comes. The genius is a genius by the first look he casts on any object. Is his eye creative? Does he not rest in angles and colors, but beholds the design,—he will presently undervalue the actual object. In powerful moments, his thought has dissolved the works of art and nature into their causes, so that the works appear heavy and faulty. He has a conception of beauty which the sculptor cannot embody. Picture, statue, temple, railroad, steam-engine, existed first in an artist's mind, without flaw, mistake, or friction, which impair the executed models. So did the church, the state, college, court, social circle, and all the institutions. It is not strange that these men, remembering what they have seen and hoped of ideas, should affirm disdainfully the superiority of ideas. Having at some time seen that the happy soul will carry all the arts in power, they say, Why cumber ourselves with superfluous realizations? and, like dreaming beggars, they assume to speak and act as if these values were already substantiated.

On the other part, the men of toil and trade and luxury,—the animal world, including the animal in the philosopher and poet also,—and the practical world, including the painful drudgeries which are never excused to philosopher or poet any more than to the rest,—weigh heavily on the other side. The trade in our streets believes in no metaphysical causes, thinks nothing of the force which necessitated traders and a trading planet to exist: no, but sticks to cotton, sugar, wool, and salt. The ward meetings, on election days, are not softened by any misgiving of the value of these ballotings. Hot life is streaming in a single direction. To the men of this world, to the animal strength and spirits, to the men of practical power, whilst immersed in it, the man of ideas appears out of his reason. They alone have reason.

Things always bring their own philosophy with them, that is, prudence. No man acquires property without acquiring with it a little arithmetic, also. In England, the richest country that ever existed, property stands for more, compared with personal ability, than in any other. After dinner, a man believes less, denies more: verities have lost some charm. After dinner, arithmetic is the only science: ideas are disturbing, incendiary, follies of young men, repudiated by the solid portion of society: and a man comes to be valued by his athletic and animal qualities. Spence relates, that Mr. Pope was with Sir Godfrey Kneller, one day, when his nephew, a Guinea trader, came in. 'Nephew,' said Sir Godfrey, 'you have the honor of seeing the two greatest men in the world.' 'I don't know how great men you may be,' said the Guinea man, 'but I don't like your looks. I have often bought a man much better than both of you, all muscles and bones, for ten guineas.'° Thus, the men of the senses revenge themselves on the professors, and repay scorn for scorn. The first had leaped to conclusions not yet ripe, and say more than is true; the others make themselves merry with the philosopher, and weigh man by the pound.—They believe that mustard bites the tongue, that pepper is hot, friction-matches are incendiary, revolvers to be avoided, and suspenders hold up pantaloons; that there is much sentiment in a chest of tea; and a man will be eloquent, if you give him good wine. Are you tender and scrupulous,—you must eat more mince-pie. They hold that Luther had milk in him when he said,

'Wer nicht liebt Wein, Weib, und Gesang,
Der bleibt ein Narr sein Leben lang;'°

and when he advised a young scholar, perplexed with foreordination
and free-will, to get well drunk. 'The nerves,' says Cabanis,° 'they are
the man.' My neighbor, a jolly farmer, in the tavern bar-room, thinks
that the use of money is sure and speedy spending. 'For his part,' he
says, 'he puts his down his neck, and gets the good of it.'

The inconvenience of this way of thinking is, that it runs into indif-
ferentism, and then into disgust. Life is eating us up. We shall be fables
presently. Keep cool: it will be all one a hundred years hence. Life's
well enough; but we shall be glad to get out of it, and they will all be
glad to have us. Why should we fret and drudge? Our meat will taste to-
morrow as it did yesterday, and we may at last have had enough of it.
'Ah,' said my languid gentleman at Oxford, 'there's nothing new or
true,—and no matter.'

With a little more bitterness, the cynic moans:° our life is like an ass
led to market by a bundle of hay being carried before him: he sees
nothing but the bundle of hay. 'There is so much trouble in coming
into the world,' said Lord Bolingbroke, 'and so much more, as well as
meanness, in going out of it, that 'tis hardly worth while to be here at
all.'° I knew a philosopher of this kidney, who was accustomed briefly to
sum up his experience of human nature in saying, 'Mankind is a
damned rascal:' and the natural corollary is pretty sure to follow,—
'The world lives by humbug, and so will I.'

The abstractionist and the materialist thus mutually exasperating
each other, and the scoffer expressing the worst of materialism, there
arises a third party to occupy the middle ground between these two, the
skeptic, namely. He finds both wrong by being in extremes. He labors
to plant his feet, to be the beam of the balance. He will not go beyond
his card. He sees the one-sidedness of these men of the street; he will
not be a Gibeonite;° he stands for the intellectual faculties, a cool head,
and whatever serves to keep it cool: no unadvised industry, no unrewarded self-devotion, no loss of the brains in toil. Am I an ox, or a
dray?—You are both in extremes, he says. You that will have all solid,
and a world of pig-lead, deceive yourselves grossly. You believe yourselves rooted and grounded on adamant; and yet, if we uncover the last
facts of our knowledge, you are spinning like bubbles in a river, you
know not whither or whence, and you are bottomed and capped and
wrapped in delusions.

Neither will he be betrayed to a book, and wrapped in a gown. The studious class are their own victims: they are thin and pale, their feet are cold, their heads are hot, the night is without sleep, the day a fear of interruption,—pallor, squalor, hunger, and egotism. If you come near them, and see what conceits they entertain,—they are abstractionists, and spend their days and nights in dreaming some dream; in expecting the homage of society to some precious scheme built on a truth, but destitute of proportion in its presentment, of justness in its application, and of all energy of will in the schemer to embody and vitalize it.

But I see plainly, he says, that I cannot see. I know that human strength is not in extremes, but in avoiding extremes. I, at least, will shun the weakness of philosophizing beyond my depth. What is the use of pretending to powers we have not? What is the use of pretending to assurances we have not, respecting the other life? Why exaggerate the power of virtue? Why be an angel before your time? These strings, wound up too high, will snap. If there is a wish for immortality, and no evidence, why not say just that? If there are conflicting evidences, why not state them? If there is not ground for a candid thinker to make up his mind, yea or nay,—why not suspend the judgment? I weary of these dogmatizers. I tire of these hacks of routine, who deny the dogmas. I neither affirm nor deny. I stand here to try the case. I am here to consider, σχεπτειν,° to consider how it is. I will try to keep the balance true. Of what use to take the chair, and glibly rattle off theories of society, religion, and nature, when I know that practical objections lie in the way, insurmountable by me and by my mates? Why so talkative in public, when each of my neighbors can pin me to my seat by arguments I cannot refute? Why pretend that life is so simple a game, when we know how subtle and elusive the Proteus is? Why think to shut up all things in your narrow coop, when we know there are not one or two only, but ten, twenty, a thousand things, and unlike? Why fancy that you have all the truth in your keeping? There is much to say on all sides.

Who shall forbid a wise skepticism, seeing that there is no practical question on which any thing more than an approximate solution can be had? Is not marriage an open question, when it is alleged, from the beginning of the world, that such as are in the institution wish to get out, and such as are out wish to get in? And the reply of Socrates, to him who asked whether he should choose a wife, still remains reasonable, 'that, whether he should choose one or not, he would repent it.' Is not the state a question? All society is divided in opinion on the subject of the state. Nobody loves it; great numbers dislike it, and suffer conscientious scruples to allegiance: and the only defence set up, is, the fear of doing worse in disorganizing. Is it otherwise with the church?

Or, to put any of the questions which touch mankind nearest,—shall the young man aim at a leading part in law, in politics, in trade? It will not be pretended that a success in either of these kinds is quite coincident with what is best and inmost in his mind. Shall he, then, cutting the stays that hold him fast to the social state, put out to sea with no guidance but his genius? There is much to say on both sides. Remember the open question between the present order of 'competition,' and the friends of 'attractive and associated labor.' The generous minds embrace the proposition of labor shared by all; it is the only honesty; nothing else is safe. It is from the poor man's hut alone, that strength and virtue come: and yet, on the other side, it is alleged that labor impairs the form, and breaks the spirit of man, and the laborers cry unanimously, 'We have no thoughts.' Culture, how indispensable! I cannot forgive you the want of accomplishments; and yet, culture will instantly destroy that chiefest beauty of spontaneousness. Excellent is culture for a savage; but once let him read in the book, and he is no longer able not to think of Plutarch's heroes. In short, since true fortitude of understanding consists 'in not letting what we know be embarrassed by what we do not know,' we ought to secure those advantages which we can command, and not risk them by clutching after the airy and unattainable. Come, no chimeras! Let us go abroad; let us mix in affairs; let us learn, and get, and have, and climb. 'Men are a sort of moving plants, and, like trees, receive a great part of their nourishment from the air. If they keep too much at home, they pine.'° Let us have a robust, manly life; let us know what we know, for certain; what we have, let it be solid, and seasonable, and our own. A world in the hand is worth two in the bush. Let us have to do with real men and women, and not with skipping ghosts.

This, then, is the right ground of the skeptic,—this of consideration, of self-containing; not at all of unbelief; not at all of universal denying, nor of universal doubting,—doubting even that he doubts; least of all, of scoffing and profligate jeering at all that is stable and good. These are no more his moods than are those of religion and philosophy. He is the considerer, the prudent, taking in sail, counting stock, husbanding his means, believing that a man has too many enemies, than that he can afford to be his own; that we can not give ourselves too many advantages, in this unequal conflict, with powers so vast and unweariable ranged on one side, and this little, conceited, vulnerable popinjay that a man is, bobbing up and down into every danger, on the other. It is a position taken up for better defence, as of more safety, and one that can be maintained; and it is one of more opportunity and range: as, when we build a house, the rule is, to set it not too high nor too low, under the wind, but out of the dirt.

The philosophy we want is one of fluxions and mobility. The Spartan and Stoic schemes are too stark and stiff for our occasion. A theory of Saint John, and of nonresistance, seems, on the other hand, too thin and aerial. We want some coat woven of elastic steel, stout as the first, and limber as the second. We want a ship in these billows we inhabit. An angular, dogmatic house would be rent to chips and splinters, in this storm of many elements. No, it must be tight, and fit to the form of man, to live at all; as a shell is the architecture of a house founded on the sea. The soul of man must be the type of our scheme, just as the body of man is the type after which a dwelling-house is built. Adaptiveness is the peculiarity of human nature. We are golden averages, volitant stabilities, compensated or periodic errors, houses founded on the sea. The wise skeptic wishes to have a near view of the best game, and the chief players; what is best in the planet; art and nature, places and events, but mainly men. Every thing that is excellent in mankind,—a form of grace, an arm of iron, lips of persuasion, a brain of resources, every one skilful to play and win,—he will see and judge.

The terms of admission to this spectacle, are, that he have a certain solid and intelligible way of living of his own; some method of answering the inevitable needs of human life; proof that he has played with skill and success; that he has evinced the temper, stoutness, and the range of qualities which, among his contemporaries and countrymen, entitle him to fellowship and trust. For, the secrets of life are not shown except to sympathy and likeness. Men do not confide themselves to boys, or coxcombs, or pedants, but to their peers. Some wise limitation, as the modern phrase is; some condition between the extremes, and having itself a positive quality; some stark and sufficient man, who is not salt or sugar, but sufficiently related to the world to do justice to Paris or London, and, at the same time, a vigorous and original thinker, whom cities can not overawe, but who uses them,—is the fit person to occupy this ground of speculation.

These qualities meet in the character of Montaigne. And yet, since the personal regard which I entertain for Montaigne may be unduly great, I will, under the shield of this prince of egotists, offer, as an apology for electing him as the representative of skepticism, a word or two to explain how my love began and grew for this admirable gossip.

A single odd volume of Cotton's translation° of the Essays remained to me from my father's library, when a boy. It lay long neglected, until, after many years, when I was newly escaped from college, I read the book, and procured the remaining volumes. I remember the delight and wonder in which I lived with it. It seemed to me as if I had myself written the book, in some former life, so sincerely it spoke to my thought and experience. It happened, when in Paris, in 1833, that, in the cemetery of Pere le Chaise, I came to a tomb of Auguste Collignon, who died in 1830, aged sixty-eight years, and who, said the monument, 'lived to do right, and had formed himself to virtue on the Essays of Montaigne.' Some years later, I became acquainted with an accomplished English poet, John Sterling;° and, in prosecuting my correspondence, I found that, from a love of Montaigne, he had made a pilgrimage to his chateau, still standing near Castellan, in Perigord, and, after two hundred and fifty years, had copied from the walls of his library the inscriptions which Montaigne had written there. That Journal of Mr. Sterling's, published in the Westminster Review, Mr. Hazlitt° has reprinted in the *Prolegomena* to his edition of the Essays. I heard with pleasure that one of the newly-discovered autographs of William Shakspeare was in a copy of Florio's translation° of Montaigne. It is the only book which we certainly know to have been in the poet's library. And, oddly enough, the duplicate copy of Florio, which the British Museum purchased, with a view of protecting the Shakspeare autograph, (as I was informed in the Museum,) turned out to have the autograph of Ben Jonson in the fly-leaf. Leigh Hunt° relates of Lord Byron, that Montaigne was the only great writer of past times whom he read with avowed satisfaction. Other coincidences, not needful to be mentioned here, concurred to make this old Gascon still new and immortal for me.

In 1571, on the death of his father, Montaigne, then thirty-eight years old, retired from the practice of law, at Bordeaux, and settled himself on his estate. Though he had been a man of pleasure, and sometimes a courtier, his studious habits now grew on him, and he loved the compass, staidness, and independence, of the country gentleman's life. He took up his economy in good earnest, and made his farms yield the most. Downright and plain-dealing, and abhorring to be deceived or to deceive, he was esteemed in the country for his sense and probity. In the civil wars of the League,° which converted every house into a fort, Montaigne kept his gates open, and his house without defence. All parties freely came and went, his courage and honor being universally esteemed. The neighboring lords and gentry brought jewels and papers to him for safe-keeping. Gibbon reckons, in these bigoted times, but two men of liberality in France,—Henry IV. and Montaigne.

Montaigne is the frankest and honestest of all writers. His French freedom runs into grossness; but he has anticipated all censure by the bounty of his own confessions. In his times, books were written to one sex only, and almost all were written in Latin; so that, in a humorist, a certain nakedness of statement was permitted, which our manners, of a literature addressed equally to both sexes, do not allow. But, though a biblical plainness, coupled with a most uncanonical levity, may shut his pages to many sensitive readers, yet the offence is superficial. He parades it: he makes the most of it: nobody can think or say worse of him than he does. He pretends to most of the vices; and, if there be any virtue in him, he says, it got in by stealth.° There is no man, in his opinion, who has not deserved hanging five or six times; and he pretends no exception in his own behalf. 'Five or six as ridiculous stories,' too, he says, 'can be told of me, as of any man living.'° But, with all this really superfluous frankness, the opinion of an invincible probity grows into every reader's mind.

'When I the most strictly and religiously confess myself, I find that the best virtue I have has in it some tincture of vice; and I am afraid that Plato, in his purest virtue, (I, who am as sincere and perfect a lover of virtue of that stamp as any other whatever,) if he had listened, and laid his ear close to himself, would have heard some jarring sound of human mixture; but faint and remote, and only to be perceived by himself.'°

Here is an impatience and fastidiousness at color or pretence of any kind. He has been in courts so long as to have conceived a furious disgust at appearances; he will indulge himself with a little cursing and swearing; he will talk with sailors and gipsies, use flash and street ballads: he has stayed in-doors till he is deadly sick; he will to the open air, though it rain bullets. He has seen too much of gentlemen of the long robe, until he wishes for cannibals; and is so nervous, by factitious life, that he thinks, the more barbarous man is, the better he is. He likes his saddle. You may read theology, and grammar, and metaphysics elsewhere. Whatever you get here, shall smack of the earth and of real life, sweet, or smart, or stinging. He makes no hesitation to entertain you with the records of his disease; and his journey to Italy is quite full of that matter. He took and kept this position of equilibrium. Over his name, he drew an emblematic pair of scales, and wrote *Que sçais je?*° under it. As I look at his effigy opposite the title-page, I seem to hear him say, 'You may play old Poz,° if you will; you may rail and exaggerate,—I stand here for truth, and will not, for all the states, and churches, and revenues, and personal reputations of Europe, overstate the dry fact, as I see it; I will rather mumble and prose about what I certainly know,—my house and barns; my father, my wife, and my tenants;

my old lean bald pate; my knives and forks; what meats I eat, and what drinks I prefer; and a hundred straws just as ridiculous,—than I will write, with a fine crow-quill, a fine romance. I like gray days, and autumn and winter weather. I am gray and autumnal myself, and think an undress, and old shoes that do not pinch my feet, and old friends who do not constrain me, and plain topics where I do not need to strain myself and pump my brains, the most suitable. Our condition as men is risky and ticklish enough. One can not be sure of himself and his fortune an hour, but he may be whisked off into some pitiable or ridiculous plight. Why should I vapor and play the philosopher, instead of ballasting, the best I can, this dancing balloon? So, at least, I live within compass, keep myself ready for action, and can shoot the gulf, at last, with decency. If there be any thing farcical in such a life, the blame is not mine: let it lie at fate's and nature's door.'

The Essays, therefore, are an entertaining soliloquy on every random topic that comes into his head; treating every thing without ceremony, yet with masculine sense. There have been men with deeper insight; but, one would say, never a man with such abundance of thoughts: he is never dull, never insincere, and has the genius to make the reader care for all that he cares for.

The sincerity and marrow of the man reaches to his sentences. I know not any where the book that seems less written. It is the language of conversation transferred to a book. Cut these words, and they would bleed; they are vascular and alive. One has the same pleasure in it that we have in listening to the necessary speech of men about their work, when any unusual circumstance gives momentary importance to the dialogue. For blacksmiths and teamsters do not trip in their speech; it is a shower of bullets. It is Cambridge men who correct themselves, and begin again at every half sentence, and, moreover, will pun, and refine too much, and swerve from the matter to the expression. Montaigne talks with shrewdness, knows the world, and books, and himself, and uses the positive degree: never shrieks, or protests, or prays: no weakness, no convulsion, no superlative: does not wish to jump out of his skin, or play any antics, or annihilate space or time; but is stout and solid; tastes every moment of the day; likes pain, because it makes him feel himself, and realize things; as we pinch ourselves to know that we are awake. He keeps the plain; he rarely mounts or sinks; likes to feel solid ground, and the stones underneath. His writing has no enthusiasms, no aspiration; contented, self-respecting, and keeping the middle of the road. There is but one exception,—in his love for Socrates. In speaking of him, for once his cheek flushes, and his style rises to passion.

Montaigne died of a quinsy, at the age of sixty, in 1592. When he came to die, he caused the mass to be celebrated in his chamber. At the age of thirty-three, he had been married. 'But,' he says, 'might I have had my own will, I would not have married Wisdom herself, if she would have had me: but 'tis to much purpose to evade it, the common custom and use of life will have it so. Most of my actions are guided by example, not choice.'° In the hour of death, he gave the same weight to custom. *Que sçais je?* What do I know?

This book of Montaigne the world has endorsed, by translating it into all tongues, and printing seventy-five editions of it in Europe: and that, too, a circulation somewhat chosen, namely, among courtiers, soldiers, princes, men of the world, and men of wit and generosity.

Shall we say that Montaigne has spoken wisely, and given the right and permanent expression of the human mind, on the conduct of life?

We are natural believers. Truth, or the connection between cause and effect, alone interests us. We are persuaded that a thread runs through all things: all worlds are strung on it, as beads: and men, and events, and life, come to us, only because of that thread: they pass and repass, only that we may know the direction and continuity of that line. A book or statement which goes to show that there is no line, but random and chaos, a calamity out of nothing, a prosperity and no account of it, a hero born from a fool, a fool from a hero,—dispirits us. Seen or unseen, we believe the tie exists. Talent makes counterfeit ties; genius finds the real ones. We hearken to the man of science, because we anticipate the sequence in natural phenomena which he uncovers. We love whatever affirms, connects, preserves; and dislike what scatters or pulls down. One man appears whose nature is to all men's eyes conserving and constructive: his presence supposes a well-ordered society, agriculture, trade, large institutions, and empire. If these did not exist, they would begin to exist through his endeavors. Therefore, he cheers and comforts men, who feel all this in him very readily. The nonconformist and the rebel say all manner of unanswerable things against the existing republic, but discover to our sense no plan of house or state of their own. Therefore, though the town, and state, and way of living, which our counsellor contemplated, might be a very modest or musty prosperity, yet men rightly go for him, and reject the reformer, so long as he comes only with axe and crowbar.

But though we are natural conservers and causationists, and reject a sour, dumpish unbelief, the skeptical class, which Montaigne represents, have reason, and every man, at some time, belongs to it. Every superior mind will pass through this domain of equilibration,—I should rather say, will know how to avail himself of the checks and balances in nature, as a natural weapon against the exaggeration and formalism of bigots and blockheads.

Skepticism is the attitude assumed by the student in relation to the particulars which society adores, but which he sees to be reverend only in their tendency and spirit. The ground occupied by the skeptic is the vestibule of the temple. Society does not like to have any breath of question blown on the existing order. But the interrogation of custom at all points is an inevitable stage in the growth of every superior mind, and is the evidence of its perception of the flowing power which remains itself in all changes.

The superior mind will find itself equally at odds with the evils of society, and with the projects that are offered to relieve them. The wise skeptic is a bad citizen; no conservative; he sees the selfishness of property, and the drowsiness of institutions. But neither is he fit to work with any democratic party that ever was constituted; for parties wish every one committed, and he penetrates the popular patriotism. His politics are those of the 'Soul's Errand' of Sir Walter Raleigh;° or of Krishna, in the Bhagavat,° 'There is none who is worthy of my love or hatred;' whilst he sentences law, physic, divinity, commerce, and custom. He is a reformer: yet he is no better member of the philanthropic association. It turns out that he is not the champion of the operative, the pauper, the prisoner, the slave. It stands in his mind, that our life in this world is not of quite so easy interpretation as churches and school-books say. He does not wish to take ground against these benevolences, to play the part of devil's attorney, and blazon every doubt and sneer that darkens the sun for him. But he says, There are doubts.

I mean to use the occasion, and celebrate the calendar-day of our Saint Michel de Montaigne, by counting and describing these doubts or negations. I wish to ferret them out of their holes, and sun them a little. We must do with them as the police do with old rogues, who are shown up to the public at the marshal's office. They will never be so formidable, when once they have been identified and registered. But I mean honestly by them,—that justice shall be done to their terrors. I shall not take Sunday objections, made up on purpose to be put down. I shall take the worst I can find, whether I can dispose of them, or they of me.

I do not press the skepticism of the materialist. I know, the quadruped opinion will not prevail. 'Tis of no importance what bats and oxen think. The first dangerous symptom I report, is, the levity of intellect; as if it were fatal to earnestness to know much. Knowledge is the knowing that we can not know. The dull pray; the geniuses are light mockers. How respectable is earnestness on every platform! but intellect kills it. Nay, San Carlo, my subtle and admirable friend, one of the most penetrating of men, finds that all direct ascension, even of lofty piety, leads to this ghastly insight, and sends back the votary orphaned. My astonishing San Carlo° thought the lawgivers and saints infected. They found the ark empty; saw, and would not tell; and tried to choke off their approaching followers, by saying, 'Action, action, my dear fellows, is for you!' Bad as was to me this detection by San Carlo, this frost in July, this blow from a bride, there was still a worse, namely, the cloy or satiety of the saints. In the mount of vision, ere they have yet risen from their knees, they say, 'We discover that this our homage and beatitude is partial and deformed: we must fly for relief to the suspected and reviled Intellect, to the Understanding, the Mephistopheles, to the gymnastics of talent.'

This is hobgoblin the first; and, though it has been the subject of much elegy, in our nineteenth century, from Byron, Goethe, and other poets of less fame, not to mention many distinguished private observers,—I confess it is not very affecting to my imagination; for it seems to concern the shattering of baby-houses and crockery-shops. What flutters the church of Rome, or of England, or of Geneva, or of Boston, may yet be very far from touching any principle of faith. I think that the intellect and moral sentiment are unanimous; and that, though philosophy extirpates bugbears, yet it supplies the natural checks of vice, and polarity to the soul. I think that the wiser a man is, the more stupendous he finds the natural and moral economy, and lifts himself to a more absolute reliance.

There is the power of moods, each setting at nought all but its own tissue of facts and beliefs. There is the power of complexions, obviously modifying the dispositions and sentiments. The beliefs and unbeliefs appear to be structural; and, as soon as each man attains the poise and vivacity which allow the whole machinery to play, he will not need extreme examples, but will rapidly alternate all opinions in his own life. Our life is March weather, savage and serene in one hour. We go forth austere, dedicated, believing in the iron links of Destiny, and will not turn on our heel to save our life: but a book, or a bust, or only the sound of a name, shoots a spark through the nerves, and we suddenly believe in will: my finger-ring shall be the seal of Solomon: fate is for imbeciles: all is possible to the resolved mind. Presently, a new experience gives a new turn to our thoughts: common sense resumes its tyranny: we say, 'Well, the army, after all, is the gate to fame, manners, and poetry: and, look you,—on the whole, selfishness plants best, prunes best, makes the best commerce, and the best citizen.' Are the opinions of a man on right and wrong, on fate and causation, at the mercy of a broken sleep or an indigestion? Is his belief in God and Duty no deeper than a stomach evidence? And what guaranty for the permanence of his opinions? I like not the French celerity,—a new church and state once a week.—This is the second negation; and I shall let it pass for what it will. As far as it asserts rotation of states of mind, I suppose it suggests its own remedy, namely, in the record of larger periods. What is the mean of many states; of all the states? Does the general voice of ages affirm any principle, or is no community of sentiment discoverable in distant times and places? And when it shows the power of self-interest, I accept that as part of the divine law, and must reconcile it with aspiration the best I can.

The word Fate, or Destiny, expresses the sense of mankind, in all ages,—that the laws of the world do not always befriend, but often hurt and crush us. Fate, in the shape of *Kinde* or nature, grows over us like grass. We paint Time with a scythe; Love and Fortune, blind; and Destiny, deaf. We have too little power of resistance against this ferocity which champs us up. What front can we make against these unavoidable, victorious, maleficent forces? What can I do against the influence of Race, in my history? What can I do against hereditary and constitutional habits, against scrofula, lymph, impotence? against climate, against barbarism, in my country? I can reason down or deny every thing, except this perpetual Belly: feed he must and will, and I cannot make him respectable.

But the main resistance which the affirmative impulse finds, and one including all others, is in the doctrine of the Illusionists. There is a painful rumor in circulation, that we have been practised upon in all the principal performances of life, and free agency is the emptiest name. We have been sopped and drugged with the air, with food, with woman, with children, with sciences, with events, which leave us exactly where they found us. The mathematics, 'tis complained, leave the mind where they find it: so do all sciences; and so do all events and actions. I find a man who has passed through all the sciences, the churl he was; and, through all the offices, learned, civil, and social, can detect the child.

We are not the less necessitated to dedicate life to them. In fact, we may come to accept it as the fixed rule and theory of our state of education, that God is a substance, and his method is illusion. The eastern sages owned the goddess Yoganidra, the great illusory energy of Vishnu, by whom, as utter ignorance, the whole world is beguiled.

Or, shall I state it thus?—The astonishment of life, is, the absence of any appearance of reconciliation between the theory and practice of life. Reason, the prized reality, the Law, is apprehended, now and then, for a serene and profound moment, amidst the hubbub of cares and works which have no direct bearing on it;—is then lost, for months or years, and again found, for an interval, to be lost again. If we compute it in time, we may, in fifty years, have half a dozen reasonable hours. But what are these cares and works the better? A method in the world we do not see, but this parallelism of great and little, which never react on each other, nor discover the smallest tendency to converge. Experiences, fortunes, governings, readings, writings, are nothing to the purpose; as when a man comes into the room, it does not appear whether he has been fed on yams or buffalo,—he has contrived to get so much bone and fibre as he wants, out of rice or out of snow. So vast is the disproportion between the sky of law and the pismire of performance under it, that, whether he is a man of worth or a sot, is not so great a matter as we say. Shall I add, as one juggle of this enchantment, the stunning non-intercourse law which makes coöperation impossible? The young spirit pants to enter society. But all the ways of culture and greatness lead to solitary imprisonment. He has been often baulked. He did not expect a sympathy with his thought from the village, but he went with it to the chosen and intelligent, and found no entertainment for it, but mere misapprehension, distaste, and scoffing. Men are strangely mistimed and misapplied; and the excellence of each is an inflamed individualism which separates him more.

There are these, and more than these diseases of thought, which our ordinary teachers do not attempt to remove. Now shall we, because a good nature inclines us to virtue's side, say, There are no doubts,—and lie for the right? Is life to be led in a brave or in a cowardly manner? and is not the satisfaction of the doubts essential to all manliness? Is the name of virtue to be a barrier to that which is virtue? Can you not believe that a man of earnest and burly habit may find small good in tea, essays, and catechism, and want a rougher instruction, want men, labor, trade, farming, war, hunger, plenty, love, hatred, doubt, and terror, to make things plain to him; and has he not a right to insist on being convinced in his own way? When he is convinced, he will be worth the pains.

Belief consists in accepting the affirmations of the soul; unbelief, in denying them. Some minds are incapable of skepticism. The doubts they profess to entertain are rather a civility or accommodation to the common discourse of their company. They may well give themselves leave to speculate, for they are secure of a return. Once admitted to the heaven of thought, they see no relapse into night, but infinite invitation on the other side. Heaven is within heaven, and sky over sky, and they are encompassed with divinities. Others there are, to whom the heaven is brass, and it shuts down to the surface of the earth. It is a question of temperament, or of more or less immersion in nature. The last class must needs have a reflex or parasite faith; not a sight of realities, but an instinctive reliance on the seers and believers of realities. The manners and thoughts of believers astonish them, and convince them that these have seen something which is hid from themselves. But their sensual habit would fix the believer to his last position, whilst he as inevitably advances; and presently the unbeliever, for love of belief, burns the believer.

Great believers are always reckoned infidels, impracticable, fantastic, atheistic, and really men of no account. The spiritualist finds himself driven to express his faith by a series of skepticisms. Charitable souls come with their projects, and ask his coöperation. How can he hesitate? It is the rule of mere comity and courtesy to agree where you can, and to turn your sentence with something auspicious, and not freezing and sinister. But he is forced to say, 'O, these things will be as they must be: what can you do? These particular griefs and crimes are the foliage and fruit of such trees as we see growing. It is vain to complain of the leaf or the berry: cut it off; it will bear another just as bad. You must begin your cure lower down.' The generosities of the day prove an intractable element for him. The people's questions are not his; their methods are not his; and, against all the dictates of good nature, he is driven to say, he has no pleasure in them.

Even the doctrines dear to the hope of man, of the divine Providence, and of the immortality of the soul, his neighbors can not put the statement so that he shall affirm it. But he denies out of more faith, and not less. He denies out of honesty. He had rather stand charged with the imbecility of skepticism, than with untruth. I believe, he says, in the moral design of the universe; it exists hospitably for the weal of souls; but your dogmas seem to me caricatures: why should I make believe them? Will any say, this is cold and infidel? The wise and magnanimous will not say so. They will exult in his far-sighted good-will, that can abandon to the adversary all the ground of tradition and common belief, without losing a jot of strength. It sees to the end of all transgression. George Fox saw 'that there was an ocean of darkness and death; but withal, an infinite ocean of light and love which flowed over that of darkness.'°

The final solution in which skepticism is lost, is, in the moral sentiment, which never forfeits its supremacy. All moods may be safely tried, and their weight allowed to all objections: the moral sentiment as easily outweighs them all, as any one. This is the drop which balances the sea. I play with the miscellany of facts, and take those superficial views which we call skepticism; but I know that they will presently appear to me in that order which makes skepticism impossible. A man of thought must feel the thought that is parent of the universe: that the masses of nature do undulate and flow.

This faith avails to the whole emergency of life and objects. The world is saturated with deity and with law. He is content with just and unjust, with sots and fools, with the triumph of folly and fraud. He can behold with serenity the yawning gulf between the ambition of man and his power of performance, between the demand and supply of power, which makes the tragedy of all souls.

Charles Fourier announced that 'the attractions of man are proportioned to his destinies;'° in other words, that every desire predicts its own satisfaction. Yet, all experience exhibits the reverse of this; the incompetency of power is the universal grief of young and ardent minds. They accuse the divine providence of a certain parsimony. It has shown the heaven and earth to every child, and filled him with a desire for the whole; a desire raging, infinite; a hunger, as of space to be filled with planets; a cry of famine, as of devils for souls. Then for the satisfaction,—to each man is administered a single drop, a bead of dew of vital power, *per day*,—a cup as large as space, and one drop of the water of life in it. Each man woke in the morning, with an appetite that could eat the solar system like a cake; a spirit for action and passion without bounds; he could lay his hand on the morning star: he could try conclusions with gravitation or chemistry; but, on the first motion to prove his strength,—hands, feet, senses, gave way, and would not serve him. He was an emperor deserted by his states, and left to whistle by himself, or thrust into a mob of emperors, all whistling: and still the sirens sang, 'The attractions are proportioned to the destinies.' In every house, in the heart of each maiden, and of each boy, in the soul of the soaring saint, this chasm is found,—between the largest promise of ideal power, and the shabby experience.

The expansive nature of truth comes to our succor, elastic, not to be surrounded. Man helps himself by larger generalizations. The lesson of life is practically to generalize; to believe what the years and the centuries say against the hours; to resist the usurpation of particulars; to penetrate to their catholic sense. Things seem to say one thing, and say the reverse. The appearance is immoral; the result is moral. Things seem to tend downward, to justify despondency, to promote rogues, to defeat the just; and, by knaves, as by martyrs, the just cause is carried forward. Although knaves win in every political struggle, although society seems to be delivered over from the hands of one set of criminals into the hands of another set of criminals, as fast as the government is changed, and the march of civilization is a train of felonies, yet, general ends are somehow answered. We see, now, events forced on, which seem to retard or retrograde the civility of ages. But the world-spirit is a good swimmer, and storms and waves can not drown him. He snaps his finger at laws: and so, throughout history, heaven seems to affect low and poor means. Through the years and the centuries, through evil agents, through toys and atoms, a great and beneficent tendency irresistibly streams.

Let a man learn to look for the permanent in the mutable and fleeting; let him learn to bear the disappearance of things he was wont to reverence, without losing his reverence; let him learn that he is here, not to work, but to be worked upon; and that, though abyss open under abyss, and opinion displace opinion, all are at last contained in the Eternal Cause.—

'If my bark sink, 'tis to another sea.'°

SHAKSPEARE; OR, THE POET

GREAT men are more distinguished by range and extent, than by originality. If we require the originality which consists in weaving, like a spider, their web from their own bowels; in finding clay, and making bricks, and building the house; no great men are original. Nor does valuable originality consist in unlikeness to other men. The hero is in the press of knights, and the thick of events; and, seeing what men want, and sharing their desire, he adds the needful length of sight and of arm, to come at the desired point. The greatest genius is the most indebted man. A poet is no rattlebrain, saying what comes uppermost, and, because he says every thing, saying, at last, something good; but a heart in unison with his time and country. There is nothing whimsical and fantastic in his production, but sweet and sad earnest, freighted with the weightiest convictions, and pointed with the most determined aim which any man or class knows of in his times.

The Genius of our life is jealous of individuals, and will not have any individual great, except through the general. There is no choice to genius. A great man does not wake up on some fine morning and say, 'I am full of life, I will go to sea, and find an Antarctic continent: to-day I will square the circle: I will ransack botany, and find a new food for man: I have a new architecture in my mind: I foresee a new mechanic power:' no, but he finds himself in the river of the thoughts and events, forced onward by the ideas and necessities of his contemporaries. He stands where all the eyes of men look one way, and their hands all point in the direction in which he should go. The church has reared him amidst rites and pomps, and he carries out the advice which her music gave him, and builds a cathedral needed by her chants and processions. He finds a war raging: it educates him, by trumpet, in barracks, and he betters the instruction. He finds two counties groping to bring coal, or flour, or fish, from the place of production to the place of consumption, and he hits on a railroad. Every master has found his materials collected, and his power lay in his sympathy with his people, and in his love of the materials he wrought in. What an economy of power! and what a compensation for the shortness of life! All is done to his hand. The world has brought him thus far on his way. The human race has gone out before him, sunk the hills, filled the hollows, and bridged the rivers. Men, nations, poets, artisans, women, all have worked for him, and he enters into their labors. Choose any other thing, out of the line of tendency, out of the national feeling and history, and he would have all to do for himself: his powers would be expended in the first preparations. Great genial power, one would almost say, consists in not being original at all; in being altogether receptive; in letting the world do all, and suffering the spirit of the hour to pass unobstructed through the mind.

Shakspeare's youth fell in a time when the English people were importunate for dramatic entertainments. The court took offence easily at political allusions, and attempted to suppress them. The Puritans, a growing and energetic party, and the religious among the Anglican church, would suppress them. But the people wanted them. Inn-yards, houses without roofs, and extemporaneous enclosures at country fairs, were the ready theatres of strolling players. The people had tasted this new joy; and, as we could not hope to suppress newspapers now,—no, not by the strongest party,—neither then could king, prelate, or puritan, alone or united, suppress an organ, which was ballad, epic, newspaper, caucus, lecture, punch,° and library, at the same time. Probably king, prelate, and puritan, all found their own account in it. It had become, by all causes, a national interest,—by no means conspicuous, so that some great scholar would have thought of treating it in an English history,—but not a whit less considerable, because it was cheap, and of no account, like a baker's-shop. The best proof of its vitality is the crowd of writers which suddenly broke into this field; Kyd, Marlow, Greene, Jonson, Chapman, Dekker, Webster, Heywood, Middleton, Peele, Ford, Massinger, Beaumont, and Fletcher.°

The secure possession, by the stage, of the public mind, is of the first importance to the poet who works for it. He loses no time in idle experiments. Here is audience and expectation prepared. In the case of Shakspeare there is much more. At the time when he left Stratford, and went up to London, a great body of stage-plays, of all dates and writers, existed in manuscript, and were in turn produced on the boards. Here is the Tale of Troy, which the audience will bear hearing some part of every week; the Death of Julius Cæsar, and other stories out of Plutarch, which they never tire of; a shelf full of English history, from the chronicles of Brut and Arthur, down to the royal Henries, which men hear eagerly; and a string of doleful tragedies, merry Italian tales, and Spanish voyages,° which all the London prentices know. All the mass has been treated, with more or less skill, by every playwright, and the prompter has the soiled and tattered manuscripts. It is now no longer possible to say who wrote them first. They have been the property of the Theatre so long, and so many rising geniuses have enlarged or altered them, inserting a speech, or a whole scene, or adding a song, that no man can any longer claim copyright on this work of numbers. Happily, no man wishes to. They are not yet desired in that way. We have few readers, many spectators and hearers. They had best lie where they are.

Shakspeare, in common with his comrades, esteemed the mass of old plays, waste stock, in which any experiment could be freely tried. Had the *prestige* which hedges about a modern tragedy existed, nothing could have been done. The rude warm blood of the living England circulated in the play, as in street-ballads, and gave body which he wanted to his airy and majestic fancy. The poet needs a ground in popular tradition on which he may work, and which, again, may restrain his art within the due temperance. It holds him to the people, supplies a foundation for his edifice; and, in furnishing so much work done to his hand, leaves him at leisure, and in full strength for the audacities of his imagination. In short, the poet owes to his legend what sculpture owed to the temple. Sculpture in Egypt, and in Greece, grew up in subordination to architecture. It was the ornament of the temple wall: at first, a rude relief carved on pediments, then the relief became bolder, and a head or arm was projected from the wall, the groups being still arranged with reference to the building, which serves also as a frame to hold the figures; and when, at last, the greatest freedom of style and treatment was reached, the prevailing genius of architecture still enforced a certain calmness and continence in the statue. As soon as the statue was begun for itself, and with no reference to the temple or palace, the art began to decline: freak, extravagance, and exhibition, took the place of the old temperance. This balance-wheel, which the sculptor found in architecture, the perilous irritability of poetic talent found in the accumulated dramatic materials to which the people were already wonted, and which had a certain excellence which no single genius, however extraordinary, could hope to create.

In point of fact, it appears that Shakspeare did owe debts in all directions, and was able to use whatever he found; and the amount of indebtedness may be inferred from Malone's laborious computations° in regard to the First, Second, and Third parts of Henry VI., in which, 'out of 6043 lines, 1771 were written by some author preceding Shakspeare; 2373 by him, on the foundation laid by his predecessors; and 1899 were entirely his own.' And the proceeding investigation hardly leaves a single drama of his absolute invention. Malone's sentence is an important piece of external history. In Henry VIII., I think I see plainly the cropping out of the original rock on which his own finer stratum was laid. The first play was written by a superior, thoughtful man, with a vicious ear. I can mark his lines, and know well their cadence. See Wolsey's soliloquy,° and the following scene with Cromwell, where,— instead of the metre of Shakspeare, whose secret is, that the thought constructs the tune, so that reading for the sense will best bring out the rhythm,—here the lines are constructed on a given tune, and the verse has even a trace of pulpit eloquence. But the play contains, through all its length, unmistakable traits of Shakspeare's hand, and some passages, as the account of the coronation, are like autographs. What is odd, the compliment to Queen Elizabeth is in the bad rhythm.

Shakspeare knew that tradition supplies a better fable than any invention can. If he lost any credit of design, he augmented his resources; and, at that day, our petulant demand for originality was not so much pressed. There was no literature for the million. The universal reading, the cheap press, were unknown. A great poet, who appears in illiterate times, absorbs into his sphere all the light which is any where radiating. Every intellectual jewel, every flower of sentiment, it is his fine office to bring to his people; and he comes to value his memory equally with his invention. He is therefore little solicitous whence his thoughts have been derived; whether through translation, whether through tradition, whether by travel in distant countries, whether by inspiration; from whatever source, they are equally welcome to his uncritical audience. Nay, he borrows very near home. Other men say wise things as well as he; only they say a good many foolish things, and do not know when they have spoken wisely. He knows the sparkle of the true stone, and puts it in high place, wherever he finds it. Such is the happy position of Homer, perhaps; of Chaucer, of Saadi.° They felt that all wit was their wit. And they are librarians and historiographers, as well as poets. Each romancer was heir and dispenser of all the hundred tales of the world,—

> 'Presenting Thebes' and Pelops' line
> And the tale of Troy divine.'°

The influence of Chaucer is conspicuous in all our early literature; and, more recently, not only Pope and Dryden have been beholden to him, but, in the whole society of English writers, a large unacknowledged debt is easily traced. One is charmed with the opulence which feeds so many pensioners. But Chaucer is a huge borrower. Chaucer, it seems, drew continually, through Lydgate and Caxton, from Guido di Colonna, whose Latin romance of the Trojan war was in turn a compilation from Dares Phrygius, Ovid, and Statius. Then Petrarch, Boccaccio, and the Provençal poets, are his benefactors: the Romaunt of the Rose is only judicious translation from William of Lorris and John of Meun: Troilus and Creseide, from Lollius of Urbino: The Cock and the Fox, from the *Lais* of Marie: The House of Fame, from the French or Italian: and poor Gower° he uses as if he were only a brick-kiln or stone-quarry, out of which to build his house. He steals by this apology,—that what he takes has no worth where he finds it, and the greatest where he leaves it. It has come to be practically a sort of rule in literature, that a man, having once shown himself capable of original writing, is entitled thenceforth to steal from the writings of others at discretion. Thought is the property of him who can entertain it; and of him who can adequately place it. A certain awkwardness marks the use of borrowed thoughts; but, as soon as we have learned what to do with them, they become our own.

Thus, all originality is relative. Every thinker is retrospective. The learned member of the legislature, at Westminster, or at Washington, speaks and votes for thousands. Show us the constituency, and the now invisible channels by which the senator is made aware of their wishes, the crowd of practical and knowing men, who, by correspondence or conversation, are feeding him with evidence, anecdotes, and estimates, and it will bereave his fine attitude and resistance of something of their impressiveness. As Sir Robert Peel and Mr. Webster vote, so Locke and Rousseau think for thousands; and so there were fountains all around Homer, Menu,° Saadi, or Milton, from which they drew; friends, lovers, books, traditions, proverbs,—all perished,—which, if seen, would go to reduce the wonder. Did the bard speak with authority? Did he feel himself overmatched by any companion? The appeal is to the consciousness of the writer. Is there at last in his breast a Delphi whereof to ask concerning any thought or thing, whether it be verily so, yea or nay? and to have answer, and to rely on that? All the debts which such a man could contract to other wit, would never disturb his consciousness of originality: for the ministrations of books, and of other minds, are a whiff of smoke to that most private reality with which he has conversed.

It is easy to see that what is best written or done by genius, in the world, was no man's work, but came by wide social labor, when a thousand wrought like one, sharing the same impulse. Our English Bible is a wonderful specimen of the strength and music of the English language. But it was not made by one man, or at one time; but centuries and churches brought it to perfection. There never was a time when there was not some translation existing. The Liturgy, admired for its energy and pathos, is an anthology of the piety of ages and nations, a translation of the prayers and forms of the Catholic church,—these collected, too, in long periods, from the prayers and meditations of every saint and sacred writer, all over the world. Grotius° makes the like remark in respect to the Lord's Prayer, that the single clauses of which it is composed were already in use, in the time of Christ, in the rabbinical forms. He picked out the grains of gold. The nervous language of the Common Law, the impressive forms of our courts, and the precision and substantial truth of the legal distinctions, are the contribution of all the sharp-sighted, strong-minded men who have lived in the countries where these laws govern. The translation of Plutarch° gets its excellence by being translation on translation. There never was a time when there was none. All the truly idiomatic and national phrases are kept, and all others successively picked out, and thrown away. Something like the same process had gone on, long before, with the originals of these books. The world takes liberties with world-books. Vedas, Æsop's Fables, Pilpay, Arabian Nights, Cid, Iliad, Robin Hood, Scottish Minstrelsy,° are not the work of single men. In the composition of such works, the time thinks, the market thinks, the mason, the carpenter, the merchant, the farmer, the fop, all think for us. Every book supplies its time with one good word; every municipal law, every trade, every folly of the day, and the generic catholic genius who is not afraid or ashamed to owe his originality to the originality of all, stands with the next age as the recorder and embodiment of his own.

We have to thank the researches of antiquaries, and the Shakspeare Society, for ascertaining the steps of the English drama, from the Mysteries celebrated in churches and by churchmen, and the final detachment from the church, and the completion of secular plays, from Ferrex and Porrex, and Gammer Gurton's Needle,° down to the possession of the stage by the very pieces which Shakspeare altered, remodelled, and finally made his own. Elated with success, and piqued by the growing interest of the problem, they have left no book-stall unsearched, no chest in a garret unopened, no file of old yellow accounts to decompose in damp and worms, so keen was the hope to discover whether the boy Shakspeare poached or not, whether he held horses at the theatre door, whether he kept school, and why he left in his will only his second-best bed to Ann Hathaway, his wife.

There is somewhat touching in the madness with which the passing age mischooses the object on which all candles shine, and all eyes are turned; the care with which it registers every trifle touching Queen Elizabeth, and King James, and the Essexes, Leicesters, Burleighs, and Buckinghams;° and lets pass without a single valuable note the founder of another dynasty, which alone will cause the Tudor dynasty to be remembered,—the man who carries the Saxon race in him by the inspiration which feeds him, and on whose thoughts the foremost people of the world are now for some ages to be nourished, and minds to receive this and not another bias. A popular player,—nobody suspected he was the poet of the human race; and the secret was kept as faithfully from poets and intellectual men, as from courtiers and frivolous people. Bacon, who took the inventory of the human understanding for his times, never mentioned his name. Ben Jonson, though we have strained his few words° of regard and panegyric, had no suspicion of the elastic fame whose first vibrations he was attempting. He no doubt thought the praise he has conceded to him generous, and esteemed himself, out of all question, the better poet of the two.

If it need wit to know wit, according to the proverb, Shakspeare's time should be capable of recognizing it. Sir Henry Wotton° was born four years after Shakspeare, and died twenty-three years after him; and I find, among his correspondents and acquaintances, the following persons: Theodore Beza, Isaac Casaubon, Sir Philip Sidney, Earl of Essex, Lord Bacon, Sir Walter Raleigh, John Milton, Sir Henry Vane, Isaac Walton, Dr. Donne, Abraham Cowley, Bellarmine, Charles Cotton, John Pym, John Hales, Kepler, Vieta, Albericus Gentilis, Paul Sarpi, Arminius; with all of whom exists some token of his having communicated, without enumerating many others, whom doubtless he saw,—Shakspeare, Spenser, Jonson, Beaumont, Massinger, two Herberts, Marlow, Chapman, and the rest. Since the constellation of great men who appeared in Greece in the time of Pericles, there was never any such society;—yet their genius failed them to find out the best head in the universe. Our poet's mask was impenetrable. You cannot see the mountain near. It took a century to make it suspected; and not until two centuries had passed, after his death, did any criticism which we think adequate begin to appear. It was not possible to write the history of Shakspeare till now; for he is the father of German literature: it was on the introduction of Shakspeare into German, by Lessing, and the translation of his works by Wieland and Schlegel,° that the rapid burst of German literature was most intimately connected. It was not until the nineteenth century, whose speculative genius is a sort of living Hamlet, that the tragedy of Hamlet could find such wondering readers. Now, literature, philosophy, and thought, are Shakspearized. His mind is the horizon beyond which, at present, we do not see. Our ears are educated to music by his rhythm. Coleridge and Goethe are the only critics who have expressed our convictions with any adequate fidelity: but there is in all cultivated minds a silent appreciation of his superlative power and beauty, which, like Christianity, qualifies the period.

The Shakspeare Society have inquired in all directions, advertised the missing facts, offered money for any information that will lead to proof; and with what result? Beside some important illustration of the history of the English stage, to which I have adverted, they have gleaned a few facts touching the property, and dealings in regard to property, of the poet. It appears that, from year to year, he owned a larger share in the Blackfriars' Theatre: its wardrobe and other appurtenances were his: that he bought an estate in his native village, with his earnings, as writer and shareholder; that he lived in the best house in Stratford; was intrusted by his neighbors with their commissions in London, as of borrowing money, and the like; that he was a veritable farmer. About the time when he was writing Macbeth, he sues Philip Rogers, in the borough-court of Stratford, for thirty-five shillings, ten pence, for corn delivered to him at different times; and, in all respects, appears as a good husband, with no reputation for eccentricity or excess. He was a good-natured sort of man, an actor and shareholder in the theatre, not in any striking manner distinguished from other actors and managers. I admit the importance of this information. It was well worth the pains that have been taken to procure it.

But whatever scraps of information concerning his condition these researches may have rescued, they can shed no light upon that infinite invention which is the concealed magnet of his attraction for us. We are very clumsy writers of history. We tell the chronicle of parentage, birth, birth-place, schooling, school-mates, earning of money, marriage, pub-lication of books, celebrity, death; and when we have come to an end of this gossip, no ray of relation appears between it and the goddess-born; and it seems as if, had we dipped at random into the 'Modern Plu-tarch,' and read any other life there, it would have fitted the poems as well. It is the essence of poetry to spring, like the rainbow daughter of Wonder, from the invisible, to abolish the past, and refuse all history. Malone, Warburton, Dyce, and Collier,° have wasted their oil. The famed theatres, Covent Garden, Drury Lane, the Park, and Tremont, have vainly assisted. Betterton, Garrick, Kemble, Kean, and Mac-ready,° dedicate their lives to this genius; him they crown, elucidate, obey, and express. The genius knows them not. The recitation begins; one golden word leaps out immortal from all this painted pedantry, and sweetly torments us with invitations to its own inaccessible homes. I remember, I went once to see the Hamlet of a famed performer, the pride of the English stage; and all I then heard, and all I now remember, of the tragedian, was that in which the tragedian had no part; simply, Hamlet's question to the ghost,—

> 'What may this mean,
> That thou, dead corse, again in complete steel
> Revisit'st thus the glimpses of the moon?'°

That imagination which dilates the closet he writes in to the world's dimension, crowds it with agents in rank and order, as quickly reduces the big reality to be the glimpses of the moon. These tricks of his magic spoil for us the illusions of the green-room. Can any biography shed light on the localities into which the Midsummer Night's Dream admits me? Did Shakspeare confide to any notary or parish recorder, sacristan, or surrogate, in Stratford, the genesis of that delicate creation? The forest of Arden, the nimble air of Scone Castle, the moonlight of Portia's villa, 'the antres vast and desarts idle,' of Othello's captivity,°—where is the third cousin, or grand-nephew, the chancellor's file of accounts, or private letter, that has kept one word of those transcendent secrets? In fine, in this drama, as in all great works of art,—in the Cyclopæan architecture of Egypt and India; in the Phidian sculpture; the Gothic minsters; the Italian painting; the Ballads of Spain and Scotland,—the Genius draws up the ladder after him, when the creative age goes up to heaven, and gives way to a new, who see the works, and ask in vain for a history.

Shakspeare is the only biographer of Shakspeare; and even he can tell nothing, except to the Shakspeare in us; that is, to our most apprehensive and sympathetic hour. He cannot step from off his tripod, and give us anecdotes of his inspirations. Read the antique documents extricated, analyzed, and compared, by the assiduous Dyce and Collier; and now read one of those skiey sentences,—aerolites,—which seem to have fallen out of heaven, and which, not your experience, but the man within the breast, has accepted as words of fate; and tell me if they match; if the former account in any manner for the latter; or, which gives the most historical insight into the man.

Hence, though our external history is so meagre, yet, with Shakspeare for biographer, instead of Aubrey and Rowe,° we have really the information which is material, that which describes character and fortune, that which, if we were about to meet the man and deal with him, would most import us to know. We have his recorded convictions on those questions which knock for answer at every heart,—on life and death, on love, on wealth and poverty, on the prizes of life, and the ways whereby we come at them; on the characters of men, and the influences, occult and open, which affect their fortunes; and on those mysterious and demoniacal powers which defy our science, and which yet interweave their malice and their gift in our brightest hours. Who ever read the volume of the Sonnets, without finding that the poet had there revealed, under masks that are no masks to the intelligent, the lore of friendship and of love; the confusion of sentiments in the most susceptible, and, at the same time, the most intellectual of men? What trait of his private mind has he hidden in his dramas? One can discern, in his ample pictures of the gentleman and the king, what forms and humanities pleased him; his delight in troops of friends, in large hospitality, in cheerful giving. Let Timon, let Warwick, let Antonio° the merchant, answer for his great heart. So far from Shakspeare's being the least known, he is the one person, in all modern history, known to us. What point of morals, of manners, of economy, of philosophy, of religion, of taste, of the conduct of life, has he not settled? What mystery has he not signified his knowledge of? What office, or function, or district of man's work, has he not remembered? What king has he not taught state, as Talma° taught Napoleon? What maiden has not found him finer than her delicacy? What lover has he not outloved? What sage has he not outseen? What gentleman has he not instructed in the rudeness of his behavior?

Some able and appreciating critics think no criticism on Shakspeare valuable, that does not rest purely on the dramatic merit; that he is falsely judged as poet and philosopher. I think as highly as these critics of his dramatic merit, but still think it secondary. He was a full man, who liked to talk; a brain exhaling thoughts and images, which, seeking vent, found the drama next at hand. Had he been less, we should have had to consider how well he filled his place, how good a dramatist he was,—and he is the best in the world. But it turns out, that what he has to say is of that weight, as to withdraw some attention from the vehicle; and he is like some saint whose history is to be rendered into all languages, into verse and prose, into songs and pictures, and cut up into proverbs; so that the occasion which gave the saint's meaning the form of a conversation, or of a prayer, or of a code of laws, is immaterial, compared with the universality of its application. So it fares with the wise Shakspeare and his book of life. He wrote the airs for all our modern music: he wrote the text of modern life; the text of manners: he drew the man of England and Europe; the father of the man in America: he drew the man, and described the day, and what is done in it: he read the hearts of men and women, their probity, and their second thought, and wiles; the wiles of innocence, and the transitions by which virtues and vices slide into their contraries: he could divide the mother's part from the father's part in the face of the child, or draw the fine demarcations of freedom and of fate: he knew the laws of repression which make the police of nature: and all the sweets and all the terrors of human lot lay in his mind as truly but as softly as the landscape lies on the eye. And the importance of this wisdom of life sinks the form, as of Drama or Epic, out of notice. 'Tis like making a question concerning the paper on which a king's message is written.

Shakspeare is as much out of the category of eminent authors, as he is out of the crowd. He is inconceivably wise; the others, conceivably. A good reader can, in a sort, nestle into Plato's brain, and think from thence; but not into Shakspeare's. We are still out of doors. For executive faculty, for creation, Shakspeare is unique. No man can imagine it better. He was the farthest reach of subtlety compatible with an individual self,—the subtilest of authors, and only just within the possibility of authorship. With this wisdom of life, is the equal endowment of imaginative and of lyric power. He clothed the creatures of his legend with form and sentiments, as if they were people who had lived under his roof; and few real men have left such distinct characters as these fictions. And they spoke in language as sweet as it was fit. Yet his talents never seduced him into an ostentation, nor did he harp on one string. An omnipresent humanity coördinates all his faculties. Give a man of talents a story to tell, and his partiality will presently appear. He has certain observations, opinions, topics, which have some accidental prominence, and which he disposes all to exhibit. He crams this part, and starves that other part, consulting not the fitness of the thing, but his fitness and strength. But Shakspeare has no peculiarity, no importunate topic; but all is duly given; no veins, no curiosities: no cow-painter, no bird-fancier, no mannerist is he: he has no discoverable egotism: the great he tells greatly; the small, subordinately. He is wise without emphasis or assertion; he is strong, as nature is strong, who lifts the land into mountain slopes without effort, and by the same rule as she floats a bubble in the air, and likes as well to do the one as the other. This makes that equality of power in farce, tragedy, narrative, and lovesongs; a merit so incessant, that each reader is incredulous of the perception of other readers.

This power of expression, or of transferring the inmost truth of things into music and verse, makes him the type of the poet, and has added a new problem to metaphysics. This is that which throws him into natural history, as a main production of the globe, and as announcing new eras and ameliorations. Things were mirrored in his poetry without loss or blur: he could paint the fine with precision, the great with compass; the tragic and the comic indifferently, and without any distortion or favor. He carried his powerful execution into minute details, to a hair point; finishes an eyelash or a dimple as firmly as he draws a mountain; and yet these, like nature's, will bear the scrutiny of the solar microscope.

In short, he is the chief example to prove that more or less of production, more or fewer pictures, is a thing indifferent. He had the power to make one picture. Daguerre° learned how to let one flower etch its image on his plate of iodine; and then proceeds at leisure to etch a million. There are always objects; but there was never representation. Here is perfect representation, at last; and now let the world of figures sit for their portraits. No recipe can be given for the making of a Shakspeare; but the possibility of the translation of things into song is demonstrated.

His lyric power lies in the genius of the piece. The sonnets, though their excellence is lost in the splendor of the dramas, are as inimitable as they: and it is not a merit of lines, but a total merit of the piece; like the tone of voice of some incomparable person, so is this a speech of poetic beings, and any clause as unproducible now as a whole poem.

Though the speeches in the plays, and single lines, have a beauty which tempts the ear to pause on them for their euphuism, yet the sentence is so loaded with meaning, and so linked with its foregoers and followers, that the logician is satisfied. His means are as admirable as his ends; every subordinate invention, by which he helps himself to connect some irreconcilable opposites, is a poem too. He is not reduced to dismount and walk, because his horses are running off with him in some distant direction: he always rides.

The finest poetry was first experience: but the thought has suffered a transformation since it was an experience. Cultivated men often attain a good degree of skill in writing verses; but it is easy to read, through their poems, their personal history: any one acquainted with parties can name every figure: this is Andrew, and that is Rachel. The sense thus remains prosaic. It is a caterpillar with wings, and not yet a butterfly. In the poet's mind, the fact has gone quite over into the new element of thought, and has lost all that is exuvial. This generosity abides with Shakspeare. We say, from the truth and closeness of his pictures, that he knows the lesson by heart. Yet there is not a trace of egotism.

One more royal trait properly belongs to the poet. I mean his cheerfulness, without which no man can be a poet,—for beauty is his aim. He loves virtue, not for its obligation, but for its grace: he delights in the world, in man, in woman, for the lovely light that sparkles from them. Beauty, the spirit of joy and hilarity, he sheds over the universe. Epicurus relates, that poetry hath such charms that a lover might forsake his mistress to partake of them. And the true bards have been noted for their firm and cheerful temper. Homer lies in sunshine; Chaucer is glad and erect; and Saadi says, 'It was rumored abroad that I was penitent; but what had I to do with repentance?' Not less sovereign and cheerful,—much more sovereign and cheerful, is the tone of Shakspeare. His name suggests joy and emancipation to the heart of men. If he should appear in any company of human souls, who would not march in his troop? He touches nothing that does not borrow health and longevity from his festal style.

And now, how stands the account of man with this bard and benefactor, when in solitude, shutting our ears to the reverberations of his fame, we seek to strike the balance? Solitude has austere lessons; it can teach us to spare both heroes and poets; and it weighs Shakspeare also, and finds him to share the halfness and imperfection of humanity.

Shakspeare, Homer, Dante, Chaucer, saw the splendor of meaning that plays over the visible world; knew that a tree had another use than for apples, and corn another than for meal, and the ball of the earth, than for tillage and roads: that these things bore a second and finer harvest to the mind, being emblems of its thoughts, and conveying in all their natural history a certain mute commentary on human life. Shakspeare employed them as colors to compose his picture. He rested in their beauty; and never took the step which seemed inevitable to such genius, namely, to explore the virtue which resides in these symbols, and imparts this power,—what is that which they themselves say? He converted the elements, which waited on his command, into entertainments. He was master of the revels to mankind. Is it not as if one should have, through majestic powers of science, the comets given into his hand, or the planets and their moons, and should draw them from their orbits to glare with the municipal fireworks on a holiday night, and advertise in all towns, 'very superior pyrotechny this evening!' Are the agents of nature, and the power to understand them, worth no more than a street serenade, or the breath of a cigar? One remembers again the trumpet-text in the Koran,—'The heavens and the earth, and all that is between them, think ye we have created them in jest?' As long as the question is of talent and mental power, the world of men has not his equal to show. But when the question is to life, and its materials, and its auxiliaries, how does he profit me? What does it signify? It is but a Twelfth Night, or Midsummer-Night's Dream, or a Winter Evening's Tale: what signifies another picture more or less? The Egyptian verdict of the Shakspeare Societies comes to mind, that he was a jovial actor and manager. I can not marry this fact to his verse. Other admirable men have led lives in some sort of keeping with their thought; but this man, in wide contrast. Had he been less, had he reached only the common measure of great authors, of Bacon, Milton, Tasso,° Cervantes, we might leave the fact in the twilight of human fate: but, that this man of men, he who gave to the science of mind a new and larger subject than had ever existed, and planted the standard of humanity some furlongs forward into Chaos,—that he should not be wise for himself,—it must even go into the world's history, that the best poet led an obscure and profane life, using his genius for the public amusement.

Well, other men, priest and prophet, Israelite, German, and Swede, beheld the same objects: they also saw through them that which was contained. And to what purpose? The beauty straightway vanished; they read commandments, all-excluding mountainous duty; an obligation, a sadness, as of piled mountains, fell on them, and life became ghastly, joyless, a pilgrim's progress, a probation, beleaguered round with doleful histories of Adam's fall and curse, behind us; with doomsdays and purgatorial and penal fires before us; and the heart of the seer and the heart of the listener sank in them.

It must be conceded that these are half-views of half-men. The world still wants its poet-priest, a reconciler, who shall not trifle with Shakspeare the player, nor shall grope in graves with Swedenborg the mourner; but who shall see, speak, and act, with equal inspiration. For knowledge will brighten the sunshine; right is more beautiful than private affection; and love is compatible with universal wisdom.

THE CONDUCT OF LIFE
(1860)

FATE

DELICATE omens traced in air
To the lone bard true witness bare;
Birds with auguries on their wings
Chanted undeceiving things
Him to beckon, him to warn;
Well might then the poet scorn
To learn of scribe or courier
Hints writ in vaster character;
And on his mind, at dawn of day,
Soft shadows of the evening lay.
For the prevision is allied
Unto the thing so signified;
Or say, the foresight that awaits
Is the same Genius that creates.

IT chanced during one winter, a few years ago, that our cities were bent on discussing the theory of the Age. By an odd coincidence, four or five noted men were each reading a discourse to the citizens of Boston or New York, on the Spirit of the Times. It so happened that the subject had the same prominence in some remarkable pamphlets and journals issued in London in the same season. To me, however, the question of the times resolved itself into a practical question of the conduct of life. How shall I live? We are incompetent to solve the times. Our geometry cannot span the huge orbits of the prevailing ideas, behold their return, and reconcile their opposition. We can only obey our own polarity. 'Tis fine for us to speculate and elect our course, if we must accept an irresistible dictation.

In our first steps to gain our wishes, we come upon immovable limitations. We are fired with the hope to reform men. After many experiments, we find that we must begin earlier,—at school. But the boys and girls are not docile; we can make nothing of them. We decide that they are not of good stock. We must begin our reform earlier still,—at generation: that is to say, there is Fate, or laws of the world.

But if there be irresistible dictation, this dictation understands itself. If we must accept Fate, we are not less compelled to affirm liberty, the significance of the individual, the grandeur of duty, the power of character. This is true, and that other is true. But our geometry cannot span these extreme points, and reconcile them. What to do? By obeying each thought frankly, by harping, or, if you will, pounding on each string, we learn at last its power. By the same obedience to other thoughts, we learn theirs, and then comes some reasonable hope of harmonizing them. We are sure, that, though we know not how, necessity does comport with liberty, the individual with the world, my polarity with the spirit of the times. The riddle of the age has for each a private solution. If one would study his own time, it must be by this method of taking up in turn each of the leading topics which belong to our scheme of human life, and, by firmly stating all that is agreeable to experience on one, and doing the same justice to the opposing facts in the others, the true limitations will appear. Any excess of emphasis, on one part, would be corrected, and a just balance would be made.

But let us honestly state the facts. Our America has a bad name for superficialness. Great men, great nations, have not been boasters and buffoons, but perceivers of the terror of life, and have manned themselves to face it. The Spartan, embodying his religion in his country, dies before its majesty without a question. The Turk, who believes his doom is written on the iron leaf in the moment when he entered the world, rushes on the enemy's sabre with undivided will. The Turk, the Arab, the Persian, accepts the foreordained fate.

> 'On two days, it steads not to run from thy grave,
>   The appointed, and the unappointed day;
> On the first, neither balm nor physician can save,
>   Nor thee, on the second, the Universe slay.'°

The Hindoo, under the wheel, is as firm. Our Calvinists, in the last generation, had something of the same dignity. They felt that the weight of the Universe held them down to their place. What could *they* do? Wise men feel that there is something which cannot be talked or voted away,—a strap or belt which girds the world.

> 'The Destiny, minister general,
> That executeth in the world o'er all,
> The purveyance which God hath seen beforne,
> So strong it is, that tho' the world had sworn
> The contrary of a thing by yea or nay,
> Yet sometime it shall fallen on a day
> That falleth not oft in a thousand year;
> For, certainly, our appetités here,
> Be it of war, or peace, or hate, or love,
> All this is ruled by the sight above.'°
>   CHAUCER: *The Knighte's Tale.*

The Greek Tragedy expressed the same sense: 'Whatever is fated, that will take place. The great immense mind of Jove is not to be transgressed.'°

Savages cling to a local god of one tribe or town. The broad ethics of Jesus were quickly narrowed to village theologies, which preach an election or favoritism. And, now and then, an amiable parson, like Jung Stilling, or Robert Huntington, believes in a pistareen-Providence,° which, whenever the good man wants a dinner, makes that somebody shall knock at his door, and leave a half-dollar. But Nature is no sentimentalist,—does not cosset or pamper us. We must see that the world is rough and surly, and will not mind drowning a man or a woman; but swallows your ship like a grain of dust. The cold, inconsiderate of persons, tingles your blood, benumbs your feet, freezes a man like an apple. The diseases, the elements, fortune, gravity, lightning, respect no persons. The way of Providence is a little rude. The habit of snake and spider, the snap of the tiger and other leapers and bloody jumpers, the crackle of the bones of his prey in the coil of the anaconda,—these are in the system, and our habits are like theirs. You have just dined, and, however scrupulously the slaughter-house is concealed in the graceful distance of miles, there is complicity,—expensive races,—race living at the expense of race. The planet is liable to shocks from comets, perturbations from planets, rendings from earthquake and volcano, alterations of climate, precessions of equinoxes. Rivers dry up by opening of the forest. The sea changes its bed. Towns and counties fall into it. At Lisbon, an earthquake° killed men like flies. At Naples, three years ago,° ten thousand persons were crushed in a few minutes. The scurvy at sea; the sword of the climate in the west of Africa, at Cayenne, at Panama, at New Orleans, cut off men like a massacre. Our western prairie shakes with fever and ague. The cholera, the small-pox, have proved as mortal to some tribes, as a frost to the crickets, which, having filled the summer with noise, are silenced by a fall of the temperature of one night. Without uncovering what does not concern us, or counting how many species of parasites hang on a bombyx; or groping after intestinal parasites, or infusory biters, or the obscurities of alternate generation;—the forms of the shark, the *labrus*,° the jaw of the sea-wolf paved with crushing teeth, the weapons of the grampus, and other warriors hidden in the sea,—are hints of ferocity in the interiors of nature. Let us not deny it up and down. Providence has a wild, rough, incalculable road to its end, and it is of no use to try to whitewash its huge, mixed instrumentalities, or to dress up that terrific benefactor in a clean shirt and white neckcloth of a student in divinity.

Will you say, the disasters which threaten mankind are exceptional, and one need not lay his account for cataclysms every day? Aye, but what happens once, may happen again, and so long as these strokes are not to be parried by us, they must be feared.

But these shocks and ruins are less destructive to us, than the stealthy power of other laws which act on us daily. An expense of ends to means is fate;—organization tyrannizing over character. The menagerie, or forms and powers of the spine, is a book of fate: the bill of the bird, the skull of the snake, determines tyrannically its limits. So is the scale of races, of temperaments; so is sex; so is climate; so is the reaction of talents imprisoning the vital power in certain directions. Every spirit makes its house; but afterwards the house confines the spirit.

The gross lines are legible to the dull: the cabman is phrenologist so far: he looks in your face to see if his shilling is sure. A dome of brow denotes one thing; a pot-belly another; a squint, a pug-nose, mats of hair, the pigment of the epidermis, betray character. People seem sheathed in their tough organization. Ask Spurzheim, ask the doctors, ask Quetelet,° if temperaments decide nothing? or if there be anything they do not decide? Read the description in medical books of the four temperaments, and you will think you are reading your own thoughts which you had not yet told. Find the part which black eyes, and which blue eyes, play severally in the company. How shall a man escape from his ancestors, or draw off from his veins the black drop which he drew from his father's or his mother's life? It often appears in a family, as if all the qualities of the progenitors were potted in several jars,—some ruling quality in each son or daughter of the house,—and sometimes the unmixed temperament, the rank unmitigated elixir, the family vice, is drawn off in a separate individual, and the others are proportionally relieved. We sometimes see a change of expression in our companion, and say, his father, or his mother, comes to the windows of his eyes, and sometimes a remote relative. In different hours, a man represents each of several of his ancestors, as if there were seven or eight of us rolled up in each man's skin,—seven or eight ancestors at least,—and they constitute the variety of notes for that new piece of music which his life is. At the corner of the street, you read the possibility of each passenger, in the facial angle, in the complexion, in the depth of his eye. His parentage determines it. Men are what their mothers made them. You may as well ask a loom which weaves huckaback, why it does not make cashmere, as expect poetry from this engineer, or a chemical discovery from that jobber. Ask the digger in the ditch to explain Newton's laws: the fine organs of his brain have been pinched by overwork and squalid poverty from father to son, for a hundred years. When each comes forth from his mother's womb, the gate of gifts closes behind him. Let him value his hands and feet, he has but one pair. So he has but one future, and that is already predetermined in his lobes, and described in that little fatty face, pig-eye, and squat form. All the privilege and all the legislation of the world cannot meddle or help to make a poet or a prince of him.

Jesus said, 'When he looketh on her, he hath committed adultery.'° But he is an adulterer before he has yet looked on the woman, by the superfluity of animal, and the defect of thought, in his constitution. Who meets him, or who meets her, in the street, sees that they are ripe to be each other's victim.

In certain men, digestion and sex absorb the vital force, and the stronger these are, the individual is so much weaker. The more of these drones perish, the better for the hive. If, later, they give birth to some superior individual, with force enough to add to this animal a new aim, and a complete apparatus to work it out, all the ancestors are gladly forgotten. Most men and most women are merely one couple more. Now and then, one has a new cell or camarilla° opened in his brain,—an architectural, a musical, or a philological knack, some stray taste or talent for flowers, or chemistry, or pigments, or story-telling, a good hand for drawing, a good foot for dancing, an athletic frame for wide journeying, &c.—which skill nowise alters rank in the scale of nature, but serves to pass the time, the life of sensation going on as before. At last, these hints and tendencies are fixed in one, or in a succession. Each absorbs so much food and force, as to become itself a new centre. The new talent draws off so rapidly the vital force, that not enough remains for the animal functions, hardly enough for health; so that, in the second generation, if the like genius appear, the health is visibly deteriorated, and the generative force impaired.

People are born with the moral or with the material bias;—uterine brothers with this diverging destination: and I suppose, with high magnifiers, Mr. Frauenhofer or Dr. Carpenter might come to distinguish in the embryo at the fourth day, this is a Whig, and that a Free-soiler.°

It was a poetic attempt to lift this mountain of Fate, to reconcile this despotism of race with liberty, which led the Hindoos to say, 'Fate is nothing but the deeds committed in a prior state of existence.' I find the coincidence of the extremes of eastern and western speculation in the daring statement of Schelling,° 'there is in every man a certain feeling, that he has been what he is from all eternity, and by no means became such in time.' To say it less sublimely,—in the history of the individual is always an account of his condition, and he knows himself to be a party to his present estate.

A good deal of our politics is physiological. Now and then, a man of wealth in the heyday of youth adopts the tenet of broadest freedom. In England, there is always some man of wealth and large connection planting himself, during all his years of health, on the side of progress, who, as soon as he begins to die, checks his forward play, calls in his troops, and becomes conservative. All conservatives are such from personal defects. They have been effeminated by position or nature, born halt and blind, through luxury of their parents, and can only, like invalids, act on the defensive. But strong natures, backwoodsmen, New Hampshire giants, Napoleons, Burkes, Broughams, Websters, Kossuths,° are inevitable patriots, until their life ebbs, and their defects and gout, palsy and money, warp them.

The strongest idea incarnates itself in majorities and nations, in the healthiest and strongest. Probably, the election goes by avoirdupois weight, and, if you could weigh bodily the tonnage of any hundred of the Whig and the Democratic party in a town, on the Dearborn balance,° as they passed the hayscales, you could predict with certainty which party would carry it. On the whole, it would be rather the speediest way of deciding the vote, to put the selectmen or the mayor and aldermen at the hayscales.

In science, we have to consider two things: power and circumstance. All we know of the egg, from each successive discovery, is, *another vesicle*;° and if, after five hundred years, you get a better observer, or a better glass, he finds within the last observed another. In vegetable and animal tissue, it is just alike, and all that the primary power or spasm operates, is, still, vesicles, vesicles. Yes,—but the tyrannical Circumstance! A vesicle in new circumstances, a vesicle lodged in darkness, Oken° thought, became animal; in light, a plant. Lodged in the parent animal, it suffers changes, which end in unsheathing miraculous capability in the unaltered vesicle, and it unlocks itself to fish, bird, or quadruped, head and foot, eye and claw. The Circumstance is Nature. Nature is, what you may do. There is much you may not. We have two things,—the circumstance, and the life. Once we thought, positive power was all. Now we learn, that negative power, or circumstance, is half. Nature is the tyrannous circumstance, the thick skull, the sheathed snake, the ponderous, rock-like jaw; necessitated activity; violent direction; the conditions of a tool, like the locomotive, strong enough on its track, but which can do nothing but mischief off of it; or skates, which are wings on the ice, but fetters on the ground.

The book of Nature is the book of Fate. She turns the gigantic pages,—leaf after leaf,—never re-turning one. One leaf she lays down, a floor of granite; then a thousand ages, and a bed of slate; a thousand ages, and a measure of coal; a thousand ages, and a layer of marl and mud: vegetable forms appear; her first misshapen animals, zoophyte, trilobium, fish; then, saurians,—rude forms, in which she has only blocked her future statue, concealing under these unwieldy monsters the fine type of her coming king. The face of the planet cools and dries, the races meliorate, and man is born. But when a race has lived its term, it comes no more again.

The population of the world is a conditional population; not the best, but the best that could live now; and the scale of tribes, and the steadiness with which victory adheres to one tribe, and defeat to another, is as uniform as the superposition of strata. We know in history what weight belongs to race. We see the English, French, and Germans planting themselves on every shore and market of America and Australia, and monopolizing the commerce of these countries. We like the nervous and victorious habit of our own branch of the family. We follow the step of the Jew, of the Indian, of the Negro. We see how much will has been expended to extinguish the Jew, in vain. Look at the unpalatable conclusions of Knox,° in his 'Fragment of Races,'—a rash and unsatisfactory writer, but charged with pungent and unforgetable truths. 'Nature respects race, and not hybrids.' 'Every race has its own *habitat*.' 'Detach a colony from the race, and it deteriorates to the crab.' See the shades of the picture. The German and Irish millions, like the Negro, have a great deal of guano° in their destiny. They are ferried over the Atlantic, and carted over America, to ditch and to drudge, to make corn cheap, and then to lie down prematurely to make a spot of green grass on the prairie.

One more fagot of these adamantine bandages, is, the new science of Statistics. It is a rule, that the most casual and extraordinary events—if the basis of population is broad enough—become matter of fixed calculation. It would not be safe to say when a captain like Bonaparte, a singer like Jenny Lind, or a navigator like Bowditch,° would be born in Boston: but, on a population of twenty or two hundred millions, something like accuracy may be had.*

* 'Everything which pertains to the human species, considered as a whole, belongs to the order of physical facts. The greater the number of individuals, the more does the influence of the individual will disappear, leaving predominance to a series of general facts dependent on causes by which society exists, and is preserved.'—QUETELET.

'Tis frivolous to fix pedantically the date of particular inventions. They have all been invented over and over fifty times. Man is the arch machine, of which all these shifts drawn from himself are toy models. He helps himself on each emergency by copying or duplicating his own structure, just so far as the need is. 'Tis hard to find the right Homer, Zoroaster, or Menu; harder still to find the Tubal Cain, or Vulcan, or Cadmus, or Copernicus, or Fust, or Fulton,° the indisputable inventor. There are scores and centuries of them. 'The air is full of men.' This kind of talent so abounds, this constructive tool-making efficiency, as if it adhered to the chemic atoms, as if the air he breathes were made of Vaucansons, Franklins, and Watts.°

Doubtless, in every million there will be an astronomer, a mathematician, a comic poet, a mystic. No one can read the history of astronomy, without perceiving that Copernicus, Newton, Laplace,° are not new men, or a new kind of men, but that Thales, Anaximenes, Hipparchus, Empedocles, Aristarchus, Pythagoras, Œnopides,° had anticipated them; each had the same tense geometrical brain, apt for the same vigorous computation and logic, a mind parallel to the movement of the world. The Roman mile probably rested on a measure of a degree of the meridian. Mahometan and Chinese know what we know of leap-year, of the Gregorian calendar, and of the precession of the equinoxes. As, in every barrel of cowries, brought to New Bedford, there shall be one *orangia*,° so there will, in a dozen millions of Malays and Mahometans, be one or two astronomical skulls. In a large city, the most casual things, and things whose beauty lies in their casualty, are produced as punctually and to order as the baker's muffin for breakfast. Punch° makes exactly one capital joke a week; and the journals contrive to furnish one good piece of news every day.

And not less work the laws of repression, the penalties of violated functions. Famine, typhus, frost, war, suicide, and effete races, must be reckoned calculable parts of the system of the world.

These are pebbles from the mountain, hints of the terms by which our life is walled up, and which show a kind of mechanical exactness, as of a loom or mill, in what we call casual or fortuitous events.

The force with which we resist these torrents of tendency looks so ridiculously inadequate, that it amounts to little more than a criticism or a protest made by a minority of one, under compulsion of millions. I seemed, in the height of a tempest, to see men overboard struggling in the waves, and driven about here and there. They glanced intelligently at each other, but 'twas little they could do for one another; 'twas much if each could keep afloat alone. Well, they had a right to their eye-beams, and all the rest was Fate.

We cannot trifle with this reality, this cropping-out in our planted gardens of the core of the world. No picture of life can have any veracity that does not admit the odious facts. A man's power is hooped in by a necessity, which, by many experiments, he touches on every side, until he learns its arc.

The element running through entire nature, which we popularly call Fate, is known to us as limitation. Whatever limits us, we call Fate. If we are brute and barbarous, the fate takes a brute and dreadful shape. As we refine, our checks become finer. If we rise to spiritual culture, the antagonism takes a spiritual form. In the Hindoo fables, Vishnu follows Maya° through all her ascending changes, from insect and crawfish up to elephant; whatever form she took, he took the male form of that kind, until she became at last woman and goddess, and he a man and a god. The limitations refine as the soul purifies, but the ring of necessity is always perched at the top.

When the gods in the Norse heaven were unable to bind the Fenris Wolf° with steel or with weight of mountains,—the one he snapped and the other he spurned with his heel,—they put round his foot a limp band softer than silk or cobweb, and this held him: the more he spurned it, the stiffer it drew. So soft and so stanch is the ring of Fate. Neither brandy, nor nectar, nor sulphuric ether, nor hell-fire, nor ichor, nor poetry, nor genius, can get rid of this limp band. For if we give it the high sense in which the poets use it, even thought itself is not above Fate: that too must act according to eternal laws, and all that is wilful and fantastic in it is in opposition to its fundamental essence.

And, last of all, high over thought, in the world of morals, Fate appears as vindicator, levelling the high, lifting the low, requiring justice in man, and always striking soon or late, when justice is not done. What is useful will last; what is hurtful will sink. 'The doer must suffer,' said the Greeks: 'you would soothe a Deity not to be soothed.' 'God himself cannot procure good for the wicked,' said the Welsh triad. 'God may consent, but only for a time,' said the bard of Spain. The limitation is impassable by any insight of man. In its last and loftiest ascensions, insight itself, and the freedom of the will, is one of its obedient members. But we must not run into generalizations too large, but show the natural bounds or essential distinctions, and seek to do justice to the other elements as well.

Thus we trace Fate, in matter, mind, and morals,—in race, in retardations of strata, and in thought and character as well. It is everywhere bound or limitation. But Fate has its lord; limitation its limits; is different seen from above and from below; from within and from without. For, though Fate is immense, so is power, which is the other fact in the dual world, immense. If Fate follows and limits power, power attends and antagonizes Fate. We must respect Fate as natural history, but there is more than natural history. For who and what is this criticism that pries into the matter? Man is not order of nature, sack and sack, belly and members, link in a chain, nor any ignominious baggage, but a stupendous antagonism, a dragging together of the poles of the Universe. He betrays his relation to what is below him,—thick-skulled, small-brained, fishy, quadrumanous,—quadruped ill-disguised, hardly escaped into biped, and has paid for the new powers by loss of some of the old ones. But the lightning which explodes and fashions planets, maker of planets and suns, is in him. On one side, elemental order, sandstone and granite, rock-ledges, peat-bog, forest, sea and shore; and, on the other part, thought, the spirit which composes and decomposes nature,—here they are, side by side, god and devil, mind and matter, king and conspirator, belt and spasm, riding peacefully together in the eye and brain of every man.

Nor can he blink the freewill. To hazard the contradiction,—freedom is necessary. If you please to plant yourself on the side of Fate, and say, Fate is all; then we say, a part of Fate is the freedom of man. Forever wells up the impulse of choosing and acting in the soul. Intellect annuls Fate. So far as a man thinks, he is free. And though nothing is more disgusting than the crowing about liberty by slaves, as most men are, and the flippant mistaking for freedom of some paper preamble like a 'Declaration of Independence,' or the statute right to vote, by those who have never dared to think or to act, yet it is wholesome to man to look not at Fate, but the other way: the practical view is the other. His sound relation to these facts is to use and command, not to cringe to them. 'Look not on nature, for her name is fatal,' said the oracle. The too much contemplation of these limits induces meanness. They who talk much of destiny, their birth-star, &c., are in a lower dangerous plane, and invite the evils they fear.

I cited the instinctive and heroic races as proud believers in Destiny. They conspire with it; a loving resignation is with the event. But the dogma makes a different impression, when it is held by the weak and lazy. 'Tis weak and vicious people who cast the blame on Fate. The right use of Fate is to bring up our conduct to the loftiness of nature.

Rude and invincible except by themselves are the elements. So let man be. Let him empty his breast of his windy conceits, and show his lordship by manners and deeds on the scale of nature. Let him hold his purpose as with the tug of gravitation. No power, no persuasion, no bribe shall make him give up his point. A man ought to compare advantageously with a river, an oak, or a mountain. He shall have not less the flow, the expansion, and the resistance of these.

'Tis the best use of Fate to teach a fatal courage. Go face the fire at sea, or the cholera in your friend's house, or the burglar in your own, or what danger lies in the way of duty, knowing you are guarded by the cherubim of Destiny. If you believe in Fate to your harm, believe it, at least, for your good.

For, if Fate is so prevailing, man also is part of it, and can confront fate with fate. If the Universe have these savage accidents, our atoms are as savage in resistance. We should be crushed by the atmosphere, but for the reaction of the air within the body. A tube made of a film of glass can resist the shock of the ocean, if filled with the same water. If there be omnipotence in the stroke, there is omnipotence of recoil.

1. But Fate against Fate is only parrying and defence: there are, also, the noble creative forces. The revelation of Thought takes man out of servitude into freedom. We rightly say of ourselves, we were born, and afterward we were born again, and many times. We have successive experiences so important, that the new forgets the old, and hence the mythology of the seven or the nine heavens. The day of days, the great day of the feast of life, is that in which the inward eye opens to the Unity in things, to the omnipresence of law;—sees that what is must be, and ought to be, or is the best. This beatitude dips from on high down on us, and we see. It is not in us so much as we are in it. If the air come to our lungs, we breathe and live; if not, we die. If the light come to our eyes, we see; else not. And if truth come to our mind, we suddenly expand to its dimensions, as if we grew to worlds. We are as lawgivers; we speak for Nature; we prophesy and divine.

This insight throws us on the party and interest of the Universe, against all and sundry; against ourselves, as much as others. A man speaking from insight affirms of himself what is true of the mind: seeing its immortality, he says, I am immortal; seeing its invincibility, he says, I am strong. It is not in us, but we are in it. It is of the maker, not of what is made. All things are touched and changed by it. This uses, and is not used. It distances those who share it, from those who share it not. Those who share it not are flocks and herds. It dates from itself;—not from former men or better men,—gospel, or constitution, or college, or custom. Where it shines, Nature is no longer intrusive, but all things make a musical or pictorial impression. The world of men show like a comedy without laughter:—populations, interests, government, history;—'tis all toy figures in a toy house. It does not overvalue particular truths. We hear eagerly every thought and word quoted from an intellectual man. But, in his presence, our own mind is roused to activity, and we forget very fast what he says, much more interested in the new play of our own thought, than in any thought of his. 'Tis the majesty into which we have suddenly mounted, the impersonality, the scorn of egotisms, the sphere of laws, that engage us. Once we were stepping a little this way, and a little that way; now, we are as men in a balloon, and do not think so much of the point we have left, or the point we would make, as of the liberty and glory of the way.

Just as much intellect as you add, so much organic power. He who sees through the design, presides over it, and must will that which must be. We sit and rule, and, though we sleep, our dream will come to pass. Our thought, though it were only an hour old, affirms an oldest necessity, not to be separated from thought, and not to be separated from will. They must always have coëxisted. It apprises us of its sovereignty and godhead, which refuse to be severed from it. It is not mine or thine, but the will of all mind. It is poured into the souls of all men, as the soul itself which constitutes them men. I know not whether there be, as is alleged, in the upper region of our atmosphere, a permanent westerly current, which carries with it all atoms which rise to that height, but I see, that when souls reach a certain clearness of perception, they accept a knowledge and motive above selfishness. A breath of will blows eternally through the universe of souls in the direction of the Right and Necessary. It is the air which all intellects inhale and exhale, and it is the wind which blows the worlds into order and orbit.

Thought dissolves the material universe, by carrying the mind up into a sphere where all is plastic. Of two men, each obeying his own thought, he whose thought is deepest will be the strongest character. Always one man more than another represents the will of Divine Providence to the period.

2. If thought makes free, so does the moral sentiment. The mixtures of spiritual chemistry refuse to be analyzed. Yet we can see that with the perception of truth is joined the desire that it shall prevail. That affection is essential to will. Moreover, when a strong will appears, it usually results from a certain unity of organization, as if the whole energy of body and mind flowed in one direction. All great force is real and elemental. There is no manufacturing a strong will. There must be a

pound to balance a pound. Where power is shown in will, it must rest on the universal force. Alaric° and Bonaparte must believe they rest on a truth, or their will can be bought or bent. There is a bribe possible for any finite will. But the pure sympathy with universal ends is an infinite force, and cannot be bribed or bent. Whoever has had experience of the moral sentiment cannot choose but believe in unlimited power. Each pulse from that heart is an oath from the Most High. I know not what the word *sublime* means, if it be not the intimations in this infant of a terrific force. A text of heroism, a name and anecdote of courage, are not arguments, but sallies of freedom. One of these is the verse of the Persian Hafiz,° ' 'Tis written on the gate of Heaven, "Wo unto him who suffers himself to be betrayed by Fate!" ' Does the reading of history make us fatalists? What courage does not the opposite opinion show! A little whim of will to be free gallantly contending against the universe of chemistry.

But insight is not will, nor is affection will. Perception is cold, and goodness dies in wishes; as Voltaire said, 'tis the misfortune of worthy people that they are cowards; '*un des plus grands malheurs des honnêtes gens c'est qu'ils sont des lâches.*' There must be a fusion of these two to generate the energy of will. There can be no driving force, except through the conversion of the man into his will, making him the will, and the will him. And one may say boldly, that no man has a right perception of any truth, who has not been reacted on by it, so as to be ready to be its martyr.

The one serious and formidable thing in nature is a will. Society is servile from want of will, and therefore the world wants saviours and religions. One way is right to go: the hero sees it, and moves on that aim, and has the world under him for root and support. He is to others as the world. His approbation is honor; his dissent, infamy. The glance of his eye has the force of sunbeams. A personal influence towers up in memory only worthy, and we gladly forget numbers, money, climate, gravitation, and the rest of Fate.

We can afford to allow the limitation, if we know it is the meter of the growing man. We stand against Fate, as children stand up against the wall in their father's house, and notch their height from year to year. But when the boy grows to man, and is master of the house, he pulls down that wall, and builds a new and bigger. 'Tis only a question of time. Every brave youth is in training to ride and rule this dragon. His science is to make weapons and wings of these passions and retarding forces. Now whether, seeing these two things, fate and power, we are permitted to believe in unity? The bulk of mankind believe in two gods. They are under one dominion here in the house, as friend and parent, in social circles, in letters, in art, in love, in religion: but in mechanics, in dealing with steam and climate, in trade, in politics, they think they come under another; and that it would be a practical blunder to transfer the method and way of working of one sphere, into the other. What good, honest, generous men at home, will be wolves and foxes on change!° What pious men in the parlor will vote for what reprobates at the polls! To a certain point, they believe themselves the care of a Providence. But, in a steamboat, in an epidemic, in war, they believe a malignant energy rules.

But relation and connection are not somewhere and sometimes, but everywhere and always. The divine order does not stop where their sight stops. The friendly power works on the same rules, in the next farm, and the next planet. But, where they have not experience, they run against it, and hurt themselves. Fate, then, is a name for facts not yet passed under the fire of thought;—for causes which are unpenetrated.

But every jet of chaos which threatens to exterminate us, is convertible by intellect into wholesome force. Fate is unpenetrated causes. The water drowns ship and sailor, like a grain of dust. But learn to swim, trim your bark, and the wave which drowned it, will be cloven by it, and carry it, like its own foam, a plume and a power. The cold is inconsiderate of persons, tingles your blood, freezes a man like a dewdrop. But learn to skate, and the ice will give you a graceful, sweet, and poetic motion. The cold will brace your limbs and brain to genius, and make you foremost men of time. Cold and sea will train an imperial Saxon race, which nature cannot bear to lose, and, after cooping it up for a thousand years in yonder England, gives a hundred Englands, a hundred Mexicos. All the bloods it shall absorb and domineer: and more than Mexicos,—the secrets of water and steam, the spasms of electricity, the ductility of metals, the chariot of the air, the ruddered balloon are awaiting you.

The annual slaughter from typhus far exceeds that of war; but right drainage destroys typhus. The plague in the sea-service from scurvy is healed by lemon juice and other diets portable or procurable: the depopulation by cholera and small-pox is ended by drainage and vaccination; and every other pest is not less in the chain of cause and effect, and may be fought off. And, whilst art draws out the venom, it commonly extorts some benefit from the vanquished enemy. The mischievous torrent is taught to drudge for man: the wild beasts he makes useful for food, or dress, or labor; the chemic explosions are controlled like his watch. These are now the steeds on which he rides. Man moves in all modes, by legs of horses, by wings of wind, by steam, by gas of balloon, by electricity, and stands on tiptoe threatening to hunt the eagle in his own element. There's nothing he will not make his carrier.

Steam was, till the other day, the devil which we dreaded. Every pot made by any human potter or brazier had a hole in its cover, to let off the enemy, lest he should lift pot and roof, and carry the house away. But the Marquis of Worcester,° Watt, and Fulton bethought themselves, that, where was power, was not devil, but was God; that it must be availed of, and not by any means let off and wasted. Could he lift pots and roofs and houses so handily? he was the workman they were in search of. He could be used to lift away, chain, and compel other devils, far more reluctant and dangerous, namely, cubic miles of earth, mountains, weight or resistance of water, machinery, and the labors of all men in the world; and time he shall lengthen, and shorten space.

It has not fared much otherwise with higher kinds of steam. The opinion of the million was the terror of the world, and it was attempted, either to dissipate it, by amusing nations, or to pile it over with strata of society,—a layer of soldiers; over that, a layer of lords; and a king on the top; with clamps and hoops of castles, garrisons, and police. But, sometimes, the religious principle would get in, and burst the hoops, and rive every mountain laid on top of it. The Fultons and Watts of politics, believing in unity, saw that it was a power, and, by satisfying it, (as justice satisfies everybody,) through a different disposition of society,—grouping it on a level, instead of piling it into a mountain,—they have contrived to make of his terror the most harmless and energetic form of a State.

Very odious, I confess, are the lessons of Fate. Who likes to have a dapper phrenologist pronouncing on his fortunes? Who likes to believe that he has hidden in his skull, spine, and pelvis, all the vices of a Saxon or Celtic race, which will be sure to pull him down,—with what grandeur of hope and resolve he is fired,—into a selfish, huckstering, servile, dodging animal? A learned physician tells us, the fact is invariable with the Neapolitan, that, when mature, he assumes the forms of the unmistakable scoundrel. That is a little overstated,—but may pass.

But these are magazines and arsenals. A man must thank his defects, and stand in some terror of his talents. A transcendent talent draws so largely on his forces, as to lame him; a defect pays him revenues on the other side. The sufferance, which is the badge of the Jew, has made him, in these days, the ruler of the rulers of the earth. If Fate is ore and quarry, if evil is good in the making, if limitation is power that shall be, if calamities, oppositions, and weights are wings and means,—we are reconciled.

Fate involves the melioration. No statement of the Universe can have any soundness, which does not admit its ascending effort. The direction of the whole, and of the parts, is toward benefit, and in proportion to the health. Behind every individual, closes organization: before him, opens liberty,—the Better, the Best. The first and worst races are dead. The second and imperfect races are dying out, or remain for the maturing of higher. In the latest race, in man, every generosity, every new perception, the love and praise he extorts from his fellows, are certificates of advance out of fate into freedom. Liberation of the will from the sheaths and clogs of organization which he has outgrown, is the end and aim of this world. Every calamity is a spur and valuable hint; and where his endeavors do not yet fully avail, they tell as tendency. The whole circle of animal life,—tooth against tooth,—devouring war, war for food, a yelp of pain and a grunt of triumph, until, at last, the whole menagerie, the whole chemical mass is mellowed and refined for higher use,—pleases at a sufficient perspective.

But to see how fate slides into freedom, and freedom into fate, observe how far the roots of every creature run, or find, if you can, a point where there is no thread of connection. Our life is consentaneous and far-related. This knot of nature is so well tied, that nobody was ever cunning enough to find the two ends. Nature is intricate, overlapped, interweaved, and endless. Christopher Wren° said of the beautiful King's College chapel, 'that, if anybody would tell him where to lay the first stone, he would build such another.' But where shall we find the first atom in this house of man, which is all consent, inosculation, and balance of parts?

The web of relation is shown in *habitat*, shown in hybernation. When hybernation was observed, it was found, that, whilst some animals became torpid in winter, others were torpid in summer: hybernation then was a false name. The *long sleep* is not an effect of cold, but is regulated by the supply of food proper to the animal. It becomes torpid when the fruit or prey it lives on is not in season, and regains its activity when its food is ready.

Eyes are found in light; ears in auricular air; feet on land; fins in water; wings in air; and, each creature where it was meant to be, with a mutual fitness. Every zone has its own *Fauna*. There is adjustment between the animal and its food, its parasite, its enemy. Balances are kept. It is not allowed to diminish in numbers, nor to exceed. The like adjustments exist for man. His food is cooked, when he arrives; his coal in the pit; the house ventilated; the mud of the deluge dried; his companions arrived at the same hour, and awaiting him with love, concert, laughter, and tears. These are coarse adjustments, but the invisible are not less. There are more belongings to every creature than his air and his food. His instincts must be met, and he has predisposing power that bends and fits what is near him to his use. He is not possible until the invisible things are right for him, as well as the visible. Of what changes, then, in sky and earth, and in finer skies and earths, does the appearance of some Dante or Columbus apprise us!

How is this effected? Nature is no spendthrift, but takes the shortest way to her ends. As the general says to his soldiers, 'if you want a fort, build a fort,' so nature makes every creature do its own work and get its living,—is it planet, animal, or tree. The planet makes itself. The animal cell makes itself;—then, what it wants. Every creature,—wren or dragon,—shall make its own lair. As soon as there is life, there is self-direction, and absorbing and using of material. Life is freedom,—life in the direct ratio of its amount. You may be sure, the new-born man is not inert. Life works both voluntarily and supernaturally in its neighborhood. Do you suppose, he can be estimated by his weight in pounds, or, that he is contained in his skin,—this reaching, radiating, jaculating fellow? The smallest candle fills a mile with its rays, and the papillæ° of a man run out to every star.

When there is something to be done, the world knows how to get it done. The vegetable eye makes leaf, pericarp, root, bark, or thorn, as the need is; the first cell converts itself into stomach, mouth, nose, or nail, according to the want: the world throws its life into a hero or a shepherd; and puts him where he is wanted. Dante and Columbus were Italians, in their time: they would be Russians or Americans to-day. Things ripen, new men come. The adaptation is not capricious. The ulterior aim, the purpose beyond itself, the correlation by which planets subside and crystallize, then animate beasts and men, will not stop, but will work into finer particulars, and from finer to finest.

The secret of the world is, the tie between person and event. Person makes event, and event person. The 'times,' 'the age,' what is that, but a few profound persons and a few active persons who epitomize the times?—Goethe, Hegel, Metternich, Adams, Calhoun, Guizot, Peel, Cobden, Kossuth, Rothschild, Astor, Brunel,° and the rest. The same fitness must be presumed between a man and the time and event, as between the sexes, or between a race of animals and the food it eats, or the inferior races it uses. He thinks his fate alien, because the copula is hidden. But the soul contains the event that shall befall it, for the event is only the actualization of its thoughts; and what we pray to ourselves for is always granted. The event is the print of your form. It fits you like your skin. What each does is proper to him. Events are the children of his body and mind. We learn that the soul of Fate is the soul of us, as Hafiz sings,

> Alas! till now I had not known,
> My guide and fortune's guide are one.

All the toys that infatuate men, and which they play for,—houses, land, money, luxury, power, fame, are the selfsame thing, with a new gauze or two of illusion overlaid. And of all the drums and rattles by which men are made willing to have their heads broke, and are led out solemnly every morning to parade,—the most admirable is this by which we are brought to believe that events are arbitrary, and independent of actions. At the conjuror's, we detect the hair by which he moves his puppet, but we have not eyes sharp enough to descry the thread that ties cause and effect.

Nature magically suits the man to his fortunes, by making these the fruit of his character. Ducks take to the water, eagles to the sky, waders to the sea margin, hunters to the forest, clerks to counting-rooms, soldiers to the frontier. Thus events grow on the same stem with persons; are sub-persons. The pleasure of life is according to the man that lives it, and not according to the work or the place. Life is an ecstasy. We know what madness belongs to love,—what power to paint a vile object in hues of heaven. As insane persons are indifferent to their dress, diet, and other accommodations, and, as we do in dreams, with equanimity, the most absurd acts, so, a drop more of wine in our cup of life will reconcile us to strange company and work. Each creature puts forth from itself its own condition and sphere, as the slug sweats out its slimy house on the pear-leaf, and the woolly aphides on the apple perspire their own bed, and the fish its shell. In youth, we clothe ourselves with rainbows, and go as brave as the zodiac. In age, we put out another sort of perspiration,—gout, fever, rheumatism, caprice, doubt, fretting, and avarice.

A man's fortunes are the fruit of his character. A man's friends are his magnetisms. We go to Herodotus and Plutarch° for examples of Fate; but we are examples. '*Quisque suos patimur manes.*'° The tendency of every man to enact all that is in his constitution is expressed in the old belief, that the efforts which we make to escape from our destiny only serve to lead us into it: and I have noticed, a man likes better to be complimented on his position, as the proof of the last or total excellence, than on his merits.

A man will see his character emitted in the events that seem to meet, but which exude from and accompany him. Events expand with the character. As once he found himself among toys, so now he plays a part in colossal systems, and his growth is declared in his ambition, his companions, and his performance. He looks like a piece of luck, but is a piece of causation;—the mosaic, angulated and ground to fit into the gap he fills. Hence in each town there is some man who is, in his brain and performance, an explanation of the tillage, production, factories, banks, churches, ways of living, and society, of that town. If you do not chance to meet him, all that you see will leave you a little puzzled: if you see him, it will become plain. We know in Massachusetts who built New Bedford, who built Lynn, Lowell, Lawrence, Clinton, Fitchburg, Holyoke, Portland, and many another noisy mart. Each of these men, if they were transparent, would seem to you not so much men, as walking cities, and, wherever you put them, they would build one.

History is the action and reaction of these two,—Nature and Thought;—two boys pushing each other on the curbstone of the pavement. Everything is pusher or pushed: and matter and mind are in perpetual tilt and balance, so. Whilst the man is weak, the earth takes up him. He plants his brain and affections. By and by he will take up the earth, and have his gardens and vineyards in the beautiful order and productiveness of his thought. Every solid in the universe is ready to become fluid on the approach of the mind, and the power to flux it is the measure of the mind. If the wall remain adamant, it accuses the want of thought. To a subtler force, it will stream into new forms, expressive of the character of the mind. What is the city in which we sit here, but an aggregate of incongruous materials, which have obeyed the will of some man? The granite was reluctant, but his hands were stronger, and it came. Iron was deep in the ground, and well combined with stone; but could not hide from his fires. Wood, lime, stuffs, fruits, gums, were dispersed over the earth and sea, in vain. Here they are, within reach of every man's day-labor,—what he wants of them. The whole world is the flux of matter over the wires of thought to the poles or points where it would build. The races of men rise out of the ground preoccupied with a thought which rules them, and divided into parties ready armed and angry to fight for this metaphysical abstraction. The quality of the thought differences the Egyptian and the Roman, the Austrian and the American. The men who come on the stage at one period are all found to be related to each other. Certain ideas are in the air. We are all impressionable, for we are made of them; all impressionable, but some more than others, and these first express them. This explains the curious contemporaneousness of inventions and discoveries. The truth is in the air, and the most impressionable brain will announce it first, but all will announce it a few minutes later. So women, as most susceptible, are the best index of the coming hour. So the great man, that is, the man most imbued with the spirit of the time, is the impressionable man,—of a fibre irritable and delicate, like iodine to light. He feels the infinitesimal attractions. His mind is righter than others, because he yields to a current so feeble as can be felt only by a needle delicately poised.

The correlation is shown in defects. Möller,° in his Essay on Architecture, taught that the building which was fitted accurately to answer its end, would turn out to be beautiful, though beauty had not been intended. I find the like unity in human structures rather virulent and pervasive; that a crudity in the blood will appear in the argument; a hump in the shoulder will appear in the speech and handiwork. If his mind could be seen, the hump would be seen. If a man has a seesaw in his voice, it will run into his sentences, into his poem, into the structure of his fable, into his speculation, into his charity. And, as every man is hunted by his own dæmon, vexed by his own disease, this checks all his activity.

So each man, like each plant, has his parasites. A strong, astringent, bilious nature has more truculent enemies than the slugs and moths that fret my leaves. Such an one has curculios, borers, knife-worms: a swindler ate him first, then a client, then a quack, then smooth, plausible gentlemen, bitter and selfish as Moloch.°

This correlation really existing can be divined. If the threads are there, thought can follow and show them. Especially when a soul is quick and docile; as Chaucer sings,

> 'Or if the soul of proper kind
> Be so perfect as men find,
> That it wot what is to come,
> And that he warneth all and some
> Of every of their aventures,
> By previsions or figures;
> But that our flesh hath not might
> It to understand aright
> For it is warned too darkly.'°—

Some people are made up of rhyme, coincidence, omen, periodicity, and presage: they meet the person they seek; what their companion prepares to say to them, they first say to him; and a hundred signs apprise them of what is about to befall.

Wonderful intricacy in the web, wonderful constancy in the design this vagabond life admits. We wonder how the fly finds its mate, and yet year after year we find two men, two women, without legal or carnal tie, spend a great part of their best time within a few feet of each other. And the moral is, that what we seek we shall find; what we flee from flees from us; as Goethe said, 'what we wish for in youth, comes in heaps on us in old age,'° too often cursed with the granting of our prayer: and hence the high caution, that, since we are sure of having what we wish, we beware to ask only for high things.

One key, one solution to the mysteries of human condition, one solution to the old knots of fate, freedom, and foreknowledge, exists, the propounding, namely, of the double consciousness. A man must ride alternately on the horses of his private and his public nature, as the equestrians in the circus throw themselves nimbly from horse to horse, or plant one foot on the back of one, and the other foot on the back of the other. So when a man is the victim of his fate, has sciatica in his loins, and cramp in his mind; a club-foot and a club in his wit; a sour face, and a selfish temper; a strut in his gait, and a conceit in his affection; or is ground to powder by the vice of his race; he is to rally on his relation to the Universe, which his ruin benefits. Leaving the dæmon who suffers, he is to take sides with the Deity who secures universal benefit by his pain.

To offset the drag of temperament and race, which pulls down, learn this lesson, namely, that by the cunning co-presence of two elements, which is throughout nature, whatever lames or paralyzes you, draws in with it the divinity, in some form, to repay. A good intention clothes itself with sudden power. When a god wishes to ride, any chip or pebble will bud and shoot out winged feet, and serve him for a horse.

Let us build altars to the Blessed Unity which holds nature and souls in perfect solution, and compels every atom to serve an universal end. I do not wonder at a snow-flake, a shell, a summer landscape, or the glory of the stars; but at the necessity of beauty under which the universe lies; that all is and must be pictorial; that the rainbow, and the curve of the horizon, and the arch of the blue vault are only results from the organism of the eye. There is no need for foolish amateurs to fetch me to admire a garden of flowers, or a sun-gilt cloud, or a waterfall, when I cannot look without seeing splendor and grace. How idle to choose a random sparkle here or there, when the indwelling necessity plants the rose of beauty on the brow of chaos, and discloses the central intention of Nature to be harmony and joy.

Let us build altars to the Beautiful Necessity. If we thought men were free in the sense, that, in a single exception one fantastical will could prevail over the law of things, it were all one as if a child's hand could pull down the sun. If, in the least particular, one could derange the order of nature,—who would accept the gift of life?

Let us build altars to the Beautiful Necessity, which secures that all is made of one piece; that plaintiff and defendant, friend and enemy, animal and planet, food and eater, are of one kind. In astronomy, is vast space, but no foreign system; in geology, vast time, but the same laws as to-day. Why should we be afraid of Nature, which is no other than 'philosophy and theology embodied'? Why should we fear to be crushed by savage elements, we who are made up of the same elements? Let us build to the Beautiful Necessity, which makes man brave in believing that he cannot shun a danger that is appointed, nor incur one that is not; to the Necessity which rudely or softly educates him to the perception that there are no contingencies; that Law rules throughout existence, a Law which is not intelligent but intelligence,—not personal nor impersonal,—it disdains words and passes understanding; it dissolves persons; it vivifies nature; yet solicits the pure in heart to draw on all its omnipotence.

POWER

His tongue was framed to music,
And his hand was armed with skill,
His face was the mould of beauty,
And his heart the throne of will.

THERE is not yet any inventory of a man's faculties, any more than a bible of his opinions. Who shall set a limit to the influence of a human being? There are men, who, by their sympathetic attractions, carry nations with them, and lead the activity of the human race. And if there be such a tie, that, wherever the mind of man goes, nature will accompany him, perhaps there are men whose magnetisms are of that force to draw material and elemental powers, and, where they appear, immense instrumentalities organize around them. Life is a search after power; and this is an element with which the world is so saturated,—there is no chink or crevice in which it is not lodged,—that no honest seeking goes unrewarded. A man should prize events and possessions as the ore in which this fine mineral is found; and he can well afford to let events and possessions, and the breath of the body go, if their value has been added to him in the shape of power. If he have secured the elixir, he can spare the wide gardens from which it was distilled. A cultivated man, wise to know and bold to perform, is the end to which nature works, and the education of the will is the flowering and result of all this geology and astronomy.

All successful men have agreed in one thing,—they were *causationists*. They believed that things went not by luck, but by law; that there was not a weak or a cracked link in the chain that joins the first and last of things. A belief in causality, or strict connection between every trifle and the principle of being, and, in consequence, belief in compensation, or, that nothing is got for nothing,—characterizes all valuable minds, and must control every effort that is made by an industrious one. The most valiant men are the best believers in the tension of the laws. 'All the great captains,' said Bonaparte, 'have performed vast achievements by conforming with the rules of the art,—by adjusting efforts to obstacles.'

The key to the age may be this, or that, or the other, as the young orators describe;—the key to all ages is—Imbecility; imbecility in the vast majority of men, at all times, and, even in heroes, in all but certain eminent moments; victims of gravity, custom, and fear. This gives force to the strong,—that the multitude have no habit of self-reliance or original action.

We must reckon success a constitutional trait. Courage,—the old physicians taught, (and their meaning holds, if their physiology is a little mythical,)—courage, or the degree of life, is as the degree of circulation of the blood in the arteries. 'During passion, anger, fury, trials of strength, wrestling, fighting, a large amount of blood is collected in the arteries, the maintenance of bodily strength requiring it, and but little is sent into the veins. This condition is constant with intrepid persons.'° Where the arteries hold their blood, is courage and adventure possible. Where they pour it unrestrained into the veins, the spirit is low and feeble. For performance of great mark, it needs extraordinary health. If Eric is in robust health, and has slept well, and is at the top of his condition, and thirty years old, at his departure from Greenland, he will steer west, and his ships will reach Newfoundland. But take out Eric, and put in a stronger and bolder man,—Biorn, or Thorfin,°—and the ships will, with just as much ease, sail six hundred, one thousand, fifteen hundred miles further, and reach Labrador and New England. There is no chance in results. With adults, as with children, one class enter cordially into the game, and whirl with the whirling world; the others have cold hands, and remain bystanders; or are only dragged in by the humor and vivacity of those who can carry a dead weight. The first wealth is health. Sickness is poor-spirited, and cannot serve any one: it must husband its resources to live. But health or fulness answers its own ends, and has to spare, runs over, and inundates the neighborhoods and creeks of other men's necessities.

All power is of one kind, a sharing of the nature of the world. The mind that is parallel with the laws of nature will be in the current of events, and strong with their strength. One man is made of the same stuff of which events are made; is in sympathy with the course of things; can predict it. Whatever befalls, befalls him first; so that he is equal to whatever shall happen. A man who knows men, can talk well on politics, trade, law, war, religion. For, everywhere, men are led in the same manners.

The advantage of a strong pulse is not to be supplied by any labor, art, or concert. It is like the climate, which easily rears a crop, which no glass, or irrigation, or tillage, or manures, can elsewhere rival. It is like the opportunity of a city like New York, or Constantinople, which needs no diplomacy to force capital or genius or labor to it. They come of themselves, as the waters flow to it. So a broad, healthy, massive understanding seems to lie on the shore of unseen rivers, of unseen oceans, which are covered with barks, that, night and day, are drifted to this point. That is poured into its lap, which other men lie plotting for. It is in everybody's secret; anticipates everybody's discovery; and if it do not command every fact of the genius and the scholar, it is because it is large and sluggish, and does not think them worth the exertion which you do.

This affirmative force is in one, and is not in another, as one horse has the spring in him, and another in the whip. 'On the neck of the young man,' said Hafiz,° 'sparkles no gem so gracious as enterprise.' Import into any stationary district, as into an old Dutch population in New York or Pennsylvania, or among the planters of Virginia, a colony of hardy Yankees, with seething brains, heads full of steam-hammer, pulley, crank, and toothed wheel,—and everything begins to shine with values. What enhancement to all the water and land in England, is the arrival of James Watt or Brunel!° In every company, there is not only the active and passive sex, but, in both men and women, a deeper and more important *sex of mind*, namely, the inventive or creative class of both men and women, and the uninventive or accepting class. Each *plus* man represents his set, and, if he have the accidental advantage of personal ascendancy,—which implies neither more nor less of talent, but merely the temperamental or taming eye of a soldier or a schoolmaster, (which one has, and one has not, as one has a black moustache and one a blond,) then quite easily and without envy or resistance, all his coadjutors and feeders will admit his right to absorb them. The merchant works by book-keeper and cashier; the lawyer's authorities are hunted up by clerks; the geologist reports the surveys of his subalterns; Commander Wilkes appropriates the results of all the naturalists attached to the Expedition; Thorwaldsen's statue is finished by stone-cutters; Dumas° has journeymen; and Shakspeare was theatre-manager, and used the labor of many young men, as well as the playbooks.

There is always room for a man of force, and he makes room for many. Society is a troop of thinkers, and the best heads among them take the best places. A feeble man can see the farms that are fenced and tilled, the houses that are built. The strong man sees the possible houses and farms. His eye makes estates, as fast as the sun breeds clouds.

When a new boy comes into school, when a man travels, and encounters strangers every day, or, when into any old club a new comer is domesticated, that happens which befalls, when a strange ox is driven into a pen or pasture where cattle are kept; there is at once a trial of strength between the best pair of horns and the new comer, and it is settled thenceforth which is the leader. So now, there is a measuring of strength, very courteous, but decisive, and an acquiescence thenceforward when these two meet. Each reads his fate in the other's eyes. The weaker party finds, that none of his information or wit quite fits the occasion. He thought he knew this or that: he finds that he omitted to learn the end of it. Nothing that he knows will quite hit the mark, whilst all the rival's arrows are good, and well thrown. But if he knew all the facts in the encyclopædia, it would not help him: for this is an affair of presence of mind, of attitude, of aplomb: the opponent has the sun and wind, and, in every cast, the choice of weapon and mark; and, when he himself is matched with some other antagonist, his own shafts fly well and hit. 'Tis a question of stomach and constitution. The second man is as good as the first,—perhaps better; but has not stoutness or stomach, as the first has, and so his wit seems over-fine or under-fine.

Health is good,—power, life, that resists disease, poison, and all enemies, and is conservative, as well as creative. Here is question, every spring, whether to graft with wax, or whether with clay; whether to whitewash or to potash, or to prune; but the one point is the thrifty tree. A good tree, that agrees with the soil, will grow in spite of blight, or bug, or pruning, or neglect, by night and by day, in all weathers and all treatments. Vivacity, leadership, must be had, and we are not allowed to be nice in choosing. We must fetch the pump with dirty water, if clean cannot be had. If we will make bread, we must have contagion, yeast, emptyings, or what not, to induce fermentation into the dough: as the torpid artist seeks inspiration at any cost, by virtue or by vice, by friend or by fiend, by prayer or by wine. And we have a certain instinct, that where is great amount of life, though gross and peccant, it has its own checks and purifications, and will be found at last in harmony with moral laws.

We watch in children with pathetic interest, the degree in which they possess recuperative force. When they are hurt by us, or by each other, or go to the bottom of the class, or miss the annual prizes, or are beaten in the game,—if they lose heart, and remember the mischance in their chamber at home, they have a serious check. But if they have the buoyancy and resistance that preoccupies them with new interest in the new moment,—the wounds cicatrize, and the fibre is the tougher for the hurt.

One comes to value this *plus* health, when he sees that all difficulties vanish before it. A timid man listening to the alarmists in Congress, and in the newspapers, and observing the profligacy of party,—sectional interests urged with a fury which shuts its eyes to consequences, with a mind made up to desperate extremities, ballot in one hand, and rifle in the other,—might easily believe that he and his country have seen their best days, and he hardens himself the best he can against the coming ruin. But, after this has been foretold with equal confidence fifty times, and government six per cents have not declined a quarter of a mill, he discovers that the enormous elements of strength which are here in play, make our politics unimportant. Personal power, freedom, and the resources of nature strain every faculty of every citizen. We prosper with such vigor, that, like thrifty trees, which grow in spite of ice, lice, mice, and borers, so we do not suffer from the profligate swarms that fatten on the national treasury. The huge animals nourish huge parasites, and the rancor of the disease attests the strength of the constitution. The same energy in the Greek *Demos* drew the remark, that the evils of popular government appear greater than they are; there is compensation for them in the spirit and energy it awakens. The rough and ready style which belongs to a people of sailors, foresters, farmers, and mechanics, has its advantages. Power educates the potentate. As long as our people quote English standards they dwarf their own proportions. A Western lawyer° of eminence said to me he wished it were a penal offence to bring an English law-book into a court in this country, so pernicious had he found in his experience our deference to English precedent. The very word 'commerce' has only an English meaning, and is pinched to the cramp exigencies of English experience. The commerce of rivers, the commerce of railroads, and who knows but the commerce of air-balloons, must add an American extension to the pond-hole of admiralty. As long as our people quote English standards, they will miss the sovereignty of power; but let these rough riders,—legislators in shirt-sleeves,—Hoosier, Sucker, Wolverine, Badger,°—or whatever hard head Arkansas, Oregon, or Utah sends, half orator, half assassin, to represent its wrath and cupidity at Washington,—let these drive as they may; and the disposition of territories and public lands, the necessity of balancing and keeping at bay the snarling majorities of German, Irish, and of native millions, will bestow promptness, address, and reason, at last, on our buffalo-hunter, and authority and majesty of manners. The instinct of the people is right. Men expect from good whigs, put into office by the respectability of the country, much less skill to deal with Mexico, Spain, Britain, or with our own malcontent members, than from some strong transgressor, like Jefferson, or Jackson, who first conquers his own government, and then uses the same genius to conquer the foreigner. The senators who dissented from Mr. Polk's Mexican war, were not those who knew better, but those who, from political position, could afford it; not Webster, but Benton and Calhoun.°

This power, to be sure, is not clothed in satin. 'Tis the power of Lynch law, of soldiers and pirates; and it bullies the peaceable and loyal. But it brings its own antidote; and here is my point,—that all kinds of power usually emerge at the same time; good energy, and bad; power of mind, with physical health; the ecstasies of devotion, with the exasperations of debauchery. The same elements are always present, only sometimes these conspicuous, and sometimes those; what was yesterday foreground, being to-day background,—what was surface, playing now a not less effective part as basis. The longer the drought lasts, the more is the atmosphere surcharged with water. The faster the ball falls to the sun, the force to fly off is by so much augmented. And, in morals, wild liberty breeds iron conscience; natures with great impulses have great resources, and return from far. In politics, the sons of democrats will be whigs; whilst red republicanism, in the father, is a spasm of nature to engender an intolerable tyrant in the next age. On the other hand, conservatism, ever more timorous and narrow, disgusts the children, and drives them for a mouthful of fresh air into radicalism.

Those who have most of this coarse energy,—the 'bruisers,' who have run the gauntlet of caucus and tavern through the county or the state, have their own vices, but they have the good nature of strength and courage. Fierce and unscrupulous, they are usually frank and direct, and above falsehood. Our politics fall into bad hands, and churchmen and men of refinement, it seems agreed, are not fit persons to send to Congress. Politics is a deleterious profession, like some poisonous handicrafts. Men in power have no opinions, but may be had cheap for any opinion, for any purpose,—and if it be only a question between the most civil and the most forcible, I lean to the last. These Hoosiers and Suckers are really better than the snivelling opposition. Their wrath is at least of a bold and manly cast. They see, against the unanimous declarations of the people, how much crime the people will bear; they proceed from step to step, and they have calculated but too justly upon their Excellencies, the New England governors, and upon their Honors, the New England legislators. The messages of the governors and the resolutions of the legislatures, are a proverb for expressing a sham virtuous indignation, which, in the course of events, is sure to be belied.

In trade, also, this energy usually carries a trace of ferocity. Philanthropic and religious bodies do not commonly make their executive officers out of saints. The communities hitherto founded by Socialists,—the Jesuits, the Port-Royalists, the American communities at New Harmony, at Brook Farm, at Zoar,° are only possible, by installing Judas as steward. The rest of the offices may be filled by good burgesses. The pious and charitable proprietor has a foreman not quite so pious and charitable. The most amiable of country gentlemen has a certain pleasure in the teeth of the bull-dog which guards his orchard. Of the Shaker society,° it was formerly a sort of proverb in the country, that they always sent the devil to market. And in representations of the Deity, painting, poetry, and popular religion have ever drawn the wrath from Hell. It is an esoteric doctrine of society, that a little wickedness is good to make muscle; as if conscience were not good for hands and legs, as if poor decayed formalists of law and order cannot run like wild goats, wolves, and conies; that, as there is a use in medicine for poisons, so the world cannot move without rogues; that public spirit and the ready hand are as well found among the malignants. 'Tis not very rare, the coincidence of sharp private and political practice, with public spirit, and good neighborhood.

I knew a burly Boniface° who for many years kept a public-house in one of our rural capitals. He was a knave whom the town could ill spare. He was a social, vascular creature, grasping and selfish. There was no crime which he did not or could not commit. But he made good friends of the selectmen, served them with his best chop, when they supped at his house, and also with his honor the Judge, he was very cordial, grasping his hand. He introduced all the fiends, male and female, into the town, and united in his person the functions of bully, incendiary, swindler, barkeeper, and burglar. He girdled the trees, and cut off the horses' tails of the temperance people, in the night. He led the 'rummies' and radicals in town-meeting with a speech. Meantime, he was civil, fat, and easy, in his house, and precisely the most public-spirited citizen. He was active in getting the roads repaired and planted with shade-trees; he subscribed for the fountains, the gas, and the telegraph; he introduced the new horse-rake, the new scraper, the baby-jumper, and what not, that Connecticut sends to the admiring citizens. He did this the easier, that the peddler stopped at his house, and paid his keeping, by setting up his new trap on the landlord's premises.

Whilst thus the energy for originating and executing work, deforms itself by excess, and so our axe chops off our own fingers,—this evil is not without remedy. All the elements whose aid man calls in, will sometimes become his masters, especially those of most subtle force. Shall he, then, renounce steam, fire, and electricity, or, shall he learn to deal with them? The rule for this whole class of agencies is,—all *plus* is good; only put it in the right place.

Men of this surcharge of arterial blood cannot live on nuts, herb-tea, and elegies; cannot read novels, and play whist; cannot satisfy all their wants at the Thursday Lecture, or the Boston Athenæum. They pine for adventure, and must go to Pike's Peak; had rather die by the hatchet of a Pawnee, than sit all day and every day at a counting-room desk. They are made for war, for the sea, for mining, hunting, and clearing; for hair-breadth adventures, huge risks, and the joy of eventful living. Some men cannot endure an hour of calm at sea. I remember a poor Malay cook, on board a Liverpool packet, who, when the wind blew a gale, could not contain his joy; 'Blow!' he cried, 'me do tell you, blow!' Their friends and governors must see that some vent for their explosive complexion is provided. The roisters who are destined for infamy at home, if sent to Mexico, will 'cover you with glory,' and come back heroes and generals. There are Oregons, Californias, and Exploring Expeditions enough appertaining to America, to find them in files to gnaw, and in crocodiles to eat. The young English are fine animals, full of blood, and when they have no wars to breathe their riotous valors in, they seek for travels as dangerous as war, diving into Maelstroms; swimming Hellesponts; wading up the snowy Himmaleh; hunting lion, rhinoceros, elephant, in South Africa; gypsying with Borrow in Spain and Algiers; riding alligators in South America with Waterton; utilizing Bedouin, Sheik, and Pacha, with Layard;° yachting among the icebergs of Lancaster Sound; peeping into craters on the equator; or running on the creases of Malays in Borneo.

The excess of virility has the same importance in general history, as in private and industrial life. Strong race or strong individual rests at last on natural forces, which are best in the savage, who, like the beasts around him, is still in reception of the milk from the teats of Nature. Cut off the connection between any of our works, and this aboriginal source, and the work is shallow. The people lean on this, and the mob is not quite so bad an argument as we sometimes say, for it has this good side. 'March without the people,' said a French deputy from the tribune, 'and you march into night: their instincts are a finger-pointing of Providence, always turned toward real benefit. But when you espouse an Orleans party, or a Bourbon, or a Montalembert party, or any other but an organic party, though you mean well, you have a personality instead of a principle, which will inevitably drag you into a corner.'

The best anecdotes of this force are to be had from savage life, in explorers, soldiers, and buccaneers. But who cares for fallings-out of assassins, and fights of bears, or grindings of icebergs? Physical force has no value, where there is nothing else. Snow in snow-banks, fire in volcanoes and solfataras is cheap. The luxury of ice is in tropical countries, and midsummer days. The luxury of fire is, to have a little on our hearth: and of electricity, not volleys of the charged cloud, but the manageable stream on the battery-wires. So of spirit, or energy; the rests or remains of it in the civil and moral man, are worth all the cannibals in the Pacific.

In history, the great moment is, when the savage is just ceasing to be a savage, with all his hairy Pelasgic strength° directed on his opening sense of beauty:—and you have Pericles and Phidias,°—not yet passed over into the Corinthian civility.° Everything good in nature and the world is in that moment of transition, when the swarthy juices still flow plentifully from nature, but their astringency or acridity is got out by ethics and humanity.

The triumphs of peace have been in some proximity to war. Whilst the hand was still familiar with the sword-hilt, whilst the habits of the camp were still visible in the port and complexion of the gentleman, his intellectual power culminated: the compression and tension of these stern conditions is a training for the finest and softest arts, and can rarely be compensated in tranquil times, except by some analogous vigor drawn from occupations as hardy as war.

We say that success is constitutional; depends on a *plus* condition of mind and body, on power of work, on courage; that it is of main efficacy in carrying on the world, and, though rarely found in the right state for an article of commerce, but oftener in the supersaturate or excess, which makes it dangerous and destructive, yet it cannot be spared, and must be had in that form, and absorbents provided to take off its edge.

The affirmative class monopolize the homage of mankind. They originate and execute all the great feats. What a force was coiled up in the skull of Napoleon! Of the sixty thousand men making his army at Eylau, it seems some thirty thousand were thieves and burglars. The men whom, in peaceful communities, we hold if we can, with iron at their legs, in prisons, under the muskets of sentinels, this man dealt with, hand to hand, dragged them to their duty, and won his victories by their bayonets.

This aboriginal might gives a surprising pleasure when it appears under conditions of supreme refinement, as in the proficients in high art. When Michel Angelo was forced to paint the Sistine Chapel in fresco, of which art he knew nothing, he went down into the Pope's gardens behind the Vatican, and with a shovel dug out ochres, red and yellow, mixed them with glue and water with his own hands, and having, after many trials, at last suited himself, climbed his ladders, and painted away, week after week, month after month, the sibyls and prophets. He surpassed his successors in rough vigor, as much as in purity of intellect and refinement. He was not crushed by his one picture left unfinished at last. Michel was wont° to draw his figures first in skeleton, then to clothe them with flesh, and lastly to drape them. 'Ah!' said a brave painter to me, thinking on these things, 'if a man has failed, you will find he has dreamed instead of working. There is no way to success in our art, but to take off your coat, grind paint, and work like a digger on the railroad, all day and every day.'

Success goes thus invariably with a certain *plus* or positive power: an ounce of power must balance an ounce of weight. And, though a man cannot return into his mother's womb, and be born with new amounts of vivacity, yet there are two economies, which are the best *succedanea*° which the case admits. The first is, the stopping off decisively our miscellaneous activity, and concentrating our force on one or a few points; as the gardener, by severe pruning, forces the sap of the tree into one or two vigorous limbs, instead of suffering it to spindle into a sheaf of twigs.

'Enlarge not thy destiny,' said the oracle: 'endeavor not to do more than is given thee in charge.'° The one prudence in life is concentration; the one evil is dissipation: and it makes no difference whether our dissipations are coarse or fine; property and its cares, friends, and a social habit, or politics, or music, or feasting. Everything is good which takes away one plaything and delusion more, and drives us home to add one stroke of faithful work. Friends, books, pictures, lower duties, talents, flatteries, hopes,—all are distractions which cause oscillations in our giddy balloon, and make a good poise and a straight course impossible. You must elect your work; you shall take what your brain can, and drop all the rest. Only so, can that amount of vital force accumulate, which can make the step from knowing to doing. No matter how much faculty of idle seeing a man has, the step from knowing to doing is rarely taken. 'Tis a step out of a chalk circle of imbecility into fruitfulness. Many an artist lacking this, lacks all: he sees the masculine Angelo or Cellini° with despair. He, too, is up to Nature and the

First Cause in his thought. But the spasm to collect and swing his whole being into one act, he has not. The poet Campbell° said, that 'a man accustomed to work was equal to any achievement he resolved on, and, that, for himself, necessity not inspiration was the prompter of his muse.'

Concentration is the secret of strength in politics, in war, in trade, in short, in all management of human affairs. One of the high anecdotes of the world is the reply of Newton to the inquiry, 'how he had been able to achieve his discoveries?'—'By always intending my mind.' Or if you will have a text from politics, take this from Plutarch: 'There was, in the whole city, but one street in which Pericles was ever seen, the street which led to the market-place and the council house. He declined all invitations to banquets, and all gay assemblies and company. During the whole period of his administration, he never dined at the table of a friend.'° Or if we seek an example from trade,—'I hope,' said a good man to Rothschild,° 'your children are not too fond of money and business: I am sure you would not wish that.'—'I am sure I should wish that: I wish them to give mind, soul, heart, and body to business,—that is the way to be happy. It requires a great deal of boldness and a great deal of caution, to make a great fortune, and when you have got it, it requires ten times as much wit to keep it. If I were to listen to all the projects proposed to me, I should ruin myself very soon. Stick to one business, young man. Stick to your brewery, (he said this to young Buxton,) and you will be the great brewer of London. Be brewer, and banker, and merchant, and manufacturer, and you will soon be in the Gazette.'

Many men are knowing, many are apprehensive and tenacious, but they do not rush to a decision. But in our flowing affairs a decision must be made,—the best, if you can; but any is better than none. There are twenty ways of going to a point, and one is the shortest; but set out at once on one. A man who has that presence of mind which can bring to him on the instant all he knows, is worth for action a dozen men who know as much, but can only bring it to light slowly. The good Speaker in the House is not the man who knows the theory of parliamentary tactics, but the man who decides offhand. The good judge is not he who does hair-splitting justice to every allegation, but who, aiming at substantial justice, rules something intelligible for the guidance of suitors. The good lawyer is not the man who has an eye to every side and angle of contingency, and qualifies all his qualifications, but who throws himself on your part so heartily, that he can get you out of a scrape. Dr. Johnson said, in one of his flowing sentences, 'Miserable beyond all

names of wretchedness is that unhappy pair, who are doomed to reduce
beforehand to the principles of abstract reason all the details of each
domestic day. There are cases where little can be said, and much must
be done.'

The second substitute for temperament is drill, the power of use and
routine. The hack is a better roadster than the Arab barb. In chemistry,
the galvanic stream, slow, but continuous, is equal in power to the electric spark, and is, in our arts, a better agent. So in human action, against
the spasm of energy, we offset the continuity of drill. We spread the
same amount of force over much time, instead of condensing it into a
moment. 'Tis the same ounce of gold here in a ball, and there in a leaf.
At West Point, Col. Buford,° the chief engineer, pounded with a hammer on the trunnions of a cannon, until he broke them off. He fired a
piece of ordnance some hundred times in swift succession, until it
burst. Now which stroke broke the trunnion? Every stroke. Which blast
burst the piece? Every blast. '*Diligence passe sens*,' Henry VIII. was wont
to say, or, great is drill. John Kemble said, that the worst provincial
company of actors would go through a play better than the best amateur
company. Basil Hall° likes to show that the worst regular troops will
beat the best volunteers. Practice is nine tenths. A course of mobs is
good practice for orators. All the great speakers were bad speakers at
first. Stumping it through England for seven years, made Cobden° a
consummate debater. Stumping it through New England for twice
seven, trained Wendell Phillips.° The way to learn German, is, to read
the same dozen pages over and over a hundred times, till you know
every word and particle in them, and can pronounce and repeat them
by heart. No genius can recite a ballad at first reading, so well as
mediocrity can at the fifteenth or twentieth reading. The rule for hospitality and Irish 'help,' is, to have the same dinner every day throughout
the year. At last, Mrs. O'Shaughnessy learns to cook it to a nicety, the
host learns to carve it, and the guests are well served. A humorous
friend of mine thinks, that the reason why Nature is so perfect in her
art, and gets up such inconceivably fine sunsets, is, that she has learned
how, at last, by dint of doing the same thing so very often. Cannot one
converse better on a topic on which he has experience, than on one
which is new? Men whose opinion is valued on 'Change, are only such
as have a special experience, and off that ground their opinion is not
valuable. 'More are made good by exercitation, than by nature,' said
Democritus.° The friction in nature is so enormous that we cannot
spare any power. It is not question to express our thought, to elect our
way, but to overcome resistances of the medium and material in every-

thing we do. Hence the use of drill, and the worthlessness of amateurs to cope with practitioners. Six hours every day at the piano, only to give facility of touch; six hours a day at painting, only to give command of the odious materials, oil, ochres, and brushes. The masters say, that they know a master in music, only by seeing the pose of the hands on the keys;—so difficult and vital an act is the command of the instrument. To have learned the use of the tools, by thousands of manipulations; to have learned the arts of reckoning, by endless adding and dividing, is the power of the mechanic and the clerk.

I remarked in England,° in confirmation of a frequent experience at home, that, in literary circles, the men of trust and consideration, bookmakers, editors, university deans and professors, bishops, too, were by no means men of the largest literary talent, but usually of a low and ordinary intellectuality, with a sort of mercantile activity and working talent. Indifferent hacks and mediocrities tower, by pushing their forces to a lucrative point, or by working power, over multitudes of superior men, in Old as in New England.

I have not forgotten that there are sublime considerations which limit the value of talent and superficial success. We can easily overpraise the vulgar hero. There are sources on which we have not drawn. I know what I abstain from. I adjourn what I have to say on this topic to the chapters on Culture and Worship. But this force or spirit, being the means relied on by Nature for bringing the work of the day about,—as far as we attach importance to household life, and the prizes of the world, we must respect that. And I hold, that an economy may be applied to it; it is as much a subject of exact law and arithmetic as fluids and gases are; it may be husbanded, or wasted; every man is efficient only as he is a container or vessel of this force, and never was any signal act or achievement in history, but by this expenditure. This is not gold, but the gold-maker; not the fame, but the exploit.

If these forces and this husbandry are within reach of our will, and the laws of them can be read, we infer that all success, and all conceivable benefit for man, is also, first or last, within his reach, and has its own sublime economies by which it may be attained. The world is mathematical, and has no casualty, in all its vast and flowing curve. Success has no more eccentricity, than the gingham and muslin we weave in our mills. I know no more affecting lesson to our busy, plotting New England brains, than to go into one of the factories with which we have lined all the watercourses in the States. A man hardly knows how much he is a machine, until he begins to make telegraph, loom, press, and locomotive, in his own image. But in these, he is forced to leave out his follies and hindrances, so that when we go to the mill, the machine is more moral than we. Let a man dare go to a loom, and see if he be equal to it. Let machine confront machine, and see how they come out. The world-mill is more complex than the calico-mill, and the architect stooped less. In the gingham-mill, a broken thread or a shred spoils the web through a piece of a hundred yards, and is traced back to the girl that wove it, and lessens her wages. The stockholder, on being shown this, rubs his hands with delight. Are you so cunning, Mr. Profitloss, and do you expect to swindle your master and employer, in the web you weave? A day is a more magnificent cloth than any muslin, the mechanism that makes it is infinitely cunninger, and you shall not conceal the sleezy, fraudulent, rotten hours you have slipped into the piece, nor fear that any honest thread, or straighter steel, or more inflexible shaft, will not testify in the web.

CONSIDERATIONS
BY THE WAY

Hear what British Merlin sung,
Of keenest eye and truest tongue.
Say not, the chiefs who first arrive
Usurp the seats for which all strive;
The forefathers this land who found
Failed to plant the vantage-ground;
Ever from one who comes to-morrow
Men wait their good and truth to borrow.
But wilt thou measure all thy road,
See thou lift the lightest load.
Who has little, to him who has less, can spare,
And thou, Cyndyllan's son! beware
Ponderous gold and stuffs to bear,
To falter ere thou thy task fulfil,—
Only the light-armed climb the hill.
The richest of all lords is Use,
And ruddy Health the loftiest Muse.
Live in the sunshine, swim the sea,
Drink the wild air's salubrity:
Where the star Canope shines in May,
Shepherds are thankful, and nations gay.
The music that can deepest reach,
And cure all ill, is cordial speech:
Mask thy wisdom with delight,
Toy with the bow, yet hit the white.
Of all wit's uses, the main one
Is to live well with who has none.
Cleave to thine acre; the round year
Will fetch all fruits and virtues here:
Fool and foe may harmless roam,
Loved and lovers bide at home.
A day for toil, an hour for sport,
But for a friend is life too short.

ALTHOUGH this garrulity of advising is born with us, I confess that life is rather a subject of wonder, than of didactics. So much fate, so much irresistible dictation from temperament and unknown inspiration enters into it, that we doubt we can say anything out of our own experience whereby to help each other. All the professions are timid and expectant agencies. The priest is glad if his prayers or his sermon meet the condition of any soul; if of two, if of ten, 'tis a signal success. But he walked to the church without any assurance that he knew the distemper, or could heal it. The physician prescribes hesitatingly out of his few resources, the same tonic or sedative to this new and peculiar constitution, which he has applied with various success to a hundred men before. If the patient mends, he is glad and surprised. The lawyer advises the client, and tells his story to the jury, and leaves it with them, and is as gay and as much relieved as the client, if it turns out that he has a verdict. The judge weighs the arguments, and puts a brave face on the matter, and, since there must be a decision, decides as he can, and hopes he has done justice, and given satisfaction to the community; but is only an advocate after all. And so is all life a timid and unskilful spectator. We do what we must, and call it by the best names. We like very well to be praised for our action, but our conscience says, 'Not unto us.' 'Tis little we can do for each other. We accompany the youth with sympathy, and manifold old sayings of the wise, to the gate of the arena, but 'tis certain that not by strength of ours, or of the old sayings, but only on strength of his own, unknown to us or to any, he must stand or fall. That by which a man conquers in any passage, is a profound secret to every other being in the world, and it is only as he turns his back on us and on all men, and draws on this most private wisdom, that any good can come to him. What we have, therefore, to say of life, is rather description, or, if you please, celebration, than available rules.

Yet vigor is contagious, and whatever makes us either think or feel strongly, adds to our power, and enlarges our field of action. We have a debt to every great heart, to every fine genius; to those who have put life and fortune on the cast of an act of justice; to those who have added new sciences; to those who have refined life by elegant pursuits. 'Tis the fine souls who serve us, and not what is called fine society. Fine society is only a self-protection against the vulgarities of the street and the tavern. Fine society, in the common acceptation, has neither ideas nor aims. It renders the service of a perfumery, or a laundry, not of a farm or factory. 'Tis an exclusion and a precinct. Sidney Smith° said, 'A few yards in London cement or dissolve friendship.' It is an unprincipled decorum; an affair of clean linen and coaches, of gloves, cards, and elegance in trifles. There are other measures of self-respect for a man, than the number of clean shirts he puts on every day. Society wishes to be amused. I do not wish to be amused. I wish that life should not be cheap, but sacred. I wish the days to be as centuries, loaded, fragrant. Now we reckon them as bank-days, by some debt which is to be paid us, or which we are to pay, or some pleasure we are to taste. Is all we have to do to draw the breath in, and blow it out again? Porphyry's° definition is better; 'Life is that which holds matter together.' The babe in arms is a channel through which the energies we call fate, love, and reason, visibly stream. See what a cometary train of auxiliaries man carries with him, of animals, plants, stones, gases, and imponderable elements. Let us infer his ends from this pomp of means. Mirabeau said, 'Why should we feel ourselves to be men, unless it be to succeed in everything, everywhere. You must say of nothing, *That is beneath me*, nor feel that anything can be out of your power. Nothing is impossible to the man who can will. *Is that necessary? That shall be:*—this is the only law of success.'° Whoever said it, this is in the right key. But this is not the tone and genius of the men in the street. In the streets, we grow cynical. The men we meet are coarse and torpid. The finest wits have their sediment. What quantities of fribbles, paupers, invalids, epicures, antiquaries, politicians, thieves, and triflers of both sexes, might be advantageously spared! Mankind divides itself into two classes,—benefactors and malefactors. The second class is vast, the first a handful. A person seldom falls sick, but the bystanders are animated with a faint hope that he will die:—quantities of poor lives; of distressing invalids; of cases for a gun. Franklin said, 'Mankind are very superficial and dastardly: they begin upon a thing, but, meeting with a difficulty, they fly from it discouraged: but they have capacities, if they would employ them.'° Shall we then judge a country by the majority, or by the minority? By the minority, surely. 'Tis pedantry to estimate nations by the census, or by square miles of land, or other than by their importance to the mind of the time.

Leave this hypocritical prating about the masses. Masses are rude, lame, unmade, pernicious in their demands and influence, and need not to be flattered but to be schooled. I wish not to concede anything to them, but to tame, drill, divide, and break them up, and draw individuals out of them. The worst of charity is, that the lives you are asked to preserve are not worth preserving. Masses! the calamity is the masses. I do not wish any mass at all, but honest men only, lovely, sweet, accomplished women only, and no shovel-handed, narrow-brained, gin-drinking million stockingers or lazzaroni° at all. If government knew how, I should like to see it check, not multiply the population. When it reaches its true law of action, every man that is born will be hailed as essential. Away with this hurrah of masses, and let us have the considerate vote of single men spoken on their honor and their conscience. In old Egypt, it was established law, that the vote of a prophet be reckoned equal to a hundred hands. I think it was much under-estimated. 'Clay and clay differ in dignity,'° as we discover by our preferences every day. What a vicious practice is this of our politicians at Washington pairing off! as if one man who votes wrong, going away, could excuse you, who mean to vote right, for going away; or, as if your presence did not tell in more ways than in your vote. Suppose the three hundred heroes at Thermopylæ had paired off with three hundred Persians: would it have been all the same to Greece, and to history? Napoleon was called by his men *Cent Mille*. Add honesty to him, and they might have called him Hundred Million.

Nature makes fifty poor melons for one that is good, and shakes down a tree full of gnarled, wormy, unripe crabs, before you can find a dozen dessert apples; and she scatters nations of naked Indians, and nations of clothed Christians, with two or three good heads among them. Nature works very hard, and only hits the white once in a million throws. In mankind, she is contented if she yields one master in a century. The more difficulty there is in creating good men, the more they are used when they come. I once counted in a little neighborhood, and found that every able-bodied man had, say from twelve to fifteen persons dependent on him for material aid,—to whom he is to be for spoon and jug, for backer and sponsor, for nursery and hospital, and many functions beside: nor does it seem to make much difference whether he is bachelor or patriarch; if he do not violently decline the duties that fall to him, this amount of helpfulness will in one way or another be brought home to him. This is the tax which his abilities pay. The good men are employed for private centres of use, and for larger influence. All revelations, whether of mechanical or intellectual or moral science, are made not to communities, but to single persons. All the marked events of our day, all the cities, all the colonizations, may be traced back to their origin in a private brain. All the feats which make our civility were the thoughts of a few good heads.

Meantime, this spawning productivity is not noxious or needless. You would say, this rabble of nations might be spared. But no, they are all counted and depended on. Fate keeps everything alive so long as the smallest thread of public necessity holds it on to the tree. The coxcomb and bully and thief class are allowed as proletaries, every one of their vices being the excess or acridity of a virtue. The mass are animal, in pupilage, and near chimpanzee. But the units, whereof this mass is composed are neuters, every one of which may be grown to a queen-bee. The rule is, we are used as brute atoms, until we think: then, we use all the rest. Nature turns all malfaisance to good. Nature provided for real needs. No sane man at last distrusts himself. His existence is a perfect answer to all sentimental cavils. If he is, he is wanted, and has the precise properties that are required. That we are here, is proof we ought to be here. We have as good right, and the same sort of right to be here, as Cape Cod or Sandy Hook° have to be there.

To say then, the majority are wicked, means no malice, no bad heart in the observer, but, simply, that the majority are unripe, and have not yet come to themselves, do not yet know their opinion. *That*, if they knew it, is an oracle for them and for all. But in the passing moment, the quadruped interest is very prone to prevail: and this beast-force, whilst it makes the discipline of the world, the school of heroes, the glory of martyrs, has provoked, in every age, the satire of wits, and the tears of good men. They find the journals, the clubs, the governments, the churches, to be in the interest, and the pay of the devil. And wise men have met this obstruction in their times, like Socrates, with his famous irony; like Bacon, with life-long dissimulation; like Erasmus, with his book 'The Praise of Folly;' like Rabelais,° with his satire rending the nations. 'They were the fools who cried against me, you will say,' wrote the Chevalier de Boufflers to Grimm; 'aye, but the fools have the advantage of numbers, and 'tis that which decides. 'Tis of no use for us to make war with them; we shall not weaken them; they will always be the masters. There will not be a practice or an usage introduced, of which they are not the authors.'°

In front of these sinister facts, the first lesson of history is the good of evil. Good is a good doctor, but Bad is sometimes a better. 'Tis the oppressions of William the Norman, savage forest-laws, and crushing despotism, that made possible the inspirations of *Magna Charta*° under John. Edward I. wanted money, armies, castles, and as much as he could get. It was necessary to call the people together by shorter, swifter ways,—and the House of Commons arose. To obtain subsidies, he paid in privileges. In the twenty-fourth year of his reign, he decreed, 'that no tax should be levied without consent of Lords and Commons;'—which is the basis of the English Constitution. Plutarch affirms that the cruel wars which followed the march of Alexander, introduced the civility, language, and arts of Greece into the savage East; introduced marriage; built seventy cities; and united hostile nations under one government. The barbarians who broke up the Roman empire did not arrive a day too soon. Schiller° says, the Thirty Years' War made Germany a nation. Rough, selfish despots serve men immensely, as Henry VIII. in the contest with the Pope; as the infatuations no less than the wisdom of Cromwell; as the ferocity of the Russian czars; as the fanaticism of the

French regicides of 1789. The frost which kills the harvest of a year, saves the harvests of a century, by destroying the weevil or the locust. Wars, fires, plagues, break up immovable routine, clear the ground of rotten races and dens of distemper, and open a fair field to new men. There is a tendency in things to right themselves, and the war or revolution or bankruptcy that shatters a rotten system, allows things to take a new and natural order. The sharpest evils are bent into that periodicity which makes the errors of planets, and the fevers and distempers of men, self-limiting. Nature is upheld by antagonism. Passions, resistance, danger, are educators. We acquire the strength we have overcome. Without war, no soldier; without enemies, no hero. The sun were insipid, if the universe were not opaque. And the glory of character is in affronting the horrors of depravity, to draw thence new nobilities of power: as Art lives and thrills in new use and combining of contrasts, and mining into the dark evermore for blacker pits of night. What would painter do, or what would poet or saint, but for crucifixions and hells? And evermore in the world is this marvellous balance of beauty and disgust, magnificence and rats. Not Antoninus,° but a poor washer-woman said, 'The more trouble, the more lion; that's my principle.'

I do not think very respectfully of the designs or the doings of the people who went to California, in 1849. It was a rush and a scramble of needy adventurers, and, in the western country, a general jail-delivery of all the rowdies of the rivers. Some of them went with honest purposes, some with very bad ones, and all of them with the very commonplace wish to find a short way to wealth. But Nature watches over all, and turns this malfaisance to good. California gets peopled and subdued,—civilized in this immoral way,—and, on this fiction, a real prosperity is rooted and grown. 'Tis a decoy-duck; 'tis tubs thrown to amuse the whale: but real ducks, and whales that yield oil, are caught. And, out of Sabine rapes, and out of robbers' forays, real Romes and their heroisms come in fulness of time.

In America, the geography is sublime,° but the men are not: the inventions are excellent, but the inventors one is sometimes ashamed of. The agencies by which events so grand as the opening of California, of Texas, of Oregon, and the junction of the two oceans, are effected, are paltry,—coarse selfishness, fraud, and conspiracy: and most of the great results of history are brought about by discreditable means.

The benefaction derived in Illinois, and the great West, from railroads is inestimable, and vastly exceeding any intentional philanthropy on record. What is the benefit done by a good King Alfred, or by a

Howard, or Pestalozzi, or Elizabeth Fry,° or Florence Nightingale, or any lover, less or larger, compared with the involuntary blessing wrought on nations by the selfish capitalists who built the Illinois, Michigan, and the network of the Mississippi valley roads, which have evoked not only all the wealth of the soil, but the energy of millions of men. 'Tis a sentence of ancient wisdom, 'that God hangs the greatest weights on the smallest wires.'

What happens thus to nations, befalls every day in private houses. When the friends of a gentleman brought to his notice the follies of his sons, with many hints of their danger, he replied, that he knew so much mischief when he was a boy, and had turned out on the whole so successfully, that he was not alarmed by the dissipation of boys; 'twas dangerous water, but, he thought, they would soon touch bottom, and then swim to the top. This is bold practice, and there are many failures to a good escape. Yet one would say, that a good understanding would suffice as well as moral sensibility to keep one erect; the gratifications of the passions are so quickly seen to be damaging, and,—what men like least,—seriously lowering them in social rank. Then all talent sinks with character.

'*Croyez moi, l'erreur aussi a son mérite,*'° said Voltaire. We see those who surmount, by dint of some egotism or infatuation, obstacles from which the prudent recoil. The right partisan is a heady narrow man, who, because he does not see many things, sees some one thing with heat and exaggeration, and, if he falls among other narrow men, or on objects which have a brief importance, as some trade or politics of the hour, he prefers it to the universe, and seems inspired, and a godsend to those who wish to magnify the matter, and carry a point. Better, certainly, if we could secure the strength and fire which rude, passionate men bring into society, quite clear of their vices. But who dares draw out the linchpin from the wagon-wheel? 'Tis so manifest, that there is no moral deformity, but is a good passion out of place; that there is no man who is not indebted to his foibles; that, according to the old oracle, 'the Furies are the bonds of men;'° that the poisons are our principal medicines, which kill the disease, and save the life. In the high prophetic phrase, *He causes the wrath of man to praise him,*° and twists and wrenches our evil to our good. Shakspeare wrote,—

"'Tis said, best men are moulded of their faults;"°

and great educators and lawgivers, and especially generals, and leaders of colonies, mainly rely on this stuff, and esteem men of irregular and passional force the best timber. A man of sense° and energy, the late head of the Farm School in Boston harbor, said to me, 'I want none of your good boys,—give me the bad ones.' And this is the reason, I suppose, why, as soon as the children are good, the mothers are scared, and think they are going to die. Mirabeau said, 'There are none but men of strong passions capable of going to greatness; none but such capable of meriting the public gratitude.' Passion, though a bad regulator, is a powerful spring. Any absorbing passion has the effect to deliver from the little coils and cares of every day: 'tis the heat which sets our human atoms spinning, overcomes the friction of crossing thresholds, and first addresses in society, and gives us a good start and speed, easy to continue, when once it is begun. In short, there is no man who is not at some time indebted to his vices, as no plant that is not fed from manures. We only insist that the man meliorate, and that the plant grow upward, and convert the base into the better nature.

The wise workman will not regret the poverty or the solitude which brought out his working talents. The youth is charmed with the fine air and accomplishments of the children of fortune. But all great men come out of the middle classes. 'Tis better for the head; 'tis better for the heart. Marcus Antoninus says, that Fronto° told him, 'that the so-called high-born are for the most part heartless;' whilst nothing is so indicative of deepest culture as a tender consideration of the ignorant. Charles James Fox° said of England, 'The history of this country proves, that we are not to expect from men in affluent circumstances the vigilance, energy, and exertion without which the House of Commons would lose its greatest force and weight. Human nature is prone to indulgence, and the most meritorious public services have always been performed by persons in a condition of life removed from opulence.' And yet what we ask daily, is to be conventional. Supply, most kind gods! this defect in my address, in my form, in my fortunes, which puts me a little out of the ring: supply it, and let me be like the rest whom I admire, and on good terms with them. But the wise gods say, No, we have better things for thee. By humiliations, by defeats, by loss of sympathy, by gulfs of disparity, learn a wider truth and humanity than that of a fine gentleman. A Fifth-Avenue° landlord, a West-End householder, is not the highest style of man: and, though good hearts and sound minds are of no condition, yet he who is to be wise for many, must not be protected. He must know the huts where poor men lie, and the chores which poor men do. The first-class minds, Æsop, Socrates, Cervantes, Shakspeare, Franklin, had the poor man's feeling and mortification. A rich man was never insulted in his life: but this man must be stung. A rich man was never in danger from cold, or hunger, or war, or ruffians, and you can see he was not, from the moderation of his ideas. 'Tis a fatal disadvantage to be cockered, and to eat too much cake. What tests of manhood could he stand? Take him out of his protections. He is a good book-keeper; or he is a shrewd adviser in the insurance office: perhaps he could pass a college examination, and take his degrees: perhaps he can give wise counsel in a court of law. Now plant him down among farmers, firemen, Indians, and emigrants. Set a dog on him: set a highwayman on him: try him with a course of mobs: send him to Kansas, to Pike's Peak, to Oregon: and, if he have true faculty, this may be the element he wants, and he will come out of it with broader wisdom and manly power. Æsop, Saadi, Cervantes, Regnard,° have been taken by corsairs, left for dead, sold for slaves, and know the realities of human life.

Bad times have a scientific value. These are occasions a good learner would not miss. As we go gladly to Faneuil Hall,° to be played upon by the stormy winds and strong fingers of enraged patriotism, so is a fanatical persecution, civil war, national bankruptcy, or revolution, more rich in the central tones than languid years of prosperity. What had been, ever since our memory, solid continent, yawns apart, and discloses its composition and genesis. We learn geology the morning after the earthquake, on ghastly diagrams of cloven mountains, upheaved plains, and the dry bed of the sea.

In our life and culture, everything is worked up, and comes in use,— passion, war, revolt, bankruptcy, and not less, folly and blunders, insult, ennui, and bad company. Nature is a rag-merchant, who works up every shred and ort and end into new creations; like a good chemist, whom I found, the other day, in his laboratory, converting his old shirts into pure white sugar. Life is a boundless privilege, and when you pay for your ticket, and get into the car, you have no guess what good company you shall find there. You buy much that is not rendered in the bill. Men achieve a certain greatness unawares, when working to another aim.

If now in this connection of discourse, we should venture on laying down the first obvious rules of life, I will not here repeat the first rule of economy, already propounded once and again, that every man shall maintain himself,—but I will say, get health. No labor, pains, temperance, poverty, nor exercise, that can gain it, must be grudged. For sickness is a cannibal which eats up all the life and youth it can lay hold of, and absorbs its own sons and daughters. I figure it as a pale, wailing, distracted phantom, absolutely selfish, heedless of what is good and great, attentive to its sensations, losing its soul, and afflicting other souls with meanness and mopings, and with ministration to its voracity of trifles. Dr. Johnson said severely, 'Every man is a rascal as soon as he is sick.' Drop the cant, and treat it sanely. In dealing with the drunken, we do not affect to be drunk. We must treat the sick with the same firmness, giving them, of course, every aid,—but withholding ourselves. I once asked a clergyman in a retired town, who were his companions? what men of ability he saw? he replied, that he spent his time with the sick and the dying. I said, he seemed to me to need quite other company, and all the more that he had this: for if people were sick and dying to any purpose, we would leave all and go to them, but, as far as I had observed, they were as frivolous as the rest, and sometimes much more frivolous. Let us engage our companions not to spare us. I knew a wise woman who said to her friends, 'When I am old, rule me.' And the best part of health is fine disposition. It is more essential than talent, even in the works of talent. Nothing will supply the want of sunshine to peaches, and, to make knowledge valuable, you must have the cheerfulness of wisdom. Whenever you are sincerely pleased, you are nourished. The joy of the spirit indicates its strength. All healthy things are sweet-tempered. Genius works in sport, and goodness smiles to the last; and, for the reason, that whoever sees the law which distributes things, does not despond, but is animated to great desires and endeavors. He who desponds betrays that he has not seen it.

'Tis a Dutch proverb, that 'paint costs nothing,' such are its preserving qualities in damp climates. Well, sunshine costs less, yet is finer pigment. And so of cheerfulness, or a good temper, the more it is spent, the more of it remains. The latent heat of an ounce of wood or stone is inexhaustible. You may rub the same chip of pine to the point of kindling, a hundred times; and the power of happiness of any soul is not to be computed or drained. It is observed that a depression of spirits develops the germs of a plague in individuals and nations.

It is an old commendation of right behavior, '*Aliis lætus, sapiens sibi*,' which our English proverb translates, 'Be merry *and* wise.' I know how easy it is to men of the world to look grave and sneer at your sanguine youth, and its glittering dreams. But I find the gayest castles in the air that were ever piled, far better for comfort and for use, than the dungeons in the air that are daily dug and caverned out by grumbling, discontented people. I know those miserable fellows, and I hate them, who see a black star always riding through the light and colored clouds in the sky overhead: waves of light pass over and hide it for a moment, but the black star keeps fast in the zenith. But power dwells with cheerfulness; hope puts us in a working mood, whilst despair is no muse, and untunes the active powers. A man should make life and Nature happier to us, or he had better never been born. When the political economist reckons up the unproductive classes, he should put at the head this class of pitiers of themselves, cravers of sympathy, bewailing imaginary disasters. An old French verse runs, in my translation:—

> Some of your griefs you have cured,
> And the sharpest you still have survived;
> But what torments of pain you endured
> From evils that never arrived!

There are three wants which never can be satisfied: that of the rich, who wants something more; that of the sick, who wants something different; and that of the traveller, who says, 'Anywhere but here.' The Turkish cadi said to Layard,° 'After the fashion of thy people, thou hast wandered from one place to another, until thou art happy and content in none.' My countrymen are not less infatuated with the *rococo* toy of Italy. All America seems on the point of embarking for Europe. But we shall not always traverse seas and lands with light purposes, and for pleasure, as we say. One day we shall cast out the passion for Europe, by the passion for America. Culture will give gravity and domestic rest to those who now travel only as not knowing how else to spend money. Already, who provoke pity like that excellent family party just arriving in their well-appointed carriage, as far from home and any honest end as ever? Each nation has asked successively, 'What are they here for?' until at last the party are shamefaced, and anticipate the question at the gates of each town.

Genial manners are good, and power of accommodation to any circumstance, but the high prize of life, the crowning fortune of a man is to be born with a bias to some pursuit, which finds him in employment and happiness,—whether it be to make baskets, or broadswords, or canals, or statutes, or songs. I doubt not this was the meaning of Socrates, when he pronounced artists the only truly wise, as being actually, not apparently so.

In childhood, we fancied ourselves walled in by the horizon, as by a glass bell, and doubted not, by distant travel, we should reach the baths of the descending sun and stars. On experiment, the horizon flies before us, and leaves us on an endless common, sheltered by no glass bell. Yet 'tis strange how tenaciously we cling to that bell-astronomy, of a protecting domestic horizon. I find the same illusion in the search after happiness, which I observe, every summer, recommenced in this neighborhood, soon after the pairing of the birds. The young people do not like the town, do not like the sea-shore, they will go inland; find a dear cottage deep in the mountains, secret as their hearts. They set forth on their travels in search of a home: they reach Berkshire; they reach Vermont; they look at the farms;—good farms, high mountain-sides: but where is the seclusion? The farm is near this; 'tis near that; they have got far from Boston, but 'tis near Albany, or near Burlington,° or near Montreal. They explore a farm, but the house is small, old, thin; discontented people lived there, and are gone:—there's too much sky, too much out-doors; too public. The youth aches for solitude. When he comes to the house, he passes through the house. That does not make the deep recess he sought. 'Ah! now, I perceive,' he says, 'it must be deep with persons; friends only can give depth.' Yes, but there is a great dearth, this year, of friends; hard to find, and hard to have when found: they are just going away: they too are in the whirl of the flitting world, and have engagements and necessities. They are just starting for Wisconsin; have letters from Bremen:°—see you again, soon. Slow, slow to learn the lesson, that there is but one depth, but one interior, and that is—his purpose. When joy or calamity or genius shall show him it, then woods, then farms, then city shopmen and cab-drivers, indifferently with prophet or friend, will mirror back to him its unfathomable heaven, its populous solitude.

The uses of travel are occasional, and short; but the best fruit it finds, when it finds it, is conversation; and this is a main function of life. What a difference in the hospitality of minds! Inestimable is he to whom we can say what we cannot say to ourselves. Others are involun-tarily hurtful to us, and bereave us of the power of thought, impound and imprison us. As, when there is sympathy, there needs but one wise man in a company, and all are wise,—so, a blockhead makes a block-head of his companion. Wonderful power to benumb possesses this brother. When he comes into the office or public room, the society dis-solves; one after another slips out, and the apartment is at his disposal. What is incurable but a frivolous habit? A fly is as untamable as a hyena. Yet folly in the sense of fun, fooling, or dawdling can easily be borne; as Talleyrand° said, 'I find nonsense singularly refreshing;' but a virulent, aggressive fool taints the reason of a household. I have seen a whole family of quiet, sensible people unhinged and beside themselves, vic-tims of such a rogue. For the steady wrongheadedness of one perverse person irritates the best: since we must withstand absurdity. But resis-tance only exasperates the acrid fool, who believes that Nature and gra-vitation are quite wrong, and he only is right. Hence all the dozen inmates are soon perverted, with whatever virtues and industries they have, into contradictors, accusers, explainers, and repairers of this one malefactor; like a boat about to be overset, or a carriage run away with,—not only the foolish pilot or driver, but everybody on board is forced to assume strange and ridiculous attitudes, to balance the vehicle and prevent the upsetting. For remedy, whilst the case is yet mild, I recommend phlegm and truth: let all the truth that is spoken or done be at the zero of indifference, or truth itself will be folly. But, when the case is seated and malignant, the only safety is in amputation; as seamen say, you shall cut and run. How to live with unfit companions?—for, with such, life is for the most part spent: and experience teaches little better than our earliest instinct of self-defence, namely, not to engage, not to mix yourself in any manner with them; but let their madness spend itself unopposed;—you are you, and I am I.

Conversation is an art in which a man has all mankind for his competitors, for it is that which all are practising every day while they live. Our habit of thought,—take men as they rise,—is not satisfying; in the common experience, I fear, it is poor and squalid. The success which will content them, is, a bargain, a lucrative employment, an advantage gained over a competitor, a marriage, a patrimony, a legacy, and the like. With these objects, their conversation deals with surfaces: politics, trade, personal defects, exaggerated bad news, and the rain. This is forlorn, and they feel sore and sensitive. Now, if one comes who can illuminate this dark house with thoughts, show them their native riches, what gifts they have, how indispensable each is, what magical powers over nature and men; what access to poetry, religion, and the powers which constitute character; he wakes in them the feeling of worth, his suggestions require new ways of living, new books, new men, new arts and sciences,—then we come out of our egg-shell existence into the great dome, and see the zenith over and the nadir under us. Instead of the tanks and buckets of knowledge to which we are daily confined, we come down to the shore of the sea, and dip our hands in its miraculous waves. 'Tis wonderful the effect on the company. They are not the men they were. They have all been to California, and all have come back millionnaires. There is no book and no pleasure in life comparable to it. Ask what is best in our experience, and we shall say, a few pieces of plain-dealing with wise people. Our conversation once and again has apprised us that we belong to better circles than we have yet beheld; that a mental power invites us, whose generalizations are more worth for joy and for effect than anything that is now called philosophy or literature. In excited conversation, we have glimpses of the Universe, hints of power native to the soul, far-darting lights and shadows of an

Andes landscape, such as we can hardly attain in lone meditation. Here are oracles sometimes profusely given, to which the memory goes back in barren hours.

Add the consent of will and temperament, and there exists the covenant of friendship. Our chief want in life, is, somebody who shall make us do what we can. This is the service of a friend. With him we are easily great. There is a sublime attraction in him to whatever virtue is in us. How he flings wide the doors of existence! What questions we ask of him! what an understanding we have! how few words are needed! It is the only real society. An Eastern poet, Ali Ben Abu Taleb,° writes with sad truth,—

> 'He who has a thousand friends has not a friend to spare,
> And he who has one enemy shall meet him everywhere.'

But few writers have said anything better to this point than Hafiz,° who indicates this relation as the test of mental health: 'Thou learnest no secret until thou knowest friendship, since to the unsound no heavenly knowledge enters.' Neither is life long enough for friendship. That is a serious and majestic affair, like a royal presence, or a religion, and not a postilion's dinner to be eaten on the run. There is a pudency about friendship, as about love, and though fine souls never lose sight of it, yet they do not name it. With the first class of men our friendship or good understanding goes quite behind all accidents of estrangement, of condition, of reputation. And yet we do not provide for the greatest good of life. We take care of our health; we lay up money; we make our roof tight, and our clothing sufficient; but who provides wisely that he shall not be wanting in the best property of all,—friends? We know that all our training is to fit us for this, and we do not take the step towards it. How long shall we sit and wait for these benefactors?

It makes no difference, in looking back five years, how you have been dieted or dressed; whether you have been lodged on the first floor or the attic; whether you have had gardens and baths, good cattle and horses, have been carried in a neat equipage, or in a ridiculous truck: these things are forgotten so quickly, and leave no effect. But it counts much whether we have had good companions, in that time;—almost as much as what we have been doing. And see the overpowering importance of neighborhood in all association. As it is marriage, fit or unfit, that makes our home, so it is who lives near us of equal social degree,— a few people at convenient distance, no matter how bad company,— these, and these only, shall be your life's companions: and all those who are native, congenial, and by many an oath of the heart, sacramented to you, are gradually and totally lost. You cannot deal systematically with this fine element of society, and one may take a good deal of pains to bring people together, and to organize clubs and debating societies, and yet no result come of it. But it is certain that there is a great deal of good in us that does not know itself, and that a habit of union and competition brings people up and keeps them up to their highest point; that life would be twice or ten times life, if spent with wise and fruitful companions. The obvious inference is, a little useful deliberation and pre-concert, when one goes to buy house and land.

But we live with people on other platforms; we live with dependents, not only with the young whom we are to teach all we know, and clothe with the advantages we have earned, but also with those who serve us directly, and for money. Yet the old rules hold good. Let not the tie be mercenary, though the service is measured by money. Make yourself necessary to somebody. Do not make life hard to any. This point is acquiring new importance in American social life. Our domestic service is usually a foolish fracas of unreasonable demand on one side, and shirking on the other. A man of wit° was asked, in the train, what was his errand in the city? He replied, 'I have been sent to procure an angel to do cooking.' A lady complained to me, that, of her two maidens, one was absent-minded, and the other was absent-bodied. And the evil increases from the ignorance and hostility of every ship-load of the immigrant population swarming into houses and farms. Few people discern that it rests with the master or the mistress what service comes from the man or the maid; that this identical hussy was a tutelar spirit in one house, and a haridan in the other. All sensible people are selfish, and nature is tugging at every contract to make the terms of it fair. If you are proposing only your own, the other party must deal a little hardly by you. If you deal generously, the other, though selfish and unjust, will make an exception in your favor, and deal truly with you. When I asked an iron-master about the slag and cinder in railroad iron,—'O,' he said, 'there's always good iron to be had: if there's cinder in the iron, 'tis because there was cinder in the pay.'

But why multiply these topics, and their illustrations, which are endless? Life brings to each his task, and, whatever art you select, algebra, planting, architecture, poems, commerce, politics,—all are attainable, even to the miraculous triumphs, on the same terms, of selecting that for which you are apt;—begin at the beginning, proceed in order, step by step. 'Tis as easy to twist iron anchors, and braid cannons, as to braid straw, to boil granite as to boil water, if you take all the steps in order. Wherever there is failure, there is some giddiness, some superstition about luck, some step omitted, which Nature never pardons. The happy conditions of life may be had on the same terms. Their attraction for you is the pledge that they are within your reach. Our prayers are prophets. There must be fidelity, and there must be adherence. How respectable the life that clings to its objects! Youthful aspirations are fine things, your theories and plans of life are fair and commendable:—but will you stick? Not one, I fear, in that Common full of people, or, in a thousand, but one: and, when you tax them with treachery, and remind them of their high resolutions, they have forgotten that they made a vow. The individuals are fugitive, and in the act of becoming something else, and irresponsible. The race is great, the ideal fair, but the men whiffling and unsure. The hero is he who is immovably centred. The main difference between people seems to be, that one man can come under obligations on which you can rely,—is obligable; and another is not. As he has not a law within him, there's nothing to tie him to.

'Tis inevitable to name particulars of virtue, and of condition, and to exaggerate them. But all rests at last on that integrity which dwarfs talent, and can spare it. Sanity consists in not being subdued by your means. Fancy prices are paid for position, and for the culture of talent, but to the grand interests, superficial success is of no account. The man,—it is his attitude,—not feats, but forces,—not on set days and public occasions, but, at all hours, and in repose alike as in energy, still formidable, and not to be disposed of. The populace says, with Horne Tooke,° 'If you would be powerful, pretend to be powerful.' I prefer to say, with the old prophet, 'Seekest thou great things? seek them not:'°— or, what was said of a Spanish prince, 'The more you took from him, the greater he looked.' *Plus on lui ôte, plus il est grand.*

The secret of culture is to learn, that a few great points steadily re-appear, alike in the poverty of the obscurest farm, and in the miscellany of metropolitan life, and that these few are alone to be regarded,—the escape from all false ties; courage to be what we are; and love of what is simple and beautiful; independence, and cheerful relation, these are the essentials,—these, and the wish to serve,—to add somewhat to the well-being of men.

ILLUSIONS

Flow, flow the waves hated,
Accursed, adored,
The waves of mutation:
No anchorage is.
Sleep is not, death is not;
Who seem to die live.
House you were born in,
Friends of your spring-time,
Old man and young maid,
Day's toil and its guerdon,
They are all vanishing,
Fleeing to fables,
Cannot be moored.
See the stars through them,
Through treacherous marbles.
Know, the stars yonder,
The stars everlasting,
Are fugitive also,
And emulate, vaulted,
The lambent heat-lightning,
And fire-fly's flight.

When thou dost return
On the wave's circulation,
Beholding the shimmer,
The wild dissipation,
And, out of endeavor
To change and to flow,
The gas become solid,
And phantoms and nothings
Return to be things,
And endless imbroglio
Is law and the world,—
Then first shalt thou know,
That in the wild turmoil,
Horsed on the Proteus,
Thou ridest to power,
And to endurance.

SOME years ago,° in company with an agreeable party, I spent a
long summer day in exploring the Mammoth Cave in Kentucky. We

traversed, through spacious galleries affording a solid masonry foundation for the town and county overhead, the six or eight black miles from the mouth of the cavern to the innermost recess which tourists visit,—a niche or grotto made of one seamless stalactite, and called, I believe, Serena's Bower. I lost the light of one day. I saw high domes, and bottomless pits; heard the voice of unseen waterfalls; paddled three quarters of a mile in the deep Echo River, whose waters are peopled with the blind fish; crossed the streams 'Lethe' and 'Styx;'° plied with music and guns the echoes in these alarming galleries; saw every form of stalagmite and stalactite in the sculptured and fretted chambers,— icicle, orange-flower, acanthus, grapes, and snowball. We shot Bengal lights into the vaults and groins of the sparry cathedrals, and examined all the masterpieces which the four combined engineers, water, limestone, gravitation, and time, could make in the dark.

The mysteries and scenery of the cave had the same dignity that belongs to all natural objects, and which shames the fine things to which we foppishly compare them. I remarked, especially, the mimetic habit, with which Nature, on new instruments, hums her old tunes, making night to mimic day, and chemistry to ape vegetation. But I then took notice, and still chiefly remember, that the best thing which the cave had to offer was an illusion. On arriving at what is called the 'Star-Chamber,' our lamps were taken from us by the guide, and extinguished or put aside, and, on looking upwards, I saw or seemed to see the night heaven thick with stars glimmering more or less brightly over our heads, and even what seemed a comet flaming among them. All the party were touched with astonishment and pleasure. Our musical friends sung with much feeling a pretty song, 'The stars are in the quiet sky,' &c., and I sat down on the rocky floor to enjoy the serene picture. Some crystal specks in the black ceiling high overhead, reflecting the light of a half-hid lamp, yielded this magnificent effect.

I own, I did not like the cave so well for eking out its sublimities with this theatrical trick. But I have had many experiences like it, before and since; and we must be content to be pleased without too curiously analyzing the occasions. Our conversation with Nature is not just what it seems. The cloud-rack, the sunrise and sunset glories, rainbows, and northern lights are not quite so spheral as our childhood thought them; and the part our organization plays in them is too large. The senses interfere everywhere, and mix their own structure with all they report of. Once, we fancied the earth a plane, and stationary. In admiring the sunset, we do not yet deduct the rounding, coördinating, pictorial powers of the eye.

The same interference from our organization creates the most of our pleasure and pain. Our first mistake is the belief that the circumstance gives the joy which we give to the circumstance. Life is an ecstasy. Life is sweet as nitrous oxide; and the fisherman dripping all day over a cold pond, the switchman at the railway intersection, the farmer in the field, the negro in the rice-swamp, the fop in the street, the hunter in the woods, the barrister with the jury, the belle at the ball, all ascribe a certain pleasure to their employment, which they themselves give it. Health and appetite impart the sweetness to sugar, bread, and meat. We fancy that our civilization has got on far, but we still come back to our primers.

We live by our imaginations, by our admirations, by our sentiments. The child walks amid heaps of illusions, which he does not like to have disturbed. The boy, how sweet to him is his fancy! how dear the story of barons and battles! What a hero he is, whilst he feeds on his heroes! What a debt is his to imaginative books! He has no better friend or influence, than Scott, Shakspeare, Plutarch, and Homer. The man lives to other objects, but who dare affirm that they are more real? Even the prose of the streets is full of refractions. In the life of the dreariest alderman, fancy enters into all details, and colors them with rosy hue. He imitates the air and actions of people whom he admires, and is raised in his own eyes. He pays a debt quicker to a rich man than to a poor man. He wishes the bow and compliment of some leader in the state, or in society; weighs what he says; perhaps he never comes nearer to him for that, but dies at last better contented for this amusement of his eyes and his fancy.

The world rolls, the din of life is never hushed. In London, in Paris, in Boston, in San Francisco, the carnival, the masquerade is at its height. Nobody drops his domino. The unities, the fictions of the piece it would be an impertinence to break. The chapter of fascinations is very long. Great is paint; nay, God is the painter; and we rightly accuse the critic who destroys too many illusions. Society does not love its unmaskers. It was wittily, if somewhat bitterly, said by D'Alembert, *'qu'un état de vapeur était un état très fâcheux, parcequ'il nous faisait voir les choses comme elles sont.'*° I find men victims of illusion in all parts of life. Children, youths, adults, and old men, all are led by one bawble or another. Yoganidra, the goddess of illusion, Proteus, or Momus, or Gylfi's Mocking,—for the Power has many names,—is stronger than the Titans, stronger than Apollo.° Few have overheard the gods, or surprised their secret. Life is a succession of lessons which must be lived to be understood. All is riddle, and the key to a riddle is another riddle.

There are as many pillows of illusion as flakes in a snow-storm. We wake from one dream into another dream. The toys, to be sure, are various, and are graduated in refinement to the quality of the dupe. The intellectual man requires a fine bait; the sots are easily amused. But everybody is drugged with his own frenzy, and the pageant marches at all hours, with music and banner and badge.

Amid the joyous troop who give in to the charivari, comes now and then a sad-eyed boy, whose eyes lack the requisite refractions to clothe the show in due glory, and who is afflicted with a tendency to trace home the glittering miscellany of fruits and flowers to one root. Science is a search after identity, and the scientific whim is lurking in all corners. At the State Fair, a friend of mine complained that all the varieties of fancy pears in our orchards seem to have been selected by somebody who had a whim for a particular kind of pear, and only cultivated such as had that perfume; they were all alike. And I remember the quarrel of another youth with the confectioners, that, when he racked his wit to choose the best comfits in the shops, in all the endless varieties of sweetmeat he could only find three flavors, or two. What then? Pears and cakes are good for something; and because you, unluckily, have an eye or nose too keen, why need you spoil the comfort which the rest of us find in them? I knew a humorist, who, in a good deal of rattle, had a grain or two of sense. He shocked the company by maintaining that the attributes of God were two,—power and risibility; and that it was the duty of every pious man to keep up the comedy. And I have known gentlemen of great stake in the community, but whose sympathies were cold,—presidents of colleges, and governors, and senators,—who held themselves bound to sign every temperance pledge, and act with Bible societies, and missions, and peace-makers, and cry *Hist-a-boy!* to every good dog. We must not carry comity too far, but we all have kind impulses in this direction. When the boys come into my yard for leave to gather horse-chestnuts, I own I enter into Nature's game, and affect to grant the permission reluctantly, fearing that any moment they will find out the imposture of that showy chaff. But this tenderness is quite unnecessary; the enchantments are laid on very thick. Their young life is thatched with them. Bare and grim to tears is the lot of the children in the hovel I saw yesterday; yet not the less they hung it round with frippery romance, like the children of the happiest fortune, and talked of 'the dear cottage where so many joyful hours had flown.' Well, this thatching of hovels is the custom of the country. Women, more than all, are the element and kingdom of illusion. Being fascinated, they fascinate. They see through Claude-Lorraines.° And how dare any one, if he could, pluck away the *coulisses*,° stage effects, and ceremonies, by which they live? Too pathetic, too pitiable, is the region of affection, and its atmosphere always liable to *mirage*.

We are not very much to blame for our bad marriages. We live amid hallucinations; and this especial trap is laid to trip up our feet with, and all are tripped up first or last. But the mighty Mother who had been so sly with us, as if she felt that she owed us some indemnity, insinuates into the Pandora-box of marriage some deep and serious benefits, and some great joys. We find a delight in the beauty and happiness of children, that makes the heart too big for the body. In the worst-assorted connections there is ever some mixture of true marriage. Teague and his jade get some just relations of mutual respect, kindly observation, and fostering of each other, learn something, and would carry themselves wiselier, if they were now to begin.

'Tis fine for us to point at one or another fine madman, as if there were any exempts. The scholar in his library is none. I, who have all my life heard any number of orations and debates, read poems and miscellaneous books, conversed with many geniuses, am still the victim of any new page; and, if Marmaduke, or Hugh, or Moosehead, or any other, invent a new style or mythology, I fancy that the world will be all brave and right, if dressed in these colors, which I had not thought of. Then at once I will daub with this new paint; but it will not stick. 'Tis like the cement which the peddler sells at the door; he makes broken crockery hold with it, but you can never buy of him a bit of the cement which will make it hold when he is gone.

Men who make themselves felt in the world avail themselves of a certain fate in their constitution, which they know how to use. But they never deeply interest us, unless they lift a corner of the curtain, or betray never so slightly their penetration of what is behind it. 'Tis the charm of practical men, that outside of their practicality are a certain poetry and play, as if they led the good horse Power by the bridle, and preferred to walk, though they can ride so fiercely. Bonaparte is intellectual, as well as Cæsar; and the best soldiers, sea-captains, and railway men have a gentleness, when off duty; a good-natured admission that there are illusions, and who shall say that he is not their sport? We stigmatize the cast-iron fellows, who cannot so detach themselves, as 'dragon-ridden,' 'thunder-stricken,' and fools of fate, with whatever powers endowed.

Since our tuition is through emblems and indirections, 'tis well to know that there is method in it, a fixed scale, and rank above rank in the phantasms. We begin low with coarse masks, and rise to the most subtle and beautiful. The red men told Columbus, 'they had an herb which took away fatigue'; but he found the illusion of 'arriving from the east at the Indies' more composing to his lofty spirit than any tobacco. Is not our faith in the impenetrability of matter more sedative than narcotics? You play with jackstraws, balls, bowls, horse and gun, estates and politics; but there are finer games before you. Is not time a pretty toy? Life will show you masks that are worth all your carnivals. Yonder mountain must migrate into your mind. The fine star-dust and nebulous blur in Orion, 'the portentous year of Mizar and Alcor,'° must come down and be dealt with in your household thought. What if you shall come to discern that the play and playground of all this pompous history are radiations from yourself, and that the sun borrows his beams? What terrible questions we are learning to ask! The former men believed in magic, by which temples, cities, and men were swallowed up, and all trace of them gone. We are coming on the secret of a magic which sweeps out of men's minds all vestige of theism and beliefs which they and their fathers held and were framed upon.

There are deceptions of the senses, deceptions of the passions, and the structural, beneficent illusions of sentiment and of the intellect. There is the illusion of love, which attributes to the beloved person all which that person shares with his or her family, sex, age, or condition, nay, with the human mind itself. 'Tis these which the lover loves, and Anna Matilda gets the credit of them. As if one shut up always in a tower, with one window, through which the face of heaven and earth could be seen, should fancy that all the marvels he beheld belonged to that window. There is the illusion of time, which is very deep; who has disposed of it? or come to the conviction that what seems the *succession* of thought is only the distribution of wholes into causal series? The intellect sees that every atom carries the whole of Nature; that the mind opens to omnipotence; that, in the endless striving and ascents, the metamorphosis is entire, so that the soul doth not know itself in its own act, when that act is perfected. There is illusion that shall deceive even the elect. There is illusion that shall deceive even the performer of the miracle. Though he make his body, he denies that he makes it. Though the world exist from thought, thought is daunted in presence of the world. One after the other we accept the mental laws, still resisting those which follow, which however must be accepted. But all our concessions only compel us to new profusion. And what avails it that science has come to treat space and time as simply forms of thought, and the material world as hypothetical, and withal our pretension of *property* and even of self-hood are fading with the rest, if, at last, even our thoughts are not finalities; but the incessant flowing and ascension reach these also, and each thought which yesterday was a finality, to-day is yielding to a larger generalization?

With such volatile elements to work in, 'tis no wonder if our estimates are loose and floating. We must work and affirm, but we have no guess of the value of what we say or do. The cloud is now as big as your hand, and now it covers a county. That story of Thor,° who was set to drain the drinking-horn in Asgard, and to wrestle with the old woman, and to run with the runner Lok, and presently found that he had been drinking up the sea, and wrestling with Time, and racing with Thought, describes us who are contending, amid these seeming trifles, with the supreme energies of Nature. We fancy we have fallen into bad company and squalid condition, low debts, shoe-bills, broken glass to pay for, pots to buy, butcher's meat, sugar, milk, and coal. 'Set me some great task, ye gods! and I will show my spirit.' 'Not so,' says the good Heaven; 'plod and plough, vamp your old coats and hats, weave a shoe-string; great affairs and the best wine by and by.' Well, 'tis all phantasm; and if we weave a yard of tape in all humility, and as well as we can, long hereafter we shall see it was no cotton tape at all, but some galaxy which we braided, and that the threads were Time and Nature.

We cannot write the order of the variable winds. How can we penetrate the law of our shifting moods and susceptibility? Yet they differ as all and nothing. Instead of the firmament of yesterday, which our eyes require, it is to-day an eggshell which coops us in; we cannot even see what or where our stars of destiny are. From day to day, the capital facts of human life are hidden from our eyes. Suddenly the mist rolls up, and reveals them, and we think how much good time is gone, that might have been saved, had any hint of these things been shown. A sudden rise in the road shows us the system of mountains, and all the summits, which have been just as near us all the year, but quite out of mind. But these alternations are not without their order, and we are parties to our various fortune. If life seem a succession of dreams, yet poetic justice is done in dreams also. The visions of good men are good; it is the undisciplined will that is whipped with bad thoughts and bad fortunes. When we break the laws, we lose our hold on the central reality. Like sick men in hospitals, we change only from bed to bed, from one folly to another; and it cannot signify much what becomes of such castaways,—wailing, stupid, comatose creatures,—lifted from bed to bed, from the nothing of life to the nothing of death.

In this kingdom of illusions we grope eagerly for stays and foundations. There is none but a strict and faithful dealing at home, and a severe barring out of all duplicity or illusion there. Whatever games are played with us, we must play no games with ourselves, but deal in our privacy with the last honesty and truth. I look upon the simple and childish virtues of veracity and honesty as the root of all that is sublime in character. Speak as you think, be what you are, pay your debts of all kinds. I prefer to be owned as sound and solvent, and my word as good as my bond, and to be what cannot be skipped, or dissipated, or undermined, to all the *éclat* in the universe. This reality is the foundation of friendship, religion, poetry, and art. At the top or at the bottom of all illusions, I set the cheat which still leads us to work and live for appearances, in spite of our conviction, in all sane hours, that it is what we really are that avails with friends, with strangers, and with fate or fortune.

One would think from the talk of men, that riches and poverty were a great matter; and our civilization mainly respects it. But the Indians say, that they do not think the white man with his brow of care, always toiling, afraid of heat and cold, and keeping within doors, has any advantage of them. The permanent interest of every man is, never to be in a false position, but to have the weight of Nature to back him in all that he does. Riches and poverty are a thick or thin costume; and our life— the life of all of us—identical. For we transcend the circumstance continually, and taste the real quality of existence; as in our employments, which only differ in the manipulations, but express the same laws; or in our thoughts, which wear no silks, and taste no ice-creams. We see God face to face every hour, and know the savor of Nature.

The early Greek philosophers Heraclitus and Xenophanes measured their force on this problem of identity. Diogenes of Apollonia° said, that unless the atoms were made of one stuff, they could never blend and act with one another. But the Hindoos, in their sacred writings, express the liveliest feeling, both of the essential identity, and of that illusion which they conceive variety to be. 'The notions, "*I am*," and "*This is mine*," which influence mankind, are but delusions of the mother of the world. Dispel, O Lord of all creatures! the conceit of knowledge which proceeds from ignorance.'° And the beatitude of man they hold to lie in being freed from fascination.

The intellect is stimulated by the statement of truth in a trope, and the will by clothing the laws of life in illusions. But the unities of Truth and of Right are not broken by the disguise. There need never be any confusion in these. In a crowded life of many parts and performers, on a stage of nations, or in the obscurest hamlet in Maine or California, the same elements offer the same choices to each new comer, and, according to his election, he fixes his fortune in absolute Nature. It would be hard to put more mental and moral philosophy than the Persians have thrown into a sentence:—

> 'Fooled thou must be, though wisest of the wise:
> Then be the fool of virtue, not of vice.'°

There is no chance, and no anarchy, in the universe. All is system and gradation. Every god is there sitting in his sphere. The young mortal enters the hall of the firmament: there is he alone with them alone, they pouring on him benedictions and gifts, and beckoning him up to their thrones. On the instant, and incessantly, fall snow-storms of illusions. He fancies himself in a vast crowd which sways this way and that, and whose movement and doings he must obey: he fancies himself poor, orphaned, insignificant. The mad crowd drives hither and thither, now furiously commanding this thing to be done, now that. What is he that he should resist their will, and think or act for himself? Every moment, new changes, and new showers of deceptions, to baffle and distract him. And when, by and by, for an instant, the air clears, and the cloud lifts a little, there are the gods still sitting around him on their thrones,—they alone with him alone.

UNCOLLECTED PROSE

THE LORD'S SUPPER

The Kingdom of God is not meat and drink, but righteousness,
and peace, and joy in the Holy Ghost.—ROMANS XIV. 17.

IN the history of the Church no subject has been more fruitful of controversy than the Lord's Supper. There never has been any unanimity
in the understanding of its nature, nor any uniformity in the mode of
celebrating it. Without considering the frivolous questions which have
been lately debated as to the posture in which men should partake of it;
whether mixed or unmixed wine should be served; whether leavened or
unleavened bread should be broken; the questions have been settled
differently in every church, who should be admitted to the feast, and
how often it should be prepared. In the Catholic Church, infants were
at one time permitted and then forbidden to partake; and, since the
ninth century, the laity receive the bread only, the cup being reserved to
the priesthood. So, as to the time of the solemnity. In the fourth
Lateran Council,° it was decreed that any believer should communicate
at least once in a year—at Easter. Afterwards it was determined that
this Sacrament should be received three times in the year—at Easter,
Whitsuntide, and Christmas. But more important controversies have
arisen respecting its nature. The famous question of the Real Pres-
ence° was the main controversy between the Church of England and
the Church of Rome. The doctrine of the Consubstantiation taught by
Luther was denied by Calvin. In the Church of England, Archbishops
Laud and Wake maintained that the elements were an Eucharist or
sacrifice of Thanksgiving to God; Cudworth and Warburton, that this
was not a sacrifice, but a sacrificial feast; and Bishop Hoadley,° that it
was neither a sacrifice nor a feast after sacrifice, but a simple commemoration. And finally, it is now near two hundred years since the Society
of Quakers denied the authority of the rite altogether, and gave good
reasons for disusing it.

I allude to these facts only to show that, so far from the supper being
a tradition in which men are fully agreed, there has always been the
widest room for difference of opinion upon this particular.

Having recently given particular attention to this subject, I was led to
the conclusion that Jesus did not intend to establish an institution for
perpetual observance when he ate the Passover with his disciples; and,
further, to the opinion, that it is not expedient to celebrate it as we do. I
shall now endeavor to state distinctly my reasons for these two opinions.

I. The authority of the rite.

An account of the last supper of Christ with his disciples is given by the four Evangelists, Matthew, Mark, Luke, and John.

In St. Matthew's Gospel (Matt. XXVI. 26–30) are recorded the words of Jesus in giving bread and wine on that occasion to his disciples, but no expression occurs intimating that this feast was hereafter to be commemorated.

In St. Mark (Mark XIV. 23) the same words are recorded, and still with no intimation that the occasion was to be remembered.

St. Luke (Luke XXII. 15), after relating the breaking of the bread, has these words: This do in remembrance of me.

In St. John, although other occurrences of the same evening are related, this whole transaction is passed over without notice.

Now observe the facts. Two of the Evangelists, namely, Matthew and John, were of the twelve disciples, and were present on that occasion.° Neither of them drops the slightest intimation of any intention on the part of Jesus to set up anything permanent. John, especially, the beloved disciple, who has recorded with minuteness the conversation and the transactions of that memorable evening, has quite omitted such a notice. Neither does it appear to have come to the knowledge of Mark who, though not an eye-witness, relates the other facts. This material fact, that the occasion was to be remembered, is found in Luke alone, who was not present. There is no reason, however, that we know, for rejecting the account of Luke. I doubt not, the expression was used by Jesus. I shall presently consider its meaning. I have only brought these accounts together, that you may judge whether it is likely that a solemn institution, to be continued to the end of time by all mankind, as they should come, nation after nation, within the influence of the Christian religion, would have been established in this slight manner—in a manner so slight, that the intention of commemorating it should not appear, from their narrative, to have caught the ear or dwelt in the mind of the only two among the twelve who wrote down what happened.

Still we must suppose that the expression, 'This do in remembrance of me,' had come to the ear of Luke from some disciple who was present. What did it really signify? It is a prophetic and an affectionate expression. Jesus is a Jew, sitting with his countrymen, celebrating their national feast. He thinks of his own impending death, and wishes the minds of his disciples to be prepared for it. 'When hereafter,' he says to them, 'you shall keep the Passover, it will have an altered aspect to your eyes. It is now a historical covenant of God with the Jewish nation. Hereafter, it will remind you of a new covenant sealed with my blood.

In years to come, as long as your people shall come up to Jerusalem to keep this feast, the connection which has subsisted between us will give a new meaning in your eyes to the national festival, as the anniversary of my death.' I see natural feeling and beauty in the use of such language from Jesus, a friend to his friends; I can readily imagine that he was willing and desirous, when his disciples met, his memory should hallow their intercourse; but I cannot bring myself to believe that in the use of such an expression he looked beyond the living generation, beyond the abolition of the festival he was celebrating, and the scattering of the nation, and meant to impose a memorial feast upon the whole world.

Without presuming to fix precisely the purpose in the mind of Jesus, you will see that many opinions may be entertained of his intention, all consistent with the opinion that he did not design a perpetual ordinance. He may have foreseen that his disciples would meet to remember him, and that with good effect. It may have crossed his mind that this would be easily continued a hundred or a thousand years—as men more easily transmit a form than a virtue—and yet have been altogether out of his purpose to fasten it upon men in all times and all countries.

But though the words, *Do this in remembrance of me,* do not occur in Matthew, Mark, or John, and although it should be granted us that, taken alone, they do not necessarily import so much as is usually thought, yet many persons are apt to imagine that the very striking and personal manner in which this eating and drinking is described, indicates a striking and formal purpose to found a festival. And I admit that this impression might probably be left upon the mind of one who read only the passages under consideration in the New Testament. But this impression is removed by reading any narrative of the mode in which the ancient or the modern Jews have kept the Passover. It is then perceived that the leading circumstances in the Gospels are only a faithful account of that ceremony. Jesus did not celebrate the Passover, and afterwards the Supper, but the Supper *was* the Passover. He did with his disciples exactly what every master of a family in Jerusalem was doing at the same hour with his household. It appears that the Jews ate the lamb and the unleavened bread, and drank wine after a prescribed manner. It was the custom for the master of the feast to break the bread and to bless it, using this formula, which the Talmudists have preserved to us, 'Blessed be thou, O Lord our God, the King of the world, who hast produced this food from the earth,'—and to give it to every one at the table. It was the custom of the master of the family to take the cup which contained the wine, and to bless it, saying, 'Blessed be Thou, O Lord, who givest us the fruit of the vine,'—and then to give the cup to all. Among the modern Jews who in their dispersion retain the Passover, a hymn is also sung after this ceremony, specifying the twelve great works done by God for the deliverance of their fathers out of Egypt.

But still it may be asked, why did Jesus make expressions so extraordinary and emphatic as these—'This is my body which is broken for you. Take; eat. This is my blood which is shed for you. Drink it.'—I reply they are not extraordinary expressions from him. They were familiar in his mouth. He always taught by parables and symbols. It was the national way of teaching and was largely used by him. Remember the readiness which he always showed to spiritualize every occurrence. He stooped and wrote on the sand. He admonished his disciples respecting the leaven of the Pharisees. He instructed the woman of Samaria respecting living water. He permitted himself to be anointed, declaring that it was for his interment. He washed the feet of his disciples. These are admitted to be symbolical actions and expressions. Here, in like manner, he calls the bread his body, and bids the disciples eat. He had used the same expression repeatedly before. The reason why St. John does not repeat his words on this occasion, seems to be that he had reported a similar discourse of Jesus to the people of Capernaum more at length already (John VI. 27). He there tells the Jews, 'Except ye eat the flesh of the Son of Man and drink His blood, ye have no life in you.' And when the Jews on that occasion complained that they did not comprehend what he meant, he added for their better understanding, and as if for our understanding, that we might not think his body was to be actually eaten, that he only meant, *we should live by his commandment.* He closed his discourse with these explanatory expressions: 'The flesh profiteth nothing; the *words* that I speak to you, they are spirit and they are life.'

Whilst I am upon this topic, I cannot help remarking that it is not a little singular that we should have preserved this rite and insisted upon perpetuating one symbolical act of Christ whilst we have totally neglected all others—particularly one other which had at least an equal claim to our observance. Jesus washed the feet of his disciples and told them that, as he had washed their feet, they ought to wash one another's feet; for he had given them an example, that they should do as he had done to them. I ask any person who believes the Supper to have been designed by Jesus to be commemorated forever, to go and read the account of it in the other Gospels, and then compare with it the account of this transaction in St. John, and tell me if this be not much more explicitly authorized than the Supper. It only differs in this, that we have found the Supper used in New England and the washing of the feet not. But if we had found it an established rite in our churches, on grounds of mere authority, it would have been impossible to have argued against it. That rite is used by the Church of Rome, and by the Sandemanians.° It has been very properly dropped by other Christians. Why? For two reasons: (1) because it was a local custom, and unsuitable in western countries; and (2) because it was typical, and all understand that humility is the thing signified. But the Passover was local too, and does not concern us, and its bread and wine were typical, and do not help us to understand the redemption which they signified.

These views of the original account of the Lord's Supper lead me to esteem it an occasion full of solemn and prophetic interest, but never intended by Jesus to be the foundation of a perpetual institution.

It appears however in Christian history that the disciples had very early taken advantage of these impressive words of Christ to hold religious meetings, where they broke bread and drank wine as symbols. I look upon this fact as very natural in the circumstances of the church. The disciples lived together; they threw all their property into a common stock; they were bound together by the memory of Christ, and nothing could be more natural than that this eventful evening should be affectionately remembered by them; that they, Jews like Jesus, should adopt his expressions and his types, and furthermore, that what was done with peculiar propriety by them, his personal friends, with less propriety should come to be extended to their companions also. In this way religious feasts grew up among the early Christians. They were readily adopted by the Jewish converts who were familiar with religious feasts, and also by the Pagan converts whose idolatrous worship had been made up of sacred festivals, and who very readily abused these to gross riot, as appears from the censures of St. Paul. Many persons consider this fact, the observance of such a memorial feast by the early disciples, decisive of the question whether it ought to be observed by us. For my part I see nothing to wonder at in its originating with them; all that is surprising is that it should exist among us. There was good reason for his personal friends to remember their friend and repeat his words. It was only too probable that among the half converted Pagans and Jews, any rite, any form, would find favor, whilst yet unable to comprehend the spiritual character of Christianity.

The circumstance, however, that St. Paul adopts these views, has seemed to many persons conclusive in favor of the institution. I am of opinion that it is wholly upon the epistle to the Corinthians, and not upon the Gospels, that the ordinance stands. Upon this matter of St. Paul's view of the Supper, a few important considerations must be stated.

The end which he has in view, in the eleventh chapter of the first epistle is, not to enjoin upon his friends to observe the Supper, but to censure their abuse of it. *We* quote the passage now-a-days as if it enjoined attendance upon the Supper; but he wrote it merely to chide them for drunkenness. To make their enormity plainer he goes back to the origin of this religious feast to show what sort of feast that was, out of which this riot of theirs came, and so relates the transactions of the Last Supper. '*I have received of the Lord,*' he says, '*that which I delivered to you.*' By this expression it is often thought that a miraculous communication is implied; but certainly without good reason, if it is remembered that St. Paul was living in the lifetime of all the apostles who could give him an account of the transaction; and it is contrary to all reason to suppose that God should work a miracle to convey information that could so easily be got by natural means. So that the import of the expression is that he had received the story of an eye-witness such as we also possess.

But there is a material circumstance which diminishes our confidence in the correctness of the Apostle's view; and that is, the observation that his mind had not escaped the prevalent error of the primitive church, the belief, namely, that the second coming of Christ would shortly occur, until which time, he tells them, this feast was to be kept. Elsewhere he tells them, that, at that time the world would be burnt up with fire, and a new government established, in which the Saints would sit on thrones; so slow were the disciples during the life, and after the ascension of Christ, to receive the idea which we receive, that his second coming was a spiritual kingdom, the dominion of his religion in the hearts of men, to be extended gradually over the whole world.

In this manner we may see clearly enough how this ancient ordinance got its footing among the early Christians, and this single expectation of a speedy reappearance of a temporal Messiah, which kept its influence even over so spiritual a man as St. Paul, would naturally tend to preserve the use of the rite when once established.

We arrive then at this conclusion, *first*, that it does not appear, from a careful examination of the account of the Last Supper in the Evangelists, that it was designed by Jesus to be perpetual; *secondly*, that it does not appear that the opinion of St. Paul, all things considered, ought to alter our opinion derived from the evangelists.

One general remark before quitting this branch of the subject. We ought to be cautious in taking even the best ascertained opinions and practices of the primitive church, for our own. If it could be satisfactorily shown that they esteemed it authorized and to be transmitted forever, that does not settle the question for us. We know how inveterately they were attached to their Jewish prejudices, and how often even the influence of Christ failed to enlarge their views. On every other subject succeeding times have learned to form a judgment more in accordance with the spirit of Christianity than was the practice of the early ages.

But it is said: 'Admit that the rite was not designed to be perpetual. What harm doth it? Here it stands, generally accepted, under some form, by the Christian world, the undoubted occasion of much good; is it not better it should remain?'

II. This is the question of expediency.

I proceed to state a few objections that in my judgment lie against its use in its present form.

1. If the view which I have taken of the history of the institution be correct, then the claim of authority should be dropped in administering it. You say, every time you celebrate the rite, that Jesus enjoined it; and the whole language you use conveys that impression. But if you read the New Testament as I do, you do not believe he did.

2. It has seemed to me that the use of this ordinance tends to produce confusion in our views of the relation of the soul to God. It is the old objection to the doctrine of the Trinity,—that the true worship was transferred from God to Christ, or that such confusion was introduced into the soul, that an undivided worship was given nowhere. Is not that the effect of the Lord's Supper? I appeal now to the convictions of communicants—and ask such persons whether they have not been occasionally conscious of a painful confusion of thought between the worship due to God and the commemoration due to Christ. For, the service does not stand upon the basis of a voluntary act, but is imposed by authority. It is an expression of gratitude to Christ, enjoined by Christ. There is an endeavor to keep Jesus in mind, whilst yet the prayers are addressed to God. I fear it is the effect of this ordinance to clothe Jesus with an authority which he never claimed and which distracts the mind of the worshipper. I know our opinions differ much respecting the nature and offices of Christ, and the degree of veneration to which he is entitled. I am so much a Unitarian as this: that I believe the human mind cannot admit but one God, and that every effort to pay religious homage to more than one being, goes to take away all right ideas. I appeal, brethren, to your individual experience. In the moment when you make the least petition to God, though it be but a silent wish that he may approve you, or add one moment to your life,—do you not, in the very act, necessarily exclude all other beings from your thought? In that act, the soul stands alone with God, and Jesus is no more present to the mind than your brother or your child.

But is not Jesus called in Scripture the Mediator? He is the mediator in that only sense in which possibly any being can mediate between God and man—that is an Instructor of man. He teaches us how to become like God. And a true disciple of Jesus will receive the light he gives most thankfully; but the thanks he offers, and which an exalted being will accept, are not *compliments*—commemorations,—but the use of that instruction.

3. Passing other objections, I come to this, that the *use of the elements*, however suitable to the people and the modes of thought in the East, where it originated, is foreign and unsuited to affect us. Whatever long usage and strong association may have done in some individuals to deaden this repulsion, I apprehend that their use is rather tolerated than loved by any of us. We are not accustomed to express our thoughts or emotions by symbolical actions. Most men find the bread and wine no aid to devotion and to some, it is a painful impediment. To eat bread is one thing; to love the precepts of Christ and resolve to obey them is quite another.

The statement of this objection leads me to say that I think this difficulty, wherever it is felt, to be entitled to the greatest weight. It is alone a sufficient objection to the ordinance. It is my own objection. This mode of commemorating Christ is not suitable to me. That is reason enough why I should abandon it. If I believed that it was enjoined by Jesus on his disciples, and that he even contemplated making permanent this mode of commemoration, every way agreeable to an eastern mind, and yet, on trial, it was disagreeable to my own feelings, I should not adopt it. I should choose other ways which, as more effectual upon me, he would approve more. For I choose that my remembrances of him should be pleasing, affecting, religious. I will love him as a glorified friend, after the free way of friendship, and not pay him a stiff sign of respect, as men do to those whom they fear. A passage read from his discourses, a moving provocation to works like his, any act or meeting which tends to awaken a pure thought, a flow of love, an original design of virtue, I call a worthy, a true commemoration.

4. Fourthly, the importance ascribed to this particular ordinance is not consistent with the spirit of Christianity. The general object and effect of this ordinance is unexceptionable. It has been, and is, I doubt not, the occasion of indefinite good; but an importance is given by Christians to it which never can belong to any form. My friends, the apostle well assures us that 'the kingdom of God is not meat and drink, but righteousness and peace and joy, in the Holy Ghost.'° I am not so foolish as to declaim against forms. Forms are as essential as bodies;

but to exalt particular forms, to adhere to one form a moment after it is out-grown, is unreasonable, and it is alien to the spirit of Christ. If I understand the distinction of Christianity, the reason why it is to be preferred over all other systems and is divine is this, that it is a moral system; that it presents men with truths which are their own reason, and enjoins practices that are their own justification; that if miracles may be said to have been its evidence to the first Christians, they are not its evidence to us, but the doctrines themselves; that every practice is Christian which praises itself, and every practice unchristian which condemns itself. I am not engaged to Christianity by decent forms, or saving ordinances; it is not usage, it is not what I do not understand, that binds me to it—let these be the sandy foundations of falsehoods. What I revere and obey in it is its reality, its boundless charity, its deep interior life, the rest it gives to my mind, the echo it returns to my thoughts, the perfect accord it makes with my reason through all its representation of God and His Providence; and the persuasion and courage that come out thence to lead me upward and onward. Freedom is the essence of this faith. It has for its object simply to make men good and wise. Its institutions, then, should be as flexible as the wants of men. That form out of which the life and suitableness have departed, should be as worthless in its eyes as the dead leaves that are falling around us.

And therefore, although for the satisfaction of others, I have labored to show by the history that this rite was not intended to be perpetual; although I have gone back to weigh the expressions of Paul, I feel that here is the true point of view. In the midst of considerations as to what Paul thought, and why he so thought, I cannot help feeling that it is time misspent to argue to or from his convictions, or those of Luke and John, respecting any form. I seem to lose the substance in seeking the shadow. That for which Paul lived and died so gloriously; that for which Jesus gave himself to be crucified; the end that animated the thousand martyrs and heroes who have followed his steps, was to redeem us from a formal religion, and teach us to seek our well-being in the formation of the soul. The whole world was full of idols and ordinances. The Jewish was a religion of forms. The Pagan was a religion of forms; it was all body—it had no life—and the Almighty God was pleased to qualify and send forth a man to teach men that they must serve him with the heart; that only that life was religious which was thoroughly good; that sacrifice was smoke, and forms were shadows. This man lived and died true to this purpose; and now, with his blessed word and life before us, Christians must contend that it is a matter of vital importance—really a duty, to commemorate him by a certain form, whether that form be agreeable to their understandings or not.

Is not this to make vain the gift of God? Is not this to turn back the hand on the dial? Is not this to make men—to make ourselves—forget that not forms, but duties; not names, but righteousness and love are enjoined; and that in the eye of God there is no other measure of the value of any one form than the measure of its use?

There remain some practical objections to the ordinance into which I shall not now enter. There is one on which I had intended to say a few words; I mean the unfavorable relation in which it places that numerous class of persons who abstain from it merely from disinclination to the rite.

Influenced by these considerations, I have proposed to the brethren of the Church to drop the use of the elements and the claim of authority in the administration of this ordinance, and have suggested a mode in which a meeting for the same purpose might be held free of objection.

My brethren have considered my views with patience and candor, and have recommended unanimously an adherence to the present form. I have, therefore, been compelled to consider whether it becomes me to administer it. I am clearly of opinion I ought not. This discourse has already been so far extended, that I can only say that the reason of my determination is shortly this:—It is my desire, in the office of a Christian minister, to do nothing which I cannot do with my whole heart. Having said this, I have said all. I have no hostility to this institution; I am only stating my want of sympathy with it. Neither should I ever have obtruded this opinion upon other people, had I not been called by my office to administer it. That is the end of my opposition, that I am not interested in it. I am content that it stand to the end of the world, if it please men and please heaven, and I shall rejoice in all the good it produces.

As it is the prevailing opinion and feeling in our religious community, that it is an indispensable part of the pastoral office to administer this ordinance, I am about to resign into your hands that office which you have confided to me.° It has many duties for which I am feebly qualified. It has some which it will always be my delight to discharge, according to my ability, wherever I exist. And whilst the recollection of its claims oppresses me with a sense of my unworthiness, I am consoled by the hope that no time and no change can deprive me of the satisfaction of pursuing and exercising its highest functions.

September 9, 1832.

SOCIETY AND SOLITUDE

I FELL in with a humorist, on my travels, who had in his chamber a cast of the Rondanini Medusa,° and who assured me that the name which that fine work of art bore in the catalogues was a misnomer, as he was convinced that the sculptor who carved it intended it for Memory, the mother of the Muses. In the conversation that followed, my new friend made some extraordinary confessions. 'Do you not see,' he said, 'the penalty of learning, and that each of these scholars whom you have met at S——, though he were to be the last man, would, like the executioner in Hood's poem, guillotine the last but one?' He added many lively remarks, but his evident earnestness engaged my attention, and, in the weeks that followed, we became better acquainted. He had good abilities, a genial temper, and no vices; but he had one defect,— he could not speak in the tone of the people. There was some paralysis on his will, such that, when he met men on common terms, he spoke weakly, and from the point, like a flighty girl. His consciousness of the fault made it worse. He envied every drover and lumberman in the tavern their manly speech. He coveted Mirabeau's *don terrible de la familiarité*,° believing that he whose sympathy goes lowest is the man from whom kings have the most to fear. For himself, he declared that he could not get enough alone to write a letter to a friend. He left the city; he hid himself in pastures. The solitary river was not solitary enough; the sun and moon put him out. When he bought a house, the first thing he did was to plant trees. He could not enough conceal himself. Set a hedge here; set oaks there,—trees behind trees; above all, set evergreens, for they will keep a secret all the year round. The most agreeable compliment you could pay him was, to imply that you had not observed him in a house or a street where you had met him. Whilst he suffered at being seen where he was, he consoled himself with the delicious thought of the inconceivable number of places where he was not. All he wished of his tailor was to provide that sober mean of color and cut which would never detain the eye for a moment. He went to Vienna, to Smyrna, to London. In all the variety of costumes, a carnival, a kaleidoscope of clothes, to his horror he could never discover a man in the street who wore anything like his own dress. He would have given his soul for the ring of Gyges.° His dismay at his visibility had blunted the fears of mortality. 'Do you think,' he said, 'I am in such great terror of being shot,—I, who am only waiting to shuffle off my corporeal jacket, to slip away into the back stars, and put diameters of the solar system and sidereal orbits between me and all souls,—there to wear out ages in solitude, and forget memory itself, if it be possible?' He had a remorse running to despair, of his social *gaucheries*, and walked miles and miles to get the twitchings out of his face, the starts and shrugs out of his arms and shoulders. God may forgive sins, he said, but awkwardness has no forgiveness in heaven or earth. He admired in Newton, not so much his theory of the moon, as his letter to Collins, in which he forbade him to insert his name with the solution of the problem in the 'Philosophical Transactions': 'It would perhaps increase my acquaintance, the thing which I chiefly study to decline.'°

These conversations led me somewhat later to the knowledge of similar cases, and to the discovery that they are not of very infrequent occurrence. Few substances are found pure in nature. Those constitutions which can bear in open day the rough dealing of the world must be of that mean and average structure,—such as iron and salt, atmospheric air, and water. But there are metals, like potassium and sodium, which, to be kept pure, must be kept under naphtha. Such are the talents determined on some specialty, which a culminating civilization fosters in the heart of great cities and in royal chambers. Nature protects her own work. To the culture of the world, an Archimedes, a Newton is indispensable; so she guards them by a certain aridity. If these had been good fellows, fond of dancing, port, and clubs, we should have had no 'Theory of the Sphere,' and no 'Principia.'° They had that necessity of isolation which genius feels. Each must stand on his glass tripod, if he would keep his electricity. Even Swedenborg, whose theory of the universe is based on affection, and who reprobates to weariness the danger and vice of pure intellect, is constrained to make an extraordinary exception: 'There are also angels who do not live consociated, but separate, house and house; these dwell in the midst of heaven, because they are the best of angels.'°

We have known many fine geniuses with that imperfection that they cannot do anything useful, not so much as write one clean sentence. 'T is worse, and tragic, that no man is fit for society who has fine traits. At a distance, he is admired; but bring him hand to hand, he is a cripple. One protects himself by solitude, and one by courtesy, and one by an acid, worldly manner,—each concealing how he can the thinness of his skin and his incapacity for strict association. But there is no remedy that can reach the heart of the disease, but either habits of self-reliance that should go in practice to making the man independent of the human race, or else a religion of love. Now he hardly seems entitled to marry; for how can he protect a woman, who cannot protect himself?

We pray to be conventional. But the wary Heaven takes care you shall not be, if there is anything good in you. Dante was very bad company, and was never invited to dinner. Michel Angelo had a sad, sour time of it. The ministers of beauty are rarely beautiful in coaches and saloons. Columbus discovered no isle or key so lonely as himself. Yet each of these potentates saw well the reason of his exclusion. Solitary was he? Why, yes; but his society was limited only by the amount of brain Nature appropriated in that age to carry on the government of the world. 'If I stay,' said Dante, when there was question of going to Rome, 'who will go? and if I go, who will stay?'°

But the necessity of solitude is deeper than we have said, and is organic. I have seen many a philosopher whose world is large enough for only one person. He affects to be a good companion; but we are still surprising his secret, that he means and needs to impose his system on all the rest. The determination of each is *from* all the others, like that of each tree up into free space. 'T is no wonder, when each has his whole head, our societies should be so small. Like President Tyler,° our party falls from us every day, and we must ride in a sulky at last. Dear heart! take it sadly home to thee,—there is no co-operation. We begin with friendships, and all our youth is a reconnoitring and recruiting of the holy fraternity they shall combine for the salvation of men. But so the remoter stars seem a nebula of united light; yet there is no group which a telescope will not resolve, and the dearest friends are separated by impassable gulfs. The co-operation is involuntary, and is put upon us by the Genius of Life, who reserves this as a part of his prerogative. 'T is fine for us to talk; we sit and muse, and are serene and complete; but the moment we meet with anybody, each becomes a fraction.

Though the stuff of tragedy and of romances is in a moral union of two superior persons, whose confidence in each other for long years, out of sight, and in sight, and against all appearances, is at last justified by victorious proof of probity to gods and men, causing joyful emotions, tears and glory,—though there be for heroes this *moral union*, yet, they, too, are as far off as ever from an intellectual union, and the moral union is for comparatively low and external purposes, like the co-operation of a ship's company or of a fire-club. But how insular and pathetically solitary are all the people we know! Nor dare they tell what they think of each other, when they meet in the street. We have a fine right, to be sure, to taunt men of the world with superficial and treacherous courtesies!

Such is the tragic necessity which strict science finds underneath our domestic and neighborly life, irresistibly driving each adult soul as with whips into the desert, and making our warm covenants sentimental and momentary. We must infer that the ends of thought were peremptory, if they were to be secured at such ruinous cost. They are deeper than can be told, and belong to the immensities and eternities. They reach down to that depth where society itself originates and disappears,—where the question is, Which is first, man or men?—where the individual is lost in his source.

But this banishment to the rocks and echoes no metaphysics can make right or tolerable. This result is so against nature, such a half-view, that it must be corrected by a common sense and experience. 'A man is born by the side of his father, and there he remains.' A man must be clothed with society, or we shall feel a certain bareness and poverty, as of a displaced and unfurnished member. He is to be dressed in arts and institutions, as well as in body-garments. Now and then a man exquisitely made can live alone, and must; but coop up most men, and you undo them. 'The king lived and ate in his hall with men, and understood men,' said Selden.° When a young barrister said to the late Mr. Mason, 'I keep my chamber to read law,'—'Read law!' replied the veteran, ''t is in the courtroom you must read law.'° Nor is the rule otherwise for literature. If you would learn to write, 't is in the street you must learn it. Both for the vehicle and for the aims of fine arts, you must frequent the public square. The people, and not the college, is the writer's home. A scholar is a candle which the love and desire of all men will light. Never his lands or his rents, but the power to charm the disguised soul that sits veiled under this bearded and that rosy visage is his rent and ration. His products are as needful as those of the baker or the weaver. Society cannot do without cultivated men. As soon as the first wants are satisfied, the higher wants become imperative.

'T is hard to mesmerize ourselves, to whip our own top; but through sympathy we are capable of energy and endurance. Concert fires people to a certain fury of performance they can rarely reach alone. Here is the use of society: it is so easy with the great to be great; so easy to come up to an existing standard;—as easy as it is to the lover to swim to his maiden through waves so grim before. The benefits of affection are immense; and the one event which never loses its romance is the encounter with superior persons on terms allowing the happiest intercourse.

It by no means follows that we are not fit for society, because *soirées* are tedious, and because the *soirée* finds us tedious. A backwoodsman, who had been sent to the university, told me that, when he heard the best-bred young men at the law-school talk together, he reckoned himself a boor; but whenever he caught them apart, and had one to himself alone, then they were the boors, and he the better man. And if we recall the rare hours when we encountered the best persons, we then found ourselves, and then first society seemed to exist. That was society, though in the transom of a brig, or on the Florida Keys.°

A cold, sluggish blood thinks it has not facts enough to the purpose, and must decline its turn in the conversation. But they who speak have no more,—have less. 'T is not new facts that avail, but the heat to dissolve everybody's facts. Heat puts you in right relation with magazines of facts. The capital defect of cold, arid natures is the want of animal spirits. They seem a power incredible, as if God should raise the dead. The recluse witnesses what others perform by their aid, with a kind of fear. It is as much out of his possibility as the prowess of Cœur-de-Lion,° or an Irishman's day's-work on the railroad. 'T is said, the present and the future are always rivals. Animal spirits constitute the power of the present, and their feats are like the structure of a pyramid. Their result is a lord, a general, or a boon companion. Before these, what a base mendicant is Memory with his leathern badge! But this genial heat is latent in all constitutions, and is disengaged only by the friction of society. As Bacon said of manners, 'To obtain them, it only needs not to despise them,'° so we say of animal spirits, that they are the spontaneous product of health and of a social habit. 'For behavior, men learn it, as they take diseases, one of another.'°

But the people are to be taken in very small doses. If solitude is proud, so is society vulgar. In society, high advantages are set down to the individual as disqualifications. We sink as easily as we rise, through sympathy. So many men whom I know are degraded by their sympathies, their native aims being high enough, but their relation all too tender to the gross people about them. Men cannot afford to live together on their merits, and they adjust themselves by their demerits,—by their love of gossip, or by sheer tolerance and animal good-nature. They untune and dissipate the brave aspirant.

The remedy is, to reinforce each of these moods from the other. Conversation will not corrupt us, if we come to the assembly in our own garb and speech, and with the energy of health to select what is ours and reject what is not. Society we must have; but let it be society, and not exchanging news, or eating from the same dish. Is it society to sit in one of your chairs? I cannot go to the houses of my nearest relatives, because I do not wish to be alone. Society exists by chemical affinity, and not otherwise.

Put any company of people together with freedom for conversation, and a rapid self-distribution takes place, into sets and pairs. The best are accused of exclusiveness. It would be more true to say, they separate as oil from water, as children from old people, without love or hatred in the matter, each seeking his like; and any interference with the affinities would produce constraint and suffocation. All conversation is a magnetic experiment. I know that my friend can talk eloquently; you know that he cannot articulate a sentence: we have seen him in different company. Assort your party, or invite none. Put Stubbs and Coleridge, Quintilian and Aunt Miriam, into pairs, and you make them all wretched.° 'T is an extempore Sing-Sing built in a parlor. Leave them to seek their own mates, and they will be as merry as sparrows.

A higher civility will re-establish in our customs a certain reverence which we have lost. What to do with these brisk young men who break through all fences, and make themselves at home in every house? I find out in an instant if my companion does not want me, and ropes cannot hold me when my welcome is gone. One would think that the affinities would pronounce themselves with a surer reciprocity.

Here again, as so often, Nature delights to put us between extreme antagonisms, and our safety is in the skill with which we keep the diagonal line. Solitude is impracticable, and society fatal. We must keep our head in the one and our hands in the other. The conditions are met, if we keep our independence, yet do not lose our sympathy. These wonderful horses need to be driven by fine hands. We require such a solitude as shall hold us to its revelations when we are in the street and in palaces; for most men are cowed in society, and say good things to you in private, but will not stand to them in public. But let us not be the victims of words. Society and solitude are deceptive names. It is not the circumstance of seeing more or fewer people, but the readiness of sympathy, that imports; and a sound mind will derive its principles from insight, with ever a purer ascent to the sufficient and absolute right, and will accept society as the natural element in which they are to be applied.

LETTERS AND SOCIAL AIMS
(1876)

QUOTATION AND ORIGINALITY

WHOEVER looks at the insect world, at flies, aphides, gnats, and innumerable parasites, and even at the infant mammals, must have remarked the extreme content they take in suction, which constitutes the main business of their life. If we go into a library or news-room, we see the same function on a higher plane, performed with like ardor, with equal impatience of interruption, indicating the sweetness of the act. In the highest civilization the book is still the highest delight. He who has once known its satisfactions is provided with a resource against calamity. Like Plato's disciple who has perceived a truth, 'he is pre-served from harm until another period.'° In every man's memory, with the hours when life culminated are usually associated certain books which met his views. Of a large and powerful class we might ask with confidence, What is the event they most desire? what gift? What but the book that shall come, which they have sought through all libraries, through all languages, that shall be to their mature eyes what many a tinsel-covered toy pamphlet was to their childhood, and shall speak to the imagination? Our high respect for a well-read man is praise enough of literature. If we encountered a man of rare intellect, we should ask him what books he read. We expect a great man to be a good reader; or in proportion to the spontaneous power should be the assimilating power. And though such are a more difficult and exacting class, they are not less eager. 'He that borrows the aid of an equal understanding,' said Burke, 'doubles his own; he that uses that of a superior elevates his own to the stature of that he contemplates.'°

We prize books, and they prize them most who are themselves wise. Our debt to tradition through reading and conversation is so massive, our protest or private addition so rare and insignificant,—and this com-monly on the ground of other reading or hearing,—that, in a large sense, one would say there is no pure originality. All minds quote. Old and new make the warp and woof of every moment. There is no thread that is not a twist of these two strands. By necessity, by proclivity, and by delight, we all quote. We quote not only books and proverbs, but arts, sciences, religion, customs, and laws; nay, we quote temples and houses, tables and chairs by imitation. The Patent-Office Com-missioner knows that all machines in use have been invented and reinvented over and over; that the mariner's compass, the boat, the pendulum, glass, movable types, the kaleidoscope, the railway, the power-loom, etc., have been many times found and lost, from Egypt,

China, and Pompeii down; and if we have arts which Rome wanted, so also Rome had arts which we have lost; that the invention of yesterday of making wood indestructible by means of vapor of coal-oil or paraffine was suggested by the Egyptian method which has preserved its mummy-cases four thousand years.

The highest statement of new philosophy complacently caps itself with some prophetic maxim from the oldest learning. There is something mortifying in this perpetual circle. This extreme economy argues a very small capital of invention. The stream of affection flows broad and strong; the practical activity is a river of supply; but the dearth of design accuses the penury of intellect. How few thoughts! In a hundred years, millions of men, and not a hundred lines of poetry, not a theory of philosophy that offers a solution of the great problems, not an art of education that fulfils the conditions. In this delay and vacancy of thought we must make the best amends we can by seeking the wisdom of others to fill the time.

If we confine ourselves to literature, 't is easy to see that the debt is immense to past thought. None escapes it. The originals are not original. There is imitation, model, and suggestion, to the very archangels, if we knew their history. The first book tyrannizes over the second. Read Tasso,° and you think of Virgil; read Virgil, and you think of Homer; and Milton forces you to reflect how narrow are the limits of human invention. The 'Paradise Lost' had never existed but for these precursors; and if we find in India or Arabia a book out of our horizon of thought and tradition, we are soon taught by new researches in its native country to discover its foregoers, and its latent, but real connection with our own Bibles.

Read in Plato, and you shall find Christian dogmas, and not only so, but stumble on our evangelical phrases. Hegel pre-exists in Proclus, and, long before, in Heraclitus and Parmenides. Whoso knows Plutarch, Lucian, Rabelais, Montaigne, and Bayle° will have a key to many supposed originalities. Rabelais is the source of many a proverb, story, and jest, derived from him into all modern languages; and if we knew Rabelais's reading, we should see the rill of the Rabelais river. Swedenborg, Behmen, Spinoza,° will appear original to uninstructed and to thoughtless persons: their originality will disappear to such as are either well-read or thoughtful; for scholars will recognize their dogmas as reappearing in men of a similar intellectual elevation throughout history. Albert, the 'wonderful doctor,' St. Buonaventura, the 'seraphic doctor,' Thomas Aquinas, the 'angelic doctor' of the thirteenth century, whose books made the sufficient culture of these ages, Dante absorbed and he survives for us. 'Renard the Fox,' a German poem of the thirteenth century, was long supposed to be the original work, until Grimm found fragments of another original a century older. M. Le Grand showed that in the old Fabliaux were the originals of the tales of Molière, La Fontaine, Boccaccio, and of Voltaire.°

Mythology is no man's work; but, what we daily observe in regard to the *bon-mots* that circulate in society,—that every talker helps a story in repeating it, until, at last, from the slenderest filament of fact a good fable is constructed,—the same growth befalls mythology: the legend is tossed from believer to poet, from poet to believer, everybody adding a grace or dropping a fault or rounding the form, until it gets an ideal truth.

Religious literature, the psalms and liturgies of churches, are of course of this slow growth,—a fagot of selections gathered through ages, leaving the worse, and saving the better, until it is at last the work of the whole communion of worshippers. The Bible itself is like an old Cremona;° it has been played upon by the devotion of thousands of years, until every word and particle is public and tunable. And whatever undue reverence may have been claimed for it by the prestige of philonic inspiration,° the stronger tendency we are describing is likely to undo. What divines had assumed as the distinctive revelations of Christianity, theologic criticism has matched by exact parallelisms from the Stoics and poets of Greece and Rome. Later, when Confucius and the Indian scriptures were made known, no claim to monopoly of ethical wisdom could be thought of; and the surprising results of the new researches into the history of Egypt have opened to us the deep debt of the churches of Rome and England to the Egyptian hierology.

The borrowing is often honest enough, and comes of magnanimity and stoutness. A great man quotes bravely and will not draw on his invention when his memory serves him with a word as good. What he quotes, he fills with his own voice and humor, and the whole cyclopædia of his table-talk is presently believed to be his own. Thirty years ago, when Mr. Webster at the bar or in the Senate filled the eyes and minds of young men, you might often hear cited as Mr. Webster's three rules: first, never to do to-day what he could defer till to-morrow; secondly, never to do himself what he could make another do for him; and, thirdly, never to pay any debt to-day. Well, they are none the worse for being already told, in the last generation, of Sheridan; and we find in Grimm's *Mémoires* that Sheridan got them from the witty D'Argenson;° who, no doubt, if we could consult him, could tell of whom he first heard them told. In our own college days we remember hearing other pieces of Mr. Webster's advice to students,—among others, this: that, when he opened a new book, he turned to the table of contents, took a pen, and sketched a sheet of matters and topics,—what he knew and what he thought,—before he read the book. But we find in Southey's 'Commonplace Book' this said of the Earl of Strafford: 'I learned one rule of him,' says Sir G. Radcliffe,° 'which I think worthy to be remembered. When he met with a well-penned oration or tract upon any subject, he framed a speech upon the same argument, inventing and disposing what seemed fit to be said upon that subject, before he read the book; then, reading, compared his own with the author's, and noted his own defects and the author's art and fulness; whereby he drew all that ran in the author more strictly, and might better judge of his own wants to supply them.' I remember to have heard Mr. Samuel Rogers, in London, relate, among other anecdotes of the Duke of Wellington,° that a lady having expressed in his presence a passionate wish to witness a great victory, he replied: 'Madam, there is nothing so dreadful as a great victory,—excepting a great defeat.' But this speech is also D'Argenson's, and is reported by Grimm. So the sarcasm attributed to Lord Eldon upon Brougham,° his predecessor on the woolsack, 'What a wonderful versatile mind has Brougham! he knows politics, Greek, history, science; if he only knew a little of law, he would know a little of everything.' You may find the original of this gibe in Grimm, who says that Louis XVI., going out of chapel after hearing a sermon from the Abbé Maury,° said, '*Si l'Abbé nous avait parlé un peu de religion, il nous aurait parlé de tout.*'° A pleasantry which ran through all the newspapers a few years since, taxing the eccentricities of a gifted family connection in New England, was only a theft of Lady Mary Wortley Montagu's° *mot* of a hundred years ago, that 'the world was made up of men and women and Herveys.'°

Many of the historical proverbs have a doubtful paternity. Columbus's egg is claimed for Brunelleschi.° Rabelais's dying words, 'I am going to see the great Perhaps' (*le grand Peut-être*), only repeats the 'IF' inscribed on the portal of the temple at Delphi.° Goethe's favorite phrase, 'the open secret,' translates Aristotle's answer to Alexander, 'These books are published and not published.'° Madame de Staël's 'Architecture is frozen music' is borrowed from Goethe's 'dumb music,'° which is Vitruvius's rule, that 'the architect must not only understand drawing, but music.' Wordsworth's hero acting 'on the plan which pleased his childish thought,' is Schiller's 'Tell him to reverence the dreams of his youth,' and earlier, Bacon's '*Consilia juventutis plus divinitatis habent.*'°

In romantic literature examples of this vamping abound. The fine verse in the old Scotch ballad of 'The Drowned Lovers,'°

> 'Thou art roaring ower loud, Clyde water,
>   Thy streams are ower strang;
> Make me thy wrack when I come back,
>   But spare me when I gang,'

is a translation of Martial's epigram° on Hero and Leander, where the prayer of Leander is the same:—

> 'Parcite dum propero, mergite dum redeo.'

Hafiz furnished Burns with the song of 'John Barleycorn,' and furnished Moore with the original of the piece,

> 'When in death I shall calm recline,
> Oh, bear my heart to my mistress dear,' etc.

There are many fables which, as they are found in every language, and betray no sign of being borrowed, are said to be agreeable to the human mind. Such are 'The Seven Sleepers,' 'Gyges's Ring,' 'The Travelling Cloak,' 'The Wandering Jew,' 'The Pied Piper,' 'Jack and his Beanstalk,' the 'Lady Diving in the Lake and Rising in the Cave,'°—whose omnipresence only indicates how easily a good story crosses all frontiers. The popular incident of Baron Munchausen,° who hung his bugle up by the kitchen fire, and the frozen tune thawed out, is found in Greece in Plato's time. Antiphanes,° one of Plato's friends, laughingly compared his writings to a city where the words froze in the air as soon as they were pronounced, and the next summer, when they were warmed and melted by the sun, the people heard what had been spoken in the winter. It is only within this century that England and America discovered that their nursery-tales were old German and Scandinavian stories; and now it appears that they came from India, and are the property of all the nations descended from the Aryan race, and have been warbled and babbled between nurses and children for unknown thousands of years.

If we observe the tenacity with which nations cling to their first types of costume, of architecture, of tools and methods in tillage, and of decoration,—if we learn how old are the patterns of our shawls, the capitals of our columns, the fret, the beads, and other ornaments on our walls, the alternate lotus-bud and leaf-stem of our iron fences,—we shall think very well of the first men, or ill of the latest.

Now shall we say that only the first men were well alive, and the existing generation is invalided and degenerate? Is all literature eavesdropping, and all art Chinese imitation? our life a custom, and our body borrowed, like a beggar's dinner, from a hundred charities? A more subtle and severe criticism might suggest that some dislocation has befallen the race; that men are off their centre; that multitudes of men do not live with Nature, but behold it as exiles. People go out to look at sunrises and sunsets who do not recognize their own quietly and happily, but know that it is foreign to them. As they do by books, so they *quote* the sunset and the star, and do not make them theirs. Worse yet, they live as foreigners in the world of truth, and quote thoughts, and thus disown them. Quotation confesses inferiority. In opening a new book we often discover, from the unguarded devotion with which the writer gives his motto or text, all we have to expect from him. If Lord Bacon appears already in the preface, I go and read the 'Instauration'° instead of the new book.

The mischief is quickly punished in general and in particular. Admirable mimics have nothing of their own. In every kind of parasite, when Nature has finished an aphis, a teredo, or a vampire bat,—an excellent sucking-pipe to tap another animal, or a mistletoe or dodder among plants,—the self-supplying organs wither and dwindle, as being superfluous. In common prudence there is an early limit to this leaning on an original. In literature quotation is good only when the writer whom I follow goes my way, and, being better mounted than I, gives me a cast, as we say; but if I like the gay equipage so well as to go out of my road, I had better have gone afoot.

But it is necessary to remember there are certain considerations which go far to qualify a reproach too grave. This vast mental indebtedness has every variety that pecuniary debt has,—every variety of merit. The capitalist of either kind is as hungry to lend as the consumer to borrow; and the transaction no more indicates intellectual turpitude in the borrower than the simple fact of debt involves bankruptcy. On the contrary, in far the greater number of cases the transaction is honorable to both. Can we not help ourselves as discreetly by the force of two in literature? Certainly it only needs two well placed and well tempered for co-operation, to get somewhat far transcending any private enterprise! Shall we converse as spies? Our very abstaining to repeat and credit the fine remark of our friend is thievish. Each man of thought is surrounded by wiser men than he, if they cannot write as well. Cannot he and they combine? Cannot they sink their jealousies in God's love, and call their poem Beaumont and Fletcher,° or the Theban Phalanx's? The city will for nine days or nine years make differences and sinister comparisons: there is a new and more excellent public that will bless the friends. Nay, it is an inevitable fruit of our social nature. The child quotes his father, and the man quotes his friend. Each man is a hero and an oracle to somebody, and to that person whatever he says has an enhanced value. Whatever we think and say is wonderfully better for our spirits and trust in another mouth. There is none so eminent and wise but he knows minds whose opinion confirms or qualifies his own: and men of extraordinary genius acquire an almost absolute ascendant over their nearest companions. The Comte de Crillon said one day to M. d'Allonville, with French vivacity, 'If the universe and I professed one opinion, and M. Necker° expressed a contrary one, I should be at once convinced that the universe and I were mistaken.'

Original power is usually accompanied with assimilating power, and we value in Coleridge his excellent knowledge and quotations perhaps as much, possibly more, than his original suggestions. If an author give us just distinctions, inspiring lessons, or imaginative poetry, it is not so important to us whose they are. If we are fired and guided by these, we know him as a benefactor, and shall return to him as long as he serves us so well. We may like well to know what is Plato's and what is Montesquieu's or Goethe's part, and what thought was always dear to the writer himself; but the worth of the sentences consists in their radiancy and equal aptitude to all intelligence. They fit all our facts like a charm. We respect ourselves the more that we know them.

Next to the originator of a good sentence is the first quoter of it. Many will read the book before one thinks of quoting a passage. As soon as he has done this, that line will be quoted east and west. Then there are great ways of borrowing. Genius borrows nobly. When Shakspeare is charged with debts to his authors, Landor° replies: 'Yet he was more original than his originals. He breathed upon dead bodies and brought them into life.' And we must thank Karl Ottfried Müller° for the just remark, 'Poesy, drawing within its circle all that is glorious and inspiring, gave itself but little concern as to where its flowers originally grew.' So Voltaire usually imitated, but with such superiority that Dubuc° said: 'He is like the false Amphitryon;° although the stranger, it is always he who has the air of being master of the house.' Wordsworth, as soon as he heard a good thing, caught it up, meditated upon it, and very soon reproduced it in his conversation and writing. If De Quincey° said, 'That is what I told you,' he replied, 'No: that is mine,—mine, and not yours.' On the whole, we like the valor of it. 'T is on Marmontel's° principle, 'I pounce on what is mine, wherever I find it'; and on Bacon's broader rule, 'I take all knowledge to be my province.'° It betrays the consciousness that truth is the property of no individual, but is the treasure of all men. And inasmuch as any writer has ascended to a just view of man's condition, he has adopted this tone. In so far as the receiver's aim is on life, and not on literature, will be his indifference to the source. The nobler the truth or sentiment, the less imports the question of authorship. It never troubles the simple seeker from whom he derived such or such a sentiment. Whoever expresses to us a just thought makes ridiculous the pains of the critic who should tell him where such a word had been said before. 'It is no more according to Plato than according to me.' Truth is always present: it only needs to lift the iron lids of the mind's eye to read its oracles. But the moment there is the purpose of display, the fraud is exposed. In fact, it is as difficult to appropriate the thoughts of others, as it is to invent. Always some steep transition, some sudden alteration of temperature, of point or of view, betrays the foreign interpolation.

There is, besides, a new charm in such intellectual works as, passing through long time, have had a multitude of authors and improvers. We admire that poetry which no man wrote,—no poet less than the genius of humanity itself,—which is to be read in a mythology, in the effect of a fixed or national style of pictures, of sculptures, or drama, or cities, or sciences, on us. Such a poem also is language. Every word in the language has once been used happily. The ear, caught by that felicity, retains it, and it is used again and again, as if the charm belonged to the word, and not to the life of thought which so enforced it. These profane uses, of course, kill it, and it is avoided. But a quick wit can at any time reinforce it, and it comes into vogue again. Then people quote so differently: one finding only what is gaudy and popular; another, the heart of the author, the report of his select and happiest hour: and the reader sometimes giving more to the citation than he owes to it. Most of the classical citations you shall hear or read in the current journals or speeches were not drawn from the originals, but from previous quotations in English books; and you can easily pronounce, from the use and relevancy of the sentence, whether it had not done duty many times before,—whether your jewel was got from the mine or from an auctioneer. We are as much informed of a writer's genius by what he selects as by what he originates. We read the quotation with his eyes, and find a new and fervent sense; as a passage from one of the poets, well recited, borrows new interest from the rendering. As the journals say, 'the italics are ours.' The profit of books is according to the sensibility of the reader. The profoundest thought or passion sleeps as in a mine, until an equal mind and heart finds and publishes it. The passages of Shakspeare that we most prize were never quoted until within this century;

and Milton's prose, and Burke, even, have their best fame within it. Every one, too, remembers his friends by their favorite poetry or other reading.

Observe, also, that a writer appears to more advantage in the pages of another book than in his own. In his own, he waits as a candidate for your approbation; in another's, he is a lawgiver.

Then another's thoughts have a certain advantage with us simply because they are another's. There is an illusion in a new phrase. A man hears a fine sentence out of Swedenborg, and wonders at the wisdom, and is very merry at heart that he has now got so fine a thing. Translate it out of the new words into his own usual phrase, and he will wonder again at his own simplicity, such tricks do fine words play with us.

'T is curious what new interest an old author acquires by official canonization in Tiraboschi, or Dr. Johnson, or Von Hammer-Purgstall, or Hallam,° or other historian of literature. Their registration of his book, or citation of a passage, carries the sentimental value of a college diploma. Hallam, though never profound, is a fair mind, able to appreciate poetry, unless it becomes deep, being always blind and deaf to imaginative and analogy-loving souls, like the Platonists, like Giordano Bruno,° like Donne, Herbert, Crashaw, and Vaughan; and Hallam cites a sentence from Bacon or Sidney, and distinguishes a lyric of Edwards or Vaux,° and straightway it commends itself to us as if it had received the Isthmian crown.°

It is a familiar expedient of brilliant writers, and not less of witty talkers, the device of ascribing their own sentence to an imaginary person, in order to give it weight,—as Cicero, Cowley, Swift, Landor, and Carlyle have done. And Cardinal de Retz,° at a critical moment in the Parliament of Paris, described himself in an extemporary Latin sentence, which he pretended to quote from a classic author, and which told admirably well. It is a curious reflex effect of this enhancement of our thought by citing it from another, that many men can write better under a mask than for themselves,—as Chatterton in archaic ballad, Le Sage in Spanish costume, Macpherson as 'Ossian,'°—and, I doubt not, many a young barrister in chambers in London, who forges good thunder for the 'Times,' but never works as well under his own name. This is a sort of dramatizing talent; as it is not rare to find great powers of recitation, without the least original eloquence,—or people who copy drawings with admirable skill, but are incapable of any design.

In hours of high mental activity we sometimes do the book too much honor, reading out of it better things than the author wrote,—reading, as we say, between the lines. You have had the like experience in conversation: the wit was in what you heard, not in what the speakers said. Our best thought came from others. We heard in their words a deeper sense than the speakers put into them, and could express ourselves in other people's phrases to finer purpose than they knew. In Moore's Diary, Mr. Hallam is reported as mentioning at dinner one of his friends who had said, 'I don't know how it is, a thing that falls flat from me seems quite an excellent joke when given at second-hand by Sheridan. I never like my own *bon-mots* until he adopts them.'° Dumont was exalted by being used by Mirabeau, by Bentham, and by Sir Philip Francis, who, again, was less than his own 'Junius';° and James Hogg (except in his poems 'Kilmeny' and 'The Witch of Fife') is but a third-rate author, owing his fame to his effigy colossalized through the lens of John Wilson,—who, again, writes better under the domino of 'Christopher North' than in his proper clothes.° The bold theory of Delia Bacon,° that Shakspeare's plays were written by a society of wits,—by Sir Walter Raleigh, Lord Bacon, and others around the Earl of Southampton,—had plainly for her the charm of the superior meaning they would acquire when read under this light; this idea of the authorship controlling our appreciation of the works themselves. We once knew a man overjoyed at the notice of his pamphlet in a leading newspaper. What range he gave his imagination! Who could have written it? Was it not Colonel Carbine, or Senator Tonitrus, or, at the least, Professor Maximilian? Yes, he could detect in the style that fine Roman hand. How it seemed the very voice of the refined and discerning public, inviting merit at last to consent to fame, and come up and take place in the reserved and authentic chairs! He carried the journal with haste to the sympathizing Cousin Matilda, who is so proud of all we do. But what dismay, when the good Matilda, pleased with his pleasure, confessed she had written the criticism, and carried it with her own hands to the post-office! 'Mr. Wordsworth,' said Charles Lamb,° 'allow me to introduce to you my only admirer.'

Swedenborg threw a formidable theory into the world, that every soul existed in a society of souls, from which all its thoughts passed into it, as the blood of the mother circulates in her unborn child; and he noticed that, when in his bed,—alternately sleeping and waking,—sleeping, he was surrounded by persons disputing and offering opinions on the one side and on the other side of a proposition; waking, the like suggestions occurred for and against the proposition as his own thoughts; sleeping again, he saw and heard the speakers as before: and this as often as he slept or waked. And if we expand the image, does it not look as if we men were thinking and talking out of an enormous antiquity, as if we stood, not in a coterie of prompters that filled a sitting-room, but in a circle of intelligences that reached through all thinkers, poets, inventors, and wits, men and women, English, German, Celt, Aryan, Ninevite, Copt,—back to the first geometer, bard, mason, carpenter, planter, shepherd,—back to the first negro, who, with more health or better perception, gave a shriller sound or name for the thing he saw and dealt with? Our benefactors are as many as the children who invented speech, word by word. Language is a city, to the building of which every human being brought a stone; yet he is no more to be credited with the grand result than the acaleph which adds a cell to the coral reef which is the basis of the continent.

Πάντα ῥεῖ: all things are in flux.° It is inevitable that you are indebted to the past. You are fed and formed by it. The old forest is decomposed for the composition of the new forest. The old animals have given their bodies to the earth to furnish through chemistry the forming race, and every individual is only a momentary fixation of what was yesterday another's, is to-day his, and will belong to a third tomorrow. So it is in thought. Our knowledge is the amassed thought and experience of innumerable minds: our language, our science, our religion, our opinions, our fancies we inherited. Our country, customs, laws, our ambitions, and our notions of fit and fair,—all these we never made; we found them ready-made; we but quote them. Goethe frankly said, 'What would remain to me if this art of appropriation were derogatory to genius? Every one of my writings has been furnished to me by a thousand different persons, a thousand things: wise and foolish have brought me, without suspecting it, the offering of their thoughts, faculties, and experience. My work is an aggregation of beings taken from the whole of nature; it bears the name of Goethe.'°

But there remains the indefeasible persistency of the individual to be himself. One leaf, one blade of grass, one meridian, does not resemble another. Every mind is different; and the more it is unfolded, the more pronounced is that difference. He must draw the elements into him for food, and, if they be granite and silex, will prefer them cooked by sun and rain, by time and art, to his hand. But, however received, these elements pass into the substance of his constitution, will be assimilated, and tend always to form, not a partisan, but a possessor of truth. To all that can be said of the preponderance of the Past, the single word Genius is a sufficient reply. The divine resides in the new. The divine never quotes, but is, and creates. The profound apprehension of the Present is Genius, which makes the Past forgotten. Genius believes its faintest presentiment against the testimony of all history; for it knows that facts are not ultimates, but that a state of mind is the ancestor of everything. And what is Originality? It is being, being one's self, and reporting accurately what we see and are. Genius is, in the first instance, sensibility, the capacity of receiving just impressions from the external world, and the power of co-ordinating these after the laws of thought. It implies Will, or original force, for their right distribution and expression. If to this the sentiment of piety be added, if the thinker feels that the thought most strictly his own is not his own, and recognizes the perpetual suggestion of the Supreme Intellect, the oldest thoughts become new and fertile whilst he speaks them.

Originals never lose their value. There is always in them a style and weight of speech, which the immanence of the oracle bestowed, and which cannot be counterfeited. Hence the permanence of the high poets. Plato, Cicero, and Plutarch cite the poets in the manner in which Scripture is quoted in our churches. A phrase or a single word is adduced, with honoring emphasis, from Pindar, Hesiod, or Euripedes,° as precluding all argument, because thus had they said: importing that the bard spoke not his own, but the words of some god. True poets have always ascended to this lofty platform, and met this expectation. Shakspeare, Milton, Wordsworth, were very conscious of their responsibilities. When a man thinks happily, he finds no foot-track in the field he traverses. All spontaneous thought is irrespective of all else. Pindar uses this haughty defiance, as if it were impossible to find his sources: 'There are many swift darts within my quiver, which have a voice for those with understanding; but to the crowd they need interpreters. He is gifted with genius who knoweth much by natural talent.'°

Our pleasure in seeing each mind take the subject to which it has a proper right is seen in mere fitness in time. He that comes second must needs quote him that comes first. The earliest describers of savage life, as Captain Cook's account of the Society Islands, or Alexander Henry's travels among our Indian tribes,° have a charm of truth and just point of view. Landsmen and sailors freshly come from the most civilized countries, and with no false expectation, no sentimentality yet about wild life, healthily receive and report what they saw,—seeing what they must, and using no choice; and no man suspects the superior merit of the description, until Chateaubriand, or Moore, or Campbell, or Byron,° or the artists arrive, and mix so much art with their picture that the incomparable advantage of the first narrative appears. For the same reason we dislike that the poet should choose an antique or far-fetched subject for his muse, as if he avowed want of insight. The great deal always with the nearest. Only as braveries of too prodigal power can we pardon it, when the life of genius is so redundant that out of petulance it flings its fire into some old mummy, and, lo! it walks and blushes again here in the street.

We cannot overstate our debt to the Past, but the moment has the supreme claim. The Past is for us; but the sole terms on which it can become ours are its subordination to the Present. Only an inventor knows how to borrow, and every man is or should be an inventor. We must not tamper with the organic motion of the soul. 'T is certain that thought has its own proper motion, and the hints which flash from it, the words overheard at unawares by the free mind, are trustworthy and fertile, when obeyed, and not perverted to low and selfish account. This vast memory is only raw material. The divine gift is ever the instant life, which receives and uses and creates, and can well bury the old in the omnipotency with which Nature decomposes all her harvest for recomposition.

POETRY AND IMAGINATION

THE perception of matter is made the common-sense, and for cause. This was the cradle, this the go-cart, of the human child. We must learn the homely laws of fire and water; we must feed, wash, plant, build. These are ends of necessity, and first in the order of nature. Poverty, frost, famine, disease, debt, are the beadles and guardsmen that hold us to common-sense. The intellect, yielded up to itself, cannot supersede this tyrannic necessity. The restraining grace of common-sense is the mark of all the valid minds,—of Æsop, Aristotle, Alfred,° Luther, Shakspeare, Cervantes, Franklin, Napoleon. The common-sense which does not meddle with the absolute, but takes things at their word,—things as they appear,—believes in the existence of matter, not because we can touch it, or conceive of it, but because it agrees with ourselves, and the universe does not jest with us, but is in earnest,—is the house of health and life. In spite of all the joys of poets and the joys of saints, the most imaginative and abstracted person never makes, with impunity, the least mistake in this particular,—never tries to kindle his oven with water, nor carries a torch into a powder-mill, nor seizes his wild charger by the tail. We should not pardon the blunder in another, nor endure it in ourselves.

But whilst we deal with this as finality, early hints are given that we are not to stay here; that we must be making ready to go;—a warning that this magnificent hotel and conveniency we call Nature is not final. First innuendoes, then broad hints, then smart taps, are given, suggesting that nothing stands still in nature but death; that the creation is on wheels, in transit, always passing into something else, streaming into something higher; that matter is not what it appears;—that chemistry can blow it all into gas. Faraday,° the most exact of natural philosophers, taught that when we should arrive at the monads, or primordial elements (the supposed little cubes or prisms of which all matter was built up), we should not find cubes, or prisms, or atoms, at all, but spherules of force. It was whispered that the globes of the universe were precipitates of something more subtle; nay, somewhat was murmured in our ear that dwindled astronomy into a toy;—that too was no finality;—only provisional,—a makeshift;—that under chemistry was power and purpose: power and purpose ride on matter to the last atom. It was steeped in thought,—did everywhere express thought; that, as great conquerors have burned their ships when once they were landed

on the wished-for shore, so the noble house of Nature we inhabit has
temporary uses, and we can afford to leave it one day. The ends of all
are moral, and therefore the beginnings are such. Thin or solid, everything is in flight. I believe this conviction makes the charm of
chemistry,—that we have the same avoirdupois matter in an alembic,
without a vestige of the old form; and in animal transformation not less,
as in grub and fly, in egg and bird, in embryo and man; everything
undressing and stealing away from its old into new form, and nothing
fast but those invisible cords which we call laws, on which all is strung.
Then we see that things wear different names and faces, but belong to
one family; that the secret cords, or laws, show their well-known virtue
through every variety,—be it animal, or plant, or planet,—and the
interest is gradually transferred from the forms to the lurking method.

This hint, however conveyed, upsets our politics, trade, customs,
marriages, nay, the common-sense side of religion and literature,
which are all founded on low nature,—on the clearest and most economical mode of administering the material world, considered as final.
The admission, never so covertly, that this is a makeshift, sets the dullest brain in ferment;—our little sir, from his first tottering steps,—as
soon as he can crow,—does not like to be practised upon, suspects that
some one is 'doing' him,—and, at this alarm, everything is compromised;—gunpowder is laid under every man's breakfast-table.

But whilst the man is startled by this closer inspection of the laws
of matter, his attention is called to the independent action of the
mind,—its strange suggestions and laws,—a certain tyranny which
springs up in his own thoughts, which have an order, method, and
beliefs of their own, very different from the order which this
common-sense uses.

Suppose there were in the ocean certain strong currents which drove
a ship, caught in them, with a force that no skill of sailing with the best
wind, and no strength of oars, or sails, or steam, could make any head
against, any more than against the current of Niagara: such currents—
so tyrannical—exist in thoughts, those finest and subtilest of all
waters,—that, as soon as once thought begins, it refuses to remember
whose brain it belongs to,—what country, tradition, or religion,—and
goes whirling off—swim we merrily°—in a direction self-chosen, by
law of thought, and not by law of kitchen clock or county committee. It
has its own polarity. One of these vortices or self-directions of thought
is the impulse to search resemblance, affinity, identity, in all its objects,
and hence our science, from its rudest to its most refined theories.

The electric word pronounced by John Hunter a hundred years

ago,—*arrested and progressive development*,°—indicating the way upward from the invisible protoplasm to the highest organisms,—gave the poetic key to Natural Science,—of which the theories of Geoffroy St. Hilaire, of Oken, of Goethe, of Agassiz, and Owen,° and Darwin, in zoölogy and botany, are the fruits,—a hint whose power is not yet exhausted, showing unity and perfect order in physics.

The hardest chemist, the severest analyzer, scornful of all but driest fact, is forced to keep the poetic curve of nature, and his result is like a myth of Theocritus.° All multiplicity rushes to be resolved into unity. Anatomy, osteology, exhibit arrested or progressive ascent in each kind; the lower pointing to the higher forms, the higher to the highest, from the fluid in an elastic sack, from radiate, mollusk, articulate, vertebrate,—up to man; as if the whole animal world were only a Hunterian museum to exhibit the genesis of mankind.

Identity of law, perfect order in physics, perfect parallelism between the laws of Nature and the laws of thought exist. In botany we have the like, the poetic perception of metamorphosis,—that the same vegetable point or eye which is the unit of the plant can be transformed at pleasure into every part, as bract, leaf, petal, stamen, pistil, or seed.

In geology, what a useful hint was given to the early inquirers on seeing in the possession of Professor Playfair° a bough of a fossil tree which was perfect wood at one end, and perfect mineral coal at the other. Natural objects, if individually described, and out of connection, are not yet known, since they are really parts of a symmetrical universe, like words of a sentence; and if their true order is found, the poet can read their divine significance orderly as in a Bible. Each animal or vegetable form remembers the next inferior, and predicts the next higher.

There is one animal, one plant, one matter, and one force. The laws of light and of heat translate each other;—so do the laws of sound and of color; and so galvanism, electricity, and magnetism are varied forms of the selfsame energy. While the student ponders this immense unity, he observes that all things in nature, the animals, the mountain, the river, the seasons, wood, iron, stone, vapor,—have a mysterious relation to his thoughts and his life; their growths, decays, quality, and use so curiously resemble himself, in parts and in wholes, that he is compelled to speak by means of them. His words and his thoughts are framed by their help. Every noun is an image. Nature gives him, sometimes in a flattered likeness, sometimes in caricature, a copy of every humor and shade in his character and mind. The world is an immense picture-book of every passage in human life. Every object he beholds is the mask of a man.

'The privates of man's heart
They speken and sound in his ear
As tho' they loud winds were';°

for the universe is full of their echoes.

Every correspondence we observe in mind and matter suggests a substance older and deeper than either of these old nobilities. We see the law gleaming through, like the sense of a half-translated ode of Hafiz.° The poet who plays with it with most boldness best justifies himself,—is most profound and most devout. Passion adds eyes,—is a magnifying-glass. Sonnets of lovers are mad enough, but are valuable to the philosopher, as are prayers of saints, for their potent symbolism.

Science was false by being unpoetical. It assumed to explain a reptile or mollusk, and isolated it,—which is hunting for life in graveyards. Reptile or mollusk or man or angel only exists in system, in relation. The metaphysician, the poet, only sees each animal form as an inevitable step in the path of the creating mind. The Indian, the hunter, the boy with his pets, have sweeter knowledge of these than the savant. We use semblances of logic until experience puts us in possession of real logic. The poet knows the missing link by the joy it gives. The poet gives us the eminent experiences only,—a god stepping from peak to peak, nor planting his foot but on a mountain.

Science does not know its debt to imagination. Goethe did not believe that a great naturalist could exist without this faculty. He was himself conscious of its help, which made him a prophet among the doctors. From this vision he gave brave hints to the zoölogist, the botanist, and the optician.

Poetry.—The primary use of a fact is low: the secondary use, as it is a figure or illustration of my thought, is the real worth. First, the fact; second, its impression, or what I think of it. Hence Nature was called 'a kind of adulterated reason.' Seas, forests, metals, diamonds, and fossils interest the eye, but 't is only with some preparatory or predicting charm. Their value to the intellect appears only when I hear their meaning made plain in the spiritual truth they cover. The mind, penetrated with its sentiment or its thought, projects it outward on whatever it beholds. The lover sees reminders of his mistress in every beautiful object; the saint, an argument for devotion in every natural process; and the facility with which Nature lends itself to the thoughts of man, the aptness with which a river, a flower, a bird, fire, day, or night, can express his fortunes, is as if the world were only a disguised man, and, with a change of form, rendered to him all his experience. We cannot utter a sentence in sprightly conversation without a similitude. Note our incessant use of the word *like*,—like fire, like a rock, like thunder, like a bee, 'like a year without a spring.' Conversation is not permitted without tropes; nothing but great weight in things can afford a quite literal speech. It is ever enlivened by inversion and trope. God himself does not speak prose, but communicates with us by hints, omens, inference, and dark resemblances in objects lying all around us.

Nothing so marks a man as imaginative expressions. A figurative statement arrests attention, and is remembered and repeated. How often has a phrase of this kind made a reputation. Pythagoras's Golden Sayings were such, and Socrates's, and Mirabeau's, and Burke's, and Bonaparte's. Genius thus makes the transfer from one part of Nature to a remote part, and betrays the rhymes and echoes that pole makes with pole. Imaginative minds cling to their images, and do not wish them rashly rendered into prose reality, as children resent your showing them that their doll Cinderella is nothing but pine wood and rags: and my young scholar does not wish to know what the leopard, the wolf, or Lucia,° signify in Dante's Inferno, but prefers to keep their veils on. Mark the delight of an audience in an image. When some familiar truth or fact appears in a new dress, mounted as on a fine horse, equipped with a grand pair of ballooning wings, we cannot enough testify our surprise and pleasure. It is like the new virtue shown in some unprized old property, as when a boy finds that his pocket-knife will attract steel filings and take up a needle; or when the old horse-block in the yard is found to be a Torso Hercules of the Phidian age. Vivacity of expression may indicate this high gift, even when the thought is of no great scope, as when Michel Angelo, praising the *terra cottas*, said, 'If this earth were to become marble, woe to the antiques!'° A happy symbol is a sort of evidence that your thought is just. I had rather have a good symbol of my thought, or a good analogy, than the suffrage of Kant or Plato. If you agree with me, or if Locke or Montesquieu agree, I may yet be wrong; but if the elm-tree thinks the same thing, if running water, if burning coal, if crystals, if alkalies, in their several fashions, say what I say, it must be true. Thus, a good symbol is the best argument, and is a missionary to persuade thousands. The Vedas, the Edda, the Koran,° are each remembered by their happiest figure. There is no more welcome gift to men than a new symbol. That satiates, transports, converts them. They assimilate themselves to it,—deal with it in all ways, and it will last a hundred years. Then comes a new genius, and brings another. Thus the Greek mythology called the sea 'the tear of Saturn.' The return of the soul to God was described as 'a flask of water broken in the sea.' Saint John gave us the Christian figure of 'souls washed in the blood of Christ.' The aged Michel Angelo indicates his perpetual study as in boyhood,—'I carry my satchel still.' Machiavel described the papacy as 'a stone inserted in the body of Italy to keep the wound open.' To the Parliament debating how to tax America, Burke exclaimed, 'Shear the wolf.' Our Kentuckian orator said of his dissent from his companion, 'I showed him the back of my hand.'° And our proverb of the courteous soldier reads: 'An iron hand in a velvet glove.'

This belief that the higher use of the material world is to furnish us types or pictures to express the thoughts of the mind is carried to its logical extreme by the Hindoos, who, following Buddha, have made it the central doctrine of their religion, that what we call Nature, the external world, has no real existence,—is only phenomenal. Youth, age, property, condition, events, persons,—self, even,—are successive *maias* (deceptions) through which Vishnu mocks and instructs the soul. I think Hindoo books the best gymnastics for the mind, as showing treatment. All European libraries might almost be read without the swing of this gigantic arm being suspected. But these Orientals deal with worlds and pebbles freely.

For the value of a trope is that the hearer is one; and indeed Nature itself is a vast trope, and all particular natures are tropes. As the bird alights on the bough,—then plunges into the air again, so the thoughts of God pause but for a moment in any form. All thinking is analogizing, and 't is the use of life to learn metonomy. The endless passing of one element into new forms, the incessant metamorphosis, explains the rank which the imagination holds in our catalogue of mental powers. The imagination is the reader of these forms. The poet accounts all productions and changes of Nature as the nouns of language, uses them representatively, too well pleased with their ulterior to value much their primary meaning. Every new object so seen gives a shock of agreeable surprise. The impressions on the imagination make the great days of life: the book, the landscape, or the personality which did not stay on the surface of the eye or ear, but penetrated to the inward sense, agitates us, and is not forgotten. Walking, working, or talking, the sole question is how many strokes vibrate on this mystic string,—how many diameters are drawn quite through from matter to spirit; for, whenever you enunciate a natural law, you discover that you have enunciated a law of the mind. Chemistry, geology, hydraulics, are secondary science. The atomic theory is only an interior process *produced*, as geometers say, or the effect of a foregone metaphysical theory. Swedenborg saw gravity to be only an external of the irresistible attractions of affection and faith. Mountains and oceans we think we understand:—yes, so long as they are contented to be such, and are safe with the geologist,—but when they are melted in Promethean alembics, and come out men, and then, melted again, come out words, without any abatement, but with an exaltation of power!—

In poetry we say we require the miracle. The bee flies among the flowers, and gets mint and marjoram, and generates a new product, which is not mint and marjoram, but honey; the chemist mixes hydrogen and oxygen to yield a new product, which is not these, but water; and the poet listens to conversation, and beholds all objects in nature, to give back, not them, but a new and transcendent whole.

Poetry is the perpetual endeavor to express the spirit of the thing, to pass the brute body, and search the life and reason which causes it to exist;—to see that the object is always flowing away, whilst the spirit or necessity which causes it subsists. Its essential mark is that it betrays in every word instant activity of mind, shown in new uses of every fact and image,—in preternatural quickness or perception of relations. All its words are poems. It is a presence of mind that gives a miraculous command of all means of uttering the thought and feeling of the moment. The poet squanders on the hour an amount of life that would more than furnish the seventy years of the man that stands next him.

The term genius, when used with emphasis, implies imagination; use of symbols, figurative speech. A deep insight will always, like Nature, ultimate its thought in a thing. As soon as a man masters a principle, and sees his facts in relation to it, fields, waters, skies, offer to clothe his thoughts in images. Then all men understand him: Parthian, Mede, Chinese, Spaniard, and Indian hear their own tongue. For he can now find symbols of universal significance, which are readily rendered into any dialect; as a painter, a sculptor, a musician, can in their several ways express the same sentiment of anger, or love, or religion.

The thoughts are few; the forms many; the large vocabulary or many-colored coat of the indigent unity. The savans° are chatty and vain,—but hold them hard to principle and definition, and they become mute and near-sighted. What is motion? what is beauty? what is matter? what is life? what is force? Push them hard, and they will not be loquacious. They will come to Plato, Proclus,° and Swedenborg. The invisible and imponderable is the sole fact. 'Why changes not the violet earth into musk?'° What is the term of the ever-flowing metamorphosis? I do not know what are the stoppages, but I see that a devouring unity changes all into that which changes not.

The act of imagination is ever attended by pure delight. It infuses a certain volatility and intoxication into all nature. It has a flute which sets the atoms of our frame in a dance. Our indeterminate size is a delicious secret which it reveals to us. The mountains begin to dislimn, and float in the air. In the presence and conversation of a true poet, teeming with images to express his enlarging thought, his person, his form, grows larger to our fascinated eyes. And thus begins that deification which all nations have made of their heroes in every kind,—saints, poets, law-givers, and warriors.

Imagination.—Whilst common-sense looks at things or visible nature as real and final facts, poetry, or the imagination which dictates it, is a second sight, looking through these, and using them as types or words for thoughts which they signify. Or is this belief a metaphysical whim of modern times, and quite too refined? On the contrary, it is as old as the human mind. Our best definition of poetry is one of the oldest sentences, and claims to come down to us from the Chaldæan Zoroaster, who wrote it thus: 'Poets are standing transporters, whose employment consists in speaking to the Father and to matter; in producing apparent imitations of unapparent natures, and inscribing things unapparent in the apparent fabrication of the world';° in other words, the world exists for thought: it is to make appear things which hide: mountains, crystals, plants, animals, are seen; that which makes them is not seen: these, then, are 'apparent copies of unapparent natures.' Bacon expressed the same sense in his definition, 'Poetry accommodates the shows of things to the desires of the mind';° and Swedenborg, when he said, 'There is nothing existing in human thought, even though relating to the most mysterious tenet of faith, but has combined with it a natural and sensuous image.' And again: 'Names, countries, nations, and the like are not at all known to those who are in heaven; they have no idea of such things, but of the realities signified thereby.' A symbol always stimulates the intellect; therefore is poetry ever the best reading. The very design of imagination is to domesticate us in another, in a celestial, nature.

This power is in the image because this power is in nature. It so affects, because it so is. All that is wondrous in Swedenborg is not his invention, but his extraordinary perception;—that he was necessitated so to see. The world realizes the mind. Better than images is seen through them. The selection of the image is no more arbitrary than the power and significance of the image. The selection must follow fate. Poetry, if perfected, is the only verity; is the speech of man after the real, and not after the apparent.

Or, shall we say that the imagination exists by sharing the ethereal currents? The poet contemplates the central identity, sees it undulate and roll this way and that, with divine flowings, through remotest things; and, following it, can detect essential resemblances in natures never before compared. He can class them so audaciously, because he is sensible of the sweep of the celestial stream, from which nothing is exempt. His own body is a fleeing apparition,—his personality as fugitive as the trope he employs. In certain hours we can almost pass our hand through our own body. I think the use or value of poetry to be the suggestion it affords of the flux or fugaciousness of the poet. The mind delights in measuring itself thus with matter, with history, and flouting both. A thought, any thought, pressed, followed, opened, dwarfs matter, custom, and all but itself. But this second sight does not necessarily impair the primary or common sense. Pindar° and Dante, yes, and the gray and timeworn sentences of Zoroaster, may all be parsed, though we do not parse them. The poet has a logic, though it be subtle. He observes higher laws than he transgresses. 'Poetry must first be good sense, though it is something better.'°

This union of first and second sight reads nature to the end of delight and of moral use. Men are imaginative, but not overpowered by it to the extent of confounding its suggestions with external facts. We live in both spheres, and must not mix them. Genius certifies its entire possession of its thought, by translating it into a fact which perfectly represents it, and is hereby education. Charles James Fox thought 'Poetry the great refreshment of the human mind,—the only thing, after all; that men first found out they had minds, by making and tasting poetry.'°

Man runs about restless and in pain when his condition or the objects about him do not fully match his thought. He wishes to be rich, to be old, to be young, that things may obey him. In the ocean, in fire, in the sky, in the forest, he finds facts adequate and as large as he. As his thoughts are deeper than he can fathom, so also are these. 'T is easier to read Sanscrit, to decipher the arrowhead character, than to interpret these familiar sights. 'T is even much to name them. Thus Thomson's 'Seasons'° and the best parts of many old and many new poets are simply enumerations by a person who felt the beauty of the common sights and sounds, without any attempt to draw a moral or affix a meaning.

The poet discovers that what men value as substances have a higher value as symbols; that Nature is the immense shadow of man. A man's action is only a picture-book of his creed. He does after what he believes. Your condition, your employment, is the fable of *you*. The world is thoroughly anthropomorphized, as if it had passed through the body and mind of man, and taken his mould and form. Indeed, good poetry is always personification, and heightens every species of force in nature by giving it a human volition. We are advertised that there is nothing to which he is not related; that everything is convertible into every other. The staff in this hand is the *radius vector* of the sun. The chemistry of this is the chemistry of that. Whatever one act we do, whatever one thing we learn, we are doing and learning all things,— marching in the direction of universal power. Every healthy mind is a true Alexander or Sesostris,° building a universal monarchy.

The senses imprison us, and we help them with metres as limitary,— with a pair of scales and a foot-rule, and a clock. How long it took to find out what a day was, or what this sun, that makes days! It cost thousands of years only to make the motion of the earth suspected. Slowly, by comparing thousands of observations, there dawned on some mind a theory of the sun,—and we found the astronomical fact. But the astronomy is in the mind: the senses affirm that the earth stands still and the sun moves. The senses collect the surface facts of matter. The intellect acts on these brute reports, and obtains from them results which are the essence or intellectual form of the experiences. It compares, distributes, generalizes, and uplifts them into its own sphere. It knows that these transfigured results are not the brute experiences, just as souls in heaven are not the red bodies they once animated. Many transfigurations have befallen them. The atoms of the body were once nebulæ, then rock, then loam, then corn, then chyme, then chyle, then blood; and now the beholding and co-energizing mind sees the same refining and ascent to the third, the seventh, or the tenth power of the daily accidents which the senses report, and which make the raw material of knowledge. It was sensation; when memory came, it was experience; when mind acted, it was knowledge; when mind acted on it as knowledge, it was thought.

This metonomy, or seeing the same sense in things so diverse, gives a pure pleasure. Every one of a million times we find a charm in the metamorphosis. It makes us dance and sing. All men are so far poets. When people tell me they do not relish poetry, and bring me Shelley, or Aikin's Poets,° or I know not what volumes of rhymed English, to show that it has no charm, I am quite of their mind. But this dislike of the books only proves their liking of poetry. For they relish Æsop,—cannot forget him, or not use him; bring them Homer's Iliad, and they like that; or the Cid,° and that rings well: read to them from Chaucer, and they reckon him an honest fellow. 'Lear' and 'Macbeth' and 'Richard III.' they know pretty well without guide. Give them Robin Hood's ballads, or 'Griselda,' or 'Sir Andrew Barton,' or 'Sir Patrick Spense,' or 'Chevy Chase,' or 'Tam O'Shanter,'° and they like these well enough. They like to see statues; they like to name the stars; they like to talk and hear of Jove, Apollo, Minerva, Venus, and the Nine. See how tenacious we are of the old names. They like poetry without knowing it as such. They like to go to the theatre and be made to weep; to Faneuil Hall, and be taught by Otis, Webster, or Kossuth, or Phillips,° what great hearts they have, what tears, what new possible enlargements to their narrow horizons. They like to see sunsets on the hills or on a lake shore. Now, a cow does not gaze at the rainbow, or show or affect any interest in the landscape, or a peacock, or the song of thrushes.

Nature is the true idealist. When she serves us best, when, on rare days, she speaks to the imagination, we feel that the huge heaven and earth are but a web drawn around us, that the light, skies, and mountains are but the painted vicissitudes of the soul. Who has heard our hymn in the churches without accepting the truth,—

> 'As o'er our heads the seasons roll,
> And soothe with *change of bliss* the soul'?°

Of course, when we describe man as poet, and credit him with the triumphs of the art, we speak of the potential or ideal man,—not found now in any one person. You must go through a city or a nation, and find one faculty here, one there, to build the true poet withal. Yet all men know the portrait when it is drawn, and it is part of religion to believe its possible incarnation.

He is the healthy, the wise, the fundamental, the manly man, seer of the secret; against all the appearance, he sees and reports the truth, namely, that the soul generates matter. And poetry is the only verity,— the expression of a sound mind speaking after the ideal, and not after the apparent. As a power, it is the perception of the symbolic character of things, and the treating them as representative: as a talent, it is a magnetic tenaciousness of an image, and by the treatment demonstrating that this pigment of thought is as palpable and objective to the poet as is the ground on which he stands, or the walls of houses about him. And this power appears in Dante and Shakspeare. In some individuals this insight, or second sight, has an extraordinary reach which compels our wonder, as in Behmen, Swedenborg, and William Blake,° the painter.

William Blake, whose abnormal genius, Wordsworth said, interested him more than the conversation of Scott or of Byron, writes thus: 'He who does not imagine in stronger and better lineaments, and in stronger and better light than his perishing mortal eye can see, does not imagine at all. The painter of this work asserts that all his imaginations appear to him infinitely more perfect and more minutely organized, than anything seen by his mortal eye. . . . I assert for myself that I do not behold the outward creation, and that to me it would be a hindrance, and not action. I question not my corporeal eye any more than I would question a window concerning a sight. I look through it, and not with it.'°

'T is a problem of metaphysics to define the province of Fancy and Imagination. The words are often used, and the things confounded. Imagination respects the cause. It is the vision of an inspired soul reading arguments and affirmations in all nature of that which it is driven to say. But as soon as this soul is released a little from its passion, and at leisure plays with the resemblances and types for amusement, and not for its moral end, we call its action Fancy. Lear, mad with his affliction, thinks every man who suffers must have the like cause with his own. 'What, have his daughters brought him to this pass?'° But when, his attention being diverted, his mind rests from this thought, he becomes fanciful with Tom, playing with the superficial resemblances of objects. Bunyan, in pain for his soul, wrote 'Pilgrim's Progress'; Quarles, after he was quite cool, wrote 'Emblems.'°

Imagination is central; fancy, superficial. Fancy relates to surface, in which a great part of life lies. The lover is rightly said to fancy the hair, eyes, complexion of the maid. Fancy is a wilful, imagination a spontaneous act; fancy, a play as with dolls and puppets which we choose to call men and women; imagination, a perception and affirming of a real relation between a thought and some material fact. Fancy amuses; imagination expands and exalts us. Imagination uses an organic classification. Fancy joins by accidental resemblance, surprises and amuses the idle, but is silent in the presence of great passion and action. Fancy aggregates; imagination animates. Fancy is related to color; imagination, to form. Fancy paints; imagination sculptures.

Veracity.—I do not wish, therefore, to find that my poet is not partaker of the feast he spreads, or that he would kindle or amuse me with that which does not kindle or amuse him. He must believe in his poetry. Homer, Milton, Hafiz, Herbert, Swedenborg, Wordsworth, are heartily enamored of their sweet thoughts. Moreover, they know that this correspondence of things to thoughts is far deeper than they can penetrate,—defying adequate expression; that it is elemental, or in the core of things. Veracity, therefore, is that which we require in poets,—that they shall say how it was with them, and not what might be said. And the fault of our popular poetry is that it is not sincere.

'What news?' asks man of man everywhere. The only teller of news is the poet. When he sings, the world listens with the assurance that now a secret of God is to be spoken. The right poetic mood is or makes a more complete sensibility,—piercing the outward fact to the meaning of the fact; shows a sharper insight: and the perception creates the strong expression of it, as the man who sees his way walks in it.

'T is a rule in eloquence, that the moment the orator loses command of his audience, the audience commands him. So, in poetry, the master rushes to deliver his thought, and the words and images fly to him to express it; whilst colder moods are forced to respect the ways of saying it, and insinuate, or, as it were, muffle the fact, to suit the poverty or caprice of their expression, so that they only hint the matter, or allude to it, being unable to fuse and mould their words and images to fluid obedience. See how Shakspeare grapples at once with the main problem of the tragedy, as in 'Lear' and 'Macbeth,' and the opening of 'The Merchant of Venice.'

All writings must be in a degree exoteric, written to a human *should* or *would*, instead of to the fatal *is*: this holds even of the bravest and sincerest writers. Every writer is a skater, and must go partly where he would, and partly where the skates carry him; or a sailor, who can only land where sails can be blown. And yet it is to be added, that high poetry exceeds the fact, or nature itself, just as skates allow the good skater far more grace than his best walking would show, or sails more than riding. The poet writes from a real experience, the amateur feigns one. Of course, one draws the bow with his fingers, and the other with the strength of his body; one speaks with his lips, and the other with a chest voice. Talent amuses, but if your verse has not a necessary and autobiographic basis, though under whatever gay poetic veils, it shall not waste my time.

For poetry is faith. To the poet the world is virgin soil: all is practicable; the men are ready for virtue; it is always time to do right. He is a true re-commencer, or Adam in the garden again. He affirms the applicability of the ideal law to this moment and the present knot of affairs. Parties, lawyers, and men of the world will invariably dispute such an application as romantic and dangerous: they admit the general truth, but they and their affair always constitute a case in bar of the statute.

Free-trade, they concede, is very well as a principle, but it is never quite the time for its adoption without prejudicing actual interests. Chastity, they admit, is very well,—but then think of Mirabeau's° passion and temperament!—Eternal laws are very well, which admit no violation,— but so extreme were the times and manners of mankind, that you must admit miracles,—for the times constituted a case. Of course, we know what you say, that legends are found in all tribes,—but this legend is different. And so, throughout, the poet affirms the laws; prose busies itself with exceptions,—with the local and individual.

I require that the poem should impress me, so that after I have shut the book, it shall recall me to itself, or that passages should. And inestimable is the criticism of memory as a corrective to first impressions. We are dazzled at first by new words and brilliancy of color, which occupy the fancy and deceive the judgment. But all this is easily forgotten. Later, the thought, the happy image which expressed it, and which was a true experience of the poet, recurs to mind, and sends me back in search of the book. And I wish that the poet should foresee this habit of readers, and omit all but the important passages. Shakspeare is made up of important passages, like Damascus steel made up of old nails. Homer has his own,—

> 'One omen is good, to die for one's country';°

and again,—

> 'They heal their griefs, for curable are the hearts of the noble.'°

Write, that I may know you. Style betrays you, as your eyes do. We detect at once by it whether the writer has a firm grasp on his fact or thought,—exists at the moment for that alone, or whether he has one eye apologizing, deprecatory, turned on his reader. In proportion always to his possession of his thought is his defiance of his readers. There is no choice of words for him who clearly sees the truth. That provides him with the best word.

Great design belongs to a poem, and is better than any skill of execution,—but how rare! I find it in the poems of Wordsworth,— 'Laodamia,' and the 'Ode to Dion,' and the plan of 'The Recluse.' We want design, and do not forgive the bards if they have only the art of enamelling. We want an architect, and they bring us an upholsterer.

If your subject do not appear to you the flower of the world at this moment, you have not rightly chosen it. No matter what it is, grand or gay, national or private, if it has a natural prominence to you, work away until you come to the heart of it: then it will, though it were a sparrow or a spider-web, as fully represent the central law, and draw all tragic or joyful illustration, as if it were the book of Genesis or the book of Doom. The subject—we must so often say it—is indifferent. Any word, every word in language, every circumstance, becomes poetic in the hands of a higher thought.

The test or measure of poetic genius is the power to read the poetry of affairs,—to fuse the circumstance of to-day; not to use Scott's antique superstitions, or Shakspeare's, but to convert those of the nine-teenth century, and of the existing nations, into universal symbols. 'T is easy to repaint the mythology of the Greeks, or of the Catholic Church, the feudal castle, the crusade, the martyrdoms of mediæval Europe; but to point out where the same creative force is now working in our own houses and public assemblies, to convert the vivid energies acting at this hour, in New York and Chicago and San Francisco, into universal symbols, requires a subtile and commanding thought. 'T is boyish in Swedenborg to cumber himself with the dead scurf of Hebrew antiquity, as if the Divine creative energy had fainted in his own cen-tury. American life storms about us daily, and is slow to find a tongue. This contemporary insight is transubstantiation, the conversion of daily bread into the holiest symbols; and every man would be a poet, if his intellectual digestion were perfect. The test of the poet is the power to take the passing day, with its news, its cares, its fears, as he shares them, and hold it up to a divine reason, till he sees it to have a purpose and beauty, and to be related to astronomy and history, and the eternal order of the world. Then the dry twig blossoms in his hand. He is calmed and elevated.

The use of 'occasional poems' is to give leave to originality. Every one delights in the felicity frequently shown in our drawing-rooms. In a game-party or picnic poem each writer is released from the solemn rhythmic traditions which alarm and suffocate his fancy, and the result is that one of the partners offers a poem in a new style that hints at a new literature. Yet the writer holds it cheap, and could do the like all day. On the stage, the farce is commonly far better given than the tra-gedy, as the stock actors understand the farce, and do not understand the tragedy. The writer in the parlor has more presence of mind, more wit and fancy, more play of thought, on the incidents that occur at table, or about the house, than in the politics of Germany or Rome. Many of the fine poems of Herrick, Jonson, and their contemporaries had this casual origin.

I know there is entertainment and room for talent in the artist's selection of ancient or remote subjects; as when the poet goes to India, or to Rome, or Persia, for his fable. But I believe nobody knows better than he, that herein he consults his ease, rather than his strength or his desire. He is very well convinced that the great moments of life are those in which his own house, his own body, the tritest and nearest ways and words and things, have been illuminated into prophets and teachers. What else is it to be a poet? What are his garland and singing robes? What but a sensibility so keen that the scent of an elder-blow, or the timber-yard and corporation-works of a nest of pismires is event enough for him,—all emblems and personal appeals to him. His wreath and robe is to do what he enjoys; emancipation from other men's questions, and glad study of his own; escape from the gossip and routine of society, and the allowed right and practice of making better. He does not give his hand, but in sign of giving his heart; he is not affable with all, but silent, uncommitted, or in love, as his heart leads him. There is no subject that does not belong to him,—politics, economy, manufactures, and stock-brokerage, as much as sunsets and souls; only, these things, placed in their true order, are poetry; displaced, or put in kitchen order, they are unpoetic. Malthus is the right organ of the English proprietors; but we shall never understand political economy, until Burns or Béranger° or some poet shall teach it in songs, and he will not teach Malthusianism.

Poetry is the *gai science*.° The trait and test of the poet is that he builds, adds, and affirms. The critic destroys: the poet says nothing but what helps somebody; let others be distracted with cares, he is exempt. All their pleasures are tinged with pain. All his pains are edged with pleasure. The gladness he imparts he shares. As one of the old Minnesingers sung,—

> 'Oft have I heard, and now believe it true,
> Whom man delights in, God delights in too.'°

Poetry is the consolation of mortal men. They live cabined, cribbed, confined, in a narrow and trivial lot,—in wants, pains, anxieties, and superstitions, in profligate politics, in personal animosities, in mean employments,—and victims of these; and the nobler powers untried, unknown. A poet comes, who lifts the veil; gives them glimpses of the laws of the universe; shows them the circumstance as illusion; shows that nature is only a language to express the laws, which are grand and beautiful,—and lets them, by his songs, into some of the realities. Socrates; the Indian teachers of the Maia;° the Bibles of the nations; Shakspeare, Milton, Hafiz, Ossian, the Welsh Bards,°—these all deal with nature and history as means and symbols, and not as ends. With such guides they begin to see that what they had called pictures are realities, and the mean life is pictures. And this is achieved by words; for it is a few oracles spoken by perceiving men that are the texts on which religions and states are founded. And this perception has at once its moral sequence. Ben Jonson said, 'The principal end of poetry is to inform men in the just reason of living.'°

Creation.—But there is a third step which poetry takes, and which seems higher than the others, namely, creation, or ideas taking forms of their own,—when the poet invents the fable, and invents the language which his heroes speak. He reads in the word or action of the man its yet untold results. His inspiration is power to carry out and complete the metamorphosis, which, in the imperfect kinds, arrested for ages,— in the perfecter, proceeds rapidly in the same individual. For poetry is science, and the poet a truer logician. Men in the courts or in the street think themselves logical, and the poet whimsical. Do they think there is chance or wilfulness in what he sees and tells? To be sure, we demand of him what he demands of himself,—veracity, first of all. But with that, he is the lawgiver, as being an exact reporter of the essential law. He knows that he did not make his thought,—no, his thought made him, and made the sun and the stars. Is the solar system good art and architecture? the same wise achievement is in the human brain also, can you only wile it from interference and marring. We cannot look at works of art but they teach us how near man is to creating. Michel Angelo is largely filled with the Creator that made and makes men. How much of the original craft remains in him, and he a mortal man! In him and the like perfecter brains the instinct is resistless, knows the right way, is melodious, and at all points divine. The reason we set so high a value on any poetry,—as often on a line or a phrase as on a poem,—is, that it is a new work of Nature, as a man is. It must be as new as foam and as old as the rock. But a new verse comes once in a hundred years; therefore Pindar, Hafiz, Dante, speak so proudly of what seems to the clown a jingle.

The writer, like the priest, must be exempted from secular labor. His work needs a frolic health; he must be at the top of his condition. In that prosperity he is sometimes caught up into a perception of means and materials, of feats and fine arts, of fairy machineries and funds of power hitherto utterly unknown to him, whereby he can transfer his visions to mortal canvas, or reduce them into iambic or trochaic, into lyric or heroic rhyme. These successes are not less admirable and astonishing to the poet than they are to his audience. He has seen something which all the mathematics and the best industry could never bring him unto. Now at this rare elevation above his usual sphere, he has come into new circulations, the marrow of the world is in his bones, the opulence of forms begins to pour into his intellect, and he is permitted to dip his brush into the old paint-pot with which birds, flowers, the human cheek, the living rock, the broad landscape, the ocean, and the eternal sky were painted.

These fine fruits of judgment, poesy, and sentiment, when once their hour is struck, and the world is ripe for them, know as well as coarser how to feed and replenish themselves, and maintain their stock alive, and multiply; for roses and violets renew their race like oaks, and flights of painted moths are as old as the Alleghanies. The balance of the world is kept, and dewdrop and haze and the pencil of light are as long-lived as chaos and darkness.

Our science is always abreast of our self-knowledge. Poetry begins, or all becomes poetry, when we look from the centre outward, and are using all as if the mind made it. That only can we see which we are, and which we make. The weaver sees gingham; the broker sees the stock-list; the politician, the ward and county votes; the poet sees the horizon, and the shores of matter lying on the sky, the interaction of the elements,—the large effect of laws which correspond to the inward laws which he knows, and so are but a kind of extension of himself. 'The attractions are proportional to the destinies.'° Events or things are only the fulfilment of the prediction of the faculties. Better men saw heavens and earths; saw noble instruments of noble souls. We see railroads, mills, and banks, and we pity the poverty of these dreaming Buddhists. There was as much creative force then as now, but it made globes, and astronomic heavens, instead of broadcloth and wine-glasses.

The poet is enamored of thoughts and laws. These know their way, and, guided by them, he is ascending from an interest in visible things to an interest in that which they signify, and from the part of a spectator to the part of a maker. And as everything streams and advances, as every faculty and every desire is procreant, and every perception is a destiny, there is no limit to his hope. 'Anything, child, that the mind covets, from the milk of a cocoa to the throne of the three worlds, thou mayest obtain, by keeping the law of thy members and the law of thy mind.'° It suggests that there is higher poetry than we write or read.

Rightly, poetry is organic. We cannot know things by words and writing, but only by taking a central position in the universe, and living in its forms. We sink to rise.

'None any work can frame,
Unless himself become the same.'°

All the parts and forms of nature are the expression or production of divine faculties, and the same are in us. And the fascination of genius for us is this awful nearness to Nature's creations.

I have heard that the Germans think the creator of Trim and Uncle Toby,° though he never wrote a verse, a greater poet than Cowper,° and that Goldsmith's title to the name is not from his 'Deserted Village,' but derived from the 'Vicar of Wakefield.' Better examples are Shakspeare's Ariel, his Caliban, and his fairies in the 'Midsummer Night's Dream.' Barthold Niebuhr° said well, 'There is little merit in inventing a happy idea, or attractive situation, so long as it is only the author's voice which we hear. As a being whom we have called into life by magic arts, as soon as it has received existence acts independently of the master's impulse, so the poet creates his persons, and then watches and relates what they do and say. Such creation is poetry, in the literal sense of the term, and its possibility is an unfathomable enigma. The gushing fulness of speech belongs to the poet, and it flows from the lips of each of his magic beings in the thoughts and words peculiar to its nature.'*

This force of representation so plants his figures before him that he treats them as real; talks to them as if they were bodily there; puts words in their mouth such as they should have spoken, and is affected by them as by persons. Vast is the difference between writing clean verses for magazines, and creating these new persons and situations,— new language with emphasis and reality. The humor of Falstaff, the terror of Macbeth, have each their swarm of fit thoughts and images, as if Shakspeare had known and reported the men, instead of inventing them at his desk. This power appears not only in the outline or portrait of his actors, but also in the bearing and behavior and style of each individual. Ben Jonson told Drummond° 'that Sidney did not keep a decorum in making every one speak as well as himself.'

This reminds me that we all have one key to this miracle of the poet, and the dunce has experiences that may explain Shakspeare to him,— one key, namely, dreams. In dreams we are true poets; we create the persons of the drama; we give them appropriate figures, faces, costume; they are perfect in their organs, attitude, manners: moreover, they speak after their own characters, not ours;—they speak to us, and we listen with surprise to what they say. Indeed, I doubt if the best poet has yet written any five-act play that can compare in thoroughness of inven-

* Niebuhr, Letters, etc., Vol. III. p. 196.

tion with this unwritten play in fifty acts, composed by the dullest snorer on the floor of the watch-house.

Melody, Rhyme, Form.—Music and rhyme are among the earliest pleasures of the child, and, in the history of literature, poetry precedes prose. Every one may see, as he rides on the highway through an uninteresting landscape, how a little water instantly relieves the monotony: no matter what objects are near it,—a gray rock, a grass-patch, an alder-bush, or a stake,—they become beautiful by being reflected. It is rhyme to the eye, and explains the charm of rhyme to the ear. Shadows please us as still finer rhymes. Architecture gives the like pleasure by the repetition of equal parts in a colonnade, in a row of windows, or in wings; gardens, by the symmetric contrasts of the beds and walks. In society, you have this figure in a bridal company, where a choir of white-robed maidens give the charm of living statues; in a funeral procession, where all wear black; in a regiment of soldiers in uniform.

The universality of this taste is proved by our habit of casting our facts into rhyme to remember them better, as so many proverbs may show. Who would hold the order of the almanac so fast but for the ding-dong,

> 'Thirty days hath September,' etc.;

or of the Zodiac, but for

> 'The Ram, the Bull, the heavenly Twins,' etc.? °

We are lovers of rhyme and return, period and musical reflection. The babe is lulled to sleep by the nurse's song. Sailors can work better for their *yo-heave-o.* Soldiers can march better and fight better for the drum and trumpet. Metre begins with pulse-beat, and the length of lines in songs and poems is determined by the inhalation and exhalation of the lungs. If you hum or whistle the rhythm of the common English metres,—of the decasyllabic quatrain, or the octosyllabic with alternate sexisyllabic, or other rhythms, you can easily believe these metres to be organic, derived from the human pulse, and to be therefore not proper to one nation, but to mankind. I think you will also find a charm heroic, plaintive, pathetic, in these cadences, and be at once set on searching for the words that can rightly fill these vacant beats. Young people like rhyme, drum-beat, tune, things in pairs and alternatives; and, in higher degrees, we know the instant power of music upon our temperaments to change our mood, and give us its own: and human passion, seizing these constitutional tunes, aims to fill them with appropriate words, or marry music to thought, believing, as we believe of all marriage, that matches are made in heaven, and that for every thought its proper melody or rhyme exists, though the odds are immense against our finding it, and only genius can rightly say the banns.

Another form of rhyme is iterations of phrase, as the record of the death of Sisera:—

'At her feet he bowed, he fell, he lay down: at her feet he bowed, he fell: where he bowed, there he fell down dead.'°

The fact is made conspicuous, nay, colossal, by this simple rhetoric.

'They shall perish, but thou shalt endure: yea, all of them shall wax old like a garment; as a vesture shalt thou change them, and they shall be changed: but thou art the same, and thy years shall have no end.'°

Milton delights in these iterations:—

> 'Though fallen on evil days,
> On evil days though fallen, and evil tongues.'°

> 'Was I deceived, or did a sable cloud
> Turn forth its silver lining on the night?
> I did not err, there does a sable cloud
> Turn forth its silver lining on the night.'°
> *Comus.*

> 'A little onward lend thy guiding hand,
> To these dark steps a little farther on.'°
> *Samson.*

So in our songs and ballads the refrain skilfully used, and deriving some novelty or better sense in each of many verses:—

> 'Busk thee, busk thee, my bonny bonny bride,
> Busk thee, busk thee, my winsome marrow.'°
> *Hamilton.*

Of course rhyme soars and refines with the growth of the mind. The boy liked the drum, the people liked an overpowering jewsharp tune. Later they like to transfer that rhyme to life, and to detect a melody as prompt and perfect in their daily affairs. Omen and coincidence show the rhythmical structure of man; hence the taste for signs, sortilege, prophecy and fulfilment, anniversaries, etc. By and by, when they apprehend real rhymes, namely, the correspondence of parts in nature,—acid and alkali, body and mind, man and maid, character and history, action and reaction,—they do not longer value rattles and ding-dongs, or barbaric word-jingle. Astronomy, Botany, Chemistry,

Hydraulics and the elemental forces have their own periods and returns, their own grand strains of harmony not less exact, up to the primeval apothegm 'that there is nothing on earth which is not in the heavens in a heavenly form, and nothing in the heavens which is not on the earth in an earthly form.'° They furnish the poet with grander pairs and alternations, and will require an equal expansion in his metres.

There is under the seeming poverty of metres an infinite variety, as every artist knows. A right ode (however nearly it may adopt conventional metre, as the Spenserian,° or the heroic blank-verse, or one of the fixed lyric metres) will by any sprightliness be at once lifted out of conventionality, and will modify the metre. Every good poem that I know I recall by its rhythm also. Rhyme is a pretty good measure of the latitude and opulence of a writer. If unskilful, he is at once detected by the poverty of his chimes. A small, well-worn, sprucely brushed vocabulary serves him. Now try Spenser, Marlow, Chapman, and see how wide they fly for weapons, and how rich and lavish their profusion. In their rhythm is no manufacture, but a vortex, or musical tornado, which falling on words and the experience of a learned mind, whirls these materials into the same grand order as planets and moons obey, and seasons, and monsoons.

There are also prose poets. Thomas Taylor,° the Platonist, for instance, is really a better man of imagination, a better poet, or perhaps I should say a better feeder to a poet, than any man between Milton and Wordsworth. Thomas Moore had the magnanimity to say, 'If Burke and Bacon were not poets (measured lines not being necessary to constitute one), he did not know what poetry meant.'° And every good reader will easily recall expressions or passages in works of pure science which have given him the same pleasure which he seeks in professed poets. Richard Owen, the eminent paleontologist, said:—

'All hitherto observed causes of extirpation point either to continuous slowly operating geologic changes, or to no greater sudden cause than the, so to speak, spectral appearance of mankind on a limited tract of land not before inhabited.'°

St. Augustine complains to God of his friends offering him the books of the philosophers:—

'And these were the dishes in which they brought to me, being hungry, the Sun and the Moon instead of Thee.'°

It would not be easy to refuse to Sir Thomas Browne's 'Fragment on Mummies'° the claim of poetry:—

'Of their living habitations they made little account, conceiving of them but as *hospitia*, or inns, while they adorned the sepulchres of the dead, and, planting thereon lasting bases, defied the crumbling touches of time, and the misty vaporousness of oblivion. Yet all were but Babel vanities. Time sadly over-cometh all things, and is now dominant, and sitteth upon a Sphinx, and looketh unto Memphis and old Thebes, while his sister Oblivion reclineth semi-somnous on a pyramid, gloriously triumphing, making puzzles of Titanian erections, and turning old glories into dreams. History sinketh beneath her cloud. The traveller as he paceth through those deserts asketh of her, Who builded them? and she mumbleth something, but what it is he heareth not.'

Rhyme, being a kind of music, shares this advantage with music, that it has a privilege of speaking truth which all Philistia° is unable to chal-lenge. Music is the poor man's Parnassus.° With the first note of the flute or horn, or the first strain of a song, we quit the world of common-sense, and launch on the sea of ideas and emotions: we pour contempt on the prose you so magnify; yet the sturdiest Philistine is silent. The like allowance is the prescriptive right of poetry. You shall not speak ideal truth in prose uncontradicted: you may in verse. The best thoughts run into the best words; imaginative and affectionate thoughts into music and metre. We ask for food and fire, we talk of our work, our tools, and material necessities in prose, that is, without any elevation or aim at beauty; but when we rise into the world of thought, and think of these things only for what they signify, speech refines into order and harmony. I know what you say of mediæval barbarism and sleighbell-rhyme, but we have not done with music, no, nor with rhyme, nor must console ourselves with prose poets so long as boys whistle and girls sing.

Let Poetry then pass, if it will, into music and rhyme. That is the form which itself puts on. We do not enclose watches in wooden, but in crystal cases, and rhyme is the transparent frame that allows almost the pure architecture of thought to become visible to the mental eye. Sub-stance is much, but so are mode and form much. The poet, like a delighted boy, brings you heaps of rainbow bubbles, opaline, air-borne, spherical as the world, instead of a few drops of soap and water. Victor Hugo says well, 'An idea steeped in verse becomes suddenly more incisive and more brilliant: the iron becomes steel.'° Lord Bacon, we are told, 'loved not to see poesy go on other feet than poetical dactyls and spondees';° and Ben Jonson said, 'that Donne, for not keeping of accent, deserved hanging.'°

Poetry being an attempt to express, not the common-sense, as the avoirdupois of the hero, or his structure in feet and inches, but the beauty and soul in his aspect as it shines to fancy and feeling,—and so of all other objects in nature,—runs into fable, personifies every fact:— 'the clouds clapped their hands,'—'the hills skipped,'—'the sky spoke.' This is the substance, and this treatment always attempts a metrical grace. Outside of the nursery the beginning of literature is the prayers of a people, and they are always hymns, poetic,—the mind allowing itself range, and therewith is ever a corresponding freedom in the style which becomes lyrical. The prayers of nations are rhythmic,—have iterations, and alliterations, like the marriage-service and burial-service in our liturgies.

Poetry will never be a simple means, as when history or philosophy is rhymed, or laureate odes on state occasions are written. Itself must be its own end, or it is nothing. The difference between poetry and stock-poetry is this, that in the latter the rhythm is given, and the sense adapted to it; while in the former the sense dictates the rhythm. I might even say that the rhyme is there in the theme, thought, and image themselves. Ask the fact for the form. For a verse is not a vehicle to carry a sentence as a jewel is carried in a case: the verse must be alive, and inseparable from its contents, as the soul of man inspires and directs the body; and we measure the inspiration by the music. In reading prose, I am sensitive as soon as a sentence drags; but in poetry, as soon as one word drags. Ever as the thought mounts, the expression mounts. 'T is cumulative also; the poem is made up of lines each of which filled the ear of the poet in its turn, so that mere synthesis produces a work quite superhuman.

Indeed, the masters sometimes rise above themselves to strains which charm their readers, and which neither any competitor could outdo, nor the bard himself again equal. Try this strain of Beaumont and Fletcher:—

> 'Hence, all ye vain delights,
> As short as are the nights
> In which you spend your folly!
> There's naught in this life sweet,
> If men were wise to see't,
> But only melancholy.
> Oh! sweetest melancholy!
> Welcome, folded arms and fixed eyes,
> A sigh that piercing mortifies,
> A look that's fastened to the ground,
> A tongue chained up, without a sound;
> Fountain-heads and pathless groves,
> Places which pale Passion loves,

Midnight walks, when all the fowls
Are warmly housed, save bats and owls;
A midnight bell, a passing groan,
These are the sounds we feed upon,
Then stretch our bones in a still, gloomy valley.
Nothing's so dainty sweet as lovely melancholy.'°

Keats disclosed by certain lines in his 'Hyperion' this inward skill; and
Coleridge showed at least his love and appetency for it. It appears in
Ben Jonson's songs, including certainly 'The faery beam upon you,'
etc., Waller's 'Go, lovely rose!' Herbert's 'Virtue' and 'Easter,' and
Lovelace's lines 'To Althea' and 'To Lucasta,' and Collins's 'Ode, to
Evening,' all but the last verse, which is academical. Perhaps this dainty
style of poetry is not producible to-day, any more than a right Gothic
cathedral. It belonged to a time and taste which is not in the world.

As the imagination is not a talent of some men, but is the health of
every man, so also is this joy of musical expression. I know the pride of
mathematicians and materialists, but they cannot conceal from me their
capital want. The critic, the philosopher, is a failed poet. Gray avows
'that he thinks even a bad verse as good a thing or better than the best
observation that was ever made on it.' I honor the naturalist; I honor the
geometer, but he has before him higher power and happiness than he
knows. Yet we will leave to the masters their own forms. Newton may
be permitted to call Terence° a play-book, and to wonder at the frivolous taste for rhymers; he only predicts, one would say, a grander
poetry: he only shows that he is not yet reached; that the poetry which
satisfies more youthful souls is not such to a mind like his, accustomed
to grander harmonies;—this being a child's whistle to his ear; that the
music must rise to a loftier strain, up to Handel, up to Beethoven, up to
the thorough-bass of the sea-shore, up to the largeness of astronomy:
at last that great heart will hear in the music beats like its own: the
waves of melody will wash and float him also, and set him into concert
and harmony.

Bards and Trouveurs.—The metallic force of primitive words makes
the superiority of the remains of the rude ages. It costs the early bard
little talent to chant more impressively than the later, more cultivated
poets. His advantage is that his words are things, each the lucky sound
which described the fact, and we listen to him as we do to the Indian, or
the hunter, or miner, each of whom represents his facts as accurately as
the cry of the wolf or the eagle tells of the forest or the air they inhabit.
The original force, the direct smell of the earth or the sea, is in these

ancient poems, the Sagas of the North, the Nibelungen Lied,° the songs and ballads of the English and Scotch.

I find or fancy more true poetry, the love of the vast and the ideal, in the Welsh and bardic fragments of Taliessin° and his successors than in many volumes of British Classics. An intrepid magniloquence appears in all the bards, as:—

> 'The whole ocean flamed as one wound.'
> *King Regner Lodbook.*°

> 'God himself cannot procure good for the wicked.'
> *Welsh Triad.*°

A favorable specimen is Taliessin's 'Invocation of the Wind' at the door of Castle Teganwy.

> 'Discover thou what it is,—
> The strong creature from before the flood,
> Without flesh, without bone, without head, without feet,
> It will neither be younger nor older than at the beginning;
> It has no fear, nor the rude wants of created things.
> Great God! how the sea whitens when it comes!
> It is in the field, it is in the wood,
> Without hand, without foot,
> Without age, without season,
> It is always of the same age with the ages of ages,
> And of equal breadth with the surface of the earth.
> It was not born, it sees not,
> And is not seen; it does not come when desired;
> It has no form, it bears no burden,
> For it is void of sin.
> It makes no perturbation in the place where God wills it,
> On the sea, on the land.'°

In one of his poems he asks:—

> 'Is there but one course to the wind?
> But one to the water of the sea?
> Is there but one spark in the fire of boundless energy?'°

He says of his hero, Cunedda,—

> 'He will assimilate, he will agree with the deep and the shallow.'°

To another,—

> 'When I lapse to a sinful word,
> May neither you, nor others hear.'°

Of an enemy,—

'The caldron of the sea was bordered round by his land, but it would not boil the food of a coward.'°

To an exile on an island he says,—

'The heavy blue chain of the sea didst thou, O just man, endure.'°

Another bard in like tone says,—

'I am possessed of songs such as no son of man can repeat; one of them is called the "Helper"; it will help thee at thy need in sickness, grief, and all adversities. I know a song which I need only to sing when men have loaded me with bonds: when I sing it, my chains fall in pieces and I walk forth at liberty.'°

The Norsemen have no less faith in poetry and its power, when they describe it thus:—

'Odin spoke everything in rhyme. He and his temple-gods were called song-smiths. He could make his enemies in battle blind or deaf, and their weapons so blunt that they could no more cut than a willow-twig. Odin taught these arts in runes or songs, which are called incantations.'*°

The Crusades brought out the genius of France, in the twelfth century, when Pierre d'Auvergne said,—

'I will sing a new song which resounds in my breast: never was a song good or beautiful which resembled any other.'°

And Pons de Capdeuil declares,—

'Since the air renews itself and softens, so must my heart renew itself, and what buds in it buds and grows outside of it.'°

There is in every poem a height which attracts more than other parts, and is best remembered. Thus, in 'Morte d'Arthur,' I remember nothing so well as Sir Gawain's parley with Merlin in his wonderful prison:—

'After the disappearance of Merlin from King Arthur's court he was seriously missed, and many knights set out in search of him. Among others was Sir Gawain, who pursued his search till it was time to return to the court. He came into the forest of Broceliande, lamenting as he went along. Presently, he heard the voice of one groaning on his right hand; looking that way, he could see nothing save a kind of smoke which seemed like air, and through which he could not pass; and this impediment made him so wrathful that it deprived him of speech. Presently he heard a voice which said, "Gawain, Gawain, be not out of heart, for everything which must happen will come to pass." And when he heard the voice which thus called him by his right name, he replied, "Who can this be who

* Heimskringla, Vol. I. p. 221.

hath spoken to me?" "How," said the voice, "Sir Gawain, know you me not? You were wont to know me well, but thus things are interwoven and thus the proverb says true, 'Leave the court and the court will leave you.' So is it with me. Whilst I served King Arthur, I was well known by you and by other barons, but because I have left the court, I am known no longer, and put in forgetfulness, which I ought not to be if faith reigned in the world." When Sir Gawain heard the voice which spoke to him thus, he thought it was Merlin, and he answered, "Sir, certes I ought to know you well, for many times I have heard your words. I pray you appear before me so that I may be able to recognize you." "Ah, sir," said Merlin, "you will never see me more, and that grieves me, but I cannot remedy it, and when you shall have departed from this place, I shall nevermore speak to you nor to any other person, save only my mistress; for never other person will be able to discover this place for anything which may befall; neither shall I ever go out from hence, for in the world there is no such strong tower as this wherein I am confined; and it is neither of wood, nor of iron, nor of stone, but of air, without anything else; and made by enchantment so strong, that it can never be demolished while the world lasts, neither can I go out, nor can any one come in, save she who hath enclosed me here, and who keeps me company when it pleaseth her: she cometh when she listeth, for her will is here." "How, Merlin, my good friend," said Sir Gawain, "are you restrained so strongly that you cannot deliver yourself nor make yourself visible unto me; how can this happen, seeing that you are the wisest man in the world?" "Rather," said Merlin, "the greatest fool; for I well knew that all this would befall me, and I have been fool enough to love another more than myself, for I taught my mistress that whereby she hath imprisoned me in such manner that none can set me free." "Certes, Merlin," replied Sir Gawain, "of that I am right sorrowful, and so will King Arthur, my uncle, be, when he shall know it, as one who is making search after you throughout all countries." "Well," said Merlin, "it must be borne, for never will he see me, nor I him; neither will any one speak with me again after you, it would be vain to attempt it; for you yourself, when you have turned away, will never be able to find the place: but salute for me the king and the queen, and all the barons, and tell them of my condition. You will find the king at Carduel in Wales; and when you arrive there you will find there all the companions who departed with you, and who at this day will return. Now then go in the name of God, who will protect and save the King Arthur, and the realm of Logres, and you also, as the best knights who are in the world." With that Sir Gawain departed joyful and sorrowful; joyful because of what Merlin had assured him should happen to him, and sorrowful that Merlin had thus been lost.'

Morals.—We are sometimes apprized that there is a mental power and creation more excellent than anything which is commonly called philosophy and literature; that the high poets,—that Homer, Milton, Shakspeare, do not fully content us. How rarely they offer us the heavenly bread! The most they have done is to intoxicate us once and again with its taste. They have touched this heaven and retain afterwards some sparkle of it: they betray their belief that such discourse is possible. There is something—our brothers on this or that side of the sea do not know it or own it; the eminent scholars of England, historians and reviewers, romancers and poets included, might deny and blaspheme it—which is setting us and them aside and the whole world also, and planting itself. To true poetry we shall sit down as the result and justification of the age in which it appears, and think lightly of histories and statutes. None of your parlor or piano verse,—none of your carpet poets, who are content to amuse, will satisfy us. Power, new power, is the good which the soul seeks. The poetic gift we want, as the health and supremacy of man,—not rhymes and sonneteering, not bookmaking and bookselling; surely not cold spying and authorship.

Is not poetry the little chamber in the brain where is generated the explosive force which, by gentle shocks, sets in action the intellectual world? Bring us the bards who shall sing all our old ideas out of our heads, and new ones in; men-making poets; poetry which, like the verses inscribed on Balder's columns in Breidablik,° is capable of restoring the dead to life;—poetry like that verse of Saadi,° which the angels testified 'met the approbation of Allah in Heaven';—poetry which finds its rhymes and cadences in the rhymes and iterations of nature, and is the gift to men of new images and symbols, each the ensign and oracle of an age; that shall assimilate men to it, mould itself into religions and mythologies, and impart its quality to centuries;— poetry which tastes the world and reports of it, upbuilding the world again in the thought;

> 'Not with tickling rhymes,
> But high and noble matter, such as flies
> From brains entranced, and filled with ecstasies.'°

Poetry must be affirmative. It is the piety of the intellect. 'Thus saith the Lord,' should begin the song. The poet who shall use nature as his hieroglyphic must have an adequate message to convey thereby. Therefore, when we speak of the Poet in any high sense, we are driven to such examples as Zoroaster and Plato, St. John and Menu,° with their moral burdens. The Muse shall be the counterpart of Nature, and equally rich. I find her not often in books. We know Nature, and figure her exuberant, tranquil, magnificent in her fertility, coherent; so that every creation is omen of every other. She is not proud of the sea, of the stars, of space or time, or man or woman. All her kinds share the attributes of the selectest extremes. But in current literature I do not find her. Literature warps away from life, though at first it seems to bind it.

In the world of letters how few commanding oracles! Homer did what he could,—Pindar, Æschylus, and the Greek Gnomic poets° and the tragedians. Dante was faithful when not carried away by his fierce hatreds. But in so many alcoves of English poetry I can count only nine or ten authors who are still inspirers and lawgivers to their race.

The supreme value of poetry is to educate us to a height beyond itself, or which it rarely reaches;—the subduing mankind to order and virtue. He is the true Orpheus who writes his ode, not with syllables, but men. 'In poetry,' said Goethe, 'only the really great and pure advances us, and this exists as a second nature, either elevating us to itself, or rejecting us.' The poet must let Humanity sit with the Muse in his head, as the charioteer sits with the hero in the Iliad. 'Show me,' said Sarona in the novel,° 'one wicked man who has written poetry, and I will show you where his poetry is not poetry; or rather, I will show you in his poetry no poetry at all.'*

I have heard that there is a hope which precedes and must precede all science of the visible or the invisible world; and that science is the realization of that hope in either region. I count the genius of Swedenborg and Wordsworth as the agents of a reform in philosophy, the bringing poetry back to nature,—to the marrying of nature and mind, undoing the old divorce in which poetry had been famished and false, and nature had been suspected and pagan. The philosophy which a nation receives, rules its religion, poetry, politics, arts, trades, and whole history. A good poem—say Shakspeare's 'Macbeth,' or 'Hamlet,' or the 'Tempest'—goes about the world offering itself to reasonable men, who read it with joy and carry it to their reasonable neighbors. Thus it draws to it the wise and generous souls, confirming their secret thoughts, and, through their sympathy, really publishing itself. It affects the characters of its readers by formulating their opinions and feelings, and inevitably prompting their daily action. If they build ships, they write 'Ariel' or 'Prospero' or 'Ophelia'° on the ship's stern, and impart a tenderness and mystery to matters of fact. The ballad and romance work on the hearts of boys, who recite the rhymes to their hoops or their skates if alone, and these heroic songs or lines are remembered and determine many practical choices which they make later. Do you think Burns has had no influence on the life of men and women in Scotland,—has opened no eyes and ears to the face of nature and the dignity of man and the charm and excellence of woman?

We are a little civil, it must be owned, to Homer and Æschylus, to

* Miss Shepard's 'Counterparts,' Vol. I. p. 67.

Dante and Shakspeare, and give them the benefit of the largest interpretation. We must be a little strict also, and ask whether, if we sit down
at home, and do not go to Hamlet, Hamlet will come to us? whether we
shall find our tragedy written in his,—our hopes, wants, pains, dis-
graces, described to the life,—and the way opened to the paradise
which ever in the best hour beckons us? But our overpraise and ideali-
zation of famous masters is not in its origin a poor Boswellism,° but an
impatience of mediocrity. The praise we now give to our heroes we
shall unsay when we make larger demands. How fast we outgrow the
books of the nursery,—then those that satisfied our youth. What we
once admired as poetry has long since come to be a sound of tin pans;
and many of our later books we have outgrown. Perhaps Homer and
Milton will be tin pans yet. Better not to be easily pleased. The poet
should rejoice if he has taught us to despise his song; if he has so
moved us as to lift us,—to open the eye of the intellect to see farther
and better.

In proportion as a man's life comes into union with truth, his
thoughts approach to a parallelism with the currents of natural laws, so
that he easily expresses his meaning by natural symbols, or uses the
ecstatic or poetic speech. By successive states of mind all the facts of
nature are for the first time interpreted. In proportion as his life departs
from this simplicity, he uses circumlocution,—by many words hoping
to suggest what he cannot say. Vexatious to find poets, who are by
excellence the thinking and feeling of the world, deficient in truth of
intellect and of affection. Then is conscience unfaithful, and thought
unwise. To know the merit of Shakspeare, read 'Faust.'° I find 'Faust' a
little too modern and intelligible. We can find such a fabric at several
mills, though a little inferior. 'Faust' abounds in the disagreeable. The
vice is prurient, learned, Parisian. In the presence of Jove, Priapus may
be allowed as an offset, but here he is an equal hero. The egotism, the
wit, is calculated. The book is undeniably written by a master, and
stands unhappily related to the whole modern world; but it is a very disagreeable chapter of literature, and accuses the author as well as the
times. Shakspeare could, no doubt, have been disagreeable, had he less
genius, and if ugliness had attracted him. In short, our English nature
and genius has made us the worst critics of Goethe,

> 'We, who speak the tongue
> That Shakspeare spake, the faith and manners hold
> Which Milton held.'°

It is not style or rhymes, or a new image more or less, that imports, but sanity; that life should not be mean; that life should be an image in every part beautiful; that the old forgotten splendors of the universe should glow again for us;—that we should lose our wit, but gain our reason. And when life is true to the poles of nature, the streams of truth will roll through us in song.

Transcendency.—In a cotillon some persons dance and others await their turn when the music and the figure come to them. In the dance of God there is not one of the chorus but can and will begin to spin, monumental as he now looks, whenever the music and figure reach his place and duty. O celestial Bacchus!° drive them mad,—this multitude of vagabonds, hungry for eloquence, hungry for poetry, starving for symbols, perishing for want of electricity to vitalize this too much pasture, and in the long delay indemnifying themselves with the false wine of alcohol, of politics, or of money.

Every man may be, and at some time a man is, lifted to a platform whence he looks beyond sense to moral and spiritual truth; and in that mood deals sovereignly with matter, and strings worlds like beads upon his thought. The success with which this is done can alone determine how genuine is the inspiration. The poet is rare because he must be exquisitely vital and sympathetic, and, at the same time, immovably centred. In good society, nay, among the angels in heaven, is not everything spoken in fine parable, and not so servilely as it befell to the sense? All is symbolized. Facts are not foreign, as they seem, but related. Wait a little and we see the return of the remote hyperbolic curve. The solid men complain that the idealist leaves out the fundamental facts; the poet complains that the solid men leave out the sky. To every plant there are two powers; one shoots down as rootlet, and one upward as tree. You must have eyes of science to see in the seed its nodes; you must have the vivacity of the poet to perceive in the thought its futurities. The poet is representative,—whole man, diamond-merchant, symbolizer, emancipator; in him the world projects a scribe's hand and writes the adequate genesis. The nature of things is flowing, a metamorphosis. The free spirit sympathizes not only with the actual form, but with the power or possible forms; but for obvious municipal or parietal uses, God has given us a bias or a rest on to-day's forms. Hence the shudder of joy with which in each clear moment we recognize the metamorphosis, because it is always a conquest, a surprise from the heart of things. One would say of the force in the works of nature, all depends on the battery. If it give one shock, we shall get to the fish form, and stop; if two shocks, to the bird; if three, to the quadruped; if four, to the man. Power of generalizing differences men. The number of successive saltations the nimble thought can make, measures the difference between the highest and lowest of mankind. The habit of saliency, of not pausing but going on, is a sort of importation or domestication of the Divine effort in a man. After the largest circle has been drawn, a larger can be drawn around it. The problem of the poet is to unite freedom with precision; to give the pleasure of color, and be not less the most powerful of sculptors. Music seems to you sufficient, or the subtle and delicate scent of lavender; but Dante was free imagination,—all wings,—yet he wrote like Euclid. And mark the equality of Shakspeare to the comic, the tender and sweet, and to the grand and terrible. A little more or less skill in whistling is of no account. See those weary pentameter tales of Dryden and others. Turnpike is one thing and blue sky another. Let the poet, of all men, stop with his inspiration. The inexorable rule in the muses' court, *either inspiration or silence*, compels the bard to report only his supreme moments. It teaches the enormous force of a few words and in proportion to the inspiration checks loquacity. Much that we call poetry is but polite verse. The high poetry which shall thrill and agitate mankind, restore youth and health, dissipate the dreams under which men reel and stagger, and bring in the new thoughts, the sanity and heroic aims of nations, is deeper hid and longer postponed than was America or Australia, or the finding of steam or of the galvanic battery. We must not conclude against poetry from the defects of poets. They are, in our experience, men of every degree of skill,—some of them only once or twice receivers of an inspiration, and presently falling back on a low life. The drop of *ichor* that tingles in their veins has not yet refined their blood, and cannot lift the whole man to the digestion and function of ichor,—that is, to godlike nature. Time will be when ichor shall be their blood, when what are now glimpses and aspirations shall be the routine of the day. Yet even partial ascents to poetry and ideas are forerunners, and announce the dawn. In the mire of the sensual life, their religion, their poets, their admiration of heroes and benefactors, even their novel and newspaper, nay, their superstitions also, are hosts of ideals,—a cordage of ropes that hold them up out of the slough. Poetry is inestimable as a lonely faith, a lonely protest in the uproar of atheism.

But so many men are ill-born or ill-bred,—the brains are so marred, so imperfectly formed, unheroically,—brains of the sons of fallen men,—that the doctrine is imperfectly received. One man sees a spark or shimmer of the truth, and reports it, and his saying becomes a legend or golden proverb for ages, and other men report as much, but none wholly and well. Poems,—we have no poem. Whenever that angel shall be organized and appear on earth, the Iliad will be reckoned a poor ballad-grinding. I doubt never the riches of nature, the gifts of the future, the immense wealth of the mind. O yes, poets we shall have, mythology, symbols, religion, of our own. We, too, shall know how to take up all this industry and empire, this Western civilization, into thought, as easily as men did when arts were few; but not by holding it high, but by holding it low. The intellect uses and is not used,—uses London and Paris and Berlin, east and west, to its end. The only heart that can help us is one that draws, not from our society, but from itself, a counterpoise to society. What if we find partiality and meanness in us? The grandeur of our life exists in spite of us,—all over and under and within us, in what of us is inevitable and above our control. Men are facts as well as persons, and the involuntary part of their life so much as to fill the mind and leave them no countenance to say aught of what is so trivial as their selfish thinking and doing. Sooner or later that which is now life shall be poetry, and every fair and manly trait shall add a richer strain to the song.

THOREAU°

HENRY DAVID THOREAU was the last male descendant of a French ancestor who came to this country from the Isle of Guernsey. His character exhibited occasional traits drawn from this blood in singular combination with a very strong Saxon genius.

He was born in Concord, Massachusetts, on the 12th of July, 1817. He was graduated at Harvard College in 1837, but without any literary distinction. An iconoclast in literature, he seldom thanked colleges for their service to him, holding them in small esteem, whilst yet his debt to them was important. After leaving the University, he joined his brother in teaching a private school, which he soon renounced. His father was a manufacturer of lead-pencils, and Henry applied himself for a time to this craft, believing he could make a better pencil than was then in use. After completing his experiments, he exhibited his work to chemists and artists in Boston, and having obtained their certificates to its excellence and to its equality with the best London manufacture, he returned home contented. His friends congratulated him that he had now opened his way to fortune. But he replied, that he should never make another pencil. 'Why should I? I would not do again what I have done once.' He resumed his endless walks and miscellaneous studies, making every day some new acquaintance with Nature, though as yet never speaking of zoölogy or botany, since, though very studious of natural facts, he was incurious of technical and textual science.

At this time, a strong, healthy youth, fresh from college, whilst all his companions were choosing their profession, or eager to begin some lucrative employment, it was inevitable that his thoughts should be exercised on the same question, and it required rare decision to refuse all the accustomed paths, and keep his solitary freedom at the cost of disappointing the natural expectations of his family and friends: all the more difficult that he had a perfect probity, was exact in securing his own independence, and in holding every man to the like duty. But Thoreau never faltered. He was a born protestant. He declined to give up his large ambition of knowledge and action for any narrow craft or profession, aiming at a much more comprehensive calling, the art of living well. If he slighted and defied the opinions of others, it was only that he was more intent to reconcile his practice with his own belief. Never idle or self-indulgent, he preferred, when he wanted money, earning it by some piece of manual labor agreeable to him, as building a boat or a fence, planting, grafting, surveying, or other short work, to any long engagements. With his hardy habits and few wants, his skill in wood-craft, and his powerful arithmetic, he was very competent to live in any part of the world. It would cost him less time to supply his wants than another. He was therefore secure of his leisure.

A natural skill for mensuration, growing out of his mathematical knowledge, and his habit of ascertaining the measures and distances of objects which interested him, the size of trees, the depth and extent of ponds and rivers, the height of mountains, and the air-line distance of his favorite summits,—this, and his intimate knowledge of the territory about Concord, made him drift into the profession of land-surveyor. It had the advantage for him that it led him continually into new and secluded grounds, and helped his studies of Nature. His accuracy and skill in this work were readily appreciated, and he found all the employment he wanted.

He could easily solve the problems of the surveyor, but he was daily beset with graver questions, which he manfully confronted. He interrogated every custom, and wished to settle all his practice on an ideal foundation. He was a protestant *à l'outrance*, and few lives contain so many renunciations. He was bred to no profession; he never married; he lived alone; he never went to church; he never voted; he refused to pay a tax to the State; he ate no flesh, he drank no wine, he never knew the use of tobacco; and, though a naturalist, he used neither trap nor gun. He chose, wisely, no doubt, for himself, to be the bachelor of thought and Nature. He had no talent for wealth, and knew how to be poor without the least hint of squalor or inelegance. Perhaps he fell into his way of living without forecasting it much, but approved it with later wisdom. 'I am often reminded,' he wrote in his journal, 'that, if I had bestowed on me the wealth of Crœsus, my aims must be still the same, and my means essentially the same.' He had no temptations to fight against,—no appetites, no passions, no taste for elegant trifles. A fine house, dress, the manners and talk of highly cultivated people were all thrown away on him. He much preferred a good Indian, and considered these refinements as impediments to conversation, wishing to meet his companion on the simplest terms. He declined invitations to dinner-parties, because there each was in every one's way, and he could not meet the individuals to any purpose. 'They make their pride,' he said, 'in making their dinner cost much; I make my pride in making my dinner cost little.' When asked at table what dish he preferred, he answered, 'The nearest.' He did not like the taste of wine, and never had a vice in his life. He said,—'I have a faint recollection of pleasure derived from smoking dried lily-stems, before I was a man. I had commonly a supply of these. I have never smoked anything more noxious.'

He chose to be rich by making his wants few, and supplying them himself. In his travels, he used the railroad only to get over so much country as was unimportant to the present purpose, walking hundreds of miles, avoiding taverns, buying a lodging in farmers' and fishermen's houses, as cheaper, and more agreeable to him, and because there he could better find the men and the information he wanted.

There was somewhat military in his nature not to be subdued, always manly and able, but rarely tender, as if he did not feel himself except in opposition. He wanted a fallacy to expose, a blunder to pillory, I may say required a little sense of victory, a roll of the drum, to call his powers into full exercise. It cost him nothing to say No; indeed, he found it much easier than to say Yes. It seemed as if his first instinct on hearing a proposition was to controvert it, so impatient was he of the limitations of our daily thought. This habit, of course, is a little chilling to the social affections; and though the companion would in the end acquit him of any malice or untruth, yet it mars conversation. Hence, no equal companion stood in affectionate relations with one so pure and guileless. 'I love Henry,' said one of his friends, 'but I cannot like him; and as for taking his arm, I should as soon think of taking the arm of an elm-tree.'°

Yet, hermit and stoic as he was, he was really fond of sympathy, and threw himself heartily and childlike into the company of young people whom he loved, and whom he delighted to entertain, as he only could, with the varied and endless anecdotes of his experiences by field and river. And he was always ready to lead a huckleberry-party or a search for chestnuts or grapes. Talking, one day, of a public discourse, Henry remarked, that whatever succeeded with the audience was bad. I said, 'Who would not like to write something which all can read, like "Robinson Crusoe"? and who does not see with regret that his page is not solid with a right materialistic treatment, which delights everybody?' Henry objected, of course, and vaunted the better lectures which reached only a few persons. But, at supper, a young girl, understanding that he was to lecture at the Lyceum, sharply asked him, 'whether his lecture would be a nice, interesting story, such as she wished to hear, or whether it was one of those old philosophical things that she did not care about.' Henry turned to her, and bethought himself, and, I saw, was trying to believe that he had matter that might fit her and her brother, who were to sit up and go to the lecture, if it was a good one for them.

He was a speaker and actor of the truth,—born such,—and was ever running into dramatic situations from this cause. In any circumstance, it interested all bystanders to know what part Henry would take, and what he would say; and he did not disappoint expectation, but used an original judgment on each emergency. In 1845 he built himself a small framed house on the shores of Walden Pond, and lived there two years alone, a life of labor and study. This action was quite native and fit for him. No one who knew him would tax him with affectation. He was more unlike his neighbors in his thought than in his action. As soon as he had exhausted the advantages of that solitude, he abandoned it. In 1847, not approving some uses to which the public expenditure was applied, he refused to pay his town tax, and was put in jail. A friend paid the tax for him, and he was released. The like annoyance was threatened the next year. But, as his friends paid the tax, notwithstanding his protest, I believe he ceased to resist. No opposition or ridicule had any weight with him. He coldly and fully stated his opinion without affecting to believe that it was the opinion of the company. It was of no consequence, if every one present held the opposite opinion. On one occasion he went to the University Library to procure some books. The librarian refused to lend them. Mr. Thoreau repaired to the President, who stated to him the rules and usages, which permitted the loan of books to resident graduates, to clergymen who were alumni, and to some others resident within a circle of ten miles' radius from the College. Mr. Thoreau explained to the President that the railroad had destroyed the old scale of distances,—that the library was useless, yes, and President and College useless, on the terms of his rules,—that the one benefit he owed to the College was its library,—that, at this moment, not only his want of books was imperative, but he wanted a large number of books, and assured him that he, Thoreau, and not the librarian, was the proper custodian of these. In short, the President found the petitioner so formidable, and the rules getting to look so ridiculous, that he ended by giving him a privilege which in his hands proved unlimited thereafter.

No truer American existed than Thoreau. His preference of his country and condition was genuine, and his aversation from English and European manners and tastes almost reached contempt. He listened impatiently to news or *bon mots* gleaned from London circles; and though he tried to be civil, these anecdotes fatigued him. The men were all imitating each other, and on a small mould. Why can they not live as far apart as possible, and each be a man by himself? What he sought was the most energetic nature; and he wished to go to Oregon, not to London. 'In every part of Great Britain,' he wrote in his diary, 'are discovered traces of the Romans, their funereal urns, their camps, their roads, their dwellings. But New England, at least, is not based on any Roman ruins. We have not to lay the foundations of our houses on the ashes of a former civilization.'

But, idealist as he was, standing for abolition of slavery, abolition of tariffs, almost for abolition of government, it is needless to say he found himself not only unrepresented in actual politics, but almost equally opposed to every class of reformers. Yet he paid the tribute of his uniform respect to the Anti-Slavery party. One man, whose personal acquaintance he had formed, he honored with exceptional regard. Before the first friendly word had been spoken for Captain John Brown,° he sent notices to most houses in Concord, that he would speak in a public hall on the condition and character of John Brown, on Sunday evening, and invited all people to come. The Republican Committee, the Abolitionist Committee, sent him word that it was premature and not advisable. He replied,—'I did not send to you for advice, but to announce that I am to speak.' The hall was filled at an early hour by people of all parties, and his earnest eulogy of the hero was heard by all respectfully, by many with a sympathy that surprised themselves.

It was said of Plotinus° that he was ashamed of his body, and 't is very likely he had good reason for it,—that his body was a bad servant, and he had not skill in dealing with the material world, as happens often to men of abstract intellect. But Mr. Thoreau was equipped with a most adapted and serviceable body. He was of short stature, firmly built, of light complexion, with strong, serious blue eyes, and a grave aspect,— his face covered in the late years with a becoming beard. His senses were acute, his frame well-knit and hardy, his hands strong and skilful in the use of tools. And there was a wonderful fitness of body and mind. He could pace sixteen rods more accurately than another man could measure them with rod and chain. He could find his path in the woods at night, he said, better by his feet than his eyes. He could estimate the measure of a tree very well by his eye; he could estimate the weight of a calf or a pig, like a dealer. From a box containing a bushel or more of loose pencils,° he could take up with his hands fast enough just a dozen pencils at every grasp. He was a good swimmer, runner, skater, boatman, and would probably outwalk most countrymen in a day's journey. And the relation of body to mind was still finer than we have indicated. He said he wanted every stride his legs made. The length of his walk uniformly made the length of his writing. If shut up in the house, he did not write at all.

He had a strong common sense, like that which Rose Flammock, the weaver's daughter, in Scott's romance,° commends in her father, as resembling a yardstick, which, whilst it measures dowlas and diaper, can equally well measure tapestry and cloth of gold. He had always a new resource. When I was planting forest-trees, and had procured half a peck of acorns, he said that only a small portion of them would be sound, and proceeded to examine them, and select the sound ones. But finding this took time, he said, 'I think, if you put them all into water, the good ones will sink'; which experiment we tried with success. He could plan a garden, or a house, or a barn; would have been competent to lead a 'Pacific Exploring Expedition'; could give judicious counsel in the gravest private or public affairs.

He lived for the day, not cumbered and mortified by his memory. If he brought you yesterday a new proposition, he would bring you to-day another not less revolutionary. A very industrious man, and setting, like all highly organized men, a high value on his time, he seemed the only man of leisure in town, always ready for any excursion that promised well, or for conversation prolonged into late hours. His trenchant sense was never stopped by his rules of daily prudence, but was always up to the new occasion. He liked and used the simplest food, yet, when some one urged a vegetable diet, Thoreau thought all diets a very small matter, saying that 'the man who shoots the buffalo lives better than the man who boards at the Graham House.' He said,—'You can sleep near the railroad, and never be disturbed: Nature knows very well what sounds are worth attending to, and has made up her mind not to hear the railroad-whistle. But things respect the devout mind, and a mental ecstasy was never interrupted.' He noted, what repeatedly befell him, that, after receiving from a distance a rare plant, he would presently find the same in his own haunts. And those pieces of luck which happen only to good players happened to him. One day, walking with a stranger, who inquired where Indian arrow-heads could be found, he replied, 'Everywhere,' and, stooping forward, picked one on the instant from the ground. At Mount Washington, in Tuckerman's Ravine, Thoreau had a bad fall, and sprained his foot. As he was in the act of getting up from his fall, he saw for the first time the leaves of the *Arnica mollis*.°

His robust common sense, armed with stout hands, keen perceptions, and strong will, cannot yet account for the superiority which shone in his simple and hidden life. I must add the cardinal fact, that there was an excellent wisdom in him, proper to a rare class of men, which showed him the material world as a means and symbol. This dis-

covery, which sometimes yields to poets a certain casual and interrupted light, serving for the ornament of their writing, was in him an
unsleeping insight; and whatever faults or obstructions of temperament
might cloud it, he was not disobedient to the heavenly vision. In his
youth, he said, one day, 'The other world is all my art: my pencils will
draw no other; my jack-knife will cut nothing else; I do not use it as a
means.' This was the muse and genius that ruled his opinions, conversation, studies, work, and course of life. This made him a searching
judge of men. At first glance he measured his companion, and, though
insensible to some fine traits of culture, could very well report his
weight and calibre. And this made the impression of genius which his
conversation sometimes gave.

He understood the matter in hand at a glance, and saw the limitations and poverty of those he talked with, so that nothing seemed concealed from such terrible eyes. I have repeatedly known young men of
sensibility converted in a moment to the belief that this was the man
they were in search of, the man of men, who could tell them all they
should do. His own dealing with them was never affectionate, but
superior, didactic,—scorning their petty ways,—very slowly conceding,
or not conceding at all, the promise of his society at their houses, or
even at his own. 'Would he not walk with them?' 'He did not know.
There was nothing so important to him as his walk; he had no walks to
throw away on company.' Visits were offered him from respectful parties, but he declined them. Admiring friends offered to carry him at
their own cost to the Yellow-Stone River,—to the West Indies,—to
South America. But though nothing could be more grave or considered
than his refusals, they remind one in quite new relations of that fop
Brummel's° reply to the gentleman who offered him his carriage in a
shower, 'But where will *you* ride, then?'—and what accusing silences,
and what searching and irresistible speeches, battering down all
defences, his companions can remember!

Mr. Thoreau dedicated his genius with such entire love to the fields,
hills, and waters of his native town, that he made them known and
interesting to all reading Americans, and to people over the sea. The
river on whose banks he was born° and died he knew from its springs to
its confluence with the Merrimack. He had made summer and winter
observations on it for many years, and at every hour of the day and the
night. The result of the recent survey of the Water Commissioners
appointed by the State of Massachusetts he had reached by his private
experiments, several years earlier. Every fact which occurs in the bed,
on the banks, or in the air over it; the fishes, and their spawning and

nests, their manners, their food; the shad-flies which fill the air on a certain evening once a year, and which are snapped at by the fishes so ravenously that many of these die of repletion; the conical heaps of small stones on the river-shallows, one of which heaps will sometimes overfill a cart,—these heaps the huge nests of small fishes; the birds which frequent the stream, heron, duck, sheldrake, loon, osprey; the snake, muskrat, otter, woodchuck, and fox, on the banks; the turtle, frog, hyla, and cricket, which make the banks vocal,—were all known to him, and, as it were, townsmen and fellow-creatures; so that he felt an absurdity or violence in any narrative of one of these by itself apart, and still more of its dimensions on an inch-rule, or in the exhibition of its skeleton, or the specimen of a squirrel or a bird in brandy. He liked to speak of the manners of the river, as itself a lawful creature, yet with exactness, and always to an observed fact. As he knew the river, so the ponds in this region.

One of the weapons he used, more important than microscope or alcohol-receiver to other investigators, was a whim which grew on him by indulgence, yet appeared in gravest statement, namely, of extolling his own town and neighborhood as the most favored centre for natural observation. He remarked that the Flora of Massachusetts embraced almost all the important plants of America,—most of the oaks, most of the willows, the best pines, the ash, the maple, the beech, the nuts. He returned Kane's 'Arctic Voyage'° to a friend of whom he had borrowed it, with the remark, that 'most of the phenomena noted might be observed in Concord.' He seemed a little envious of the Pole, for the coincident sunrise and sunset, or five minutes' day after six months: a splendid fact, which Annursnuc° had never afforded him. He found red snow in one of his walks, and told me that he expected to find yet the Victoria regia° in Concord. He was the attorney of the indigenous plants, and owned to a preference of the weeds to the imported plants, as of the Indian to the civilized man,—and noticed, with pleasure, that the willow bean-poles of his neighbor had grown more than his beans. 'See these weeds,' he said, 'which have been hoed at by a million farmers all spring and summer, and yet have prevailed, and just now come out triumphant over all lanes, pastures, fields, and gardens, such is their vigor. We have insulted them with low names, too,—as Pigweed, Wormwood, Chickweed, Shad-Blossom.' He says, 'They have brave names, too,—Ambrosia, Stellaria, Amelanchia, Amaranth, etc.'

I think his fancy for referring everything to the meridian of Concord did not grow out of any ignorance or depreciation of other longitudes or latitudes, but was rather a playful expression of his conviction of the indifferency of all places, and that the best place for each is where he stands. He expressed it once in this wise:—'I think nothing is to be hoped from you, if this bit of mould under your feet is not sweeter to you to eat than any other in this world, or in any world.'

The other weapon with which he conquered all obstacles in science was patience. He knew how to sit immovable, a part of the rock he rested on, until the bird, the reptile, the fish, which had retired from him, should come back, and resume its habits, nay, moved by curiosity, should come to him and watch him.

It was a pleasure and a privilege to walk with him. He knew the country like a fox or a bird, and passed through it as freely by paths of his own. He knew every track in the snow or on the ground, and what creature had taken this path before him. One must submit abjectly to such a guide, and the reward was great. Under his arm he carried an old music-book to press plants; in his pocket, his diary and pencil, a spy-glass for birds, microscope, jack-knife, and twine. He wore straw hat, stout shoes, strong gray trousers, to brave shrub-oaks and smilax, and to climb a tree for a hawk's or a squirrel's nest. He waded into the pool for the water-plants, and his strong legs were no insignificant part of his armor. On the day I speak of hc looked for the Menyanthes,° detected it across the wide pool, and, on examination of the florets, decided that it had been in flower five days. He drew out of his breast-pocket his diary, and read the names of all the plants that should bloom on this day, whereof he kept account as a banker when his notes fall due. The Cypripedium° not due till to-morrow. He thought, that, if waked up from a trance, in this swamp, he could tell by the plants what time of the year it was within two days. The redstart was flying about, and presently the fine gros-beaks, whose brilliant scarlet makes the rash gazer wipe his eye,° and whose fine clear note Thoreau compared to that of a tanager which has got rid of its hoarseness. Presently he heard a note which he called that of the night-warbler, a bird he had never identified, had been in search of twelve years, which always, when he saw it, was in the act of diving down into a tree or bush, and which it was vain to seek; the only bird that sings indifferently by night and by day. I told him he must beware of finding and booking it, lest life should have nothing more to show him. He said, 'What you seek in vain for, half your life, one day you come full upon all the family at dinner. You seek it like a dream, and as soon as you find it you become its prey.'

His interest in the flower or the bird lay very deep in his mind, was connected with Nature,—and the meaning of Nature was never attempted to be defined by him. He would not offer a memoir of his observations to the Natural History Society. 'Why should I? To detach the description from its connections in my mind would make it no longer true or valuable to me: and they do not wish what belongs to it.' His power of observation seemed to indicate additional senses. He saw as with microscope, heard as with ear-trumpet, and his memory was a photographic register of all he saw and heard. And yet none knew better than he that it is not the fact that imports, but the impression or effect of the fact on your mind. Every fact lay in glory in his mind, a type of the order and beauty of the whole.

His determination on Natural History was organic. He confessed that he sometimes felt like a hound or a panther, and, if born among Indians, would have been a fell hunter. But, restrained by his Massachusetts culture, he played out the game in this mild form of botany and ichthyology. His intimacy with animals suggested what Thomas Fuller records of Butler the apiologist, that 'either he had told the bees things or the bees had told him.' Snakes coiled round his leg; the fishes swam into his hand, and he took them out of the water; he pulled the woodchuck out of its hole by the tail, and took the foxes under his protection from the hunters. Our naturalist had perfect magnanimity; he had no secrets: he would carry you to the heron's haunt, or even to his most prized botanical swamp,—possibly knowing that you could never find it again, yet willing to take his risks.

No college ever offered him a diploma, or a professor's chair; no academy made him its corresponding secretary, its discoverer, or even its member. Whether these learned bodies feared the satire of his presence. Yet so much knowledge of Nature's secret and genius few others possessed, none in a more large and religious synthesis. For not a particle of respect had he to the opinions of any man or body of men, but homage solely to the truth itself; and as he discovered everywhere among doctors some leaning of courtesy, it discredited them. He grew to be revered and admired by his townsmen, who had at first known him only as an oddity. The farmers who employed him as a surveyor soon discovered his rare accuracy and skill, his knowledge of their lands, of trees, of birds, of Indian remains, and the like, which enabled him to tell every farmer more than he knew before of his own farm; so that he began to feel a little as if Mr. Thoreau had better rights in his land than he. They felt, too, the superiority of character which addressed all men with a native authority.

Indian relics abound in Concord,—arrow-heads, stone chisels, pestles, and fragments of pottery; and on the river-bank, large heaps of clam-shells and ashes mark spots which the savages frequented. These, and every circumstance touching the Indian, were important in his eyes. His visits to Maine were chiefly for love of the Indian. He had the satisfaction of seeing the manufacture of the bark-canoe, as well as of trying his hand in its management on the rapids. He was inquisitive about the making of the stone arrow-head, and in his last days charged a youth setting out for the Rocky Mountains to find an Indian who could tell him that: 'It was well worth a visit to California to learn it.' Occasionally, a small party of Penobscot Indians would visit Concord, and pitch their tents for a few weeks in summer on the river-bank. He failed not to make acquaintance with the best of them; though he well knew that asking questions of Indians is like catechizing beavers and rabbits. In his last visit to Maine he had great satisfaction from Joseph Polis, an intelligent Indian of Oldtown, who was his guide for some weeks.

He was equally interested in every natural fact. The depth of his perception found likeness of law throughout Nature, and I know not any genius who so swiftly inferred universal law from the single fact. He was no pedant of a department. His eye was open to beauty, and his ear to music. He found these, not in rare conditions, but wheresoever he went. He thought the best of music was in single strains; and he found poetic suggestion in the humming of the telegraph-wire.

His poetry might be bad or good; he no doubt wanted a lyric facility and technical skill; but he had the source of poetry in his spiritual perception. He was a good reader and critic, and his judgment on poetry was to the ground of it. He could not be deceived as to the presence or absence of the poetic element in any composition, and his thirst for this made him negligent and perhaps scornful of superficial graces. He would pass by many delicate rhythms, but he would have detected every live stanza or line in a volume, and knew very well where to find an equal poetic charm in prose. He was so enamored of the spiritual beauty that he held all actual written poems in very light esteem in the comparison. He admired Æschylus and Pindar;° but, when some one was commending them, he said that 'Æschylus and the Greeks, in describing Apollo and Orpheus, had given no song, or no good one. They ought not to have moved trees, but to have chanted to the gods such a hymn as would have sung all their old ideas out of their heads, and new ones in.' His own verses are often rude and defective. The gold does not yet run pure, is drossy and crude. The thyme and marjoram are not yet honey. But if he want lyric fineness and technical merits, if he have not the poetic temperament, he never lacks the causal thought, showing that his genius was better than his talent. He knew the worth of the

Imagination for the uplifting and consolation of human life, and liked to throw every thought into a symbol. The fact you tell is of no value, but only the impression. For this reason his presence was poetic, always piqued the curiosity to know more deeply the secrets of his mind. He had many reserves, an unwillingness to exhibit to profane eyes what was still sacred in his own, and knew well how to throw a poetic veil over his experience. All readers of 'Walden' will remember his mythical record of his disappointments:—

'I long ago lost a hound, a bay horse, and a turtle-dove, and am still on their trail. Many are the travellers I have spoken concerning them, describing their tracks, and what calls they answered to. I have met one or two who had heard the hound, and the tramp of the horse, and even seen the dove disappear behind a cloud; and they seemed as anxious to recover them as if they had lost them themselves.'*

His riddles were worth the reading, and I confide, that, if at any time I do not understand the expression, it it yet just. Such was the wealth of his truth that it was not worth his while to use words in vain. His poem entitled 'Sympathy' reveals the tenderness under that triple steel of stoicism, and the intellectual subtilty it could animate. His classic poem on 'Smoke' suggests Simonides,° but is better than any poem of Simonides. His biography is in his verses. His habitual thought makes all his poetry a hymn to the Cause of causes, the Spirit which vivifies and controls his own.

> 'I hearing get, who had but ears,
> And sight, who had but eyes before;
> I moments live, who lived but years,
> And truth discern, who knew but learning's lore.'

And still more in these religious lines:—

> 'Now chiefly is my natal hour,
> And only now my prime of life;
> I will not doubt the love untold,
> Which not my worth or want hath bought,
> Which wooed me young, and wooes me old,
> And to this evening hath me brought.'°

Whilst he used in his writings a certain petulance of remark in reference to churches or churchmen, he was a person of a rare, tender, and absolute religion, a person incapable of any profanation, by act or by thought. Of course, the same isolation which belonged to his original

* Walden, p. 20.

thinking and living detached him from the social religious forms. This is neither to be censured nor regretted. Aristotle long ago explained it, when he said, 'One who surpasses his fellow-citizens in virtue is no longer a part of the city. Their law is not for him, since he is a law to himself.'

Thoreau was sincerity itself, and might fortify the convictions of prophets in the ethical laws by his holy living. It was an affirmative experience which refused to be set aside. A truth-speaker he, capable of the most deep and strict conversation; a physician to the wounds of any soul; a friend, knowing not only the secret of friendship, but almost worshipped by those few persons who resorted to him as their confessor and prophet, and knew the deep value of his mind and great heart. He thought that without religion or devotion of some kind nothing great was ever accomplished: and he thought that the bigoted sectarian had better bear this in mind.

His virtues, of course, sometimes ran into extremes. It was easy to trace to the inexorable demand on all for exact truth that austerity which made this willing hermit more solitary even than he wished. Himself of a perfect probity, he required not less of others. He had a disgust at crime, and no worldly success would cover it. He detected paltering as readily in dignified and prosperous persons as in beggars, and with equal scorn. Such dangerous frankness was in his dealing that his admirers called him 'that terrible Thoreau,' as if he spoke when silent, and was still present when he had departed. I think the severity of his ideal interfered to deprive him of a healthy sufficiency of human society.

The habit of a realist to find things the reverse of their appearance inclined him to put every statement in a paradox. A certain habit of antagonism defaced his earlier writings,—a trick of rhetoric not quite outgrown in his later, of substituting for the obvious word and thought its diametrical opposite. He praised wild mountains and winter forests for their domestic air, in snow and ice he would find sultriness, and commended the wilderness for resembling Rome and Paris. 'It was so dry, that you might call it wet.'

The tendency to magnify the moment, to read all the laws of Nature in the one object or one combination under your eye, is of course comic to those who do not share the philosopher's perception of identity. To him there was no such thing as size. The pond was a small ocean; the Atlantic, a large Walden Pond. He referred every minute fact to cosmical laws. Though he meant to be just, he seemed haunted by a certain chronic assumption that the science of the day pretended completeness, and he had just found out that the *savans* had neglected to discriminate a particular botanical variety, had failed to describe the seeds or count the sepals. 'That is to say,' we replied, 'the blockheads were not born in Concord; but who said they were? It was their unspeakable misfortune to be born in London, or Paris, or Rome; but, poor fellows, they did what they could, considering that they never saw Bateman's Pond, or Nine-Acre Corner, or Becky-Stow's Swamp. Besides, what were you sent into the world for, but to add this observation?'

Had his genius been only contemplative, he had been fitted to his life, but with his energy and practical ability he seemed born for great enterprise and for command; and I so much regret the loss of his rare powers of action, that I cannot help counting it a fault in him that he had no ambition. Wanting this, instead of engineering for all America, he was the captain of a huckleberry-party. Pounding beans is good to the end of pounding empires one of these days; but if, at the end of years, it is still only beans!

But these foibles, real or apparent, were fast vanishing in the incessant growth of a spirit so robust and wise, and which effaced its defeats with new triumphs. His study of Nature was a perpetual ornament to him, and inspired his friends with curiosity to see the world through his eyes, and to hear his adventures. They possessed every kind of interest.

He had many elegances of his own, whilst he scoffed at conventional elegance. Thus, he could not bear to hear the sound of his own steps, the grit of gravel; and therefore never willingly walked in the road, but in the grass, on mountains and in woods. His senses were acute, and he remarked that by night every dwelling-house gives out bad air, like a slaughter-house. He liked the pure fragrance of melilot.° He honored certain plants with special regard, and, over all, the pond-lily,—then, the gentian, and the *Mikania scandens*,° and 'life-everlasting,' and a bass-tree which he visited every year when it bloomed, in the middle of July. He thought the scent a more oracular inquisition than the sight,— more oracular and trustworthy. The scent, of course, reveals what is concealed from the other senses. By it he detected earthiness. He delighted in echoes, and said they were almost the only kind of kindred voices that he heard. He loved Nature so well, was so happy in her solitude, that he became very jealous of cities, and the sad work which their refinements and artifices made with man and his dwelling. The axe was always destroying his forest. 'Thank God,' he said, 'they cannot cut down the clouds!' 'All kinds of figures are drawn on the blue ground with this fibrous white paint.'

I subjoin a few sentences taken from his unpublished manuscripts, not only as records of his thought and feeling, but for their power of description and literary excellence.

'Some circumstantial evidence is very strong, as when you find a trout in the milk.'

'The chub is a soft fish, and tastes like boiled brown paper salted.'

'The youth gets together his materials to build a bridge to the moon, or, perchance, a palace or temple on the earth, and at length the middle-aged man concludes to build a wood-shed with them.'

'The locust z–ing.'

'Devil's-needles zigzagging along the Nut-Meadow brook.'

'Sugar is not so sweet to the palate as sound to the healthy ear.'

'I put on some hemlock-boughs, and the rich salt crackling of their leaves was like mustard to the ear, the crackling of uncountable regiments. Dead trees love the fire.'

'The bluebird carries the sky on his back.'

'The tanager flies through the green foliage as if it would ignite the leaves.'

'If I wish for a horse-hair for my compass-sight, I must go to the stable; but the hair-bird, with her sharp eyes, goes to the road.'

'Immortal water, alive even to the superficies.'

'Fire is the most tolerable third party.'

'Nature made ferns for pure leaves, to show what she could do in that line.'

'No tree has so fair a bole and so handsome an instep as the beech.'

'How did these beautiful rainbow-tints get into the shell of the fresh-water clam, buried in the mud at the bottom of our dark river?'

'Hard are the times when the infant's shoes are second-foot.'

'We are strictly confined to our men to whom we give liberty.'

'Nothing is so much to be feared as fear. Atheism may comparatively be popular with God himself.'

'Of what significance the things you can forget? A little thought is sexton to all the world.'

'How can we expect a harvest of thought who have not had a seed-time of character?'

'Only he can be trusted with gifts who can present a face of bronze to expectations.'

'I ask to be melted. You can only ask of the metals that they be tender to the fire that melts them. To nought else can they be tender.'

There is a flower known to botanists, one of the same genus with our summer plant called 'Life-Everlasting,' a *Gnaphalium*° like that, which grows on the most inaccessible cliffs of the Tyrolese mountains,° where the chamois dare hardly venture, and which the hunter, tempted by its beauty, and by his love, (for it is immensely valued by the Swiss maidens,) climbs the cliffs to gather, and is sometimes found dead at the foot, with the flower in his hand. It is called by botanists the *Gnaphalium leontopodium*, but by the Swiss *Edelweisse*, which signifies *Noble Purity*. Thoreau seemed to me living in the hope to gather this plant, which belonged to him of right. The scale on which his studies proceeded was so large as to require longevity, and we were the less prepared for his sudden disappearance. The country knows not yet, or in the least part, how great a son it has lost. It seems an injury that he should leave in the midst his broken task, which none else can finish,— a kind of indignity to so noble a soul, that it should depart out of Nature before yet he has been really shown to his peers for what he is. But he, at least, is content. His soul was made for the noblest society; he had in a short life exhausted the capabilities of this world; wherever there is knowledge, wherever there is virtue, wherever there is beauty, he will find a home.

POEMS

To-day

I rake no coffined clay, nor publish wide
The resurrection of departed pride.
Safe in their ancient crannies, dark and deep,
Let kings and conquerors, saints and soldiers sleep—
Late in the world,—too late perchance for fame,
Just late enough to reap abundant blame,—
I choose a novel theme, a bold abuse
Of critic charters, an unlaurelled Muse.

Old mouldy men and books and names and lands
Disgust my reason and defile my hands.   10
I had as lief respect an ancient shoe,
As love old things *for age*, and hate the new.
I spurn the Past, my mind disdains its nod,
Nor kneels in homage to so mean a God.
I laugh at those who, while they gape and gaze,
The bald antiquity of China praise.
Youth is (whatever cynic tubs pretend)
The fault that boys and nations soonest mend.

                                                        1824.

The River

And I behold once more
My old familiar haunts; here the blue river,
The same blue wonder that my infant eye
Admired, sage doubting whence the traveller came,—
Whence brought his sunny bubbles ere he washed
The fragrant flag-roots° in my father's fields,
And where thereafter in the world he went.
Look, here he is, unaltered, save that now
He hath broke his banks and flooded all the vales
With his redundant waves.   10

Here is the rock where, yet a simple child,
I caught with bended pin my earliest fish,
Much triumphing,—and these the fields
Over whose flowers I chased the butterfly,
A blooming hunter of a fairy fine.
And hark! where overhead the ancient crows
Hold their sour conversation in the sky:—
These are the same, but I am not the same,
But wiser than I was, and wise enough
Not to regret the changes, tho' they cost   20
Me many a sigh. Oh, call not Nature dumb;
These trees and stones are audible to me,
These idle flowers, that tremble in the wind,
I understand their faery syllables,
And all their sad significance. The wind,
That rustles down the well-known forest road—
It hath a sound more eloquent than speech.
The stream, the trees, the grass, the sighing wind,
All of them utter sounds of 'monishment
And grave parental love.   30
They are not of our race, they seem to say,
And yet have knowledge of our moral race,
And somewhat of majestic sympathy,
Something of pity for the puny clay,
That holds and boasts the immeasurable mind.
I feel as I were welcome to these trees
After long months of weary wandering,
Acknowledged by their hospitable boughs;
They know me as their son, for side by side,
They were coeval with my ancestors,   40
Adorned with them my country's primitive times,
And soon may give my dust their funeral shade.

CONCORD, June, 1827.

A Letter

Dear brother, would you know the life,
Please God, that I would lead?
On the first wheels that quit this weary town
Over yon western bridges I would ride

And with a cheerful benison forsake
Each street and spire and roof, incontinent.
Then would I seek where God might guide my steps,
Deep in a woodland tract, a sunny farm,
Amid the mountain counties, Hants, Franklin, Berks,
Where down the rock ravine a river roars,   10
Even from a brook, and where old woods
Not tamed and cleared cumber the ground
With their centennial wrecks.
Find me a slope where I can feel the sun
And mark the rising of the early stars.
There will I bring my books,—my household gods,
The reliquaries of my dead saint, and dwell
In the sweet odor of her memory.
Then in the uncouth solitude unlock
My stock of art, plant dials in the grass,   20
Hang in the air a bright thermometer
And aim a telescope at the inviolate sun.

CHARDON ST., BOSTON, 1831.

Webster

1831

Let Webster's lofty face
Ever on thousands shine,
A beacon set that Freedom's race
Might gather omens from that radiant sign.

From the Phi Beta Kappa Poem

1834

Ill fits the abstemious Muse a crown to weave
For living brows; ill fits them to receive:
And yet, if virtue abrogate the law,
One portrait—fact or fancy—we may draw;
A form which Nature cast in the heroic mould
Of them who rescued liberty of old;   10
He, when the rising storm of party roared,

Brought his great forehead to the council board,
There, while hot heads perplexed with fears the state,
Calm as the morn the manly patriot sate;
Seemed, when at last his clarion accents broke,
As if the conscience of the country spoke.
Not on its base Monadnoc° surer stood,
Than he to common sense and common good:
No mimic; from his breast his counsel drew,
Believed the eloquent was aye the true;   20
He bridged the gulf from th' alway good and wise
To that within the vision of small eyes.
Self-centred; when he launched the genuine word
It shook or captivated all who heard,
Ran from his mouth to mountains and the sea,
And burned in noble hearts proverb and prophecy.

1854

Why did all manly gifts in Webster fail?
He wrote on Nature's grandest brow, For Sale.

Each and All

Little thinks, in the field, yon red-cloaked clown,°
Of thee from the hill-top looking down;
The heifer that lows in the upland farm,
Far-heard, lows not thine ear to charm;
The sexton, tolling his bell at noon,
Deems not that great Napoleon
Stops his horse, and lists with delight,
Whilst his files sweep round yon Alpine height;
Nor knowest thou what argument
Thy life to thy neighbor's creed has lent.   10
All are needed by each one;
Nothing is fair or good alone.
I thought the sparrow's note from heaven,
Singing at dawn on the alder bough;
I brought him home, in his nest, at even;
He sings the song, but it pleases not now,
For I did not bring home the river and sky;—

He sang to my ear,—they sang to my eye.
The delicate shells lay on the shore;
The bubbles of the latest wave   20
Fresh pearls to their enamel gave;
And the bellowing of the savage sea
Greeted their safe escape to me.
I wiped away the weeds and foam,
I fetched my sea-born treasures home;
But the poor, unsightly, noisome things
Had left their beauty on the shore,
With the sun, and the sand, and the wild uproar.
The lover watched his graceful maid,
As 'mid the virgin train she strayed,   30
Nor knew her beauty's best attire
Was woven still by the snow-white choir.
At last she came to his hermitage,
Like the bird from the woodlands to the cage;—
The gay enchantment was undone,
A gentle wife, but fairy none.
Then I said, 'I covet truth;
Beauty is unripe childhood's cheat;
I leave it behind with the games of youth.'—
As I spoke, beneath my feet   40
The ground-pine curled its pretty wreath,
Running over the club-moss burrs;
I inhaled the violet's breath;
Around me stood the oaks and firs;
Pine-cones and acorns lay on the ground,
Over me soared the eternal sky,
Full of light and of deity;
Again I saw, again I heard,
The rolling river, the morning bird;—
Beauty through my senses stole;   50
I yielded myself to the perfect whole.

The Problem

I like a church; I like a cowl;
I love a prophet of the soul;

And on my heart monastic aisles
Fall like sweet strains, or pensive smiles;
Yet not for all his faith can see
Would I that cowled churchman be.

Why should the vest on him allure,
Which I could not on me endure?

Not from a vain or shallow thought
His awful Jove young Phidias° brought;   10
Never from lips of cunning fell
The thrilling Delphic oracle;°
Out from the heart of nature rolled
The burdens of the Bible old;
The litanies of nations came,
Like the volcano's tongue of flame,
Up from the burning core below,—
The canticles of love and woe;
The hand that rounded Peter's dome,
And groined the aisles of Christian Rome,   20
Wrought in a sad sincerity;
Himself from God he could not free;
He builded better than he knew;—
The conscious stone to beauty grew.

Know'st thou what wove yon woodbird's nest
Of leaves, and feathers from her breast?
Or how the fish outbuilt her shell,
Painting with morn each annual cell?
Or how the sacred pine-tree adds
To her old leaves new myriads?   30
Such and so grew these holy piles,
Whilst love and terror laid the tiles.
Earth proudly wears the Parthenon,
As the best gem upon her zone;
And Morning opes with haste her lids,
To gaze upon the Pyramids;
O'er England's abbeys bends the sky,
As on its friends, with kindred eye;
For, out of Thought's interior sphere,
These wonders rose to upper air;   40
And Nature gladly gave them place,

Adopted them into her race,
And granted them an equal date
With Andes and with Ararat.°

These temples grew as grows the grass;
Art might obey, but not surpass.
The passive Master lent his hand
To the vast soul that o'er him planned;
And the same power that reared the shrine,
Bestrode the tribes that knelt within.   50
Ever the fiery Pentecost°
Girds with one flame the countless host,
Trances the heart through chanting choirs,
And through the priest the mind inspires.
The word unto the prophet spoken
Was writ on tables yet unbroken;
The word by seers or sibyls told,
In groves of oak, or fanes of gold,
Still floats upon the morning wind,
Still whispers to the willing mind.   60
One accent of the Holy Ghost
The heedless world hath never lost.
I know what say the fathers wise,—
The Book itself before me lies,
Old *Chrysostom*, best Augustine,°
And he who blent both in his line,
The younger *Golden Lips* or mines,
Taylor,° the Shakspeare of divines.
His words are music in my ear,
I see his cowled portrait dear;   70
And yet, for all his faith could see,
I would not the good bishop be.

To Rhea

Thee, dear friend, a brother soothes,
Not with flatteries, but truths,
Which tarnish not, but purify
To light which dims the morning's eye.
I have come from the spring-woods,
From the fragrant solitudes;—

Listen what the poplar-tree
And murmuring waters counselled me.

If with love thy heart has burned;
If thy love is unreturned;   10
Hide thy grief within thy breast,
Though it tear thee unexpressed;
For when love has once departed
From the eyes of the false-hearted,
And one by one has torn off quite
The bandages of purple light;
Though thou wert the loveliest
Form the soul had ever dressed,
Thou shalt seem, in each reply,
A vixen to his altered eye;   20
Thy softest pleadings seem too bold,
Thy praying lute will seem to scold;
Though thou kept the straightest road,
Yet thou errest far and broad.

But thou shalt do as do the gods
In their cloudless periods;
For of this lore be thou sure,—
Though thou forget, the gods, secure,
Forget never their command,
But make the statute of this land.   30
As they lead, so follow all,
Ever have done, ever shall.
Warning to the blind and deaf,
'Tis written on the iron leaf,
Who drinks of Cupid's nectar cup
Loveth downward, and not up;
Therefore, who loves, of gods or men,
Shall not by the same be loved again;
His sweetheart's idolatry
Falls, in turn, a new degree.   40
When a god is once beguiled
By beauty of a mortal child,
And by her radiant youth delighted,
He is not fooled, but warily knoweth
His love shall never be requited.

And thus the wise Immortal doeth.—
'Tis his study and delight
To bless that creature day and night;
From all evils to defend her;
In her lap to pour all splendor;   50
To ransack earth for riches rare,
And fetch her stars to deck her hair:
He mixes music with her thoughts,
And saddens her with heavenly doubts:
All grace, all good his great heart knows,
Profuse in love, the king bestows:
Saying, 'Hearken! Earth, Sea, Air!
This monument of my despair
Build I to the All-Good, All-Fair.
Not for a private good,   60
But I, from my beatitude,
Albeit scorned as none was scorned,
Adorn her as was none adorned.
I make this maiden an ensample
To Nature, through her kingdoms ample,
Whereby to model newer races,
Statelier forms, and fairer faces;
To carry man to new degrees
Of power, and of comeliness.
These presents be the hostages   70
Which I pawn for my release.
See to thyself, O Universe!
Thou art better, and not worse.'—
And the god, having given all,
Is freed forever from his thrall.

The Visit

Askest, 'How long thou shalt stay,'
Devastator of the day?
Know, each substance, and relation,
Thorough nature's operation,
Hath its unit, bound, and metre;
And every new compound
Is some product and repeater,—

Product of the early found.
But the unit of the visit,
The encounter of the wise,—   10
Say, what other metre is it
Than the meeting of the eyes?
Nature poureth into nature
Through the channels of that feature.
Riding on the ray of sight,
More fleet than waves or whirlwinds go,
Or for service, or delight,
Hearts to hearts their meaning show,
Sum their long experience,
And import intelligence.   20
Single look has drained the breast;
Single moment years confessed.
The duration of a glance
Is the term of convenance,
And, though thy rede° be church or state,
Frugal multiples of that.
Speeding Saturn cannot halt;
Linger,—thou shalt rue the fault;
If Love his moment overstay,
Hatred's swift repulsions play.   30

Uriel

It fell in the ancient periods,
   Which the brooding soul surveys,
Or ever the wild Time coined itself
   Into calendar months and days.

This was the lapse of Uriel,
Which in Paradise befell.
Once, among the Pleiads° walking,
Said° overheard the young gods talking;
And the treason, too long pent,
To his ears was evident.   10
The young deities discussed
Laws of form, and metre just,
Orb, quintessence, and sunbeams,

What subsisteth, and what seems.
One, with low tones that decide,
And doubt and reverend use defied,
With a look that solved the sphere,
And stirred the devils everywhere,
Gave his sentiment divine
Against the being of a line.   20
'Line in nature is not found;
Unit and universe are round;
In vain produced, all rays return;
Evil will bless, and ice will burn.'
As Uriel spoke with piercing eye,
A shudder ran around the sky;
The stern old war-gods shook their heads;
The seraphs frowned from myrtle-beds;
Seemed to the holy festival
The rash word boded ill to all;   30
The balance-beam of Fate was bent;
The bounds of good and ill were rent;
Strong Hades could not keep his own,
But all slid to confusion.
A sad self-knowledge, withering, fell
On the beauty of Uriel;
In heaven once eminent, the god
Withdrew, that hour, into his cloud;
Whether doomed to long gyration
In the sea of generation,   40
Or by knowledge grown too bright
To hit the nerve of feebler sight.
Straightway, a forgetting wind
Stole over the celestial kind,
And their lips the secret kept,
If in ashes the fire-seed slept.
But now and then, truth-speaking things
Shamed the angels' veiling wings;
And, shrilling from the solar course,
Or from fruit of chemic force,   50
Procession of a soul in matter,
Or the speeding change of water,
Or out of the good of evil born,
Came Uriel's voice of cherub scorn,

And a blush tinged the upper sky,
And the gods shook, they knew not why.

The Sphinx

The Sphinx is drowsy,
    Her wings are furled;
Her ear is heavy,
    She broods on the world.
'Who'll tell me my secret,
    The ages have kept?—
I awaited the seer,
    While they slumbered and slept;—

'The fate of the man-child;
    The meaning of man;   10
Known fruit of the unknown;
    Dædalian plan;°
Out of sleeping a waking,
    Out of waking a sleep;
Life death overtaking;
    Deep underneath deep?

'Erect as a sunbeam,
    Upspringeth the palm;
The elephant browses,
    Undaunted and calm;   20
In beautiful motion
    The thrush plies his wings;
Kind leaves of his covert,
    Your silence he sings.

'The waves, unashamed,
    In difference sweet,
Play glad with the breezes,
    Old playfellows meet;
The journeying atoms,
    Primordial wholes,   30
Firmly draw, firmly drive,
    By their animate poles.

'Sea, earth, air, sound, silence,
   Plant, quadruped, bird,
By one music enchanted,
   One deity stirred,—
Each the other adorning,
   Accompany still;
Night veileth the morning,
   The vapor the hill.   40

'The babe by its mother
   Lies bathed in joy;
Glide its hours uncounted,—
   The sun is its toy;
Shines the peace of all being,
   Without cloud, in its eyes;
And the sum of the world
   In soft miniature lies.

'But man crouches and blushes,
   Absconds and conceals;   50
He creepeth and peepeth,
   He palters and steals;
Infirm, melancholy,
   Jealous glancing around,
An oaf, an accomplice,
   He poisons the ground.

'Outspoke the great mother,
   Beholding his fear;—
At the sound of her accents
   Cold shuddered the sphere:—   60
"Who has drugged my boy's cup?
   Who has mixed my boy's bread?
Who, with sadness and madness,
   Has turned the man-child's head?" '

I heard a poet answer,
   Aloud and cheerfully,
'Say on, sweet Sphinx! thy dirges
   Are pleasant songs to me.

Deep love lieth under
  These pictures of time;   70
They fade in the light of
  Their meaning sublime.

'The fiend that man harries
  Is love of the Best;
Yawns the pit of the Dragon,
  Lit by rays from the Blest.
The Lethe° of nature
  Can't trance him again,
Whose soul sees the perfect,
  Which his eyes seek in vain.   80

'Profounder, profounder,
  Man's spirit must dive;
To his aye-rolling orbit
  No goal will arrive;
The heavens that now draw him
  With sweetness untold,
Once found,—for new heavens
  He spurneth the old.

'Pride ruined the angels,
  Their shame them restores;   90
And the joy that is sweetest
  Lurks in stings of remorse.
Have I a lover
  Who is noble and free?—
I would he were nobler
  Than to love me.

'Eterne alternation
  Now follows, now flies;
And under pain, pleasure,—
  Under pleasure, pain lies.   100
Love works at the centre,
  Heart-heaving alway;
Forth speed the strong pulses
  To the borders of day.

'Dull Sphinx, Jove keep thy five wits!
    Thy sight is growing blear;
Rue, myrrh, and cummin° for the Sphinx—
    Her muddy eyes to clear!'—
The old Sphinx bit her thick lip,—
    Said, 'Who taught thee me to name?   110
I am thy spirit, yoke-fellow,
    Of thine eye I am eyebeam.

'Thou art the unanswered question;
    Couldst see thy proper eye,
Alway it asketh, asketh;
    And each answer is a lie.
So take thy quest through nature,
    It through thousand natures ply;
Ask on, thou clothed eternity;
    Time is the false reply.'   120

Uprose the merry Sphinx,
    And crouched no more in stone;
She melted into purple cloud,
    She silvered in the moon;
She spired into a yellow flame;
    She flowered in blossoms red;
She flowed into a foaming wave;
    She stood Monadnoc's head.

Thorough a thousand voices
    Spoke the universal dame: 130
'Who telleth one of my meanings,
    Is master of all I am.'

Mithridates

I cannot spare water or wine,
    Tobacco-leaf, or poppy, or rose;
From the earth-poles to the line,
    All between that works or grows,
Every thing is kin of mine.

Give me agates for my meat;
Give me cantharids to eat;
From air and ocean bring me foods,
From all zones and altitudes;—

From all natures, sharp and slimy,　　　　　　　10
　　Salt and basalt, wild and tame:
Tree and lichen, ape, sea-lion,
　　Bird, and reptile, be my game.

Ivy for my fillet band;
Blinding dog-wood in my hand;
Hemlock for my sherbet cull me,
And the prussic juice to lull me;
Swing me in the upas boughs,
Vampyre-fanned, when I carouse.°

Too long shut in strait and few,　　　　　　　20
Thinly dieted on dew,
I will use the world, and sift it,
To a thousand humors shift it,
As you spin a cherry.
O doleful ghosts, and goblins merry!
O all you virtues, methods, mights,
Means, appliances, delights,
Reputed wrongs and braggart rights,
Smug routine, and things allowed,
Minorities, things under cloud!　　　　　　　30
Hither! take me, use me, fill me,
Vein and artery, though ye kill me!
God! I will not be an owl,
But sun me in the Capitol.

Hamatreya

Minott, Lee, Willard, Hosmer, Meriam, Flint°
Possessed the land which rendered to their toil
Hay, corn, roots, hemp, flax, apples, wool, and wood.
Each of these landlords walked amidst his farm,

Saying, "Tis mine, my children's, and my name's:
How sweet the west wind sounds in my own trees!
How graceful climb those shadows on my hill!
I fancy these pure waters and the flags°
Know me, as does my dog: we sympathize;
And, I affirm, my actions smack of the soil.'   10
Where are these men? Asleep beneath their grounds;
And strangers, fond as they, their furrows plough.
Earth laughs in flowers, to see her boastful boys
Earth-proud, proud of the earth which is not theirs;
Who steer the plough, but cannot steer their feet
Clear of the grave.

They added ridge to valley, brook to pond,
And sighed for all that bounded their domain.
'This suits me for a pasture; that's my park;
We must have clay, lime, gravel, granite-ledge,   20
And misty lowland, where to go for peat.
The land is well,—lies fairly to the south.
'Tis good, when you have crossed the sea and back,
To find the sitfast acres where you left them.'
Ah! the hot owner sees not Death, who adds
Him to his land, a lump of mould the more.
Hear what the Earth says:—

Earth-Song

    'Mine and yours;
    Mine, not yours.
    Earth endures;   30
    Stars abide—
    Shine down in the old sea;
    Old are the shores;
    But where are old men?
    I who have seen much,
    Such have I never seen.

    'The lawyer's deed
    Ran sure,
    In tail,

To them, and to their heirs   40
Who shall succeed,
Without fail,
Forevermore.

'Here is the land,
Shaggy with wood,
With its old valley,
Mound, and flood.
But the heritors?
Fled like the flood's foam,—
The lawyer, and the laws,   50
And the kingdom,
Clean swept herefrom.

'They called me theirs,
Who so controlled me;
Yet every one
Wished to stay, and is gone.
How am I theirs,
If they cannot hold me,
But I hold them?'

When I heard the Earth-song,   60
I was no longer brave;
My avarice cooled
Like lust in the chill of the grave.

The Rhodora:

ON BEING ASKED, WHENCE IS THE FLOWER?

In May, when sea-winds pierced our solitudes,
I found the fresh Rhodora in the woods,
Spreading its leafless blooms in a damp nook,
To please the desert and the sluggish brook.
The purple petals, fallen in the pool,
Made the black water with their beauty gay;
Here might the red-bird come his plumes to cool,
And court the flower that cheapens his array.

Rhodora! if the sages ask thee why
This charm is wasted on the earth and sky,   10
Tell them, dear, that if eyes were made for seeing,
Then Beauty is its own excuse for being:
Why thou wert there, O rival of the rose!
I never thought to ask, I never knew;
But, in my simple ignorance, suppose
The self-same Power that brought me there brought you.

The Humble-Bee

Burly, dozing, humble-bee,
Where thou art is clime for me.
Let them sail for Porto Rique,°
Far-off heats through seas to seek;
I will follow thee alone,
Thou animated torrid-zone!
Zigzag steerer, desert cheerer,
Let me chase thy waving lines;
Keep me nearer, me thy hearer,
Singing over shrubs and vines.   10

Insect lover of the sun,
Joy of thy dominion!
Sailor of the atmosphere;
Swimmer through the waves of air;
Voyager of light and noon;
Epicurean of June;
Wait, I prithee, till I come
Within earshot of thy hum,—
All without is martyrdom.

When the south wind, in May days,   20
With a net of shining haze
Silvers the horizon wall,
And, with softness touching all,
Tints the human countenance
With a color of romance,

And, infusing subtle heats,
Turns the sod to violets,
Thou, in sunny solitudes,
Rover of the underwoods,
The green silence dost displace   30
With thy mellow, breezy bass.

Hot midsummer's petted crone,
Sweet to me thy drowsy tone
Tells of countless sunny hours,
Long days, and solid banks of flowers;
Of gulfs of sweetness without bound
In Indian wildernesses found;
Of Syrian peace, immortal leisure,
Firmest cheer, and bird-like pleasure.

Aught unsavory or unclean   40
Hath my insect never seen;
But violets and bilberry bells,
Maple-sap, and daffodels,
Grass with green flag half-mast high,
Succory to match the sky,
Columbine with horn of honey,
Scented fern, and agrimony,
Clover, catchfly, adder's tongue,
And brier roses, dwelt among;
All beside was unknown waste,   50
All was picture as he passed.

Wiser far than human seer,
Yellow-breeched philosopher!
Seeing only what is fair,
Sipping only what is sweet,
Thou dost mock at fate and care,
Leave the chaff, and take the wheat.
When the fierce north-western blast
Cools sea and land so far and fast,
Thou already slumberest deep;   60
Woe and want thou canst outsleep;
Want and woe, which torture us,
Thy sleep makes ridiculous.

The Snow-Storm

Announced by all the trumpets of the sky,
Arrives the snow, and, driving o'er the fields,
Seems nowhere to alight: the whited air
Hides hills and woods, the river, and the heaven,
And veils the farm-house at the garden's end.
The sled and traveller stopped, the courier's feet
Delayed, all friends shut out, the housemates sit
Around the radiant fireplace, enclosed
In a tumultuous privacy of storm.

Come see the north wind's masonry.   10
Out of an unseen quarry evermore
Furnished with tile, the fierce artificer
Curves his white bastions with projected roof
Round every windward stake, or tree, or door.
Speeding, the myriad-handed, his wild work
So fanciful, so savage, nought cares he
For number or proportion. Mockingly,
On coop or kennel he hangs Parian wreaths;°
A swan-like form invests the hidden thorn;
Fills up the farmer's lane from wall to wall,   20
Maugre the farmer's sighs; and, at the gate,
A tapering turret overtops the work.
And when his hours are numbered, and the world
Is all his own, retiring, as he were not,
Leaves, when the sun appears, astonished Art
To mimic in slow structures, stone by stone,
Built in an age, the mad wind's night-work,
The frolic architecture of the snow.

Woodnotes

I

I

For this present, hard
Is the fortune of the bard,

Born out of time;
All his accomplishment,
From Nature's utmost treasure spent,
    Booteth not him.
When the pine tosses its cones
To the song of its waterfall tones,
He speeds to the woodland walks,
To birds and trees he talks: 10
Cæsar of his leafy Rome,
There the poet is at home.
He goes to the river-side,—
Not hook nor line hath he;
He stands in the meadows wide,—
Nor gun nor scythe to see;
With none has he to do,
And none seek him,
Nor men below,
Nor spirits dim.   20
Sure some god his eye enchants:
What he knows nobody wants.
In the wood he travels glad,
Without better fortune had,
Melancholy without bad.
Planter of celestial plants,
What he knows nobody wants;
What he knows he hides, not vaunts.
Knowledge this man prizes best
Seems fantastic to the rest: 30
Pondering shadows, colors, clouds,
Grass-buds, and caterpillar-shrouds,
Boughs on which the wild bees settle,
Tints that spot the violets' petal,
Why Nature loves the number five,
And why the star-form she repeats:
Lover of all things alive,
Wonderer at all he meets,
Wonderer chiefly at himself,—
Who can tell him what he is?   40
Or how meet in human elf
Coming and past eternities?

2

And such I knew, a forest seer,
A minstrel of the natural year,
Foreteller of the vernal ides,
Wise harbinger of spheres and tides,
A lover true, who knew by heart
Each joy the mountain dales impart;
It seemed that Nature could not raise
A plant in any secret place,   50
In quaking bog, on snowy hill,
Beneath the grass that shades the rill,
Under the snow, between the rocks,
In damp fields known to bird and fox
But he would come in the very hour°
It opened in its virgin bower,
As if a sunbeam showed the place,
And tell its long-descended race.
It seemed as if the breezes brought him;
It seemed as if the sparrows taught him;   60
As if by secret sight he knew
Where, in far fields, the orchis grew.
Many haps fall in the field
Seldom seen by wishful eyes,
But all her shows did Nature yield,
To please and win this pilgrim wise.
He saw the partridge drum in the woods;
He heard the woodcock's evening hymn;
He found the tawny thrush's broods;
And the shy hawk did wait for him;   70
What others did at distance hear,
And guessed within the thicket's gloom,
Was showed to this philosopher,
And at his bidding seemed to come.

3

In unploughed Maine he sought the lumberers' gang,
Where from a hundred lakes young rivers sprang;
He trode the unplanted forest floor, whereon
The all-seeing sun for ages hath not shone;
Where feeds the moose, and walks the surly bear,
And up the tall mast runs the woodpecker.   80

He saw beneath dim aisles, in odorous beds,
The slight Linnæa° hang its twin-born heads,
And blessed the monument of the man of flowers,
Which breathes his sweet fame through the northern
      bowers.
He heard, when in the grove, at intervals,
With sudden roar the aged pine-tree falls,—
One crash, the death-hymn of the perfect tree,
Declares the close of its green century.
Low lies the plant to whose creation went
Sweet influence from every element;   90
Whose living towers the years conspired to build,
Whose giddy top the morning loved to gild.
Through these green tents, by eldest Nature dressed,
He roamed, content alike with man and beast.
Where darkness found him he lay glad at night;
There the red morning touched him with its light.
Three moons his great heart him a hermit made,
So long he roved at will the boundless shade.
The timid it concerns to ask their way,
And fear what foe in caves and swamps can stray,   100
To make no step until the event is known,
And ills to come as evils past bemoan.
Not so the wise; no coward watch he keeps
To spy what danger on his pathway creeps;
Go where he will, the wise man is at home,
His hearth the earth,—his hall the azure dome;
Where his clear spirit leads him, there's his road,
By God's own light illumined and foreshowed.

4

    'Twas one of the charmed days,
    When the genius of God doth flow,   110
    The wind may alter twenty ways,
    A tempest cannot blow;
    It may blow north, it still is warm;
    Or south, it still is clear;
    Or east, it smells like a clover-farm;
    Or west, no thunder fear.
    The musing peasant lowly great
    Beside the forest water sate;

The rope-like pine roots crosswise grown
Composed the network of his throne;   120
The wide lake, edged with sand and grass,
Was burnished to a floor of glass,
Painted with shadows green and proud
Of the tree and of the cloud.
He was the heart of all the scene;
On him the sun looked more serene;
To hill and cloud his face was known,—
It seemed the likeness of their own;
They knew by secret sympathy
The public child of earth and sky.   130
'You ask,' he said, 'what guide
Me through trackless thickets led,
Through thick-stemmed woodlands rough and wide?
I found the water's bed.
The watercourses were my guide;
I travelled grateful by their side,
Or through their channel dry;
They led me through the thicket damp,
Through brake and fern, the beavers' camp,
Through beds of granite cut my road,   140
And their resistless friendship showed;
The falling waters led me,
The foodful waters fed me,
And brought me to the lowest land,
Unerring to the ocean sand.
The moss upon the forest bark
Was polestar when the night was dark;
The purple berries in the wood
Supplied me necessary food;
For Nature ever faithful is   150
To such as trust her faithfulness.
When the forest shall mislead me,
When the night and morning lie,
When sea and land refuse to feed me,
'Twill be time enough to die;
Then will yet my mother yield
A pillow in her greenest field,
Nor the June flowers scorn to cover
The clay of their departed lover.

Fable

The mountain and the squirrel
Had a quarrel;
And the former called the latter 'Little Prig.'
Bun replied,
'You are doubtless very big;
But all sorts of things and weather
Must be taken in together,
To make up a year
And a sphere.
And I think it no disgrace   10
To occupy my place.
If I'm not so large as you,
You are not so small as I,
And not half so spry.
I'll not deny you make
A very pretty squirrel track;
Talents differ; all is well and wisely put;
If I cannot carry forests on my back,
Neither can you crack a nut.'

Ode,

INSCRIBED TO W. H. CHANNING.

Though loath to grieve
The evil time's sole patriot,
I cannot leave
My honied thought
For the priest's cant,
Or statesman's rant.

If I refuse
My study for their politique,
Which at the best is trick,
The angry Muse   10
Puts confusion in my brain.

But who is he that prates
Of the culture of mankind,
Of better arts and life?
Go, blindworm, go,
Behold the famous States
Harrying Mexico
With rifle and with knife!

Or who, with accent bolder,
Dare praise the freedom-loving mountaineer?   20
I found by thee, O rushing Contoocook!°
And in thy valleys, Agiochook!°
The jackals of the negro-holder.

The God who made New Hampshire
Taunted the lofty land
With little men;°—
Small bat and wren
House in the oak:—
If earth-fire cleave
The upheaved land, and bury the folk,   30
The southern crocodile would grieve.
Virtue palters; Right is hence;
Freedom praised, but hid;
Funeral eloquence
Rattles the coffin-lid.

What boots thy zeal,
O glowing friend,
That would indignant rend
The northland from the south?
Wherefore? to what good end?   40
Boston Bay and Bunker Hill
Would serve things still;—
Things are of the snake.

The horseman serves the horse,
The neatherd serves the neat,
The merchant serves the purse,
The eater serves his meat;
'Tis the day of the chattel,

Web to weave, and corn to grind;
Things are in the saddle,   50
And ride mankind.

There are two laws discrete,
Not reconciled,—
Law for man, and law for thing;
The last builds town and fleet,
But it runs wild,
And doth the man unking.

'Tis fit the forest fall,
The steep be graded,
The mountain tunnelled,   60
The sand shaded,
The orchard planted,
The glebe tilled,
The prairie granted,
The steamer built.

Let man serve law for man;
Live for friendship, live for love,
For truth's and harmony's behoof;
The state may follow how it can,
As Olympus follows Jove.   70

   Yet do not I invite
The wrinkled shopman to my sounding woods,
Nor bid the unwilling senator
Ask votes of thrushes in the solitudes.
Every one to his chosen work;—
Foolish hands may mix and mar;
Wise and sure the issues are.
Round they roll till dark is light,
Sex to sex, and even to odd;—
The over-god   80
Who marries Right to Might,
Who peoples, unpeoples,—
He who exterminates
Races by stronger races,
Black by white faces,—

Knows to bring honey
Out of the lion;°
Grafts gentlest scion
On pirate and Turk.

The Cossack eats Poland,   90
Like stolen fruit;
Her last noble is ruined,
Her last poet mute:
Straight, into double band
The victors divide;
Half for freedom strike and stand;—
The astonished Muse finds thousands at her side.

Suum Cuique

The rain has spoiled the farmer's day;
Shall sorrow put my books away?
   Thereby are two days lost:
Nature shall mind her own affairs;
I will attend my proper cares,
   In rain, or sun, or frost.

Compensation

Why should I keep holiday
   When other men have none?
Why but because, when these are gay,
   I sit and mourn alone?

And why, when mirth unseals all tongues,
   Should mine alone be dumb?
Ah! late I spoke to silent throngs,
   And now their hour is come.

Forerunners

Long I followed happy guides,
I could never reach their sides;
Their step is forth, and, ere the day,

Breaks up their leaguer, and away.
Keen my sense, my heart was young,
Right good-will my sinews strung,
But no speed of mine avails
To hunt upon their shining trails.
On and away, their hasting feet
Make the morning proud and sweet;   10
Flowers they strew,—I catch the scent;
Or tone of silver instrument
Leaves on the wind melodious trace;
Yet I could never see their face.
On eastern hills I see their smokes,
Mixed with mist by distant lochs.
I met many travellers
Who the road had surely kept;
They saw not my fine revellers,—
These had crossed them while they slept.   20
Some had heard their fair report,
In the country or the court.
Fleetest couriers alive
Never yet could once arrive,
As they went or they returned,
At the house where these sojourned.
Sometimes their strong speed they slacken,
Though they are not overtaken;
In sleep their jubilant troop is near,—
I tuneful voices overhear;   30
It may be in wood or waste,—
At unawares 'tis come and past.
Their near camp my spirit knows
By signs gracious as rainbows.
I thenceforward, and long after,
Listen for their harp-like laughter,
And carry in my heart, for days,
Peace that hallows rudest ways.

Give All to Love

Give all to love;
Obey thy heart;

Friends, kindred, days,
Estate, good-fame,
Plans, credit, and the Muse,—
Nothing refuse.

'Tis a brave master;
Let it have scope:
Follow it utterly,
Hope beyond hope: 10
High and more high
It dives into noon,
With wing unspent,
Untold intent;
But it is a god,
Knows its own path,
And the outlets of the sky.

It was not for the mean;
It requireth courage stout,
Souls above doubt,   20
Valor unbending;
Such 'twill reward,—
They shall return
More than they were,
And ever ascending.

Leave all for love;
Yet, hear me, yet,
One word more thy heart behoved,
One pulse more of firm endeavor,—
Keep thee to-day,   30
To-morrow, forever,
Free as an Arab
Of thy beloved.

Cling with life to the maid;
But when the surprise,
First vague shadow of surmise
Flits across her bosom young
Of a joy apart from thee,
Free be she, fancy-free;

Nor thou detain her vesture's hem,   40
Nor the palest rose she flung
From her summer diadem.

Though thou loved her as thyself,
As a self of purer clay,
Though her parting dims the day,
Stealing grace from all alive;
Heartily know,
When half-gods go,
The gods arrive.

Merlin

I

Thy trivial harp will never please
Or fill my craving ear;
Its chords should ring as blows the breeze,
Free, peremptory, clear.
No jingling serenader's art,
Nor tinkle of piano strings,
Can make the wild blood start
In its mystic springs.
The kingly bard
Must smite the chords rudely and hard,   10
As with hammer or with mace;
That they may render back
Artful thunder, which conveys
Secrets of the solar track,
Sparks of the supersolar blaze.
Merlin's blows are strokes of fate,
Chiming with the forest tone,
When boughs buffet boughs in the wood;
Chiming with the gasp and moan
Of the ice-imprisoned flood;   20
With the pulse of manly hearts;
With the voice of orators;
With the din of city arts;
With the cannonade of wars;
With the marches of the brave;
And prayers of might from martyrs' cave.

Great is the art,
Great be the manners, of the bard.
He shall not his brain encumber
With the coil of rhythm and number;   30
But, leaving rule and pale forethought,
He shall aye° climb
For his rhyme.
'Pass in, pass in,' the angels say,
In to the upper doors,
Nor count compartments of the floors,
But mount to paradise
By the stairway of surprise.

Blameless master of the games,
King of sport that never shames,   40
He shall daily joy dispense
Hid in song's sweet influence.
Things more cheerly live and go,
What time the subtle mind
Sings aloud the tune whereto
Their pulses beat,
And march their feet,
And their members are combined.

By Sybarites° beguiled,
He shall no task decline;   50
Merlin's mighty line
Extremes of nature reconciled,—
Bereaved a tyrant of his will,
And made the lion mild.
Songs can the tempest still,
Scattered on the stormy air,
Mould the year to fair increase,
And bring in poetic peace.

He shall not seek to weave,
In weak, unhappy times,   60
Efficacious rhymes;
Wait his returning strength.
Bird, that from the nadir's floor
To the zenith's top can soar,

The soaring orbit of the muse exceeds that journey's length.
Nor profane affect to hit
Or compass that, by meddling wit,
Which only the propitious mind
Publishes when 'tis inclined.
There are open hours   70
When the God's will sallies free,
And the dull idiot might see
The flowing fortunes of a thousand years;—
Sudden, at unawares,
Self-moved, fly-to the doors
Nor sword of angels could reveal
What they conceal.

Merlin

II

The rhyme of the poet
Modulates the king's affairs;
Balance-loving Nature   80
Made all things in pairs.
To every foot its antipode;
Each color with its counter glowed;
To every tone beat answering tones,
Higher or graver;
Flavor gladly blends with flavor;
Leaf answers leaf upon the bough;
And match the paired cotyledons.
Hands to hands, and feet to feet,
Coeval grooms and brides;   90
Eldest rite, two married sides
In every mortal meet.
Light's far furnace shines,
Smelting balls and bars,
Forging double stars,
Glittering twins and trines.
The animals are sick with love,
Lovesick with rhyme;
Each with all propitious time
Into chorus wove.   100

Like the dancers' ordered band,
Thoughts come also hand in hand;
In equal couples mated,
Or else alternated;
Adding by their mutual gage,
One to other, health and age.
Solitary fancies go
Short-lived wandering to and fro,
Most like to bachelors,
Or an ungiven maid,   110
Not ancestors,
With no posterity to make the lie afraid,
Or keep truth undecayed.
Perfect-paired as eagle's wings,
Justice is the rhyme of things;
Trade and counting use
The self-same tuneful muse;
And Nemesis,°
Who with even matches odd,
Who athwart space redresses   120
The partial wrong,
Fills the just period,
And finishes the song.

Subtle rhymes, with ruin rife,
Murmur in the house of life,
Sung by the Sisters° as they spin;
In perfect time and measure they
Build and unbuild our echoing clay,
As the two twilights of the day
Fold us music-drunken in.   130

Bacchus

Bring me wine, but wine which never grew
In the belly of the grape,
Or grew on vine whose tap-roots, reaching through
Under the Andes to the Cape,
Suffered no savor of the earth to scape.

Let its grapes the morn salute
From a nocturnal root,
Which feels the acrid juice
Of Styx and Erebus;°
And turns the woe of Night,   10
By its own craft, to a more rich delight.

We buy ashes for bread;
We buy diluted wine;
Give me of the true,—
Whose ample leaves and tendrils curled
Among the silver hills of heaven,
Draw everlasting dew;
Wine of wine,
Blood of the world,
Form of forms, and mould of statures,   20
That I intoxicated,
And by the draught assimilated,
May float at pleasure through all natures;
The bird-language rightly spell,
And that which roses say so well.

Wine that is shed
Like the torrents of the sun
Up the horizon walls,
Or like the Atlantic streams, which run
When the South Sea calls.   30

Water and bread,
Food which needs no transmuting,
Rainbow-flowering, wisdom-fruiting
Wine which is already man,
Food which teach and reason can.

Wine which Music is,—
Music and wine are one,—
That I, drinking this,
Shall hear far Chaos talk with me;
Kings unborn shall walk with me;   40

And the poor grass shall plot and plan
What it will do when it is man.
Quickened so, will I unlock
Every crypt of every rock.

I thank the joyful juice
For all I know;—
Winds of remembering
Of the ancient being blow,
And seeming-solid walls of use
Open and flow.   50

Pour, Bacchus! the remembering wine;
Retrieve the loss of me and mine!
Vine for vine be antidote,
And the grape requite the lote!
Haste to cure the old despair,—
Reason in Nature's lotus drenched,
The memory of ages quenched;
Give them again to shine;
Let wine repair what this undid;
And where the infection slid,   60
A dazzling memory revive;
Refresh the faded tints,
Recut the aged prints,
And write my old adventures with the pen
Which on the first day drew,
Upon the tablets blue,
The dancing Pleiads° and eternal men.

Merops

What care I, so they stand the same,—
    Things of the heavenly mind,—
How long the power to give them name
    Tarries yet behind?

Thus far to-day your favors reach,
    O fair, appeasing presences!
Ye taught my lips a single speech,
    And a thousand silences.

Space grants beyond his fated road
   No inch to the god of day;   10
And copious language still bestowed
   One word, no more, to say.

Xenophanes

By fate, not option, frugal Nature gave
One scent to hyson° and to wall-flower,
One sound to pine-groves and to waterfalls,
One aspect to the desert and the lake.
It was her stern necessity: all things
Are of one pattern made; bird, beast, and flower,
Song, picture, form, space, thought, and character,
Deceive us, seeming to be many things,
And are but one. Beheld far off, they differ
As God and devil; bring them to the mind,   10
They dull its edge with their monotony.
To know one element, explore another,
And in the second reappears the first.
The specious panorama of a year
But multiplies the image of a day,—
A belt of mirrors round a taper's flame;
And universal Nature, through her vast
And crowded whole, an infinite paroquet,
Repeats one note.

Blight

      Give me truths;
For I am weary of the surfaces,
And die of inanition. If I knew
Only the herbs and simples of the wood,
Rue, cinquefoil, gill, vervain, and agrimony,
Blue-vetch, and trillium, hawkweed, sassafras,
Milkweeds, and murky brakes, quaint pipes, and sundew,°
And rare and virtuous roots, which in these woods
Draw untold juices from the common earth,

Untold, unknown, and I could surely spell   10
Their fragrance, and their chemistry apply
By sweet affinities to human flesh,
Driving the foe and stablishing the friend,—
O, that were much, and I could be a part
Of the round day, related to the sun
And planted world, and full executor
Of their imperfect functions.
But these young scholars, who invade our hills,
Bold as the engineer who fells the wood,
And travelling often in the cut he makes,   20
Love not the flower they pluck, and know it not,
And all their botany is Latin names.°
The old men studied magic in the flowers,
And human fortunes in astronomy,
And an omnipotence in chemistry,
Preferring things to names, for these were men,
Were unitarians of the united world,
And, wheresoever their clear eye-beams fell,
They caught the footsteps of the SAME. Our eyes
Are armed, but we are strangers to the stars,   30
And strangers to the mystic beast and bird,
And strangers to the plant and to the mine.
The injured elements say, 'Not in us;'
And night and day, ocean and continent,
Fire, plant, and mineral say, 'Not in us,'
And haughtily return us stare for stare.
For we invade them impiously for gain;
We devastate them unreligiously,
And coldly ask their pottage, not their love.
Therefore they shove us from them, yield to us   40
Only what to our griping toil is due;
But the sweet affluence of love and song,
The rich results of the divine consents
Of man and earth, of world beloved and lover,
The nectar and ambrosia, are withheld;
And in the midst of spoils and slaves, we thieves
And pirates of the universe, shut out
Daily to a more thin and outward rind,
Turn pale and starve. Therefore, to our sick eyes,
The stunted trees look sick, the summer short,   50

Clouds shade the sun, which will not tan our hay,
And nothing thrives to reach its natural term;
And life, shorn of its venerable length,
Even at its greatest space is a defeat,
And dies in anger that it was a dupe;
And, in its highest noon and wantonness,
Is early frugal, like a beggar's child;
With most unhandsome calculation taught,
Even in the hot pursuit of the best aims
And prizes of ambition, checks its hand,　　　　　60
Like Alpine cataracts frozen as they leaped,
Chilled with a miserly comparison
Of the toy's purchase with the length of life.

Threnody

The South-wind brings
Life, sunshine, and desire,
And on every mount and meadow
Breathes aromatic fire;
But over the dead he has no power,
The lost, the lost, he cannot restore;
And, looking over the hills, I mourn
The darling who shall not return.

I see my empty house,
I see my trees repair their boughs;　　　　　10
And he, the wondrous child,
Whose silver warble wild
Outvalued every pulsing sound
Within the air's cerulean° round,—
The hyacinthine boy,° for whom
Morn well might break and April bloom,—
The gracious boy, who did adorn
The world whereinto he was born,
And by his countenance repay
The favor of the loving Day,—　　　　　20
Has disappeared from the Day's eye;
Far and wide she cannot find him;
My hopes pursue, they cannot bind him.

Returned this day, the south wind searches,
And finds young pines and budding birches;
But finds not the budding man;
Nature, who lost him, cannot remake him;
Fate let him fall, Fate can't retake him;
Nature, Fate, Men, him seek in vain.

And whither now, my truant wise and sweet,   30
O, whither tend thy feet?
I had the right, few days ago,
Thy steps to watch, thy place to know;
How have I forfeited the right?
Hast thou forgot me in a new delight?
I hearken for thy household cheer,
O eloquent child!
Whose voice, an equal messenger,
Conveyed thy meaning mild.
What though the pains and joys   40
Whereof it spoke were toys
Fitting his age and ken,
Yet fairest dames and bearded men,
Who heard the sweet request,
So gentle, wise, and grave,
Bended with joy to his behest,
And let the world's affairs go by,
Awhile to share his cordial game,
Or mend his wicker wagon-frame,
Still plotting how their hungry ear   50
That winsome voice again might hear;
For his lips could well pronounce
Words that were persuasions.

Gentlest guardians marked serene
His early hope, his liberal mien;
Took counsel from his guiding eyes
To make this wisdom earthly wise.
Ah, vainly do these eyes recall
The school-march, each day's festival,
When every morn my bosom glowed   60
To watch the convoy on the road;
The babe in willow wagon closed,

With rolling eyes and face composed;
With children forward and behind,
Like Cupids studiously inclined;
And he the chieftain paced beside,
The centre of the troop allied,
With sunny face of sweet repose,
To guard the babe from fancied foes.
The little captain innocent   70
Took the eye with him as he went;
Each village senior paused to scan
And speak the lovely caravan.
From the window I look out
To mark thy beautiful parade,
Stately marching in cap and coat
To some tune by fairies played;—
A music heard by thee alone
To works as noble led thee on.

Now Love and Pride, alas! in vain,   80
Up and down their glances strain.
The painted sled stands where it stood;
The kennel by the corded wood;
The gathered sticks to stanch the wall
Of the snow-tower, when snow should fall;
The ominous hole he dug in the sand,
And childhood's castles built or planned;
His daily haunts I well discern,—
The poultry-yard, the shed, the barn,—
And every inch of garden ground   90
Paced by the blessed feet around,
From the roadside to the brook
Whereinto he loved to look.
Step the meek birds where erst they ranged;
The wintry garden lies unchanged;
The brook into the stream runs on;
But the deep-eyed boy is gone.
On that shaded day,
Dark with more clouds than tempests are,
When thou didst yield thy innocent breath   100
In birdlike heavings unto death,
Night came, and Nature had not thee;

I said, 'We are mates in misery.'
The morrow dawned with needless glow;
Each snowbird chirped, each fowl must crow;
Each tramper started; but the feet
Of the most beautiful and sweet
Of human youth had left the hill
And garden,—they were bound and still.
There's not a sparrow or a wren,   110
There's not a blade of autumn grain,
Which the four seasons do not tend,
And tides of life and increase lend;
And every chick of every bird,
And weed and rock-moss is preferred.
O ostrich-like forgetfulness!
O loss of larger in the less!
Was there no star that could be sent,
No watcher in the firmament,
No angel from the countless host   120
That loiters round the crystal coast,
Could stoop to heal that only child,
Nature's sweet marvel undefiled,
And keep the blossom of the earth,
Which all her harvests were not worth?
Not mine,—I never called thee mine,
But Nature's heir,—if I repine,
And seeing rashly torn and moved
Not what I made, but what I loved,
Grow early old with grief that thou   130
Must to the wastes of Nature go,—
'Tis because a general hope
Was quenched, and all must doubt and grope.
For flattering planets seemed to say
This child should ills of ages stay,
By wondrous tongue, and guided pen,
Bring the flown Muses back to men.
Perchance not he but Nature ailed,
The world and not the infant failed.
It was not ripe yet to sustain   140
A genius of so fine a strain,
Who gazed upon the sun and moon
As if he came unto his own,

And, pregnant with his grander thought,
Brought the old order into doubt.
His beauty once their beauty tried;
They could not feed him, and he died,
And wandered backward as in scorn,
To wait an æon to be born.
Ill day which made this beauty waste,   150
Plight broken, this high face defaced!
Some went and came about the dead;
And some in books of solace read;
Some to their friends the tidings say;
Some went to write, some went to pray;
One tarried here, there hurried one;
But their heart abode with none.
Covetous death bereaved us all,
To aggrandize one funeral.
The eager fate which carried thee   160
Took the largest part of me:
For this losing is true dying;
This is lordly man's down-lying,
This his slow but sure reclining,
Star by star his world resigning.

O child of paradise,
Boy who made dear his father's home,
In whose deep eyes
Men read the welfare of the times to come,
I am too much bereft.   170
The world dishonored thou hast left.
O truth's and nature's costly lie!
O trusted broken prophecy!
O richest fortune sourly crossed!
Born for the future, to the future lost!

The deep Heart answered, 'Weepest thou?
Worthier cause for passion wild
If I had not taken the child.
And deemest thou as those who pore,
With aged eyes, short way before,—   180
Think'st Beauty vanished from the coast
Of matter, and thy darling lost?

Taught he not thee—the man of eld,°
Whose eyes within his eyes beheld
Heaven's numerous hierarchy span
The mystic gulf from God to man?
To be alone wilt thou begin
When worlds of lovers hem thee in?
To-morrow, when the masks shall fall
That dizen° Nature's carnival,   190
The pure shall see by their own will,
Which overflowing Love shall fill,
'Tis not within the force of fate
The fate-conjoined to separate.
But thou, my votary, weepest thou?
I gave thee sight—where is it now?
I taught thy heart beyond the reach
Of ritual, bible, or of speech;
Wrote in thy mind's transparent table,
As far as the incommunicable;   200
Taught thee each private sign to raise,
Lit by the supersolar blaze.
Past utterance, and past belief,
And past the blasphemy of grief,
The mysteries of Nature's heart;
And though no Muse can these impart,
Throb thine with Nature's throbbing breast,
And all is clear from east to west.°

'I came to thee as to a friend;
Dearest, to thee I did not send   210
Tutors, but a joyful eye,
Innocence that matched the sky,
Lovely locks, a form of wonder,
Laughter rich as woodland thunder,
That thou might'st entertain apart
The richest flowering of all art:
And, as the great all-loving Day
Through smallest chambers takes its way,
That thou might'st break thy daily bread
With prophet, Savior, and head;   220
That thou might'st cherish for thine own
The riches of sweet Mary's Son,

Boy-Rabbi,° Israel's paragon.
And thoughtest thou such guest
Would in thy hall take up his rest?
Would rushing life forget her laws,
Fate's glowing revolution pause?
High omens ask diviner guess;
Not to be conned to tediousness.
And know my higher gifts unbind   230
The zone that girds the incarnate mind.
When the scanty shores are full
With Thought's perilous, whirling pool;
When frail Nature can no more,
Then the Spirit strikes the hour:
My servant Death, with solving rite,
Pours finite into infinite.

'Wilt thou freeze love's tidal flow,
Whose streams through nature circling go?
Nail the wild star to its track   240
On the half-climbed zodiac?
Light is light which radiates,
Blood is blood which circulates,
Life is life which generates,
And many-seeming life is one,—
Wilt thou transfix and make it none?
Its onward force too starkly pent
In figure, bone, and lineament?
Wilt thou, uncalled, interrogate,
Talker! the unreplying Fate?   250
Nor see the genius of the whole
Ascendant in the private soul,
Beckon it when to go and come,
Self-announced its hour of doom?
Fair the soul's recess and shrine,
Magic-built to last a season;
Masterpiece of love benign;
Fairer that expansive reason
Whose omen 'tis, and sign.
Wilt thou not ope thy heart to know   260
What rainbows teach, and sunsets show?

Verdict which accumulates
From lengthening scroll of human fates,
Voice of earth to earth returned,
Prayers of saints that inly burned,—
Saying, *What is excellent,*
As God lives, is permanent:
Hearts are dust, hearts' loves remain;
Heart's love will meet thee again.
Revere the Maker; fetch thine eye   270
Up to his style, and manners of the sky.
Not of adamant° and gold
Built he heaven stark and cold;
No, but a nest of bending reeds,
Flowering grass, and scented weeds;
Or like a traveller's fleeing tent,
Or bow above the tempest bent;
Built of tears and sacred flames,
And virtue reaching to its aims;
Built of furtherance and pursuing,   280
Not of spent deeds, but of doing.
Silent rushes the swift Lord
Through ruined systems still restored,
Broadsowing, bleak and void to bless,
Plants with worlds the wilderness;
Waters with tears of ancient sorrow
Apples of Eden ripe to-morrow.
House and tenant go to ground,
Lost in God, in Godhead found.'

Hymn:

SUNG AT THE COMPLETION OF THE CONCORD MONUMENT,
April 19, 1836.

By the rude bridge that arched the flood,
    Their flag to April's breeze unfurled,
Here once the embattled farmers stood,
    And fired the shot heard round the world.

The foe long since in silence slept;
    Alike the conqueror silent sleeps;
And Time the ruined bridge has swept
    Down the dark stream which seaward creeps.

On this green bank, by this soft stream,
  We set to-day a votive stone;   10
That memory may their deed redeem,
  When, like our sires, our sons are gone.

Spirit, that made those heroes dare
  To die, or leave their children free,
Bid Time and Nature gently spare
  The shaft we raise to them and thee.

Brahma

If the red slayer think he slays,
  Or if the slain think he is slain,
They know not well the subtle ways
  I keep, and pass, and turn again.

Far or forgot to me is near;
  Shadow and sunlight are the same;
The vanished gods to me appear;
  And one to me are shame and fame.

They reckon ill who leave me out;
  When me they fly, I am the wings;   10
I am the doubter and the doubt,
  And I the hymn the Brahmin° sings.

The strong gods pine for my abode,
  And pine in vain the sacred Seven;°
But thou, meek lover of the good!
  Find me, and turn thy back on heaven.

Voluntaries

I

Low and mournful be the strain,
Haughty thought be far from me;

Tones of penitence and pain,
Moanings of the tropic sea;
Low and tender in the cell
Where a captive sits in chains,
Crooning ditties treasured well
From his Afric's torrid plains.
Sole estate his sire bequeathed—
Hapless sire to hapless son—   10
Was the wailing song he breathed,
And his chain when life was done.
    What his fault, or what his crime?
Or what ill planet crossed his prime?
Heart too soft and will too weak
To front the fate that crouches near,—
Dove beneath the vulture's beak;—
Will song dissuade the thirsty spear?
Dragged from his mother's arms and breast,
Displaced, disfurnished here,   20
His wistful toil to do his best
Chilled by a ribald jeer.
Great men in the Senate sate,
Sage and hero, side by side,
Building for their sons the State,
Which they shall rule with pride.
They forbore to break the chain
Which bound the dusky tribe,
Checked by the owners' fierce disdain,
Lured by 'Union' as the bribe.   30
Destiny sat by, and said,
'Pang for pang your seed shall pay,
Hide in false peace your coward head,
I bring round the harvest-day.'

II

Freedom all winged expands,
Nor perches in a narrow place;
Her broad van seeks unplanted lands;
She loves a poor and virtuous race.
Clinging to a colder zone
Whose dark sky sheds the snow-flake down,   40

The snow-flake is her banner's star,
Her stripes the boreal streamers are.
Long she loved the Northman well;
Now the iron age is done,
She will not refuse to dwell
With the offspring of the Sun;
Foundling of the desert far,
Where palms plume, siroccos blaze,
He roves unhurt the burning ways
In climates of the summer star.   50
He has avenues to God
Hid from men of Northern brain,
Far beholding, without cloud,
What these with slowest steps attain.
If once the generous chief arrive
To lead him willing to be led,
For freedom he will strike and strive,
And drain his heart till he be dead.

III

In an age of fops and toys,
Wanting wisdom, void of right,   60
Who shall nerve heroic boys
To hazard all in Freedom's fight,—
Break sharply off their jolly games,
Forsake their comrades gay,
And quit proud homes and youthful dames,
For famine, toil, and fray?
Yet on the nimble air benign
Speed nimbler messages,
That waft the breath of grace divine
To hearts in sloth and ease.   70
So nigh is grandeur to our dust,
So near is God to man,
When Duty whispers low, *Thou must*,
The youth replies, *I can*.

IV

O, well for the fortunate soul
Which Music's wings infold,

Stealing away the memory
Of sorrows new and old!
Yet happier he whose inward sight,
Stayed on his subtile thought,   80
Shuts his sense on toys of time,
To vacant bosoms brought.
But best befriended of the God
He who, in evil times,
Warned by an inward voice,
Heeds not the darkness and the dread,
Biding by his rule and choice,
Feeling only the fiery thread
Leading over heroic ground,
Walled with mortal terror round,   90
To the aim which him allures,
And the sweet heaven his deed secures.

Stainless soldier on the walls,
Knowing this,—and knows no more,—
Whoever fights, whoever falls,
Justice conquers evermore,
Justice after as before,—
And he who battles on her side,
God, though he were ten times slain,
Crowns him victor glorified,   100
Victor over death and pain;
Forever: but his erring foe,
Self-assured that he prevails,
Looks from his victim lying low,
And sees aloft the red right arm
Redress the eternal scales.
He, the poor foe, whom angels foil,
Blind with pride, and fooled by hate,
Writhes within the dragon coil,
Reserved to a speechless fate.   110

V

Blooms the laurel which belongs
To the valiant chief who fights;
I see the wreath, I hear the songs
Lauding the Eternal Rights,

Victors over daily wrongs:
Awful victors, they misguide
Whom they will destroy,
And there coming triumph hide
In our downfall, or our joy:
They reach no term, they never sleep,   120
In equal strength through space abide;
Though, feigning dwarfs, they crouch and creep,
The strong they slay, the swift outstride:
Fate's grass grows rank in valley clods,
And rankly on the castled steep,—
Speak it firmly, these are gods,
All are ghosts beside.

Days

Damsels of Time, the hypocritic Days,
Muffled and dumb like barefoot dervishes,°
And marching single in an endless file,
Bring diadems and fagots in their hands.
To each they offer gifts after his will,
Bread, kingdoms, stars, and sky that holds them all.
I, in my pleached garden,° watched the pomp,
Forgot my morning wishes, hastily
Took a few herbs and apples, and the Day
Turned and departed silent. I, too late,   10
Under her solemn fillet° saw the scorn.

Song of Nature

Mine are the night and morning,
The pits of air, the gulf of space,
The sportive sun, the gibbous moon,
The innumerable days.

I hide in the solar glory,
I am dumb in the pealing song,
I rest on the pitch of the torrent,
In slumber I am strong.

No numbers have counted my tallies,
No tribes my house can fill,   10
I sit by the shining Fount of Life,
And pour the deluge still;

And ever by delicate powers
Gathering along the centuries
From race on race the rarest flowers,
My wreath shall nothing miss.

And many a thousand summers
My apples ripened well,
And light from meliorating stars
With firmer glory fell.   20

I wrote the past in characters
Of rock and fire the scroll,
The building in the coral sea,
The planting of the coal.

And thefts from satellites and rings
And broken stars I drew,
And out of spent and aged things
I formed the world anew;

What time the gods kept carnival,
Tricked out in star and flower,   30
And in cramp elf and saurian° forms
They swathed their too much power.

Time and Thought were my surveyors,
They laid their courses well,
They boiled the sea, and baked the layers
Of granite, marl, and shell.

But he, the man-child glorious,—
Where tarries he the while?
The rainbow shines his harbinger,
The sunset gleams his smile.   40

My boreal lights leap upward,
Forthright my planets roll,
And still the man-child is not born,
The summit of the whole.

Must time and tide forever run?
Will never my winds go sleep in the west?
Will never my wheels which whirl the sun
And satellites have rest?

Too much of donning and doffing,
Too slow the rainbow fades,   50
I weary of my robe of snow,
My leaves and my cascades;

I tire of globes and races,
Too long the game is played;
What without him is summer's pomp,
Or winter's frozen shade?

I travail in pain for him,
My creatures travail and wait;
His couriers come by squadrons,
He comes not to the gate.   60

Twice I have moulded an image,
And thrice outstretched my hand,
Made one of day, and one of night,
And one of the salt sea-sand.

One in a Judæan manger,
And one by Avon stream,
One over against the mouths of Nile,°
And one in the Academe.°

I moulded kings and saviours,
And bards o'er kings to rule;—   70
But fell the starry influence short,
The cup was never full.

Yet whirl the glowing wheels once more,
And mix the bowl again;
Seethe, Fate! the ancient elements,
Heat, cold, wet, dry, and peace, and pain.

Let war and trade and creeds and song
Blend, ripen race on race,
The sunburnt world a man shall breed
Of all the zones, and countless days.   80

No ray is dimmed, no atom worn,
My oldest force is good as new,
And the fresh rose on yonder thorn
Gives back the bending heavens in dew.

Two Rivers

Thy summer voice, Musketaquit,
Repeats the music of the rain;
But sweeter rivers pulsing flit
Through thee, as thou through Concord Plain.

Thou in thy narrow banks art pent:
The stream I love unbounded goes
Through flood and sea and firmament;
Through light, through life, it forward flows.

I see the inundation sweet,
I hear the spending of the stream   10
Through years, through men, through nature fleet,
Through passion, thought, through power and
        dream.

Musketaquit, a goblin strong,
Of shard and flint makes jewels gay;
They lose their grief who hear his song,
And where he winds is the day of day.

So forth and brighter fares my stream,—
Who drink it shall not thirst again;°
No darkness stains its equal gleam,
And ages drop in it like rain.   20

Waldeinsamkeit

I do not count the hours I spend
In wandering by the sea;
The forest is my loyal friend,
Like God it useth me.

In plains that room for shadows make
Of skirting hills to lie,
Bound in by streams which give and take
Their colors from the sky;

Or on the mountain-crest sublime,
Or down the oaken glade,   10
O what have I to do with time?
For this the day was made.

Cities of mortals woe-begone
Fantastic care derides,
But in the serious landscape lone
Stern benefit abides.

Sheen will tarnish, honey cloy,
And merry is only a mask of sad,
But, sober on a fund of joy,
The woods at heart are glad.   20

There the great Planter plants
Of fruitful worlds the grain,
And with a million spells enchants
The souls that walk in pain.

Still on the seeds of all he made
The rose of beauty burns;
Through times that wear, and forms that fade,
Immortal youth returns.

The black ducks mounting from the lake,
The pigeon in the pines,   30
The bittern's° boom, a desert make
Which no false art refines.

Down in yon watery nook,
Where bearded mists divide,
The gray old gods whom Chaos know,
The sires of Nature, hide.

Aloft, in secret veins of air,
Blows the sweet breath of song,
O, few to scale those uplands dare,
Though they to all belong! 40

See thou bring not to field or stone
The fancies found in books;
Leave authors' eyes, and fetch your own,
To brave the landscape's looks.

And if, amid this dear delight,
My thoughts did home rebound,
I well might reckon it a slight
To the high cheer I found.

Oblivion here thy wisdom is,
Thy thrift, the sleep of cares; 50
For a proud idleness like this
Crowns all thy mean affairs.

Terminus

It is time to be old,
  To take in sail:—
The god of bounds,
Who sets to seas a shore,
Came to me in his fatal rounds,
And said: 'No more!
No farther spread
Thy broad ambitious branches, and thy root.
Fancy departs: no more invent,
Contract thy firmament 10
To compass of a tent.
There's not enough for this and that,
Make thy option which of two;
Economize the failing river,
Not the less revere the Giver,

Leave the many and hold the few.
Timely wise accept the terms,
Soften the fall with wary foot;
A little while
Still plan and smile,   20
And, fault of novel germs,
Mature the unfallen fruit.
Curse, if thou wilt, thy sires,
Bad husbands of their fires,
Who, when they gave thee breath,
Failed to bequeath
The needful sinew stark as once,
The Baresark° marrow to thy bones,
But left a legacy of ebbing veins,
Inconstant heat and nerveless reins,—   30
Amid the Muses, left thee deaf and dumb,
Amid the gladiators, halt and numb.'
As the bird trims her to the gale,
I trim myself to the storm of time,
I man the rudder, reef the sail,
Obey the voice at eve obeyed at prime:
'Lowly faithful, banish fear,
Right onward drive unharmed;
The port, well worth the cruise, is near,
And every wave is charmed.'   40

April

The April winds are magical,
And thrill our tuneful frames;
The garden-walks are passional
To bachelors and dames.
The hedge is gemmed with diamonds,
The air with Cupids full,
The clews of fairy Rosamonds°
Guide lovers to the pool.
Each dimple in the water,
Each leaf that shades the rock,   10
Can cozen, pique, and flatter,

Can parley and provoke.
Goodfellow, Puck,° and goblins
Know more than any book;
Down with your doleful problems,
And court the sunny brook.
The south-winds are quick-witted,
The schools are sad and slow,
The masters quite omitted
The lore we care to know.   20

Grace

How much, preventing God, how much I owe
To the defences thou hast round me set;
Example, custom, fear, occasion slow,—
These scorned bondmen were my parapet.
I dare not peep over this parapet
To gauge with glance the roaring gulf below,
The depths of sin to which I had descended,
Had not these me against myself defended.

Insight

Power that by obedience grows,
Knowledge which its source not knows,
Wave which severs whom it bears
From the things which he compares,
Adding wings through things to range,
To his own blood harsh and strange.

The Enchanter

In the deep heart of man a poet dwells
Who all the day of life his summer story tells:
Scatters on every eye dust of his spells,
Scent, form and color: to the flowers and shells
Wins the believing child with wondrous tales;
Touches a cheek with colors of romance,

And crowds a history into a glance;
Gives beauty to the lake and fountain,
Spies over-sea the fires of the mountain;
When thrushes ope their throat, 't is he that sings,   10
And he that paints the oriole's fiery wings.
The little Shakspeare in the maiden's heart
Makes Romeo of a plough-boy on his cart;
Opens the eye to Virtue's starlike meed
And gives persuasion to a gentle deed.

QUATRAINS

Memory

Night-dreams trace on Memory's wall
Shadows of the thoughts of day,
And thy fortunes, as they fall,
The bias of the will betray.

Nature in Leasts

As sings the pine-tree in the wind,
So sings in the wind a sprig of the pine;
Her strength and soul has laughing France
Shed in each drop of wine.

ELEMENTS AND MOTTOES

Compensation

I

The wings of Time are black and white,
Pied with morning and with night.
Mountain tall and ocean deep
Trembling balance duly keep.
In changing moon and tidal wave
Glows the feud of Want and Have.
Gauge of more and less through space,
Electric star or pencil plays,
The lonely Earth amid the balls
That hurry through the eternal halls,   10
A makeweight flying to the void,
Supplemental asteroid,
Or compensatory spark,
Shoots across the neutral Dark.

II

Man's the elm, and Wealth the vine;
Stanch and strong the tendrils twine:
Though the frail ringlets thee deceive,
None from its stock that vine can reave.
Fear not, then, thou child infirm,
There's no god dare wrong a worm;   20
Laurel crowns cleave to deserts,
And power to him who power exerts.
Hast not thy share? On winged feet,
Lo! it rushes thee to meet;
And all that Nature made thy own,
Floating in air or pent in stone,
Will rive the hills and swim the sea,
And, like thy shadow, follow thee.

Spiritual Laws

The living Heaven thy prayers respect,
House at once and architect,
Quarrying man's rejected hours,
Builds therewith eternal towers;
Sole and self-commanded works,
Fears not undermining days,
Grows by decays,
And, by the famous might that lurks
In reaction and recoil,
Makes flame to freeze, and ice to boil;   10
Forging, through swart arms of Offence,
The silver seat of Innocence.

Heroism

Ruby wine is drunk by knaves,
Sugar spends to fatten slaves,
Rose and vine-leaf deck buffoons;
Thunder-clouds are Jove's festoons,
Drooping oft in wreaths of dread,
Lightning-knotted round his head;
The hero is not fed on sweets,
Daily his own heart he eats;
Chambers of the great are jails,
And head-winds right for royal sails.   10

Wealth

Who shall tell what did befall,
Far away in time, when once,
Over the lifeless ball,
Hung idle stars and suns?
What god the element obeyed?
Wings of what wind the lichen bore,
Wafting the puny seeds of power,
Which, lodged in rock, the rock abrade?

And well the primal pioneer
Knew the strong task to it assigned   10
Patient through Heaven's enormous year
To build in matter home for mind.
From air the creeping centuries drew
The matted thicket low and wide,
This must the leaves of ages strew
The granite slab to clothe and hide,
Ere wheat can wave its golden pride.
What smiths, and in what furnace, rolled
(In dizzy æons dim and mute
The reeling brain can ill compute)   20
Copper and iron, lead, and gold?
What oldest star the fame can save
Of races perishing to pave
The planet with a floor of lime?
Dust is their pyramid and mole:
Who saw what ferns and palms were pressed
Under the tumbling mountain's breast,
In the safe herbal of the coal?
But when the quarried means were piled,
All is waste and worthless, till   30
Arrives the wise selecting will,
And, out of slime and chaos, Wit
Draws the threads of fair and fit.
Then temples rose, and towns, and marts,
The shop of toil, the hall of arts;
Then flew the sail across the seas
To feed the North from tropic trees;
The storm-wind wove, the torrent span,
Where they were bid the rivers ran;
New slaves fulfilled the poet's dream,   40
Galvanic wire, strong-shouldered steam.
Then docks were built, and crops were stored,
And ingots added to the hoard.
But, though light-headed man forget,
Remembering Matter pays her debt:
Still, through her motes and masses, draw
Electric thrills and ties of Law,
Which bind the strengths of Nature wild
To the conscience of a child.

Culture

Can rules or tutors educate
The semigod whom we await?
He must be musical,
Tremulous, impressional,
Alive to gentle influence
Of landscape and of sky,
And tender to the spirit-touch
Of man's or maiden's eye:
But, to his native centre fast,
Shall into Future fuse the Past, 10
And the world's flowing fates in his own mould recast.

Worship

This is he, who, felled by foes,
Sprung harmless up, refreshed by blows:
He to captivity was sold,
But him no prison-bars would hold:
Though they sealed him in a rock,
Mountain chains he can unlock:
Thrown to lions for their meat,
The crouching lion kissed his feet:
Bound to the stake, no flames appalled,
But arched o'er him an honoring vault. 10
This is he men miscall Fate,
Threading dark ways, arriving late,
But ever coming in time to crown
The truth, and hurl wrong-doers down.
He is the oldest, and best known,
More near than aught thou call'st thy own,
Yet, greeted in another's eyes,
Disconcerts with glad surprise.
This is Jove, who, deaf to prayers,
Floods with blessings unawares. 20
Draw, if thou canst, the mystic line
Severing rightly his from thine,
Which is human, which divine.

NOTES

I am grateful to Mark Richardson and James Barszcz, both of Rutgers University, for their assistance in the preparation of these notes and to Mark Richardson, again, for preparing the chronology. Grateful acknowledgement is due also to the editors of *The Collected Works of Ralph Waldo Emerson* (4 vols. to date), and of *The Journals and Miscellaneous Notebooks of Ralph Waldo Emerson* (16 vols.; referred to in the notes as *JMN*); their work has made ours immeasurably easier. In preparing these notes I have relied also on the biographical, bibliographical, and reference works noted in the 'Further Reading' section of this volume, below, pp. 615–18.

NATURE; ADDRESSES AND LECTURES

NATURE

7 *More servants . . . notice of.* From George Herbert's poem 'Man' (1633).

Aeolus's bag. In the *Odyssey*, Book 10, Aeolus gives Odysseus a bag containing all the winds unfavourable to Odysseus' journey home.

10 *Leonidas.* Leonidas, King of Sparta, killed at Thermopylae in 480 BC as he led the defence against the invading Persian army.

Arnold Winkelried. Swiss patriot and knight (d. 1386), whose sacrifice of himself helped the Swiss defeat the Austrians at the Battle of Sempach on 9 July 1386.

11 *Sir Harry Vane.* English statesman (1613–62), appointed fourth Governor of Massachusetts (1636–7); Puritan leader during the English Civil War; executed on Tower Hill by order of Charles II.

Lord Russell. Lord William Russell (1639–83), Whig statesman and Parliamentary opponent of Charles II; executed for treason.

12 *il piu nell' uno.* The many in the one.

14 *Linnaeus . . . Buffon.* Carl Linnaeus (1707–78), Swedish botanist, founder of the system of botanical classification by sexual characteristics. George Louis Leclerc, Comte de *Buffon* (1707–88), French naturalist, member of the Academy and director of the Jardin du Roi.

It is sown a natural body. 1 Cor. 15: 44.

16 *The visible . . . invisible.* From Emanuel Swedenborg (1668–1772), Swedish mystic and theologian.

17 *Can these things . . . wonder? Macbeth,* III. iv. 110–12.

'Material objects', said a French philosopher. From G. Oegger, *The True Messiah; or the Old and New Testaments, Examined According to the Principles of Language and Nature,* trans. Elizabeth Peabody (Boston, 1842). Emerson read the book in manuscript, and copied the passage here quoted into his journal for July 1835.

scoriae. Refuse from the melting of metals; dross.

Every scripture . . . forth. The remark is George Fox's (1624–91), the English founder of the Society of Friends, better known as Quakers. Emerson found it in William Sewell's *History of the Rise, Increase, and Progress of the Christian People Called Quakers*, 2 vols. (Philadelphia, 1823), i. 115 (cf. *JMN*, iii, 236).

every object . . . soul. Emerson quotes from Coleridge's *Aids to Reflection*, ed. James Marsh (Burlington, Vermont, 1829), pp. 150–1 (cf. *JMN*, vi, 64).

18 *good thoughts . . . executed!* Emerson quotes loosely from Bacon's essay 'Of Great Place': 'For good thoughts (though God accept them) yet towards men are little better than good dreams, except they be put in act . . .'

19 *What we . . . know.* Emerson copied the remark into his journal for November 1827. He takes it from Robert Plumer Ward's (1765–1846) novel *Tremaine* (Philadelphia, 1825), iii. 125–6, where it is attributed to Bishop Joseph Butler (cf. *JMN*, vi, 64).

21 *Xenophanes.* Greek philosopher (570–480 BC).

The fable of Proteus. In classical mythology, Proteus is a sea deity who can assume different forms at will.

Thus architecture . . . Vitruvius. Cf. note to 'Quotation and Originality' (p. 430) for Madame de Staël's and Goethe's use of this remark. Vitruvius was a Roman architect of the 1st century BC.

Omne . . . consonat. All truth accords with truth.

Ens. A term used by philosophers to denote abstract being; existence in itself.

The wise man . . . rightly. Emerson quotes loosely from Goethe's *Wilhelm Meister's Travels*, chap. 6, in Thomas Carlyle's translation. Cf. *The Works of Thomas Carlyle* (New York, 1901), xxiv. 228.

25 *The ornament . . . air.* From Shakespeare's sonnet 70.

No, it . . . politic. From Shakespeare's sonnet 124.

Take those . . . morn. From *Measure for Measure*, IV. i. 1–4.

26 *The strong based . . . foul and muddy.* All these lines are spoken by Prospero, in *The Tempest*, V. i.

The problem . . . absolute. Not from Plato, but from Coleridge's *The Friend* (London, 1818). Cf. vol. iii, Section the Second, Essay V, para. 4. Coleridge is describing the 'final object' of Plato's philosophy.

27 *The sublime remark of Euler . . . true.* Leonhard Euler (1707–83), Swiss mathematician and physicist. Emerson found the remark in Coleridge's *Aids to Reflection*, ed. James Marsh (1829), p. 274 (cf. *JMN*, iv, 332).

Turgot. Anne Robert Jacques Turgot (1727–81), French statesman and economist.

These are . . . counsel. Emerson closely paraphrases Prov. 8: 23–30.

28 *The things . . . eternal.* 2 Cor. 4: 18.

Berkeley and Viasa. George Berkeley (1685–1753), Irish bishop and idealist philosopher. *Viasa,* legendary author of the *Vedas,* the most ancient sacred writings of the Hindus.

the Manichean and Plotinus. Manicheanism, originated by Mani, a 3rd-century Persian, posited a cosmic conflict between darkness (evil) and light (good). Matter, including the body, belonged to the realm of darkness. *Plotinus* (?205–70), Egyptian-born neo-Platonic philosopher.

these flesh-pots of Egypt. Cf. Exod. 16: 2–3.

it is . . . time. Emerson may have had in mind the platonic treatment of beauty in Michelangelo's sonnet 52 ('I saw no mortal beauty with these eyes', trans. J. A. Symonds), or in the conjoined sonnets treating the same themes.

30 *The golden key . . . eternity.* From Milton's *Comus,* 13–14.

32–3 *Man is . . . attend him.* Emerson modernizes some spellings, and omits several stanzas.

33 *the sentence of Plato.* Not Plato, but Aristotle. Cf. *Poetics,* sect. 9 (1451b): 'Hence poetry is something more philosophic and of graver import than history, since its statements are of the nature rather of universals . . .' (trans. Ingram Bywater) in *The Rhetoric and the Poetics of Aristotle* (New York, 1984).

a certain poet. Some scholars suppose this 'certain poet' to be A. Bronson Alcott (1799–1888), American teacher, philosopher, and friend of Emerson.

Nebuchadnezzar. Cf. Dan. 4: 25, 32–3.

34 *if his word . . . nature.* Adapted from *Richard II,* IV. i. 264. In the first edition of *Nature* (1836), this phrase appears in quotes.

Hohenlohe, and the Shakers. Hohenloe, German priest of the 19th century, well known for his 'miraculous' cures. The *Shakers* were a communistic, celibate religious society, named for the shaking dance that was a part of their worship.

35 *Deep calls unto . . . deep.* Cf. Pss. 42: 7.

THE AMERICAN SCHOLAR

37 *the Phi Beta Kappa Society.* An American academic honorary society, founded in 1766.

the constellation Harp. The editors of the *Collected Works* point out that there is apparently no astronomical evidence for Emerson's claim that this star 'shall one day be the pole-star'.

one of those fables. Told in Plato's *Symposium*; and in Plutarch's *Morals,* 'Of Brotherly Love'.

38 *All things . . . one.* Cf. Epictetus' *Enchiridion,* 43: 'Everything has two handles, by one of which it ought to be carried and by the other not' (Loeb Classical Library, Cambridge, Mass., 1928).

44 *Savoyards*. Natives or inhabitants of the Savoy region in south-eastern France.

45 *Berserkirs*. 'Berserker', a Scandinavian warrior of old who fought without armour and was especially fierce.

Alfred. Alfred the Great (849–99), King of the West Saxons, who brought England closer to unity. He also translated classical works into the vernacular.

Flamsteed and Herschel. John *Flamsteed* (1646–1719), English astronomer. Sir William *Herschel* (1738–1822), German-born English astronomer.

48 *Linnaeus . . . Davy . . . Cuvier*. *Linnaeus*, see p. 14 n. Sir Humphrey *Davy* (1778–1829), English chemist. Léopold Chrétien Frédéric Dagobert *Cuvier* (1769–1832), French anatomist who studied fossils, better known by his literary name, George Cuvier.

49 *Sicklied o'er . . . thought*. *Hamlet*, III. i. 87.

51 *Pestalozzi*. Johann Heinrich Pestalozzi (1746–1827), Swiss educator and philanthropist.

THE DIVINITY SCHOOL ADDRESS

58 *A pagan . . . outworn*. From Wordsworth's sonnet 'The World Is Too Much With Us'.

59 *not disobedient . . . vision*. Cf. Acts 26: 19.

Epaminondas. Theban general (418–362 BC).

63 *a devout person*. Emerson's second wife, Lidian. He records her remark in his journal for 3 December 1837.

64 *the God . . . secret*. Cf. Matt. 6: 4, 18.

Zeno . . . Zoroaster. Zeno of Citium (?342–?270 BC), founder of the Stoic school of philosophy in Greece. Little is known about Zoroaster, or, more commonly, Zarathustra, the ancient prophet of the Parsee religion in Persia. He is believed to have lived in the 5th century BC.

George Fox. See p. 17 n.

Wesleys and Oberlins. John *Wesley* (1703–91), with his brother Charles (1707–88), founded the Methodist movement in England. Jean Frédéric *Oberlin* (1740–1826), Alsatian clergyman and philanthropist, often called the 'saint' of the Protestant church.

66 *Massena*. André Masséna (1758–1817), field marshal under Napoleon.

THE CONSERVATIVE

68 *Saturn*. Saturn was an ancient Roman deity, the god of seeds and sowing, and was identified with the Greek god Kronos, father of Neptune, Pluto, and Jupiter.

72 *Chaldeans*. An ancient people of southern Babylonia (now southern Iraq).

73 *the Persian noble of old.* The editors of the *Collected Works* identify him as Otanes, a Greek nobleman who figures in the histories of Herodotus. Otanes' remark is recorded in Book III, sect. 83, of Herodotus. Cf. A. D. Godley's translation in the Loeb Classical Library, 4 vols. (New York, 1921), ii. 111.

76 *The Friar Bernard.* Probably St Bernard of Clairvaux (1090–1153), theologian and reformer, considered by the Catholic Church as the last of the fathers. Emerson records this anecdote in a journal entry for December 1841, though he does not there identify the man as St Bernard.

77 *Anacharsis . . . Othman the Turk. Anacharsis,* a Scythian prince (*fl. c.*600 BC); he was famous for his wit. *Clovis* (465–511), King of the Salian Franks and a brilliant military commander. *Alfred* the Great, see p. 45 n. In the year of his death, *Alaric* I (?370–410), King of the Visigoths, conquered Rome. *Ali* (?600–661), Fourth Caliph and head of the Shiite sect. *Omar* (581–644), Second Caliph; his empire comprised Persia, Syria, and North Africa. *Saladin* (1137–93), Sultan of Egypt and Syria. *Othman* or Osman I (1259–1326), founder of the Ottoman Empire.

80 *Montaigne.* Michel Eyquem de Montaigne (1533–92), French author of the *Essais,* succeeded to his father's estate in 1571. He was much admired by the people of Bordeaux, where he served as mayor.

THE METHOD OF NATURE

82 *Where there . . . perish.* Cf. Prov. 29: 18.

85 *Empedocles.* It is said that Empedocles, a Greek philosopher of the 5th century BC, threw himself into volcanic Mount Etna as a test of his divinity, and that Etna threw back his sandals.

86 *Memoires pour servir.* A genre of personal memoirs.

87 *pericarp.* Covering of the seeds of plants.

88 *saurians . . . palaiotheria. Saurians*: reptiles. *Palaiotheria*: members of an extinct genus of mammals.

Raphael . . . Salvator. Raffaello Santi (1483–1520) and *Salvator* Rosa (1615–73), Italian painters.

92 *Zoroaster.* See p. 64 n.

Heraclitus. Pre-Socratic Greek philosopher (?540–480 BC).

95 *Emanuel Swedenborg.* Swedish mystic and theologian (1688–1772), upon whose doctrines the New Jerusalem Church was founded in 1788.

Ali the Caliph. See p. 77 n.

THE TRANSCENDENTALIST

97 *January, 1842.* Actually, Emerson delivered the lecture in December, 1841.

98 *Condillac.* Étienne Bonnot de Condillac (1715–80), French philosopher and associate of Rousseau and Diderot.

100 *You heard . . . not I. Othello,* v. ii. 127.

The more . . . devil. Othello, v. ii. 130.

Jacobi. Friedrich Heinrich Jacobi (1743–1819), German philosopher. Coleridge quotes Jacobi's 'Letter to Fichte' at the head of 'Section the First' of Essay 15 of his *Friend* (London, 1818). Cf. *The Complete Works of Samuel Taylor Coleridge*, ed. Barbara E. Rooke (Princeton, 1969), iv, 313.

Fichte. Johann Gottlieb Fichte (1762–1814), German philosopher.

Pylades . . . Cato. In Greek legend, *Pylades* helped his friend *Orestes* murder Clytemnestra (Orestes' mother) to avenge her murder of her husband, Agamemnon. *Timoleon* (d. 337 BC), Greek statesman and general, assassinated his brother Timophanes, the would-be tyrant of Corinth. *Epaminondas*, see p. 59 n. *Johann de Witt* (1625–72), chief official of the Dutch Republic, fell from the grace of his countrymen when he offered concessions to Louis XIV in a desperate attempt to establish a stable peace with France; he and his brother Cornelis were murdered by a mob in August 1672. *Cato* the Younger (95–46 BC) committed suicide on hearing of Caesar's victory at Thapsus.

101–2 *Kant . . . Locke.* Immanuel *Kant* (1724–1804), greatest of the German idealist philosophers. John *Locke* (1632–1704), English empiricist and philosopher.

102 *Gnostics . . . Reformers.* The *Gnostics* were a sect of early Christian thinkers whose mystical doctrines, which combined elements of Christian theology with Greek and Eastern philosophy, were denounced as heretical by the early church. The *Essenes* were an ancient sect of Jewish mystics and ascetics, existing from the 2nd century BC to the 2nd century AD. Manicheanism, see p. 28 n. With '*Reformers*' Emerson refers to the leaders of the Protestant Reformation, e.g. Martin Luther, John Calvin.

106 *in the heat . . . detachment.* Emerson quotes loosely from sect. 117 of Walter Savage Landor's *Pericles and Aspasia* (1836). Cleone is reporting (in a letter to Aspasia) this exchange between an Athenian general and Xanthus, a soldier. Emerson had long admired Landor, whom he met in 1833 while travelling through Florence.

ESSAYS: FIRST SERIES

HISTORY

114 *Asdrubal . . . Caesar.* Perhaps *Hasdrubal*, the name of several Carthaginian soldiers of the 3rd century BC. *Caesar Borgia* (1476–1507), Italian general and statesman.

Alcibiades, and Catiline. Alcibiades (450–404 BC), Athenian general and statesman, and one-time student of Socrates. At one point in his tumultuous career, Alcibiades sought the overthrow of the democratic government of Athens. *Catilina* (?108–62 BC) conspired unsuccessfully to assassinate Cicero.

116 *Ferguson.* James Ferguson (1710–76), Scottish astronomer.

Sidney . . . Marmaduke Robinson. Emerson probably refers to Algernon Sidney (1622–83), who served in the Parliamentary forces during the English Civil War, and was executed at the behest of Charles II. Charles Eliot Norton was the first to suggest that, with 'Marmaduke Robinson', Emerson is probably confusing two men: Marmaduke Stevenson and William Robinson. Both were Quakers executed by the Puritans in 1659.

Ohio Circles. Ancient earthworks built by American Indians in southern Ohio.

Belzoni. Giovanni Battista Belzoni (1778–1823), Italian traveller and archaeologist. In 1817, he discovered the tomb of Seti I at Thebes.

118 *'tongue on the balance of expression'.* A 'tongue' is the index on a balance or scale. The editors of the *Collected Works* trace the phrase to Johann Joachim Winckelmann (1717–68), Prussian scholar of ancient architecture.

Pindar. Greek lyric poet (522–440 BC).

Phocion. Athenian general of the 4th century BC. He was condemned and executed for treason. Plutarch records his 'last action' and remarks in his *Lives.*

119 *Guido's Rospigliosi Aurora.* Guido Reni (1575–1642), Italian painter and engraver. Carlyle gave a print of his 'Aurora' to Emerson.

Roos. Probably Johann Heinrich Roos (1631–85), German etcher and painter of animals and landscapes. However, there lived several painters by the name.

Erwin of Steinbach. German architect of the 13th century. He planned and directed the construction of Strasburg Cathedral.

120 *Heeren.* Arnold H. L. Heeren (1760–1842), German historian. Emerson quotes from his *Historical Researches into the Politics, Intercourse, and Trade of the Carthaginians, Ethiopians, and Egyptians* (1832), upon which he draws indirectly in the next few paragraphs. For specific references see the note to this passage prepared by the editors of the *Collected Works.*

121 *Astaboras.* The Atbara, a river in East Africa flowing into the Nile.

123 *After the army . . . like.* From Xenophon's *Anabasis*, IV. iv. 8–14. Xenophon (?435–354 BC), Greek general and historian.

the Philoctetes. A play by Sophocles.

124 *Zoroaster . . . Menu. Zoroaster*, see p. 64 n. *Menu* or Manu is the figure to whom is attributed a body of ancient Indian writings on moral philosophy. Emerson had in his library a copy of *The Institutions of Law; Or, the Ordinances of Menu*, trans. Sir William Jones (London, 1825).

Simeon the Stylite, the Thebais. Simeon Stylites (387–459), Syrian monk. First of the 'Pillar saints', Simeon established himself upon a pillar, from which he preached for some 30 years. Thebais is the Latin name for southern Egypt, the site of early Christian monasteries.

Belus. Emerson probably refers to Baal, the deity of Canaan in the Old Testament. Denounced by the Hebrew prophets, members of the cult of Baal practised holy prostitution and child sacrifice.

Champollion. Jean François Champollion (1790–1832), French Egyptologist.

125 *Hafiz . . . Ariosto*. *Hafiz*, pseudonym of Shams ed-Din Muhammed (d. 1388), Persian lyric poet. Ludovico *Ariosto* (1475–1533), Italian poet.

126 *Chirons . . . Leda*. The Chirons, Griffins, Phorkyas, Helen, and Leda all appear in Goethe's *Faust*.

127 *Hence Plato said . . . understand*. From the *Apology*, 22.

to bend . . . the mind. A favourite expression of Emerson's, this sentence appears in Bacon's *Advancement of Learning*, Book 2, chap. 4.

Perceforest and Amadis de Gaul. Romances from medieval sources relating the adventures of chivalric heroes.

the story . . . Mantle. Familiar to Emerson from Thomas Percy's *Reliques of Ancient English Poetry* (1765).

the Bride of Lammermoor. Scott's novel was published 23 years earlier in 1819. The persons Emerson mentions in this paragraph are characters in the novel.

128 *His substance . . . contain it*. From *1 Henry VI*, II. iii. 50–6. Emerson quotes Talbot's lines loosely.

Davy . . . Gay-Lussac. Davy, see p. 48 n. Joseph-Louis *Gay-Lussac* (1778–1850), French chemist.

Watt . . . Arkwright. James *Watt* (1736–1819), Scottish inventor who contributed greatly to the development of the steam engine. Robert *Fulton* (1765–1815), American engineer and inventor who developed the first practical steam-boats. Amos *Whittemore* (1759–1828), American inventor and gunsmith. Sir Richard *Arkwright* (1732–92), English inventor who developed spinning machines for the textile industry.

SELF-RELIANCE

131 Stephen Whicher has compiled a useful 'table of sources' for this essay, which traces passages to their sources in lectures and journals. Cf. Whicher (ed.), *Selections from Ralph Waldo Emerson* (Boston, 1957), pp. 482–3.

133 *Lethe*. The river Lethe is in the underworld of classical mythology. The dead drink its waters to forget their earthly lives.

134 *Barbadoes*. Slavery was abolished in Barbados in 1834.

I shun . . . me. Cf. Matt. 10: 37.

the lintels of the door-post. Cf. Exod. 12: 23.

136 *the foolish face of praise*. From Pope's *Epistle to Dr Arbuthnot*, l. 212.

137 *as Joseph . . . flee*. Cf. Gen. 39.

an acrostic or Alexandrian stanza. A palindrome, which reads the same backwards and forwards.

138 *Chatham's voice . . . Adams's eye.* William Pitt, 1st Earl of *Chatham* (1708–78), English statesman and renowned orator. The *Adams* in question may be Samuel Adams (1722–1803), American leader of the revolutionary movement in Massachusetts, or John Quincey Adams (1767–1848), sixth President of the United States.

Let the words be gazetted. Taken out of use. When an official military newspaper or gazette announces the retirement of an officer, he is said to be 'gazetted out'.

Monachism . . . Rome. 'Monachism' or monasticism, founded by St *Antony* (251–356). Thomas *Clarkson* (1769–1846), English philanthropist and polemicist, worked for the abolition of the British slave trade, which Parliament outlawed in 1807. Milton makes this remark of *Scipio* (237–183 BC), Roman general and statesman, in *Paradise Lost,* ix. 510.

139 *That popular fable of the sot.* Best known from the 'induction' to *The Taming of the Shrew.*

Alfred . . . Scanderberg . . . Gustavus. Revered early rulers of, respectively, England (see p. 45 n.), Albania, and Sweden.

143 *Bid the invaders . . . within.* Cf. Exod. 3: 5.

Come out unto us. Cf. Isa. 36: 16.

What we love . . . love. In a journal entry for June 1839, Emerson attributes this remark to Johann Christoph Friedrich von Schiller (1759–1805), German poet and dramatist.

Thor and Woden. Norse gods associated with, respectively, courage and constancy.

145 *the word made flesh . . . nations.* Cf. John 1: 14 and Rev. 22: 2.

prayer in all action. It was on this theme that Emerson preached his first sermon, entitled 'Pray Without Ceasing', in October 1826.

146 *His hidden . . . gods.* From Francis Beaumont and John Fletcher's (see p. 432 n.) play *Bonduca,* iii. 1. 84–5.

To the persevering . . . swift. One of the so-called 'Chaldean Oracles' of Zoroaster (see p. 64 n.).

Let not God . . . obey. Exod. 20: 19.

Lavoisier . . . Fourier. Antoine *Lavoisier* (1726–97), French chemist. James *Hutton* (1726–97), Scottish geologist. Jeremy *Bentham* (1748–1832), English philosopher of utilitarianism. Charles *Fourier* (1772–1837), French theorist of socialism, upon whose doctrine the Brook Farm (see p. 266 n.) experiment was founded.

148 *Phidias.* Greek sculptor of the 5th century BC.

149 *Phocion . . . Anaxagoras . . . Diogenes. Phocion,* see p. 118 n. *Anaxagoras,* Greek philosopher of the 5th century BC. *Diogenes,* Greek philosopher of the 4th century BC.

Hudson . . . Franklin. That is, the explorers Sir William Edward *Parry* (1790–1855) and Sir John *Franklin* (1786–1847) were astonished by the achievements of Henry *Hudson* in the 17th century and Vitus *Bering* in the early 18th century.

149–50 *Las Casas.* Napoleon dictated part of his memoirs to Comte Emmanuel Las Casas (1766–1842), who accompanied the emperor into exile.

150 *the Caliph Ali.* See p. 77 n.

THE OVER-SOUL

152 *But souls . . . eternity.* From Henry More's 'Psychozia, or, the Life of the Soul', in *Philosophical Poems* (1647), canto 2.

155 *Can crowd . . . eternity.* From Byron's play *Cain* I. i. 536–7.

The wind . . . whither. Cf. John 3: 8.

156 *Zeno and Arrian.* Zeno, see p. 64 n. Flavius *Arrianus* (95–180), Greek historian and disciple of Epictetus, the Stoic philosopher of the 1st century AD.

158 *Emanuel Swedenborg.* See p. 95 n.

159 *blasted with excess of light.* Cf. Thomas Gray's 'Progress of Poesy', l. 101.

Plotinus . . . Porphyry . . . Behmen. Plotinus and *Porphyry* were neo-Platonic philosophers of the 3rd century AD. Jakob *Boehme* (1575–1624), German mystic and theologian.

Moravian . . . Quietist . . . New Jerusalem Church. Moravians, a Protestant sect in Saxony in the 18th century. *Quietists,* a 17th-century sect denounced as heretics by the Roman Catholic Church. The *New Jerusalem Church,* see p. 95 n.

patois. Dialect.

161 *Paley, Mackintosh, and Stewart.* William *Paley* (1743–1805), English theologian and utilitarian philosopher. Sir James *Mackintosh* (1765–1832), Scottish writer and utilitarian. Dugald *Stewart* (1753–1828), Scottish philosopher of the 'common sense' school.

163 *Their 'highest praising . . . praising'.* From *Areopagitica,* para. 4.

164 *go into . . . door.* Cf. Matt. 6: 6.

165 *the ancient.* Probably Plotinus (see p. 28 n.) in his 'On Beauty'. For details, see the note to this passage prepared by the editors of the *Collected Works.*

CIRCLES

166 *St. Augustine described.* The editors of the *Collected Works* point out that the idea, as expressed here, is not Augustine's. Emerson encountered it in several writers: Coleridge, Sir Thomas Browne, and John Norris. In an entry for 2 July 1835 Emerson copied into his journal the following phrase from Norris's *An Essay Towards the Theory of the Ideal or Intelligible World* (1701–4): 'the sphere of truth whose centre is everywhere and whose circumference is nowhere.'

One moral . . . deduced. Emerson refers to his essay 'Compensation', in the same volume.

another dawn risen on mid-noon. An allusion to *Paradise Lost* v. 308–11.

170 *Pentecost.* The descent of the Holy Spirit described in Acts 2, to which Emerson alludes in the following sentences.

171 *'Then shall . . . in all.* 1 Cor. 15: 28.

173 *'Forgive . . . right'.* From Edward Young's *Night Thoughts* (1742–45), ix. 2316–17. The first line should read: 'His crimes forgive, forgive his virtues too . . . '

lively stones . . . God! Cf. 1 Pet. 2: 5: 'Ye also, as lively stones, are built up a spiritual house . . . '

175 *Nothing great . . . enthusiasm.* Emerson takes this sentence from Coleridge's *The Statesman's Manual*, para. 21.

INTELLECT

176 *Heraclitus looked upon . . . mists.* No such figure is among the fragments of Heraclitus (92 n.); the expression is apparently Emerson's. For some speculation about possible sources for the figure, cf. the note to this passage prepared by the editors of the *Collected Works*.

177 *take no . . . morrow.* Cf. Matt. 6: 34, where Jesus says: 'Take therefore no thought for the morrow: for the morrow shall take thought for the things of itself.'

179 *No man . . . live.* Cf. Exod. 33: 20: 'and the Lord said, "Thou canst not see my face: for there shall no man see me and live" '.

184 *Socrates . . . Lysis . . . Menexenus.* Socrates, Lysis, and Menexenus appear in Plato's *Lysis* dialogue.

Leave father . . . me. Matt. 19: 29.

Cousin. Victor Cousin (1792–1867), French philosopher and follower of Hegel, Kant, and Schelling.

185 *The cherubim . . . most.* Adapted from Byron's play *Cain* I. i. 420–1.

the Trismegisti. Those who write or comment on the books ascribed to Hermes Trismegistus ('thrice great Hermes'), a name given by neo-Platonic philosophers to the Egyptian god Thoth. Hermetic philosophy affirms the unity of all beings and objects.

persuasion . . . intellect. The editors of the *Collected Works* have traced this to Plotinus' *Enneades* (see p. 28 n.).

ART

191 *barbaric pearl and gold.* Cf. *Paradise Lost*, ii. 4.

Raphael . . . Titian. Raffaello Santi (1483–1520), Italian painter. *The Transfiguration*, to which Emerson refers below, was his last work. *Angelo* is short for *Michelangelo.* Emerson probably means Andrea *Sacchi* (1598–1661),

Italian painter; his father, Benedetto Sacchi, was also a painter, though of less renown. *Titian* (1477–1576), Italian painter.

What, old mole . . . fast? Cf. *Hamlet*, I. v. 162.

192 *Earl of Pembroke*. Thomas Herbert, Earl of Pembroke (1656–1733), English statesman, naval commander, President of the Royal Society 1689–90. He collected statues.

194 *the Lena*. Actually the river Neva.

ESSAYS: SECOND SERIES

THE POET

197 *Orpheus . . . Swedenborg*. Emerson, like many of his contemporaries, believed *Orpheus* to have been a historical figure and the actual author of the 'Orphic Hymns', familiar to Emerson in the translations of Thomas Taylor. The *Dictionary of National Biography* points out that 'no doubt of the historic personality of Orpheus or the authenticity of the hymns ascribed to him ever crossed [Taylor's] mind' Emerson followed him in this respect. *Empedocles*, see p. 85 n. *Heraclitus*, see p. 92 n. *Swedenborg*, see p. 95 n.

198 *These stand . . . service*. An allusion to the last line of Milton's sonnet 19: 'They also serve who only stand and wait.'

200 *a Chimborazo under the line*. Chimborazo is an inactive volcano in central Ecuador, located near the equator—or 'under the line'.

the yellow leaf. Emerson alludes to *Macbeth*, v. iii. 22–3 where Macbeth says: 'my way of life / Is fall'n into the sere, the yellow leaf . . . '.

201 *Jamblichus*. Iamblichus (d. *c.*330), a Syrian neo-Platonic philosopher.

202 *'So every . . . body make'*. Stanza 19 of Edmund Spenser's 'An Hymne in Honour of Beautie' (1594).

Proclus. A Greek neo-Platonist of the 5th century AD, familiar to Emerson in the translations of Thomas Taylor.

203 *See the great ball . . . palmetto*. In the presidential campaign of 1840, the Whigs staged such events as this to make memorable their slogan, 'Keep the Ball Rolling'. Emerson lists the towns of Lowell, Lynn, and Salem, Massachusetts, each associated with its chief product. The 'cider-barrel' and 'log cabin' were the emblems of W. H. Harrison's 1840 campaign for the presidency. The 'hickory stick' was the symbol of Andrew 'Old Hickory' Jackson, seventh President of the USA. The state flag of South Carolina features a palmetto tree, which became associated with Senator John Caldwell Calhoun, who had earlier served as vice-president under John Quincey Adams and under Jackson.

204 *Lord Chatham . . . Bailey's Dictionary*. William Pitt, 1st Earl of Chatham (see p. 138 n.), known, apparently, for his reading in the *Universal Etymological English Dictionary*, published by Nathaniel Bailey in 1721.

205 *the eyes of Lynceus*. In Greek mythology, Lyncaeus is a sharp-eyed crew-man on Jason's ship, the *Argo*.

206 *Phosphorus*. Phosphorus ('light bringer'), Greek god identified with the morning star.

207 *alter idem*. A second self; the same yet different.

208 *Milton says . . . bowl*. Cf. Milton's sixth *Latin Elegy*.

209 *Vitruvius*. See p. 21 n.

When Socrates, in Charmides. Cf. the *Charmides* of Plato, sect. 157.

So in our tree . . . top. Lines 132–3 of the dedicatory epistle to Chapman's *Iliad*, 'To the High Borne Prince of Men, Henrie'.

210 *Chaucer, in his praise*. In the 'Wife of Bath's Tale', ll. 278–81.

when John saw. Cf. Rev. 6: 13.

Pythagoras . . . Oken. Pythagoras, Greek philosopher of the 6th century BC. *Paracelsus*, 16th-century Swiss physician and alchemist. *Cornelius Agrippa*, 16th-century German philosopher. Jerome *Cardan*, 16th-century Italian mathematician and naturalist. Johann *Kepler* (1571–1630), German astronomer. Friedrich Wilhelm Joseph von *Schelling* (1775–1854), German philosopher. Lorenz *Oken* (1779–1851), German naturalist and proponent of the theory that the cell is the fundamental unit of living matter.

211 *Jacob Behmen*. See p. 159 n.

213 *Chalmers's collection*. Alexander Chalmers (1759–1834), Scottish journalist and biographer, editor of *The Works of the English Poets, from Chaucer to Cowper* (1810).

EXPERIENCE

216 *gives us the lethe to drink*. See p. 133 n.

217 *like those that Hermes won*. Hermes was a lover of Rhea and won five days from the Moon so that she could give birth to Osiris. Rhea's husband, Saturn, had placed her under a curse which prevented her giving birth on any day of the year.

Tiraboschi, Warton, or Schlegel. Girolano *Tiraboschi* (1731–94), Italian literary historian. Thomas *Warton* (1728–90), historian of English poetry. Emerson could have had in mind either Friedrich von *Schlegel* (1772–1829) or his brother August Wilhelm (1767–1845): both men were historians of German literature.

Ate Dea . . . so soft. Emerson quotes from Robert Burton's *Anatomy of Melancholy*: there is 'not one [man] of a thousand . . . whom that *Ate Dea*, "Over men's heads walking aloft, / With tender feet treading so soft," Homer's goddess *Ate*, hath not involved into this discontented rank, or plagued with some misery or other' (First Partition, section 2, member 3, subsection 10). Burton translated the quoted lines from Lucian's *Podagra*.

Ate is the goddess of infatuation, associated with moral blindness; in the *Iliad* (ix. 502–12), she pursues and punishes sinners.

218 *Boscovich*. Ruggerio Giuseppe Boscovich (1711–87), Italian mathematician, astronomer, and physicist, advocate of Newton's theories.

The Indian who . . . us all. Emerson takes the story from Robert Southey's poem *The Curse of Kehama* (1810), Part 2, sect. 14.

Para coats. Coats made from the Para rubber of South America.

221 *Pero si muove*. 'Still, it moves'—the words of Galileo upon his being forced by the ecclesiastical authorities to deny his heretical observation that the earth orbits the sun.

Plotinus. See p. 28 n.

Bettine. Elizabeth (Brentano) von Arnim (1785–1859), German writer who adapted for publication her correspondence with Goethe and with Beethoven.

Labrador spar. A kind of feldspar, known as labradorite, found in the Labrador peninsula of Canada.

222 *Education-Farm*. An allusion to the Brook Farm Institute of Agriculture and Education, a commune founded in 1841 near West Roxbury, Massachusetts.

There is now . . . Iranis. Emerson quotes from the *Desatir*, a collection of Persian prophetic writings. For a description of this work and how Emerson came to know it see the note prepared by the editors of the *Collected Works*, iii, 185–7.

224 *Poussin . . . Communion of St. Jerome*. Nicolas *Poussin* (1594–1665), French painter. *Rosa*, see p. 88 n. Raphael's (see p. 88 n.) *The Transfiguration of Christ* is in the Vatican. Michelangelo's *Last Judgment* is in the Sistine Chapel, Rome. Domenichinio's *Communion of St. Jerome* is in the Louvre.

Gentoos and Grahamites. *Gentoos*: Hindus. *Grahamites*, followers of Sylvester Graham (1794–1851), a Presbyterian minister and advocate of vegetarianism.

225 *Life itself . . . sleep*. Cf. Prospero's speech in *The Tempest*, IV. i. 156–8: 'We are such stuff / As dreams are made on; and our little life / Is rounded with a sleep.'

226 *the kingdom . . . observation*. Cf. Luke 17: 20: 'the kingdom of God cometh not with observation . . . '.

227 *Sir Everard Home*. A Scottish surgeon, author of *Lectures on Comparative Anatomy* (1814–28).

228 *Since neither . . . knew*. Cf. ll. 455–7 of *Antigone*, in the 17th-century translation by Samuel White.

Thales . . . Zoroaster. *Thales*, Greek natural philosopher of the 6th century BC. *Anaximenes*, Greek philosopher of the 6th century BC. *Anaxagoras*, Greek philosopher of the 5th century BC. *Zoroaster*, see p. 64 n.

Mencius. The 3rd-century BC Confucian philosopher.

231 *Hermes, Cadmus. Hermes*, the Greek god of invention. *Cadmus*, mythical founder of Thebes.

232 *Flaxman's drawing.* John Flaxman (1755–1826), English illustrator. *Eumenides* is a tragedy by Aeschylus.

233 *that every soul . . . period.* Cf. Plato's *Phaedrus*, 248c.

NATURE

236 *Gabriel and Uriel.* Angels in Milton's *Paradise Lost.*

houstonia. A genus of North American herbs with blue, lilac, or white flowers; bluet.

237 *villeggiatura.* A holiday in the country, especially a visit to a villa.

master of revels. In the court of Elizabeth I, and in some later courts, the Master of Revels organized the royal entertainments.

Paphos, or Ctesiphon. Ctesiphon, a large city on the Tigris near Baghdad, and the site of the splendid palace built by Chosroes I in the 6th century AD. *Paphos*, an ancient city in Cyprus, and site of one of the temples of Venus.

Notch Mountains. Mountains near Franconia, New Hampshire.

238 *a prince of the power of the air.* Cf. Eph. 2: 2: 'in time past ye walked according to the course of this world, according to the prince of the power of air . . .'.

Tempes. Tempe is a beautiful valley in Greece; its name has become generic for its kind.

Como Lake, or the Madeira Islands. The *Madeira Islands* lie off the coast of Morocco. *Lake Como* is in Lombardy, northern Italy; famous for its beauty, and for the abundant game and vegetation that grace its shores, the lake figures in the writings of Virgil and others.

the Campagna. The Campagna di Roma, a lowland plain surrounding Rome.

natura naturata. 'Created nature'.

239 *'Wreaths' and 'Flora's chaplets'.* Emerson has in mind the annual 'gift-book' anthologies of verse and short fiction popular in America in the early and mid-19th century, usually published for the Christmas season. They commonly bore such names as 'Magnolia', 'The Snow-flake', etc.

differential thermometer. A U-shaped coupling of two thermometers, used to measure the difference between the temperatures of the substances in which its two tines are immersed.

Proteus. In classical mythology, a sea deity, son of Poseidon and 'shepherd' of the seals.

240 *Ceres, and Pomona.* In classical mythology, respectively, the goddess of grain, and the guardian of the apple orchards.

241 *Franklin . . . Black.* Benjamin *Franklin* (1706–90), American statesman, scientist, and author. John *Dalton* (1766–1844), English chemist. *Davy*, see p. 48 n. Joseph *Black* (1728–99), Scottish chemist.

243 *Luther declares*. The editors of the *Collected Works* point out that Luther made no such declaration.

Jacob Behmen and George Fox. Boehme, see p. 159 n. Fox, see p. 17 n.

James Naylor. James Nayler (?1617–60), an eminent English Quaker. In 1656, he rode into Bristol accompanied by his followers who chanted 'Holy, holy, holy, Lord God of Israel'. For this, he was tried by Parliament, convicted, branded with a hot iron, and fined.

246 *tickled trout*. Trout taken in the manner described by Richard Jeffries (1848–87) in his *Red Deer* (London, 1884): 'Groping for trout (or tickling) is tracing it to the stone it lies under, then rubbing it gently beneath, which causes the fish to gradually move backwards into the hand, till the fingers suddenly close in the gills.' Cf. also *Twelfth Night* II. v. 19–20, where Maria says upon Malvolio's entrance: 'for here comes the trout that must be caught with tickling.'

POLITICS

250 *Laban . . . the officer*. Cf. Gen. 28–31.

calling that . . . just. A quotation from Plutarch's 'Symposiacs', in his *Morals*, Book 8, question 2, para. 2. Emerson prepared an introduction for an edition of the *Morals* collected and revised by William H. Goodwin (Boston, 1870).

253 *Botany Bay*. Great Britain established a penal colony at Botany Bay, New South Wales, Australia, in 1788.

254 *one foreign observer . . . among us*. Probably Alexis de Tocqueville, who described the relation between 'equality of conditions' and marriage in *Democracy in America* (first US edition, 1838); notably, in the chapter on 'How Equality Helps to Maintain Good Morals in America'. From the *Journals* it is clear that Emerson had read de Tocqueville by April 1841. Emerson met him in Paris in 1848.

Fisher Ames. Fisher Ames (1758–1808), a Federalist, served in the US House of Representatives 1789–97.

256 *Annual Register . . . Conversations' Lexicon*. Contemporary encyclopedias of history.

NOMINALIST AND REALIST

262 *Eleusinian mysteries*. Eleusis was a prehistoric settlement in Greece which remained independent of Athens until about the 7th century BC. The 'Mysteries' were mystical ceremonies associated with the gods Demeter and Dionysius.

Pope's Odyssey. Alexander Pope (1688–1744) published his *Odyssey* in 1725–6. William Broome and Elijah Fenton assisted in the translation.

263 *Handel's Messiah*. George Frederick Handel (1685–1759), German-born British composer. The *Messiah* (1742) is the most famous of his oratorios. Emerson attended a performance of it in Boston on Christmas Day 1843.

Mesmerism . . . the Millennial Church. Mesmerism is the general term for the para-psychological theories of animal magnetism associated with Friedrich Anton Mesmer (1734–1815), the Austrian physician. *Swedenborgism* is the theology of the followers of Emanuel Swedenborg (1688–1772), Swedish mystic and theologian. *Fourierism*, see p. 146 n. *Millennialists* believe in a future thousand-year period of blessedness.

264 *Nick Bottom.* One of the 'rude mechanicals' who perform the play 'Pyramus and Thisbe' before Duke Theseus in Shakespeare's *A Midsummer Night's Dream.* Bottom wants to play all the parts. Cf. I. ii.

265 *Alphonso of Castille.* Alfonso X (?1226–84) was King of Castile and Leon from 1252 until his death. Edward W. Emerson observes that Alphonso 'is reported to have said that, had God consulted him in the making of the world, he would have made it differently'.

hellebore. 'A name given by the ancients to certain plants having poisonous and medicinal properties, and especially reputed as specifics for mental disease' (*OED*).

266 *Brook Farm . . . Shakers. Brook Farm* was a commune established near West Roxbury, Massachusetts, in 1841; it was disbanded six years later. *Skaneateles* was a similar experiment near Skaneateles Lake in New York State, begun in 1844. The *Northampton* Association of Education and Industry communally operated a silk factory at what is now Florence, Massachusetts, from 1842 to 1846. *Essenes*, see p. 102 n. The *Port-Royalists* were a community of intellectuals at a convent near Paris, in the 17th century. The *Shakers* were a Protestant sect founded by Ann Lee (1736–84), properly called the United Society of Believers in Christ's Second Coming. The 'Shakers' earned their nickname for the ecstatic dance that was part of their worship.

Into paint . . . bride. Emerson quotes l. 110 of Washington Allston's poem, 'The Paint King', published in *Sylphs of the Seasons, with Other Poems* (1813). Allston (1779–1843), an American, was himself a celebrated painter.

268 *Lord Eldon.* John Scott, 1st Earl of Eldon (1751–1838), English statesman and jurist. By no means an 'agitator', Lord Eldon vigorously opposed parliamentary reform throughout his career.

NEW ENGLAND REFORMERS

271 *when a church censured.* Not uncommon in Emerson's day.

272 *the party of Free Trade.* The Democratic Party, whose power lay, in Emerson's day, in the anti-tariff South.

the Globe newspaper. Published in Washington, D.C.

275 *St. Simon . . . Fourier . . . Owen.* Charles Henri, Comte de Saint-Simon (1760–1825), French socialist. Fourier, see p. 146‡ n. Robert Owen (1771–1858), Welsh reformer and socialist. Edward W. Emerson suggests that Emerson had in mind such social experiments in Massachusetts as Brook Farm, which was organized according to Fourier's principles; the

communally operated silk factory of the Northampton Association; and the Hopedale community, founded by Adin Ballou.

278 *You remember the story.* As the editors of the *Collected Works* point out, Emerson's audience would have remembered the story, which appeared in a number of Latin primers of the 19th century.

the good-hearted word . . . truth. Cf. *Republic*, iii. 413a.

279 *Warton relates . . . Berkeley.* Joseph *Warton* (1722–1800), English literary critic and classical scholar. *Berkeley*, see p. 28 n. The aim of the *Scriblerus Club*— which counted among its members Swift, Pope, and Gay—was to criticize and ridicule 'all the false tastes in learning' (*Oxford Companion to English Literature*, ed. Margaret Drabble. Oxford: OUP, 1985). It was active chiefly in 1714, 14 years before Bishop Berkeley embarked for the Bermudas. Allen *Bathurst*, 1st Earl (1684–1775), Tory statesman and friend of Swift and Pope.

280 *Mirabeau, Charles Fox.* Honoré Gabriel Riquetti, Comte de *Mirabeau* (1749–91), French Revolutionary statesman and renowned orator. *Charles James Fox* (1749–1806), English liberal statesman, accomplished orator and debater.

Cimon, Themistocles, Alcibiades. Cimon (d. 449 BC), Athenian statesman and military commander who destroyed the attacking Persian fleet in 466 or 467. *Themistocles* (*c.*523–458 BC), Athenian general and statesman, instrumental in the defeat of the Persian army in 480 BC. *Alcibiades* (?450–404 BC), Athenian statesman and general, see p. 114 n.

282 *Dandini.* This story is told of an Indian sage named Dandimis (or Dandamys) in Montaigne's essay 'Of Profit and Honesty'.

REPRESENTATIVE MEN

PLATO; OR, THE PHILOSOPHER

289 *Omar.* See p. 77 n.

Boethius . . . Alfieri. Boethius (475–525), neo-Platonist philosopher and Roman statesman. François *Rabelais* (1490–1533), French physician and satirist, author of *Gargantua* and *Pantagruel*. Desiderius *Erasmus* (?1466–1536), Dutch humanist, classical scholar, author of *Praise of Folly*. Giordano *Bruno* (1548–1600), Italian philosopher. Vittorio, Conte *Alfieri* (1749–1803), Italian poet.

Behmen. See p. 159 n.

Henry More . . . Picus Mirandola. Henry More (1614–87), English philosopher of the 'Cambridge Platonist' school; as were *Ralph Cudworth* (1617–88) and *John Smith* (1618–52). *John Hales* (1584–1656), English clergyman. *Jeremy Taylor* (1613–67), Anglican bishop renowned for his eloquence. Floyer *Sydenham* (1710–87), English classical scholar and translator of Plato. *Thomas Taylor* (1758–1835), English scholar whose translations of Plato, and of the neo-Platonists Plotinus and Proclus, Emerson much admired. *Marsilio Ficino* (1433–99), Italian Platonic philosopher. Giovanni, Conte Pico della *Mirandola* (1463–94), Italian neo-Platonist.

290 *Solon . . . Sophron . . . Philolaus. Solon* (?639–?559 BC), Athenian statesman and reformer. *Sophron* of Syracuse (5th century BC), writer whose descriptions of the Sicilian Greeks are said to have been admired by Plato. *Philolaus*, Pythagorean philosopher of the 5th century BC.

Timæus, Heraclitus, Parmenides. Timæus, possibly a fictitious figure, is supposed to have been a contemporary and countryman of Philolaus (above); he appears in Plato's *Timaeus* dialogue. *Heraclitus*, see p. 92 n. *Parmenides*, Greek philosopher of the 5th century BC, who appears in Plato's dialogue of the same name.

Such a genius . . . persons. Republic, vi. 503.

291 *He ground them all into paint.* Emerson alludes to l. 110 of Allston's poem, 'The Paint King' (see p. 266 n.).

He was born 430 BC. . . . Emerson's remarks on Plato's biography agree with the scholarship of his day, though later scholars have emended some of what he recounts here; for which see the note to this passage in the Harvard Belknap Press edition of Emerson's *Collected Works*, iv. 179–80.

292 *the Seven Wise Masters.* Bias, Chilon, Cleobulus, Periander, Pittacus, Solon, and Thales: statesmen of ancient Greece. A number of proverbs and maxims are attributed to them.

He shall . . . define. Phaedrus, 266.

293 *the Vedas.* Sacred writings of the Hindus, familiar to Emerson in the 18th-century translations of Sir William Jones, and of Henry Thomas Colebrook.

293–4 *You are fit . . . am I, I.* The editors of the *Collected Works* have traced this quotation to several passages in the *Vishnu Purana, a System of Mythology and Tradition*, trans. H. H. Wilson (London, 1840), pp. 596, 659, 253, 132, 225.

294 *Tartarus.* An abyss in the underworld of classical mythology.

295 *Malthus.* Thomas Malthus (1706–1834), English economist who predicted that global population growth would outstrip food production, bringing about widespread famine.

Pentelican marble. Marble quarried at Mount Pentelicus, Greece.

Medford . . . Lowell. Towns in Massachusetts.

296 *Let us declare . . . truth. Timaeus*, 29e.

All things . . . beautiful. The editors of the *Collected Works* trace these sentences to Thomas Taylor's translation of *The Six Books of Proclus*, 2 vols. (London, 1816), i. 125.

297 *alar bones.* Bones of the wing.

One would say . . . too bold. Emerson alludes to *The Faerie Queene*, Book 3, canto 11, stanzas 50–4.

298 *Socrates' profession.* Cf. *Theaetetus*, 148e, where Socrates says to Theaetetus, who is working through a testy philosophical problem: 'Yes, you are suffering the pangs of labor . . . because you are not empty, but pregnant.' The 'cooking' and 'adulatory art' figures appear in the *Gorgias*, 464e–466a.

For philosophy . . . the man. In an appendix to their text of *Representative Men*, the editors of the *Collected Works* reprint Emerson's revisions of the book's manuscript. There, Emerson places this remark in Thomas Taylor's *Works of Plato*, 5 vols. (London, 1804), iv, 400.

I, therefore . . . here. Gorgias, 526d–e.

299 *The essence . . . human form. Phaedrus,* 249.

300 *The whole . . . these. Republic,* v. 450b.

Isocrates. Isocrates (436–338 BC), Athenian orator, renowned teacher of rhetoric. He was a student of Socrates.

By us . . . blunders. Timaeus, 47a–c.

By each . . . alone. Republic, 527e.

301 *In the Republic.* Cf. *Republic,* 374–6.

Socrates declares . . . may happen. Theages, 129e–130e, now believed spurious.

301–2 *Let there be . . . of truths.* Adapted from *Republic,* 509e–511.

302 *When an artificer . . . from beautiful. Timaeus,* 28a–b.

the Banquet. Better known as *The Symposium.*

Body cannot . . . God only. Cf. *Phaedo,* 65–6.

304 *the Hippiases and Gorgiases.* Both renowned teachers in Socrates' day, each appears in Plato's dialogues. Cf. *Greater Hippias, Lesser Hippias, Gorgias.*

Meno. A disciple of Gorgias, he appears in Plato's dialogue *Meno.* Emerson adapts this sentence from 80a.

Whatever inconvenience . . . you say. Crito, 54d.

306 *Karnac.* A village in central Egypt, and the site of the ruins of the Temple of Amon.

Etrurian remains. Etruria was an ancient settlement in central Italy, whose people produced magnificent frescos and sculptures.

PLATO: NEW READINGS

307 *Mr. Bohn's 'Serial Library'.* A series of inexpensive editions published by Henry George Bohn in London.

Phidias, Menu. Phidias (500–?432 BC), Greek sculptor. *Menu,* see p. 124 n.

Laplace. Pierre Simon, Marquis de Laplace (1749–1827), French mathematician and astronomer.

308 *His perception . . . new creation.* Cf. *Phaedrus,* 72.

the cave of Trophonius . . . Fates. The allegory of the cave is told in *Republic*, vii. The oracle of *Trophonius* is at Boethia, and he appears in many Greek writings; he is not, however, associated with the cave of Plato's allegory. The story of the *ring of Gyges* is told in *Republic*, 359; of the *temperaments* in *Republic*, 415; of *Hades and the Fates* in *Republic*, 619 ff.

soliform . . . boniform. Soliform: resembling the sun. *Boniform*: promoting, perceiving, or akin to the good.

that it is better . . . do it. Cf. *Gorgias*, 474c, where Socrates argues this point.

that the sinner . . . punishment. Cf. *Gorgias*, 480c–d, where Socrates argues this point.

that the lie . . . homicide. Socrates' arguments in *Republic*, 451.

that the soul . . . willingly. Cf. *Republic*, 413a.

308–9 *that the order . . . best possible.* Cf. *Republic*, 403c–d.

309 *the fine . . . a worse man.* Cf. *Republic*, 347c.

that his guards . . . they need. Cf. *Republic*, 416e.

Of all . . . greatest good. Republic, 366e.

Thus the fact . . . explication. Emerson has in mind Socrates' arguments that the soul is immortal in *Phaedo*, 72–3.

310 *The names of things . . . illustration.* Cf. *Cratylus*, 390e, 408c; *Philebus*, 30d.

when he paints. Cf. *Timaeus*, 30a.

Nature is . . . the story. Emerson quotes from *The Winter's Tale*, IV. iv. 88–90, and from *Antony and Cleopatra*, III. xiii. 43–6.

MONTAIGNE; OR, THE SKEPTIC

312 *Plotinus . . . Fénelon . . . Pindar. Plotinus*, see p. 28 n. François de Salignac de la Mothe Fénelon (1651–1715), French divine and writer. *Pindar*, see p. 118 n.

313 *Spence relates . . . guineas.* The anecdote is recorded in *Joseph Spence: Observations, Anecdotes, and Characters of Books and Men*, ed. J. M. Osborne, 2 vols. (Clarendon Press, Oxford, 1966), i. 47, no. 111. References to Spence below are to this edition. The painter Sir Godfrey Kneller (1646–1723) was a friend of Pope.

314 *Wer nicht . . . Leben lang.* 'He who doesn't love wine, women, and song / Remains a fool his whole life long.'

Cabanis. Pierre Jean Georges Cabanis (1757–1808), French physician and philosopher.

the cynic moans. The editors of the *Journals and Miscellaneous Notebooks* point out, in a note to the 1845 entry in which this remark appears, that the 'cynic' is Emerson's second wife, Lidian. Cf. *JMN*, ix. 201.

There is . . . at all. Henry St John, 1st Viscount Bolingbroke (1678–1751), Tory statesman, renowned orator, and an intimate of Pope. Emerson takes the anecdote from Spence's *Anecdotes*, op. cit., i. 266, no. 646.

a Gibeonite. The people of Gibeon, in ancient Palestine, were condemned by the prophet Joshua to be the hewers of wood and drawers of water because they deceived the Israelites. Cf. Josh. 9.

315 σχεπτειν. To look out.

316 *Men are . . . pine.* From Spence's *Anecdotes*, op. cit., ii. 499, no. 1359.

317 *Cotton's translation.* Charles Cotton (1630–87) published his translation of Montaigne's *Essays* in 1685. It went through a number of later editions.

318 *John Sterling.* British essayist, poet, and friend of Carlyle (1806–44), corresponded with Emerson; the two never met.

Mr. Hazlitt. William Hazlitt (1811–93), editor of *The Complete Works of Montaigne* (1842), to whom Emerson alludes, was the son of William Hazlitt the critic and essayist.

Florio's translation. John Florio (?1553–1625) published his translation of Montaigne's *Essays* in 1603.

Leigh Hunt. English essayist and poet (1784–1859), author of *Lord Byron and Some of His Contemporaries* (1828).

the civil wars of the League. The Holy League was an alliance of French Catholics who took up arms to suppress Protestantism and Protestant influence in politics.

319 *He pretends . . . stealth.* Cf. Montaigne's essay 'Of Presumption', ii. 17 in his *Essays*. Hereafter references to Montaigne's *Essays* will be given simply by book and chapter number.

Five or six . . . living. From *Essays*, iii. 3: 'Of Three Kinds of Association'.

When I . . . himself. Essays, ii. 20: 'We Taste Nothing Pure'.

Que sçais je? What do I know?

old Poz. In the children's stories of Maria Edgeworth (1767–1849), the character Old Poz was very sure ('positive') of his opinions.

321 *But . . . not choice. Essays*, iii. 5: 'On Some Verses of Virgil'.

322 *'Soul's Errand' of Sir Walter Raleigh.* Raleigh's poem is better known as 'The Lie'.

the Bhagavat. The *Bhagavadgita*, sacred Hindu writings.

323 *San Carlo.* Edward W. Emerson identifies him as Charles K. Newcomb, an idealistic friend of Emerson who lived at Brook Farm.

327 *George Fox saw . . . darkness.* The remark is recorded in chap. 1 of Fox's (p. 17 n.) *Journals.*

Charles Fourier . . . destinies. The phrase Emerson quotes is engraved on Fourier's tomb (see p. 146 n.).

328 *If my bark . . . sea.* The last line of 'A Poet's Hope', by William Ellery Channing (1817–1901), a friend of Emerson; not to be confused with his uncle of the same name, the distinguished Unitarian minister.

330 *punch*. Emerson may have had in mind *Punch*, an English weekly begun in 1841.

Kyd . . . Fletcher. Dramatists contemporary with Shakespeare.

Brut . . . Spanish voyages. *Brut* or Brutus is the legendary father of the Britons, whose story is told in Geoffrey of Monmouth's *History of the Kings of Britain* (1136). Michael Drayton (1563–1631) retells the legend in his *Poly-Olbion* (1622), but no plays on Brut survive. Raphael Holinshed (d.? 1580) was the most famous historian of the *Henries*, and his *Chronicles* (1577) is a major source for Shakespeare's English history plays. Hazlitt points out in his *Lectures on Elizabethan Literature* that, in Shakespeare's day, translators had for the first time made widely available such *Italian tales, and Spanish voyages* as Emerson mentions here.

331 *Malone's laborious computations*. Edmond Malone (1741–1812), Irish scholar, undertook pioneer studies in the composition history of Shakespeare's plays. His views on the authorship of the Henry VI plays are now generally discredited. A number of scholars still suppose *Henry VIII* to be the collaborative work of Shakespeare and John Fletcher.

332 *See Wolsey's soliloquy*. *Henry VIII*, III. ii. 350 ff.

Saadi. 13th-century Persian poet much admired by Emerson.

Presenting Thebes' . . . divine. From Milton's 'Il Penseroso', ll. 99–100.

332–3 *Lydgate and Caxton . . . poor Gower*. Emerson is mistaken here. John *Lydgate* (?1370–1451) was an imitator of Chaucer, who died when Lydgate was about 30. Lydgate's work dates from 1412–38. William *Caxton* (?1422–91) is still less plausible as a predecessor of Chaucer. Much of the rest of what Emerson says here is misleading, where it is not incorrect. (Cf. the note to this passage in the *Collected Works*, iv. 220–1, in which the editors set the record straight in detail.) *Guido delle Colone* was a 13th-century Sicilian poet, whose *Historia Troiana* (in Latin, 1282) is based on an earlier work by the 12th-century French poet Benoît de Sainte-Maure, who had himself borrowed from the works of *Dares Phrygius* and Dictys Cretensis. Giovanni *Boccaccio* (1313–75), Italian author of the *Decameron*, borrowed from Guido's work, and it is to him that Chaucer owes the greater debt. *Romaunt of the Rose* is a translation into Middle English of *Roman de la Rose*, by Guillaume de *Lorris* and Jean de *Meun*, 13th-century French poets; Chaucer is thought to have supplied about 1,700 lines of the translation. The *Lollius of Urbino* whom Emerson mentions as the source for *Troilus and Cressida* is in fact a fictitious figure; Emerson apparently takes in earnest l. 394 of the first book of Chaucer's poem: 'As writ myn auctour called Lollius.' The connection between '*The Cock and the Fox*' ('The Nun's Priest's Tale') and the *Lais* of the 12th-century French poet *Marie* de France is considered specious by modern scholars. Chaucer did take a few stories from his contemporary John *Gower* (?1330–1408), the English poet.

333 *Sir Robert Peel . . . Mr. Webster . . . Menu*. Sir Robert *Peel* (1788–1850), Prime Minister of Great Britain 1834–5, 1841–6. Daniel *Webster*

(1782–1852), American lawyer, accomplished orator, Whig statesman, served at the US House of Representatives and in the Senate. *Menu*, see p. 124 n.

334 *Grotius*. Hugo Grotius (1583–1645), Dutch jurist and statesman.

The translation of Plutarch. Emerson has in mind the 1579 translation of the *Lives* by Sir Thomas North, not from the original Greek, but from the French of Jacques Amyot.

Vedas . . . Scottish Minstrelsy. The *Vedas*, a body of ancient Hindu writings. *Pilpay*, usually Bidpai, is both the title and the supposed author of a collection of Indian fables. An Arabic version of the fables appeared in about 750; from this a number of English and Continental translations have been made. *The Thousand and One Nights* (*Arabian Nights*), a collection of tales originally in Arabic, appeared in Europe first in the French translation of Antoine Galland, published 1704–17. The Spanish *Poema del Cid* dates from the 12th century, and its hero Rodrigo Díaz, el Cid Campeador (?1030–99), figures in numerous Spanish ballads. Sir Walter Scott published his *Minstrelsy of the Scottish Border* in 1802–3. His friend Joseph Ritson (1752–1802), the British antiquarian, published *Robin Hood: a Collection of all the Ancient Poems, Songs, and Ballads Now Extant Relative to that Outlaw* in 1795.

Ferrex . . . Needle. *Ferrex and Porrex*, another name for *Gorboduc*, one of the earliest English tragedies, written by Thomas Norton and Thomas Sackville and performed first in 1561. *Gammer Gurton's Needle* is an early English comedy attributed to John Still. It was first performed in 1566.

Essexes . . . Buckinghams. Eminent families of the Elizabethan aristocracy.

335 *Ben Jonson . . . his few words*. Emerson is thinking of the two poems by Jonson that appeared in the First Folio edition of Shakespeare's plays in 1623: 'To the Reader', and 'To the Memory of My Beloved, the Author Mr. William Shakespeare; and What he has Left Us'.

Sir Henry Wotton. English poet and diplomat (1568–1639). Emerson discussed Wotton in his 1835–6 lecture series on English Literature. The details of Wotton's acquaintance with the persons mentioned here were familiar to Emerson from Izaak Walton's *The Lives of Donne, Wotton, Hooker, Herbert and Sanderson*, which he owned in a two-volume edition (Boston, 1832); and from Wotton's own *Reliquiae Wottonianae*, also in Emerson's library.

Lessing . . . Wieland . . . Schlegel. Gotthold Ephraim *Lessing* (1729–81), German dramatist and critic, published articles in praise of Shakespeare. Christoph Martin *Wieland* (1733–1813) published the first German prose translations of 22 of Shakespeare's plays between 1762 and 1766. The first of August Wilhelm von *Schlegel*'s (1767–1845) translations of Shakespeare's plays into German verse appeared in 1798.

336 *Malone . . . Collier*. Editors and critics of Shakespeare's works.

Betterton . . . Macready. Renowned actors of the 17th, 18th, and 19th centuries.

337 *What may ... moon? Hamlet*, I. iii. 51–3.

The forest of Arden ... captivity. The *Forest of Arden* is part of the setting for *As You Like It*. Emerson has Macbeth's Inverness castle, not *Scone*, in mind: 'This castle hath a pleasant seat, the air / Nimbly and sweetly recommends itself / Unto our gentle senses' (I. vi. 1–3). *Portia* is a character in *The Merchant of Venice*. Emerson quotes from *Othello*'s retelling of his life and times before the Duke of Venice: 'of antres vast and desarts idle ... It was my hint to speak' (I. iii. 140–2).

Aubrey and Rowe. John *Aubrey* (1626–97), English antiquarian and biographer, collected anecdotes about Shakespeare and other writers and eminent persons. Nicholas *Rowe* (1674–1718), English playwright and editor of Shakespeare.

338 *Timon ... Warwick ... Antonio.* Timon is the protagonist of *Timon of Athens*. *Warwick* could be one of two characters: Richard Beauchamp, Earl of Warwick, appearing in *2 Henry IV*, *Henry V*, and *1 Henry VI*; or his son-in-law Richard Neville, Earl of Warwick, in *1–2 Henry VI*. *Antonio* appears in *The Merchant of Venice*.

Talma. François Joseph Talma (1763–1826), considered the greatest tragedian of his day, whose company was enjoyed by Napoleon.

340 *Daguerre.* Louis Jacques Mandé Daguerre (1789–1851), French pioneer of photography after whom the process 'daguerreotype' is named.

342 *Tasso.* Torquato Tasso (1544–95), Italian poet.

THE CONDUCT OF LIFE

FATE

346 *On two days ... slay.* Emerson's translation of a German translation of a poem attributed to the Persian poet Pindar of Rei.

The Destiny ... above. Cf. ll. 805–14. Spellings and usages have been modernized in the text from which Emerson quotes.

347 *Whatever is ... transgressed.* Cf. Aeschylus, *The Suppliant Maidens*, ll. 1047–9.

Jung Stilling ... pistareen-Providence. Johann H. *Jung Stilling* (1740–1817), German mystic. *Robert Huntington* may be a mistake for William Huntington (1745–1813), an eccentric English minister. *Pistareen*, a Spanish coin of little value in the USA.

an earthquake. In 1755.

three years ago. 17 December 1857.

bombyx ... infusory biters ... labrus. Bombyx, the moth of the silkworm. *Infusory biters*, microscopic animal life. *Labrus*, a predatory fish.

348 *Spurzheim ... Quetelet.* Johann Gaspar *Spurzheim* (1766–1832), German phrenologist. Emerson probably heard him lecture in Boston in 1832. Lambert Adolphe Jacques *Quételet* (1796–1874), Belgian statistician who applied probability theories to social and political questions.

349 *When he . . . adultery.* Cf. Matt. 5: 28.

camarilla. A small chamber.

Mr. Frauenhofer . . . Free-soiler. Joseph von *Frauenhofer* or Fraunhofer (1787–1826), Bavarian optician, astronomer, and physicist. William B. *Carpenter* (1813–85), English biologist who promoted the use of the microscope in research. *Free-soiler,* a member of the Free-Soil Party, active in 1848–54, which demanded that no more territories be admitted to the Union as slave-states.

Schelling. See p. 210 n.

350 *Broughams . . . Kossuths.* Henry Peter, Baron *Brougham* and Vaux (1778–1868), English jurist, Member of Parliament, and Lord Chancellor, the highest judicial post in the kingdom. Lajos *Kossuth* (1802–94), Hungarian patriot, leader of the nationalist uprising in 1848.

Dearborn balance. A balance named after Henry Dearborn.

vesicle. A fluid-filled sac.

Oken. See p. 210 n.

351 *Knox.* Dr Robert Knox (1791–1862), Scottish anatomist, author of *The Races of Man, a Fragment* (1850), which argues that the races of man are biologically distinct.

guano. Bird droppings used as fertilizer.

Jenny Lind . . . Bowditch. Jenny Lind (1820–87), Swedish-born British soprano. Nathaniel *Bowditch* (1773–1838), American mathematician, author of *New American Practical Navigator* (1802).

352 *Zoroaster . . . Fulton. Zoroaster,* see p. 64 n. *Menu,* see p. 124 n. *Tubal Cain,* 'an instructor of every artificer in brass and iron' (Gen. 4: 22). *Vulcan,* Roman god of fire and metal-working. *Cadmus,* legendary founder of Thebes. Johann *Fust* (?1400–?1466), an associate of Gutenberg, contributed to the invention of movable type. *Fulton,* see p. 128 n.

Vaucansons . . . Watts. Jacques de *Vaucanson* (1709–82), French inventor, mathematician. *Watt,* see p. 128 n.

Laplace. See p. 307 n.

Thales . . . Œnopides. Thales, see p. 228 n. *Anaximenes,* see p. 228 n. *Hipparchus,* Greek astronomer of the 2nd century BC. *Empedocles,* see p. 85 n. *Aristarchus* of Samos, Greek astronomer of the 3rd century BC. *Pythagoras,* see p. 210 n. *Oenopides,* Greek astronomer of the 5th century BC.

orangia. An especially valuable cowrie, or seashell.

Punch. An English satirical weekly, begun in 1841.

353 *Vishnu . . . Maya. Vishnu,* a Hindu god, the saviour of mankind. *Maya,* Hindu goddess of illusion.

the gods in the Norse . . . Fenris Wolf. In Norse mythology, Fenris was a wolf-like monster, the offspring of Loki and Angerboda, destined to destroy Odin.

356 *Alaric.* See p. 77 n.

357 *Hafiz.* See p. 125 n.

358 *on change.* That is, on the floor of the stock exchange.

359 *Marquis of Worcester.* Edward Somerset, Marquis of Worcester (1601–67), English inventor.

360 *Christopher Wren.* English architect (1632–1723). The chapel is at Cambridge University.

361 *papillæ.* Small, nipple-like protuberances of connective tissue.

Hegel . . . Brunel. Georg Wilhelm Friedrich *Hegel* (1770–1831), German philosopher. Prince Clemens *Metternich* (1773–1859), Austrian statesman. John *Adams* (1735–1826), American statesman, delegate to the first Continental Congress in 1774, President of the USA 1796–1800. John C. *Calhoun* (1782–1850), senator from South Carolina, Vice-president of the USA 1825–32. François *Guizot* (1787–1874), French historian and statesman. *Peel,* see p. 333 n. Richard *Cobden* (1804–65), English free-trade economist, politician, and founding member of the Anti-Corn Law League. *Kossuth,* see p. 350 n. Meyer *Rothschild* (1743–1812), German financier. John Jacob *Astor* (1763–1848), American capitalist. Isambard Kingdom *Brunel* (1806–59), English engineer, designer of the first Atlantic steamer.

362 *Herodotus and Plutarch. Herodotus,* Greek historian of the 5th century BC. *Plutarch,* Greek biographer and philosopher of the 1st century AD.

Quisque suos patimur manes. 'Each of us suffers his own spirit' (*Aeneid,* vi. 743), trans. H. Rushton Fairclough, in the Loeb Classical Library (Cambridge, Mass. 1960).

364 *Möller.* Georg *Möller* (1784–1852), German architect, author of *Essay on the Origin and Progress of Gothic Architecture* (1825).

Moloch. Phoenician god, to whom children were offered in sacrifice.

Or if the soul . . . darkly. From the Proem to the *House of Fame,* ll. 43–51.

365 *what we . . . old age.* Epigraph to Part 2 of his *Poetry and Truth.*

POWER

368 *During passion . . . persons.* From Swedenborg (see p. 95 n.), *The Animal Kingdom, Considered Anatomically, Physically, and Philosophically,* trans. James Garth Wilkinson, 2 vols. (Boston, 1843–4), ii. 205 (cf. *JMN,* ix, 293).

Eric . . . Biorn . . . Thorfin. Eric the Red, Norwegian sailor and explorer, founded Norse colonies in Greenland in 986. Karlsenfi *Thorfinn* (*fl.* 1002–16), Scandinavian navigator and explorer. *Biorn* is unidentified.

369 *Hafiz.* See p. 125 n.

James Watt or Brunel. Watt, see p. 128 n. *Brunel,* see p. 361 n.

Commander Wilkes . . . Thorwaldsen . . . Dumas. Charles *Wilkes* (1798–1877), American naval officer and explorer of the South Seas. The published account of his 1838–42 expedition won him acclaim, though he actually wrote only part of it. Bertel *Thorwaldsen* (1770–1844), Danish sculptor. Alexandre *Dumas* (1802–70), French novelist and playwright, is said to have employed collaborators, for the most part without acknowledgement.

371 *A Western lawyer.* Edward W. Emerson identifies him as Judge Halmer Hull Emmons (1815–77).

Hoosier . . . Badger. Nicknames, respectively, for the residents of Indiana, Illinois, Michigan, and Wisconsin.

372 *Benton and Calhoun.* Thomas Hart *Benton* (1782–1858), senator from North Carolina. John Caldwell *Calhoun* (1782–1850), senator from South Carolina. Both opposed President James K. Polk's war policy. Perhaps Emerson's enmity toward the chief protector of Southern and slave-holders' interests brought him to the misleading conclusion that Calhoun could 'afford' to oppose Polk's popular policy. A colleague of Calhoun's wrote: 'By his self-sacrificing course particularly over the Mexican War he has lost the presidency, and he has put himself in a position where not a friend he had out of Carolina could sustain him *and live.*' Cf. Gerald Capers, *John C. Calhoun: Opportunist* (Gainesville, 1960), p. 234.

373 *Port-Royalists . . . Zoar.* The Abbey at *Port-Royal,* near Paris, was the retreat of a number of 17th-century scholars, including Pascal and Arnauld. *New Harmony* was on the Wabash River in Indiana. It was founded in 1814 by the Rappists, a communistic sect led by the German George Rapp (1757–1847). It failed in 1825, and Robert Owen (see p. 275 n.) purchased it and oversaw the settlement of some 1,000 people. It lasted two years more. *Brook Farm,* see p. 266 n. In 1819, a society of German separatists founded the community at *Zoar* in Ohio. This experiment enjoyed a happier fate than the others, lasting until 1898.

the Shaker society. See p. 266 n.

Boniface. The proprietor of an inn; so-called after the jovial innkeeper Boniface in George Farquhar's play *The Beaux's Stratagem* (1707).

374 *Borrow . . . Waterton . . . Layard.* George Henry *Borrow* (1803–81), English author and adventurer, wandered through England from 1825 to 1832, often in the company of gypsies, and travelled as an agent for the Bible Society from St Petersburg to Spain to Morocco. Charles *Waterton* (1782–1865), British naturalist, published his *Wanderings in South America* in 1825. Sir Austin Henry *Layard* (1817–94), English archaeologist and politician, author of *Nineveh and its Remains* (1848).

375 *Pelasgic strength.* The Pelasgians were an ancient people of Greece and the eastern isles of the Mediterranean.

Pericles and Phidias. Pericles (490–429 BC), Athenian statesman and military commander. He commissioned *Phidias,* the Greek sculptor of the 5th century BC, to construct the Parthenon.

Corinthian civility. Corinth, Greece, was famous for its elegance and luxury.

376 *Michel was wont*. Emerson was familiar with the anecdote from Giorgio Vasari's life of Michelangelo. Vasari was a contemporary of the great artist.

succedanea. A substitute.

Enlarge not . . . charge. Emerson copied this into his journal for Fall 1848 from Thomas Stanley's *History of the Chaldaick Philosophy* (1701), p. 52.

Cellini. Benvenuto Cellini (1500–71), Italian goldsmith, sculptor, and engineer.

377 *Campbell*. Thomas Campbell (1777–1844), Scottish poet.

There was . . . friend. Emerson copied this remark into his journal from Arnold H. L. Heeren's *Reflections on the Politics of Ancient Greece*, trans. George Bancroft (1824), pp. 267–8 (see p. 120 n.).

Rothschild. See p. 361 n.

378 *Col. Buford*. Probably Napoleon Bonaparte Buford (1807–83), American soldier and engineer, graduate of West Point, where he taught natural philosophy 1834–5.

Basil Hall. British naval commander and author (1788–1844).

Cobden. See p. 361 n.

Wendell Phillips. American abolitionist and renowned orator (1811–84).

Democritus. Greek philosopher of the 5th century BC.

379 *I remarked in England*. It is worth mentioning that in the March 1848 journal entry from which this sentence is taken Emerson offers John Henry Newman as an example of such a 'working talent'.

CONSIDERATIONS BY THE WAY

382 *Sidney Smith*. English journalist and clergyman (1771–1845).

383 *Porphyry*. See p. 159 n.

Mirabeau said . . . success. See p. 280 n. Emerson takes the remark from *Mirabeau's Letters During His Residence in England*, 2 vols. (1832), ii. 288–9 (cf. *JMN*, xiii, 224).

Franklin said . . . employ them. See p. 241 n. Emerson found Franklin's remark reported by John Adams in a journal entry for March 1786. Cf. *The Works of John Adams*, ed. Charles Francis Adams, 10 vols. (Boston, 1850–6), iii. 395.

lazzaroni. Beggars.

384 *Clay . . . dignity*. From *Cymbeline*, IV. ii. 4: 'But clay and clay differ in dignity, / Whose dust is both alike.'

385 *Cape Cod or Sandy Hook*. Capes in, respectively, Massachusetts and New Jersey.

Erasmus . . . Rabelais. See p. 289 n.

They were the fools . . . authors. Stanislaus Jean, Marquis de Boufflers (1738–1815), French author known for his romances. Emerson found the remark in Arsène Houssaye's *Men and Women of the Eighteenth Century* (1852), i. 183 (cf. *JMN*, xiii, 125).

Magna Charta. King John signed the Magna Charta on 15 June 1215, 151 years after William the Conqueror defeated Harold II at Hastings on 14 October 1066. Edward I (1239–1307) reigned from 1272 until his death. He called an assembly of the estates in 1295, considered to be the first 'parliament'.

Schiller. See p. 143 n.

386 *Antoninus.* Emerson has in mind either the tumultuous career of Marcus Antonius—Mark Antony—(83–30 BC), or that of Marcus Aurelius Antonius (121–80), Emperor of Rome, who saw his nation through several wars, plagues, and earthquakes.

In America . . . sublime. Compare these lines from Emerson's 'Ode Inscribed to W. H. Channing': 'The God who made New Hampshire / Taunted the lofty land / With little men.'

387 *Howard . . . Pestalozzi . . . Elizabeth Fry.* Probably John *Howard* (1726–90), the English humanitarian who devoted much of his life to prison reform. *Pestalozzi*, see p. 51 n. *Elizabeth Fry* (1780–1845), English Quaker and prison reformer.

Croyez . . . mérite. 'Believe me, error also has its value.'

the old oracle . . . bonds of men. Emerson found this among Thomas Taylor's 'Collection of the Chaldean Oracles', published in the *Monthly Magazine and British Register* iii (June 1797), pp. 509–26 (cf. *JMN*, xiii, 400).

He causes . . . praise him. Cf. Pss. 76: 10.

'Tis said . . . faults. Measure for Measure, v. i. 439.

A man of sense. Daniel Chandler, the superintendent of the Boston Asylum and Farm School for Indigent Boys.

388 *Fronto.* Marcus Cornelius Fronto (100–70), Roman rhetorician and teacher of Marcus Aurelius Antonius.

Charles James Fox. See p. 280 n.

Fifth-Avenue. Fashionable section of Manhattan, New York City.

389 *Æsop . . . Regnard. Aesop*, the Greek fabulist of the 6th century BC, was born a slave. *Saadi*, Persian poet of the 13th century, was taken prisoner by the Crusaders. *Cervantes* (1547–1616), author of *Don Quixote*, was held captive in Algiers for five years. Jean François *Regnard* (1655–1709), French comic dramatist, was also held captive by Algerian corsairs.

Faneuil Hall. A market in Boston, Massachusetts, Faneuil Hall was the site of revolutionary meetings and is sometimes called the 'cradle of liberty'.

391 *Layard.* See p. 374 n.

392 *Berkshire . . . Albany . . . Burlington.* The *Berkshire* mountain range is in western Massachusetts. *Albany* is the capital of the state of New York. *Burlington* is a town in northern Vermont.

Bremen. Almost certainly a mistake for Fredrika Bremer (1801–65), Swedish novelist, whose two-year visit to America is chronicled in her immensely popular volume of 'letters', *Homes of the New World; Impressions of America* (1853). Bremer stayed at the Emerson house twice during her travels.

Talleyrand. Charles Maurice Talleyrand de Périgord, Prince de Bénévent (1754–1838), French statesman, famous for his cynical wit.

394 *Ali Ben Abu Taleb.* Ali ibu-abi-Talib died in 661.

Hafiz. See p. 125 n.

395 *A man of wit.* Emerson identifies him in the April 1852 journal entry from which he takes the remark as the Revd Francis Parkman (1788–1852), father of the famous historian.

396 *Horne Tooke.* John Horne Tooke (1736–1812), English radical politician. Emerson found the remark in Coleridge's *Table Talk* in an entry for 1 May 1832.

Seekest thou . . . not. Cf. Jer. 45: 5.

ILLUSIONS

397 *Some years ago.* Emerson spent two days at the Mammoth Cave in Kentucky while on a lecture tour in July 1850. On the first day, he spent some 14 hours in the cave, hiking 18 miles.

398 *the streams 'Lethe' and 'Styx'.* The Lethe and the Styx are the chief rivers in the Hades of Greek mythology. The many rivulets and passages in the Mammoth Cave bear names taken from diverse contexts. In addition to the 'Lethe' and 'Styx', there is a 'Purgatory', a 'Cleveland Cabinet', a 'Black Hole of Calcutta', etc. The 'Star Chamber' which Emerson describes was named after the English court of civil and criminal jurisdiction at Westminster in the 16th and early 17th centuries. 'Serena's Bower' is actually 'Serena's Arbor'. Cf. Horace Hovey and Richard Call's *Mammoth Cave of Kentucky; an Illustrated Manual* (Louisville, 1901). The cave depends as much upon allusion as illusion for its charms.

399 *It was wittily . . . elles sont.* Jean le Rond d'Alembert (?1717–83), French mathematician and philosopher, and, with Diderot, an editor of the *Encyclopédie.* The sentence reads, roughly: 'the misty condition of things is vexing because it makes us see them as they are', i.e. as hazy or misty.

Yoganidra . . . Apollo. Yoganidra is the goddess of illusion in Hindu mythology. *Proteus* is the Greek sea god capable of rapidly assuming different forms; *Momus*, the Greek god of mockery and laughter. *Gylfi* is a King of Sweden in Norse mythology. Snorri Sturluson (1178–1241), the Icelandic historian and folklorist, writes in his *Prose Edda* of the 'beguiling of Gylphi'.

Cf. *The Prose Edda*, trans. Arthur Brodeur (New York, 1929), pp. 13 ff. The *Titans* are the giant deities of ancient mythology, whom the Olympian gods usurped. *Apollo* is the Greek and Roman god of sunlight, prophecy, music, and poetry.

400 *Claude-Lorraines*. 'A somewhat convex dark or coloured hand-mirror, used to concentrate the features of a landscape in subdued tones. Sometimes applied to coloured glasses through which a landscape is viewed' (*OED*). Named after the French landscape painter, Claude Lorraine (1600–82).

401 *coulisses*. The side-scenes or wings of a theatrical stage.

402 *the portentous year of Mizar and Alcor*. Mizar and Alcor are two of the seven fixed stars in the constellation Ursa Major. Ptolemy rated the influence of Mizar as equal to that of Mars. Cf. Fred Gettings, *Dictionary of Astrology* (London, 1985).

403 *That story of Thor*. Thor is the Norse god of thunder. Snorri Sturluson tells his story in his *Prose Edda*, op. cit.

404 *Heraclitus . . . Apollonia. Heraclitus*, see p. 92 n. *Xenophanes*, see p. 21 n. *Diogenes of Apollonia* was a Greek natural philosopher of the 5th century BC.

The notions . . . ignorance. Emerson is quoting from the *Vishnu Purana, a System of Hindu Mythology and Tradition*, trans. H. H. Wilson (London, 1840), p. 585 (cf. *JMN*, ix, 320).

405 *Fooled thou . . . vice*. Emerson takes the couplet from *Practical Philosophy of the Muhammudan People, exhibited in its professed connexion with the European, so as to render either an introduction to the other; being a translation of the Akh-lak-I-Jalaly, the most esteemed ethical work of the Middle Ages, from the Persian of Fakir Jany Muhammad Asaad*, trans. W. F. Thompson (London, 1839), p. 95 (cf. *JMN*, ix, 263).

THE LORD'S SUPPER

409 *fourth Lateran Council*. The Fourth Lateran Council was convened by Pope Innocent III at the Lateran Palace, Rome, in 1215. This council defined the doctrine of the Eucharist, introducing the term 'transubstantiate' into official church vocabulary.

Real Presence. In Eucharistic doctrine, the term used to denote the actual, as opposed to the symbolic, presence of the body and blood of Christ in the sacrament.

Archbishops Laud and Wake . . . Bishop Hoadley. William *Laud* (1573–1645), Archbishop of Canterbury 1633–45. William *Wake* (1657–1737), Archbishop of Canterbury 1716–37. Ralph *Cudworth* (1617–88), English philosopher of the 'Cambridge Platonist' school. William *Warburton* (1698–1779), English theologian, Bishop of Gloucester 1759–79. Benjamin *Hoadley* (1676–1761), English theologian, Bishop of Bangor 1715, of Hereford 1721, of Salisbury 1723, and of Winchester 1734–61.

410 *Two of the Evangelists . . . occasion.* Subsequent biblical scholarship generally agrees that none of the four 'evangelists' was an acquaintance of Jesus, and that 'Mark' is probably of the earliest authorship, written *c.* AD 65.

413 *Sandemanians.* Members of the religious sect founded by Scottish theologian Robert Sandeman (1718–71).

416 *the kingdom . . . Holy Ghost.* Rom. 14: 17, Emerson's epigraph to 'The Lord's Supper'.

418 *I am about . . . to me.* The proprietors of the Second Church, Boston, accepted Emerson's resignation on 28 October 1832, some six weeks after he delivered this sermon. He had been ordained pastor of the Second Church on 11 March 1829.

SOCIETY AND SOLITUDE

419 *the Rondanini Medusa.* The Palazzo Rondanini is in Rome. Inlaid above one of its portals is a bust of the Medusa.

Mirabeau's . . . familiarité. Mirabeau, see p. 280 n. Emerson had read his *Letters* (1832). The phrase reads in English: 'the terrible gift of familiarity'.

the ring of Gyges. Gyges (*fl.* 7th century BC), King of Lydia, an ancient nation in west Asia Minor. In Book 2 of *The Republic*, Plato recounts the legend that Gyges found a magic ring which had the power to render him invisible. Gyges thus got access to his predecessor on the throne and murdered him.

420 *It would . . . decline.* Isaac Newton (1642–1727), English natural philosopher and mathematician, makes this remark in a letter to John Collins of 18 February 1670 (Julian calendar). Collins (1652–83) was an English mathematician and member of the Royal Society. Cf. *The Correspondence of Isaac Newton,* ed. H. W. Turnbull (Cambridge, 1959), i. 27.

Archimedes . . . Principia. Archimedes (?287–212 BC), Greek geometer, wrote a treatise on spheres, among other works. *Principia* (1687), Newton's great work, in which he sets forth the theory of gravitation.

Swedenborg . . . angels. Emerson is quoting from Swedenborg's (see p. 95 n.) *Heaven and Its Wonders and Hell,* published in Latin in 1758. The book has often been translated into English.

421 *If I stay . . . will stay?* In 1301, Dante was sent from Florence to Rome as an emissary.

President Tyler. John Tyler (1790–1862), tenth President of the United States, born in Virginia. In his early career, Tyler was a state-rights Democrat, serving in the Virginia State Legislature, the US House of Representatives; then as Governor of Virginia; and later as a US senator. President Jackson's authoritarian handling of the South Carolina nullification movement of the early 1830s alienated Tyler from the Democratic Party. He then became associated with the newly formed Whigs, and ran on the ticket in 1840 with William Henry Harrison. Tyler became president when Harrison died a month after his inauguration. But differences with Henry Clay, the powerful Whig Party leader and senator from Kentucky, again forced him out of the party. All but one member of Tyler's Cabinet resigned in 1841.

422 *The king . . . said Selden.* John Selden (1584–1654), English historian. Emerson quotes loosely from his *Table-talk*, apothegms and remarks taken from Selden's conversation, and first published in 1689, 35 years after his death.

When a young . . . read law. In his journal for 1852 Emerson records this exchange between Jeremiah Mason (1768–1848), a New Hampshire lawyer and US senator, and Richard Henry Dana (1815–82): 'Jere. Mason said to R H Dana;——"law school! a man must read law in the court house" ' (*JMN*, xiii. 14).

423 *That was society . . . Keys.* Edward W. Emerson remarks that this is an allusion to Emerson's trip to Florida in 1826–7, which he took for his health. It was on this trip that Emerson met Achille Murat, the nephew of Napoleon.

Cœur-de-Lion. Richard the Lion Heart (1157–99) became King of England in 1189, and reigned until his death.

'To obtain . . . despise them'. Emerson quotes loosely from Bacon's essay 'Of Ceremonies and Respects'.

'For behavior . . . another'. A paraphrase of Shakespeare, *2 Henry IV*, v. i. 75–7.

424 *Put Stubbs . . . wretched.* Marcus Fabius *Quintilianus* (*fl.* 1st century AD), Roman rhetorician and author of *Institutio Oratoria*, a treatise on rhetoric and education. *Stubbs* and *Aunt Miriam* are, of course, generics.

LETTERS AND SOCIAL AIMS

QUOTATION AND ORIGINALITY

427 *he is . . . period.* From Plato's *Phaedrus*, 247d. A modern translation reads: the soul contemplating truth 'is nourished and prospers, until the heaven's revolution brings her back full circle'. Cf. *Plato: Collected Dialogues*, ed. Edith Hamilton and Huntington Cairns (Princeton, 1963), p. 494.

He that borrows . . . contemplates. In *The Works of the Right Honorable Edmund Burke*, 12 vols. (Boston, 1865–7), iii. 219.

428 *Tasso.* See p. 342 n.

Hegel . . . Bayle. Hegel, see p. 361 n. *Proclus*, see p. 202 n. *Heraclitus*, see p. 92 n. *Parmenides*, see p. 290 n. *Plutarch*, see p. 362 n. *Lucian* (117–80), Greek satirist. *Rabelais*, see p. 289 n. *Montaigne*, see p. 80 n. Pierre *Bayle* (1647–1706), French philosopher and literary critic.

Swedenborg, Behmen, Spinoza: Swedenborg, see p. 95 n. *Boehme*, see p. 159 n. Baruch *Spinoza* (1632–77), Dutch-Jewish philosopher and theologian.

428–9 *Albert . . . Voltaire*. *Albertus* Magnus (?1193–1280), Count of Bollstadt, Dominican priest and theological philosopher whose learning was legendary; teacher of Aquinas. John of Fidanza (1221–74), priest of the order of St Francis, canonized *St Bonaventura*. St *Thomas Aquinas* (1226–74), Italian scholastic theologian. *Dante* Alighieri (1265–1321), Italian poet, author of the *Inferno*. Jakob Ludwig Karl *Grimm* (1785–1863) and his brother Wilhelm Karl (1786–1859), German folklorists and philologists. Pierre Jean Baptiste *le Grand* d'Aussy (1737–1800), French poet, critic, historian, and editor of a volume of fabliaux of the 12th and 13th centuries. Fabliaux were short, often bawdy, tales in verse. Jean Baptiste Poquelin *Molière* (1622–73), French playwright. Jean de *La Fontaine* (1621–95), French poet. Giovanni *Boccaccio* (1313–75), Italian writer of verse and prose, author of the *Decameron*. François Marie Arouet de *Voltaire* (1694–1778), French writer and intellectual, author of *Candide*.

429 *Cremona*. Name of an Italian town renowned for its violin-makers.

philonic inspiration. Philo Judaeus (*fl.* 1st century AD), born at Alexandria, fused Platonism and Judaic scripture in an effort to show that the roots of Greek philosophy lie in the Pentateuch.

Mr. Webster's three rules . . . D'Argenson. *Webster*, see p. 333 n. Richard Brinsley *Sheridan* (1751–1816), Irish dramatist. Marc Antonie René de Paulmy *d'Argenson* (1722–87), member of the French Academy, editor of *Bibliothèque universelle des romans*.

430 *Southey's Commonplace Book . . . Radcliffe*. Robert *Southey* (1774–1843), English poet, critic, historian, and biographer. His *Commonplace Book* was published posthumously in 1849–51. Thomas Wentworth, Earl of *Strafford* (1593–1641), English statesman. Sir George *Radcliffe* (1593–1657) managed Strafford's affairs from 1627 until they were both imprisoned on charges of treason in 1640. Strafford was executed and Radcliffe passed the rest of his days in exile at Flushing.

Mr. Samuel Rogers . . . Duke of Wellington. Samuel *Rogers* (1763–1855), English poet and art collector, whom Emerson had met in London in 1847. Arthur Wellesley, 1st *Duke of Wellington* (1769–1852), British field marshal, best remembered for his defeat of Napoleon at Waterloo in 1815. Emerson records Rogers's anecdote in his journal for October 1847. Cf. *JMN*, x. 179.

Lord Eldon . . . Brougham. *Eldon*, see p. 268 n. *Brougham*, see p. 350 n.

the Abbé Maury. Jean Siffrein Maury (1746–1817), French prelate, Archbishop of Paris under Napoleon.

Si l'Abbé . . . de tout. 'If the Abbé had told us a little about religion, he'd have told us about everything.'

Lady Mary Wortley Montagu. English writer and intimate of Pope, Addison, and others (1689–1762).

Herveys. Distinguished English family, friends of Lady Wortley Montagu. The comment is in her *Letters*, i. 67.

Columbus's egg . . . Brunelleschi. Christopher *Columbus* (1451–1506), the great explorer, is said to have balanced an egg on end to persuade the Indians that he had supernatural powers. Filippo *Brunelleschi* (1377–1446), Italian sculptor and architect.

Rabelais . . . Delphi. Rabelais's (see p. 289 n.) last words were reputedly: 'I am going to seek a grand perhaps; draw the curtain, the farce is played.' Edward W. Emerson points out that there is a chapter in Plutarch's *Morals* called 'Of the Word *EI* Engraven Over the Gate of Apollo's Temple at Delphi'. Cf. vol. iv in William Goodwin's edition of the *Morals* (Boston, 1871) for which Emerson supplied an introduction.

Goethe's favorite . . . published. Aristotle's remark is reported in chap. 7 of Plutarch's *Alexander.* Cf. p. 243 of the Loeb Classical Library edition of Plutarch's *Lives,* trans. Bernadotte Perrin (Cambridge, Mass., 1958).

Madame de Staël's . . . dumb music. Anne Louise Germaine Necker, Madame de Staël (1766–1817), French writer, met Goethe in 1803. Emerson apparently has the genealogy of the remark wrong. In de Staël's novel *Corinne* is the remark: 'La vue d'un tel monument est comme une musique continuelle et fixée . . . ' (Book 4, chap. 3), p. 61 of the edition published in New York in 1857. ('The sight of such a monument is like a continuous and stationary music.') Emerson had borrowed an earlier edition of the novel from the Boston Atheneum in 1839. In *Conversations of Goethe with Eckerman and Soret* (London, 1882) this remark of Goethe's appears in the entry dated 23 March 1829: 'I have found a paper of mine among some others . . . in which I call architecture "petrified music" ' (p. 378). Some translations of the remark read 'frozen' for 'petrified'.

Wordsworth's . . . habent. The *Wordsworth* line is from 'Character of the Happy Warrior' (1807), l. 5. *Schiller,* see p. 143 n. The sentence from *Bacon* reads: 'Youthful plans are more prophetic.'

431 *The Drowned Lovers.* In *English and Scottish Ballads,* Francis James Child (Boston, 1857–8), iv. 189. Child prints several versions of the ballad.

Martial's epigram. This is epigram 25. 'Spare me while I hasten [to her], overwhelm me when I return.' Cf. Walter Ker's translation in the Loeb Classical Library edition of Martial's epigrams, 2 vols. (London, 1919), i. 19.

Such are . . . Cave. The *Seven Sleepers* of Ephesus were Christian youths who fled the persecution of the Emperor Decius in the 3rd century AD. They hid in a cave and slept until found and awakened 200 years later by a shepherd. *Gyges,* see p. 419 n. The *Wandering Jew* is a legendary figure who was condemned to walk the earth forever because he mocked Jesus at the Crucifixion. The *Pied Piper* was summoned by the Mayor of Hamelin to rid his town of rats. Playing an enchanting tune on his fife, he led the rats out of the city into a river where they drowned. But the mayor refused to pay the Piper. In retaliation, the Piper enchanted the children of Hamelin as he had the rats, leading them into a cave outside the town, whence they never returned. *Jack* bartered an ox for a sack of magic beans that grew into a beanstalk reaching beyond the clouds. The *Lady of the Lake* is from Arthurian lore. I have not located the legend of the *Travelling Cloak*.

Baron Munchausen. Karl Friedrich Hieronymus, Baron von Münchausen (1720–97), German soldier who became something of a legendary figure. He was famous for his tall tales, some of which appear in *Baron Münchausen's Narrative of his Marvellous Travels and Campaigns in Russia* (1785).

Antiphanes. The editors of the *JMN* point out that this anecdote appears in *An Introduction to the Dialogues of Plato* (1841), p. 201.

432 *the 'Instauration'*. Allusion to Bacon's *Great Instauration*, published in Latin as the *Instauratio Magna* in 1620. It memorably begins: 'Francis of Verulam reasoned thus with himself, and judged it to be for the interest of the present and future generations that they should be made acquainted with his thoughts.' Bacon also applied the phrase 'great instauration' to his whole philosophical enterprise.

Beaumont and Fletcher. Francis *Beaumont* (1584–1616), and John *Fletcher* (1579–1625), Elizabethan dramatists, collaborated on a number of plays.

433 *Comte de Crillon . . . M. Necker*. Probably François Felix Dorothée, Duc de Crillon (1748–1820), a French general. Probably Armond-François, Comte *d'Allonville* (1764–1832), a French military officer. Jacques *Necker* (1732–1804), Swiss-born banker, was twice Minister of Finance in France, until he fell from favour for opposing the seizure of church properties in the early days of the Revolution.

Landor. Walter Savage Landor (1775–1864), English poet whom Emerson much admired, and whom he met in Florence in 1833.

Karl Ottfried Müller. German classical philologist and archaeologist (1797–1840).

Dubuc. Not identified.

the false Amphitryon. Amphitryon is a character in Molière's play of the same name. Amphitryon, a Theban general, returns to Thebes to celebrate a successful campaign with a great feast. The evening before, Jupiter has assumed the form of the general and presented himself to his wife, with whom he is in love. The comedy turns upon the appearance at the feast of both the true and the 'false' Amphitryon.

De Quincey. Thomas De Quincey (1785–1859), English essayist and critic. De Quincey told this anecdote to Emerson during Emerson's stay in London in the winter of 1848.

Marmontel. Jean François Marmontel (1723–99), French poet and dramatist.

Bacon's . . . province. Bacon makes this remark in a letter to Lord Burghley in 1592. Cf. Spedding's edition of *The Works of Francis Bacon* (1862), viii. 109: 'Lastly, I confess that I have as vast contemplative ends, as I have moderate civil ends: for I have taken all knowledge to be my province . . .'

435 *Tiraboschi . . . Hallam. Tiraboschi*, see p. 217 n. Joseph, Baron *von Hammer-Purgstall* (1774–1856), Austrian historian of Asian literature. Henry *Hallam* (1777–1859), English historian of Europe and European literature, author of *Introduction to the Literature of Europe in the Fifteenth, Sixteenth and Seventeenth Centuries* (1837–9).

Giordano Bruno. See p. 289 n.

Vaux. Thomas Vaux (1510–56), English poet.

Isthmian crown. The Isthmus of Corinth in Greece was the site of the ancient Isthmian Games and Festival.

Cardinal de Retz. Jean Paul de Goudi, Cardinal de Retz (1614–79), French churchman, whose *Memoirs* Emerson had borrowed from the Boston Atheneum in 1854.

Chatterton . . . 'Ossian'. Thomas *Chatterton* (1752–70), English poet, author of forged archaic verse. He claimed that his 'Rowley' poems were the work of an imaginary 15th-century poet, Thomas Rowley. Alain-René *Le Sage* (1668–1747), French novelist and dramatist. The hero of his masterpiece, *Gil Blas*, is a Spaniard. James *Macpherson* (1736–96), Scottish historian, and forger of archaic poems. He forged *Fingal, an Ancient Epic Poem, in Six Books* (1762), and *Temora* (1763), also an epic—both purportedly from Gaelic originals. Ossian was a legendary Gaelic bard, to whom Macpherson attributed *Fingal*.

436 *Moore's Diary . . . adopts them.* Thomas *Moore* (1779–1852), Irish poet. The anecdote appears in a journal entry for 20 October 1823. Cf. *Memoirs, Journal and Correspondence of Thomas Moore*, 8 vols., ed. Lord John Russell (Boston, 1853), iv. 144. Emerson had borrowed a number of volumes of the *Memoirs* from the Boston Atheneum in 1853 and 1855. *Sheridan*, see p. 429 n.

Dumont . . . 'Junius'. Pierre Étienne Louis *Dumont* (1759–1829), Swiss-born writer. He was secretary to Jeremy *Bentham* (1748–1832), the English utilitarian philosopher, and edited Bentham's unpublished writings. Dumont also worked for *Mirabeau* (p. 280 n.), assisting in the preparation of his speeches and reports to the National Assembly in 1789–90. In his *Souvenirs sur Mirabeau*, Dumont all but claimed Mirabeau for his puppet. While in England, Dumont was an active proponent of Whig liberalism, as was Sir Philip *Francis* (1740–1818), Irish politician and writer. Francis is the reputed author of the *'Junius'* letters, which attacked the policies of George III and his partisans.

James Hogg . . . clothes. James Hogg (1770–1835), Scottish poet. *John Wilson* (1785–1854), Scottish poet, critic, and friend of Hogg. He appears in the person of 'Christopher North' in *Noctes Ambrosianae*, a series of dialogues first published in *Blackwood's Edinburgh Magazine* (1822–35).

The bold theory of Delia Bacon. Delia Bacon (1811–59), American author and early proponent of the 'Baconian theory', which held that Francis Bacon wrote Shakespeare's plays. Nathaniel Hawthorne supplied an introduction to her *Philosophy of the Plays of Shakespeare Unfolded* (1857). Henry

Wriothesley, 3rd Earl of Southampton (1573–1624), was Shakespeare's patron, to whom the poet dedicated his *'Venus and Adonis'*. Sir Walter Raleigh (1552–1618), courtier, poet, historian, and explorer, was beheaded on a 15-year-old charge of treason.

436 *Charles Lamb.* English essayist, literary critic, and poet (1775–1834).

437 *all things are in flux.* An allusion to the doctrines of Heraclitus (see p. 116‡ n.). Emerson here translates Fragment 20.

Goethe frankly . . . Goethe. Passage unlocated. But Eckerman and Soret record in their *Conversations of Goethe* a similar remark the poet made on 12 May 1825: 'People are always talking about originality; but what do they mean? As soon as we are born, the world begins to work upon us, and this goes on to the end. And, after all, what can we call our own except energy, strength, and will? If I could give an account of all that I owe to great predecessors and contemporaries, there would be but a small balance in my favour.' In *Conversations of Goethe with Eckerman and Soret* (London, 1882), p. 164. 21–5.

438 *Pindar, Hesiod, or Euripides. Pindar,* see p. 149 n. *Hesiod (fl.* 8th century BC), Greek poet. *Euripides* (?480–406 BC), Greek tragedian.

There are many . . . talent. From Pindar's second 'Olympian Ode'. Cf. p. 27 of the Loeb Classical Library *Pindar,* trans. Sir John Sandys (Cambridge, Mass., 1961).

Captain Cook's . . . tribes. James *Cook* (1728–79), English navigator and explorer of the South Pacific. Accounts of his first voyage can be found in Hawkesworth's *Voyages* (1773), and of his second voyage in the two volumes Cook wrote and published in 1777; Cook and King wrote an account and his third voyage in 1784. The *Society Islands* form an archipelago in the South Pacific; the largest among them is Tahiti. *Alexander Henry* (1739–1834), American fur-trader and explorer, published his *Travels and Adventures in Canada and the Indian Territories Between the Years 1760 and 1776* in 1809.

Chateaubriand . . . Byron. François René, Vicomte de *Chateaubriand* (1769–1848), French writer and politician, who spent eight months in America in 1791. He describes the journey in *Voyage en Amérique.* Thomas Moore (1779–1852), Irish poet, *Moore* published a series of Oriental tales in verse and prose, *Lalla Rookh* (1817). Thomas *Campbell* (1777–1844), Scottish poet, whose *Gertrude in Wyoming* (1809), a poem in Spenserian stanzas, narrates the destruction of a settlement at Wyoming, Pennsylvania, by Indians. *Byron's* pilgrim Childe Harold, in the poem of the same name, travels from Portugal to Albania and elsewhere.

POETRY AND IMAGINATION

440 *Alfred.* Alfred the Great (848–99), see p. 45 n.

Faraday. Michael Faraday (1791–1867), English chemist and natural philosopher. Emerson heard Faraday lecture on electricity at the Royal Institute, London, in 1848.

441 *swim we merrily.* Emerson takes the phrase from the White Lady of Ave-nel's song, 'Merrily We Swim', in Walter Scott's *The Monastery*, chap. 5. Or cf. *Scott: Poetical Works*, ed. J. Logie Robertson (London, 1904), p. 784. It begins: 'Merrily we swim, the moon shines bright, / Both current and ripple are dancing in the light.'

442 *John Hunter . . . progressive development.* John Hunter (1728–93), Scottish physiologist and surgeon. He founded the Hunterian Museum in 1785, which Emerson visited in 1833. Several scholars have made considerable efforts to trace this 'electric word' to its source in Hunter's writings, without success. Moncure Conway located the apparent source of the *idea* in a note to p. 265 in Vol. i of Palmer's edition if Hunter's works. Cf. Conway's *Auto-biography* (Boston, 1904), i. 168 n. The phrase 'arrested and progressive development' seems to be Emerson's own. Conway enlisted the help of Professors Huxley, Tyndall, and others, but none could find it in Hunter. Cf. also Gay Wilson Allen's *Waldo Emerson* (New York, 1981), p. 575.

Geoffrey Saint-Hilaire . . . Owen. Étienne *Geoffrey Saint-Hilaire* (1772–1844), French zoologist who began the zoological collection at the Jardin des Plantes in Paris, author of *Philosophie anatomique. Oken*, see p. 259‡ n. Johann Wolfgang von *Goethe* (1749–1832), the German poet and dramatist, was also a scientist, and did research in geology, anatomy, and botany. Jean Louis Rodolphe Agassiz (1807–73), Swiss naturalist, who lectured at Harvard during the 1840s and 1850s; he also lectured in Concord each year, where he was a guest of the Emersons. Sir Richard *Owen* (1804–92), English zoologist and curator of the Museum of the Royal College of Surgeons, whose work *Paleontology* (1860) Emerson borrowed from the Boston Atheneum in 1860 and 1868. Owen guided Emerson through the Hunterian Museum in London.

Theocritus. 4th century BC, Greek pastoral poet whose early poems treated heroic legend.

Professor Playfair. John Playfair (1748–1819), Scottish mathematician and geologist, whose *Works* (Edinburgh, 1822) Emerson borrowed from the Boston Atheneum in 1834.

443 *The privates of man's heart . . . were.* Emerson takes these lines from John Gower's (p. 405 n.) *Confessio Amantis* (?1383). (I. 2806–8).

Hafiz. see p. 157 n. Emerson read Hafiz in the German translations of Joseph von Hammer-Purgstall, *Der Diwan von Mohammed Schenseddin Hafis* (1812–13), and of Georg Friedrich Daumer. Emerson himself trans-lated a few of the odes of Hafiz into English from the German. Two of his translations are reprinted in *Anthology of World Poetry*, ed. Mark Van Doren (New York, 1928).

444 *the leopard, the wolf, or Lucia.* Emerson alludes to the first two cantos of Dante's *Inferno*. The leopard and the she-wolf appear in ll. 33 ff. of canto I; Lucia, in ll. 96 ff. of canto II. John Ciardi observes in the notes to his translation of the poem (New York, 1954) that the leopard and the

she-wolf are the first and third of the 'Three Beasts' in Jer. 5: 6. Lucia is the patron saint of eyesight.

Michel Angelo . . . antiques! Giorgio Vasari, a contemporary of Michelangelo (1475–1564), reports the remark in his chapter on the life of the artist in *The Great Masters.* Cf. Gaston du C. de Vere's translation, ed. Michael Sonino (New York, 1986), p. 322. Michelangelo is speaking of the figures in terracotta, coloured to look like marble, by Antonio Begarelli (1499–?1565) at Modena. John Addington Symonds repeats the anecdote in his *Life of Michelangelo Buonarotti* (New York, 1911), ii. 353.

The Vedas, the Edda, the Koran. The *Vedas* are the ancient, sacred books of the Hindus. The *Edda* is a collection of ancient Icelandic poetry and myth. The *Koran* is the sacred scripture of Islam.

444–5 *Thus the Greek mythology . . . glove. St John* makes several such remarks; cf. Rev. 1: 5: 'And from Jesus Christ, who is the faithful witness, and the first begotten of the dead, and the prince of the kings of the earth. Unto him that loved us, and washed us from our sins in his own blood.' Richard Duppa writes in his life of *Michelangelo*, which Emerson had read:

> Lomazzo tells an anecdote, that cardinal Farnese one day found him, when an old man, walking alone in the Colosseum, and expressed his surprise at finding him solitary amidst the ruins; to which he replied, 'I go yet to school, that I may continue to learn.' Whether the anecdote be correctly true or not, it is evident he entertained this feeling, for there is still remaining a design by him, of an old man, with a long beard, in a child's go-cart, and an hour-glass before him, emblematical of the last stage of life, and a scroll over his head ANCHORA INPARO, in Roman capitals, denoting that no state of bodily decay or approximation to death was incompatible with intellectual development (*Lives and Works of Michel Angelo and Raphael*, London, 1856).

Emerson copied the motto 'Anchora Inparo' into his journal, and used the anecdote in its entirety in his lecture 'Michel Angelo Buonaroti', first given on 5 Feb. 1835. The lecture is reprinted in vol. i of *The Early Letters of Ralph Waldo Emerson*, eds. Stephen Whicher and Robert Spiller (Cambridge, Mass., 1966). There, he translates the motto thus: 'I still learn.' The 'satchel' is apparently Emerson's embellishment. Niccolò *Machiavelli* (1469–1527), Italian statesman and political theorist, author of *The Prince* (1532). Edmund *Burke* (1729–97), British statesman and philosopher, addressed Parliament on 'American Taxation', arguing against the repressive policies of Lord North's administration. Burke published the address in 1774. The *Kentuckian orator* to whom Emerson alludes is Davy Crockett (1786–1836), distinguished soldier and US Congressman.

446 *savans.* Parlour sages; specious intellectuals.

Proclus. See p. 202 n.

Why changes . . . musk? From a poem by Hafiz, which Emerson read in *Der Diwan von Mohammed Schemsed-din Hafis*, op. cit., i. 316 (cf. *JMN*, xi, 107).

447 *The Chaldæan Zoroaster . . . the world. Zoroaster*, see p. 64 n. Emerson quotes from Thomas Taylor's translation, 'Collection of the Chaldean Oracles', in *Monthly Magazine and Register* (1797), No. 29, III, p. 520. the Chaldeans were a semitic people related to the Babylonians. Taylor only tentatively assigns this 'oracle' to Zoroaster.

Bacon expressed . . . mind. Emerson quotes from James Spedding's English translation of the *De Augmentis* (Bacon's Latin translation and expansion of *The Advancement of Learning*), Book II, chap. 13; or, p. 316 of vol. iv of Spedding's edition of the *Works* (London, 1860). The sentence occurs in *The Advancement* in much the same form: poetry 'doth raise and erect the mind, by submitting the shews of things to the desires of the mind' (iii. 343–4 of Spedding's edition).

448 *Pindar.* Greek lyric poet (*c.*522–440 BC).

Poetry must first . . . better. Emerson is apparently paraphrasing Coleridge: 'Poetry is something more than good sense, but it must be good sense, at all events.' The remark is recorded in Coleridge's *Table Talk* in the entry for 9 May 1830.

Charles James Fox . . . poetry. Fox, see p. 280 n. Fox's correspondence with Gilbert Wakefield (1756–1801), English classical scholar, was published in 1813, and bears the subtitle 'chiefly on subjects of classical literature'. Emerson borrowed the book from the Boston Atheneum in 1830.

Thomson's 'Seasons'. James Thomson (1700–48), Scottish poet and precursor of the Romantics, whose long poem *The Seasons* appeared in 1726–30.

449 *Sesostris.* An Egyptian monarch, perhaps legendary, whose empire, at its apogee, purportedly reached India. Three emperors by the name sat on the throne of Egypt between *c.*1980 and 1850 BC. The Sesostris of legend may have been one of them, or a fictional composite of the three.

Aikin's Poets. John Aikin (1747–1822), English author, biographer, and physician. He wrote critical and biographical introductions to an edition of the British poets.

the Cid. See p. 334 n.

450 *Robin Hood's ballads . . . 'Tam O'Shanter'.* Joseph Ritson (see p. 334 n.) published *Robin Hood: a Collection of all the Ancient Poems, Songs and Ballads now extant relative to that Outlaw* in 1795. *Griselda* is the type of the patient and long-suffering woman. Versions of the character appear in Boccaccio's *Decameron* (day 10, tale 10), and in Chaucer's 'Clerk's Tale'. *Sir Andrew Barton, Sir Patrick Spens*, and *Chevy Chase* are the titles/heroes of traditional English ballads. *'Tam O'Shanter'* (1791) is a narrative poem by Robert Burns.

Faneuil Hall . . . Phillips. Faneuil Hall is a market in Boston, often called 'the cradle of liberty'. James *Otis* (1725–83), American statesman, member of the Massachusetts Assembly, and popular advocate of civil rights. *Webster*, see p. 333 n. *Kossuth*, see p. 350 n. *Phillips*, see p. 378 n.

As o'er our heads . . . the soul. Edward W. Emerson traces these lines to a hymn by Helen Maria Williams (1762–1827), which begins 'My God, all Nature owns thy sway'.

Behmen . . . William Blake. Jakob *Boehme*, see p. 159 n. *William Blake* (1757–1827), the English poet and mystic, was also an accomplished engraver and painter.

451 *He who . . . with it.* Emerson is quoting from two works by Blake. The sentences which precede the ellipse are from *A Descriptive Catalogue of Pictures, Poetical and Historical Inventions, Painted by William Blake . . .* (1809). Blake makes the remarks in his commentary on painting number four, 'The Bard, from Gray'. Cf. *Blake: the Complete Writings, with Variant Readings*, ed. Geoffrey Keynes (New York, 1966), pp. 576–7. The sentences which follow the ellipse are from *A Vision of the Last Judgment* (1810), p. 617 of Keynes's edition. Blake's text reads 'Corporeal or Vegetative Eye' for 'corporeal eye'.

Lear . . . this pass? Emerson alludes to *King Lear*, III. iv, and quotes l. 63.

Quarles . . . 'Emblems'. Francis Quarles (1592–1644), English poet, published his *Emblems*, a book of devotional poems, in 1635.

453 *Mirabeau.* see p. 280 n.

One omen . . . country. Homer, *Iliad*, xii. 245.

They heal . . . noble. Homer, *Iliad*, xiii. 116.

455 *Malthus . . . Burns . . . Béranger. Malthus*, see p. 295 n. Robert *Burns* (1759–96), Scottish poet. Pierre-Jean de *Béranger* (1789–1857), French poet often translated in England and America.

gai science. The phrase to which Nietzsche, a great reader of Emerson, alludes with the title of his *Frohliche Wissenschaft* (1882). The epigraph from that book is also taken from Emerson. Elsewhere, in 'Prospects', Emerson speaks of 'professors of the joyous science'.

As one . . . in too. The 'Minnesinger' Emerson quotes is Pons de Capdueil, a French troubadour of the 12th century. Emerson found the lines in *Lays of the Minnesingers or German Troubadours of the Twelfth and Thirteenth Centuries*, ed. Edgar Taylor (London, 1825), p. 220 (cf. *JMN*, xiv, 412).

the Maia. 'Maya' is a term from Hindu philosophy, denoting the power of a god to produce illusion; or, more generally, the illusory nature of all sensory experience. The term is usually not capitalized.

Welsh Bards. Emerson alludes to the emergence of a poetic tradition in Wales in the 6th century AD, in which Taliesin is the central figure.

456 *Ben Jonson . . . living.* Ben Jonson (1572–1637), English playwright and poet. Emerson quotes from the dedicatory epistle to his play *Volpone* (1607): ' . . . the principall end of poesie, to informe men, in the best reason of living.' Cf. C. H. Herford and Percy Simpson's edition of *Ben Jonson* (London, 1937), v. 20.

457 *The attractions . . . destinies.* This is an axiom of Fourier (p. 327 n.).

Anything, child . . . thy mind. Emerson quotes loosely from the *Vishnu Purana, a System of Hindu Mythology and Tradition*, trans. H. H. Wilson (London, 1840), pp. 88–9 (cf. *JMN*, ix, 300).

458 *None any work . . . the same.* The editors of the *JMN* have traced the couplet to Thomas Stanley's *History of Philosophy* (1701), p. 179. Stanley attributes it to a translation from Dante by Mirandola.

the creator of Trim and Uncle Toby. Trim and Uncle Toby appear in Laurence Sterne's (1713–68) novel *Tristram Shandy* (1759–67).

Cowper. William Cowper (1731–1800), English poet.

and that Goldsmith's title . . . Barthold Niebuhr. Oliver *Goldsmith* (1730–74), English poet, essayist, novelist, and dramatist. His poem *The Deserted Village* appeared in 1770; his novel *The Vicar of Wakefield* in 1766. *Ariel* and *Caliban* are characters in Shakespeare's *The Tempest*; the *fairies* appear in *A Midsummer Night's Dream*. Barthold Niebuhr (1776–1831), Danish historian.

Ben Jonson . . . Drummond. William Drummond of Hawthornden (1585–1649), Scottish writer and poet, who published notes on his conversations with Jonson (i. 132, cf. note to 456 above for a full citation).

459 *The Ram, the Bull . . . etc.* Emerson alludes to a rhyme by Isaac Watts. Cf. his *Works*, ed. D. Jennings and P. Doddridge, 6 vols. (London, 1753), iv. 706–7 (cf. *JMN*, xi, 419).

460 *At her feet . . . dead.* Judg. 5: 27.

They shall . . . no end. Pss. 102: 26–7.

Though fallen . . . tongues. Milton, *Paradise Lost*, vii. 25–6.

Was I . . . the night. Milton, *Comus*, 221–4.

A little . . . farther on. Milton, *Samson Agonistes*, 1–2.

Busk thee . . . marrow. William Hamilton (1704–54), Scottish poet. Emerson quotes from his song 'The Braes of Yarrow', ll. 1–2.

461 *that there is . . . form.* Perhaps he has Swedenborg (see p. 95 n.) in mind. Sections 87–115 of his *Heaven and Hell* treat of 'the correspondence between all things belonging to Heaven, and all things belonging to man', and 'between all things belonging to Heaven and all things belonging to the earth'.

the Spenserian. The stanza in which Spenser wrote *The Faerie Queen*, consisting of nine lines. The first eight are in iambic pentameter; the ninth is an alexandrine. The rhyme scheme is: ababbcbcc.

Thomas Taylor. See p. 289 n.

Thomas Moore . . . meant. See p. 436 n. Emerson takes the comment on Burke and Bacon from Moore's *Memoirs, Journals and Correspondence*, ed. John Russell (Edinburgh, 1853), iii. 344. Moore makes the comment to Henry Richard Fox, 3rd Baron Holland (1773–1840).

Richard Owen . . . inhabited. Emerson quotes from Owen's (see p. 442 n.) *Paleontology; or, a Systematic Summary of Extinct Animals and their Geological Relations* (Edinburgh, 1860), p. 399.

St. Augustine . . . Thee. Aurelius Augustinus, St Augustine (354–430), the greatest of the early Christian thinkers. Emerson takes the sentence from his *Confessions*, Book III, chap. 6. Cf. the Loeb Classical Library edition of the 1631 William Watts translation (Cambridge, Mass., 1912), p. 115.

Sir Thomas Browne's 'Fragment on Mummies'. Sir Thomas Browne (1605–82), English physician and writer. The 'Fragment on Mummies' was printed first in Simon Wilkin's edition of Browne's writings in 1836. Geoffrey Keynes reprints it in his *The Works of Sir Thomas Browne*, 4 vols. (Chicago, 1964), iii. 472. Keynes discusses briefly in his preface the controversy over Browne's authorship of the fragment.

462 *Philistia.* A region on the east coast of the Mediterranean, homeland of the Old Testament Philistines.

Parnassus. Mountain in Greece said, in the old legends, to be the haunt of the Muses. Emerson titled the anthology of verse he edited *Parnassus* (1874).

Victor Hugo . . . steel. Victor Hugo (1802–85), French poet and novelist. Emerson quotes from his preface to *Cromwell* (1827): 'l'idée, trempée dans la vers, prend soudain quelque chose de plus incisif et de plus éclatant. C'est le fer qui devient acier.' Cf. *Cromwell* (Paris, 1936), p. 55. The translation is probably Emerson's. Hugo's 'Preface' became something of a manifesto for the French Romantic writers.

Lord Bacon . . . spondees. Ben Jonson said this of Bacon to William Drummond of Hawthornden (i. 141, cf. p. 456 n. for a full citation).

Ben Jonson . . . hanging. Also from *Notes on Ben Jonson's Conversations with William Drummond.* Cf. i. 133 of Herford and Simpson, op. cit.

463–4 *Beaumont and Fletcher . . . melancholy.* The song appears in their play *Nice Valour*, III. iii. 40–58.

464 *Newton . . . Terence. Newton*, see p. 420 n. *Terence* (190–159 BC), Roman comic poet.

465 *Sagas . . . Nibelungen Lied.* The *Sagas* are a group of Icelandic and Scandinavian narratives dating from the Middle Ages. They recount the histories of the first peoples of the region, of the old Icelandic kings, and of legendary persons. The *Nibelungenlied* is a German epic poem of the 13th century, which tells the story of Siegfried and Sieglind, King and Queen of the Netherlands. Wagner adapted it in his *Ring des Nibelungen*.

Taliessin. See p. 455 n.

The whole ocean . . . King Regner Lodbook. Ragnar Lodbrok was a Danish king of the 8th century, perhaps legendary. In his *Northern Antiquities, or an Historical Account of the manners, customs, religion and laws, Maritime expeditions and Discoveries, Language and Literature of the Ancient Scandinavians* (Bishop Percy trans., I. A. Blackwell ed., London, 1847). Paul Henri

Mallet reprints two stanzas of the 'Death Song of Ragnar Lodbrok', the last two lines of which read: 'All was Ocean swollen / Though oozed blood went to raven' (p. 385).

God himself . . . Welsh Triad. The 'Welsh Triad' is an ancient form of proverbs in verse. Edward Davies writes in his *Mythology and Rites of the British Druids* (London, 1809): 'Some praise must be due to the ingenuity of the device, which was calculated . . . to lead the mind, imperceptibly, from a trivial remark upon the screaming of hungry birds, the state of the weather, or a dry leaf tossed about by the wind, to the contemplation of moral truth . . . And the triplets, which the people learned by rote, were peculiarly adapted to produce such a salutary effect' (p. 77). The triad from which Emerson takes the line reads: 'Snow of the mountain! the birds are tame—the discreetly happy needs only to be born—God himself cannot procure good for the wicked' (Davies, p. 79).

Discover thou . . . land. Taliesin's 'Song to the Wind' is collected in William F. Skene's *The Four Ancient Books of Wales* (Edinburgh, 1868), i. 535. Emerson had read Skene, but the lines he quotes here differ from Skene's translation in a number of minor details.

Is there . . . energy? From a poem attributed to Taliesin entitled 'Preiddeu Annwn' ('The Spoils of the Deep'), reprinted in Davies, op. cit., p. 525. The line breaks and punctuation are Emerson's.

Cunedda . . . shallow. Cunedda is said to have expelled the invading Scots from Wales. The line is from *The Book of Taliesin*, poem XLVI. Cf. Skene, op. cit., i. 47.

When I lapse . . . hear. Emerson quotes the last lines of 'The Elegy of the Thousand Sons' from *The Book of Taliesin*. Cf. Skene, op. cit., i. 550. As before, his and Emerson's renderings of the lines differ slightly.

466 *The caldron . . . coward.* Again from the Taliesinian poem 'Preiddeu Annwn'. Cf. Davies, op. cit., p. 518.

The heavy . . . endure. From 'Preiddeu Annwn'. Cf. Davies, op. cit., p. 515; Skene, op. cit., i. 264. The phrase 'of the sea' occurs in neither Skene's nor Davies's translations. Emerson adapted this line into a short poem titled 'The Exile / (After Taliessin)': 'The heavy blue chain / Of the boundless main / Didst thou, just man, endure.' Cf. vol. ix, p. 376, of the 'Centenary' edition of Emerson's *Works* (1904).

I am possessed . . . liberty. Emerson quotes from Mallet, op. cit., p. 371. He omits the following sentences which fall between 'adversities' and 'I know a song which . . . ': 'I know a song, which the sons of man ought to sing, if they would become skilful physicians. I know a song, by which I soften and enchant the arms of my enemies; and render their weapons of no effect!'

Odin . . . incantations. Odin is chief among the gods of Icelandic mythology. Emerson quotes from the 'Ynglinga Saga' of the *Heimskringla*. Cf. *The Heimskringla, or Sagas of the Norse Kings*, translated from the Icelandic of Snorri Sturluson by Samuel Laing, ed. Rasmus B. Anderson, 4 vols. (New York, 1889), i. 276.

Pierre d'Auvergne . . . other. Pierre d'Auvergne, a 12th-century Provençal troubadour. Emerson takes the lines from Claude Charles Faureil's *Historie de la Poésie Provençal* (Paris, 1846), ii. 13. Or cf. G. J. Adler's English translation of Faureil (New York, 1860), p. 358.

Pons de Capdeuil . . . of it. This is the declaration of Pierre d'Auvergne, not of his compatriot Pons de Capdeuil (see p. 455 n.). Cf. Faureil, op. cit., ii. 13–14; or Adler, op. cit., p. 359.

468 *Balder's columns in Breidablik.* Balder, a son of Odin, is an Icelandic deity of eminent beauty, wisdom, and eloquence; Briedablik is his mansion in heaven, whose name means 'wide-shining'. The 'Grimnismol' poem of the *Poetic Edda* reports: 'The seventh [mansion] is Breithablik; Balder has there / For himself a dwelling set, In the land I know that lies so fair, / And from evil fate is free', trans. Henry Adams Bellows (Princeton, 1936), p. 90. No reference is made in the *Poetic Edda* or in Mallet's *Northern Antiquities* to magical verses inscribed on the columns of Balder's mansion.

Saadi. See p. 332 n.

Not with . . . ecstasies. From Ben Jonson's 'Epistle to Elizabeth Countesse of Rutland', number XXII of the poems in *The Forrest* (1616). Emerson omits a line. The complete extract reads:

> . . . not with tickling rimes,
> Or common places, filch'd, that take these times,
> But high, and noble matter, such as flies
> From braines entranc'd, and fill'd with extasies (ll. 87–90).

Menu. See p. 124 n.

469 *the Greek Gnomic poets.* Gnomic poetry was an early form of proverbs in verse. Phocylides (6th century BC) is chief among the Gnomic poets.

Show me, said Sarona in the novel . . . at all. Emerson quotes from *Counterparts; Or, the Cross of Love* (1854), by the English novelist Elizabeth Sara Sheppard (1830–62). Her works are now largely forgotten. However, Edward W. Emerson observes that Sheppard was 'one of the few novelists that interested Mr. Emerson.'

Ariel . . . Prospero . . . Ophelia. Ariel and Prospero are characters in Shakespeare's *The Tempest*; Ophelia, a character in *Hamlet*.

470 *Boswellism.* James Boswell (1740–95) published his *Life of Samuel Johnson* in 1791. For two centuries the work has stood as the type of its genre—the study of 'the great man'.

Faust. Goethe's *Faust*, which appeared in two parts, in 1808 and 1832 respectively.

We, who . . . held. From Wordsworth's sonnet 'It is not to be thought of', number 16 in Part I of his *Poems Dedicated to National Independence and Liberty*. The original reads 'morals' for 'manners'.

471 *O celestial Bacchus!* In classical mythology, Bacchus is one of the names of Dionysius, son of Zeus, and god of wine. Many of the Greek dramatic masterpieces were first presented at the literary contests of the Bacchanalian festivals in Attica.

THOREAU

475 *Thoreau.* Henry David Thoreau (b. 1817) died of tuberculosis on 6 May 1862, and was buried at the New Burial Ground, Concord, three days later. Emerson gave the address 'Thoreau' at the service in the First Church, and published it with some additions and revisions in the *Atlantic Monthly* in August of the same year. Emerson and Thoreau began their friendship in 1837, and Thoreau lived in the Emerson house in 1841–3 and in 1847–8. It was on Emerson's property at Walden Pond that Thoreau built his cabin.

477 *'I love Henry . . . elm-tree.'* The remark is Emerson's. Cf. his journal for July–August 1848.

479 *Captain John Brown.* American abolitionist (1800–59) who, with a small force of armed men, seized the US arsenal at Harper's Ferry, Virginia, on 18 October 1859. He was tried in a Virginia court, convicted of treason and murder, and executed. Emerson heard Brown speak in Boston in 1857, and Emerson himself spoke before assemblies organized for the relief of Brown's family after his execution.

Plotinus. See p. 28 n.

From a box . . . pencils. Thoreau's family manufactured and sold pencils. His father had taken over the business from Charles Dunbar, his brother-in-law, in 1823.

480 *Scott's romance.* Walter Scott's *The Betrothed* (1825).

Arnica mollis. A herb used medicinally for sprains and bruises.

481 *that fop Brummel.* George (Beau) Brummell (1778–1840), a British gentleman, distinguished himself by his dandyish dress and manners.

The river on whose banks he was born. The Concord River in Massachusetts.

482 *Kane's 'Arctic Voyage'.* Elisha Kent Kane (1820–57), American naval surgeon and Arctic explorer. He published his *Arctic Explorations* in 1856.

Annursnuc. A hill in Concord.

Victoria regia. Water-lily native to South America.

483 *the Menyanthes.* A genus of bog plants known colloquially as 'buckbean'.

the Cypripedium. A genus of terrestrial orchids known colloquially as 'lady's slipper'.

gros-beaks, whose . . . eye. Emerson alludes to 'Vertue', a poem by George Herbert (1593–1633): 'Sweet rose, whose hue angrie and brave / Bids the rash gazer wipe his eye' (ll. 5–6). The grosbeak is a finch found in Europe and America.

485 *Æschylus and Pindar. Aeschylus* (525–456 BC), Greek tragedian. *Pindar*, see p. 118 n.

486 *Simonides.* Greek lyric poet of the 6th century BC.

I hearing get . . . brought. Emerson takes these lines from Thoreau's poem 'Inspiration'. But he quotes from the selections of the poem Thoreau printed in *A Week on the Concord and Merrimack Rivers.* The quatrain appears in the 'Friday' chapter (New York: The Library of America, 1985, p. 284); the six-line verse in the 'Monday' chapter (p. 140). These last six lines appear, with changes, in two distinct quatrains of the complete version of 'Inspiration'; the first four lines here quoted appear intact. Cf. *The Collected Poems of Henry Thoreau*, ed. Carl Bode (Baltimore, 1964), pp. 230–3.

488 *melilot.* A sweet clover.

Mikania scandens. A woody vine found in America, known colloquially as 'climbing hempweed'.

489 *Gnaphalium.* A herb, known colloquially as 'balsamweed'.

490 *Tyrolese mountains.* In western Austria.

POEMS

Unless otherwise indicated, the dates of composition, and the sources in journals and notebooks, here listed for the poems are those established by Ralph H. Orth *et al.* in *The Poetry Notebooks of Ralph Waldo Emerson* (Columbia, Missouri, 1986); the book has been most helpful to me in preparing these notes.

491 *To-day.* Emerson set down a draft of this poem in his journal for 1824. Never published by Emerson, it appeared first in the 'Centenary' edition of his *Works*, edited by his son Edward Waldo and published in 1904.

The River. A notebook draft of this poem bears the superscription 'Concord, June 1827'. Emerson had returned to Massachusetts in June after having spent the winter and spring in South Carolina and Florida recovering from respiratory ailments. Emerson neither published the poem nor gave it a title. It appears first in the 'Centenary' edition of his *Works* (1904).

l. 6. *flagroots.* The sweet flag or *calamus* is a perennial marsh herb, with long leaves and pungent roots.

492 *A Letter.* An early draft of this poem bears the heading 'Lines written in 1831 Boston'; a later draft, the heading 'Chardon Street 1830'—though the earlier date is apparently a mistake. It was in Emerson's Chardon Street house that his first wife, Ellen Tucker Emerson, died on 8 February 1831. 'A Letter' was first published in *Poems* (1904)—the 'Centenary' edition.

493 *Webster.* Emerson never published these lines. The three fragments, from three sources, first bore collectively the title 'Webster' in the 'Centenary' edition (1904), the text reprinted here. The lines dated 1831 are the last

lines of the poem 'Has God on thee conferred', as printed in *Poems* (1884). In 1834, Emerson composed and gave the Harvard Phi Beta Kappa poem, from which the lines bearing that date were selected and published as 'Webster' in *Poems* (1884). The couplet dated 1854 appears first in his journal for 1852, and reflects Emerson's disillusionment with the Whig senator from Massachusetts, who, to his disgust, had supported the Fugitive Slave Law of 1850. Daniel Webster (1782–1852) was one of the antebellum 'senate giants', with John C. Calhoun of South Carolina and Henry Clay of Kentucky.

494   l. 17. *Monadnoc.* A mountain in New Hampshire, the state in which Webster was born.

Each and All. Emerson first published this poem in the *Western Messenger* (February 1839). He collected it in *Poems* (1847).

l. 1. *red-cloaked clown.* A peasant; Emerson is probably thinking of a scene from his European travels in 1834, when he recorded in his journal: 'the shepherd or the beggar in his red-cloak little knows what a charm he gives to the wide landscape . . . '

495   *The Problem.* The germ of this poem appears in the journal for August 1838: 'It is very grateful to me to go into an English Church & hear the liturgy read. Yet nothing would induce me to be the English priest . . . ' Emerson dates an early notebook draft of 'The Problem' 10 November 1839. He published it first in *The Dial* for July 1840, and collected it in *Poems* (1847).

496   l. 10. *Phidias.* See p. 307 n.

l. 12. *Delphic oracle.* The oracle at the Temple of Apollo, near Delphos, Greece.

ll. 19–20. *The hand . . . Rome.* The hand of Michelangelo (1475–1564), who held the post of chief architect at St Peter's Cathedral in Rome.

497   l. 44. *With Andes and with Ararat.* Mountain chains in, respectively, South America and Asia Minor.

l. 51. *Pentecost.* The time of the descent of the Holy Spirit described in Acts 2.

l. 65. *Chrysostom, best Augustine.* St John *Chrysostom* (?347–407), whose surname means 'golden-mouthed', in recognition of his eloquence. He was Archbishop of Constantinople. St *Augustine*, see p. 461 n.

l. 68. *Taylor.* See p. 289 n.

To Rhea. Edward Emerson places the composition of the poem in 1843, and it appeared in *The Dial* for July of the same year. Emerson collected it in *Poems* (1847). In classical mythology, Rhea is 'the mother goddess', and both wife and sister to Kronos. Heeding a prophecy that his son would usurp him, Kronos swallows each of the children Rhea bears him, until she deceives him by giving birth to Zeus in seclusion on Mount Lycaeus.

499 *The Visit.* Composed in 1843, this poem first appeared in *The Dial* (April 1844). Emerson collected it in *Poems* (1847).

500 l. 25. *rede.* Counsel in which one places trust.

Uriel. Emerson probably wrote 'Uriel' in the early 1840s, though Stephen Whicher traces it to a journal entry for 30 October 1838: 'At the first entering ray of light, society is shaken with fear & anger from side to side. Who opened that shutter? they cry, Wo to him! They belie it, they call it darkness that comes in, affirming that they were in light before. Before the man who has spoken to them the dread word, they tremble & flee.' Some three months earlier, Emerson had delivered his unorthodox and controversial 'Divinity School Address'. Whicher suggests that the journal entry and the later treatment of the same theme in 'Uriel' are in part responses to the hostility with which the address was received; one reviewer called it 'the latest form of infidelity'. Emerson first published 'Uriel' in *Poems* (1847).

l. 7. *Pleiads.* In classical mythology, the daughters of Atlas and Pleione. Jupiter placed them in the heavens as stars.

l. 8. *Said.* The Persian poet Saadi, see p. 332 n.

502 *The Sphinx.* Emerson first published 'The Sphinx' in *The Dial* (January 1841), shortly after finishing it. It was the first poem in *Poems* (1847), as in all collections until Edward Emerson placed it eighth in the 1904 edition. Ralph Rusk remarks in his life of Emerson: 'The little volume, called simply *Poems* [1847], began defiantly with "The Sphinx". Many prospective purchasers at the bookstores must have been too dismayed to read further.'

l. 12. *Dædalian plan.* Daedalus, the legendary Athenian, built the labyrinth at Crete which imprisoned the Minotaur.

504 l. 77. *Lethe.* The river in Hades whose waters the dead drink to forget their earthly lives.

505 l. 107. *Rue, myrrh, and cummin. Rue,* a woody herb native to Europe, known commonly as the 'herb of grace'. *Myrrh,* a resin obtained from a tree native to Arabia and Africa, used in perfumes and for medicinal purposes in ancient times. *Cumin,* a dwarf plant native to Syria and Egypt, whose seeds are used as spice.

Mithridates. Written in 1846, the poem was first published in *Poems* (1847); the last two lines are omitted in later editions. Mithridates VI, King of Pontus in Asia Minor in the 1st century BC, daily administered to himself small doses of poisons so as to acquire immunity to them all.

506 ll. 6–19. *Give me agates . . . carouse. Agates* are a variety of quartz. *Cantharids* are a family of beetles whose bodies are dried and pulverized to make cantharis, a compound believed to have aphrodisiac and medicinal properties; it is toxic in high doses. Cantharis is known colloquially as 'Spanish Fly'. A *fillet* is a strip of ornamental cloth usually worn about the head; Emerson probably has in mind for this fillet 'poison' ivy. The *dogwood* is a tree or shrub of the genus *cornus*; but, in this connection, Emerson

probably means 'poison sumac', a member of the dogwood genus, known commonly as 'blind-your-eyes'. *Prussic* acid is a hydrocyanic acid used in rat poison and insecticide. The *upas* tree, native to South-east Asia and the Philippines, produces a highly toxic sap used in the preparation of poison darts. Mere proximity to this tree is popularly supposed to be fatal. *Vampyre-fanned*: fanned, perhaps, by the wings of the vampire bat, falsely supposed to subsist on the blood of men.

Hamatreya. The germ of this poem is in a series of passages Emerson copied into his journal from the *Vishnu Purana, a System of Hindu Mythology and Tradition*, trans. H. H. Wilson (London, 1840) in 1845; as, for example, this sentence: 'Foolishness has been the characteristic of every king who has boasted, "All this earth is mine—everything is mine—it will be in my house forever";—for he is dead.' The poem first appeared in *Poems* (1847), and has been reprinted in all later editions. 'Hamatreya' is apparently Emerson's variant of Maitreya, a character in the *Vishnu Purana* whose name means 'friendly'. The second Buddha is expected to bear the name.

l. 1. *Minott . . . Flint*. The names of some of the early settlers of the Concord area.

507 l. 8. *flags*. The sweet flag, a marsh herb with long slender leaves and pungent roots.

508 *The Rhodora*. Written in 1834, the poem appeared first in the *Western Messenger* (July 1839). Emerson collected it in *Poems* (1847), and chose it for *Selected Poems* (1876). The 'rhodora' is an early-blooming shrub related to the rhododendron.

509 *The Humble-Bee*. Two journal entries date the composition of the poem in May 1837: 'Yesterday in the woods I followed the fine humble-bee with rhymes & fancies fine . . . Yesterday afternoon I stirred the earth about my shrubs & trees & quarreled with piper-grass and now I have slept, & no longer am morose nor feel twitchings in the muscles of my face when a visiter is by. The humble-bee & the pine-warbler seem to me the proper objects of attention in these disastrous times.' America was in the thick of an economic depression in 1837. The *Western Messenger* published the poem in February 1839, and Emerson collected it in *Poems* (1847).

l. 3. *Porto Rique*. Emerson's brother Edward had sought 'the far-off heats' of Puerto Rico in 1830, suffering from consumptive symptoms. He died there in 1834.

511 *The Snow-Storm*. On 29 December 1834 heavy snow fell over Concord, and several entries in Emerson's journal suggest that he began 'The Snow-Storm' in the ensuing days. It appeared in *The Dial* (January 1841), and Emerson collected it in *Poems* (1847).

l. 18. *Parian wreaths*. An allusion to the ancient marble quarries on the Aegean isle of Paros, whose stone supplied sculptors in Greece.

Woodnotes I. Written probably between 1835 and 1839, the poem first appeared in *The Dial* (October 1840). Emerson collected it in *Poems* (1847). Edward Emerson writes of the second section of the poem: 'The passage about the forest seer fits Thoreau so well that the general belief that Mr. Emerson had him in mind may be accepted, but one member of the family recalls his saying a part of this picture was drawn before he knew Thoreau's gifts and experiences.' The two men became friends in 1837. Emerson published a second part to the poem in *The Dial* (October 1841), titling it 'Woodnotes II'. The two parts appear contiguously in *Poems* (1847).

513 l. 55. *But . . . hour.* Emerson writes in his sketch of Thoreau: 'He thought that, if waked up from a trance, in this swamp, he could tell by the plants what time of year it was within two days.'

514 l. 82. *Linnæa.* A genus of creeping evergreen shrubs, known commonly as 'twin-flower' for the blooms it bears in pairs.

516 *Fable.* Edward Emerson assigns the composition of this poem to 1845. It was published first in *The Diadem* (1846), a gift anthology of verse. Emerson collected it in *Poems* (1847).

Ode, Inscribed to W. H. Channing. William Henry Channing (1810–84), Unitarian clergyman, Christian socialist, and abolitionist. Emerson's 'Ode' dates to 1845–6, during which time Channing, in appearances at Concord on behalf of the anti-slavery campaign, urged Emerson, who had long supported abolition, to become an activist in the cause. Emerson collected the 'Ode' in *Poems* (1847).

517 l. 21. *Contoocook.* A river in New Hampshire.

l. 22. *Agiochook.* A mountain in New Hampshire.

l. 26. *little men.* These often quoted lines reflect Emerson's growing disillusionment with Daniel Webster, a native of New Hampshire. Webster had compromised with Democratic and pro-slavery demands, and would three years later support the Fugitive Slave Law of 1850.

519 l. 87. *honey Out of the lion.* Emerson alludes to Judg. 14: 8.

Suum Cuique. 'Suum Cuique' means 'to each his own'. Emerson first published it in *The Dial* (January 1841), and collected it in *Poems* (1847). He omitted it, however, from *Selected Poems* (1876), which omission both James Cabot and Edward Emerson respected in their editions of the poetry. The 'Suum Cuique' reprinted here is not to be confused with the couplet of the same title that appears in the poem 'Life' in *May-Day* (1867) and later collections.

Compensation. An early draft of this poem appears in a journal entry for 1 December 1834. The doctrine of 'compensation' is the extension into the field of morals of the axiom that every action implies or produces its opposite and complementary reaction. Emerson writes in 'Compensation', from *Essays: First Series* (1841): 'Every excess causes a defect; every defect an excess. Every sweet hath its sour; every evil its good. Every faculty which is a receiver of pleasure has an equal penalty put on its abuse.' The idea is everywhere encountered in Emerson's writings. He collected the poem in *Poems* (1847).

Forerunners. Probably written in 1845, this poem was published first in the gift-book *The Diadem* (1846). Emerson collected it in *Poems* (1847), and chose it for *Selected Poems* (1876).

520 *Give All to Love*. Completed in 1846, this poem appears first in *Poems* (1847). Emerson chose it for his *Selected Poems* (1876).

522 *Merlin I and II*. Emerson finished writing the poem in 1846, and published it first in *Poems* (1847). He had in mind the 'Merlin' to whom a body of ancient Welsh verse is attributed, not the sorcerer of Arthurian legend.

523 l. 32. *aye*. Always.

l. 49. *Sybarites*. The inhabitants of the Greek city of Sybaris in southern Italy, notorious for their love of luxury.

525 l. 118. *Nemesis*. In Greek mythology, the agent of divine retribution, or compensation.

l. 126. *Sisters*. Clotho, Lachesis, and Atropos, the three Fates of Greek mythology who were said to 'spin the threads' of our destinies.

Bacchus. Emerson completed the poem in 1846 and published it first in *Poems* (1847), choosing it as well for his *Selected Poems* (1876). Bacchus is one of the names of Dionysius, the god of wine, associated, too, with poetic inspiration. The Bacchanalian festivals in Attica included prestigious literary contests. An apposite passage in prose to this poem occurs in the last section of Emerson's 'Poetry and Imagination', the section beginning 'O celestial Bacchus!'.

526 l. 9. *Styx and Erebus*. The river Styx forms part of the border of Hades. Erebus is the region of darkness that lies beneath the Earth.

527 l. 67. *Pleiads*. The Pleiades were the seven daughters of Atlas. Jupiter changed them into stars, placing them in the heavens among the constellations.

Merops. It is not known when Emerson wrote this poem, which he first published in *Poems* (1847). 'Merops' is from a Greek compound word meaning 'articulate speech'.

528 *Xenophanes*. Probably written in 1834, the poem first appeared in *Poems* (1847). Emerson chose it for *Selected Poems* (1876). Xenophanes was a Greek philosopher of the 6th century BC who held that God and universe were one.

l. 2. *hyson*. A Chinese green tea.

Blight. Emerson published this first under the name 'The Times—A Fragment' in *The Dial* (January 1844). He collected it with its new title in *Poems* (1847). Edward Emerson supposes that Emerson wrote it in the summer of 1843.

ll. 5–7. *Rue . . . sundew*. Rue, a strong-scented woody herb. *Cinquefoil*, a genus of plants of the rose family. *Gill*, 'short for Gill-go-round' (*OED*), a variety of ground ivy. *Vervain*, a plant of the genus *verbena*, thought to have medicinal properties. *Agrimony*, herb of the rose family which bears a yellow flower. *Blue-vetch*, a twining plant which bears dense clusters of flowers. *Trillium*, a genus of North American herbs once used as an astringent. *Hawkweed*, a plant bearing red and orange flowers. *Sassafras*, a tree of the laurel family, whose aromatic roots are used in teas. *Milkweeds*, any one of several plants that secrete latex. *Brakes*, a common name for ferns. *Quaint pipes*, probably 'pipe-trees', any of several varieties of tree or shrub whose twigs were once used for pipe-stems. *Sundew*, an insectivorous herb found in bogs.

529 l. 22. *Latin names*. Compare this and the preceding lines to this journal entry for June–August 1845: 'Literature has been before us, wherever we go. When I come in the secretest recess of a swamp, to some obscure, and rare, and to me unknown plant, I know that its name and the number of its stamens, every bract and awn, is carefully described and registered in a book on my shelf.'

530 *Threnody*. Emerson wrote the first part of this elegy for his son Waldo—up to 'The deep Heart answered, "Weepest thou?" ' (l. 176)—soon after the boy died on 27 January 1842. Apparently, he did not write the second part until a year or more had elapsed. A 'threnody' is a lamentation for the dead.

l. 14. *cerulean*. The blue tint of the sky.

l. 15. *hyacinthine boy*. A mythical Greek youth beloved of Apollo.

535 l. 183. *eld*. Antiquity.

l. 190. *dizen*. Adorn.

ll. 207–8. *Throb . . . west*. Emerson used these lines also in the brief poem beginning 'The rounded world is fair to see', the second of two mottoes titled 'Nature'.

536 l. 223. *Boy-Rabbi*. An allusion to Luke 2: 41–52, which tells the story of the young Jesus lagging behind with the elders in the temple at Jerusalem after Mary and Joseph had left for Nazareth.

537 l. 272. *adamant*. A stone believed to be unbreakable.

Concord Hymn. Emerson wrote the poem in 1837, and it was sung by the townspeople of Concord at the dedication of the monument commemorating the Battle of Concord. The ceremony was held on 4 July 1837. Emerson himself was not present.

538 *Brahma*. The poem dates to 1845–6, when Emerson was reading the *Vishnu Purana*, the *Bhagavadgita*, and the *Upanishads*. He published it first in *Atlantic Monthly* (November 1857), and collected it in *May-Day and Other Pieces* (1867). Brahma is the highest deity of Hinduism.

l. 12. *Brahmin*. Member of the highest or priestly caste of Hindus.

l. 14. *the sacred Seven*. The 'Seven Seers' or Maharsis of ancient Hindu poetry. 'Seers' or 'rsis' were singers of the sacred songs.

Voluntaries. Emerson composed this poem in 1863, partly in honour of Colonel Robert Gould Shaw and the Massachusetts regiment in his command. The regiment was among the first to enlist blacks, many of them ex-slaves, and Shaw had resigned the command of a prestigious all-white regiment to lead them. He and many of his men were killed in an assault on Fort Wagner in South Carolina, 18 July 1863. The poem first appeared in *Atlantic Monthly* (October 1863), and was reprinted in *Memorial: Robert Gould Shaw* (1864). Emerson collected it in *May-Day* (1867).

542 *Days*. The germ of this poem is a journal entry for 27 May 1847, the eve of Emerson's forty-fourth birthday: 'The days come and go like muffled and veiled figures sent from a distant friendly party, but they say nothing, and if we do not use the gifts they bring, they carry them as silently away.' Emerson rated the poem among his best, though he wrote of it some months later: 'I find one state of mind does not remember or conceive of another state. Thus I have written within a twelvemonth verses ("Days") which I do not remember the composition or correction of . . . ' He published the poem first in *Atlantic Monthly* (November 1857), and collected it in *May-Day* (1867).

l. 2. *dervishes*. Muslim ascetics.

l. 7. *pleached garden*. That is, a garden beneath a canopy of laced branches or slats.

l. 11. *fillet*. Ornamental headband.

Song of Nature. The sources for this poem in the journals and poetry note-books are too numerous to mention here, and they span some 14 years between 1845 and 1859. See Carl F. Straunch, 'The Sources of Emerson's "Song of Nature" ', *Harvard Library Bulletin* 9 (Autumn 1955), pp. 300–34. Emerson published the poem first in *Atlantic Monthly* (January 1860), and revised it slightly for *May-Day* (1867).

543 l. 31. *saurian*. Reptilian.

544 l. 67. *One . . . Nile*. Several critics have suggested that Emerson had in mind Plotinus, the 3rd-century neo-Platonic philosopher.

l. 68. *And . . . Academe*. Probably Plato.

545 *Two Rivers*. A prose version of the first few stanzas appears in his journal for spring 1856. The conceit of the poem, however, may date much earlier to an entry for June 1840: 'We see the river glide below us but we see not the river that glides over us & envelopes us in its floods.' Emerson published it first in *Atlantic Monthly* (January 1858), and collected it in *May-Day* (1867).

l. 18. *Who . . . again*. An allusion to John 4: 14, which records Jesus's reply to the Samaritan woman at the well: 'But whosoever drinketh of the water that I shall give him shall never thirst.'

546 *Waldeinsamkeit*. Emerson probably wrote this poem in autumn 1857. He published it first in *Atlantic Monthly* (October 1858), and collected it in *May-Day* (1867). As Edward Emerson points out, the title is German for

'forest solitude'. Emerson may have been the more attracted to it for its suggestion of 'Walden', whose woods he loved.

l. 31. *bittern*. A small heron which frequents bogs.

547 *Terminus*. Probably begun in 1850, the poem remained unfinished until 1866. Edward Emerson writes of his first hearing of it: 'In the last days of the year 1866, when I was returning from a long stay in the Western states, I met my father in New York just starting for his usual winter lecturing trip . . . We spent the night together at the St. Denis Hotel, and as we sat by the fire he read me two or three of his poems for the new May-Day volume, among them "Terminus". It almost startled me. No thought of his aging had ever come to me, and there he sat, with no apparent abatement of bodily vigor, and young in spirit, recognizing with serene acquiescence his failing forces; I think he smiled as he read.' Emerson published it first in *Atlantic Monthly* (January 1867), and collected it in *May-Day* (1867).

548 l. 28. *Baresark*. The 'berserker' was an ancient Scandinavian warrior of especial strength and ferocity.

April. The germ of the poem is a letter Emerson wrote to Margaret Fuller on 21 February 1840: 'These spring winds are magical in their operation on our attuned frames. These are the days of passion when the air is full of cupids and devils for eyes that are still young . . . ' Emerson first published it in *Selected Poems* (1876).

l. 7. *Rosamonds*. Rosamond Clifford (d. ?1176), who earned the epithet 'Fair' for her beauty and charm. It is said that she was a mistress of Henry II.

549 l. 13. *Goodfellow, Puck*. Both are names for the mischievous sprite who figured in the popular superstitions of the 16th century. Puck appears in Shakespeare's *Midsummer Night's Dream*.

Grace. Written probably about 1830, the poem first appeared in *The Dial* (January 1842), and was reprinted as an epigraph to a chapter in *Memoirs of Margaret Fuller Ossoli* (1852), of which Emerson was a co-author. He never collected it in a volume of his own, and it appeared next in *Poems* (1884).

Insight. Edward Emerson first printed (1904) and titled these lines, which Emerson himself never published.

The Enchanter. It is not known when Emerson composed these lines. He never published them, and they appeared first in *Poems* (1884) under the non-authorial title 'The Enchanter'.

551 Both 'Memory' and 'Nature in Leasts' appeared first in *May-Day* (1867). The dates of composition are unknown.

553 *Compensation*. Lines 1–14 were probably written in 1841; ll. 15–24 in 1847. The stanzas first appeared as the two mottoes to 'Compensation' in *Essays: First Series* (1847)—the second edition of the book. Emerson collected them in *May-Day* (1867).

554 *Spiritual Laws* and *Heroism*. Both written in 1846–7, the poems first appeared as the mottoes to the essays of the same names in the 1847 edition of *Essays: First Series*. Emerson collected them in *May-Day* (1867).

554–6 *Wealth*, *Culture*, and *Worship*. Each appeared first as the motto to the
essay bearing its name in *Conduct of Life* (1860). 'Wealth' remained uncol-
lected by Emerson, but he did reprint 'Culture' and 'Worship' in *May-Day*
(1867), choosing the latter also for *Selected Poems* (1876).

FURTHER READING

EDITIONS

The standard edition of Emerson's works has until recently been the 'Centenary' edition, edited by Emerson's son, Edward Waldo Emerson. The twelve-volume collection was published first in 1903–4 (Boston: Houghton Mifflin). The AMS Press of New York reprinted it in 1968, and again in 1979 with an introduction by Joel Myerson. Though still widely used, this edition has been superseded by the following: *The Collected Works of Ralph Waldo Emerson*, 4 vols. to date, ed. Robert Spiller, Joseph Slater *et al.* (Cambridge, Mass., and London: The Belknap Press of Harvard University Press, 1971–); *The Early Lectures of Ralph Waldo Emerson*, 3 vols., ed. Stephen Whicher, Robert Spiller, and Wallace E. Williams (Cambridge, Mass., and London: The Belknap Press of Harvard University Press, 1966–72); *Ralph Waldo Emerson: Essays and Lectures*, ed. Joel Porte (New York: Library of America, 1983, with additional volumes planned); and *Young Emerson Speaks: Unpublished Discourses on Many Subjects*, ed. Arthur C. McGiffert (Boston: Houghton Mifflin, 1938).

The first comprehensive edition of Emerson's journals (standard until 1960) was *The Journals of Ralph Waldo Emerson*, 10 vols., ed. Edward Waldo Emerson and Waldo Emerson Forbes (Boston and New York: Houghton Mifflin, 1909–14). It has been superseded by *Journals and Miscellaneous Notebooks of Ralph Waldo Emerson*, 16 vols., ed. William H. Gilman *et al.* (Cambridge, Mass., and London: The Belknap Press of Harvard University Press, 1960–84). A single-volume selection made from the 1909–14 edition appeared in 1926 as *The Heart of Emerson's Journals*, ed. Bliss Perry (Boston and New York: Houghton Mifflin). More recently published is the useful one-volume selection *Emerson in His Journals*, ed. Joel Porte (Cambridge, Mass., and London: The Belknap Press of Harvard University Press, 1982). Recently published also is *The Poetry Notebooks of Ralph Waldo Emerson* (Columbia, Missouri: University of Missouri Press, 1986).

Editions of the letters of Emerson and his family include:

The Letters of Ralph Waldo Emerson, 6 vols., ed. Ralph Rusk (New York: Columbia University Press, 1939).

The Correspondence of Emerson and Carlyle, ed. Joseph Slater (New York and London: Columbia University Press, 1964).

The Letters of Lidian Jackson Emerson, ed. Delores Bird Carpenter (Columbia, Missouri: University of Missouri Press, 1987).

The Letters of Ellen Tucker Emerson, 2 vols., ed. Edith E. W. Gregg (Kent, Ohio: Kent State University Press, 1982).

One First Love: The Letters of Ellen Louisa Tucker to Ralph Waldo Emerson, ed. Edith E. W. Gregg (Cambridge, Mass.: Harvard University Press, 1962).

BIOGRAPHIES

Important biographies and memoirs include:

Allen, Gay Wilson, *Waldo Emerson* (New York: Viking Press, 1981).

Cabot, James Elliot, *A Memoir of Ralph Waldo Emerson*, 2 vols. (Boston: Houghton Mifflin, 1887).

Emerson, Edward Waldo, *Emerson in Concord* (Boston: Houghton Mifflin, 1889).

Emerson, Ellen Tucker, *The Life of Lidian Jackson Emerson*, ed. Delores Bird Carpenter (Boston: Twayne, 1980).

McAleer, John, *Ralph Waldo Emerson: Days of Encounter* (Boston: Little, Brown, 1984).

Rusk, Ralph L., *The Life of Ralph Waldo Emerson* (New York: Scribners, 1949).

BIBLIOGRAPHY

Burkholder, Robert E., and Joel Myerson (eds.), *Emerson: An Annotated Secondary Bibliography* (Pittsburgh: University of Pittsburgh Press, 1985).

Myerson, Joel (ed.), *Ralph Waldo Emerson: A Descriptive Bibliography* (Pittsburgh: University of Pittsburgh Press, 1982).

SOURCE STUDIES AND REFERENCE WORKS

Berry, Edward G., *Emerson's Plutarch* (Cambridge, Mass.: Harvard University Press, 1961).

Cameron, Kenneth Walker, *Emerson the Essayist*, 2 vols. (Raleigh: Thistle Press, 1945).

——, *Emerson's Reading* (New York: Haskell House, 1973; Reprint of 1941 Thistle Press edition).

——, *Emerson's Workshop: An Analysis of His Reading in Periodicals Through 1836* (Hartford, Conn.: Transcendental Books, 1964).

Carpenter, Frederick Ives, *Emerson and Asia* (Cambridge, Mass.: Harvard University Press, 1930).

Harding, Walter, *Emerson's Library* (Charlottesville: University Press of Virginia, 1967).

Hubbell, George S., *Concordance to the Poems of Ralph Waldo Emerson* (New York: H. W. Wilson, 1932).

Irey, Eugene F., *A Concordance to Five Essays of Ralph Waldo Emerson: Nature, The American Scholar, The Divinity School Address, Self-Reliance, and Fate* (New York: Garland Publishers, 1981).

Ihrig, Mary Alice, *Emerson's Transcendental Vocabulary: A Concordance* (New York: Garland Publishers, 1981).

Whicher, Stephen, *Selections from Ralph Waldo Emerson* (Boston: Houghton Mifflin, 1957, 1960).

Young, Charles Lowell, *Emerson's Montaigne* (New York: Macmillan, 1941).

Zink, Harriet Rodgers, *Emerson's Use of the Bible* (Lincoln: University of Nebraska Press, 1935).

CRITICISM

Anderson, Quentin, *The Imperial Self, An Essay in American Literary and Cultural History* (New York: Alfred Knopf, 1971).

Bishop, Jonathan, *Emerson on the Soul* (Cambridge, Mass.: Harvard University Press, 1964).

Bloom, Harold, *A Map of Misreading* (New York: Oxford University Press, 1975).

——, *The Ringers in the Tower* (Chicago: University of Chicago Press, 1971).

Burke, Kenneth, 'I, Eye, Ay—Concerning Emerson's Early Essay on "Nature" and the Machinery of Transcendence', in his *Language As Symbolic Action* (Berkeley and Los Angeles: University of California Press, 1966).

Cameron, Sharon, 'Representing Grief: Emerson's "Experience" ', *Representations* 15 (Summer 1986), pp. 15–41.

Cavell, Stanley, *The Quest of the Ordinary* (Chicago: University of Chicago Press, 1988).

——, *This New Yet Unapproachable America* (Albuquerque: Living Branch Press, 1989).

Chapman, John Jay, 'Emerson', in *Selected Writings of John Jay Chapman*, ed. Jacques Barzun (New York: Funk and Wagnalls, Minerva Press, 1968).

Cheyfitz, Eric, *The Trans-Parent: Sexual Politics in the Language of Emerson* (Baltimore: Johns Hopkins University Press, 1981).

Ellison, Julie, *Emerson's Romantic Style* (Princeton: Princeton University Press, 1984).

Feidleson, Charles Jr., *Symbolism and American Literature* (Chicago: University of Chicago Press, 1953).

Firkins, O. W., *Ralph Waldo Emerson* (Boston: Houghton Mifflin, 1915).

Horowitz, Howard, 'The Standard Oil Trust as Emersonian Hero', *Raritan* 4 (Spring 1987), pp. 97–120.

Hughes, Gertrude Reif, *Emerson's Demanding Optimism* (Baton Rouge: Louisiana State University Press, 1984).

James, Henry Jr., 'Emerson', in *Partial Portraits* (London and New York, Macmillan 1888). Repr. in *Henry James: Literary Criticism*, vol. i, ed. Leon Edel (New York: Library of America, 1984).

Jehlen, Myra, *American Incarnation: The Individual, the Nation, and the Continent* (Cambridge, Mass.: Harvard University Press, 1986).

Matthiessen, F. O., *American Renaissance: Art and Expression in the Age of Emerson and Whitman* (New York: Oxford University Press, 1941).

Miller, Perry, 'From Edwards to Emerson', pp. 184–203 in his *Errand Into the Wilderness* (Cambridge, Mass.: Harvard University Press, 1956).

Packer, Barbara, *Emerson's Fall: A New Interpretation of the Major Essays* (New York: Continuum, 1982).

Paul, Sherman, *Emerson's Angle of Vision: Men and Nature in the American Experience* (Cambridge, Mass.: Harvard University Press, 1952).

Pease, Donald, *Visionary Compacts: American Renaissance Writings in Cultural Context* (Madison: University of Wisconsin Press, 1987).

Poirier, Richard, *A World Elsewhere: the Place of Style in American Literature* (New York: Oxford University Press, 1966).

Poirier, Richard, *Robert Frost: the Work of Knowing* (New York: Oxford University Press, 1977).

——, *The Renewal of Literature: Emersonian Reflections* (New York: Random House, 1987).

Porte, Joel, *Representative Man: Ralph Waldo Emerson in His Time* (New York: Oxford University Press, 1979).

Porter, David, *Emerson and Literary Change* (Cambridge, Mass.: Harvard University Press, 1978).

Weisbuch, Robert, *Atlantic Double-Cross: American Literature and British Influence in the Age of Emerson* (Chicago: University of Chicago Press, 1987).

Whicher, Stephen, *Freedom and Fate: An Inner Life of Ralph Waldo Emerson* (Philadelphia: University of Pennsylvania Press, 1953).

Winters, Ivor, *In Defense of Reason* (Denver: Alan Swallow, 1943).

Yoder, R. A., *Emerson and the Orphic Poet in America* (Berkeley and Los Angeles: University of California Press, 1978).

COLLECTIONS OF ESSAYS

Bloom, Harold (ed.), *Ralph Waldo Emerson: Modern Critical Views* (New York: Chelsea House, 1985).

Konvitz, Milton R. (ed.), *The Recognition of Ralph Waldo Emerson: Selected Criticism Since 1837* (Ann Arbor: University of Michigan Press, 1972).

——, and Stephen E. Whicher (eds.), *Emerson: a Collection of Critical Essays* (Englewood Cliffs, N.J.: Prentice Hall, 1962).

Levin, David (ed.), *Emerson: Prophecy, Metamorphosis, and Influence* (New York: Columbia University Press, 1975).

Myerson, Joel (ed.), *Emerson Centennial Essays* (Carbondale: Southern Illinois University Press, 1982).

Porte, Joel (ed.), *Emerson: Prospect and Retrospect* (Cambridge, Mass.: Harvard University Press, 1982).

INDEX OF PROSE

INDEX OF POEM TITLES AND FIRST LINES